# SOCIOLOGY:

## AN INTRODUCTION

# SOCIOLOGY:
## AN INTRODUCTION

EDITED BY *Neil J. Smelser*

*John Wiley & Sons, Inc.* NEW YORK LONDON SYDNEY

# Contributing Authors

Peter L. Berger
*The New School for Social Research*

A. H. Halsey
*Oxford University*

George C. Homans
*Harvard University*

S. M. Lipset
*Harvard University*

Wilbert Moore
*Russell Sage Foundation*

Leonard Reissman
*Tulane University*

Leo F. Schnore
*University of Wisconsin*

Philip E. Slater
*Brandeis University*

Neil J. Smelser
*University of California, Berkeley*

William N. Stephens
*Florida Atlantic University*

Arthur L. Stinchcombe
*Johns Hopkins University*

Stanton Wheeler
*Russell Sage Foundation*

# PREFACE

In my office in Barrows Hall at the University of California, Berkeley, one and one half large shelves of the bookcase are filled with books with very similar titles: *Sociology; Introduction to Sociology; Basic Readings in Sociology;* and others. These books have accumulated during the past dozen years that encompass my graduate-training and teaching career. I have bought only a few of them. Most of them were sent to me by their publishers, in the hope that I would use them for an introductory course, or that I would perhaps persuade a colleague to use them. If I had made a point of systematically collecting introductory works published in the past decade, I imagine they would occupy twice the space in my study. On the basis of this little survey of my library, I have concluded that the publication of textbooks is a very thriving business in America, and that there are many books to choose from if one wishes to introduce himself to sociology.[1]

Now I am publishing a book that will find its place among the others. Because there are so many on the shelves already, and because I believe this volume differs sharply from almost all of them, my initial obligation is to indicate to my sociological colleagues and to students the ways in which this text differs from the dozens of others that have appeared in the past couple of decades. I see four key differences.

1. Traditional textbooks, like the introductory courses in which they are used, are very comprehensive in their coverage of sociological concepts and information. In some ways this is a positive feature. But a frequent cost of comprehensiveness is a degree of superficiality. Consequently, the student is likely to emerge from his introductory course with a nodding acquaintance with a diversity of sociological materials, but with too little grasp of the subtleties of sociological theory and research and too little

---

[1] Apparently, textbooks have occupied an important place in American sociology for a long time. Pitirim Sorokin, writing in 1929, noted that in contrast to the European tradition, "American literature in sociology has been composed largely out of the text-books. . . . No other country can rival the United States in [the text-book] field—not only quantitatively but qualitatively." Pitirim A. Sorokin, "Some Contrasts of Contemporary European and American Sociology: I," *Social Forces,* **8,** 57–60 (1929–1930).

appreciation of the power of sociology to illuminate and explain fundamental social facts. These combined features of comprehensiveness and superficiality have earned unflattering labels for many introductory texts, such as "seed catalogue," "dustbin," or "smorgasbord."

In preparing this book, the contributors and I have attempted to avoid this problem. No contributor has tried to cover his whole subject. Each chapter has two objectives—first, to give the student a selective and representative (but not exhaustive) exposure to a branch of sociology; and, second, to intensify and deepen his grasp of the core theoretical frameworks and empirical findings in the discipline.

2. Another common result of the effort to be comprehensive in preparing a text is that the author tends to give every subfield and developmental trend in sociology more or less "equal representation." Every traditional area—family, race relations, delinquency, stratification, and everything else—must be included. Frequently, however, this practice obscures the true character of the field. Some of its branches are vital; others are stagnant at any given time; and some activities are more on the frontiers of theory and research than others. I have encouraged the current contributors not to take a completely "democratic" approach to the field. As a result, I believe that while their approach does give the student a representative view, it also reflects a selective emphasis on at least three kinds of frontier activity in sociology.

The first frontier involves not so much a new development as a continuation of a long-term trend in sociology. In general, the main historical roots of sociology have been the European traditions of social and political philosophy and the American traditions of social concern with pressing problems such as, for instance, crime, slum life, divorce, and the assimilation of immigrants. Although the forerunners of modern sociology were certainly interested in understanding social phenomena, their overwhelming concern was in ameliorating social conditions and improving society. However, in more recent times, the focus of sociology has moved in the direction of understanding the workings of social life within the framework of scientific theory and method, and away from the immediate practical applications of this understanding to social life.[2] Some critics have decried this trend and called for a return to a more problem-centered sociology.[3] Whether these critics are right or wrong is probably a matter for history to decide, but it is certainly true that the trend toward a scientific sociology is evident

[2] See Seymour Martin Lipset and Neil J. Smelser, "Change and Controversy in Recent American Sociology," *British Journal of Sociology,* **12,** 41–51 (1961); Talcott Parsons, "Some Problems Confronting Sociology as a Profession," *American Sociological Review,* **24,** 547–559 (1959). I do not wish to exaggerate the drift away from practical preoccupations in sociology; the recent surge of sociological interest in mental illness and poverty shows their continuing importance.

[3] C. Wright Mills, *The Sociological Imagination* (New York: Oxford University Press, 1959).

in mid-twentieth century. This trend is reflected in the contents of this book.

Even though the contributors treat social phenomena within a scientific framework instead of in terms of the significance of these phenomena as social or philosophical problems, their choice of topics and issues for analysis reveals a continued preoccupation with problems faced by modern civilization. For example, Leo Schnore raises the much-debated question of whether the modern urban center is a source of human alienation. Both Leonard Reissman and Seymour Martin Lipset ask whether a complex, advanced industrial civilization gives rise to an exaggerated concentration of political power. Peter Berger analyzes what many have called the "decline of religion" in modern times in terms of processes like bureaucratization and privatization. And William Stephens attacks the issue of whether the modern urban-industrial complex leads to a loss of functions, or even a disintegration in family life. Every one of these issues reveals a legitimate scientific problem. And each contributor deals with his issue as dispassionately as possible. But it is also true that every issue is the subject of extensive ideological commentary and controversy at the present time. The centrality of these issues in contemporary sociology reflects the fact that the sociologist's selection of scientific problems is still profoundly affected by the social and ideological preoccupations of the civilization in which he lives.

The second frontier involves the systematic study of social change. At the beginning of this century, sociology and anthropology—under the influence of a number of different versions of evolutionary thought—were preoccupied with the problem of how societies had evolved from their original primitive state to their contemporary advanced state. These theories of change proved to be vulnerable, however, on both theoretical and empirical grounds; and, by World War I, evolutionary sociology and anthropology had been more or less thoroughly discredited by their critics.[4] Between the two World Wars, the systematic study of long-term social and cultural change was, with few exceptions, in a state of stagnation. This state of affairs caused sociology to be criticized as being static and ahistorical in its emphasis—a criticism that persists to the present day in some quarters. However, since World War II, sociologists once again have quickened their interest in the systematic analysis of social change. There are many reasons for this renaissance but, in my opinion, the main one is the visible ferment and flux in the recently independent and developing countries of the world. This rebirth of interest in the study of change has been so significant that, in a recent interview study of about three dozen leading American sociologists, social change and economic development were most often mentioned

---

[4] For a sketch of some of the criticisms of classical evolutionary thought, and some of the new approaches to social change that developed from these criticisms, see *infra*, pp. 699–710.

as the most important problems in sociology today.[5] This book reflects the revitalization of interest in change, not only in my own chapter but in the chapters of other contributors: for instance, by Schnore, who devotes nearly half of his space to the "dynamics of the contemporary community"; by Reissman, who includes a final section on "stratification and social change"; by Lipset, who writes on the relations between "economic development and political systems"; and by Berger, A. H. Halsey, and Stephens who, respectively, focus on recent transformations in religious, educational, and familial institutions.

The third frontier involves the systematic comparative study of societies. In the history of American sociology in particular, scholars have concentrated mainly on social phenomena within the boundaries of the United States. A certain amount of ethnocentrism is probably to be expected in any social science, since its scholars are bound to be disproportionately influenced by the conditions of their own country and their own historical epoch. Nevertheless, the preoccupation with things American has earned for sociology the criticism that it is parochial, a criticism that also persists to some degree. However, since World War II and particularly in the past decade, this domestic emphasis has begun to give way to a more genuinely comparative approach in many of the subfields of sociology.[6] Again, the reasons for this shift are numerous, but the recent emergence of America as an unequivocally internationalist power, and its interest and involvement in the affairs of nations throughout the world have probably been as important as anything else in stimulating comparative studies.

The "comparativist" perspective is apparent throughout this book. Arthur Stinchcombe, for example, illustrates the features of formal organizations by reference to Chilean and Soviet as well as American data; Reissman illuminates the principles of stratification by means of a brief comparative analysis of the American, classical Indian, and British systems of social ranking; Stanton Wheeler gives appropriate Norwegian data to illustrate the general features of social deviance; Lipset, in a brief essay, attempts to account for the structure of the major types of political parties throughout the world and, in this way, throws light on the nature and functions of the American party system; and hardly a page without a comparative reference can be found in the chapter by Wilbert E. Moore on economic and professional institutions, the chapter by Halsey on educational institutions, and the chapter by Stephens on family and kinship.

---

[5] Mihailo Popovich, "What the American Sociologists Think about Their Science and Its Problems," *The American Sociologist*, 1, 134–135 (1966).

[6] For example, Reinhard Bendix and Seymour Martin Lipset, in their introduction to the second edition (1966) of their reader in social stratification (the first was published in 1953), state that in the dozen years that have intervened between the editions the field of social stratification showed a "major shift of emphasis" in the direction of comparative studies. *Class, Status, and Power: Social Stratification in Comparative Perspective,* second edition (New York: The Free Press, 1966), p. xiii.

3. Many texts on sociology are written at a very elementary level. In one respect this is an understandable practice, since many students study sociology only after they come to college. But a frequent cost of elementary exposition is that the subject matter becomes oversimplified and watered down and, therefore, less likely to provoke the student's imagination. Moreover, I am convinced that in the late 1960's most introductory textbooks in sociology are too easy for freshmen college students. Many freshmen have already been exposed to some sociological concepts and data, since more and more courses in social science are working their way into high-school curricula. And, at the college level, educational standards are continuing to rise; the quality of students is improving steadily; and most departments in most colleges are trying to upgrade, radically, their instruction and training.

On the basis of these considerations I have urged all of the contributors to write their chapters on a more sophisticated level than is found in most sociology texts but, at the same time, to keep the exposition within the reach of the intelligent and interested college freshman. I think that the relative difficulty of this book is an asset rather than a liability. After almost a decade of teaching, I have concluded that the greatest danger in the college classroom is not, as some believe, that the student is overworked, but that he is bored with unchallenging materials. This danger becomes more apparent each year, as a greater proportion of students entering institutions of higher learning are intelligent, serious, and ambitious individuals.

4. Although most texts on sociology are written by one or sometimes two authors, most symposia or readers are collections of already published articles that were originally prepared for purposes other than undergraduate instruction. In this book, an intermediate strategy has been adopted. All of the chapters were especially commissioned, and I worked closely with all of the contributors. This strategy has advantages over the single-author text, since it allows established authorities in the different subfields of sociology to give a more definitive treatment of their specialties than is possible when one man tries to cover the field. On the other hand, a book with chapters by different authors necessarily creates problems of conceptual unity and integration. The danger is that each author will simply write in his own language and within his own perspective, with the result that the student reads a dozen discrete essays and emerges with an unintegrated, shreds-and-patches view of the field. From the outset I have been aware of this danger, and have attempted to deal with it in the following ways.

First, before any author was asked to contribute, I gave the most careful consideration to the division of the book into parts, the outline of chapters, and the choice of contributors. On pp. xv–xvii I outline the logic of the organization of the book. The broad outline was suggested originally by Professor Morris Janowitz of the University of Chicago, consulting editor to the publisher. I reorganized and elaborated this outline before its final adaptation. The decision on the authors for the chapters was mine, and I am happy that each one selected found it possible to prepare a chapter on his own specialty.

Second, before any chapter was drafted, I sent a letter to each contributor, describing the objectives and emphases of the text, and requested that he keep these in mind while preparing his contribution. Also, I asked each author to emphasize special topics and issues, so that there would be representativeness of coverage, no repetitiveness and overlapping, but a measure of conceptual continuity throughout the book. Furthermore, I encouraged him to make his contribution his own distinctive product, so that the student would not get the erroneous impression that sociology is a really unified field.

Third, I kept in close contact with each contributor during the preparation of his manuscript. In most cases, he sent me an outline of his chapter, then a polished first draft, and then a reasonably final version. I read all of these with great care, evaluating them both as a sympathetic but critical professional colleague and as an editor interested in substantive and sylistic continuity.

Finally, in my introduction to the book (pp. 2–22), I offer a view of contemporary sociological inquiry in broad perspective. Within this perspective I attempt to locate the work of the several contributors, and to relate the main themes of their chapters to one another and to the sociological enterprise in general.

I hope that this plan and its execution result in an advanced and challenging introduction to sociology for new students—an introduction that capitalizes on the skills of men established in their fields, and that balances the themes of both diversity and unity in the discipline of sociology.

NEIL J. SMELSER

*Berkeley, California*
*1967*

# Acknowledgments

I am grateful for the thorough editorial treatment given to this book by the staff of the publisher. I express my appreciation to William Gum, editor for Wiley, who not only supervised the editing but carried the lion's share of responsibility for recruiting authors, for prodding them when deadlines approached, and for generally maintaining good rapport among all persons involved in bringing this volume into print. Malcolm B. Easterlin handled the final editing of the text with skill and tact. On several occasions I exchanged suggestions and advice with Nancy Unger who is mainly responsible for arranging the book's design and the artwork for each section and chapter.

The format of the illustrations was planned by Lenord Bethel, Michael Edelson, and the Wiley staff. Lenord Bethel is responsible for all of the artwork and for the general design of each illustration. Michael Edelson is responsible for all of the photographs with these exceptions: the photograph in George C. Homans' chapter is by Wayne Miller from Magnum; the photograph of the suburban community in Leo F. Schnore's chapter is by Eve Arnold from Magnum; the photograph of the stock exchange in Wilbert Moore's chapter is by Charles Harbutt from Magnum; and the photograph of the mother and child in Philip E. Slater's chapter is by Eve Arnold from Magnum.

The cover design is by Lenord Bethel.

N. J. S.

# Organization of the Book

Two principles guided me in organizing the headings and chapters. (1) For purposes of developing a science of sociology, it is more fruitful to conceive of the field in terms of analytic aspects of social behavior instead of in terms of concrete social phenomena. (2) In introducing the student to sociology, it is best to proceed from simple to complex matters. Let me illustrate how I applied these principles.

1. As the student becomes more familiar with sociology, he will discover that the field can be divided according to several different criteria. Some subdivisions appear to be named after concrete social groups and social structures—for example, rural sociology, race relations, and sociology of the family. Other subdivisions appear to follow the names of the basic social institutions—for example, sociology of religion, sociology of education, and sociology of law. Finally, some subdivisions refer to analytic aspects of social life that do not correspond to any concrete group or structure. Stratification, for example, refers to the principle of hierarchy, not to any particular arrangements of social classes; political sociology refers to the distribution and exercise of power, not to any particular governmental structures; and deviance and social control refers to a set of fundamental social processes that pervade all concrete social arrangements.

While criteria of naming subdivisions after concrete social groups and basic social institutions have the advantage of referring to readily identifiable social phenomena, subdivisions of sociology in terms of groups and institutions are too often restricted in their reference to particular historical circumstances. Race relations seems to be a very good subfield for countries like the United States, South Africa, and Indonesia where racial groupings play a salient role; but this subfield does not seem to apply readily to racially and ethnically homogeneous societies. Again, the sociology of law seems to be an appropriate subfield for societies like ours, where law is such an important social institution; but, for societies governed largely by unwritten mores, the sociology of law has little relevance. A more general, analytic characterization, such as social control, would be preferable, since it encompasses both legal and nonlegal types of social regulation. Indeed, it might be argued that unless sociology is ultimately conceived in terms of the analytic aspects of social behavior, a discipline with truly general principles is not possible, since its subdivisions will be restricted to particular historical circumstances.

Any meaningful subdivision of a textbook into parts and chapters necessarily involves a compromise among the three principles of division just discussed. This book represents such a compromise. But, in addition, I have leaned toward emphasizing the analytic aspects of social behavior rather than its historically specific manifestations. For example, instead of listing a whole string of concrete social problems—such as delinquency, suicide, mental illness, and divorce—I asked the contributors to analyze these problems within the framework of basic sociological concepts, such as deviance and social control,[1] the relations between social and personal integration,[2] and the effects of social stratification on individual behavior.[3] Instead of treating race relations as a subject in itself, I asked several contributors to consider it within a framework of basic sociological variables—community organization,[4] social stratification,[5] social control,[6] and socialization within educational structures.[7] By following this strategy, I attempted to develop an approach that permits the student to appreciate the power of general sociological variables and principles to illuminate many varieties of concrete social phenomena.

2. The several parts of the book constitute a progression from the simple to the complex. Part I contains an account of *several basic ingredients of social life.* Homans examines some of the fundamental psychological principles of human behavior, and attempts to use them as building blocks for analyzing quite complex social activity. Schnore traces the implications of the fundamental fact that man's social existence is bounded in spatial relations. Stinchcombe explores the ways in which human and nonhuman resources are combined into purposive organizational action. And Reissman isolates the universal facet of social existence that both persons and roles are evaluated in hierarchical terms.

In Part II, the contributors deal with a more complex task—the task of spelling out the ways in which the basic ingredients *combine into institutions.* Four important institutional complexes were selected—the economic, the religious, the educational, and the political. This part makes no pretense at exhaustiveness, but attempts to provide the student with a selective introduction to the insights that sociologists can generate about institutional life.

Although the contributors to Parts I and II do analyze processes of social

---

[1] See Wheeler, *infra,* pp. 604–610.
[2] See Slater, *infra,* pp. 570–576.
[3] See Reissman, *infra,* pp. 253–261.
[4] See Schnore, *infra,* pp. 128–133.
[5] See Reissman, *infra,* pp. 240–244.
[6] See Wheeler, *infra,* p. 625.
[7] See Halsey, *infra,* pp. 421–423.

adjustment and change to a degree, the overall emphasis is structural. Part III is devoted more explicitly to *processes within social structures.* Stephens' chapter on family and kinship introduces the student to the social settings that are built around the processes of procreating human beings and creating social personalities. Slater focuses more specifically on the processes by which society forms the personality and influences its functioning. And Wheeler considers the social processes that emerge when individuals deviate from standards of social conduct and counteractive mechanisms come into play. Finally, Part IV—Social Change—adds the last dimension of complexity by raising questions of *changes in social structures themselves.* In this way, each part of the book builds on the parts that have gone before.

N. J. S.

# CONTENTS

Introduction                                           1
  Neil J. Smelser

**Part I.  BASIC SOCIAL STRUCTURES**                   23

  1  Fundamental Social Processes                      27
     George C. Homans
  2  Community                                         79
     Leo F. Schnore
  3  Formal Organizations                             151
     Arthur L. Stinchcombe
  4  Social Stratification                            203
     Leonard Reissman

**Part II.  SOCIAL INSTITUTIONS**                     269

  5  Economic and Professional Institutions           273
     Wilbert E. Moore
  6  Religious Institutions                           329
     Peter L. Berger
  7  The Sociology of Education                       381
     A. H. Halsey
  8  Political Sociology                              435
     Seymour Martin Lipset

**Part III.  SOCIALIZATION PROCESS**                  501

  9  Family and Kinship                               505
     William N. Stephens
 10  Social Bases of Personality                      545
     Philip E. Slater
 11  Deviant Behavior                                 601
     Stanton Wheeler

**Part IV.  SOCIAL CHANGE**                    **667**

12   Processes of Social Change                 671
     *Neil J. Smelser*

Author Index                                    729

Subject Index                                   737

# INTRODUCTION

*Neil J. Smelser*

## The Substance of Sociology

It is difficult to describe the main features of sociology in a few paragraphs. Like many other social sciences, it is characterized by a proliferation of overlapping and sometimes competing "schools of thought" [1] and, consequently, there is great disagreement among sociologists about the fundamental problems, concepts, theories, and methods of research in the discipline. Moreover, the field displays an increasing number of subdivisions—for instance, sociology and the family, stratification, religion, medicine, leisure, law, deviance, and collective behavior—each of which differs in one or more respects from the other. Because of this internal diversity, it is presumptuous to try to develop a single view of the field. Necessarily, then, my characterization of the substance of sociology and of the nature of sociological explanation is an approximate one; it overemphasizes some aspects of the field and underemphasizes other aspects; and it glosses over many disagreements.

A good starting point is the definition of sociology given by Max Weber (1864–1920), who stands as one of the giants of the sociological tradition and whose work is discussed in many chapters of this text. Weber considers the proper subject matter of sociology as the "understanding of social action" in order that we may arrive at a "causal explanation of its course and effects." [2] The key term is "social action." [3] By "action" Weber meant "all human behavior when and insofar as the acting individual attaches a subjective meaning to it." Thus, a purely reflex action such as a knee jerk would not be "action" because no "subjective meaning" is involved in its occurrence.[4] Action can be considered "social" insofar as "by virtue of the subjective meaning attached to it by the acting individual (or individuals), it takes acount of the behavior of others and is thereby oriented in its course." [5] According to Weber's definition, then, the subject matter of sociology is very broad, covering all items of the individual's social

[1] For two contrasting efforts to classify the major schools of sociological thought, see Don Martindale, *The Nature and Types of Sociological Theory* (Boston, Houghton Mifflin, 1960), and Helmut R. Wagner, "Types of Sociological Theory: Toward a System of Classification," *American Sociological Review*, 28, 735–742 (1963).

[2] Max Weber, *The Theory of Social and Economic Organization*, translated by A. M. Henderson and Talcott Parsons (New York: Oxford University Press, 1947), p. 88.

[3] For all intents and purposes, the terms "social action" and "social behavior" can be construed as having identical meanings.

[4] Weber's definition of "action" seems very close to George Homans' definition of "activity," which Homans uses as the starting point of his analysis of fundamental social processes. Homans' definition is "some intelligible unit of voluntary behavior— voluntary in the sense that it is not a mere reflex action like the familiar knee jerk." *Infra,* p. 32.

[5] Max Weber, *op. cit.*, p. 88.

behavior, and has both a psychological (subjective meaning) and an inter-personal (oriented to others) dimension.

On closer examination, however, Weber's definition requires some nar-rowing down, since it appears to apply to other branches of inquiry besides sociology. Consider an item of behavior such as a businessman's decision to invest in a new product. Normally we would think of this act as being "economic" in that it concerns the allocations of scarce re-sources for purposes of production and consumption of commodities. But the decision to invest can also be considered as being within sociology's legitimate scope, since it certainly has subjective meaning for the investor, and it is oriented to the actual and expected behavior of other actors—bankers, other businessmen, and consumers, for example. Similarly, we would normally consider an individual's vote for a candidate for local office to be a political act in the first instance, since it is directly related to the distribution and exercise of political power. But it, too, has a sub-jective aspect and an interpersonal reference; therefore, it can be regarded as a proper item for sociological analysis.

From these observations we must conclude that sociology does not deal with a special class of behavioral data; instead, it deals with behavioral data *as interpreted within a special type of conceptual framework*. To illustrate this important point, let us consider another item of behavior —the act of a man purchasing tickets for four to Hawaii, where he plans to spend two weeks on vacation. To interpret this act in terms of its *psychological* significance, we would examine the man's motives for pur-chasing the tickets, the particular reasons for his choice of Hawaii as a vacation spot, and perhaps the place of his attitudes toward leisure in his total psychic system. To interpret the act in its *economic* significance, we would consider the purchase of the tickets in terms of alternatives that the individual might have chosen; we might also wish to total it with similar purchases by others and assess its impact as a demand on the airline industry. To interpret the act in its *sociological* significance, we would note that the other three passengers are the purchaser's wife and children, and we might want to analyze the decision-making process within the family that led to the choice of Hawaii as a vacation spot. My task here is to demarcate the subject matter of sociology by outlining the distinctive conceptual frameworks to which behavioral data are referred for assess-ment. In the next section I shall discuss the manner in which sociological explanations are generated within these frameworks.

One common conceptual framework is found in Weber's notion of the "subjective meaning" of human behavior. This expression suggests that behavior is described in terms of its psychological significance to the actor considered as an individual person. Stated another way, the conceptual framework that is used to organize the description of behavior is the psychological system of the human being—for example, his motives, his attitudes, his emotions, his skills, and his sense of identity. Properly speaking, this framework is the focus of psychology. But it has also served in one form or another as the focus of a long-standing (if still indefinite) subdivision of sociology—social psychology.

Several contributors to this book make explicit use of the psychological framework. George Homans, in the opening chapter, first indicates that the kind of data of interest to him is "voluntary activity," and gives as an example a man casting for fish. Then Homans assesses this activity in terms of its psychological significance to the individual—that is, how frequently he is rewarded in the activity, how important the activity is to him, and how he reacts to obstacles that arise in his pursuit of the activity. Next, Homans turns to social interaction—those kinds of activities in which human beings influence one another—and analyzes this according to the same psychological concepts and propositions used in examining nonsocial behavior.[6] As another example, Philip Slater asserts that if we are to understand human behavior, we must grasp the principle that "[psychological] ambivalance [is] the keystone of individual motivation." That is, we should not conceive of any individual as simply loving or hating objects or persons but, instead, we should conceive of him as continually attempting to deal with the fact that he simultaneously loves and hates all objects and persons that are meaningful to him. Then, using the concept of ambivalence, Slater accounts for why some people are more authoritarian and intolerant of deviance than others, and why some people are more rebellious than others.[7] In both of these illustrations, behavior is described and analyzed by reference to some version of an individual's psychological system.

Sociologists frequently speak in terms of *groups* of persons instead of individual persons. When they do this, they are extending their conceptualization to a higher level of abstraction. In other words, the main basis for the concept of the group is a number of individual persons who are linked together as members. But, nevertheless, the ultimate organizing concept is still the individual, because it is the person that is considered as the unit of the group. When sociologists refer to a family as a group, for example, they refer an adult man, an adult woman, and their several children as its members. William Stephens calls this as a "small residential kin group."[8] Or, when sociologists refer to voluntary associations, such as trade unions or political parties, they think of them as being made up

---

[6] *Infra,* pp. 32–45.

[7] *Infra,* pp. 572–576.

[8] *Infra,* p. 516.

of numbers of persons who are considered as members.[9] Sometimes sociologists study social groups as units in their own right, interacting with one another without particular reference to their individual members. S. M. Lipset, for example, discusses competition among political parties; and Leonard Reissman, in his treatment of Marx, discusses conflict among entire social class groupings.[10] Certainly it is legitimate to analyze social processes in terms of interactions among groups. But it is also important to realize that the concept of group life rests on a conceptual progression involving several steps—beginning with behavioral data, moving to the level of individual persons, then to the level of aggregates of persons considered in their significance as members and, finally, to the level of the aggregates considered in relation to one another.

This conceptual progression—from behavior to person to group—provides a number of frameworks that have found widespread use in the sociological tradition. Now let us examine a second type of progression, similar to the first one in that it begins with behavioral data, but different in that it moves up a different line of abstraction. The second type of progression is suggested in Weber's definition of the *social* dimension of action—"action [that] takes account of the behavior of others." As before, let us take a particular behavioral example as a starting point; Homans' illustration of a person asking advice of another person and subsequently receiving information from him is an appropriate one. On the one hand, it is possible to assess this interaction, as Homans does, in terms of the mutual rewards and costs to each individual. This would constitute a social-psychological approach. But, on the other hand, it is also possible to assess the event in terms of the interaction itself—that is, what is going on *between* the two individuals, without explicit reference to psychological processes occurring *within* either of the individuals. In the example given, we might wish to characterize the transaction in terms of the relations between "receiver" and "giver" of information, or between "subordinate" and "superordinate." In this way we describe the event in terms of the quality of the relation between persons rather than the quality of persons themselves. The notion of the relation or interaction thus becomes the basic conceptual unit.

Sociologists use the term *role* to refer to situations in which interactions between individuals repeat themselves in a regular way over a period of time. Accordingly, we refer to the roles of husband and wife, politician and voter, employer and employee, and businessman and consumer. Notice particularly that the concept of a person and the concept of role are very

---

[9] See the discussions of trade unions and political parties by Stinchcombe and Lipset, respectively, *Infra,* pp. 188–192 and 456–462.

[10] *Infra,* pp. 462–468 and 213–218.

different things, even though both are conceptualizations based on a common body of behavioral data. Actually, the two concepts cut across one another. A person occupies many different roles; and a role cannot refer to the complete person, but only to selected aspects of his behavior. The two concepts, in short, are different ways of organizing our thinking about human behavior.

Continuing the progression from behavioral data to role interaction, we move next to the concept of *social structure* which, for many sociologists, constitutes the chief conceptual focus of the discipline. Social structure can be defined as identifiable patterns of roles that are organized primarily around the fulfillment of some social function or activity. Following A. H. Halsey's formulation, for example, educational structure refers to that cluster of roles organized around the functions of transmitting culture and forming social personalities.[11] Following Wilbert Moore, economic structure refers to that cluster of roles organized around the production and distribution of scarce goods and services.[12] An even more abstract concept used by sociologists is *social system*, which refers to a set of patterned relations among structural elements so that changes in one element set up pressures for adjustment or other types of change in remaining units. Even concepts as abstract as social system, however, rest ultimately on abstractions from the relatively simple notion of role or patterned interaction.[13]

Now we can see how the central sociological concepts of "group" and "social structure" result from different progressions of conceptual abstraction. The two concepts refer to different aspects of social behavior. Or, to emphasize the conceptual aspects, they are different ways of looking at social behavior. Furthermore, the same concrete behavioral phenomena can be legitimately characterized according to both aspects. For example, a voluntary organization such as a trade union can be described *both* as a group with individual members *and* as a system of interrelated roles —officers, shop stewards, representatives of locals, and the like. In the present state of development of the field, sociologists focus more or less equally on both of these aspects; it has not yet been settled definitely whether either, both, or neither is the best basis for organizing sociological knowledge.

Sociologists think of all social behavior—whether this behavior is

[11] *Infra*, p. 385.

[12] *Infra*, p. 281.

[13] In speaking of social systems, for example, Parsons and Shils state that "[for] most purposes the conceptual unit of the social system is the role." Talcott Parsons and Edward A. Shils, "Values, Motives, and Systems of Action," in Parsons and Shils, eds., *Toward a General Theory of Action* (Cambridge, Mass.: Harvard University Press, 1951), p. 190.

conceptualized according to the progression involving individuals and groups or according to progression involving interaction and social structure—as being subject to certain kinds of *constraints* or *social regulation.* These constraints are also considered as part of the subject matter of sociology. Although the constraints are clearly geared to the control of behavior, they are not, of course, always effective. Sociologists usually divide the constraints on social behavior into three categories—sanctions, norms, and value orientations.

The notion of *sanctions* is vividly represented in the fable of the master who induces his donkey to move forward both by dangling a carrot in front of his nose and by prodding him with a stick from behind. Stated a little more formally, sanctions refer to both gratifications (carrots) and deprivations (sticks) that control behavior with varying degrees of effectiveness. An example of a positive or gratifying sanction is an insurance company's practice of reducing premium payments for automobile owners who have an accident-free record during the preceding year; a corresponding example of a negative or depriving sanction is the company's practice of canceling policies of drivers who habitually become involved in costly accidents. An objective of both sanctions is to exercise control over owners' driving habits. Sanctions can take many forms—money, political coercion, ridicule, appeal to a person's sense of duty, snubbing, and winking, to name a few. The psychological aspects of sanctions are outlined by Homans in his discussion of the ways in which rewards and punishments determine how and why an individual behaves the way he does.[14] The social significance of sanctions is outlined in Moore's discussion of how money and other media of exchange facilitate the distribution of commodities through the economy.[15]

*Norms* refer to expectations and standards that regulate the interaction among people. Stephens gives some of the clearest illustrations of norms in his account of rules governing relations among kinsmen: brothers and sisters should not have sexual relations; a child should defer to his father; and an uncle should joke with his nieces and nephews.[16] Other illustrations of norms are found in a society's legal codes; still others are found in informal, unwritten expectations that grow up between two persons as they form a friendship. Norms stand in a very definite relation to sanctions; they specify the occasions on which sanctions should be withheld or applied. This means that a person is normally rewarded or not punished when he behaves in accordance with normative expectations, and is normally punished or not rewarded when he fails to do so.

[14] *Infra,* pp. 33–39.
[15] *Infra,* pp. 305–311.
[16] *Infra,* pp. 508–516.

*Value orientations* are cultural standards that indicate the general goals deemed desirable for organized social life. They provide the ultimate meaning and legitimacy for social arrangements and social behavior. An example of an important value in American society is "equality of opportunity." It is widely considered to be a desirable end in itself. Reissman demonstrates the importance of such a value in social life in his discussion of race in America and caste in India. He observes that many Americans are outraged by the notion of a Negro caste, and many persons in classical India were perfectly content with the existence of castes. He explains

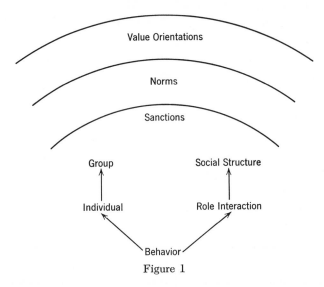

Figure 1

that this difference results from the fact that the value of equality of opportunity is institutionalized in America, but was not in classical India. For this reason, caste arrangements seem offensive and illegitimate in one country and not in the other.[17] (I do not mean to exaggerate the uniformity of value consensus by this example; some Americans do not fully accept the value of equality of opportunity, and some persons in classical India found caste to be an undesirable institution.) Value orientations stand in the same relation to norms as norms stand to sanctions; just as norms justify and specify the occasions for the application of sanctions, so values legitimize and give meaning to norms.

These are some of the main ingredients of the sociological perspective, viewed as progressions of conceptual abstraction from behavioral data. The relations among these ingredients are represented graphically in Figure 1. Viewed another way, these ingredients constitute the subject

---

[17] *Infra,* pp. 241, 244–246.

matter, or the *dependent variables*, for sociology. A dependent variable in sociology is a social phenomenon (such as an item of behavior, a regularity in social structure), variations in which the sociologist wishes to explain. Typical sociological variables are rates of migration, rates of divorce, and distinctive forms of family structure. The sociologist is interested in explaining variations in these kinds of phenomena—why they persist and why they change.

The student will discover again and again in this book that the contributors are concerned with the explanation of regularities and variations in the ingredients shown in Figure 1. Consider the following examples. Both Homans and Wheeler ask under what conditions individuals' behavior conforms to group norms.[18] Both Berger and Slater generalize this question, and raise the classical sociological problem of how social order or cohesion is possible at all, in view of pervasive human tendencies for conflict and deviance.[19] Schnore asks why people of similar socioeconomic status and racial background live close to one another in urban communities.[20] Stinchcombe asks why people in some occupations work longer hours than people in other occupations.[21] Reissman asks why India's traditional caste system appears to be giving way to a less rigid system of stratification in modern times.[22] Moore asks what factors determine the different mixtures of the free-market principle and the state-control principle of distribution of goods and services in various societies.[23] Berger asks what social forces make for the secularization of religious life in modern times.[24] Stephens asks why the norm prohibiting incest is so nearly universal in its occurrence.[25] Halsey asks why the children of some social groups perform better in schools than the children of others.[26] In a nutshell, then, the sociological enterprise is to account for regularities and variations in those phenomena that constitute the sociological framework.

Before discussing what sociologists do when they actually attempt to explain social phenomena, let us examine a few of the tasks that a sociologist must face as he poses scientific problems—the tasks of defining, classifying, and describing the phenomena that are to be explained. Although these tasks assume a special form in sociological inquiry, they are not limited to sociology; indeed, they are encountered in every kind of scientific investigation.

The sociologist, before attempting to explain any social phenomenon,

[18] *Infra*, pp. 47–51 and 633–638.
[19] *Infra*, pp. 339–343 and 555–558.
[20] *Infra*, pp. 122–133.
[21] *Infra*, pp. 180–183.
[22] *Infra*, pp. 247–249.

[23] *Infra*, pp. 289–291.
[24] *Infra*, pp. 369–378.
[25] *Infra*, pp. 524–530.
[26] *Infra*, pp. 414–432.

must *define* his dependent variables as clearly and distinctly as possible, or he will find himself in the embarrassing position of not knowing what it is he wishes to explain. To define a phenomenon is to draw conceptual boundaries around it and thus to indicate what qualifies as a legitimate item for study and what does not. The importance of the definition is illustrated in Schnore's chapter on communities. Schnore's ultimate task is the general sociological one: to account for the major lines of empirical variation in community life. But a necessary preliminary is to arrive at a definition of community. Early in his chapter, Schnore discusses a number of different definitions that have been offered by sociologists—community as a psychological entity, community as a simple geographical entity, and the like. After reviewing the relative advantages and disadvantages of each, he proposes his own definition: "the localized population which is interdependent on a daily basis, and which carries on a highly generalized set of activities in and through a set of institutions which provides on a day-to-day basis the full range of goods and services necessary for its continuity as a social and economic entity." [27] This definition provides Schnore with a basis for including and excluding various kinds of social groupings under the heading "community." For example, the city and environs of Terre Haute, Indiana, would readily qualify as a community, since it meets all of the requirements called for in the definition—localization, self-sufficiency, and others. But the definition also excludes other groupings that have conventionally been termed "communities." For instance, a "community of scholars" would not qualify because it is not geographically located; and a "prison community" would not qualify because its goals are too specific.[28] Regardless of the ultimate merits of Schnore's particular definition, *some* definition of community is necessary if the sociologist is to know what kinds of social groupings count as communities and what kinds do not.

The sociologist must establish some ways of *classifying* the respects in which the social phenomenon under study actually varies. To classify is to set up criteria for the subdivision of the phenomenon (the external boundaries of which have already been established by the definition). Again, Schnore selects a number of dimensions that he considers particularly important in community life—the degree to which a community is dependent of other communities, the size of a community, its density of population, its age, and its composition according to sex, age, and occupation.[29] In selecting these bases for classifying variation in community life, Schnore is simultaneously establishing a number of terms to describe communities.

Finally, the sociologist must actually *describe* the variations in the

[27] *Infra*, p. 95.    [29] *Infra*, pp. 96–100.
[28] *Infra*, pp. 90–95.

phenomena under study, so that he knows what kind of variations he is to explain or predict. To describe is to apply combinations of the available classificatory terms to the empirical instances of a phenomenon. Thus, much of Schnore's attention in the latter part of his chapter is devoted to describing community changes according to the classificatory dimensions developed earlier—changes in size, density, and composition.[30] In connection with the description of variations in empirical phenomena, the sociologist is confronted with a great many methodological problems: Has he selected adequate empirical indicators for his general descriptive concepts? Are the empirical indicators properly coded? Are they quantifiable? The contributors to this text do not give a great deal of explicit consideration to these methodological questions—many of which are often reserved for courses in statistics and research methods—but Stinchcombe discusses of the kinds of empirical information that can be gathered in order to describe various structures and processes in formal organizations.[31]

The tasks of defining, classifying, and describing variables are intimately related to one another. These relations can be illustrated briefly by a single dependent variable that sociologists frequently wish to explain—the rate of divorce. Suppose the sociological investigator defines divorce simply as "the dissolution of the marriage relation." The objective of such a definition is apparent—to circumscribe the boundaries of divorce and to set it off clearly from other phenomena that are not to be regarded as cases of divorce (in this case, intact marriages and nonmarital relations). When the investigator regards the definition in this way, however, it is immediately evident that in defining a variable he is simultaneously establishing a system of classification containing at least two classes: one class including instances of the variable (divorces) and one class including instances that are excluded from the scope of the variable (nondivorces). Thus the very process of defining a variable entails the operation of classifying it relative to the phenomena falling outside the scope of the definition. Indeed, definition and classification are simply different aspects of the same conceptual operation.

When defining a variable, it is essential that the sociologists demarcate its boundaries carefully. Consider again the definition of divorce as "the dissolution of the marriage relation." This definition refers without ambiguity to legally dissolved marriage relations. But in its simple form the definition does not reveal whether two other kinds of dissolutions should be included or excluded from consideration—first, legal separations (such as arrangements for temporary maintenance) that are not finally

[30] *Infra,* pp. 115–150.
[31] *Infra,* pp. 197–201.

dissolved marriages in the eyes of the law; and, second, desertions and other informal separations that have no special legal status as dissolutions. Furthermore, the definition does not indicate whether the divorce rate should be based on all persons ever divorced, or only on those who have been divorced but who have not remarried. The investigator may wish to include or exclude these categories of separation, depending on the scientific problems guiding his research; but no matter what his decision is, the boundaries of the dependent variable should be drawn precisely and unambiguously.

Suppose the investigator wishes to study all types of marital separations, but for purposes of the study he wishes to distinguish among the four categories implied in the preceding paragraph: (1) legally divorced persons who have never remarried; (2) legally divorced persons who have re-married; (3) persons legally separated but not divorced; and (4) persons informally separated. In this case he is dividing the major dependent variable (marital separations) into several subclasses, each of which receives a definition and is set off from the other subclasses. This operation once again reveals the intimate connection between definition and classification. Each time an investigator divides a variable into a number of classes, he simultaneously establishes a number of subdefinitions; and each time he defines a variable, he simultaneously classifies it relative to a larger class of phenomena.

The description of a variable depends very much on how it has been defined and classified. Suppose an investigator defines divorce as "the dissolution of the marriage relation" but restricts the reference of the definition to legally dissolved marriages. Suppose, further, that he wishes to describe the course of change in the divorce rate during the past 100 years. In keeping with his definition, he decides to measure the change by using divorce-court records as an indicator. For some purposes this descriptive measure may be a satisfactory one. But suppose, finally, that while the divorce rate as measured by this indicator shows a steady increase over the century, informal desertions—which are not measured by the index—underwent a corresponding decline, as social groups formally relying on informal desertion made more and more regular use of the divorce courts. In this hypothetical case, the apparent increase of "dissolution of the marriage relation" would actually be only a change in the *form* of marital dissolution, and would therefore misrepresent the true course of the rate of marital dissolution. Therefore, the sociologist would be led to generate an explanation for an increase which had not actually occurred! This example shows how important it is for the sociologist to make sure that his definitions, classifications, and empirical descriptions stand in proper relation to one another.

## The Nature of Sociological Explanation

The sociologist creates a scientific problem when he poses a "why" question about the observed or predicted variation in some sociological phenomenon—for instance, social behavior, social roles, norms, and values. To put it another way, the sociologist interested in explanation asks under what conditions a certain type of variation in a sociological phenomenon occurs. Explanation involves a search for conditions associated with changes in the dependent variable; these conditions are also frequently referred to as factors, causes, or *independent variables*. For example, given an accurately measured increase in the divorce rate over the past 100 years, the sociologist might look at the following conditions to explain this increase—the degree to which urbanization and industrialization had changed the family structure in the meantime; the degree to which inter-religious marriage had increased in the meantime; and the degree to which laws and norms concerning divorce had become more permissive in the meantime. Changes in these independent variables would then be related to changes in the rate of divorce.

Explanation breaks down into two distinguishable operations: formulating *hypotheses*, or establishing discrete relations between independent and dependent variables; and logically ordering the independent and dependent variables into more complicated conceptual systems, known as *models* or *theories*. I shall discuss these two operations separately.

### Sociological Hypotheses

What kinds of independent variables does the sociologist usually use to explain variations in social phenomena? Again, it is not easy to answer this question definitively, since sociologists differ greatly among themselves in the explanatory variables that they stress. It is possible, however, to illustrate systematically from the chapters in this text how sociologists have gone about their search for causes. In doing this (if I may anticipate the discussion in advance), I shall reach the apparently—but not really—paradoxical conclusion that sociologists find most of their explanations by turning to those very phenomena that, in other contexts, they may wish to explain.

The history of sociological thought has witnessed the rise and fall of many theories that might be called "nonsociological"—theories that attempt to explain the characteristics of social life on the basis of some biological, climatological, geographical, or other nonsocial factors. Some theorists interested in suicide in the late nineteenth century, for example, attempted to attribute differences in suicide rates to differences in climate and seasonal temperature.[32] By and large, these kinds of theories—especially those that are advanced as single-factor explanations—have been discredited in modern times. Nevertheless, most sociologists remain cognizant of the fact that physical and biological conditions affect social structures and social processes in important ways. To choose an obvious example, the social needs to transmit culture and socialize new personalities in families and educational institutions rest in part on the ultimate biological facts that human organisms are born immature and that they must be replaced when they die. Or, at a much more concrete level, the political fortunes of a nation may be profoundly shaken by a biological fact—when its powerful national leader is assassinated. Turning to the less obvious influences, it might be asked—as Schnore asks—to what extent the physical arrangements imposed by urban living create distinctive patterns of bureaucratization, stratification, human alienation, and social disorganization.[33] Or, as Stinchcombe points out, the age structure of a formal organization influences behavior within it in various ways; for example, if all of the available professorships in a university department are filled by men of forty, young men of twenty-five may be discouraged from competing for advancement, since there is little room at the top in the foreseeable future.[34]

Many sociologists—especially those who go by the name of social psychologists—turn to psychological concepts and principles as explanatory variables. Homans' chapter is a particularly clear illustration. His starting point is the pair of psychological assumptions that "the basic units of social behavior are the actions of individual men" and "that the actions are a function of their [psychological] payoffs [in terms of rewards and costs]." Homans asserts not only that elementary forms of behavior can be explained by these principles, but also that assertions about complex social behavior are reducible to these propositions. Even "human institutions and human societies . . . are the products of something that we think of as being weaker than water—individual human choices."[35] Indeed, Homans' whole chapter is a cumulative progression of explanations—beginning with simple items of human behavior and moving to complicated power and status structures—all presumably derived from a few simple psychological laws. Homans acknowledges that not all sociologists accept his particular type of

[32] For a criticism of these theories, see Émile Durkheim, *Suicide*, translated by John A. Spaulding and George Simpson (Glencoe, Ill.: The Free Press, 1951), pp. 104–122.
[33] *Infra*, pp. 132–150.
[34] *Infra*, pp. 193–194.
[35] *Infra*, pp. 31–32.

explanations. In fact, he is probably a spokesman for only a minority. However, his theory, no matter what its degree of acceptance, represents a particularly forceful statement of the role of psychological principles in understanding social phenomena.

Sociologists usually locate their explanatory variables in group memberships and positions in the social structure. Some would insist that these variables, being social, constitute the true focus of the discipline of sociology. This kind of explanation is illustrated by the following statements: blue-collar workers tend to vote Democratic more than white-collar workers; men tend to vote Democratic more than women; college professors tend to vote Democratic more than secondary-school teachers. In each case a dependent variable (voting behavior) is explained by referring to people's positions in the social structure.

Many instances of the social influence on individual behavior are cited in this text. Stinchcombe, for example, demonstrates how involvement in formal bureaucracies determines how much a person works, how specialized this work is, how satisfied he is with his work, and what kinds of political attitudes he might have.[36] Reissman, commenting on the stratification system as an explanatory focus, asserts that "a person's class position probably tells us more about the person than any other single fact." He illustrates this assertion by citing evidence that people who occupy different positions in the social ranking system are conscious of their class positions in differing degrees; they treat their children differently; and they show different propensities to develop mental disorders.[37]

Sociologists also attempt to account for the characteristics of one kind of social structure by relating it to another kind of social structure. Karl Marx's social theory, for example, maintains that the social class system of any society is determined by the society's distinctive mode of economic production. According to this theory, the core of the class system of a capitalist society is formed by the middle class or bourgeoisie, who control the means of production, and the working class or proletarians, who do not.[38] This approach—commonly referred to as "economic determinism"—has been criticized in many quarters. Moore offers a number of these criticisms in his chapter. But Moore cites many ways in which the structure of the economy and the structure of other parts of the society are related to one another. For example, he develops the familiar sociological argument that industrialization gives rise to an increased specialization of social

[36] *Infra*, pp. 173–188.
[37] *Infra*, pp. 252–261.
[38] For a brief exposition of the Marxian theory of stratification, see Reissman, *infra*, pp. 212–218.

roles and more complicated systems for coordinating these roles.[39] Lipset attributes some of the differences among national political systems to differences among stratification systems.[40] And Halsey attempts to account for some of the modern changes in the structure of educational institutions by referring to the demands for occupational and cultural specialization imposed by industrial society.[41] These illustrative connections among social structures, taken together, reveal a common sociological viewpoint: society is a number of different social structures that constitute a complex system of mutual dependence and mutual influence.

Hypotheses that link positions in the social structure with behavior always rest on at least implicit psychological assertions. Consider once again the hypothesis that blue-collar workers tend to vote Democratic more than white-collar workers. This hypothesis probably implies the psychological statement that blue-collar workers feel that the policies of the Democratic party are more favorable to their socioeconomic circumstances. To choose another example, most theories of social mobility—the movement of people from one layer of the socioeconomic hierarchy to another—rest on the psychological assumption that people prefer to occupy higher rather than lower positions in the stratification system. In some cases, however, the psychological underpinnings of hypotheses are not so simple. For instance, the psychological variables that may intervene between a person's position in the class structure and his disposition to develop mental disorders are very complex and seldom understood. I shall have more to say about the problem of handling a multiplicity of social and psychological variables in my discussion of the nature of sociological models and theories.

Sociologists also regard sanctions, norms, and value orientations—the major social constraints on behavior—as independent variables in many hypotheses. I have already mentioned the important place that Homans gives to rewards and punishments (sanctions) in his treatment of fundamental social processes. Stinchcombe also reviews the ways that resources are used in formal organizations "to motivate people—by payment, force, or moral suasion—to carry out the organizations' activities." [42] The chapter by Wheeler is the best illustration of the influence of norms on human behavior. This influence is obvious when people conform to normative expectations. But even when people deviate from norms, it is essential to regard the norms as important determinants of their behavior, since they constitute what is being deviated *from* and, in this way, influence the direction of behavior.[43] Finally, with regard to value orientations, several contributors to this book outline ways in which these cultural standards influence social

---

[39] *Infra*, pp. 293–300.
[40] *Infra*, pp. 458–462.
[41] *Infra*, pp. 399–410.

[42] *Infra*, pp. 160–164.
[43] *Infra*, pp. 605–609.

behavior and social structure. Berger analyzes what is the most famous sociological example of the independent influence of values—Max Weber's thesis that religious (especially ascetic) Protestantism constituted a cultural framework that was very conducive to the rise of rational bourgeois capitalism in Europe and the United States.[44] In addition, both Stinchcombe and Lipset deal with another theme developed by Weber and apply it to their special topics—how values provide a basis of legitimacy for different kinds of social and political organizations, and thus influence processes within them.[45]

As these many illustrations indicate, sociological hypotheses are formed when investigators attempt to establish causally meaningful relations between the various ingredients of the sociological framework—social behavior, group life, social structure, and the various constraints on social action. Depending on the scientific problem at hand, any of these variables may be treated either as independent (cause) or dependent (effect). Sociological explanation—at least, as we have analyzed it up to this point— is thus constituted by a multiplicity of hypotheses that have been established with varying degrees of confidence.

But adequate sociological explanation involves more than a long list of causally meaningful statements about social life. Sociologists also attempt to *organize* these statements into models and theories. Now I shall sketch some of the problems involved in generating these kinds of knowledge.

### Sociological Models and Theories

Sociologists frequently find that their efforts to explain social phenomena are made difficult by the fact that a given sociological variable is causally related not to one or two but to a myriad of other variables. Consequently, the sociologist cannot be content with establishing a few explanatory hypotheses, but must try to organize a great many associations among variables into a coherent framework. The difficulty of adequately explaining social phenomena can be illustrated by selecting a few issues from this book. Let us examine the ones below.

Sometimes the sociologist finds that one dependent variable is apparently explained by a great many different causes. Consider as a dependent variable, for example, the human attitude described under the heading "distributive justice." The essence of this attitude, as characterized by Homans, is that people in equal status positions should receive equal rewards and that people in unequal positions should receive unequal rewards.

[44] *Infra,* pp. 352–356.
[45] *Infra,* pp. 169–172 and 442–448.

A further aspect of the attitude is that the many different kinds of rewards received by a person should be more or less "in line" with one another. How can we account for the widespread existence of this attitude? Homans accounts for it in terms of his several basic psychological hypotheses involving reward, cost, value, and frustration-aggression.[46] Another explanation is offered by Freud in his work on the social psychology of groups. He maintained that all members of a group are desirous of the love of the leader (who represents a father), and are envious of one another for the leader's love. However, since all members cannot possibly gain his exclusive love, they renounce their selfish desires and believe that the leader does and should love all of them equally. "No one must want to put himself forward, and every one must be the same and have the same.[47] For Freud, this attitude underlies the growth of social justice in groups. Several contributors to this book besides Homans discuss distributive justice, but give still different explanations for it. Reissman, for example, cites the finding that attitudes favoring changes in the distribution of power in American society (that is, distributive justice) are stronger among people who experience status inconsistency in their lives (people, for example, who are high on one status reward, such as money, and low on another, such as education).[48] Moore also stresses the importance of distributive justice as an economic attitude, but traces its importance to a fundamentally religious origin.[49] The first thing a sociologist must do is to attempt to establish the validity of each of these explanatory hypotheses on its own merit. But—assuming that more than one of these hypotheses has validity—he must ask a series of further questions: Do the different explanatory hypotheses contradict one another? Or are they consistent? If consistent, how can their various contributions to the total explanation of the phenomenon of distributive justice be related to one another?

Consider another dependent variable—the tendency for some individuals to become more alienated from their social environment than others. Schnore asks in what way the conditions of urban living contribute to this tendency;[50] Stinchcombe raises the question of whether a person's position in formal organizations might offer an explanation;[51] and Moore considers the Marxian assertion that a man's relation to a machine-and-factory technology gives rise to alienation.[52] Again, the sociologist must

[46] *Infra*, pp. 62–67. See Stinchcombe's similar remarks on distributive justice, *infra*, p. 166.
[47] Sigmund Freud, *Group Psychology and the Analysis of the Ego*, Standard Edition (London: The Hogarth Press and the Institute of Psycho-analysis), Vol. 18, p. 120.
[48] *Infra*, pp. 256–257.         [51] *Infra*, pp. 179–180.
[49] *Infra*, pp. 312–313.         [52] *Infra*, pp. 295–297.
[50] *Infra*, pp. 144–145.

ask to what extent each of these is valid, and in what way the various factors might interact with one another to produce alienation.

At other times the sociologist finds that one independent variable exercises many different kinds of influences on other variables. In discussing the social effects of religion, for example, Berger notices that under some circumstances (for instance, in a small religious colony of hermits) religion may have no special effects at all on the larger society. Under other circumstances, religion may be a chief source of solidarity and control in a society. And under still other circumstances, religion may foster group cleavage and conflict, and may lead ultimately to some kind of social disorganization.[53] Faced with this apparent multiplicity of effects, the sociologist must undertake to sort them out in some way, asking under what conditions each kind becomes manifest. In short, he must *organize* as well as *accumulate* knowledge about the social effects of religion.

As a result of the principles of multiple causes for one effect and multiple effects of one cause, the sociologist often faces a situation in which a great array of determinants affects many different kinds of behavior. Consider, for example, the arguments put forth in Lipset's chapter on political institutions. With respect to the *dependent variables,* much of his chapter is devoted to generating explanations of people's political behavior. But, during the course of his exposition, it becomes clear that political behavior manifests itself in not one but many ways—expressing political attitudes verbally, voting in elections, working through party machinery, and joining radical political movements. In addition, while these several kinds of behavior are, from one standpoint, simply alternative ways of achieving political ends, it is also true that each activity is affected by a different pattern of determinants. On the side of the *independent variables,* Lipset considers the effects of political-party systems, social class, and religious groupings on political behavior. It also, the independent variables influence one another; stratification systems determine in part whether governments and political parties are democratically organized.[54] And, finally, political behavior itself affects the very same independent variables that originally gave rise to the behavior; for example, if a radical political movement succeeds in seizing power by violent revolution, this very event will certainly modify the class and religious systems of the society. All of this leads to the conclusion that the complexity of the empirical world makes life very difficult for the sociologist interested in generating coherent explanations of social phenomena.

How do sociologists deal with this interplay of social causes and effects?

---

[53] *Infra,* pp. 338–342.
[54] *Infra,* pp. 456–492.

Many times, of course, they do not deal with it at all, remaining content to seek connections among only a few variables. Sometimes, however, they attempt to assess the relative importance of different variables, and to combine numerous variables into a single explanatory framework. This framework is known as a *model* or—if it is a little more ambitious in scope— a *theory*. In this brief introduction I cannot pretend to give a survey, much less a critical evaluation of the numerous models and theories that have been created by sociologists. I can merely illustrate a few things that sociologists attempt to do in order to build manageable explanations when faced with a causal network containing a multiplicity of variables.

A social researcher frequently engages in what is known as multivariate analysis, the aim of which is to discover whether all of the *apparent* causes of a phenomenon are actually *real* causes. Let me illustrate this. In the early 1950's just at the time when McCarthyism was at its height in America, Stouffer surveyed a sample of the American population to discover some of the social factors that influence attitudes of political intolerance and anticommunism.[55] One of the findings that emerged from the study is that age is positively correlated with intolerance; older people tend to be more intolerant than younger ones. A second finding is that the level of education is negatively correlated with intolerance; the more education, the less intolerance. But since age and educational level are themselves negatively correlated (above the age of completed education, young people are more educated than old people), it is impossible to know, on the basis of the two correlations considered alone, whether either age or education, both, or neither is a determinant of intolerance. To gain this knowledge, Stouffer applied methods of analysis that hold education constant to determine whether age is still related to intolerance, and the applied methods of analysis that hold age constant to determine whether education is still related to intolerance. If Stouffer, in carrying out these operations, had found that the apparent influence of age disappears when education is held constant, he might well have concluded that the correlation between age and intolerance is apparent rather than real. That is, the reason why old people are more intolerant does not reflect the fact of their age as such but, instead, the fact that old people are less educated than young people.[56] By carrying out a series of these operations, the investigator is able to eliminate some of the apparent causal connections among social phenomena, and thus simplify his explanatory task.

[55] Samuel A. Stouffer, *Communism, Conformity and Civil Liberties: A Cross-section of the Nation Speaks Its Mind* (Garden City, N. Y.: Doubleday, 1955). Also, see *infra*, pp. 673–674.
[56] Actually, Stouffer found both age and education correlated with intolerance, even after he corrected for the influence of each on the other.

Suppose, however, that the sociologist uncovers a number of relations which are, in his estimation, genuinely causal. How might these relations be organized? One way of handling them is to consider them in causal sequence rather than as a simple list of causes. For example, if the sociologist wishes to assess the impact of social class on individual behavior,[57] his reasoning might be as follows. An individual's class-linked experiences—his income and his education, for example—place restrictions of the kind of style of life that his family can enjoy.[58] This style of life, in turn, conditions the way in which his children are reared.[59] As a result of this distinctive pattern of socialization, certain personality dispositions are laid down in his children.[60] And, finally, these dispositions will operate as important determinants of the children's subsequent adult behavior—both as individuals and in groups—including their behavior toward *their* class situations.[61] By viewing the causal sequence in this way, the sociologist organizes the several variables in systematic relation to one another, instead of representing them as a list of correlations. In addition, he deals with the complexity of causality by incorporating the principle of feedback—in this case, the principle that the stratification system (which is, in the first instance, considered as the independent variable) is itself ultimately affected by the consequences that it originally helped to produce.

One final example is appropriate. Wheeler outlines three broad classes of determinants of deviant behavior—the character of the society's normative order, the characteristics of the persons who become deviants, and the ways in which organized society reacts against deviant behavior, once it appears.[62] This list of determinants contains a theoretical order, even though Wheeler does not make this altogether explicit. The theoretical order is as follows. The starting point of any analysis of deviance is the normative demands made by society on individuals and groups. These demands define what kinds of behavior are deemed deviant and what kinds are not. Given this starting point, the next question is: What variables determine whether an individual will deviate—his family background, his attitudes toward authority, and matters of this kind? But this question cannot be asked or answered without reference to the normative structure. Otherwise an individual's behavior could not be classed as either deviant or nondeviant. Stated differently, the causal connections producing deviant behavior are only significant *within*—not outside—the already-specified normative context. To put it still

[57] See Reissman, *infra*, pp. 252ff.
[58] See Reissman, *infra*, pp. 260–261.
[59] See Reissman, *infra*, pp. 257–260.
[60] See Homans and Slater, *infra*, pp. 34–35 and 589–600.
[61] See Reissman, *infra*, pp. 254–257.
[62] *Infra*, pp. 608–610.

another way, the specification of the normative context is *logically prior* to the specification of the deviants' deviance-producing characteristics.

Now let us consider the third class of determinants affecting deviant behavior—social control. The sanctions exercised against this kind of behavior certainly affect the course taken by the behavior. But, in order for this influence to be intelligible, the deviant tendencies must have become manifest. As before, the other determinants of deviance are logically prior to the establishment of meaningful causal connections between deviant behavior and social control. In view of these observations, it is clear that Wheeler is dealing with more than a list of determinants of deviance; he is dealing with determinants organized in logical relation to one another. It is the specification of these logical relations that constitutes the work of the theorist in social science.

I have implied in this introduction that if the sociological enterprise is to move forward, work must proceed on several fronts at once. It is not sufficient only to define and classify sociological variables; nor only to specify the logical relations among variables and thereby create theories and models; nor only to generate testable hypotheses; nor only to use the best research techniques to bring empirical data to bear on these hypotheses. All these activities must be prosecuted simultaneously. And they must be carried out with reference to one another. Data unrelated to hypotheses and hypotheses unrelated to theory are meaningless; and theory that is not empirically informed is barren. Only by the constant interplay among theory, hypotheses, research methods, and data can scientific sociology achieve both rapid and balanced growth.

# I

# BASIC
# SOCIAL STRUCTURES

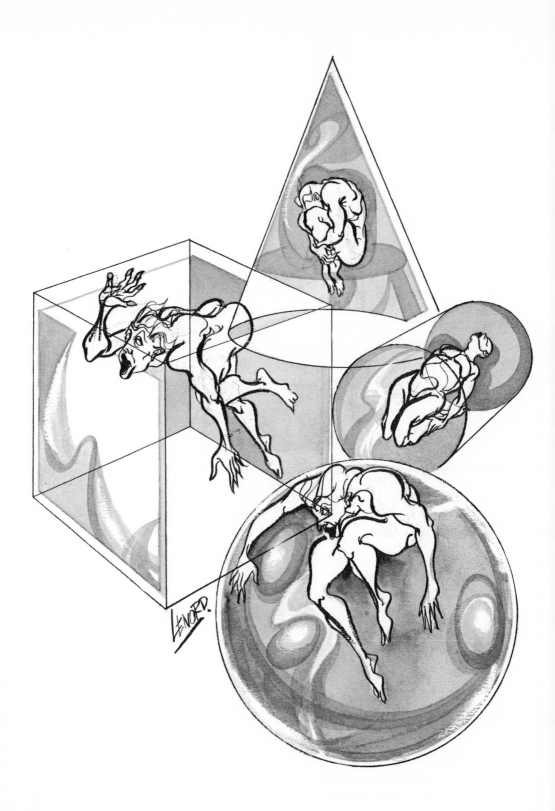

# BASIC
# SOCIAL STRUCTURES

# 1

# FUNDAMENTAL
# SOCIAL PROCESSES

*George C. Homans*

# FUNDAMENTAL
# SOCIAL PROCESSES

Any science—and this includes social science—has two related tasks: discovery and explanation. Discovery is the process of perceiving, stating clearly, and testing against data relationships between properties of nature—relationships that were previously unknown or were grasped only intuitively. For instance, the finding that there are two high tides in the ocean every day and that one of them follows the passage of the moon across the meridian was a discovery, although it was made long before science existed in the modern sense. The discovery related the tides to a span of time and to the movement of the moon. Explanation is the process of showing that the particular relationships discovered follow logically from more general relationships under specified given conditions. As an example, the explanation why there are two tides—an explanation reached long after their discovery—consists in showing that the phenomena follow from the law of gravitation under the given conditions that the earth is mostly covered with water, that the earth rotates on its axis, and that the moon moves in orbit around the earth. Explanation, in turn, may lead to new discoveries, when the general relationships, combined with new givens, suggest hypotheses that are as yet untested.

This chapter is more concerned with explanation than with discovery because the relationships that we deal with are, to a great extent, familiar to us, and need not be discovered. Here, our main topic is the fundamental processes of social behavior—the behavior that occurs when at least two persons are in contact with one another. When a young physicist begins his study of the atom, he is not even intuitively familiar with the phenomena; but when a young sociologist begins to study sociology, he has had many years of intimate familiarity with social behavior. Indeed, there is nothing that man has had *more* personal experience with than social behavior. All of us have been members of groups; we have conformed to at least a few norms; and we have taken our place in status systems—over and over again.

This familiarity with the subject matter does not mean, in the least, that no research is needed on it. Our intuitive knowledge, although it may often allow us to act successfully, is based on pure horse sense—vaguely formulated and seldom systematically tested. Research will make this knowledge more explicit and rigorous. But the results of research (and they will be cited here) seldom seem very new and surprising, especially when we think about them for a while. In fact, a common accusation is that they are obvious. Nevertheless, in light of our long experience with social behavior, it would be surprising if we *were* surprised.

What is more, the particular aspects of social behavior that we study here are the most familiar to us. What do we mean by fundamental social processes? Let us take an example. Few Americans know much about the special features of the caste system of India. But this caste system belongs to the more general class of status systems and—as just mentioned—we have all taken part in status systems. We have, wittingly or unwittingly, helped develop them. We have watched them grow up and wither away in the course of the associations that we form in everyday life. And the same is true with respect to cooperation among men, or conflict, or power, or authority, or conformity. These processes are going on everywhere at all times and in all societies. Sometimes the results are ephemeral; but sometimes the processes build up into great structures, like caste in India, that may perpetuate themselves for centuries. Because we are mainly interested in the underlying nature of the processes (which appear to be much the same everywhere) rather than in the social structures that sometimes result from them (which differ from society to society and from group to group within any one society), we shall call these processes fundamental. The study of sociology should properly begin with these features; the more structural aspects of society should come later, as they do in this book.

While the elementary features of social behavior do not need discovery—except in the important sense of confirming rigorously what we already know intuitively—they certainly do need explanation. No matter how sound our intuitive knowledge may be in other respects, it certainly is not organized. At best we apply maxims of common sense *ad hoc* to particular situations without worrying about the limitations of the maxims or their relations to one another. Explanation helps organize our knowledge by showing how a variety of familiar processes follows from a few general principles under particular given conditions. Some degree of organized knowledge may also speed up the process of trial and error by which we usually learn about social behavior. At any rate, the purpose of this chapter is to provide organization through explanation.

The kind of explanation offered here is, in one sense, very old. But, in another sense, it has been made more rigorous by recent work in psychology. It assumes, first, that the basic units of social behavior are the actions of individual men and, second, that the actions are a function of their payoffs. (We shall discuss at length the rewards and the costs of action in the pages that follow.) We shall start with general propositions, statements of relationships involving the behavior of individual men, and try to show how the characteristics of the principal social processes follow from these propositions under usual given conditions. But, again, although we try to explain the fundamental processes, we do not, for instance, try to explain how they combine in the behavior of men of varying backgrounds, in varying numbers, and in varying environments to produce the particular structures of particular groups.

Although most human behavior is social behavior—behavior influenced by the behavior of other men—no new principles are required to explain social behavior that were not needed to explain how a man acts when he is alone with the physical environment. This does not mean that nothing new emerges from social behavior. New social phenomena are coming forth all the time. The problem is not whether new phenomena emerge but how to explain the nature of what emerges. Since behavior is social, endless complexities arise in explanation, but they are complexities that involve the interweaving of a few fundamental principles.

However, a note of warning: this kind of explanation of social phenomena is accepted by some sociologists, but not by all. There are many able sociologists who believe that the explanation should start from propositions about the characteristics of groups or societies as such, rather than from propositions about the behavior of individual men. These sociologists also tend to draw a sharp line between sociology and psychology. We do not do that here. Since propositions about individual behavior are psychological propositions in the sense that they are usually stated and tested by psychologists, we recognize no line between sociology and psychology or, indeed, between sociology and the other social sciences such as economics.

Human institutions and human societies often appear so well established and so powerful that they dominate individual men and escape human control altogether. Yet these leviathans are the products of something that we think of as being weaker than water—individual human choices. Every last one of them consists of human actions, including those uniquely human ones: the things men say. It is not true that these monsters consist of the actions of men and something more. They *are* the actions of men: they can be analyzed into individual actions with nothing left over. And if they consist of individual actions, they must be finally explained by the principles of individual behavior. Here, our purpose is to show how the weak creates the strong, and how human choice creates social institutions.

## The Basic Propositions

Consider a person performing what we call an activity; that is, some intelligible unit of voluntary behavior—voluntary in the sense that it is not a mere reflex action like the familiar knee jerk. Suppose the activity is baiting a hook on a fishing line and casting it into a pool. The first question we ask about such an activity is whether it is successful. Is the cast rewarded by a bite or at least a rise? If the fisherman does get a bite, he is likely to repeat the activity. We sum up what happens in this and other examples of rewarded activity by stating our first proposition which, like all explanatory propositions, presents a relationship between at least two variables.[1] In this case, the variables are the frequency with which the activity is rewarded and the probability that a person will perform it.

PROPOSITION I. *The more often a person's activity is rewarded, the more likely he is to perform the activity.*

We call this the *success* proposition. Like our other propositions, it is only approximately true. It implies that if an activity, once rewarded, is never rewarded thereafter, the probability that a person will perform it will, sooner or later, decrease to zero; that is, the person will cease to perform it at all. In the language of psychologists, the activity will become *extinguished*. But the proposition does not specify just how long "sooner or later" will be. Much depends on the pattern in which the reward comes. For a given number of rewards within a given period of time, the evidence is that a person will perform an activity less often if the rewards come at regular ratios—in our case, for example, a bite at every third cast—than if they come at irregular and random ratios. Furthermore, an activity once rewarded at regular ratios will, when the reward ceases, become extinguished sooner than one rewarded at irregular ratios. One of the reasons why people work so hard at fishing and keep on fishing even when they have little success is that this activity is almost always rewarded at irregular ratios. Yet Proposition I, although only approximately true, is true enough for our purposes.

An activity and its reward are always accompanied by other circumstances, which may affect the frequency with which the person repeats the activity. For instance, the pool into which our fisherman casts his line may be shady. If he gets a bite there, he is more likely to cast his line into other shady pools in the future. We say that he has "perceived" the shadiness of the pool, and "sees" that shady pools are good places in which to catch fish. The circumstances that accompany an activity and its reward are called *stimuli*. They may be many and varied and may come in complex patterns, but they are always likely to make a difference to behavior. We sum up what happens in the next proposition.

PROPOSITION II. *If in the past the occurrence of a particular stimulus, or set of stimuli, has been the occasion in which a person's activity has been rewarded, then the more similar the present stimuli are to the past ones,*

---

[1] For the basic propositions of behavioral psychology as applied to social behavior, see especially B. F. Skinner, *Science and Human Behavior* (New York: Macmillan, 1953); A. W. and C. K. Staats, *Complex Human Behavior* (New York: Holt, Rinehart, and Winston, 1963); G. C. Homans, *Social Behavior: Its Elementary Forms* (New York: Harcourt, Brace and World, 1961).

*the more likely the person is to perform the activity, or some similar activity, now.*

We call this the *stimulus* proposition. Like the success proposition, the stimulus proposition is only approximately true. The crucial variable is the similarity of stimuli, but similarity may have many more than one dimension—things may be similar in different ways—and the subtleties of the psychology of perception are beyond the scope of this chapter. Moreover, the proposition as stated here says nothing about the relationship in time between the stimulus and the activity. If the original stimulus coincided with the rewarded activity in time, it is apt to be more effective in eliciting future activity than if it had occurred much earlier or later. If we use ordinary language, we say that the person would be more likely to perceive the connection.

The first two propositions imply an important tendency toward *generalization* in a person's behavior. Both the stimulus and the activity may be generalized. The fisherman, if he has been successful in fishing in a shady pool, will fish in other shady pools or even in pools that are quite dark. If he has been successful at one kind of fishing, he will be more eager to try other kinds, and even sports that are similar to fishing, such as hunting. In time, of course, the tendency toward generalization may run into difficulty. The fisherman may find that he does well in shady pools but poorly in pools that are positively dark, and thus he may, in time, come to discriminate between the stimuli of shadiness and darkness. The process of *discrimination* accompanies the process of generalization.

Propositions I and II imply that a person's behavior is learned, and that his past experience—both his past history of success in his activities and the past circumstances attending them—has an enormous effect on his present behavior. Men, of course, have been aware of this fact for a long time, but modern psychology has reemphasized its importance. We now know that a person's past experiences (such as those of his early childhood) and his unconscious experiences (unconscious in the sense that he cannot talk about them) may influence the likelihood that he will perform certain activities and respond to certain stimuli today. Also his experience may be vicarious rather than immediate. At the outset the fisherman may fish in shady pools because someone has advised him to do this, or because he has read about fishing in a book. Nevertheless, immediate experience must enter the picture at some point. The angler is unlikely to take advice about fishing without question unless he has had an earlier experience in which he took advice and actually found it rewarding. The fact that a long and complex past history conditions everyone's present behavior creates a great deal of trouble for any social science. Even if we know the general principles of learning, we usually do not know the details of a particular man's experience; consequently we cannot apply the general principles to explain or predict his behavior in the present circumstances, except within a wide margin of error. Often the best we can do is assume that, if this particular man is similar in some respect to others whose actual behavior we know better, he will behave in similar ways, since he is apt to have undergone similar experiences. But even this assumption may fail. Then we have to try to discover what made this man's experience different from that of others whom he superficially resembles. If we look, we shall surely find an answer.

In stating Propositions I and II we assumed that a person's activity was rewarded, but we did not comment upon the degree of the reward. The fact is, of course, that the degree of a reward is a variable, which we call its *value*, and we must state a proposition describing the effect of this variable on other behavioral variables. If fish is the only food a hungry person can get, fish becomes very valuable to him, and he is likely to work harder at fishing than if he had just eaten his fill. Accordingly, we state the next proposition.

PROPOSITION III. *The more valuable the reward of an activity is to a person, the more likely he is to perform the activity.*

We call this the *value* proposition. We must recognize that the value in question is the value per unit of the reward, no matter how that unit is defined, since (as we shall see) the values of successive units may change.

The success proposition and the value proposition must be considered together. Some social scientists talk as if the only thing that determines whether a man performs an activity is his motivation: his need for the reward, his drive to get the reward—what we call its *value*. But a man may need a certain reward very much and still take no action to get it if, in his past experience, he never has been successful in getting it. Only if success presents no problem does value alone determine the probability of a man's performing an activity.

The value proposition, simple as it looks, runs into many difficulties. Although it is hard to think of performing an activity at a negative frequency, it is easy to think of rewards of negative values, which we call punishments. Our hypothetical fisherman is punished if he has to struggle through brambles to get to his pool, if he gets his line tangled in a tree, or if he slips off a rock and falls headlong in the water. The value proposition has this implication: the more punishing is the result of an activity (that is, the more negative its value), the more likely a man is *not* to perform it.

What is much more important: any activity that permits a person to escape or avoid the punishment becomes, by that fact, a rewarded activity

—and the more painful is the punishment avoided, the more valuable is the reward. Note that I have said *any* activity. This has crucial implications for the use of punishment in controlling behavior. The effect of a positive reward usually is to render the performance of a specific activity more likely, but punishment has the effect of rendering more likely the performance of any activity, and there may be a wide variety of such activities, that allows a person to avoid the punishment. If we propose to get a man to perform a specific action by punishing him if he does *not* do it, we must take care that he cannot perform any other action that might avoid the punishment. Closing the other avenues of escape may be very costly.

Values are always relative. We cannot speak of the degree of reward that a man gets from an activity except in relation to some alternative reward to be obtained from some alternative activity. That is, a man compares activities and their rewards and chooses between them, whether consciously or unconsciously. Our fisherman may either go fishing or stay in camp and play bridge; he may fish in one pool rather than in another. What we mean by an alternative reward is something that he must give up, or forego, if he chooses to do something else. Man's greatest tragedy is that he really cannot do two things at once. In terms of relative values, the value proposition implies that the probability of a man's performing an activity depends on the relation between the reward of the activity that he performs and the reward to be obtained from some alternative activity, relinquished by the fact that he performs the first one. We call the foregone reward the *cost* of the activity, and the probability that a man will perform the activity depends on its net value, or reward less cost. But we must be careful in interpreting this statement. It does not imply, in the least, that as the reward less the cost of an activity approaches zero, the probability that a man will perform the activity also approaches zero. It implies only that the probability that the man will perform the activity tends to become equal to the probability that he will perform the alternative activity.

There are many activities from which a man cannot reap a reward without, at the same time, incurring some punishment. The fisherman may be unable to fish a certain pool without first scrambling through a bramble patch. Our statement about relative values still applies to such activities. Since any activity that permits a man to avoid punishment is, by that fact, rewarded, the cost of fishing the pool is the foregone value of avoiding the brambles. And the greater the cost (in this case, perhaps, the greater the extent of the brambles), the less likely it is that the man will fish the pool.

The doctrine that all values are relative may seem to imply that a man, when he acts, compares the rewards of all of the activities that he conceivably might perform. In explaining human behavior we can, in practice, forget about this possibility. In practice a man compares only the alternatives open to him at any given time. But what does "open to him" mean? It means, naturally, that once an activity or course of activities has been chosen and started, the act of choosing and starting the activity changes the net rewards of future activities, making the costs of some of them prohibitive. Once our fisherman has committed himself to fishing and has gone upstream, he has, for the moment, greatly increased the cost of his alternative activity—playing bridge—since he must now get back to camp before he can play. The fact that present choices affect future rewards and costs is another inescapable tragedy of the human condition. Think of something more important than fishing, such as commitment to a career. No one should sell his freedom of choice except for a high price.

The proposition that the probability of a person's performing an activity varies with the net reward of the activity is, like our other propositions, only approximately true. It implies that action depends only on the excess of reward over cost, and not at all on the absolute size of either. Yet if the value of a reward becomes very high to a man, but the punishment that he incurs in getting it is very high also, especially when neither the reward nor the punishment is certain, he may become so anxious that he is incapable of any action whatsoever: he may freeze up. A fuller explanation of human behavior than we shall attempt here should include propositions about the causes and effects of anxiety. But the value proposition is good enough for our purposes, since it holds true over a wide range of behaviors.

Finally, there is the question whether the value proposition is a tautology. This amounts to asking whether the value of a reward can be measured independently of the amount of activity expended to get it. If its value cannot be measured independently, the proposition is a tautology. In one important class of cases, value can be measured independently. If the only food our fisherman can get is fish, the value of fish to him is measured by the amount of time he has gone without fish: the longer he has gone without fish, the more valuable it becomes. On the other hand, the more fish he catches and eats, the less valuable, for the moment, any further fish becomes to him; which means, of course, that other kinds of reward become relatively more valuable. The same principle holds true for many rewards and, accordingly, we state the next proposition.

PROPOSITION IV. *The more often in the recent past a person has received a particular reward, the less valuable any further unit of that reward becomes to him.*

We call this the *deprivation-satiation* proposition. We emphasize the "recent past" because there are many rewards that a man can only temporarily be satiated with: when our fisherman gets hungry again, fish soon recovers its value.

But suppose that we are not assessing the value to a man of a single type of reward on two separate occasions but the relative value that he sets on two different rewards on the same occasion. Suppose also there is no obvious difference between the rewards in the degree to which the man has been deprived of them or satiated with them. Clearly, the problem is very common. For instance, suppose that the fisherman prefers catching salmon to catching trout. Is it really true that we have no measure of the relative value to him of the two fish other than the fact that he will do more to catch one than the other so that, in this case, the value proposition becomes tautological? It might be true if the fisherman were a member of a native tribe that we had just begun to study, and all we knew about him was his actual fishing habits. But if we knew that he was an Eastern sports fisherman, and that Eastern sports fishermen assigned a higher prestige to salmon than to trout, then we should have in these facts a measure of the relative value to him of the two fish—at least in the sense of his ranking them in order of value—and the measure would be independent of the fact that he did more to catch one than the other. Someone might argue that we had only driven the problem of tautology back one step. For how can we measure the value that our man sets on prestige? Is not, perhaps, what he is really deprived of prestige and not fish? But one step back is far enough to get the problem out of the way, at least for an approximate treatment like this one.

One reason why it is so hard to assess men's values and thus predict or explain their behavior is that many values are not innate but are acquired. The value of things like food in general—although not certain kinds of food such as olives—may be born in men, but men acquire other values in the course of satisfying their innate needs. Our man may have learned to value prestige for its own sake because in his very early childhood his mother rewarded him with love when he behaved better than his sister. Many rewards acquire value, as we say, for their own sake when they repeatedly have been the means of acquiring other rewards (like mother-love) that may be innately valuable. With value, as with success and stimulation, past experience makes a big difference.

With the exception of anxiety, we have thus far treated man as if he never displayed what we usually call emotional behavior. Actually he is one of the most emotional of animals. Think of the parts played in a man's life, even his social life, by love and hatred, joy and sorrow, hope and fear, euphoria and melancholy, and even ease and constraint. Take, for example, the anxiety that arises when a highly valued result is uncertain and long deferred. Under these conditions almost any activity that is, in fact, followed by the desired result is, by the success proposition, likely to be repeated, no matter how fortuitous the origin of the action and no matter how little it really has to do with producing the result. An old-time seaman longed for a wind to fill his sails; he happened to whistle, and the wind came. It always does come sooner or later. Also whistling as a stimulus is similar to the sound of the wind. Thus whistling became reinforced as an activity that brings wind to seamen. It became established as wind-magic. Think of the part played in society by magic and superstitious behavior in general. It flourishes even today in an age of science, although it is not always recognized as being what it is.

Even though we recognize the enormous range and weight of emotional behavior, we shall introduce here only a single proposition about emotionality. Our justification is a desire not to complicate unnecessarily an introductory treatment. The proposition that follows is particularly important for explaining social processes. Suppose our fisherman, after fishing successfully for a while, ceases to catch fish. Suppose he goes to what used to be a good pool and fails to get a rise. Suppose he gets his line fouled in a tree more often than usual. Suppose he has a fish almost landed and at the last moment it gets away. In all of these events, he is likely to get angry to some degree and take out his anger in aggressive behavior: at the worst he may break his fishing rod over his knee. We say that he is angry because he did not get what he expected, and is frustrated. We sum up this sort of behavior in the next proposition.

PROPOSITION V: *When a person's activity does not receive the reward he expected, or receives punishment he did not expect, he will be angry, and in anger, the results of aggressive behavior are rewarding.*

We call this the *frustration-aggression* proposition. Perhaps we should add that when the person *does* get what he expected, he still will have an emotional reaction, which we might call satisfaction. But satisfaction is seldom as spectacular as anger.

The terms in Proposition V need further definition. What a man expects is defined by Proposition II: when a set of stimuli are present, similar to that in which a man's activity was rewarded in the past, he expects that the activity will be rewarded again now, and to the extent that it is not, he will be frustrated and angry. He is apt to be more angry the more often he was successful in these circumstances in the past (Proposition I) and the more valuable the reward is to him (Proposition III). But note that his failure to get the reward now will change his expectations for the future, so that the next time he fails in these circumstances he may well get less angry. Finally, aggressive behavior is behavior that apparently hurts something or somebody, especially the something or somebody that looks like the source or reason for the frustration, but in a pinch almost anything will do. The proposition says that in anger the results of aggressive behavior become relatively more valuable than they were before.

These five propositions certainly do not exhaust the findings of behavioral psychology. Instead, they represent the very minimum needed in explaining the simpler features of social behavior. Of equal importance with the propositions themselves is the fact that they hold true simultaneously, each limiting, modifying, or masking in particular circumstances the features of behavior that the others would lead us to expect. We have given some examples of this, but let us consider one more. According to Proposition I, the more often a man's activity is rewarded, the more often he performs it. But, by Proposition IV, the more often an activity is rewarded, the less valuable any further unit of the reward becomes and, by Proposition III, the less valuable the reward, the less often a man performs the activity. In effect, the propositions combined imply (which, of course, we know) that if a man's activity is successful often enough, this fact will create the conditions that lead to his ceasing to perform it. The propositions also imply that if a man is to keep on working hardest to get a particular reward, he must be successful just often enough to satiate partly, but not wholly, his need for the reward. If he is working to appease his hunger, he should be just successful enough to keep him a little hungry all the time. No success would lead, by Proposition I, to apathy; too much success would lead, by Proposition IV, to satiation. Since all of the propositions are simultaneously true, we should, in principle, either use them all in explaining any particular feature of behavior or show why, under the circumstances, one or more of them do not apply. In practice we do not make this effort when the reasons for the omissions are obvious.

Some of the preceding discussion (such as the comment on net reward) and much of what follows may sound as if we were treating human behavior as being more (or less) "rational" than it really is. But the word *rational* has many meanings. If it is construed as meaning that human behavior is both conscious and calculating, then we believe that our propositions hold true for unconscious as well as for conscious behavior: if our propositions imply calculation, then calculation may be unconscious. If rational behavior is limited to behavior *best* calculated to attain a particular result, then much of the behavior that we describe may be irrational. But, by this definition, someone other than the actor himself is deciding what would have been the "best" behavior. The actor may neither be aware of this standard of judgment nor, if he is aware, possess the knowledge or experience that would allow his behavior to attain the standard. We are interested in how people actually behave and not how by someone else's standard, they ought to behave. Finally, the word *rational* may refer to the kinds of values that people pursue. By this standard it might be irrational to smoke cigarettes or even to show aggression, but it might be rational to be altruistic. Here, we make no such distinction between values. No matter what values men hold, we are interested in how they behave in trying to attain these values. For us, words like *rational* and *irrational* are good words to shy away from.

## Social Interaction

Although our subject is social behavior (that is, when a man's activity is rewarded or punished directly or indirectly by one or more other men), we have stated our propositions about a man's behavior under the influence of reward as if it made no difference where the reward came from: our fisherman was not rewarded by other men but by fish. And, in one sense, it does indeed make no difference, since no new propositions are needed to explain social behavior. But it does make a difference to the complexity of the explanation. When a man's activity is rewarded by the nonhuman environment, he acts in accordance with the laws of human psychology, but the environment does not. When a man's activity is rewarded by the activity of another man, both are acting in accordance with these laws. The activity of each is influencing the activity of the other, and in human ways. The two are (to use a common term of sociology) *interacting*, and it is this reciprocal influence that causes complexity.

To replace fishing, let us find a typical example of social interaction. Suppose that at least two men, whom we shall call Person and Other, are working in the same office.[2] Person, who is inexperienced in the job, needs some advice about how to do his paper work. He goes to Other, who is an old hand at the game, and asks for help. Other gives the advice, and Person thanks him. Person's activity has been rewarded by advice, and Other's activity by thanks. Or, stated another way, they have exchange advice for thanks.

How do we explain why the interaction—the exchange—takes place? The answers are obvious, but unless we make them explicit we shall never be able to explain the more complicated cases of social interaction. Let us first go back to our propositions, and reexamine the stimulus proposi-

---

[2] This example is taken from P. M. Blau, *The Dynamics of Bureaucracy* (Chicago: University of Chicago Press, 1955), pp. 99–179.

tion (II). In social behavior the most important stimuli are those presented by persons. Assume that Person considers Other as being the kind of experienced man who could give him good advice, and that Person has had previous success in getting help of some kind from those more knowledgeable than he is himself. Most of us have had some such experience from childhood onward. Therefore, there is some likelihood that Person will ask Other for help. Assume also that, as far as Other is concerned, there is nothing about Person to suggest that he will be ungrateful.

Now let us turn to the value proposition (III). Since values are relative to alternatives, we must look at the alternative rewards open to each man. Person can either ask for advice or keep on doing his own work. Since he is inexperienced in the ways of the office, we assume that getting advice is more valuable to him than doing his own work—indeed, it will ultimately help him do his own work better—and that, for the time being, he is not satiated with advice (Proposition IV). But we must also consider the costs of getting advice, costs that he would avoid incurring if he simply did his own work. One of the costs is low. Person's friend, Other, is near at hand, so that Person does not have to spend much time finding him. Physical proximity is one of the chief factors reducing the costs, and thus increasing the probability of human interaction.[3] Another kind of cost may be heavier. If Person asks Other for advice he, by so doing, admits to Other (and, indeed, to any spectator) that, in at least this respect, he is inferior to Other and, for some men, this is a heavy cost indeed. We shall consider this kind of cost in more detail later but, for the moment, assume that it is not too great to prevent Person from asking for advice.

In the same way, Other may either give advice or keep on doing his own work. If he gives advice, he expects to be rewarded by thanks, or, to speak more generally, with social approval. All of the evidence suggests that for many men social approval is a valuable reward, and that it is difficult to satiate them with it. Other's cost in giving advice is, of course, the time he takes off from doing his own work, but this cost may not be great, since he is an experienced man and therefore can do his own work quickly.

Sociologists often sum up the relative values of two men in interaction by means of a payoff matrix such as Matrix 1.[4] The matrix is divided into four squares, representing four contingencies. Square $o1p1$ repre-

---

[3] For a good example, see L. Festinger, S. Schachter, and K. Back, *Social Pressures in Informal Groups* (New York: Harper, 1950), pp. 33–59.

[4] See, especially, J. W. Thibaut and H. M. Kelley, *The Social Psychology of Groups* (New York: Wiley, 1959).

sents the contingency in which each man does his own work; $o2p1$ represents the contingency in which Person does his own work while Other gives him advice; $o1p2$ represents the contingency in which Other does his own work and Person gives him approval; and, finally, $o2p2$ shows the contingency in which Other gives advice and Person gives approval. Each square is divided by a diagonal into two halves, the number in the northeast half represents the payoff (value of the reward) to Other in the contingency in question, and the number in the southwest half represents the value of the reward to Person. The figures are chosen in order to make $o2p2$ the best joint payoff and to make the numbers equal for the two men in $o1p1$ and in $o2p2$.

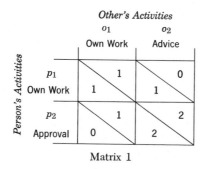

Matrix 1

In part, the matrix is quite unrealistic. Contingencies $o1p2$, when Other does his own work and Person gives him approval, and $o2p1$, when Person does his own work and Other gives him advice, are highly unlikely to occur. The reason, of course, is that the full interaction consists of three activities and not just two. The exchange of advice for approval is preceded by Person's request for advice, without which Other would be unlikely to give advice at all. But there are situations in which all four contingencies represent real possibilities, situations in which each of two men act in ways that may affect the other, but without previous communication between them. In the present situation, we assume that the activities represented by $o2p2$ get the most valuable net reward for both men: each gets a reward worth 2 at the cost of foregoing his next best alternative $o1p1$, which is worth 1. Accordingly, by the value proposition (III), these are the activities that they are likely to perform.

Once it has taken place, the exchange—the interaction—has consequences for the future. By Propositions I and II (the success and the stimulus propositions), the probability increases that each party will, in the future, exchange the same rewards with the same other person, so long as the attendant circumstances remain favorable. In the short run, they may not remain favorable. The more advice Other gives Person in the course of a day's work at the office, the less time he has left for doing his own work; the cost of giving advice becomes prohibitive, and he will break off the exchange. In the same way, Person may have gotten all the advice he needs for the time being (Proposition IV). But by the next morning these drawbacks may have disappeared. That is, in the long run the probability that the exchanges will continue has increased. Note that many of the most persistent features of social life consist of repeated interactions between individuals in families, in other small groups, and in large organizations. A repeated exchange of the same kinds of reward between two persons may be called a *relationship* between them.

A repeated interaction also makes a difference to future behavior because it changes expectations. Suppose that Other has been giving Person advice whenever he has asked for it, and then suddenly refuses. Person has come to expect the advice and is angry when he fails to get it. Generally speaking, if Person has performed an activity that has been repeatedly rewarded by Other in the past, and finds on a new and similar occasion that the reward is not forthcoming, he is, by the frustration-aggression proposition (V), apt to be angry; and, in anger, hostile activities become rewarding to him, especially activities that punish Other. Since the withholding of an expected reward is a punishment, these activities may include Person's refusal to enter into future exchanges with Other, even if he still needs advice. He is cutting off his nose to spite his face but, in anger, it is worth it if he can get back at Other. Insofar as Other values his future exchanges with Person, he may learn to avoid the punishment by living up to Person's expectations. He is the more likely to do so, the more the punishment would hurt him, which may mean that there is no alternative way by which he could get the kind of reward (social approval) that Person would deny him. To sum up: expectations may arouse aggressive reactions if they are not met, and thus bring in a new reward—precisely the reward of avoiding the aggression—that may help maintain the relationship.

Note that we have just introduced a new meaning of *alternative*. Besides alternative rewards, there are alternative ways of getting the same kind of reward. These ways may be activities directed at alternative persons. If there is some third man who can provide Other with the approval that Person denies him, Other will have less to fear from Person's anger. We shall deal at length with alternative persons later.

To avoid his anger, Other must know what Person expects, but how does he know? He may learn by experience what makes Person mad. But there is, of course, a quicker way. Whatever else men may be, they are at least great talkers. Person may say: "I expected you to do that for me, and you wouldn't!" Or, "It isn't fair not to help me now!" Or, "I've done a lot for you, you ought to do this for me!" When Person uses words like *ought* or the equivalent, he is stating what sociologists call a norm: a statement about how persons are expected to behave in given circumstances. When Person states what he expects, he is presenting a signal, a stimulus, to Other. If for Other in the past the statement of a norm has accompanied occasions in which his conformity to the norm has been rewarded, or his disregard for it has been punished by hostility, then by the stimulus proposition (II) he is a little more likely to conform to what he recognizes as a norm on the present occasion. If the rewards for an alternative activity are great enough, he may still disregard the norm, but at least he will not do so by sheer inadvertence: he knows that he will have to reckon with Person's anger.

But we must be careful not to imply that the avoidance of a particular person's hostility is the only reason why Other might conform to the norm. Generalized values may be acquired through being paired with more specific ones, and if in Other's past experience, perhaps in his family, conformity to a norm of fairness has been generally rewarded, being fair may come to be for him, as we say, rewarding in itself. And he may, especially if appealed to, be happy to do justice for its own sake, without a conscious thought for the further gains it might bring him.

Now let us turn to Person. We must recognize and always remember that the statement of a norm by one man to another and, more generally, the presentation of stimuli are themselves activities and, like other activities, may be repeated if they are rewarded. If Person appeals to a norm and is rewarded by getting what he wants from Other (or someone else), and if he incidentally avoids the very real costs of his own aggressive behavior, then he is likely to repeat norm-stating activity. Indeed, the formulation of norms may have rewards for both parties to the exchange. If the exchange now breaks down, it will at least have done so by the more or less conscious choice of one party or the other, and this certainly furthers, although it does not guarantee, the maintenance of the relationship between the two.

## The Elaboration of Interaction

Thus far, from our discussion, it would seem as if the two persons in interaction each rewarded the other with only one kind of activity and as if the activities were essentially dissimilar: Other gives advice; Person gives approval. But persons who interact repeatedly are apt to enter into more than one kind of exchange, and some of the activities exchanged may not be entirely dissimilar. In the course of giving and getting advice,

Other and Person may begin talking about matters of common interest outside the office, exchanging opinions about the affairs of the day. Sociologists would say that their relationship has become *elaborated*. The reasons for the elaboration should be obvious. A man who rewards another in one way is, by the stimulus proposition, perceived as the kind of man who may be more generally rewarding. And the very fact that the two have already been brought together by one kind of exchange may make it less costly for them to enter into a new kind of exchange with one another than with third parties. Elaboration is a common feature of social relationships.

The new exchanges may affect the original one, and vice versa. Let us examine the exchange of opinions. It may be cynical but it is often true that what rewards a man's expression of opinion is another's agreement with it, and the second party's agreement is more apt to be forthcoming if the first party's opinion is, in fact, similar to that of the second party. Now suppose that in the course of their conversation, Person expresses disagreement with Other's opinion. To some degree he has frustrated Other, deprived him of an expected reward. As usual, in anger, any activity that hurts the offender becomes, by that fact, rewarded. And one way in which Other can now hurt Person is by withdrawing from the original exchange: he may cease to give Person advice. If a man values his own opinions strongly enough, he may break off all previous relations with a person who disagrees with them.

But Person may readily learn to forestall this result. The higher the value he sets on getting advice from Other, the more likely he is to change his expressed opinion in order to make it more like Other's, and he may even, eventually, believe sincerely what he says. The total result of the many situations of this kind is a certain strain toward consistency in human relations: either two persons reward one another in more than one way, like each other on more than one count, and increase their interaction, or they will hurt one another in more than one way, dislike one another, and decrease interaction. It appears to be rather difficult, although not impossible, to keep on interacting with a person who rewards in one way and punishes in another. This strain toward consistency has been widely discussed by psychologists under the heading of *balance theory*.[5] It should also be clear why persons who interact frequently with one another are apt to become similar in some respect: to express similar opinions, to share common interests, and even to dress

[5] See, especially, F. Heider, *The Psychology of Interpersonal Relations* (New York: Wiley, 1958); L. Festinger, *A Theory of Cognitive Dissonance* (Evanston, Ill.: Row, Peterson, 1957).

alike. To summarize: the elaboration of a relationship tends either to strengthen it or to weaken it, but not to leave it unchanged.


## The Group and Conformity

We have been progressing systematically to complicate our picture of human interaction. We have moved from a single kind of exchange between two persons to multiple exchanges, and we have added the exchange of similar activities to the exchange of dissimilar ones. Now we turn from what might be called direct exchange to indirect exchange or *cooperation*. And we shall enlarge our interactors by at least one, and add the Third Man to Person and Other.

With three interactors, two sets of patterns may occur. Person may interact with Other, and Other with the Third Man, but the Third Man may not interact with Person. On the other hand, the triangle may be closed, and each individual may interact with every other one. The first pattern may be analyzed as a series of pairs, but the second introduces complications beyond pair relations. When, within a given period of time, each of a number of individuals interacts with every other individual, we say that they form a *group*, of which each of them is a *member*.

When Person and Other exchanged advice for approval in the office, each man's activity rewarded the activity of the other directly. But suppose that in the same office Person, Other, and the Third Man conspire to keep secret from the boss some of the things that they do; if he knew about them, he might try to put a stop to them. Here we might argue that the men are not rewarding one another directly, since the relevant activity of each—and, in this situation, *not* telling is an activity—is addressed not to one another but to the boss. We might argue further that they are rewarded by the activity of the boss, again by his *not* taking action, although he may not take action for reasons quite different from the fact that they have failed to tell him. Since the activity of each man contributes to this result, we might also argue that each man has, indeed, rewarded the others. Certainly they act as if this were the case, rewarding, in turn, with social approval the persons who keep their mouths shut. Here the social exchange takes the following form: each person rewards others with approval for activity not addressed to him personally but to an outsider. And each person is rewarded, in turn, not only by social approval but by the boss's silence. By the same token, a man who tells hurts all of the others (it is almost as bad for one to tell as for all to tell), and is punished by loss of social approval or possibly something worse.

When a man rewards successive activities addressed directly to himself, his deeds alone may make his expectations sufficiently obvious to another. He may need something more when the activities in question are directed to an outsider, when he has more than one associate, when he wants them all to behave in the same way, and when a single mistake may be as bad as many. Under these conditions, his statement of a norm like "Don't squeal!" is particularly rewarding—rewarding in that the persons to whom the norm is addressed may become less likely to violate it by inadvertence or by not knowing what is expected of them. The norm puts them on notice that compliance will bring approval or, at least, that noncompliance will bring punishment. Normative statements are especially apt to be made in situations like this.

It is always possible to describe the larger social structures as sets of rules to which the actual behavior of people, more or less, conforms. The question why people conform to norms, insofar as they do conform, has always been a crucial one for social scientists. Certainly many people conform without finding the direct result particularly rewarding. In our example, suppose that Person, himself, finds it valuable that the boss should be told nothing, and states the norm, "Don't squeal!" Other may feel the same way, and may conform to the norm for that reason, the approval that he gets for doing so being an extra, added attraction. The Third Man may not agree at all; he may think that no harm whatever would be done if the boss knew what was going on, but he may, nevertheless, conform. He may value the approval that others give him for conforming; he may value the other exchanges that he has entered into with members of the group—exchanges that may be cut off if he does not conform. Above all, most men value companionship, sheer interaction with others, and the most severe punishment that a group can inflict on an erring member is "sending him to Coventry" and not talking to him at all. The one finding that has been repeatedly confirmed by research on small groups is this: the larger the number of members that are rewarded, directly or indirectly, by membership in a group, the larger is the number that conform to its norms.[6]

A man's conformity may depend on the other exchanges that he has entered into with members of the group, but these exchanges take time to build up. Accordingly, people who value strict conformity to group norms should, if possible, keep the members of a group together for some time, without a considerable turnover in personnel. This is well recognized by military officers who want the members of their units to work well

[6] See, for example, L. Festinger, S. Schachter, and K. Back, *Social Pressures in Informal Groups* (New York: Harper, 1950), pp. 60–113.

together. A group can keep good control over its members only when it has something to offer them for conformity and, therefore, has something to take away from them for nonconformity.

The higher the value a member sets on the rewards he receives from other members of his group, the more likely he is to conform. But remember: this value is always relative to the alternatives open to him, especially the other persons who may be alternative sources of reward. For instance, if there is another group that he can easily join for some companionship, he is less likely to miss the companionship he might lose by failure to conform to the norms of his original group, and thus he is less likely to conform. Isolated groups in hostile environments, such as many primitive tribes, are notorious for the control that they are able to exercise over their members.

A man who joins an alternative group is lost to the original one. The more interesting case is the man who stays. Suppose he has some inclination not to conform to a norm. The larger the number of other members who are themselves prepared to conform and to withdraw approval from him for not doing so, the more valuable [by the deprivation-satiation proposition (IV)] approval becomes to him. The sources of approval are becoming fewer and fewer; approval is becoming a scarce reward; the value of what he is losing by further nonconformity is increasing and, hence, he becomes more likely to conform. The result is that there is a kind of "critical mass"—a critical number of members of a group who, if they are prepared to conform, make the conformity of additional members increasingly likely. Certainly there is evidence that if a single other member will join a man in nonconformity, the man is less likely to conform: a person being absolutely alone with no one to love him is the worst situation.[7] Note that companions in nonconformity are apt to hold similar values and thus to have, in some respect, similar backgrounds. The members of a nonconformist subgroup are apt to be more similar to one another, in ways other than their nonconformity, than they are to the remaining members of the group.

When, by this means, the majority (large or small) of the members of a group change the behavior of other members without changing their own—the majority continues to conform, while the others change toward conformity—we say that the group has exerted *power* over the individual. This case, in which many exert power over the few, is different from the case where the few exert power over the many, which we shall discuss later. But, as we shall see, both group power and individual power are apt

[7] See G. C. Homans, *Social Behavior* (New York: Harcourt, Brace and World, 1961), pp. 100–105.

to depend on a single principle: a reward becomes scarce; therefore, it becomes more valuable to the person who gets it, and its loss becomes more costly to the person who foregoes it. In the case of group power, the group creates the scarcity by all of its members' behaving in the same way: all conform, and all deny some reward to the nonconformist. They may reach this similarity spontaneously and unconsciously; they may also reach it by deliberate and conscious combination.

This tendency for the group to exercise control over the individual may be counteracted by another tendency, and the actual degree of nonconformity may be a result of the two. Consider, once more, the behavior of the members who believe in the norm, and who have, consciously or unconsciously, the choice of whether to punish the nonconformist. If they punish him by withdrawing approval from him and, for any reason, he still persists in his deviance, they may be left with no further approval to withdraw. They will have done their worst, and will have lost control over him, unless they are prepared to resort to threats of more violent punishment. But more violent punishment may, strangely, increase the probability that he will persist in nonconformity. Punishment always sets up some degree of emotional reaction in the person punished. Even if the punishment is just—and we shall have much to say about justice later—the person punished seldom has trouble persuading himself that the punishment did not fit the crime. He will feel some anger, and want to get back at his punishers. What better way of doing this than by violating their cherished norm once more? Thus the punishment of nonconformity may lead to further nonconformity. If the members value the norm highly enough, they may, of course, drive him out of the group altogether; but if they do not, and if they value his services in other capacities than that of a conformist, they may grow to tolerate him. His standing as an approved member of the group may not be high, but he will not be actively persecuted.

An enormous amount has been written about conformity and nonconformity. Some writers, and particularly the modern ones who cannot bear to leave people alone, have waxed indignant and talked as if men were positively immoral if they ever did what somebody else told them they should do. And some early anthropologists and recent sociologists have taken conformity for granted, almost assuming that obedience to norms was automatic. Actually the basic findings about conformity are simple. At the end of their recent study of the subject, Walker and Heyns reach the following general conclusion:

The greater and more valued the reward, the oftener it is achieved through conformity behavior, the more conformist the behavior is likely to become, and the more likely it is to become a generalized way of behaving in new situations. The person need not be aware of these effects.[8]

The "generalized way of behaving in new situations" refers to the mechanism that we have described in the stimulus proposition (II). If in the past, under the special kind of stimulus that we call the enunciation of a norm, a man's activity in conformity to the norm has been rewarded, then upon the occurrence on new occasions of similar stimuli—the enunciation of other norms—he is more likely to conform again. This does not mean that he necessarily will conform, but the strength of one of the forces contributing to his conformity has increased.

Since we have considered cooperation in conformity to a norm, we should now take a quick look at competition. Competition occurs when the activities of at least two persons are directed toward getting the same reward, and, to the degree that one of them is successful in getting it, the other is denied it. Since failure to get an anticipated reward is apt to arouse anger—the firmer the anticipation, the more violent the anger— and since, in anger, anything that hurts the source of frustration is rewarding, competition (as we all know) has a tendency to lead to hostilities between the competitors. These hostilities may drive one of the competitors out of the field altogether. But if they have reasons, in the other aspects of their relationship, for not carrying matters that far, their continued competition may, strangely, have about the same effect as conformity to a norm: their activities may become more and more alike. For if the activities of one of the parties have been successful in getting the reward, the other party must also adopt those activities in self-defense. If this similarity should continue, it may in time give rise to a norm, since whatever is always becomes what ought to be. If neither competitor can finally be driven from the field, and the reward is divisible, both competitors may learn to divide it between them according to some principle of distributive justice.

## Power

In discussing indirect reward (that is, when the members of a group reward one another by concerted action on the environment, physical or social), we have considered only the case in which all of the members are expected to conform to a norm—they are all expected not to squeal to their boss. In other words, all are expected to adopt the *same* kind of

[8] E. L. Walker and R. W. Heyns, *An Anatomy for Conformity* (Englewood Cliffs, N.J.: Prentice-Hall, 1962), p. 98.

behavior. But a group may also secure rewards from the environment by concerting its action in another way. The members may perform *different* actions; they may specialize in doing different things, which jointly contribute to attaining a common goal. Here, the big problem is one of coordinating the specialized activities and, to understand it, we must first deal with individual power.

Let us revert to our original payoff matrix for the exchange between Person and Other of approval for advice (see p. 43). The matrix showed that both persons gained equally by entering into the exchange—indeed, we set up the matrix purposely to show just that. By entering into the exchange, each man increased the value of his reward by one unit $(2 - 1)$ over his alternative of not entering into the exchange. The two men benefited equally, and thus, by the value proposition (III), each was equally likely to change his behavior in this way. (*Note.* Each person influenced the other, but influence is not power: power is concerned not just with influence but with inequalities of influence. )

Now suppose that Matrix 1 had looked like Matrix 2. (From now on we shall disregard the unlikely contingencies $o2p1$ and $o1p2$.) Compared with

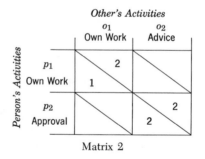

Matrix 2

the first matrix, the value to Other of doing his own work has gone up; perhaps he has been taking too much time off from his own work. At any rate, he would now be just as willing to do his own work as give advice: $2 - 2 = 0$. This means that the net reward Other gets for giving advice is now less than the net reward Person gets for giving approval: $2 - 1 = 1$. Both men may still enter into the exchange but, by the value proposition (III), the probability that Other will do so is now much less than the probability that Person will do so.

Person is now faced with the problem of increasing the likelihood that Other will give him advice. He can easily learn—and, undoubtedly, has learned in similar situations in the past (proposition II)—that he may be able to do so by increasing the value of the reward he gives Other, by offering him, for instance, a warmer grade of approval or a greater recognition of his superior abilities. That is, he can learn behaviorally, if not consciously, to make the value proposition (III) work for him. Suppose that he makes the approval he gives Other worth 3 to the latter instead of 2. (As usual, the absolute values of the figures are only illustrative.) In doing this, he may, of course, increase his own costs, since in giving increased recognition to Other he has, in the eyes of any bystander, confessed more blatantly his inferiority to Other. But, for the moment, we shall assume that he has not increased his costs significantly.

At any rate, let us assume that Matrix 3 looks like this:

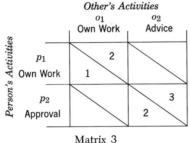

Matrix 3

Under these conditions Person has changed his behavior from what it formerly was in the original exchange: he is giving Other a better grade of approval; but Other, for his part, has not changed at all: he is, we assume, giving Person the same old advice. That is, Other is now getting approval on better terms. It is this difference in the ability to change the behavior of others in one's own favor that we refer to when we say that one man is more powerful than another. He need not, of course, have intended the change: Other may not have planned to get more approval from Person, be he gets it nevertheless. The general condition for differences in power is this: the party to the exchange who gets the lesser net reward from it is less likely to change his behavior than is the other party. This principle, like most principles governing human behavior, has often been recognized. It has been called "the principle of least interest": "that person is able to dictate the conditions of association whose interest in the continuation of the affair is least." [9] We have tried to show here how the principle follows, under given conditions, from more general psychological propositions.

The principle applies to pair relations. If a man has power over a large number of men, he may have a very great interest in maintaining this power over the group—more interest, perhaps, than any one of the group has in remaining under his control; but in exchange with any one of them, he has less to gain. This may make it rewarding for the members of the

[9] J. W. Thibaut and H. M. Kelley, *The Social Psychology of Groups* (New York: Wiley, 1959), p. 103.

group to combine and deal with him collectively on more nearly equal terms. But now a new pair relation has been established: the powerful man against the group.

Note that *after* Person has changed his behavior in order to give Other more approval, the power of the two men is shown in the matrix to be once more equal, in that each is now getting equal net reward out of the exchange: Person's 3 − 2 equals Other's 2 − 1. We have deliberately set the figures so that the rewards are equal. This was done to indicate that in repeated exchanges between persons, provided that there is no other change in the conditions, power differences tend to disappear, and neither party unilaterally will change his behavior any further. Person, for instance, will not make his approval any more fulsome, since it would cost him too much in the way of confessing his inferiority. But exchanges need not be repeated, and the other conditions need not remain unchanged.

Differences in power are differences in the capacity to reward others, and the bases for the differences in the capacity to reward others are many and varied. Some are acquired by special experience or practice, and make for differences in power only in special circumstances. Other's superiority in power to Person depends on the fact that he has acquired expert knowledge of office procedures, which Person has not had the time to acquire and which he badly needs. Some of the bases make for differences in power in a wide range of circumstances, such as differences in physical strength or in intellectual ability. Also included, although we often tend to forget them, are differences in the ability to live up to a moral code: the capacity to help others be good, when they want to be good, is a vital basis for power. And sometimes, and perhaps most often, a man may acquire one kind of power as a result of first acquiring another kind. If one man will obey him out of loyalty, he can use this person's actions to get another man to obey him out of fear. Power has a tendency to generalize.

Differences in power may, of course, depend on differences in the capacity to punish as well as on differences in the capacity to reward. For the capacity to punish entails the capacity to withhold punishment—and this is rewarding. But we must always remind ourselves of the difficulties inherent in the use of punishment to control behavior: unless the other ways of escaping the punishment are blocked, the threat of punishment may not be sufficient to elicit the particular behavior desired. Although when we speak of power we almost always think of the capacity to punish—power somehow is not really power unless it can hurt—power is, in fact, much more often exercised through providing positive rewards than through withholding punishment.

Now let us look at one very general condition that helps establish differences in power. In Matrix 2 the reason why Other has more power than

Person is that he sets a lower value on approval than Person sets on advice. This relation between the values may be brought about by the behavior of the Third Man. Suppose that the Third Man resembles Person in being unskilled, so that he too sets a high value on getting advice and is prepared to give approval in return. Now two sets of exchanges are taking place where only one did before, and this condition affects the net rewards of all persons concerned. As Other begins to advise both men, the cost of giving advice in terms of time taken from Other's own work goes up rapidly and, since he is getting more approval in return, the value of getting further approval goes down, through satiation. On the other side of the exchange, since two men are now asking for advice where only one did before, neither may be getting as much advice as one did earlier. They are in danger of becoming relatively deprived of advice, and thus, by Proposition IV, the value of advice goes up for each of them. Both effects tend to make exchanges in the immediate future less rewarding to Other than to either Person or the Third Man, and it is this that gives Other power over both of them. Both of them may respond by giving Person a warmer grade of approval in order to induce him to keep them adequately supplied with advice in this new situation.

Power, then, depends on an ability to provide rewards that are valuable because they are scarce. In the office, many men can provide approval, but we have assumed that only Other can give good advice. Yet the objective scarcity of the reward is not what counts. The ability to whistle well may be scarce, but probably no one has ever acquired power through the ability to whistle well. Only if a large number of persons found it valuable to listen to concert whistling would the ability to whistle be a basis for power—a means, for instance, of getting people to pay money. What determines the scarcity value of a reward is the relation between the supply of it and the demand for it.

But we are still not being realistic enough. We have talked as if Other had power over Person because he set a lower value on approval than Person set on advice. This way of putting things is a convenience in getting the exposition started, but it seems to violate a cardinal principle of social science, which says that there can be no comparison of subjective values. For example, one man may well know that another is getting the same amount of pay that he is getting himself, but he cannot tell whether that amount "means more" (that is, is subjectively more valuable) to the other than to himself.

In actual social behavior, no comparison of values, as such, need in fact be made. When Person responds to Other's superior power by increasing the approval he gives Other, he has not compared his own subjective values with Other's. Instead, he has responded to the perfectly overt stimuli that

Other has presented. Person, for instance, can see that Other has had many demands made on him for advice and that he has taken much time from his own work. His past history is likely to have included experience in which persons who presented similar stimuli were reluctant to give help unless they were praised very warmly. Accordingly, by the stimulus proposition (II), Person is likely on the present occasion to increase the approval he gives to Other.

In any small group where people are able to see and hear what others do, and in larger social units where information spreads by verbal communication, the stimuli presented by two persons in interaction may affect the future behavior of others not immediately concerned. After all, paying attention to stimuli is itself an activity that may get its reward in successful action on some future occasion. The Third Man may be watching Person and Other and perceive that Other is able and willing to give advice but that he will do so less often if he has taken off much time from his own work. And this perception may increase the likelihood that the Third Man will, like Person, go to Other for advice when he needs it, and increase the warmth of approval that he gives in return. Even in the United States, which is very much aware of advertising, the importance of publicity cannot be overstated.

## Bargaining

If the kind of stimuli a person presents makes a difference to the behavior of others toward him and, through publicity, to the behavior of perhaps many others, then a man may learn to manipulate the stimuli so as to obtain results favorable to himself. We shall call this kind of activity *secondary* activity, because its nature depends on the fact that men have previously learned more fundamental relationships.[10] If, in general, the person who has more power in an exchange is the person more reluctant to enter the exchange, then Other may learn to put on an act suggesting that he is very reluctant to give advice, when in fact he is perfectly ready to do so, and his activity may be rewarded by Person's giving him a better grade of approval than he would have gotten otherwise. Or Person himself may act as if he were not really very anxious to get advice although, in fact, he is panting for it. In effect (and whether both men recognize it or not, since the process may go on unconsciously on both sides), the two men are bargaining with one another over the terms of exchange of

[10] See, especially, E. Goffman, *The Presentation of the Self in Everyday Life* (Garden City, N.Y.: Doubleday, 1959).

advice for approval. And instead of saying that power is determined by "the principle of least interest," we should say that it is determined by "the principle of least *perceived* interest." But we should always remember that a fact is usually more effective than an act, and that real reluctance is likely to be more effective in bargaining than feigned reluctance.

We might mention here a bizarre but interesting factor that in some circumstances makes a difference in establishing power. It is "irrationality." Suppose that two persons are trying to influence one another by threats of punishment. If, from threats, the two should actually proceed to overt acts, both would be hurt, and therefore each would ordinarily like to get what he can by threats alone. Under these circumstances, by the principle of least interest, the person who acts as if he did not care what happened to him so long as he got his whack in, is apt to have the greater power. As we sometimes say, "He might really do it!" But not to care what happens is irrational, in the sense of not being normal human behavior. It is an odd kind of irrationality that, in fact, increases power! Anger, of course, makes more probable this kind of irrational behavior, and consequently a convincing act of being mad with rage may have great leverage. More generally, unpredictable behavior is often a source of power, and we often feel helpless in the hands of unsocialized persons like children and lunatics.[11]

The conditions in which bargaining behavior, conscious or unconscious, is likely to occur are the following ones.

1. When at least one of the parties can, in fact, control the stimuli that he presents, revealing those favorable to him and concealing those that are unfavorable. If Person has independent ways of knowing, for instance, that Other has plenty of time on his hands, Other's act of being reluctant to give advice becomes less convincing.

2. When at least one of the parties has no alternative source from which he can get the reward he is bargaining for. If there is some other skillful man in the office who is willing to give good advice on good terms, Person has less need to bargain with Other, and Other has less chance of success in bargaining with Person.

3. When the rewards that are being bargained for are highly valuable. If they are not, bargaining becomes less probable because bargaining, like other activities, always entails costs, if only in time; and for rewards of low value, the costs may outweigh the gains. A classic example is the disappearance of bargaining in big modern stores, where the volume of business is high, so that no single purchase makes a great difference to the

[11] See T. C. Schelling, *The Strategy of Conflict* (Cambridge, Mass.: Harvard University Press, 1960).

stores, and bargaining over each purchase would cost a great deal in time and thus in manpower.


## Status

We have now laid the groundwork for understanding what sociologists call differences in *status*. The ultimate bases of status differences are power differences, but perceived power often makes as much difference as real power, and it is this business of perception that we must deal with now. As we have seen, the members of our group cannot compare the "subjective value" to each of them of the rewards they receive or, for that matter, of the costs they incur. Person and the Third Man cannot judge what it means personally to Other to receive approval or to take time off from his own work. But they certainly do see that both of them go to him for advice, that both give him approval, and that he takes much time off from his own work to advise them. They can compare themselves with him in the sense that they can see that he gives more advice than they do and gets more approval. What is just as important, other people present in the office can see these things too and make the comparisons. Although they may not ask Other for advice themselves, they may well compare him with themselves, and perceive that he is more skilled than they are.

We know that they make the comparisons because they talk about them. Thus far we have not emphasized the part played by language in human affairs. We have wanted to suggest that many of the phenomena are more primitive than language itself, and may occur wholly without the use of speech. But, of course, the most marked difference between man and other animals is man's unique command of this complex means of communication. All human languages have words for ranking things along a number of dimensions: one thing is "better" than another in some respect or "bigger" or "higher"—the actual words used vary, of course, from language to language. Or one thing is "good," another "better," another "best," in some respect. Or two things are "about the same" or "equal." Men may not be able to perceive or express very well just how much better one thing is than another, but at least they can put them in rank order.

Among the things that men rank are the things people do and what they get for what they do—their outward and visible signs, if not their inward and spiritual values. They certainly rank the outward and visible signs of differences in power. And from ranking these things, it is but a step to ranking the man himself. Other gives more advice than Person or the Third Man; he gets more approval; he provides them with knowledge they cannot provide for themselves. Therefore, he himself is a "better" or "bigger" or "higher" man than they are. And since both Person and the Third Man need advice and both give approval for it in return, the two men may be called equals. From ranking persons it is another short step to ranking classes of persons. With respect to skill, at least, skilled persons are "better" than unskilled persons, and unskilled persons are "equal" to one another. After actual differences in power, the verbal ranking of persons is the crucial feature of differences in status.

The next question is why, in any group, status differences should form a system. When we talk of a system, we refer to some kind of consistency; in the case of status, two kinds are at stake. First, why should not a person rank high on one dimension of status but not another, so that it would be difficult to rank him as a whole, so to speak, as higher or lower than other persons? Many cases like this, of course, occur, cases of what sociologists call *status incongruence;* for instance, a person who is wealthy, because he has inherited money, but who appears to have almost no intelligence to go with it. But at least in small groups some tendency toward consistency is built into the underlying power relationships. A powerful person like Other gives more advice and gets more approval than either Person or the Third Man: on the two dimensions, or two counts, if you like—what he gives and what he gets—he is better than they are. There are other forces making for status congruence, including the tendency for persons who command one source of power to acquire additional sources, but we must postpone these other forces until we get further in our argument.

The second problem of consistency is this: Why should all the members of a group rank others in the same way? Why should not one man rank Other high and another man rank him low? Again, perfect consistency of this sort is never attained, but there is a tendency toward it. The origin of differences in status is differences in power, and men are powerful when many want what they, the few, are able to supply or many fear what they, the few, are able to withhold. Consequently, if there are any differences in power in the group, there will be a relatively large number of persons, at least an important nucleus, who will be in no position to deny that the few are of higher rank than they. Generally, the more similar the members of the group are in their values, the more likely they are to be similar in their rankings of others.

But how about other persons, members of the group, perhaps in the sense of being present in the same room, who do not happen to want what the few are able to supply, and who therefore are not in the least in the power of the few? Why should they also accord high status to the few? Status is a matter of the use of language, and one of the forces making for consistency in status is a force that helps bring about consistency in the use of language generally. The uttering of a form of words is an activity like any other, and it is unlikely to be repeated indefinitely if it is not rewarded by assent or at least understanding. If the persons who would not otherwise accord high status to the few, when talking to the persons who do accord it, refer to the few in words implying that they are just ordinary members of the group, they may not command the assent or even the understanding of their listeners, who may not, as we say, know what they are talking about. Accordingly the dissenters have some tendency to shift to a form of words that does communicate. More generally, a status system need not command the emotional assent of every member of a group. All that is needed for a status system is that members talk as if it were generally recognized that people like Other were "big men."

Thus so far we have seen why some persons in a group have high status and others have ordinary status. The persons of high status are persons of high power, like Other; the persons of ordinary status are men like Person and the Third Man, who do not command scarce powers to reward but are not otherwise objectionable. Yet in most groups, besides persons of high and ordinary status, there are usually persons of distinctly low status, so that the group has three main types of status—upper, middle, and lower—instead of just two. What are the characteristics of lower-status persons? They certainly do not command rare capacities to reward—or, for that matter, to punish, since this kind of capacity might well earn them high status. They are apt to be people who, with a low ability to reward other members, also punish them—but, again, to a rather low degree. They are the kind of persons who violate some of the norms of a group, but not violently enough to be driven out altogether. Like persons of high status, those of low status will be relatively few in number; for if they were numerous, their behavior would probably become the norm of the group instead of a deviation from it.

## Status Symbols

As a status system develops it alters the rewards available in a group and the costs of obtaining them. To be called a "big man," or at least "bigger" than someone else, becomes itself rewarding, not only directly but also indirectly, through its effects on the future behavior of other persons. As a result, a man may be more ready to perform the kinds of activity that win him high status than he would have been before the system developed. Other's giving good advice not only wins him approval from those who actually get it, but also becomes what we shall now call a *symbol*, reinforcing his status in the eyes of those who are merely spectators of, or witnesses to, his behavior. Indeed, *not* giving advice would now lower him in the eyes of the group. This is the phenomenon that is called *noblesse oblige*. Not all of the *noblesse* do in fact oblige, as we well know, since the cost of obliging may be too high. But the performance of activities congruent with high status has now acquired an extra value, which may make these activities a little more probable.

A status symbol is, of course, a stimulus. If a man is recognized as being a "big shot," and big shots are people who can provide valuable rewards, then, by the stimulus proposition (II), persons who do not want these rewards now may come to him when they need them in the future; and if they come to him, he may be able to extend his power over them. (*Note.* They may come to him *rather than* to somebody else: what is not done is as important in social behavior as what is done.) A certain man in the office may have great ability to give good advice; but if nobody comes to him and asks for it, because he does not present the symbols (stimuli) of being an able and experienced person, he may never be able to show others what he can do, increase his power, and raise his status. We laugh at the language of the advertising industry and its preoccupation with the "image" that a prominent person presents to the public, but many men, not all of them cheap *arrivistes*, have good reason to act, if not to talk, as if their image made a difference. And the public need not be the loser when they do so; in living up to their image, these men may behave "better" than they otherwise would have done.

The developing status system may also change the rewards and costs of persons of low status. If a person of low status is one who goes to others for rewards that they can supply and he cannot, then a man whose status was previously indefinite may, by going to another to ask for help, lower his status in his own eyes and in the eyes of others who witness the event. Indeed, we assumed earlier that this was the chief cost to Person in going to Other to ask for advice. The cost of Person is lower, the more fully he is already established as inferior to Other on the other visible aspects of status, for then his asking for advice will not lower his status still further: it will be congruent with his existing inferiority. By the same token, offering to help a man who thinks he is your equal may earn you no gratitude. You have in fact threatened him, for if he should accept the help, he would destroy the equality. This often comes as a surprise to high-minded persons.

In speaking of the symbolic behavior made possible by a status system, we have considered only the kinds of behavior that originally determined the differences in power. But as status systems develop, almost anything at all about a man, even things only indirectly related to power, may, by the operation of the stimulus proposition (II), become associated with status. Thus, if older men are in many groups able to provide scarce rewards, because in the course of years they have acquired more experience and knowledge than younger men, then people are apt to go first for help to any older man, and age has become symbolically associated with status. Depending on the circumstances of particular groups, many things besides age may become the external symbols of status: sex, or race, or seniority (years in a particular job).

A man cannot easily change his age or sex, but other symbols of status are more easily manipulated, and he may have an interest in manipulating them. Suppose that in a particular group powerful persons are apt to wear purple clothes. Then a man who, without being powerful, is able to acquire and wear purple clothes may by presenting this stimulus to others achieve some of the effects of status. This is the sort of thing that the social climber tries to do. But since one of the features of high status is the relatively small number of high-status persons, the smallness in number may itself become a symbol of status; and high-status persons may seek to deny to the social climber any symbol that, in the eyes of others, would tend to add him to their number. Many groups of high status tend toward exclusiveness, but they cannot always succeed, and they may be short-sighted in trying to do so. One of the best ways of maintaining one's own high status is to admit to the status persons of potential power.

More important, once the association between the symbol and the status is established, a man who is in fact of high status may become especially careful to wear purple clothes for fear that the failure to do this will throw his status in doubt. Consider, for instance, a man—and there have been many—whose high status rests, among other things, on a monopoly of physical force. A person in interaction with him may be more ready to risk activities that might be punished by physical force if the man of high status fails to display the symbols of power. He may be more ready, as we say, to challenge the authority of the man of high status. To defeat the challenge, it may be necessary for the man of high status actually to use his force, and this in general is costly: among other things, it may arouse the resentment of the man who is hurt. The resources that give power must always be husbanded, and especially the ability to punish: an effective threat of punishment is much cheaper than punishment itself. Consequently, it is more rewarding to a person of high status that others should avoid challenging his authority at all, and the display of the appropriate symbol may make a challenge less probable. Like the statement of a norm, it renders less likely any challenge made by inadvertence, by lack of awareness of the risks. This manipulation of symbols is, of course, a form of bargaining, and is likely to occur in the same circumstances: when the stakes are high and when the status as perceived without the symbol might be ambiguous. A man who is absolutely secure in his status can afford to worry less about the symbols of status, but, alas! anything may become a status symbol, and a conspicuous lack of concern about status may be the best status symbol of all. The honest determination of some very great men not to throw their weight around may only give them more weight to throw.

The association between status and its symbols seems often to be arbitrary, but we can generally find the reason for it if we look. Take the example we have used—purple clothes. In many societies one of the concomitants of high power and hence of high status is the control of wealth. The control, the ability to grant it or deny it to others, and not its mere possession is the important thing. Therefore, anything that is expensive is a good symbol of wealth and hence of status. In Rome and Constantinople, where purple was a symbol of high status, indeed of the imperial throne, the purple dye was especially rare and costly. One of the difficulties of maintaining status symbols today is that many things once rare and costly are now relatively cheap.

We have, thus far, considered high-status persons and their symbols, but the capacity to manipulate symbols is not limited to persons of high status. If high-status persons find rewarding, as many of them do, the sheer recognition by others of their status, then these other persons can deliberately exhibit behavior that underlines their own inferiority—*deferential behavior,* as we often call it—and thus get rewards from high-status persons at a cheaper rate than they might otherwise be able to do. Doing so will naturally cost them something, as the behavior that recognizes the superiority of others acknowledges at the same time one's own inferiority. But the cost may not be great if the inferiority is already well established, apart from the deference.

## Distributive Justice

In connection with status we must now return to Proposition V, which bears repeating. *When a person's activity does not receive the reward he expected, or receives punishment he did not expect, he will be angry, and in anger, the results of aggressive behavior are rewarding.* In discussing pair relations without differences in power, we observed that the failure of one party to an exchange to provide as much reward as the other expected would tend to complicate the relationship by adding new values: on the one part, the rewards of aggressive behavior, and on the other, the rewards of avoiding the aggression. And it is not just a matter of reward: a cost greater than expected may have the same effect as a reward less than expected. The same certainly holds true of pair relations between persons of unequal power. If Other suddenly implies by his behavior that he wants even more approval as the price of his help, Person may say: "That guy won't help me unless I crawl. I've got too much self-respect to do that any more. It isn't worth it."

The development of status complicates what a man expects in the way of reward. It increases the importance of the outward and visible signs of what men give and get: Other is now established as "better" than Person and the Third Man, both in what he gives (advice) and in what he gets (approval). And it makes the rewards and costs of third parties relevant to the original pair exchange: the fact that the Third Man, as well as Person, now wants what Other alone is ready to supply is the basis for Other's superior status. Whether Person gets angry with the terms of his exchange now depends on the answers to two questions, two comparisons: Am I getting what I expect to get, what I ought to get, in relation to someone who is "better" than I (Other)? And am I getting what I expect to get, what I ought to get, in relation to someone who is similar to me (the Third Man)? The comparison always brings in costs as well as rewards: Am I getting as much from the other as I ought to get, in view of his costs? Naturally the comparison is not made in terms of "subjective values" but in terms of the outward stimuli that behavior presents. This is the problem of distributive justice (justice in the distribution of rewards among members of a group) and of its reverse, *distributive injustice* or, as sociologists call it, *relative deprivation.* Justice is what men expect, and injustice, above all other things in social behavior, is what leads to anger.

What a man expects is determined, above all, by what has actually happened to him: by his own experience and by the experience of others, transmitted to him in words. The more common and general the experience has been, the more firm is the expectation. Now many men have had actual experience, and often many experiences, with differences in power, and they know what the general rule is. It is that a man like Other who gives relatively much of what few are able to supply, like advice, gets relatively much of what many are able to supply, like approval, and that a man who gives relatively little gets relatively little. Of course, not all men have had this experience; some have been rewarded so much at random that they hardly have any expectations at all: life to them is a matter of chance, of getting the breaks. But many men have had it—and what *is* determines what always *ought* to be. It is this actual, common experience that provides the basis for the general rule of justice: If a man is better than I in what he gives, which always entails costs, he ought to be better than I in what he gets, his rewards. But the rule works both ways, and if he is better than I in what he gets, he also ought to be better in what he gives. More generally, if he is better on one count, he ought to be better on both: his rankings on the two counts should be in line with one another. By the same token, if a man is equal to me in what he gives, he ought to be equal to me in what he gets. Aristotle's is the first general writing on distributive justice to come down to us: these two rules—two aspects of a single rule—appear in his *Nichomachean Ethics.*[12]

When two persons are interacting in isolation, there may be a problem of justice, but often each person can do something to produce what he conceives to be just conditions, because each is dependent on the other. The problem of achieving justice becomes more difficult when three persons are interacting. There are at least two cases. Suppose Other provides advice to both Person and the Third Man, but only the latter gives him approval. Then Person is being unjust to Other: Other is better than Person in the advice he gives, but Person does not recognize his superiority in return. In this case, however, Other is in the position of superior power, and may easily restore just conditions by denying Person advice until he gives approval. If one has power, he need not worry much about getting justice for himself.

Much more common is the case in which the person to whom injustice has been done is in the weaker power position. Suppose both Person and the Third Man are ready and willing to give Other approval, but Other gives advice only to the Third Man. Then injustice has been done to Person: he is similar to the Third Man in what he can give, but inferior to him in what he gets. And, in this case, he is less powerful than Other, so that he is less able to force him to be just. A great deal of experience shows that problems of injustice are especially apt to arise over distributions of rewards made by superiors to inferiors. The superior may not, of course, be an individual but an organized unit like "the company," as when the company is unfair to individuals and groups, as they see it, in the relative wages it pays them.

By the same token, a man who does justice *not* under compulsion is particularly apt to be one's superior, and hence, in the usual way, the doing of justice is apt to become a symbol of superior status. A noble who is unfair puts his *noblesse* in doubt. And when two persons are in conflict and need someone to arbitrate between them, they are apt to choose a person already established as their superior, since to choose an inferior would be to raise his status above theirs. Judgment by their peers is the least they will accept.

There is much more to be said about justice. The first version of the rule is that if a man is better than another in what he gives, he ought to be better also in what he gets. He ought to be better on two counts. But the problems of injustice may, by the ramifications of status, be extended to

[12] Book V, Chapters 3 and 4.

more than these two counts. Returning to a point we made earlier, suppose that in a particular group older men in general have more responsible jobs and get paid better than younger men. Then a particular older man may feel that he has been unjustly treated if he, too, does not have a more responsible job than younger ones and get paid better. Here the expectation has been extended to three counts: what he gives (his job), what he gets (his pay), but also his age (a background characteristic). And conditions are unjust if all three are not "in line" with one another. As we know, there may be many other dimensions besides age that, depending on the group in question, can enter into the assessment of justice. On the other side of the coin, a younger man in this group may stand low in what he gives and what he gets, but may still consider that justice has been done him. Since he is younger, he has no right to expect anything more.

Note that this "in-line-ness," besides being the condition of distributive justice, is also the condition of status congruence. When a man is angry at injustice, he is often angry at incongruence too. When an older man does not get the rewards that other older men do, he not only has been treated unfairly but his overall status has been symbolically put in doubt. This relation between justice and status congruence is not at all surprising, since justice is a question of the distribution of rewards, and the symbols of status are rewards too.

Although many men, in what they do as much as in what they say, show that they have in their minds a rule of justice similar in form to the one we have stated, the rule is in fact a very abstract one. The problem arises in applying it to particular cases. It is notorious that one man may feel that another has treated him unjustly, when the other does not think so at all, even though both men would subscribe to the same abstract rule. For instance, should seniority count more than mere ability in determining a man's rate of pay? All we can say is that the conditions that lead the members of a group to agree on the way the rule of justice should be applied are the same conditions that lead to similarity in opinions in general: the length of time the members of the group have been together and the degree to which they are similar in their backgrounds, and hence, usually, in their values. But full consensus is never attained, and the degree of consensus that is attained is always in danger of being upset by changes in the external circumstances of the group and in its internal organization. Perfect justice is a chimera.

Again, the rule of justice, as we have stated it, implies a series of rank-order correlations, a series of ordinal differences rather than cardinal ones. A man who is better than another man in what he gives should be better than the other in what he gets. But *how much* better in either respect? Here, there is no general rule, but considerable evidence that, in justice, an inch is almost as good as an ell. In one department of a business firm the members of one job group said that they ought to get "just a few dollars" more pay than another group "just to show that our job is more important." Symbolically, it was the ordinal difference that counted.[13]

Justice is a matter of human expectations; when the expectations are unrealized, men are apt to feel angry and, in anger, the results of aggressive behavior become rewarding—a fact that adds new values and new possibilities of behavior to the original ones. A man who feels he has been unjustly treated may be angry not only at the powerful man who caused the injustice but also at his own equal, who is the beneficiary of injustice by getting more reward than he does himself. A powerful man is better able to maintain injustice than most men, but even he may have good practical reasons for wanting to avoid it insofar as he can. A man to whom the powerful man has done wrong is a fellow who may want to get back at him, and what better way is there than *not* doing what the powerful man says, just because he says it? Insofar as the powerful man wants his inferiors to work well together, he will want to avoid creating jealousies between them. Finally, doing justice is the prerogative of high status, so that a man who is unfair to his inferiors may, to a degree, render his status less legitimate. He is in special danger when he has been unjust to many people in the same way, for then they may not only want to get back at him but combine together to do so. There are many good reasons for doing justice, but when there are good reasons for doing something, there are usually also good reasons for not doing it; and justice is often both difficult to do and costly. How is the best net advantage achieved? Injustice in its multifarious forms has always been the great social problem.

Remember: in the end, and always, the sense of injustice is invariably grounded on a defeat of expectations, and expectations in the long run are always grounded on what actually happens. Reexamining one of our examples: if, over a period of time, older persons do not generally get better jobs than younger ones, then an older man's sense of injustice, when he does not get a good job, will eventually disappear. Whatever is, is right—if only what is will stay put long enough, which it usually does not. It is change that makes the trouble. Thus a person or group that has, for any reason, come to expect a steady increase in rewards will, when the increase is checked or reversed, feel angry, even if they are better off absolutely than they were in the beginning. In psychologists' language, their *level of aspiration* has risen. This is a fertile source of revolt and one very hard to cope with, for how can anyone go on increasing rewards indefinitely?

[13] G. C. Homans, *Sentiments and Activities* (New York: The Free Press of Glencoe, 1962), pp. 61–74.

## Leadership and Cooperation

It is now appropriate to return to a matter that we postponed earlier. In discussing indirect reward—when the members of a group reward one another by activities directed to the external environment, human or non-human—we examined the case in which the activities of the members were similar and unchanging, as in their conformity to a norm. But there is obviously another case, in which the members of a group combine to effect a change in the environment that no single member could effect by himself, and in which their activities need neither be similar nor persist without change over time. Suppose the members combine to build a house, contributing different, specialized activities toward a total result, and changing their activities from time to time as the work progresses. If this kind of result is to be accomplished, someone must coordinate the different activities so as to time them and mesh them properly. He must give what are in fact orders, whether couched as such or only as mild suggestions, and these orders must, to some degree, be obeyed. In the next few paragraphs we shall be concerned with *leadership*, which is both an effect of status and a cause.

The basic rule of leadership is a direct application of the success (I) and value (III) propositions: people are more apt to obey a man's orders the more often obedience to his orders brings them rewards, and the more valuable are the rewards compared with some alternative. But this rule cannot come into effect unless they obey him at least once, for if they never obey him at all, they will have no way of learning whether the results of obedience would have been rewarding. How does a potential leader get people to obey him in the first place? This is an important question, since there are undoubtedly many potential leaders who never get a chance to show what they can do.

There are many possible reasons why a potential leader gets his chance, but the most important one is that he already possesses some power and status in his group. Let us look again at our original situation. Both Person and the Third Man go to Other for advice on how to do their work. We have assumed that the advice he gives is good, and that they find that complying with his advice actually helps them with their work. In one area, at least, they have already done what he has told them to do, and they have found the result rewarding, thus establishing by the stimulus proposition (II), the initial presumption that doing what he says will be rewarding in other areas too. The most important stimuli to social action are persons themselves. The fact that it is Other, and not somebody else, whom they have obeyed with good results on one occasion makes it more likely that they will perform similar obedient behavior when he gives other instructions on another occasion.

It is true that we have rigged the situation in our favor, since we have had Other give advice, and advice closely resembles giving orders. But, in general, persons get power and status by providing services that are rare and much in demand. In so doing, they tend to establish the presumption— to be accepted until it is proved mistaken—that what they do and say will be found rewarding across the board. It is this presumption that gives a man the first leverage for extending his leadership.

The fact that others have had good previous experience with him is not the only condition that helps a potential leader get his orders initially obeyed. Because he commands a scarce and valuable reward, Other has power over Person and the Third Man, so that he can increase the amount of approval he gets from them. But there is no reason why, instead of getting approval, he cannot ask for, and get, obedience itself, especially if their sense of justice suggests that they owe him a good return for his services. A person of high status usually has the power to command initial obedience.

Many studies have tried to find correlations between leadership and various personality traits. The correlations are usually low: no very specific traits of character are especially likely to make men leaders. The highest correlations, although even these are not very high, are with rather general traits, such as overall intelligence or energy. The reason is that the initial basis for leadership is the same as the basis for status: the ability to provide rewards that are low in supply but high in demand, and the nature of these rewards varies with the circumstances of particular groups. An ability that would give a man high status in one group may not do so in another.

We say that a man whose orders are in fact obeyed has *authority*. Notice that power and authority need not be identical: people may obey a man simply because they have obtained good results in the past from doing what he said and not because he has any power to compel obedience. So long as the followers obey him at least once, they will have an opportunity of discovering whether the results of obeying him are, indeed, good. Remember always that it is net reward that counts—reward in relation to some foregone alternative. Thus the results of leadership in war may not look particularly rewarding—there may have been heavy losses—but the alternative might have been worse still. If the followers do find the results of obedience satisfactory, the probability that they will obey the leader again has of course increased. In leadership, as in so many social processes, nothing succeeds like success. By the same token, if obedience to a man's orders does not bring net reward but net punishment, his orders in the long run will not be obeyed. The only general rule is that a man will obey if, "at the time of his decision, he believes it to be compatible with his personal interest as a whole." [14] Finally, if a man's order is not obeyed, that fact will undermine the presumption that his orders are to be obeyed on the next occasion, and thus wise leaders try to avoid giving orders that will not be obeyed. To give an order is always to take a risk: a leader puts his social capital on the line, to be restored and increased only by success.

Why should the followers find the results of obedience rewarding? We already know the answer. If the leader uses his authority in order to initiate action by the group as a whole, and in order to coordinate the activities of the individual members so as to accomplish a result that could not have been reached without this initiative and coordination, then the followers may find obedience to his orders very rewarding indeed. In fact, the leader has acquired a new source of power, a new and rare ability to reward many members. And his authority, the presumption that his orders are to be obeyed, may eventually extend far beyond the area in which he first demonstrated his competence.

An order and a norm are the same sort of thing. And just as men may conform to a norm without finding the direct results of conformity rewarding, the same is true with obedience to an order. Some of the followers may not find the results of obedience particularly rewarding to them personally, but they obey, nonetheless. For so long as other followers do value the results, any disobedience is a threat to these others, which they may punish by withdrawing their friendship from the disobedient. Consequently, to the extent that friendly relationships have been built up in the group, so that there is some friendship to withdraw, even members not personally interested in the goal of the group may obey the orders of the leader. A wise leader will do what he can to foster close ties not only between himself and his followers but between the followers themselves, since even these latter ties may help to maintain his authority.

How does the leader foster these ties? It is not easy. As he extends his authority he acquires new responsibilities. Since he is a person of high status, he will be expected to do justice, and his orders may now have a big effect on the course of justice within the group. In coordinating the activities of the members to accomplish the group goal, he may have to assign members to special jobs. If he does not assign to the "better" jobs—no matter how "better" is defined in the group—the persons who have higher status in the group in other respects, he will arouse their resentment against him and their jealousy of those he has favored. Again, the rewards for at-

[14] C. I. Barnard, *The Functions of the Executive* (Cambridge, Mass.: Harvard University Press, 1938), p. 165.

taining a group goal are sometimes indivisible: each member must get such satisfaction out of it as he can. But sometimes the rewards may be divisible among the members. For instance, the leader may get paid for attaining the goal, and then he is in a position to distribute money or other booty to his followers—and to himself. If he does not distribute the money and booty so as to give the "better" rewards to the "better" contributors, he will once more arouse resentment and jealousy; and these are just the things that will put the collaboration of the members and their future obedience to his orders in danger.

Thus the leader of a group always has two problems: external and internal.[15] He must lead the group to its external goal and internally preserve the rule of justice. The solutions to the two problems are often in conflict. Suppose, for instance, that he has recognized some special ability in one of the members who has previously held low status, and promotes him to one of the better jobs on the grounds that the group's effort would then be more effective. In so doing he may arouse resentment because he has given this upstart a better job than he deserved. The ablest leader will make mistakes or, more often, reach impasses where anything he does is going to hurt somebody. His best hope lies in increasing his authority enough so that the group will begin to accept, together with his orders, his definitions of what is right and fair.

If authority, the presumption that a man's orders are to be obeyed, is associated with high status in fact, then authority becomes also a symbol of status, with all the usual consequences. Thus if a man, already established as of low status, tries to give an order, he is symbolically putting himself ahead of others. They may ask, "Who is he to tell us what to do?" and disregard the order, regardless of its prima facie wisdom. After a few experiences of this sort, a man may well hesitate before making further suggestions. If he wants the group to do something, he does not now tell the members himself but takes the matter first to the leader. Only if the leader accepts the suggestion, and puts out the order as his own, will the group act. In this way, regular channels of communication tend to become established even in groups that outwardly appear very informal. But an order not given is an order that cannot be obeyed; and as the man in question becomes reluctant to give orders, he lessens his chances of getting established as a leader in his own right. This does not mean in the least that a person once established as holding low status cannot rise to leadership, for we have all seen it happen. It does mean that such a man will have initial difficulties in doing so that a higher man need not face. If

---

[15] This is C. I. Barnard's distinction between effectiveness and efficiency in *The Functions of the Executive* (cited in footnote 14), pp. 55–59.

by the principle of congruence, a person of low status is not expected to give orders, and may be resented if he tries to do so, then by the same token, a person of high status is positively expected to take the lead and will lose status if, on occasions calling for it, he does not do so. Indeed, one main reason why persons of high status try to display the symbols appropriate to their position is that they hereby help maintain the presumption that it is they, and not somebody else, who are to give orders, and that obedience to their orders will be rewarded.

When a person in a certain position (in this case, a person of high status) is expected to behave in a certain way (in this case, to lead), and, indeed, to behave in a number of other ways (in this case, for instance, to do justice) that differentiate him from persons in other positions in a group, then he has what sociologists call a *role*. Some sociologists maintain that the role is the fundamental unit of sociological analysis, and do not undertake to go behind it. For many purposes it is indeed convenient to describe social structures, especially the big and complicated ones, by speaking not of the behavior of individuals but of roles. In describing American society, for instance, it saves time to speak of the role of the father in the family, or of the role of the foreman in a factory. But for those of us who are interested in explaining fundamental phenomena, it is unsatisfactory to start with roles. Why should there be roles at all? And why should a particular role, like that of a leader, be what it is? We have made a start at answering these questions here. Then again, many persons do not behave in the ways their roles call for, do not live up very well to what is expected of them. Why? The answer is finally given by the psychological propositions we started with. The question is especially important if many men start deviating from their roles in the same way; for then they are on their way toward establishing new roles, in a process of social change. A sociology that limits itself to the description of roles will have no capacity to explain social change.

## Equality and "Social" Interaction

We must now turn to some of the back effects of the differentiation of members in status and authority on the other features of the organization of a group. One of the most striking features of social organization in groups, large and small, is the tendency for persons to interact with others who are more or less their equals in status on occasions that we usually call "social"—such occasions as spending leisure time or going to parties. In different degrees in different groups, this tendency divides persons into the layers or strata that in larger societies are called classes or castes.

How shall we explain this tendency? We must first remind ourselves that in all social interaction persons receive rewards but also incur costs—cost being defined as the reward a person would have gotten from some alternative activity that he foregoes when he performs the activity he does perform. This is just as true of interaction between superiors and inferiors in status as it is of other interaction: one never gets something for nothing. When an inferior goes to a superior for help, one cost he incurs is precisely the confession he thereby makes of his own inferiority. He may still go for help since the reward may outweigh in the cost, but there is a cost, nevertheless. In the same way, the superior may incur costs in helping the inferior, for instance, in time taken from his own work.

Moreover, the rewards of the interaction tend to decrease in value over time and the costs tend to increase. By the satiation proposition (IV), the superior, temporarily at least, may tend to become satiated with the approval he gets from inferiors, and to miss more and more the time taken from his own work. And the inferior may tend to become satiated with help and find the costs of confessing his inferiority increasingly more galling. Under these circumstances there may come a time—not necessarily the same time for both parties—when each finds that some alternative provides a greater net reward than continuing the exchange between superior and inferior. The unwillingness to exchange may not last: on the next day they both may be as ready to exchange as ever. But all we need for our argument is a temporary cessation.

The same tendency holds true with respect to what often goes with superior status—the exercise of authority. If the superior wants sooner or later to escape the real burdens of responsibility, the inferior wants sooner or later to escape from control. Obedience to orders is always in some degree constraining: if one obeys, one often does something different from what one otherwise would have wanted to do. One may still obey because one values the ultimate result, or fears the immediate punishment for disobedience, but a cost is always incurred and, in the short run, the cost mounts. Indeed, authorities are apt to be dangerous and must be approached with circumspection. One does not know where or when lightning will strike. "If the boss sees me, he may think up something for me to do."

We now set up a very rough division between two spheres of human activity, more sharply distinct in some groups than in others, but distinguished in practice, to some degree, in every one. The two spheres are contrasted in a number of different pairs of terms: the public sphere versus the private, the sphere of work versus that of leisure, the business sphere versus the "social."

The first sphere encompasses work and business in the sense that it is the one in which the initially more valuable rewards of life are exchanged, those connected with making a living in the broadest sense of the phrase. It is also a public sphere, because these valuable rewards are often the ones that many men demand but few are able to supply and because they often cannot be secured without the cooperation of many men. This is the sphere in which (as we have seen) power, status, and authority are won and lost. The second sphere—the private, the leisure, the "social" sphere—is the one in which the initially less important rewards are exchanged. This does not mean that they are absolutely unimportant or that they are not highly valued. But their value becomes relatively high only to the degree that the demand for the other kinds of reward is satiated or, for the moment, nothing further can be done to get them. Only after a man has gotten enough to eat do the rewards of play, of leisure, of "social life" (in the narrow sense of "social") become relatively valuable.

The rewards of interaction in the business sphere are initially high, but they are also purchased at high cost, precisely the cost of accepting inferiority or superiority; and as the opportunity of getting these rewards temporarily comes to an end, and men turn to the other sphere, they will seek out for interaction the kinds of men with whom they can exchange rewards that were not initially very valuable but, at least, were not purchased at the cost of differences in status. In the nature of the case, these men are going to be their equals in status. With such men one can relax, be one's self, and exchange the easy give-and-take of conversation, of conviviality, of sport. To such men one can give the easy, unconstrained liking that is a little different from the respect one accords to one's betters. With his equals the man of high status can escape the importunities of his inferiors, and the man of low status can escape from superior authority, since his equals are people whose behavior is similar to his own and who therefore are in no position to criticize him. For these reasons, "social" interaction between equals tends to be a feature of status systems everywhere.

We say "tends to be" because the very fact that social interaction tends to go toward social equals brings into play forces tending to modify the relationship. For social interaction itself will then become a symbol of status. A social climber may seek out interaction with his superiors outside the business sphere in the effort to establish symbolic equality with them, not only in their eyes but in the eyes of other beholders: he may want "to be seen with them." On their part, the superiors may try to exclude him from social interaction, for fear that allowing it might lower their own status as perceived by others. On the other hand, a superior who is secure in his status, whose position of superior power is beyond doubt, may allow his inferiors to interact with him socially, and thus acquire a new capacity to provide rare and valuable rewards. The way social behavior develops can often be summed up in the old rule: "To him that hath there shall also be given, but from him that hath not shall be taken away even that which he hath."

Another result of the tendency of persons to interact in the social sphere with their equals may tend to reinforce the relationship. Social equals, in any event, are apt to be similar in some respect, and social interaction may make them even more so. As they interact with one another in leisure-time pursuits, parties, and sports, they tend, by the process we previously called *elaboration*, to develop their own special interests, opinions, ways of doing things, and even ways of speech. Under these conditions an inferior who undertakes to establish social interaction with his superiors encounters additional difficulties. He may not have learned to do what they consider "the right things." He may not be able "to speak the same language." And thus by all he says and does he reveals himself to be an outsider. Then he may be embarrassed himself and a source of embarrassment to others; and since the essential charm of social interaction lies in persons' being at ease with one another, the embarrassment is an extra cost of interaction between superiors and inferiors and may discourage it further. Some men may still seek it out, but they are apt to be men for whom a rise in symbolic social status has a high value, who have a high tolerance for initial humiliation, and who can quickly pick up new ways of behaving. The persons that we call social climbers tend to have just these characteristics.

## Status and Conformity

We must now turn to one last back effect of the development of a status system on the other features of social behavior in a group. This is the often-observed tendency for persons at the bottom of a status system as well as those at the top to be somewhat less subject to group influences, to be in some ways less ready to conform than persons in the middle. Consider those experiments in which the members of a group have to choose between ambiguous stimuli.[16] Members may, for instance, be asked to decide which of two squares contains the larger number of dots, and they are led to believe that other members of the group think one square does, but the visual evidence suggests the other one, although not with absolutely certainty. Under these circumstances, both members of high

[16] A summary of these experiments is given in G. C. Homans, *Social Behavior* (New York: Harcourt, Brace, and World, 1961), pp. 336–358. See also E. P. Hollander, *Leaders, Groups, and Influence* (New York: Oxford University Press, 1964).

and low status are less likely to go along with the group's apparent judgment than those of middle status. The reasons for nonconformity may be somewhat different for those of high status than for those of low. Let us take up the persons of low status first.

There is something special about being at the bottom of the status heap: one has no more status to lose. If he violates very highly valued norms, the other members may drive him physically out of the group but, short of that, there is little they can do to him. If they try to punish him for nonconformity in lesser things by lowering their opinion of him, they will fail, because his status could not be lower already. Therefore, he has nothing to lose by nonconformity. On the other hand, perhaps he has something to gain by conformity, and it is true that persons who have recently entered a group at the bottom, but who may hope in time to become fully accepted, are apt to be compulsive conformists to any rule of behavior that the others value. This condition does not hold true for persons who have been long in the group and whose "bad" behavior in some respect has definitely won them low status. The others expect any new action they perform to be bad too—it is, in a way, their role to be bad. The others may even have trouble recognizing a change for the better when they see it, and thus may not give the ex-sinners credit for it. Some of us have been members of groups in which we "could not do anything right; everything we did was wrong." Now if one has nothing to lose by nonconformity and nothing to gain by conformity, he might as well act without reference to the group. If nonconformity will at least save a person his self-respect, let him be a nonconformist. True, his nonconformity may serve to confirm him in his low status in the eyes of others. To expect a man's behavior to be bad is to increase the probability that it will, in fact, be bad: social behavior is full of these "self-fulfilling prophecies." Actually, groups tend to lose control of their low-status members, and this is not all loss to the lowly. What they have lost in status they gain precisely in freedom from control, in irresponsibility. "The Lord tempers the wind to the shorn lamb."

Something of the same sort may hold true for high-status persons. They may conform to well-established and highly valued norms of the group. Indeed, they may have taken the lead in establishing them. But conformity in lesser matters, especially conformity to group judgments on new issues, when it is not at all certain that the group is right, does not offer much advantage to a person of high status. After all, he won his status by being different from and better than the others in what he does. To be different and better may be expected of him: it has become his role, and if he cannot be better, he may settle for at least being different. Merely to conform to some new group judgment is certainly not to play this role. But if he takes the risk of reaching an independent judgment, and he turns out to be right, he has done his job brilliantly. It is not his job to conform but to decide what is to be conformed to. Even if he turns out to be wrong, who will bring him to account? The person of middle status who undertakes to judge him will, by that fact, set himself up as superior to his fellows, and they may not be ready to accord him superiority. We need not claim in the least that revolts never take place in a group, or that an established leader is never dethroned. We need only recognize that the man who would dethrone a leader usually faces some difficulties in beginning his task. In social (as in physical) phenomena, starting friction is greater than sliding friction. For these reasons a member of high status may be a little less ready than ordinary members to go along with the gang.

As for the members of middle status, there is apt to be a relatively large number of them in any group, none being much better or worse than the others but all being about the same. Unlike low-status members, they have something to lose by nonconformity. Unlike high-status ones, they have little to gain by it, unless they are prepared to take the risks of setting themselves up above their former fellows and challenging the leadership. Their best ordinary bet is conformity. Again, this does not mean that all persons of middle status are conformists, but the tendency certainly exists.

We have described and explained some fundamental social processes as they occur in small, ephemeral groups, in which all the members can interact with one another face to face. It was not within our province to show how these processes build up into the larger social structures. But it may be suggestive, here at the conclusion, to ask what it would take to turn a group such as ours into a minimal version of what sociologists call a society. All it would take—and that, admittedly, is a great deal—would be the perpetuation of the group from one generation to another. That would mean bringing in children, and women to bear them. There would be norms regulating the distribution of that very valuable reward, sexual intercourse; and the differences of age and sex, with their accompanying differences in capacities, would become the basis for a structure of status, the adult men holding the superior positions. All of these things would complicate the given conditions in which the fundamental social processes operate, but they would not change the nature of the processes themselves. Thus the development of status does not change its nature just because the underlying differences in power rest on differences in sex and age rather than on, for instance, seniority in an office. Remember that all human societies for untold millennia were independent small groups, and many of them still are today.

## Selected Bibliography

Bales, R. F., *Interaction Process Analysis* (Boston: Addison-Wesley, 1950).

Bass, B. M., *Leadership, Psychology, and Organizational Behavior* (New York: Harper, 1960).

Bennis, W. G., Schein, E. H., Berlew, D. E., and Steele, F. I., eds., *Interpersonal Dynamics* (Homewood, Ill.: Dorsey Press, 1964).

Blau, P. M., *The Dynamics of Bureaucracy* (Chicago: University of Chicago Press, 1955).

Blau, P. M., *Exchange and Power in Social Life* (New York: Wiley, 1964).

Bonner, H., *Group Dynamics: Principles and Applications* (New York: Ronald Press, 1959).

Browne, C. G., and Cohn, T. S., eds., *The Study of Leadership* (Danville, Ill.: The Interstate Printers and Publishers, 1958).

Cartwright, D., and Zander, A., eds., *Group Dynamics: Research and Theory*, 2nd ed. (Evanston, Ill.: Row, Peterson, 1960).

Cartwright, D., ed., *Studies in Social Power* (Ann Arbor: University of Michigan, 1959).

Festinger, L., Schachter, S., and Back, K., *Social Pressures in Informal Groups* (New York: Harper, 1950).

Goffman, E., *The Presentation of Self in Everyday Life* (Garden City, N.Y.: Doubleday, 1959).

Golombiewski, R. T., *The Small Group* (Chicago: University of Chicago Press, 1962).

Hare, A. P., Borgatta, E. F., and Bales, R. F., eds., *Small Groups: Studies in Social Interaction* (New York: Knopf, 1955).

Hare, A. P., *Handbook of Small Group Research* (New York: The Free Press of Glencoe, 1962).

Heider, F., *The Psychology of Interpersonal Relations* (New York: Wiley, 1958).

Hollander, E. P., *Leaders, Groups, and Influence* (New York: Oxford, 1964).

Homans, G. C., *The Human Group* (New York: Harcourt, Brace, and World, 1950).

Homans, G. C., *Social Behavior: Its Elementary Forms* (New York: Harcourt, Brace, and World, 1961).

Jennings, H. H., *Leadership and Isolation*, 2nd ed. (New York: Longmans, Green, 1950).

Klein, J., *The Study of Groups* (London: Routledge and Kegan Paul, 1956).

Kuhn, A., *The Study of Society: A Unified Approach* (Homewood, Ill.: Richard D. Irwin, 1963).

Newcomb, T. M., *The Acquaintance Process* (New York: Holt, Rinehart, and Winston, 1961).

Olmsted, M. S., *The Small Group* (New York: Random House, 1959).

Shepherd, C. R., *Small Groups: Some Sociological Perspectives* (San Francisco: Chandler, 1964).

Sherif, M., and Sherif, C. W., *Reference Groups* (New York: Harper and Row, 1964).

Sprott, W. J. H., *Human Groups* (London: Penguin Books, 1958).

Staats, A. W., and C. K., *Complex Human Behavior* (New York: Holt, Rinehart, and Winston, 1963).

Stogdill, R. M., *Individual Behavior and Group Achievement* (New York: Oxford, 1959).

Thibaut, J. W., and Kelley, H. M., *The Social Psychology of Groups* (New York: Wiley, 1969).

Walker, E. L., and Heyns, R. W., *An Anatomy for Conformity* (Englewood Cliffs, N.J.: Prentice-Hall, 1962).

Zaleznik, A., and Moment, D., *The Dynamics of Interpersonal Behavior* (New York: Wiley, 1964).

# 2

# COMMUNITY

*Leo F. Schnore*

# COMMUNITY

The community is a basic unit of social structure, but it is a matter that concerns more writers than sociologists alone. Indeed, modern intellectuals have expended vast amounts of ink and paper in discussing the contemporary community, usually regarding it with a mixture of puzzlement and alarm, and at least implicitly contrasting its present condition with some ideal "state of nature"—past or future—in which the raucous problems of the day are not heard, or are somehow muted.

What is the contemporary view of the community? I shall sketch that view in a manner that is brief but familiar. We are told that in the United States more and more of us are destined to live in "the exploding metropolis," a sprawling mosaic of social worlds—grim slums at the core, violent and tense—an "asphalt jungle," surrounded by a spreading and blighted "gray area," very much in need of "renewal" or "rehabilitation." Beyond this area lies the false promised land of "suburbia," a place chiefly inhabited by harassed commuters in gray-flannel suits, linked to each other only in the lock-step of mindless conformity to bureaucratic rules and uniform standards of taste.

As a community form, "the city" is viewed as a hotbed of "alienation" and "anomie," an impersonal and unsatisfying world of "mass culture," perhaps best symbolized by a jungle of TV antennas. The city, full of racial and ethnic tensions, is portrayed as a "powder keg" with an ever-shorter fuse. Its inhabitants are engaged in a virtual war of each against all, divided by differing backgrounds and loyalties, and altogether lacking in any sense of unity that might cause the inhabitants to act in the interests of the community at large. Each man, intent only upon his own concerns—whether these concerns involve career, family, or ethnic group—is supposed to have lost that "sense of community" that unites him with his fellows in the pursuit of rational collective goals.

The main image of the contemporary community conveyed by those who contemplate today's cities is this one: an alienated, anonymous, bureaucratized mass of mankind, either densely packed in aging tenements and deteriorating houses or sprawled in chaotic array over the nearby suburbs, but—in either case—bereft of all that is good and wholesome and virtuous.

Meanwhile, in the countryside, things are not too bright either, if we may believe what we read. Aside from rural "pockets of poverty"—such as the Great Lakes cutover region and Appalachia—there is everywhere the long-term decline in the family farm, the steady attrition of rural neighborhoods, the loss of rural youth to the city, and the general disappearance of "the rural community" as a viable entity.

What may we conclude? "Things are tough everywhere?" I must admit that my sketch is a deliberate caricature of the popular literature on the contemporary community. But behind the exaggerations and polemics of that literature we find a series of very important questions.

Does the modern community alienate the mass of men from a common culture: Is life in the city an impersonal and anonymous round of meaningless motions? Does bureaucratization leave the individual hopelessly vulnerable to forces outside of his community and (as a result) outside of his control? Are we becoming increasingly segregated in terms of social class, type of family, and racial or ethnic background, so that we are increasingly conscious of differences between, rather than similarities among, members of the communities in which we live?

Now there is no lack of quick and easy "answers" to such queries as these. I could list answers at length, simply by quoting the words of the dozens of writers who have offered observations on these topics. But the list would be full of contradictions. Writers dealing with the community have raised a haze of conflicting opinion, largely speculative in nature; and, as a result, the topic has become more obscure with each contribution. In my view, even the most tentative answers to the questions that I asked above—answers based on any kind of sound evidence—are very hard to attain. And this is where the sociologist comes in.

Sociology is groping its way toward scientific status by two principal means: (1) by sharpening its *conceptual* focus, and (2) by dealing with social life in *empirical* terms. In other words, "theory" and "research" provide the two bases for approaching any sociological subject. In the case of the community, sociologists have grappled for years with the concept "community" and have reached at least a limited degree of theoretical consensus on the meaning of the term, the aspects of community life that can be treated sociologically, and the main intellectual problems that can be confronted by sociologists. On the empirical side, they have been even more successful. Despite terminological disagreements, the more research-oriented sociologists have amassed a considerable body of evidence on the community and its various facets. I do not intend to imply that we have produced a series of scientific "laws," but we have accumulated an impressive array of empirical regularities—orderly relations between sociological variables—in a community context. (Very few of these have been tested cross-culturally, of course, and a disappointingly large fraction of our knowledge of the community relates to mid-twentieth century American cities, but efforts in the direction of comparative and historical analysis are increasingly frequent.)

My procedure in this chapter is very simple. I first give an approximate chronological summary of sociological theory relating to the concept of the community, and then provide a fairly representative sample of empirical research on the community. In other words, I try to deal with both community theory and research, but without any pretense of complete coverage of the topic. It must be recognized that the literature on the subject is enormous, and any brief treatment must be highly selective.

## Community: The Concept and its Sociological Meanings

"Community," like most terms borrowed from everyday language, is a sociological concept that displays a number of facets. Sociologists are not entirely consistent in their usage, and the term takes on different meanings in different contexts. Here, we consider in approximate chronological order some of the shades of meaning that have attached to the term. The primary purpose, of course, is to delineate a manageable area of investigation and to report some of the main results of sociological research on the subject.

### Some Classical Views

The traditional sociological conception of the community does not depart radically from the common-sense meaning of the term. One of the earliest and most influential treatments of the subject in modern sociology, for example, defined the community as "a social unity whose members recognize as common a sufficiency of interests to allow of the interactivities of common life." [1] This definition embraces the familiar notion of a "community of interest" or a viewpoint shared by a number of individuals. It refers to which might be called a "psychological community." The difficulty is that such a sense of likeness, when it occurs, may have innumerables bases—familial, ethnic, occupational, and others—and that different members of the "social unity" (whatever its bases) may have quite different perceptions of their degrees of likeness with their fellows. One result is that a careful examination of 94 different definitions of community has led to the conclusion that "beyond the concept that people are involved in community, there is no complete agreement as to the nature of community." [2]

Over the years, however, the concept did undergo a subtle kind of metamorphosis, in which *one basis of commonality* came to be emphasized. That was the territorial factor. In the years between World War I and World War II, in particular, the sociological conception of the community was markedly influenced by the thinking of a group of sociologists at the University of Chicago. In their view, the most salient basis of

---

[1] Robert M. MacIver, *Community* (London: Macmillan, 1917), p. 107.
[2] George A. Hillery, Jr., "Definitions of Community: Areas of Agreement," *Rural Sociology*, **20**, 119 (June, 1955).

commonality in action and outlook was provided in the sheer co-occupancy of a given territory. The acknowledged leader of the "Chicago School" was Robert E. Park. Writing in 1929, he held as follows:

> Community, in the broadest sense of that term, has a spatial and a geographical connotation. Every community has a location, and the individuals who compose it have a place of residence within the territory which the community occupies.[3]

Some of the ambiguities in this conception are suggested, however, by Park's subsequent remark that "Towns, cities, hamlets, and, under modern conditions, the whole world, with all its differences of race, of culture, and of individual interests—all these are communities." [4] If this is the case, the concept of community is uncommonly elastic, and can be stretched to include almost any territorial aggregate in which the investigator happens to be interested—from the local neighborhood to the world at large.

Subsequent efforts by writers working in the Chicago tradition sought to reduce the scope of the territory to which the term might be meaningfully applied. Louis Wirth, for example, attempted to identify "The Scope and Problems of the Community" in an essay written in 1933:

> A territorial base, distribution in space of men, institutions, and activities, close living together on the basis of kinship and organic interdependence, and a common life based upon the mutual correspondence of interests tends to characterize a community." [5]

Requiring "close living together" and "a common life" means that a fairly limited and localized unit is being specified; the world as a whole could hardly qualify as a community under these restrictive conditions. Still, the problem of establishing meaningful boundaries remains. Writers in the Chicago tradition were trying to identify some sort of areally bounded collectivity that is larger than (for instance) the family and smaller than the world. But what are its limits?

Amos H. Hawley, in the Chicago tradition, has stated the question most clearly and has offered a tentative resolution of the boundary problem. In the course of developing "a theory of community structure," he has made these comments:

> From a spatial standpoint, the community may be defined as comprising that area the resident population of which is interrelated and integrated with reference to its daily requirements, whether contacts be direct or indirect. Arbitrary as this definition may seem, it is consistent with common usage. Participation in a daily

[3] Robert E. Park, "Sociology, Community and Society," in Wilson Gee, ed., *Research in the Social Sciences* (New York: Macmillan, 1929), p. 7.

[4] *Ibid.*

[5] Louis Wirth, "The Scope and Problems of the Community," *Publications of American Sociological Society*, **27**, 62 (May, 1933).

rhythm of collective life is the factor which distinguishes and gives unity to the population of a locality.[6]

It should also be observed that the emphasis on "daily" interaction brings time as well as space into consideration. What this definition omits is any concern with a possible "community of interest," for it represents an ecological conception. Elsewhere, however, Hawley has called attention to alternative conceptions:

> The human community, of course, is more than just an organization of symbiotic relationships and to that extent there are limitations to the scope of human ecology. Man's collective life involves, in greater or less degree, a psychological and a moral as well as a symbiotic integration. But these, so far as they are distinguishable, should be regarded as complementing aspects of the same thing rather than as separate phases or segments of the community. Sustenance activities and interrelations are inextricably interwoven with sentiments, value systems, and other ideational constructs.[7]

The ecologist, then, does not deny the existence or importance of the psychological aspect of community life. He simply prefers to regard it as a separate facet of the object under investigation, and to leave its study to others.

In any case, the areally based conception of the community, stressing the ecological aspect, has achieved a considerable degree of acceptance on the part of sociologists. Even those writers who work within intellectual traditions other than those of the Chicago School have adopted this areal or territorial emphasis in their thinking about the community. Thus Talcott Parsons, writing in 1951, held that "A community is that collectivity the members of which share a common territorial area as their base of operations for daily activities." [8] Note the striking similarity between the Parsons and Hawley definitions.

Some writers retain the areal emphasis, but insist on adding the subjective *psychological* dimension. Blaine E. Mercer offers the following definition:

> A human community is a functionally related aggregate of people who live in a particular geographic locality at a particular time, share a common culture, are arranged in a social structure, and exhibit an awareness of their uniqueness and separate identity as a group.[9]

[6] Amos H. Hawley, *Human Ecology: A Theory of Community Structure* (New York: Ronald Press, 1950), pp. 257–258.
[7] Amos H. Hawley, "Ecology and Human Ecology," *Social Forces,* **22,** 404 (May, 1944).
[8] Talcott Parsons, *The Social System* (Glencoe, Ill.: Free Press, 1951), p. 91; see also Talcott Parsons, "The Principal Structures of Community: A Sociological View," in Carl J. Friedrich, ed., *Community* (New York: Liberal Arts Press, 1959), pp. 152–179.
[9] Blaine E. Mercer, *The American Community* (New York: Random House, 1956), p. 27.

As we shall see, this kind of insistence upon subjective criteria raises more problems than it solves. The degree of "awareness" on the part of the inhabitants is a question of fact, and when this matter is put to an empirical test, the results suggest a high degree of variability. Residents conceive the community in different ways, and recognize different boundaries.[10]

Consequently, many sociologists now feel that a more serviceable definition of the community is a "stripped-down" model, consisting of the fewest possible elements. For example, Sjoberg, modifying Parsons' definition for his own purposes, has recently offered the following definition:

> . . . a community is a collectivity of actors sharing a limited territorial area as the base for carrying out the greatest share of their daily activities. This definition implies that persons interact within a *local* institutional complex which provides a wide range of basic services, yet it also takes into consideration the fact that the community is not necessarily a self-sufficient unit.[11]

Without suggesting that Sjoberg's definition should be regarded as some kind of "official" and definitive statement, I point out that it was prepared for *A Dictionary of the Social Sciences* compiled under the auspices of the United Nations Educational, Scientific, and Cultural Organization (UNESCO) and that it is not tailored to a specific problem. Instead, it is an effort to present a highly general conception that is suitable to a range of uses. Sjoberg's main contribution, however, is the clear identification of a number of *issues* involved in sociological treatments of the concept. Some of these issues have only arisen in recent years, as new perspectives have been brought to bear upon the concept of community, and it is these new views that we now consider.

### Some New Perspectives

Recent writers have questioned the utility of the community concept as it has evolved over the years, arguing that new conditions have rendered it obsolete. These criticisms must be assessed, since our concepts must display a high degree of correspondence with current realities if they are to be useful in our analyses of contemporary social life.

In a book published in 1960 under the provocative title, *The Eclipse*

[10] Jiri Kolaja, "The Image of the Whole Community," in Institut International de Sociologie, *La Sociologia y Las Sociedades en Desarrollo Industrial* (Universidad Nacionel de Cordoba: Communicaciones al XX Congreso Internacional de Sociologia, Tomo III, 1963), pp. 113–123.

[11] Gideon Sjoberg, "Community," in Julius Gould and William L. Kolb, eds., *A Dictionary of the Social Sciences* (New York: The Free Press, 1964), pp. 114–115; italics in original.

*of Community*, Maurice R. Stein launched what amounted to the first in a series of attacks on the traditional concept. Basing his criticism on a review of a number of well-known American community studies—those of Chicago, Middletown, and Yankee City—Stein attempted to assess the impact upon the community of urbanization, industrialization, and bureaucratization, which he saw as the dominant trends in twentieth-century America.

Unfortunately, he did not make quite clear just what aspect of the community has been affected. The promise of the title—with "eclipse" suggesting a significant change—was never fulfilled. The closest Stein came to specifying the nature of the changes that he had in mind is represented in the following passages.

As urbanization spread, individuals [in Middletown] lost their sense of the whole community. . . . The old system of social organization [in Yankee City] in which local economic, political, and social positions were in regular alignment had broken down as people in all positions of the local hierarchy found themselves dependent on extra-local influences. Simultaneously, their sense of belonging to a common enterprise, whether it be the shoe factory or the city itself, seriously declined. . . . The old feeling of solidarity based on a sense that everyone in town belongs to a common community gives way to subcommunities with hostile attitudes toward each other. . . . The classes in Yankee City—once joint participants in a common communal system—now confront each other as embodiments of collectivities under the control of remote power centers which determine their relationships to each other far more than factors arising in local life. . . . There is one underlying community trend to which all three of the studies [of Chicago, Middletown, and Yankee City] refer. That is the trend toward increased interdependence and decreased local autonomy.[12]

These passages give the impression that the community in "eclipse" is a *psychological* community, that is, a community that is perceived by the residents. I have already mentioned this conception, and we shall consider it later. Here, it is simply sufficient to note that this is not the only conception of the community, and is not necessarily the most fruitful one. Stein's main contribution, from my standpoint, is his provision of a set of hypotheses concerning some of the psychological correlates of the increasing *interdependence* of communities following upon the increasing ease of transportation and communication.

These technological trends play the key roles in another recent critique of traditional thinking about the community—this one by a sociologist who became an urban planner. Melvin M. Webber has attacked the notion of the community as an areally bounded social entity, and has spoken of

[12] Maurice R. Stein, *The Eclipse of Community* (Princeton, N.J.: Princeton University Press, 1960), pp. 65, 90–93, and 107.

the "community without propinquity," a new form permitted by "a chain of technological development that permit spatial separation of closely related people." [13] In his view, the contemporary American urbanite "really lives" in many communities:

The communities with which he associates and to which he "belongs" are no longer only the *communities of place* to which his ancestors were restricted; Americans are becoming more closely tied to various *interest communities* than to place communities, whether the interest be based on occupational activities, leisure pastimes, social relationships, or intellectual pursuits. Members of *interest communities* within a freely communicating society need not be spatially concentrated (except, perhaps, during the formative stages of the interest community's development), for they are increasingly able to interact with each other wherever they may be located. . . . Spatial separation or propinquity is no longer an accurate indicator of functional relations; and, hence, mere locational pattern is no longer an adequate symbol of order.[14]

This view highlights the importance of an individual's basic conception of the community in any assessment of major trends in community phenomena. Webber, like Stein, sees a decline in local autonomy as the inevitable accompaniment of the increased interdependence among communities. Again, however, it is the stress on the *psychological* dimension—a focus on "interest communities"—that leads to this conclusion. An individual's place of residence probably does have a reduced significance in this narrow sense; in a mobile society like our own, the probabilities that a person will live and die near his birthplace grow less and less, along with the probabilities that his relatives, friends, and valued colleagues will be found just around the corner. But does this mean that a territorially based conception of the community has no utility? I shall deal with this question in the next subsection.

Perhaps the most ambitious effort at criticizing the traditional conception of the community is that of Roland L. Warren. He has brought out very clearly the multidimensional character of sociological thinking on the subject, as follows.

The term "community" implies something both psychological and geographical. Psychologically, it implies shared interests, characteristics, or association, as in the expression "community of interest," or "the business community." Geographically, it denotes a specific area where people are clustered. Sociologically, the

---

[13] Melvin M. Webber, "Order in Diversity: Community without Propinquity," in Lowdon Wingo, Jr., ed., *Cities and Space* (Baltimore: Johns Hopkins Press, 1963), p. 23; see also Melvin M. Webber, "The Urban Place and the Nonplace Urban Realm," in Melvin M. Webber et al., *Explorations into Urban Structure* (Philadelphia: University of Pennsylvania Press, 1964), pp. 79–153.

[14] *Ibid.*, pp. 29 and 49; italics added.

term combines these two connotations. It relates to the shared interests and behavior patterns which people have by virtue of their common locality.[15]

However, after reviewing a number of the alleged inadequacies of older conceptions of the community, Warren concluded by offering a definition that is not markedly different from the traditional view:

> We shall consider a community to be *that combination of social units and systems which perform the major social functions having locality relevance*. This is another way of saying that by "community" we mean the organization of social activities to afford people daily local access to those broad areas of activity which are necessary in day-to-day living.[16]

Despite all of the criticism, then, recent writers seem to have advanced no further in helping us understand the phenomenon "community." Their own answers to the problem of definition seem no more compelling than those of earlier writers on the subject. This situation has caused one logician to assert that the problem is basically insoluble. "In the course of a discussion of community," John Ladd says, "it seems quite natural to ask for a definition of the term 'community.' Yet all attempts to define it appear doomed to failure." [17]

My own view is not quite so gloomy. It is my feeling that a manageable conception *can* be offered, in order to direct attention to a range of sociological problems that might otherwise be ignored or obscured. While such a definition might not be satisfactory to all sociologists, whose interests in the community display an almost bewildering variety, it should help to provide a framework within which we can examine some results of modern sociological research on the subject. Before I give my own working definition, however, it is helpful to review some of the issues brought out in the debate over the community, and to examine some of the applications of the concept in sociology and related social sciences.

### Some Issues and Applications

The first issue concerns the necessity for dealing with the areal or territorial dimension. *Is a community necessarily a geographic entity?* Opinions on this matter are divided. George A. Hillery, Jr., in his review of 94 definitions of community, carried out in 1955, remarked that "it is significant that no author encountered in the survey denied that area could be an

---

[15] Roland L. Warren, *The Community in America* (Chicago: Rand McNally and Co., 1963), p. 6.

[16] *Ibid.*, p. 9; italics in original.

[17] John Ladd, "The Concept of Community: A Logical Analysis," in Carl J. Friedrich, ed., *Community* (New York: Liberal Arts Press, 1959), p. 269.

element of community.[18] Subsequent writers, however, have denied the necessity for an areally based conception. Perhaps the most explicit denial is that of Don Martindale, who has spoken of the community "not as a term for an area where people live but for a kind of integrated system of social life in which geographical area is secondary or irrelevant." [19] Martindale clearly prefers a conception of community that emphasizes the psychological dimension, stressing a "community of interest" and neglecting the requirement of areal co-occupancy.

This view stems very naturally from such usages as those of William J. Goode, who has identified professionals as "a community within a community" in the following way:

Each profession is a community without physical locus and, like other communities with heavy in-migration, one whose founding fathers are linked only rarely by blood with the present generation. It may nevertheless be called a community by virtue of these characteristics: (1) Its members are bound by a sense of identity. (2) Once in it, few leave, so that it is a terminal or continuing status for the most part. (3) Its members share values in common. (4) Its role definitions vis-à-vis both members and non-members are agreed upon and are the same for all members. (5) Within the areas of communal action there is a common language, which is understood only partially by outsiders. (6) The Community has power over its members. (7) Its limits are reasonably clear, though they are not physical and geographical, but social. (8) Though it does not produce the next generation biologically, it does so socially through its control over the selection of professional trainees, and through its training processes it sends these recruits through an adult socialization process.[20]

This conception of the community is not confined to the professions. In a study of *Union Democracy* among printers, for example, Seymour Martin Lipset, Martin A. Trow, and James S. Coleman devoted considerable attention to the factors contributing to the development of a distinctive "occupational community" in this highly skilled craft.[21] Like Goode, they regard the presence of "community" as *a variable characteristic of occupations or professions.* Some occupations exhibit more community, some less. Without questioning this judgment, I must emphasize again that these applications of the term "community" represent a substantial departure from traditional usage, wherein the community is regarded as "a social

[18] George A. Hillery, Jr., "A Critique of Selected Community Concepts," *Social Forces,* **37,** 117 (March, 1959).
[19] Don Martindale, *American Social Structure* (New York: Appleton-Century-Crofts, 1960), p. 133.
[20] William J. Goode, "Community within a Community: The Professions," *American Sociological Review,* **22,** 194 (April, 1957).
[21] Seymour Martin Lipset, Martin A. Trow, and James S. Coleman, *Union Democracy* (Glencoe, Ill.: Free Press, 1956).

group inhabiting a common territory and having one or more additional common ties." [22] The issue, however, is not whether the application of the term to such groups as occupations is "correct." Definitions and usages are inevitably arbitrary. The issue is whether the applications are fruitful, and whether they add anything to our knowledge of the subject under study. In my opinion, there is little to be gained by proliferating the number of referents for the term. I believe that it is preferable, in other words, to devise some other terms for referring to such matters as the extent of interaction within a particular group and the bonds of common identity that may or may not develop around a given occupation. Theodore Caplow, for example, has suggested that the word "ambience" be used for such purposes. [23]

My preference, then is the retention of the areal connotation when speaking of communities. But this is easier said than done. It so happens that the term "community" has been affixed to some territorially bounded social units that are quite special in their characteristics. In other words, while the boundaries of these units may be easily discerned, the units deviate rather substantially from the ordinary connotations of the term "community."

The following examples suggest the wide range of social entities to which the term has been applied. In particular, these include prisons [24] and mental hospitals. [25] The fact that these institutions have also been described as "societies" [26] only adds to the verbal confusion. In my view, it is preferable to treat such relatively self-contained places—together with similar establishments, such as monasteries, special-purpose asylums, and military barracks—under a different heading; one applicable term that has gained some currency is the "total institution." [27] This label has the

[22] George A. Hillery, Jr., "A Critique of Selected Community Concepts," *Social Forces,* **37**, 237 (March, 1959).

[23] Theodore Caplow, "The Definition and Measurement of Ambiences," *Social Forces,* **34**, 28–33 (October, 1955).

[24] Norman S. Hayner and Ellis Ash, "The Prison as a Community," *American Sociological Review,* **5**, 577–583 (August, 1940); Donald Clemmer, *The Prison Community* (New York: Rinehart, 1958).

[25] J. Fremont Bateman and H. Warren Dunham, "The State Mental Hospital as a Specialized Community," *American Journal of Psychiatry,* **105**, 445–448 (December 1948); Maxwell Jones, A. Baker, Thomas Freeman, Julius Merry, B. A. Pomryn, Joseph Sandler, and Joy Tuxford, *The Therapeutic Community* (New York: Basic Books, 1953); David Mechanic, "Community Psychiatry: Some Sociological Perspectives and Implications," in Leigh M. Roberts, Seymour L. Halleck, and Martin B. Loeb, eds., *Community Psychiatry* (Madison: University of Wisconsin Press, 1966).

[26] William Caudill, *The Psychiatric Hospital as a Small Society* (Cambridge, Mass.: Harvard University Press, 1958); Gresham M. Sykes, *The Society of Captives: A Study of a Maximum Security Prison* (Princeton, N.J.: Princeton University Press, 1958).

[27] Erving Goffman, "Characteristics of Total Institutions," in *Symposium on Preventive and Social Psychiatry* (Washington, D.C.: Walter Reed Army Institute of Research,

virtue of suggesting that the entire round of life can be pursued within the institution's walls, but the label does not imply that life in the institution is somehow the same as life in the community outside those walls.

Still other "units" that have a distinct territorial base have been called communities. Entire regions, collections of nation-states, and even the world as a whole have been so labeled. Thus we find fairly frequent reference to "the Atlantic community" [28] and occasional mention of "the world community." [29] It is clear, however, that these usages simply reflect the familiar notion of a "community of interest," whether it is actually in being or simply thought to be desirable by the writer.

The issues raised by these contradictory uses of the term "community" may now be summarized. Should the term "community" refer to an identifiable area? My answer is "yes." Not only does this usage conform to the everyday connotations of the term, but it also reflects the dominant emphasis in the sociological literature over the years. Without suggesting that scientific definitions are best established by precedent or by majority vote, I believe that there is considerable virtue in maintaining some continuity in usage.

Should the term "community" be applied to such aggregates as occupational groups? My inclination is to say "no." It strikes me that the idea of a common outlook on the part of individuals, and strong bonds of identification, may be conveyed by means of other terms. Usages such as "the scientific community" [30] and "the jazz community" [31] tend to be metaphorical efforts to convey a kind of psychological unity. Moreover, it seems generally agreed that this "sense of community" is a highly variable condition when it does occur, differing from one individual to another and from group to group. As such, it might be preferable to regard it as wholly problematic and subject to empirical determination.

Should the term "community" be applied to special-purpose institutions, such as prisons, mental hospitals, and the like? Again, my inclination is to say "no." The concept of the "total institution" seems more adequate to encompass the key characteristics of such establishments, and the notion of the "community" might better be reserved for those *multipurpose social systems* that have more than a single goal. As Edward O.

---

1957), pp. 43–84; see also George A. Hillery, Jr., "Villages, Cities, and Total Institutions," *American Sociological Review*, 28, 779–791 (October, 1963).

[28] George E. G. Catlin, *The Atlantic Community* (London: Coram, 1959); Francis O. Wilcox and H. Field Haviland, Jr., eds., *The Atlantic Community: Progress and Prospects* (New York: Praeger, 1963).

[29] Quincy Wright, *The World Community* (Chicago: University of Chicago Press, 1948).

[30] Warren O. Hagstrom, *The Scientific Community* (New York: Basic Books, 1965).

[31] Alan P. Merriam and Raymond W. Mack, "The Jazz Community," *Social Forces*, 38, 211–222 (March, 1960).

Moe has suggested, "*The community is not structurally and functionally centralized in the same sense as a formal organization.* The great range and diversity of the needs, interests, goals and activities of people of the community are met through a variety of separate institutions and groups —no one of which holds a completely dominant position in relation to the others." [32] Hillery, speaking of "the distinction between community and noncommunity," concluded that "The implication is strong that the distinction is between systems designed to attain specific goals and those which have no such purposes, whose goals are at best diffuse." [33]

Should the term "community" be extended to refer to such large areas as whole regions, or the entire globe? I prefer a much more restrictive usage. Following Hawley and Parsons (quoted above), I would emphasize the *temporal* as well as the *spatial* aspect, and reserve the term "community" for application to areas in which *daily* interaction is possible. Even with this restriction, the sheer area encompassed within the boundaries of a given community may be quite extensive.

The boundaries of communities, in fact, appear in varying degrees of distinctness. In regions of simple agricultural occupancy the concentration of settlement at village centers combined with local self-sufficiency makes for clearly defined community areas. . . . But in advanced agricultural and industrial regions, where settlement is scattered over the space intervening between centers and where the division of labor is highly ramified, the community area lacks definiteness.

In principle, however, the boundary of every community is determined in the same manner. It is fixed by the maximum radius of routine daily movement to and from a center. Thus the community includes the area the population of which, however widely distributed, regularly turns to a common center for the satisfaction of all or a major part of its needs. That distance may differ considerably, depending on the kind of transportation facility in use. . . .

Certain great cities perform various specialized services for vast areas, often worldwide in scope. . . . New York and London are the world's financial centers; and Hollywood, New York, and Paris are fashion centers for the world. Scarcely any part of the world's population today, civilized or preliterate, fails to be touched by the influences exerted from such centers. . . . But while such influences may pulsate to remote extremities with relatively high frequency, actual movements [of persons] between centers and peripheries seldom average more often than once a month or once a season per inhabitant. . . .

Defined on the basis of interdependence alone, it is apparent that the community may be coextensive with the world, at least in some respects. Yet it is general practice to use the term to denote an area of local life. If we are to

[32] Edward O. Moe, "Consulting with a Community System: A Case Study," *Journal of Social Issues,* **15** (No. 2, 1959), 29; italics in original.
[33] George A. Hillery, "Villages, Cities, and Total Institutions" (cited in footnote 27), p. 791.

avoid the dilemma with which the modern situation presents us, it appears that we must incur the risk of doing violence to certain facts and adopt a working definition.[34]

## A Working Definition

Since we have briefly reviewed the development of the community concept, and have examined some of its applications and the issues that they raise, I now offer a working definition designed to serve the main purposes of this chapter. I do this with some hesitancy, but it is essential that I make clear at the outset just what I regard as "the community." If the review of research undertaken here is to have meaning, some boundaries must be established, and this is most readily accomplished by means of a working definition. In other words, we need to delineate a manageable area of inquiry.

For the purposes of this chapter, then, I shall regard "the community" as *the localized population which is interdependent on a daily basis, and which carries on a highly generalized series of activities in and through a set of institutions which provides on a day-to-day basis the full range of goods and services necessary for its continuity as a social and economic entity.*

As we shall see, this kind of omnibus definition encounters some difficulties in use. One difficulty is that communities differ in the extent to which they depend upon other populations: some communities are virtually "independent" entities, while others are involved in a complex network of relations with still other communities. Nevertheless, the terms in this definition refer to variables whose meanings are reasonably straightforward. Following Hawley and Parsons, the restriction of attention to "daily" interaction clearly excludes regional and global applications. The emphasis on "a highly generalized series of activities" means that the term cannot be properly applied to such "total institutions" as prisons and mental hospitals, where activities are narrowly focussed. Reference to "a set of institutions which provide on a day-to-day basis the full range of goods and services" also serves to exclude these single-purpose establishments. Finally, the stress upon "continuity as a social and economic entity" brings out the salient fact that the life span of the community normally exceeds that of its members, and suggests that it is a unit in its own right, with a history that is something more than the sum total of its inhabitants' biographies.

This definition advances no judgments concerning the extent to which residents of the community share a common culture, or—more particularly—

[34] Amos H. Hawley, *Human Ecology* (cited in footnote 6), 245–246 and 256–257.

the extent to which they experience some kind of "we-feeling" or sense of uniqueness. I contend that these matters are better left open for empirical assessment. At our present state of knowledge, these features are more properly regarded as variables, with some populations exhibiting them quite clearly and others failing to display manifestations of these particular psychological traits in any significant degree.

However, one remaining issue that has yet to be seriously confronted in the sociological literature is the extent to which communities, as defined here, might contain other social units that are *themselves* properly regarded as communities. Specifically, are such areas as New York's Harlem, Chicago's Bronzeville, and San Francisco's Chinatown to be regarded as "communities" in their own right? These are localized populations which seem to display many, if not all, of the characteristics that I have specified in my definition. Moreover, they display a high degree of visibility and persistence over time.

The thin literature dealing with these areas, and others like them, suggests a wide degree of variation in the extent to which they should be regarded as communities *per se*. In many instances, it is difficult to discern any substantial degree of agreement concerning their boundaries, and the extent to which their constituent institutions fully provide for the daily needs of their members remains open to question.[35]

One solution, although not a fully satisfactory one, is simply to regard these areas as distinctive *subcommunities*, the unity and integrity of which may vary from case to case. These areas are something more than "neighborhoods," but something less than communities in the fullest sense of the term. That is, they are parts of a larger whole; while they may be amenable to the same kind of analysis as the community at large, they are not the same kind of "complete" social unit in the sense with which MacIver spoke of the community when he remarked that "The mark of a community is that one's life may be lived wholly within it."[36]

## Types of Community

It is now apparent that the concept of "community" is not a simple one. The concept has been applied to a wide variety of social units, and there

[35] E. Franklin Frazier, "Negro Harlem: An Ecological Study," *American Journal of Sociology*, **43**, 72–88 (July, 1937); Laurence H. Ross, "The Local Community: A Survey Approach," *American Sociological Review*, **27**, 75–84 (February, 1962); Herbert J. Gans, *The Urban Villagers* (New York: Free Press, 1962).
[36] Robert M. MacIver, *Society, Its Structure and Changes* (New York: Long and Smith, 1931), p. 10.

is not a perfect consensus among sociologists concerning its essential features. Even a narrow conception of the community, such as the one advanced in this chapter, encounters some difficulties in use simply because one community differs considerably from another. Experience has shown, however, that knowledge of these variations is a very important part of the study of communities.

### Some Ways in which Communities Differ

I have stressed the idea that communities are social entities in their own right. As such, they exhibit distinctive but variable characteristics, not all of which are immediately derivable from the individual traits of the people who inhabit them. What are some of these characteristics?

I have spoken of the community as a "localized population." The first of the many ways in which communities vary is in the extent to which they are truly "localized," that is, the degree to which they are *independent* of, or *dependent* upon, close ties with other communities. The primitive situation reveals numerous instances in which communities are largely isolated from contacts with other communities. In contrast, the modern situation involves a network of interdependence among individual communities, small and large; no one community stands alone, for it is caught up in a web of sustained relationships with other parts of the world. This is particularly evident in the case of large urban communities, but it is equally true of small rural communities, not one of which exists in perfect isolation.

If the community is to be regarded as a "localized population," this also suggests that the sheer *size* of the organized aggregate is a variable characteristic of communities that deserves attention. At least in the modern situation, a localized population aggregate might be small or large, ranging from a mere handful of individuals to many millions. Indeed, as we shall see, population size turns out to be quite an important characteristic of communities, and one that influences still other characteristics, directly and indirectly. Changes in size, or the *rate* of population growth or decline, are also relevant here.

These two characteristics—population size and degree of interdependence —are themselves related. Clearly, an independent community cannot be very large in population numbers, although its area of occupancy may be of considerable size. The primitive community, existing in virtual isolation and limited in its technological repertoire, is necessarily a small social unit. It cannot support great numbers. When a high degree of interdependence is attained, however, some communities may reach considerable size, while others remain relatively small. This relationship is summarized in Table 2.1.

**Table 2.1   Relationship between Population Size and Degree of Interdependence of Communities**

| Degree of Interdependence | Population Size | |
|---|---|---|
| | Small | Large |
| Independent | Primitive communities, small and highly isolated | |
| Interdependent | Small "rural" and "urban" communities | Large "urban" communities |

As the empty cell in the upper right-hand corner emphasizes, truly "independent" (isolated) communities cannot achieve large population size. The degree of independence, then, influences the population size that a community may attain. Isolation places an upper limit upon the numbers of people who can live together on a daily basis.

Still another population characteristic of communities is *density*, or numbers per unit of area. Population size is an absolute measure, while density (like rate of growth) is relative; numbers relative to land area determines the density ratio, just as changes in size relative to time units determines the rate of growth. As with size, this density ratio varies widely, ranging from quite small to very large values. A community's population may be spread quite thinly over the territory it occupies, resulting in a low density, or it may be packed very tightly in a limited space with a high density. Although these two characteristics—size and density—tend to be correlated, it is important to notice that they may vary. A small population may live at high densities (as in the case of agricultural villages in Asia and other underdeveloped areas), and large populations may exhibit low densities. In other words, at any given size, widely different densities may be observed. Density levels depend on other factors, particularly the kind of technology in use, and, despite a gross correlation, size is not a perfectly accurate predictor of density. A community may grow in population size, for example, while its density falls. All that is required is that the occupied area be extended more rapidly than the population increments being added. Suburban "sprawl" in the United States is a good example of this phenomenon. Whole population aggregates are growing in absolute size, but they are being spread more thinly over the landscape.

Another population characteristic worthy of attention is the sheer *age of the settlement.* I am not referring here to the ages of the inhabitants, which is another matter of interest in its own right, but to the number of years that the localized population has existed as a distinguishable entity. In one sense, communities have lives of their own, and some are older than others. Unlike the individual, however, the community has no fixed "life span." It may exist for hundreds of years. Presumably this variable characteristic—the community's age—also affects other traits of the community. An old community necessarily experienced a considerable proportion of its growth in an earlier technological era, and it might be expected to bear the marks of this earlier development. A familiar example is the difference between urban communities that grew up in the United States before and after the onset of "the auto age." In general, the pre-auto communities are much more densely settled, because the more limited means of transportation available in earlier eras required people to live close together, and earlier patterns of residential density have survived.

In addition to population size, growth and density, and the age of the aggregate as a distinguishable entity, there are important differences among communities that stem from their "make-up" or population composition. In fact, this matter of the composition of the population opens up a large number of possibilities for the classification of communities. As the simplest example, consider the "biological make-up" of the community, or its age-sex composition.

Consider first the matter of *age composition*. We might expect quite a few differences between, for instance, a community of oldsters and one that contains an overwhelming majority of young adults and children. Many small rural communities in the United States consist mainly of old people who have remained behind after many years of out-migration by younger persons. However, many new suburbs are largely inhabited by young families. Obviously, these differences alone may have important consequences for the two types of community. The range of activities performed, and services required, by such dissimilar population aggregates might be expected to be quite different.

As in the case of age differences, *sex composition* can also be important. Although most communities exhibit an approximate numerical balance between the sexes, all of us know of some instances in which radical imbalances have occurred. In the development of the American West, for example, mining and lumbering communities emerged in which males were overwhelmingly predominant. Consequently, these communities developed distinctive services, institutions, and "styles of life" that departed in significant ways from the usual patterns on view in more "normal" communities of the time.

Recognition of differences in institutional patterning, however, requires that we deal with still other facets of population composition. Communities differ in more than simple "biological" traits such as age and sex; they differ in important social and economic traits. Now we examine some of the differences in these social and economic traits.

### Community Forms and Functions

It has become customary to distinguish and classify communities according to their major functions, that is, the main activities in which their inhabitants are engaged. In this classificatory work, sociologists have been joined by economists, geographers, and political scientists, but most attention has been given to the "economic" functions through which the community gains its livelihood. Perhaps the broadest classification appropriate to the modern context. is the following one, adapted from the economist Colin Clark's distinction between primary, secondary, and tertiary activities.[37]

1. *Primary* activities are extractive in nature; they are "primary" in the sense that the physical environment is confronted directly, and raw materials are extracted from it. Examples are agriculture, forestry, fishing, mining and oil production. A community may be specialized in one or another of these lines of work; its "economic base" may be the production of raw materials, with minimal attention to fabrication or distribution. Farm communities, fishing villages, and mining towns are examples of specialization in extractive pursuits.

2. Fabricating and processing activities are commonly labeled *secondary*, in the sense that extracted raw or semiprocessed materials are further altered in form by manufacturing. Today, many communities—both small and large—are mainly devoted to manufacturing, or "secondary" production. The type of manufactured product may serve to distinguish communities; thus "heavy-industry" and "light-industry" towns are commonly recognized. A community may even be identified by the specific product that it makes: Detroit is known as an auto center; Pittsburgh and Birmingham are known as steel towns; and Akron is recognized as a rubber producer.

3. Finally, the *tertiary* class contains all of the activities that consist of "services" in the broadest sense. These include the distribution of raw materials and processed goods, together with a wide range of other services such as finance, communication, government, defense, recreation, education, and the like. A community may be narrowly specialized in one or another of these lines of activity. Thus a railhead or a port city (like Galves-

[37] Colin Clark, *The Conditions of Economic Progress* (London: Macmillan, 1940).

ton, Texas) may be essentially a transportation center, devoted mainly to transshipment of goods. A regional or national capital may be narrowly focussed upon the provision of governmental services, as in the case of Washington, D.C. There are many "college towns"—like Ann Arbor, Michigan, Ithaca, New York, and Bloomington, Indiana. Or the dominant focus may be upon recreation, as in the case of Miami, Florida. As was true with the primary and secondary categories, the tertiary class contains a number of distinguishable subtypes.

The inference should not be drawn that each community has one and only one specialization. A particular community may combine a number of specialties; for instance, it may be highly diversified, carrying on simultaneously a large number of important activities. This is especially true of the very largest communities. Thus, New York City concurrently is an important center of heavy and light manufacturing as well as a center of trade and services of every description. It is an important port and railhead, a massive manufacturing complex, a key hub in the communications network, a wholesale and retail center, and a focus of financial transactions, education, recreation, and the arts.

Nevertheless, it should be recognized that the functional specialization of a community is not unrelated to its other key characteristics. Again, the sheer size of the aggregate appears to be especially crucial. A general idea of the relationship between size and function is conveyed in Table 2.2, which gives data for the United States. As Otis D. Duncan, the compiler of the statistics in the table, observes:

> It is obvious that specialization in one major industry category—the extractive [primary] industries—will be inversely related to size of community. . . . However, there is no pronounced relationship between size of place and the proportion of the labor force engaged in either of the other two broad industry sectors, the processing and fabricating [secondary] industries, and the service [tertiary] industries. . . . More significant than the figures for these broad categories are the figures . . . showing that, irrespective of industry structure, a much higher proportion of workers in large places are engaged in clerical and similar jobs. This finding accords with the supposition that large cities are focal points for administrative and coordinating functions, requiring a sizable complement of personnel to keep records and channel communications.[38]

Communities, then, do not vary in a kind of random fashion. Their functional specialization exhibits a high degree of order. These patterned differences in function according to size (shown in Table 2.2) illustrate one

---

[38] Otis Dudley Duncan, "Population Distribution and Community Structure," *Cold Spring Harbor Symposia on Quantitative Biology,* **22,** 366 (1957).

**Table 2.2  Selected Characteristics of the Employed Labor Force, by Size of Community, for the United States, 1950** [38]

| Size Class | Percent Employed in: | | | |
| --- | --- | --- | --- | --- |
| | Extractive Industries [a] | Processing and Fabricating Industries [b] | Service Industries [c] | Clerical and Kindred Occupations [d] |
| *Urbanized areas* | | | | |
| 1. 3,000,000 or more | 0.7 | 36.8 | 61.1 | 17.8 |
| 2. 1,000,000 to 3,000,000 | 0.6 | 38.0 | 60.1 | 17.8 |
| 3. 250,000 to 1,000,000 | 1.4 | 34.1 | 63.3 | 16.7 |
| 4. 50,000 to 250,000 | 1.6 | 37.0 | 60.2 | 14.6 |
| *Other urban places* | | | | |
| 5. 25,000 or more [e] | 2.3 | 34.0 | 62.5 | 13.6 |
| 6. 10,000 to 25,000 | 4.2 | 33.4 | 61.2 | 12.0 |
| 7. 2500 to 10,000 | 6.9 | 31.5 | 60.1 | 10.6 |
| *Rural territory* | | | | |
| 8. Rural nonfarm | 14.4 | 34.0 | 49.6 | 7.5 |
| 9. Rural farm | 72.3 | 12.5 | 13.4 | 2.4 |

[a] Agriculture, forestry, fisheries, and mining.
[b] Manufacturing and construction.
[c] Transportation, trade, finance, administration, and personal, professional, and business services.
[d] Includes clerical occupations in *all* industries.
[e] Includes a few places with slightly more than 50,000 inhabitants.
*Note.* The sum of the three industry categories is less than 100% because of non-reporting.

kind of relationship sought by the sociologist who specializes in the study of the community. However, they do not exhaust the interests of the sociologist, who is typically concerned with more than such gross characteristics as size and function.

The data in Table 2.2 are organized according to community size. But notice that the full range of sizes extends from "urbanized areas" with more than three million inhabitants to "rural farm" territory. This subject— the rural-urban dimension—has exerted a continuing fascination for community sociologists over the years. It is appropriate here to consider the matter in detail.

## The Rural-Urban Dimension [39]

The distinction between "rural" and "urban" is a familiar one. It is commonly recognized in everyday language, although the criteria employed are not very exact and certainly are not scientifically precise. The basis of the distinction, however, is ordinarily conceived as occupational and industrial. That is, "rural" communities are usually thought of as agricultural in character (or essentially devoted to primary activities), while "urban" communities are considered to be centers of manufacturing, trade, and services (secondary and tertiary activities).

These everyday connotations of the two terms have been carried over into the sociological literature. One of the earliest and most influential works dealing with rural and urban communities was by Pitirim Sorokin and Carle C. Zimmerman, who had this to say regarding the distinction:

> The principal criterion of the rural society or population is *occupational*, collection and cultivation of plants and animals. Through it rural society differs from other, particularly urban, populations engaged in different occupational pursuits. . . . Such is the first and fundamental criterion of difference between the rural and other, and particularly urban, communities. From it follows a series of other differences between the rural and the urban communities, most of which are causally connected with the above difference in occupation.[40]

These writers enumerate a number of other ways in which rural and urban communities differ: in community size, in density, in heterogeneity, in social differentiation and stratification, in mobility, in environment, and in systems of interaction. They argue as follows:

> [These "fundamental characteristics," or variables,] are all causally connected, or interrelated. As soon as one takes the agricultural occupation and the people engaged in it, he finds the other differences enumerated. The first "variable," so to speak, carries the others with it.[41]

It is important to recognize that each of the traits identified by Sorokin and Zimmerman are literally *variables*, that is, the traits differ in degree and not in kind. As these authors observe:

> In reality the transition from a purely rural community to an urban one, whatever may be the definition, is not abrupt but gradual; from an open farm through a small settlement of agriculturalists, a hamlet with a slight admixture of a few

[39] This section draws heavily upon Leo F. Schnore, "The Rural-Urban Variable: An Urbanite's Perspective," *Rural Sociology*, 31, 131–143 (June, 1966).
[40] Pitirim Sorokin and Carle C. Zimmerman, *Principles of Rural-Urban Sociology* (New York: Holt, 1929), p. 16; italics in original.
[41] *Ibid.*, p. 57.

non-farming people, a village, a small town, to larger and larger towns and cities. Each step is associated with a proportionately decreasing agricultural population and an increasing of the proportion of the people engaged in other than agricultural pursuits. There is no absolute boundary line which would show a clearly cut cleavage between the rural and the urban community. Correspondingly, many differential characteristics of the rural and urban community would consist not so much in the presence of certain traits in rural, and their absence in urban communities, as much as in a quantitative increase of these characteristics. . . .[42]

More recently, a number of other writers have called this conception the "rural-urban continuum," suggesting that the differences between the two polar types of community are gradual and continuous, and not qualitative differences *per se*, resulting in a simple dichotomy. Thus, Stuart A. Queen and David B. Carpenter claim that "there is a continuous gradation in the United States from rural to urban rather than a simple rural-urban dichotomy and . . . as human communities are arrayed along this rural-urban continuum, consistent variations occur in patterns of behavior." [43] Although it is certainly preferable to a purely dichotomous conception, this notion also represents something of an oversimplification, as empirical research has shown. According to Otis Dudley Duncan:

> [The rural-urban continuum] perhaps has some heuristic value in suggesting one kind of intercommunity variation. But it is highly doubtful that the unidimensional continuum, in any rigorous, mathematical sense, is a sufficiently realistic model for research on intercommunity variation. Realistic classifications will almost necessarily be multidimensional ones.[44]

Duncan based this criticism upon an examination of characteristics associated with variations in community size in the United States. A review here of all of the elements of the controversy surrounding the conceptions of "rural" and "urban" would be lengthy. Therefore, let us simply remember that even the simple rural *versus* urban dichotomy, despite its obvious deficiencies, has some utility as a first approximation. Its use permits the assemblage of masses of data in immediately comprehensible form, and suggests some of the major differences between these two types of community.

However, as was the case with other aspects of the community, the rural-urban dimension has been the source of considerable confusion in the sociological literature. Just as the community is difficult to define with

---

[42] *Ibid.*, p. 14.

[43] Stuart A. Queen and David B. Carpenter, *The American City* (New York: McGraw-Hill, 1953), p. 38.

[44] Otis Dudley Duncan, "Community Size and the Rural-Urban Continuum," in Paul K. Hatt and Albert J. Reiss, Jr., eds., *Cities and Society* (Glencoe, Ill.: Free Press, 1957), p. 45.

perfect precision, and in a way that is satisfactory to all students of the subject, so are terms like "rural" and "urban." These terms have been given a variety of meanings. It is helpful to consider at least a few of the alternative interpretations advanced by sociologists in discussing "urban," "urbanism," and "urbanization."

A classic conception of the city, or the urban community, was the one given by Louis Wirth in a 1938 essay on "Urbanism as a Way of Life":

> For sociological purposes a city may be defined as a relatively large, dense, and permanent settlement of socially heterogeneous individuals. . . . The central problem of the sociologist of the city is to discover the forms of social action and organization that typically emerge in relatively permanent, compact settlements of large numbers of heterogeneous individuals. . . . On the basis of the three variables, number, density of settlement, and degree of homogeneity, of the urban population, it appears possible to explain the characteristics of urban life and to account for the differences between cities of various sizes and types.[45]

Although Wirth's general approach has been severely criticized,[46] I think that his definition of the city remains useful, at least as a starting point in the analysis of urban and rural communities.

However, the identification of urban communities as large, dense, and heterogeneous, and the identification of rural communities as small, less dense, and homogeneous, is satisfactory only up to a certain point. While the extremes are easy enough to identify, there are inevitable problems encountered in drawing a hard and fast line. Communities range in size from small to large; they vary in density from low to high; and they extend in character from perfectly homogeneous to heterogeneous. We must set arbitrary limits in making judgments as to what shall be regarded as rural and urban. Thus the United States Bureau of the Census has used size and legal status as criteria, and has traditionally drawn the line by identifying urban communities as incorporated places of 2500 or more inhabitants. However, this definition has been a matter of administrative convenience, and a number of exceptions have been introduced over the years (for example, by recognizing certain unincorporated areas as being urban by means of special rules, and by creating "urbanized areas" whose boundaries are set by the application of density criteria).

Although size is not a perfectly adequate criterion, the use of criteria

[45] Louis Wirth, "Urbanism as a Way of Life," *American Journal of Sociology*, **44**, 8, 9, 18 (July, 1938).
[46] William L. Kolb, "The Social Structure and Functions of Cities," *Economic Development and Cultural Change*, **3**, 30–46 (October, 1954); Gideon Sjoberg, "Comparative Urban Sociology" in Robert K. Merton, Leonard Broom, and Leonard S. Cottrell, Jr., eds., *Sociology Today: Problems and Prospects* (New York: Basic Books, 1959), pp. 334–359.

other than size would involve an equal degree of arbitrariness and also would necessitate the special treatment of anomalous cases. If density were employed, for example, what is the precise man-land ratio that should qualify a place as being urban? Certainly there would be instances—regardless of the particular limit decided upon—that would raise problems, such as densely settled agricultural villages that were overwhelmingly rural in occupation and "way of life," but that exhibited urban densities.

Even the use of occupational and industrial criteria (as urged by Sorokin and Zimmerman) would not eliminate all the problems of definition. At what point should the proportion engaged in agriculture be set in order to determine whether a community was urban or rural? For example, should a simple majority be regarded as sufficient to classify a community one way or the other? There are no easy answers.

Definitions, as always, have an inevitable component of arbitrariness. In this case, the major difficulties stem from the fact that the characteristics that have been singled out for attention—size, density, and heterogeneity—are literally *variables;* that is, they exhibit differences in degree from place to place and time to time. The only reasonable solution is to recognize this great amount of variation as an inescapable empirical fact and to confront it directly. Thus our conceptions of rural and urban must include an awareness that these are *polar* types, and that communities may be found at many points on the so-called "continuum" that extends from one extreme pole to the other. In the contemporary world, sharp and absolute divisions between community forms do not exist, and it is futile to pretend that they can be found. Despite these facts, however, the basic concepts of rural and urban remain useful. They point to differences between communities that are too important to be ignored.

Now, two related notions should be introduced: "urbanism" and "urbanization." The concept of *urbanism* refers to *a state or quality* or—to use Wirth's phrase—"a way of life" thought to be especially characteristic of cities. On the other hand, urbanization refers to *a process.*

A number of typical features have been identified as constituting urbanism. A representative list of these features includes the following ones.

(a) A complex division of labour with a diversified occupational structure which forms a major basis of the system of social stratification; (b) high territorial and social mobility; (c) marked functional dependence of the population; (d) substantial personal anonymity in interpersonal contacts and segmentalization of social roles and role interactions; (e) reliance on indirect modes of social control; (f) normative deviance.[47]

[47] Albert J. Reiss, Jr., "Urbanism," in Julius Gould and William L. Kolb, eds., *A Dictionary of the Social Sciences* (New York: Free Press, 1965), pp. 738–739.

Such a conception does not limit these phenomena to cities. It is often argued, in fact, that these characteristics have spread or diffused from the city to the countryside, resulting in an urbanization of formerly rural areas. The difficulty, however, is that such a view intermixes characteristics of individual behavior (for example, anonymity and deviance) with characteristics of organized social systems (for example, a complex division of labor and functional dependence).

The process of *urbanization* has been viewed in less complex terms. Rather than referring to behavioral and organizational changes that may or may not follow upon the growth and spread of cities, it has been given a narrower demographic interpretation. In other words, it has been viewed as purely a process of population redistribution. Perhaps the most widely cited definition of urbanization in these terms is that of Hope Tisdale:

> Urbanization is a process of population concentration. It proceeds in two ways: the multiplication of points of concentration and the increase in size of individual concentrations. . . .
>
> Urbanization is a process of becoming. It implies a movement, not necessarily direct or steady or continuous, from a state of . . . less concentration toward a state of more concentration.[48]

These "points of concentration," of course, are cities, and the process is regarded as purely a matter of the redistribution of population in space. Tisdale does not accept the conception of urbanization as a diffusion of urban traits outward from cities:

> This is an objectionable definition because it makes the city the cause of urbanization rather than the result or the product of urbanization. It does not explain the appearance and growth of cities. It posits the preexistence of cities.[49]

Cities themselves, according to Tisdale, are simply to be regarded as "points of concentration," with their lower limits unspecified.

> There is no need at this juncture to fix lower limits to the size and density which qualify a concentration as a city. There is no clear-cut level of concentration at which a city suddenly springs into being. It is convenient from time to time arbitrarily to name certain levels beyond which concentrations are designated as cities. This is necessary in analyzing data and identifying characteristics of various size groups, but it does not alter the validity of the original concept.[50]

In the following discussion, I shall adopt Tisdale's conception of urbanization as the best one available. As she notes, "It eliminates or throws into different

[48] Hope Tisdale, "The Process of Urbanization," *Social Forces*, **20**, 311–312 (March, 1942).
[49] *Ibid.*, p. 311.
[50] *Ibid.*

categories other processes which, though associated with urbanization, may have opposing effects upon it. The concomitants of urbanization are not to be ignored; they are simply to be distinguished from it." [51] One such concomitant in the modern world is the emergence of a new form—the "metropolitan community."

### Urbanization and Metropolitanization

In recent decades, a number of writers have sought to identify a new type of community—one that includes both urban and rural sectors, but that differs from each of these earlier forms. This is called the metropolitan community, and its evolution is commonly recognized as most advanced in the United States. The metropolitan community is basically regarded as a great city together with its immediately surrounding territory, including many rural and urban communities that may have been largely self-sufficient at some time in the past. Quoting one of the earliest students of metropolitanization, the economic historian N. S. B. Gras:

> We may think of metropolitan economy as an organization of people having a large city as a nucleus. . . . Mere agglomeration of individuals, important as that is, does not constitute a metropolis. . . . What counts most is commercial dominance over a wide area . . .[52]

Gras did not mean to imply that this "dominance" was unilateral. It is true that the outlying areas—rural and urban—are dependent on the great city for a great many things, but the metropolis itself is also dependent on its surrounding hinterland. In his words, "Interdependence of the parts is really the key to the whole situation." [53] Another early student of metropolitanization, the sociologist R. D. McKenzie, described the emerging form as a "new type of super community organized around a dominant focal point and comprising a multiple of differentiated centers of activity." [54]

The metropolitan community is to be distinguished, then, from the city, which is a continuously built-up and densely settled territory whose inhabitants are engaged in a wide variety of secondary and tertiary activities. The metropolitan community is composed of cities, it is true, but it also contains large stretches of rural territory and a full range of settlement types, ranging from crossroad hamlets through villages and towns to large

[51] *Ibid.*

[52] Norman Scott Brien Gras, *An Introduction to Economic History* (New York: Harper, 1922), p. 186.

[53] *Ibid.*, p. 187.

[54] R. D. McKenzie, *The Metropolitan Community* (New York: McGraw-Hill, 1933), pp. 6–7.

cities. While the large cities are most dramatically visible, the entire social unit is a highly differentiated congeries, or agglomeration, of dissimilar parts. The great city—the metropolis, or central city—plays a key role in integrating and coordinating the various activities spread over the vast territory that it "dominates," but it is only one of many highly specialized parts of the whole community.

In one respect, the emergence of the metropolitan community has made the concepts of rural and urban communities virtually obsolete. The metropolitan community has merged the two concepts, creating a new kind of entity in which rural and urban sectors may be distinguished, but in which they cannot be regarded as somehow standing alone as separate entities. This is most evident in the economic aspects of contemporary life, where the fate of the rural area is intimately tied up with the fate of the urban community with which it deals. But this interdependence also extends to social and political aspects of daily existence, and the metropolitan community must be viewed as a new kind of social unit that has absorbed and reintegrated previously isolated areas which, at one time, may have been semi-independent communities in their own right.

How did such a "supercommunity" come into being? It seems commonly agreed that modern means of transportation and communication were the crucial factors. McKenzie, for example, stressed the role of the automobile and the truck:

By reducing the scale of local distance, the motor vehicle extended the horizon of the community and introduced a territorial division of labor among local institutions and neighboring centers which is unique in the history of settlement. The large center has been able to extend the radius of its influence; its population and many of its institutions, freed from the dominance of rail transportation, have become widely dispersed throughout surrounding territory. Moreover, formerly independent towns and villages and also rural territory have become part of this enlarged city complex. . . . The metropolitan community, therefore, comprises a cluster or constellation of centers. Smaller cities and towns tend to group themselves around larger ones somewhat as planets group themselves around a sun.[55]

In addition to transportation technology, modern means of communication (for example, the telephone and the radio) also played a key role, permitting widely dispersed activities to be carried on jointly.

In the remaining sections of this chapter, we shall focus our attention on the modern metropolitan community. We shall deal mainly with metropolitan communities in the United States. Whatever is lost by this deliberate

[55] *Ibid.*, pp. 6 and 71. For empirical data, see Donald J. Bogue, *The Structure of the Metropolitan Community* (Ann Arbor: University of Michigan Press, 1949).

limitation will be offset by the advantages of stressing the kind of community that has provoked the most attention from empirical researchers interested in the sociological aspects of the modern community.

## Sociological Aspects of the Community: A Static View

Recognizing that there is enormous variation in communities, how do we begin to grasp the significance of such a complex and ever-changing social phenomenon? Some deliberate simplification is required. One device is to ignore the temporal dimension, for the moment, and to consider the community as it appears to the observer at any one point in time. In this way, some of the most salient aspects of the community will become evident.

### Demographic Aspects: Size, Composition, and Distribution

Perhaps the most fundamental aspect of the community involves human numbers. As already mentioned, community size is a key feature, in that it often seems to be associated with variations in other community characteristics. But there is more than size at issue when we examine the *demographic* aspects of a community. "Demography is the study of the size, territorial distribution, and composition of population, changes therein, and the components of such changes, which may be identified as natality, mortality, territorial movement (migration), and social mobility (change of status)." [56]

In addition to size, then, population composition and distribution are at issue. It is important to notice that these three features are *static* characteristics. They are subject to measurement by means of a census, that is, an enumeration—whether complete or partial (via sampling)—of the number and characteristics of a given population at a given point in time. The cross-sectional character of a census is critical; it yields a snapshot, or an essentially static portrait of a population.

When a community is subjected to a census enumeration, all three of these features—size, composition, and distribution—are simultaneously ascertained. We learn the number of persons within the community, what their characteristics are, and how they are distributed in space. Thus, in addition to size, the "make-up" or composition of the community is determined. We also learn the major facts concerning the distributional pattern of the community, for example, its population density.

[56] Philip M. Hauser and Otis Dudley Duncan, eds., *The Study of Population* (Chicago: University of Chicago Press, 1959), p. 2.

A concern with the distribution of people and activities in space, however, leads quite naturally to another and more complex kind of inquiry. People are not randomly distributed, nor are their activities. People and activities tend to clump or cluster at certain points, and to be spread thinly at other points. The patterns assumed by these distributions are the key subject for "ecological" investigation.

## Ecological Aspects: The Spatial and Temporal Dimensions of Community Life

Human ecology has been traditionally concerned with the spatial and temporal aspects of the community. As I have stated, human activities are dissimilarly distributed in space. The same is true of time; just as spatial patterns can be observed, there are distinct temporal patterns on view in the human community. In particular, there is a daily rhythm to community life that lends a high degree of predictability to community affairs. Like spatial patterns, these temporal patterns are not the same from one community to another. They vary, and often vary in an orderly fashion.

Community size is one of the key factors in determining what the temporal pattern will look like. As Hawley has observed:

The rhythms of collective life . . . vary considerably in different-sized communities. In small communities there is well-defined staggering in the operating times of work and recreational units. Work is restricted to the daylight hours and recreation to the evening hours. . . . But as the size of the community increases marked temporal divisions tend to disappear. Every increase in size increases the number of individuals requiring a service at any given time. Thus in the large city many different units function simultaneously and some continuously around the clock. Technological changes, notably the development of electric illumination, have exerted an important influence to this end. . . . The nocturnal phase of the daily round has steadily approached equivalence to the diurnal phase, especially in the larger communities. As periodicity gives way to continuity the community acquires greater temporal and functional symmetry.[57]

Thus, time serves as a dimension on which community structure can be observed and even measured.

As in the case of time, space is employed differently in varying community contexts. In the small agricultural village, for example, there is a notable homogeneity of land uses. On the other hand, the giant metropolis is an intricate mosaic of highly differentiated land uses, in keeping with the rich variety of highly specialized activities that are carried on there.

[57] Amos H. Hawley, *Human Ecology: A Theory of Community Structure* (New York: Ronald Press, 1950), p. 305.

Every change in community size, then, might be expected to yield changes in the occupancy of space. Not only is the total occupied territory likely to be increased with each major increment in population size, but different pieces of that space are apt to be put to different uses. A dwindling amount of area is left to primary production, and more space is devoted to secondary and tertiary activities of many varieties. The residential uses of space grow and come to be differentiated, too, and we shall see that there is initiated a "sifting and sorting" process that yields a marked spatial segregation of activities and elements within the population at large.

Although I have veered into a kind of sequential description of spatial and temporal patterns, it is important to realize that these patterns can be observed at any one point in time, so that the uses of space and time (particularly the recurrent daily rhythms) are also *static* aspects of the community. Even though the patterns are subject to change, they can be instantaneously observed. These ecological patterns in time and space are also evidence, along with certain demographic data, of another kind of order or structure.

### Structural Aspects: The Organization of Communities and Their Parts

The spacing and timing of human activities reveal something about the organization of communities, that is, about their *structural* features. It is the distinctive task of the sociologist, however, to investigate all facets of social organization. Not all of these facets are readily subjected to ecological mapping in space, nor are they amenable to strict ordering in time, but they are nonetheless crucial in determining the structural aspects of communities.

A review of all the various "institutional" arrangements on view within communities is beyond the scope of this chapter. These matters are dealt with in their own right in Chapters 5 to 8, where economic, religious, educational, and political institutions are examined in detail. My discussion here is confined to a general orientation to the subject of social organization.

A community is, in itself, a unit of social organization. But it is more than that, since it contains numerous other organized units. To appraise the matter in its simplest form, consider the familiar roster of units that make up the typical contemporary American community. First, these communities consist of a congeries of families and households. In addition, most of them contain a large number of business establishments engaged in the production of goods and the provision of services. Beyond that, a majority of them support a large complement of specialized units of a public or quasipublic character: governmental agencies, schools, churches, hospitals, and the like. Finally, besides these numerous operating units, there are substantial numbers of formal and informal associations. These associations draw upon the families and other units for their membership, and they may be loosely or tightly linked to each other in still other and larger associations, such as the Red Cross, the Chamber of Commerce, neighborhood associations, and similar organizations.

This bewildering array of units is what sociologists usually have in mind when they speak of the "social organization" of a contemporary community. But the complications in the analysis of community structure do not arise merely from the sheer number and variety of units. There is the additional complication of understanding the *linkages* between these units. Some of these linkages are relatively simple and straightforward. The ties between the family and the retail business establishment, for example, are not difficult to comprehend. The families of the community constitute the market for the goods and service offered, and at least a few families provide the manpower required for staffing the enterprise. The business establishment provides needed goods or services for families, and thus there are many reciprocal relations between the two types of unit. In other instances, however, the links between two or more organized units are not so easy to determine. The ties between families making up a "social class," for instance, may be extremely tenuous, with limited interaction between one family and another. Indeed, some writers assert that social classes are not groups but are statistical artifacts, created by the observer, with members lacking in self-conscious awareness of their common circumstances and rarely coacting in any concerted fashion.[58]

Another complication in the analysis of contemporary community structure arises from the fact that communities today are not perfectly insulated from the world beyond their borders. No community is an island, entire of itself. The links with the outside world are many and various. Kinship ties bind local conjugal families to other families, often over great distances. Local business establishments may be linked to dozens or hundreds of other similar units in other communities through the corporate ties of common ownership and operation. Labor unions are parts of nonlocal wholes. Churches are usually members of regional or national groups. And even the most ostensibly "local" units—those of government—may be members of state leagues of municipalities and the like. Even if they are not, state and national governmental policy is likely to impinge at many points in their day-to-day operations. All these manifold threads of interrelationships make the community a very complex system, indeed, and it is no wonder

---

[58] Werner S. Landecker, "Class Boundaries," *American Sociological Review*, **25**, 868–877 (December, 1960).

that the sociological understanding of community organization is at a fairly primitive level.

Because of present ignorance, the analysis of community structure remains an important task of sociological effort. Viewed in its internal and external relations, the community is structurally complex; not only are the parts of the whole many and diverse, but the ties that bind these parts into a coherent whole internally—and that link the community to other areas externally—are equally numerous and varied.

## Behavioral Aspects: Social-Psychological Facets of the Community

It may seem odd to speak of the "parts" of the community as consisting of social groups—families, business establishments, institutions, organizations, associations, and the like. From another perspective, communities simply consist of individual persons. Indeed they do, and that fundamental fact has not been ignored by sociologists concerned with the community. As suggested earlier, the social-psychological aspect of the community has received considerable attention. Previously, in discussing alternative definitions of the community, we noted that many sociologists actually stress the psychological dimension, and conclude that a community without self-consciousness is no community at all.

Perhaps the most fundamental assumption made by social psychologists is that an individual's group memberships are vital factors in influencing his behavior. Attitudes and values are formed in a group context and, according to this view, concrete individual behavior is best understood in that context. The person and his actions, then, are to be studied with particular reference to the group—past and present—with which he has been and is now affiliated.

This assumption raises a number of questions. First, what are the most salient group memberships? Granting (for the sake of argument) that group membership makes a difference in a person's behavior, which groups make the most difference? The answer, of course, may vary according to such things as the stage of the life cycle. The family may be most crucial to a person in the formative years of his childhood; the peer group may be more important to him in adolescence; and the occupational group may be most salient in his adulthood. The particular type of behavior may be crucial, too, so that an individual's religious group affiliation may be vitally important in fertility behavior, somewhat less relevant in political behavior, and of virtually no consequence in economic affairs in general.

However, the question that is most vital for our present purposes may be phrased more generally: To what extent is membership in a local *community* significant in the understanding of an individual's behavior? The answer depends on the particular area of behavior that is being explored but, generally, the community of residence is fairly useful in many ways for the prediction of individual behavior. One reason is that the community context will determine in a general way the number and variety of group experiences and opportunities for group memberships.

Consider only the question of community homogeneity. If the area of residence should be a "one-class" community (as many of our small towns and suburbs are alleged to be), an individual's exposure to a variety of ways of life is likely to be sharply curtailed. The same is true with respect to racial and religious homogeneity; if all the other members of a community are of the same racial or ethnic group, or adhere to the same religious tenets, the behavioral consequences for the individual are likely to be different from the behavioral consequences in a more heterogeneous setting.

Or consider the matter of community size, which I have frequently mentioned in earlier sections. A large community offers far more variety in personal opportunities and experience than a small one. Differences of this kind are highly relevant, particularly in the formative years of an individual. Consequently, social psychologists frequently ask for information concerning the kind of community in which the individual grew up. As we shall see, there are a number of interesting and important differences between people, in outlook and behavior, according to whether their origin is rural or urban. Some of these differences are discussed in the next section.

The social-psychological aspect of the community clearly warrants attention in any full-scale examination of this social unit. The community is more than a population, arrayed in space, and organized into subunits. It is also an assemblage of people, thinking, feeling, and behaving as individuals.

## Selected Processes: Dynamics of the Contemporary Community

In this section, my purpose is to provide an overview of some of the more significant *processes* currently involving the community. We shall depart from a purely static conception, from which only cross-sectional "snapshots" can be derived, and examine some of the actual dynamic processes of change going on in communities. However, we shall find that the four aspects of the community that we just discussed—the demographic, the ecological, the structural, and the behavioral aspects—are very useful in identifying the major processes of community change. In my previous discussion, I have underscored the fact that communities are constantly changing. Now let us consider some of the major processes of change.

### Demographic Change: Urbanization in the Modern World

The most important change being wrought in communities around the world today can be easily identified. From my standpoint, this change is urbanization—the massing of men in increasingly large agglomerations. As already stated, urbanization is essentially a process of population concentration. This process actually has been taking place for many centuries, and it is now worldwide in scope.

When did cities first appear? Simple as this question seems, it is the source of a great deal of controversy. The answer obviously depends upon one's conception of the "city," and there is no universally accepted definition. Therefore, some writers date the first appearance of urban communities as early as 8000 B.C., but others view the emergence of cities as being much more recent.

The best available evidence points toward the first appearance of true "cities" soon after 3500 B.C. in Sumer or Mesopotamia, near the confluence of the Tigris and the Euphrates Rivers (the "Fertile Crescent") and just to the north in Akkad. There is common agreement, in fact, that at least two areas witnessed the independent development of cities. In addition to Mesopotamia, cities emerged in Mesoamerica. More particularly, indigenous urban centers appeared on the Yucatan peninsula and in the area that is now Guatemala. Although the precise dates of these developments are not known, urban centers may have existed as early as 1000 B.C., and certainly existed by 300 A.D.[59]

There were three other sites of early urbanization, although it is not absolutely certain whether these were fully independent developments or whether they were mainly the products of cultural diffusion from Mesopotamia. These three additional sites were (1) the Nile Valley in Egypt, where cities developed around 3100 B.C., and where there is some evidence of diffusion and borrowing from Mesopotamia; (2) the Indus Valley, in what is now West Pakistan, where an urban civilization flourished between 2500 and 1500 B.C.; and (3) the Huang Ho (Yellow River) Valley in China, where cities appeared in the fourteenth century B.C. or perhaps earlier.

It is a striking paradox that all five of these sites are in the presently "underdeveloped" areas of the world, where current levels of urbaniza-

---

[59] Gordon R. Willey, "Mesoamerica," in Robert J. Braidwood and Gordon R. Willey, eds., *Courses Toward Urban Life* (Chicago: Aldine Publishing Co., 1962), pp. 84–101.

tion are relatively low. More important, however, are certain other features that these areas has in common. Following Sjoberg's analysis, it is possible to identify at least three important "preconditions" for city life.[60] The first requirement was obviously a "favorable ecological base," including climate, soil, and water conditions approprate to agriculture. The development of agriculture permitted relatively large populations to be supported on small land areas. Another important aspect of the ecological base was a situation conducive to repeated contacts between peoples of dissimilar cultures, permitting the rapid diffusion of social and technological innovations. Note that four of the five earliest urban sites were fertile river valleys, with their waterways affording easy access to other areas.

A second precondition identified by Sjoberg is "an advanced technology." In particular, technological developments in agriculture were apparently crucial. These developments—and the domestication of grains stands out in all five instances—multiplied the yield of food beyond bare subsistence needs and thus freed at least some people from purely extractive pursuits. Except in Mesoamerica, other related developments included animal husbandry, large-scale irrigation works, metallurgy, and the invention of such devices as the wheel and the plow. In addition, writing and other systems for the rational ordering of life and experience came into being, including mathematical systems and time-reckoning devices such as the clock and the calendar.

Finally, a third factor was the emergence of a well-developed system of social organization and social control, or what Sjoberg calls a "power structure." Storage and distribution of surplus, especially, required centralized social control. Taxation and tribute were common forms of wresting a surplus from the agricultural population. In Mesopotamia, for example, the first urban centers were actually independent "city-states." Each was ruled by a king who was simultaneously the chief priest. Land supporting the city was viewed as belonging to the local god, and tribute in the form of agricultural surplus was stored in public granaries, attached to the local temples, and subsequently distributed, apparently according to need.

In some respects, all of these early urban developments were "premature." They faced internal contradictions and external threats. Internally, there were problems of sanitation, difficulties in transportation and communication, and apparent conflicts arising out of a "top-heavy" power structure in which ultimate authority resided in the hands of a few. Externally, there were constant threats from neighboring peoples; in most

[60] Gideon Sjoberg, *The Preindustrial City: Past and Present* (Glencoe, Ill.: Free Press, 1960).

instances, those at the margins of these early urban civilizations were living in simple agricultural economies, and any marked population increase on their part was likely to lead to conflict with the early urban centers. It is no surprise to learn that all of the latter ultimately collapsed.

In any case, it is important to realize that the first "urban revolution" —the very emergence of cities—was preceded by an "agricultural revolution," that is, the founding of settled agriculture. This involved the controlled use of seeds and breeds, and permanent settling on the soil rather than nomadic hunting and gathering. Until very recently, no people moved directly from nomadism to an urban way of life; agriculture always intervened. Finally, it is paramount to realize that none of these early urban developments were able to support more than 5 or (at the very most) 10% of the total population as "urbanites."

This upper limit upon urbanization was only exceeded in the modern period, dating from the seventeenth century A.D., and then only in certain societies. There was, in fact, a *second* "urban revolution," in which truly urban societies came into existence, with urban majorities, and city growth began on a sustained basis. We are much more concerned here with this more recent set of developments, since these developments formed the beginning of urbanization in the modern sense, and set in motion a whole series of related processes that are still going on around the world.

In the modern era, urbanization started in Europe and it spread with the extension of the European sphere of influence. Although perfectly adequate data are not available, there are estimates for the most recent portion of the modern period. Table 2.3 shows the proportions of population living in large cities in the major regions of the world between 1800

**Table 2.3   Percent of Total Population Living in Cities of 100,000 or More, by Major World Regions, 1800 to 1950**

| Region | Percent in Cities of 100,000 or More | | | |
|---|---|---|---|---|
| | 1800 | 1850 | 1900 | 1950 |
| Asia (excluding USSR) | 1.6 | 1.7 | 2.1 | 7.5 |
| Europe (including USSR) | 2.9 [a] | 4.9 | *11.9* | *19.9* |
| Africa | 0.3 | 0.2 | 1.1 | 5.2 |
| America | 0.4 | *3.0* | *12.8* | *22.6* |
| Oceania | — | — | *21.7* | *39.2* |
| World | 1.7 | 2.3 | 5.5 | 13.1 |

[a] The regional percentages above the world average at each date are italicized.
*Source.* Kingsley Davis and Hilda Hertz, unpublished manuscript.

and 1950. The table indicates that Europe was the only region with any degree of concentration in large cities at the beginning of the nineteenth century and, even there, less than three out of every hundred persons lived in large cities. By the end of the nineteenth century, however, regions of European settlement (the Americas and Oceania) had actually surpassed Europe in achieving higher levels of urbanization. Other measures of urbanization, of course, would yield different details about this historical process, but the main results would be the same. Urbanization, which first matured centuries earlier in non-European areas, grew to be an intrinsic part of modern European development and colonization, and advanced farthest and most rapidly in portions of the New World.

It is also important to bear in mind that all of the major regions of the world—including those that are still relatively "underdeveloped"—have shared in this process of urbanization. Even Asia and Africa, where levels of urbanization are far lower than in other portions of the globe, are urbanizing rapidly. Actually, the whole process has been going on at an accelerated rate during the past two centuries. The rate of urbanization has continued to outstrip the rate of world population growth, and the gap is growing. If we break the period from 1800 to 1950 into three equal parts, and compute growth rates for the world and for cities of a given size, the results are as given in Table 2.4. World population is enlarg-

Table 2.4  Growth Rates in Three Periods for Cities of Different Size

|  | Percent Increase in Population of: | | | |
| --- | --- | --- | --- | --- |
| Period | Total World | Cities 5000 Plus | Cities 20,000 Plus | Cities 100,000 Plus |
| 1800–1850 | 29 | 175 | 132 | 76 |
| 1850–1900 | 37 | 192 | 194 | 222 |
| 1900–1950 | 49 | 228 | 240 | 254 |

ing at an increasing rate, and the same is true of urban population. With the passage of time, the most rapid rates of increase have been registered in the very largest size class, that is, cities of 100,000 or more inhabitants. Furthermore, there is no solid indication that the rate of urbanization will slow down in the very near future, although it must ultimately slow down.

In the more advanced industrial areas, where a high level of urbanization has already been achieved, there is obviously a lesser chance for dramatic shifts in that level. Urban communities are large and numerous, and their sheer size means that it is difficult for rapid percentage gains to occur. It is in the less-developed areas of the world, and particularly in Asia and Africa, that future upsurges of urbanization may be expected. The rates of urban growth in these areas actually are already the highest in the world. An examination of Table 2.5 reveals this very clearly. The

**Table 2.5   Levels of Metropolitanization (about 1940) and Measures of Metropolitan Growth (about 1940 to about 1952), by Major World Regions**

| Region | Percent of Total Population in Metropolitan Areas (about 1940) | Average Annual Percent Increase in Metropolitan Population (about 1940 to about 1952) | Percent of Total Regional Growth Claimed by Metropolitan Areas (about 1940 to about 1952) |
|---|---|---|---|
| North America | 51.6 | 2.1 | 77.2 |
| Oceania | 53.3 | 2.4 | 55.0 |
| Europe | 33.7 | 1.1 | 55.1 |
| USSR | 17.7 | 1.9 | 84.7 |
| South America | 17.7 | 3.7 | 37.7 |
| Middle America | 16.0 | 4.3 | 32.1 |
| Africa | 9.0 | 3.9 | 23.2 |
| Asia | 10.5 | 3.8 | 24.2 |

*Source.* Jack P. Gibbs and Leo F. Schnore, "Metropolitan Growth: An International Study," *American Journal of Sociology,* **66,** 164 (September, 1962).

regions with the lowest *levels* of "metropolitanization" exhibited the highest rates of metropolitan growth in the period under study. Meanwhile, the metropolitan areas were accumulating very large proportions of the total population increase in the more advanced regions. (If the average annual rates of growth shown in Table 2.5 seem rather low, remember that a population growing at a rate of 1% per year will double in 69 years; at 2% per year, doubling will occur in about 35 years, at 3% in 23 years, and at 4% in about 17 years.)

Urbanization has proceeded farthest in Europe and in those other areas (such as North America and Oceania) that were settled by Europeans. Starting from a virtual zero point, Europe in the modern period rapidly reached the upper limits achieved by ancient and classical civilizations and quickly passed them. England, for example, had about 9% of her population in cities over 100,000 in 1801 but, by 1901, the figure had reached 35%.

It is not easy to identify all of the factors responsible for this historically unprecedented upsurge in urbanization. Certainly they include these items: Major improvements in agriculture, sanitation, and transportation; the opening of new lands and new trade routes; and an enormous rise in productivity, especially by means of factories run by machinery and fossil fuels. The list could be extended considerably, but the conclusion would still be the same: "true" urbanization was achieved only through industrialization. Immediately following the Industrial Revolution, urbanization meant more than a light scattering of small towns; it meant that substantial portions, and even majorities, of the total population in some regions and nations came to live in cities.

However, it must be recognized that industrialization no longer plays the same key role in other parts of the world. Cities may grow to enormous size without an industrial impetus. In many respects, urbanization in the less-developed areas represents a "flight from the countryside," a mass migration to escape rural poverty and not a movement in the direction of city jobs and expanding employment opportunities in urban industry. Poverty is transferred from country to city in the process, but the cities continue to grow.

The fastest rates of urbanization are therefore found in the less-developed countries, while the pace of urbanization is necessarily slowing down in the older industrial countries. There is nothing mysterious in this seemingly paradoxical situation. As Kingsley Davis and Hilda Golden, two leading students of the subject, have observed:

As the proportion of the population living in cities becomes greater and greater, the chance of maintaining the *rate* of increase in that proportion becomes less and less. . . . As the rural proportion declines to a small fraction of the total population, the cities have an even smaller pool of people to draw on for the maintenance of growth rates.[61]

Indeed, it is instructive to consider the periods in which the fastest urban growth occurred in various countries. In England, which led the way, the most rapid urban increase took place in the first half of the nineteenth century, between 1811 and 1851. In the United States, it was in the second half of that century, between 1860 and 1890. In contrast, Egypt has only registered rapid urban gains since 1920, Mexico since 1921, and India since 1941.[62] As a result, the gap between the modern and the underdeveloped areas is narrowing, and perhaps both will ultimately reach a kind of urban "saturation point" beyond which further urbanization is impossible.

[61] Kingsley Davis and Hilda Hertz Golden, "Urbanization and the Development of Pre-Industrial Areas," *Economic Development and Cultural Change*, **3**, 11 (October, 1954).
[62] Kingsley Davis, "The Origin and Growth of Urbanization in the World," *American Journal of Sociology*, **60**, 435 (March, 1955).

It is obviously hazardous to speculate about the future course of urbanization. No one knows what the upper limit may be, although it is not entirely unreasonable to expect that 85 or 90% of the population may come to live in cities, at least if agriculture continues to undergo mechanization and rationalization. Yet, we do know that the continuation of recent world-wide rates of urbanization would mean that about one fourth of the world's population would live in cities of 100,000 or over by the end of the present century, and that at least one half of the population would live in cities of this size by 2050 A.D.[63] These projections may be too high or too low, but the inference is the same: the world is urbanizing very rapidly, and there is no evidence of a slackening in the near future of the rate at which this crucial demographic process is going on.

### Ecological Change: Spatial Segregation of Activities and Groups

In the course of urbanization, many profound ecological changes are set in motion. The spatial and temporal pattern of the community undergo significant alterations. Of all the many ecological processes that have been identified, let us focus on one as being of special interest: *segregation*.

By "segregation," I simply mean the physical separation of activities and population groups in space. In the small-community setting (such as the agricultural village), segregation is minimal. Since the population is fairly homogeneous, and the activities carried on are highly similar, there is little spatial differentiation. For most persons, place of residence and place of work are close at hand. The villagers may live in a central cluster of dwellings, and may travel a short distance to peripheral fields each day. Even those who are not engaged in agriculture, such as local artisans and merchants, live very near their workplaces; indeed, home and workplace may be one and the same. Moreover, there is no pronounced segregation of residential areas according to income or other attributes.

In the course of urbanization, however, the various activities and elements in the population begin to undergo a "sifting and sorting" into definite subareas. With any substantial increase in population size, we may expect the emergence of distinct areas devoted to narrower ranges of land uses. Generally, a separation of home and work occurs—one portion of the total occupied territory eventually being set aside for residence and other portions being given over to productive activities.[64]

Within the total area devoted to "economic" activities, there appears an even more elaborate differentiation. Areas devoted to commerce

---

[63] *Ibid.*

[64] Leo F. Schnore, "The Separation of Home and Work: A Problem for Human Ecology," *Social Forces,* **32,** 336–343 (May, 1954).

emerge, and industrial areas spring up. Actually, this process may continue to the point where each of these broad classes of activity are further subdivided in space. As for commerce, a retail district may develop, with a different area devoted to wholesaling, storage, and transshipment. There may even appear distinct subdistricts devoted to narrow lines of retailing, such as clothing or furniture. As for industry, different subareas may be set aside for heavy industry, as opposed to light industry. Again, a particular industry may be highly segregated, with a number of factories making a particular product concentrated in one specialized area. For example, a garment district may emerge. Even such services as recreation and entertainment may ultimately have their own distinct subareas, such as the theater district.

Human ecologists, urban land economists, and urban geographers year after year have attempted to develop various principles to account for such segregation, by trying to identify the forces that might attract similar units to a given area, and the factors that might make highly dissimilar activities tend to repel each other. More recently, of course, planned shopping centers and industrial parks have become prominent elements in the urban landscape. But in earlier years the process of segregation apparently operated on a more spontaneous basis, without centralized control, and firms located more freely in accordance with private judgments concerning locational advantage.

As we have observed, the process of urbanization has entailed a broad segregation between workplaces on the one hand and residences on the other. In early stages of urbanization, this separation was often minimal. Commercial activities, for example, were typically carried on in the merchant's home, with the family living behind or above the shop; survivals of this pattern are evident today, in even the largest cities, and particularly in places such as neighborhood groceries, taverns, and drugstores. As urbanization has proceeded, however, this has become a less-typical arrangement. With industrialization, the factory became solely a workplace, and employees lived elsewhere rather than on the premises. The distance separating home and work was initially slight, since prior to the development of modern means of transportation workers were obliged to live within walking distance of the factory. As a result, huge industrial slums emerged in many cities, with workers and their families living in tenements and other high-density assemblages near the factories.

But modern transportation has relaxed the necessity for a person to live very near his workplace, and in the course of time residential areas have spread over the urban landscape. As these areas have diffused, they have also undergone a process of differentiation that yields another kind of segregation—a kind that is familiar to any resident of a modern city. Different housing areas are devoted to different subgroups; that is, the residential population is sifted and sorted into subareas just as surely as commercial enterprises are segregated one from the other. Each neighborhood therefore tends to have a distinctive character.

There are three main *principles of residential segregation* operating in the modern urban community in the United States. These are (1) type of household, (2) socioeconomic status, and (3) racial or ethnic status. For example, some areas of the city, are almost exclusively occupied by individuals living alone (as in rooming-house districts) or by childless couples (as in areas devoted to small apartments). Other areas, however, are overwhelmingly devoted to providing larger quarters for families with children; today, in the United States, most "suburban" developments are of this type.

Segregation according to socioeconomic status has received considerable attention by sociologists working in the ecological tradition. As Otis Dudley Duncan and Beverly Duncan have demonstrated, "ecological analysis has provided strong support for the proposition that spatial distances between occupation groups are closely related to their social distances." [65] Some of the data of these authors is shown in Table 2.6. In the table, employed males are classified according to the "census tract" in which they reside. (Census tracts are small and relatively homogeneous urban subareas delineated for statistical purposes by the United States Bureau of the Census.) The "indexes of dissimilarity" in the table indicate the minimum proportion of individuals in any given occupational group that would have to move to another census tract in order for there to be perfect conformity with the tract-by-tract residential distribution of any other particular occupational group.

The various occupational groups are arranged in Table 2.6 from top to bottom and from left to right, according to socioeconomic status, ranging from the highest status group (professionals) to the lowest (laborers). We can therefore quickly compare the residential distributions of, for instance, professionals with each of the remaining occupational groups. Reading across the first line of the table, we can quickly see that the groups most like the professionals in residential distribution are those nearest them in socioeconomic status (the managers, officials, and proprietors and the sales workers), while the group least like the professionals in residential distribution are the laborers, who are at the opposite end of the status hierarchy. Similar comparisons can be made among all

[65] Otis Dudley Duncan and Beverly Duncan, "Residential Distribution and Occupational Stratification," *American Journal of Sociology,* **60,** 502 (March, 1955).

Table 2.6   Indexes of Dissimilarity in Residential Distribution among Major Occupational Groups, for Employed Males in the Chicago Metropolitan District, 1950

| Major Occupational Group | Major Occupational Group: | | | | | | | |
|---|---|---|---|---|---|---|---|---|
| | Professional | Managers, etc. | Sales workers | Clerical workers | Craftsmen and foremen | Operatives | Service workers | Laborers |
| Professional | — | 13 | 15 | 28 | 35 | 44 | 41 | 54 |
| Managers, etc. | | — | 13 | 28 | 33 | 41 | 40 | 52 |
| Sales workers | | | — | 27 | 35 | 42 | 38 | 54 |
| Clerical workers | | | | — | 16 | 21 | 24 | 38 |
| Craftsmen and foremen | | | | | — | 17 | 35 | 35 |
| Operatives | | | | | | — | 26 | 25 |
| Service workers | | | | | | | — | 28 |
| Laborers | | | | | | | | — |

*Source.* Otis D. Duncan and Beverly Duncan, "Residential Distribution and Occupational Stratification," *American Journal of Sociology,* **60,** 498 (March, 1955), Table 3.

the other groups represented in the table. Generally, "social distance" is a good predictor of spatial distance, since men who are most like each other in occupational terms tend to reside in the same areas.

Other measures of socioeconomic status besides occupation are frequently employed by sociologists interested in stratification, and these alternative indicators have been used in ecological research on segregation processes. As one example, consider the data for Detroit shown in Table 2.7. In this table, the segregation of educational groups is measured in a much more gross fashion; educational classes are simply considered according to residence in the city of Detroit or its surrounding suburban ring, rather than in individual tracts or neighborhoods. Data are provided for adult males with varying amounts of formal schooling at each of the three most recent census dates. The first panel shows the proportion of each educational class residing within the city; thus, of all males in the metropolitan area without any formal schooling in 1940, 76.5% resided within the city limits. All of the various education groups have become increasingly suburbanized, but a basic question to which an answer is sought in Table 2.7 is: Are the various educational classes becoming more or less like

**Table 2.7   Indexes of Centralization for Educational Groups in the Detroit Metropolitan Area, 1940 to 1960**

| Males 25 Years of Age or Older, by Years of School Completed | Percent of Each Educational Group Living in City: | | | Index of Centralization: [a] | | | Differences in Index: 1940 to 1960 |
|---|---|---|---|---|---|---|---|
| | 1940 | 1950 | 1960 | 1940 | 1950 | 1960 | |
| All Males | 69.6 | 63.4 | 46.9 | 100.0 | 100.0 | 100.0 | |
| None | 76.5 | 73.7 | 69.3 | 109.9 | 116.2 | 147.7 | 37.8 |
| Grade: 1–4 | 72.1 | 71.3 | 64.9 | 103.6 | 112.4 | 138.3 | 34.7 |
| Grade: 5–6 | 71.5 | 69.3 | 59.3 | 102.7 | 109.3 | 126.4 | 23.7 |
| Grade: 7–8 | 69.1 | 62.8 | 51.4 | 99.3 | 98.8 | 109.5 | 10.2 |
| High: 1–3 | 69.0 | 62.2 | 45.9 | 99.1 | 98.1 | 97.8 | −1.3 |
| High: 4 | 70.4 | 61.2 | 40.5 | 101.2 | 96.5 | 86.3 | −14.9 |
| College: 1–3 | 69.9 | 63.3 | 40.1 | 100.4 | 99.8 | 85.5 | −14.9 |
| College: 4 + | 69.0 | 59.2 | 34.9 | 99.1 | 93.3 | 74.4 | −24.7 |

[a] The "index of centralization" is the value for each educational subgroup in a given year (the percent living in the city) divided by the same value for the total male population aged 25 and over. Thus, the index of 147.7 for those without any formal schooling in 1960 was obtained by dividing 69.3 by 46.9, and so on. *Source.* Leo F. Schnore, "Urban Structure and Suburban Selectivity," *Demography,* 1 (1964), Table 3.

each other with respect to city-suburban residence? In other words, has residential segregation by social class been increasing, remaining essentially the same, or decreasing? Most of the scholarly and semipopular literature on the subject lead to the conclusion that there has been a trend toward a "polarization" of social classes, with the central city increasingly being given over to disadvantaged groups (educationally and otherwise), and with the suburbs more and more being occupied by the well-to-do groups. Table 2.7 shows a clear-cut instance of such a case. The 20-year interval between 1940 and 1960 was characterized by a distinctly patterned "sifting and sorting" of the various educational classes between the city of Detroit and its surrounding suburbs. Notice that the index values for the lowest educational groups mounted sharply, especially between 1950 and 1960, indicating an increased concentration of these groups in the center. However, the index values fell off sharply for those with highest education.

The 20-year shifts are summarized in the last column. The process of increasing class segregation is clearly documented here.[66]

Now this kind of pattern—low-status groups in the city and high-status groups in the suburbs—is precisely what we have come to expect in considering the segregation of social classes in American cities and suburbs. But there is good evidence that this familiar pattern does not characterize all urban communities in the United States. It is primarily the larger and older cities that reveal this particular "polarization" of classes between cities and suburbs. Smaller and newer communities frequently show precisely the opposite pattern.

This reversal can be seen in Table 2.8, where 200 urbanized areas in 1960 are classified according to population size and according to a crude measure of their age, and where city-suburban status comparisons are made by means of three separate but interrelated measures of socioeconomic status: occupation, education, and income. In each instance, regardless of the measure of socioeconomic status, population size and the age of the city contribute toward important and systematic variations. The older and larger the area, the more likely that suburbs will contain the higher classes. The city-suburban segregation of social classes clearly varies according to the surrounding community context; it is not always and not everywhere the same.

Now the fact that community size and age show decidedly pronounced and regular patterns may tempt the observer to draw some inferences about the process of class segregation over time; that is, as a community grows older and larger, it might be expected to recapitulate the sequence suggested by the data in Table 2.8. Higher status groups, then, might be expected to shift from city residence to suburban location. Unfortunately, it is extremely hazardous to make such historical or "longitudinal" inferences from purely "cross-sectional" data (such as those discussed here), gathered at one point in time. The information in Table 2.8 refers to a single date (1960), and we cannot directly infer that the older and larger areas resembled the currently newer and smaller areas at some point in the historical past. It so happens that there is some scattered evidence that does suggest just such a historical transition in both North and South America, but it is not possible to document this process statistically at this time.[67] It is also difficult to predict that currently newer and smaller

[66] Leo F. Schnore, "Urban Structure and Suburban Selectivity," *Demography*, 1, 164–176 (1964); see also Leo F. Schnore, *The Urban Scene: Human Ecology and Demography* (New York: Free Press, 1965).
[67] Leo F. Schnore, "On the Spatial Structure of Cities in the Two Americas," in Philip M. Hauser and Leo F. Schnore, eds., *The Study of Urbanization* (New York: Wiley, 1965), pp. 347–398.

**Table 2.8    City-Suburban Differentials in Socioeconomic Status, by Size of Urbanized Area, and by Age of Central City, 1960**

| | Percent of Urbanized Areas with Suburban Values Higher in: | | | |
| --- | --- | --- | --- | --- |
| | Median Family Income | Percent Completing High School | Percent in White-Collar Occupations | Number of Areas |
| *Size of urbanized area in 1960* | | | | |
| 1,000,000 and over | 100.0 | 100.0 | 87.5 | 16 |
| 500,000–1,000,000 | 100.0 | 100.0 | 86.4 | 22 |
| 250,000–500,000 | 79.3 | 75.9 | 55.2 | 29 |
| 150,000–250,000 | 72.1 | 62.8 | 48.8 | 43 |
| 100,000–150,000 | 70.3 | 64.9 | 40.5 | 37 |
| 50,000–100,000 | 56.6 | 49.1 | 30.2 | 53 |
| *Census year in which central city first reached 50,000* | | | | |
| 1800–1860 | 100.0 | 100.0 | 100.0 | 14 |
| 1870–1880 | 100.0 | 100.0 | 100.0 | 17 |
| 1890–1900 | 86.1 | 75.0 | 58.3 | 36 |
| 1910–1920 | 75.0 | 75.0 | 54.2 | 48 |
| 1930–1940 | 71.9 | 56.3 | 31.3 | 32 |
| 1950–1960 | 50.9 | 47.2 | 24.3 | 53 |
| All areas | 74.0 | 68.5 | 50.5 | 200 |

*Source.* Leo F. Schnore, "The Socioeconomic Status of Cities and Suburbs," *American Sociological Review,* **28,** 78, 80 (February, 1963), Tables 1 and 2.

urban areas will—as they age and grow in population size—assume the patterns displayed by currently older and larger areas. Nevertheless, these cross-sectional differences that are now observable are worthy of attention in their own right. They are among the pieces of evidence that we have at our disposal concerning *systematic* variations in ecological characteristics of the community.

The third principle of residential segregation—racial and ethnic status—has received perhaps more consideration than the other two principles combined. In the United States, in particular, this subject has attracted increasing attention in recent years. The residential segregation of American

Negroes has been especially interesting to social scientists and others concerned with the board topic of "civil rights" in the United States.

At least some "racial" segregation is a reflection of segregation according to socioeconomic status. This is especially evident in the case of the American Negro. Quite apart from racial considerations, there would probably be some degree of residential separation of Negroes and whites simply because most Negroes cannot afford the same kind of housing accommodations as the majority of whites. In short, the low income of many Negroes bars them from some areas of occupancy (as does the low income of some whites).

The amount of Negro-white segregation observable, however, is clearly much more than can be accounted for in simple economic terms. It is only too evident that color operates as an additional barrier. Even those Negroes with high income, education, and occupational standing experience great difficulty in exercising "free choice" in the housing market. Indeed, most urban areas are characterized by the existence of two separate—and far from equal—housing markets.

The effects of the operation of these separate markets have been extensively studied by Karl E. Taeuber and Alma Taeuber in their recent book, *Negroes in Cities*.[68] These writers show that a high degree of residential segregation according to color characterizes all American cities of any substantial size. The Taeubers, in addition to presenting detailed case studies of segregation in 10 Northern and Southern cities, furnish statistical data for about 200 cities, giving each city a segregation score, thus permitting the kind of needed comparative analysis in which levels of segregation are related to other community characteristics. The analysis of trends over time is also made possible by these data.

The measure of segregation that the Taeubers use is one already encountered earlier in this chapter: the index of dissimilarity. (Table 2.6 showed indexes of this kind for occupational groups in Chicago, based on 1950 census tract data.) The Taeubers calculated similar indexes comparing the residential distributions of whites and nonwhites on a block-by-block basis. The numerical values of the index range between zero (indicating no segregation) and 100 (indicating complete segregation). If every block in a city contained only whites or only nonwhites, and if there were no blocks of mixed occupancy, the index would be 100, indicating complete dissimilarity, or maximum unevenness in residential distribution. On the other hand, if each block contained each of the two

[68] Karl E. Taeuber and Alma F. Taeuber, *Negroes in Cities* (Chicago: Aldine Publishing Co., 1965).

groups, and if both groups were represented in the same proportions as in the city as a whole, there would be no residential segregation and the index value for the city would be zero. Any particular value (between zero and 100) can be interpreted as the minimum percentage of people in either group who would have to change their blocks of residence in order for a totally unsegregated distribution to appear.

The most striking result of the comparative analysis by the Taeubers is the high level of segregation that could be found in most American cities of any size in 1960. The range in index values was very limited: from a minimum of 60.1 to a maximum of 98, which is very close to the theoretical maximum. In each of the three years that the Taeubers considered (1940, 1950, and 1960) at least one half the cities studied had index values of 90 or above, and 5 out of every 6 showed scores of 80 or above. High levels of segregation, therefore, are very general in the United States.

Having established an index value for each of a large number of cities, the Taeubers then analyzed the possible reasons for the variation from city to city. They examined a number of factors that prior research and theory had suggested might account for the observable differences in segregation. Among these factors were ones such as the total size of the city population and both the absolute and relative sizes of the nonwhite population.

The result was that none of these factors was successful in accounting for variations in the level of segregation. Actually, sharp differences were not observable. Table 2.9 gives an example. In this table, 207 cities were subdivided into approximately equal subgroups, according to three variables, and average segregation scores were calculated for each subgroup. If the variable under examination is really important in influencing the level of segregation, we would expect a clear-cut pattern in the segregation scores, with a systematic increase or decrease being evident. In reality, however, such sharp patterns are not generally observable in the data; only the percentage nonwhite (in the bottom panel) shows a clear and systematic pattern of variations. As the percentage nonwhite increases, there is a tendency in the direction of higher segregation scores. (However, this same pattern did not appear in cross-sectional observations for 1940 and 1950.)

Despite the Taeubers' inability to account for the cross-sectional variations from city to city in level of segregation, their work yields some very important information with respect to trends over time. The principal findings are summarized in Table 2.10, where data are given for 109 cities with information permitting the computation of segregation scores for each of the three most recent census dates. The first row of the table (for the United States as a whole) shows that the average value of the segregation index increased slightly over the 20-year interval. This change came about,

Table 2.9 Average Indexes of Residential Segregation for 207 Cities Grouped According to Size of Total Population, Size of Nonwhite Population, and Percentage Nonwhite, 1960 [a]

| Variable and Quintile | Number of Cities | Mean Segregation Index |
|---|---|---|
| *Size of total population:* | | |
| Smallest fifth | 41 | 87.2 |
| Second fifth | 41 | 86.0 |
| Middle fifth | 42 | 87.0 |
| Fourth fifth | 41 | 84.5 |
| Largest fifth | 42 | 86.4 |
| | | |
| *Size of nonwhite population:* | | |
| Smallest fifth | 41 | 84.3 |
| Second fifth | 41 | 84.7 |
| Middle fifth | 42 | 86.2 |
| Fourth fifth | 41 | 87.2 |
| Largest fifth | 42 | 88.7 |
| | | |
| *Percentage nonwhite:* | | |
| Smallest fifth | 41 | 83.2 |
| Second fifth | 41 | 84.7 |
| Middle fifth | 42 | 85.0 |
| Fourth fifth | 41 | 87.8 |
| Largest fifth | 42 | 90.4 |

[a] The classifications by size of nonwhite population and percentage nonwhite are based on occupied housing units rather than population.
*Source.* Karl E. Taeuber and Alma F. Taeuber, *Negroes in Cities* (Chicago: Aldine Publishing Co., 1965), p. 38, Table 3.

however, through an increase between 1940 and 1950 that was followed by a slight decrease between 1950 and 1960. Thus, the trends during the two decades were in opposite directions.

The trends in the various regions of the United States are more interesting, and perhaps more important. There were slight increases in segregation in Northern and Western cities during the 1940's. In the South, there were more marked increases during the same period. In the 1950's, Southern cities continued to exhibit fairly sizable increases in segregation as measured by the index of dissimilarity. In the North and West, however, there was a notable decline, on the average. The index values fell off most

Table 2.10    Average Values of Indexes of Residential Segregation for Regions and Census Divisions, and Changes in Indexes, 109 Cities, 1940, 1950, and 1960

| | | Average Values of Segregation Indexes | | | | |
| Region and Division | Number of Cities | 1940 | 1950 | 1960 | Change 1940– 1950 | Change 1950– 1960 |
|---|---|---|---|---|---|---|
| Total, all regions | 109 | 85.2 | 87.3 | 86.1 | 2.1 | −1.2 |
| Northeast | 25 | 83.2 | 83.6 | 78.9 | 0.4 | −4.7 |
| New England | 7 | 81.9 | 81.9 | 75.8 | 0.0 | −6.1 |
| Middle Atlantic | 18 | 83.7 | 84.3 | 80.0 | 0.6 | −4.3 |
| North Central | 29 | 88.4 | 89.9 | 88.4 | 1.5 | −1.5 |
| East North Central | 20 | 88.3 | 90.0 | 88.4 | 1.7 | −1.6 |
| West North Central | 9 | 88.6 | 89.8 | 88.3 | 1.2 | −1.5 |
| West [a] | 10 | 82.7 | 82.9 | 76.4 | 0.2 | −6.5 |
| South | 45 | 84.9 | 88.5 | 90.7 | 3.6 | 2.2 |
| South Atlantic | 22 | 86.9 | 88.7 | 90.6 | 1.8 | 1.9 |
| East South Central | 9 | 84.8 | 88.1 | 91.4 | 3.3 | 3.3 |
| West South Central | 14 | 81.7 | 88.5 | 90.5 | 6.8 | 2.0 |

[a] Census divisions within the West are not shown because there is only one city (Denver) included in the study from the Mountain Division.
*Source.* Karl E. Taeuber and Alma F. Taeuber, *Negroes in Cities* (Chicago: Aldine Publishing Co., 1965), p. 44, Table 5.

markedly in the West, dropped to a considerable degree in the Northeast, and declined more gradually in cities of the North Central region.

During the 1940's, according to the Taeubers, the housing supply lagged behind population growth, and neither the pressures of rapidly growing Negro population nor Negro socioeconomic gains really altered patterns of residential segregation. In the 1950's, the urban housing supply increased rapidly, and Negro residential areas expanded substantially. In most Northern and Western cities, the historical trend toward increasing segregation was halted or reversed, but in Southern cities Negro economic gains and population growth were insufficient to overcome this trend. Residential segregation is clearly a tenacious social problem that is not very responsive to improvements in the economic status of Negroes. This is the justification for regarding "race" as a third dimension of residential segregation, at least in the United States. I do not mean to suggest that these are somehow "universal" principles of segregation, although scattered evidence from other societies does intimate that all three factors—type of family, socioeconomic status, and racial or ethnic membership—make a difference in the spatial arrangements of people according to place of residence.

### Structural Changes: Bureaucratization, Stratification, and the Rise of Voluntary Associations

During urbanization, still other changes are set in motion, although whether they are causally related to population concentration is not clear. Not all of these changes are so conveniently measured as the process of segregation, which can be simply handled in a quantitative fashion. Now we consider some of the broad alterations in community structure that have captured the attention of sociologists interested in the community.

The first of these changes is labeled "bureaucratization," and it refers to the emergence of giant organizations—hierarchically arranged, and operated according to rational rules—organizations in which a larger and larger proportion of the economically active population is becoming involved. In popular language, the "bureaucrat" is a governmental functionary but, as we shall see, the major elements of bureaucratic organization also extend to business enterprises, the church, the military, and many formal organizations such as those devoted to public welfare. Indeed, very few aspects of contemporary urban life lie beyond the purview of bureaucratic organization.

What are the chief attributes of bureaucratic organization? The classic characterization of bureaucracy was given by Max Weber. Weber contended that the spread of the bureaucratic form of organization was one of the key structural transformations of modern times. Other authors have linked bureaucratic organization more specifically with urbanization.

In the city, "bureaucracy" becomes a ubiquitous form of organization. It is a rational-formal-legal organization which is an inevitable and indispensable concomitant of populations of large size and density and high levels of interaction. It is a form of complex organization involving (1) the distribution in a fixed way of regular activities, (2) the distribution in a fixed way of authority in accordance with rules, (3) the methodical provision for fulfillment of duties and execution of rights, and (4) the selection of personnel on the basis of qualifications rather than of birth or status. Bureaucracy in this sense is found not only in government but also in business enterprise, in labor unions, in religious organizations, in educational institutions, in fraternal organizations—in brief, in all aspects of the mass society in which collective activity is required on a continuing basis.[69]

How does the development of the bureaucratic form of organization affect the organization of the community? The community is affected in

[69] Philip M. Hauser, "Urbanization: An Overview," in Philip M. Hauser and Leo F. Schnore, eds., *The Study of Urbanization* (New York: Wiley, 1965), p. 25.

many specific areas, according to Roland L. Warren, who asserts that "The development of impersonal bureaucratic structures to coordinate the complex systems growing out of specialization and the division of labor has an important impact on local community life." [70] Indeed, Warren is only one of a number of modern scholars who have stressed the numerous ways in which bureaucratically organized activities have impinged on the contemporary community.

On the community level, whether we confront bureaucracy in the business enterprise, the labor union, the government office, or the voluntary association, [it] . . . is a form which accommodates the complex division of labor by instituting an impersonal, secondary-group type of structure to perform functions which are either new or were earlier performed in many instances under the primary-group auspices of family, friendship group, neighborhood, and church.

Bureaucratic organization is important at the community level in another respect. It provides the structural and procedural vehicle through which various types of decision-making behavior can be deliberately "administered" rather than left to the decisions of individuals in the "market" . . . Thus, the individual gift choice becomes administered through the community chest; the individual work choice becomes administered through a union; the individual motion picture choice becomes administered through the censorship activities of a religious organization or patriotic society; the individual activity in cooperating with one's neighbor becomes administered through a neighborhood association. [71]

Thus, more and more facets of community life come under bureaucratic purview in the contemporary urban setting. In addition, many more phases of local life are subject to outside influence; an increasing number of important decisions are made somewhere far beyond the local community's boundaries. "At the community level, many units which perform important functions, whether they be chain stores, or local offices of the state welfare department, or schools, are more likely to be oriented toward extracommunity systems than were the auspices which they replaced." [72]

Bureaucratization really was one of the major forces identified by Stein as bringing about "the eclipse of community." According to his thesis, "it is the growth of absentee ownership which proves most significant." [73] In Stein's view, this is most clearly apparent with respect to the community's stratification system:

Managers of local plants are not part of local prestige structures and they look to extra-local agencies, especially the higher executives of their corporations, for confirmation of their status claims. To be successful, they eventually have to leave

[70] Roland L. Warren, *The Community in America* (Chicago: Rand McNally and Co., 1963), p. 66.

[71] *Ibid.*, p. 69.

[72] *Ibid.*, p. 74.

[73] Maurice R. Stein, *The Eclipse of Community* (Princeton, N.J.: Princeton University Press, 1960), pp. 83–84.

local plants for the higher reaches of the corporate hierarchy. Their interest in the community remains primarily focused on the extent to which it provides a tractable labor force. Basic policy decisions, some of which can drastically affect community affairs, are made at top echelons, leaving local managers to enforce unpopular policies without giving them much discretion in determining their character.[74]

Some of the historical consequences of the bureaucratic trend are demonstrated by Robert O. Schulze in a case study of a small midwestern community. This community—Ypsilanti, Michigan, an industrial satellite of Detroit—experienced a "gradual absorption of its major industrial plants by large, absentee-owned corporations, a trend sharply accelerated during the World War II period." [75] Schulze was able to reconstruct the main outlines of the local "power structure" from the time of the community's founding in 1823 until 1955, and his principal finding was that *"The historical drift has been characterized by the withdrawal of the economic dominants from active and overt participation in the public life of Cibola* [Ypsilanti]." [76]

It was hypothesized that in the community *relatively* self-contained and un-involved in the larger social and economic system, the community with few and scattered commitments beyond its borders, local power would tend to be structured as a pyramid and heavily concentrated at the apex. More specifically, it was surmised that those persons who exercised major control over the community's economic system would tend to be the same persons who exercised preponderant control over its socio-political system, and that this latter control would be reflected, at least in part, by their active leadership and participation in the political and civic life of the community.[77]

But with the increasing importance of nonlocal bureaucracies, Schulze hypothesized, the new "economic dominants" would begin to withdraw their interest and active attention from local affairs.

Although the major economic units would have grown in size and potential influence, it was hypothesized that several factors would militate against the effective exercise, the actual "cashing-in," of their power in the community. The most significant of these would be the fact that the local community would have become ever less important to the survival and prosperity of its dominant economic units. As the activities of these units became increasingly directed toward—and by—populations and groups other than the local ones, the relevance of local community organizations and the impact of local political influences on the major economic units would accordingly diminish. As this occurred, the local power structure would, in effect, bifurcate—with those who exercised primary

<hr />

[74] *Ibid.*, pp. 85–86.
[75] Robert O. Schulze, "The Role of Economic Dominants in Community Power Structure," *American Sociological Review*, **23**, 4 (February, 1958).
[76] *Ibid.*, p. 5; italics in original.
[77] *Ibid.*, p. 4.

direction over its socio-political system no longer being essentially the same set of persons who exercised primary control over its economic system.[78]

Schulze was able to confirm these broad historical hypotheses. For example, he shows that "*none* of the most recent type of economic dominant—the managers of the absentee-owned corporations—has held any public office (elective or appointive) in the community." [79]

The main trends in bureaucratization and their impact on the local community are dealt with in more detail in Chapter 3. Here, it is sufficient to realize that the spread of bureaucratic forms has apparently made the local community increasingly vulnerable to outside influences. Local control seems to have declined in almost every sphere of activity, so that the local community is less than ever an "island," cut off from the other communities with which it is interrelated in an increasingly complex division of labor. (Some writers regard this trend as being fraught with psychological consequences for the individual; we consider this matter in the next section.)

I have already discussed the fact that bureaucratization has had a crucial impact on the local stratification system. As is true with other aspects of social life, outside influences are growing in importance, and the individual's position in the status hierarchy is affected less and less by such considerations as length of residence in the local community. Being a member of an "old family" does not necessarily carry the same guarantees of prestige and deference as it carried in the past. Sheer size of the community, together with the fluidity entailed by easy mobility, renders the system difficult to delineate. As Leonard Reissman has suggested, "Interaction of individuals from different backgrounds destroyed the rigid divisions of the smaller integrated society and introduced a more complex pattern of social stratification." [80]

In any event, it is difficult to sketch the main outlines of the stratification system as it has evolved in the modern America community context, except for such limited topics as residential segregation. One reason is that the research on the topic has been overwhelmingly devoted to smaller American communities. No one is able to provide more than guesses about the class systems that characterize the communities that concern us most —the gigantic metropolitan centers of our nation. A good guess is that these class systems are different from those found in smaller communities, and are notably more complex. The details of the social transformations of the stratification system that have occurred are more properly covered in another part of this book (Chapter 4).

---

[78] *Ibid.*
[79] *Ibid.*, p. 5.
[80] Leonard Reissman, *The Urban Process: Cities in Industrial Societies* (New York: Free Press of Glencoe, 1964), p. 141.

However, one final aspect of structure should be examined here: the subject of "voluntary associations," which currently are viewed as urban forms of organization *par excellence*. Wirth, in "Urbanism as a Way of Life," offered the following thesis: "Reduced to a stage of virtual impotence as an individual, the urbanite is bound to exert himself by joining with others of similar interest into organized groups to obtain his ends. This results in the enormous multiplication of voluntary organizations directed toward as great a variety of objectives as there are human needs and interests." [81] The rise of voluntary associations is consequently regarded as an intrinsic structural concomitant of the process of urbanization.

The extent to which there are observable differences between communities in voluntary association membership is shown in Table 2.11. Charles R. Wright and Herbert H. Hyman, the authors of this study, have summarized their main findings as follows:

Voluntary associations customarily have been identified as characteristic of the urban way of life, and membership in such associations has been assumed to be more common for city residents than rural people. . . .

From the 1953 national survey it is possible to determine the number of associational affiliations of family members living in counties of varying degrees of urbanization, taking the size of the largest city in the county as a crude index of its degree of urbanism. . . .

But the type of county is only a crude index of the social atmosphere within which the citizen lives. Within each county, for example, there are areas of more *and* less urban nature. Therefore a finer breakdown is desirable in order to determine more precisely the relationship between urbanism and membership in voluntary associations. Table 2.11 presents data on membership according to urban, rural non-farm, and rural farm residences within each type of county.

Several interesting findings emerge. First, it appears that, with one exception (rural farm residents in moderately urbanized counties) the relationship between urbanization of county and membership in voluntary associations persists. That is, more of the residents of highly urbanized counties belong to organizations than do persons living in similar types of neighborhoods but in less urbanized counties. For example, only 42 per cent of the urbanites in highly urbanized counties belong to no organization, in contrast with 46 per cent of the urbanites in moderately urbanized counties, and 54 per cent in the least urbanized.

Secondly, within each type of county, rural farm residence is more closely associated with non-membership than is either rural non-farm or urban residence. . . .

Third, there is *no* appreciable difference between the membership rates of urbanites and rural non-farm residents within any type of county.[82]

[81] Louis Wirth, "Urbanism as a Way of Life," *American Journal of Sociology,* **44,** 22 (July, 1938).
[82] Charles R. Wright and Herbert H. Hyman, "Voluntary Association Memberships of American Adults: Evidence from National Sample Surveys," *American Sociological Review,* **23,** 289–291 (June, 1958).

**Table 2.11   Voluntary Association Memberships by Place of Residence, United States, 1953**

| Percent of Families Whose Members Belong to: | Metropolitan Counties (with City of 50,000 or More) | | | Other Urbanized Counties (with City of 10,000 to 50,000) | | | Primarily Rural Counties (Having No Town of 10,000) | | |
|---|---|---|---|---|---|---|---|---|---|
| | Urban | Rural Nonfarm | Rural Farm | Urban | Rural Nonfarm | Rural Farm | Urban | Rural Nonfarm | Rural Farm |
| No organization | 42 | 40 | 67 | 46 | 46 | 53 | 54 | 52 | 70 |
| One organization | 33 | 37 | 21 | 36 | 34 | 28 | 27 | 24 | 21 |
| Two or more organizations | 25 | 23 | 12 | 18 | 20 | 19 | 19 | 24 | 9 |
| Total (%) | 100 | 100 | 100 | 100 | 100 | 100 | 100 | 100 | 100 |
| Number of cases | 1394 | 193 | 48 | 294 | 115 | 134 | 110 | 264 | 252 |

*Source.* Charles R. Wright and Herbert H. Hyman, "Voluntary Association Memberships of American Adults: Evidence from National Sample Surveys," *American Sociological Review,* **23**, 290, Table 4 (June, 1958).

These findings are from a cross-sectional study, of course, and they can tell us nothing about *trends* in the number and importance of voluntary associations with increasing urbanization. However, they are consistent with the Wirth hypothesis, and do not contradict the idea that urbanization has been accompanied by a rise of voluntary associations.

Moreover, there is other evidence that supports this basic notion. For example, Basil G. Zimmer finds that the level of participation of migrants in voluntary associations is related to their experience prior to having entered their community of current residence. In particular, persons born on farms are less likely to maintain memberships in urban voluntary associations. Some of his data are shown in Table 2.12, where a sample

Table 2.12  **Percent Belonging to Formal Organizations by Type of Background and by Amount of Farm Experience—Ypsilanti, Michigan, 1952 and 1953**

| Background | Percent Belonging | Number of Cases |
|---|---|---|
| (1) *Place of birth* | | |
| Farm | 33 | 244 |
| Other urban | 46 | 256 |
| Native (Ypsilanti) | 55 | 94 |
| (2) *Number of years lived on farm* [a] | | |
| Under 10 | 50 | 54 |
| 10–19 | 34 | 118 |
| 20–29 | 30 | 101 |
| 30 and over | 18 | 39 |
| (3) *Age when last lived on farm* [a] | | |
| Under 15 | 45 | 56 |
| 15–19 | 41 | 82 |
| 20–39 | 29 | 145 |
| 40 and over | 4 | 26 |

[a] Includes all persons who have ever lived on a farm.
*Source.* Basil G. Zimmer, "Farm Background and Urban Participation," *American Journal of Sociology,* **61,** 471, 474 (March, 1956), Tables 1 and 4.

of residents of Ypsilanti, Michigan, are classified according to background and current associational memberships (with church organizations and labor unions excluded from consideration). Place of birth (Panel 1) appears to make a significant difference, with persons born on farms exhibiting the lowest levels of participation. Moreover, the length of experience on the farm plays a role in affecting current memberships; in fact, these differences, shown in Panels 2 and 3 of Table 2.12 persist when age, occupation, and education are held constant. As Zimmer says, "it is evident that the amount of experience in a dissimilar environment is an important deterrent to participation in city life. As farm experience increases, the level of participation [in urban formal organization] decreases."[83]

Social life consists of more than membership in the kinds of *formal* organizations commonly treated as "voluntary associations." Within each community, there are networks of *informal* associations, such as those among family members, friends, neighbors, and co-workers. These activities have also been subjected to sociological analysis in a community context. One of the leading hypotheses of the "Chicago School" was that such formal affiliations tend to decline in the urban setting, and to be replaced by the more formal contacts offered by voluntary associations. Recent research, however, has produced evidence that tends to contradict this rather over-simplified view of life in the contemporary urban community.

A study of the Detroit metropolitan area sheds some light on this issue. In this research, both formal *and* informal associations were examined. It was found that *formal* membership were widespread (almost two thirds of the population) but were far from inclusive of the whole adult population; in contrast, *informal* group association was almost universal, with only a small segment of the population failing to participate in fairly frequent contact with family, friends, neighbors, and co-workers. Moreover, formal and informal group participation varied in a similar fashion, particularly in accordance with socioeconomic status. Table 2.13 shows some of the principal findings on this point. Formal memberships tend to vary directly with income; the higher the income, the greater is the proportion of people who are members. And, as the author—Morris Axelrod—points out:

The rank order of the comparative importance of the types of informal groups is (1) relatives, (2) friends, (3) neighbors, (4) co-workers.

Not only does this pattern of relatives, friends, neighbors and co-workers, in that order, hold for the general population, but it is also true for almost every segment of the population we have studied. . . .

It seems clear that the school of urban sociologists which has emphasized the decline of the kinship relationship has exaggerated a trend to an extreme which is inconsistent with the facts obtained here.[84]

[83] Basil G. Zimmer, "Farm Background and Urban Participation," *American Journal of Sociology,* **61,** 474 (March, 1956).
[84] Morris Axelrod, "Urban Structure and Social Participation," *American Sociological Review,* **21,** 17 (February, 1956).

**Table 2.13  Extent of Formal Group Participation, and Types of Informal Groups with Which People Have Frequent Association, by Family Income—Detroit Metropolitan Area, 1952**

| Family Income (Dollars) | Formal organizations | | Informal Associations | | | | Number of Cases |
|---|---|---|---|---|---|---|---|
| | Percent Who Are Members | Percent Who Are Very Active | Frequent Contacts with: | | | | |
| | | | Relatives | Friends | Neighbors | Co-workers | |
| Under 3000 | 42 | 8 | 52 | 37 | 37 | 12 | 106 |
| 3000–3999 | 66 | 9 | 68 | 50 | 39 | 19 | 164 |
| 4000–4999 | 67 | 14 | 67 | 48 | 40 | 22 | 138 |
| 5000–5999 | 62 | 12 | 74 | 43 | 35 | 25 | 102 |
| 6000–6999 | 65 | 12 | 64 | 44 | 29 | 23 | 77 |
| 7000 and over | 81 | 21 | 54 | 57 | 44 | 28 | 116 |

*Source.* Morris Axelrod, "Urban Structure and Social Participation," *American Sociological Review*, **21**, 15, 17 (February, 1956), Tables 3 and 6.

Unfortunately, Axelrod's data represent a "snapshot" of the situation at one point in time, and it is impossible to make sound inferences concerning trends in the matters with which he is dealing. As frequently happens, we must be content with a purely cross-sectional comparison between sub-groups, such as socioeconomic strata or residents of different types of area. Nevertheless, there are a large number of studies of American cities showing the continued importance of kinship ties to urbanites. Marvin B. Sussman and Lee Burchinal refer to "the lag between apparently antiquated family theory and empirical reality," and argue as follows:

> The theory stresses the social isolation of the nuclear family while findings from empirical studies reveal an existing and functioning extended kin system closely integrated within a network of relationships and mutual assistance along bilateral kinship lines and encompassing several generations.[85]

These authors do not deny that the nuclear family, living apart from relatives, is the dominant form in American cities.[86] However, they do question: (1) the assumption that living arrangements tell us all that there is to know about the sociological structure and functioning of families; and (2) the assumption that urban industrialization produced a radical change in the direction of true isolation of one nuclear family from another.

Actually, a great deal more of historically sophisticated research is required. This is clearly implied in these observations:

> Was the extended classical type [of family] found in rural society replaced by a nuclear one, or did it evolve into the modified kin form described in this paper? It is suggested that the notion of the isolated nuclear family stems from theory and research on immigrant groups coming into the city to work during the period of urbanization in Western society. Anomie in family behavior resulted from individual and institutional failure to make appropriate adjustments required by this migration. The coldness and indifference of the workplace and the city as a steel and concrete bastion contributed to a feeling of aloneness and isolation. . . . One assumption of this position is that early urban man had little time for concern or activity with kinsmen. A more logical assumption is that isolation, a depressive workplace, and uncertainty produced greater reliance upon kin. Once new immigrants became established in the city they served as informants, innkeepers, and providers for later kin arrivals.[87]

---

[85] Marvin B. Sussman and Lee G. Burchinal, "Kin Family Network: Unheralded Structure in Current Conceptualizations of Family Functioning," *Marriage and Family Living*, 24, 231 (August, 1962); see also Marvin B. Sussman and Lee G. Burchinal, "Intergenerational Family Continuity and Economic Activity," in H. Lee Jacobs, ed., *The Older Person in the Family* (Iowa City: The Institute of Gerontology, The University of Iowa, 1965), pp. 19–33.

[86] John Mogey, "Family and Community in Urban-Industrial Societies," in Harold T. Christensen, ed., *Handbook of Marriage and the Family* (Chicago: Rand McNally, 1964), pp. 501–534.

[87] Marvin B. Sussman and Lee G. Burchinal, "Kin Family Network" (cited in footnote 85), p. 239.

No matter what the facts may be—and many of them are forever lost behind the veil of history—it is clear that we cannot blithely assume that "the family" has undergone some kind of "breakdown" in the urban community context.

Another study of the Detroit metropolitan area enlightens us on the matter of informal group participation according to place of residence. In this study, Aida K. Tomeh distinguished three subareas: (1) the inner city, located within six miles of Detroit's central business district; (2) the outer-city zone, more than six miles from the center but still inside of Detroit's city limits; (3) the suburban area lying outside of the city limits but within "greater Detroit." As she observes, "most studies contrasting degrees of participation in the suburb and the city have not adjusted for differences in population characteristics which contribute to differences in rates of informal participation. Ideally, if after accounting for the effect of [variations in the population composition of city and suburb] we still find differences, then these must be associated with residential location itself." [88] Her procedure, therefore, was to examine three areal subgroups matched on a number of relevant characteristics, such as age, marital status, socioeconomic standing, and migrant status—all of which are factors that previous research has shown to be influential in affecting informal participation.

Tomeh's results suggest that place of residence, particularly in the suburbs, does exercise an independent influence on the amount of informal participation:

In general, the findings seem to suggest, first, that although participation differences between the inner and outer zones are quite small and inconsistent, participation increases as one moves across Detroit's city limits, and second, that participation is facilitated when relatively many persons of similar characteristics live in the same area.

The matching procedure provides some evidence that place of residence is one of several variables *independently* related to the degree of *total informal participation* because differences in participation by zone persist even when seven population characteristics are controlled. . . .

The data show that suburban residence is often associated with an increase in informal participation. This immediately poses the problem of whether the rich informal sociability of the suburb is fostered by the residence location itself or by the population composition of the area. Evidence presented here points out the importance of both factors.[89]

Thus, *place of residence* once again emerges as an important factor in social life. Just as a person's place of origin (for example, farm versus non-

[88] Aida K. Tomeh, "Informal Group Participation and Residential Patterns," *American Journal of Sociology*, **70**, 29 (July, 1964).
[89] *Ibid.*, p. 34.

farm) appears to affect his behavior, his current place of residence is also a relevant influence upon his conduct. We shall see that this variable has also been considered as a factor in individual psychology, as we now examine a final substantive topic: the behavioral aspect of the contemporary community.

### Behavioral Changes: Alienation, Anomie, and Aspirations

Here, we discuss briefly a set of processes operating in the community that have received a great deal of attention but relatively limited research —the processes concerning individuals as individuals. Much has been written on this subject, but little of it is based on empirical work. Instead, speculation and conjecture are the main bases of most discussions.

The presumed psychological results of urbanization have received perhaps the most attention. In the treatment of this topic, however, there has been a marked emphasis upon a viewpoint that depends on a particular set of values. One kind of community has been regarded as anathema. More specifically, much of the writing dealing with the consequences of urbanization has been marred by a distinct "antiurban" bias. As Oscar Lewis has said:

> It is in the evaluation of the personality of the urban dweller that urban theory has gone furthest afield. It leaps from the analysis of the social system to conjecture about individual personality; it is based not on solid psychological theory but on personal values, analogies, and outmoded physio-psychological concepts. Some of the description of the modern urbanite reads like another version of the fall of man.[90]

Despite these shortcomings, it is useful to review some of the main themes that have appeared in the social science literature dealing with the psychological consequences of urbanization. Actually, they are not radically different from the notions that now permeate much of the popular discussion of the contemporary urban community by writers outside the social sciences.

The first major subject involves the idea that urban man has been subjected to increasing alienation. Since this is such a prominent theme in today's literature, it is worthwhile briefly to consider the original source of this conception: Karl Marx. Marx was concerned with the "alienation of labor," but his view has been extended and generalized to such an extent that a direct quotation from him is in order here.

---

[90] Oscar Lewis, "The Folk-Urban Ideal Types: Further Observations on the Folk-Urban Continuum and Urbanization with Special Reference to Mexico City," in Philip M. Hauser and Leo F. Schnore, eds., *The Study of Urbanization* (New York: Wiley, 1965), p. 497.

What constitutes the *alienation of labor?* The fact that labor is external to the worker, i.e., it does not belong to his essential being; that in his work, therefore, he does not affirm himself but denies himself, does not feel content but unhappy, does not develop freely his physical and mental energy but mortifies his body and ruins his mind. The worker therefore only feels himself outside his work, and in work feels outside himself. He is at home when he is not working, and when he is working he is not at home. His labor is therefore not voluntary, but coerced; it is forced labor. It is therefore not the satisfaction of a need; it is merely a means to satisfy needs external to it.[91]

This viewpoint about labor has been extended to virtually all facets of modern existence. The urbanite, in particular, is regarded more and more as being cut off from his fellow men. He not only is caught in a meaningless work situation, but is also deprived of sustaining ties when he is off the job. The urban community is pictured as a formless anonymous mass, in which detached individuals live empty lives in psychological isolation from each other. In advocating this view, the social scientist has joined the humanist and the artist, who also portray a ceaseless "search for identity," with the beleaguered urbanite not being considered as a full member of the community in any meaningful psychological sense.

A closely related theme has involved the idea of *anomie* or normlessness (this term is frequently given as "anomy" or "anomia"). As in the case of alienation, this concept was first specifically applied by one writer, and then generalized by subsequent writers. In our case, the writer was the famous French sociologist, Émile Durkheim. Quoting him briefly:

But whence comes this state?
Since a body of rules [norms] is the definite form which spontaneously established relations between social functions take in the course of time, we can say, *a priori*, that the state of *anomy* is impossible wherever solidary organs are sufficiently prolonged. . . . For the same reason the exchanges take place among them easily, they take place frequently; being regular, they regularize themselves accordingly, and in time the work of consolidation is achieved. . . . But, on the contrary, if some opaque environment is interposed, then only stimuli of a certain intensity can be communicated. . . .

As the market extends, great industry appears. But it results in changing the relations of employers and employees. The great strain upon the nervous system and the contagious influence of great agglomeration increase the needs of the latter. Machines replace men; manufacturing replaces hard-work. The worker is regimented, separated from his family throughout the day. He always lives apart from his employer, etc. These new conditions of industrial life naturally demand a new organization, but as these changes have been accomplished with

[91] Karl Marx, quoted in Morris Stockhammer, ed., *Karl Marx Dictionary* (New York: Philosophical Library, 1965), p. 6.

great rapidity, the interests in conflict have not yet had the time to be equilibrated.[92]

As was true with alienation, it is never clear whether anomie should be attributed to urbanization, to industrialization, to some combination of the two processes, or to something else, such as bureaucratization. However, contemporary life is viewed as being starkly contrasted with some earlier, more "natural" order, or with some form of community life that might be achieved in the future.

From a research standpoint, it is astonishing that neither of these two processes—important as they presumably are—has been given extended empirical examination in a comparative community context. A recent survey of 86 studies of anomie, for example, reveals only one case in which the investigators considered the postulated link between anomie and urbanization.[93]

In this single study, Lewis M. Killian and Charles M. Grigg found that the degree of urbanization was *not* systematically related to anomie. These authors computed "anomia scores" for Negroes and whites in two southeastern communities; one was a city of more than 300,000 inhabitants and the other was a rural county seat of less than 3000 inhabitants.

The first hypothesis was derived from the theory that the city constitutes an anomic milieu in contrast to the small town. It was hypothesized that, in both Negro and white samples, city-dwellers would have higher anomia scores than small-town residents. . . .

[However] we find that level of education rather than urban residence accounts for apparent urban-rural differences in anomia among whites. Moreover, with Negro samples no significant urban-rural differences is found. The small difference that does exist actually shows a higher percentage of rural than of urban Negroes displaying high anomia. . . .

It is position in the social [class] structure of either type that is most likely to be associated with differences in anomia.[94]

Thus the only presently available empirical examination of the hypothesis provides evidence that is directly contrary to the main line of reasoning found in the more speculative literature.

There are other facets of individual behavior, however, that have been subjected to careful empirical scrutiny in a comparative community context. Perhaps the best example concerns the subject of educational and oc-

[92] Émile Durkheim, *The Division of Labor in Society*, translated by George Simpson (New York: Macmillan, 1933), pp. 368 and 370.
[93] Marshall B. Clinard, ed., *Anomie and Deviant Behavior* (New York: Free Press, 1964), pp. 243–289.
[94] Lewis M. Killian and Charles M. Grigg, "Urbanism, Race, and Anomia," *American Journal of Sociology*, **67**, 661, 664 (May, 1962).

cupational *aspirations*, which has been studied most intensively by William
H. Sewell and his associates. Despite the gloomy pattern of the literature
created by intellectuals contemplating the contemporary urban scene, individuals do continue to be motivated to take their places in the urban
social system. The educational and occupational goals of rural and urban
youth have therefore been examined in some detail.

With respect to educational aspirations, Table 2.14 provides some evidence concerning the college plans of a large sample of Wisconsin high

**Table 2.14  Percentage Planning to go to College by Place of Residence and
Intelligence—for Male and Female Wisconsin High School Seniors**

| Sex and Place of Residence | Intelligence | | | |
|---|---|---|---|---|
| | Low | Middle | High | Total |
| *Males* | | | | |
| Farm | 7.7 | 22.4 | 43.8 | 22.0 |
| Village (under 2500) | 14.3 | 31.5 | 55.1 | 31.8 |
| Small city (2500–25,000) | 13.0 | 32.3 | 66.1 | 38.4 |
| Medium city (25,000–100,000) | 18.3 | 39.8 | 65.2 | 41.7 |
| Large city (100,000 and more) | 22.9 | 47.0 | 69.4 | 50.7 |
| *Females* | | | | |
| Farm | 11.1 | 19.8 | 35.8 | 21.1 |
| Village (under 2500) | 11.1 | 25.9 | 38.5 | 23.9 |
| Small city (2500–25,000) | 13.2 | 26.3 | 50.8 | 29.5 |
| Medium city (25,000–100,000) | 12.1 | 30.3 | 52.5 | 32.8 |
| Large city (100,000 and more) | 13.4 | 32.8 | 57.4 | 35.7 |

*Source.* William H. Sewell, "Community Residence and College Plans," *American
Sociological Review,* **29,** 31 (February, 1964), Table 4.

school seniors. It is apparent that the community of residence is a fairly
good predictor of educational aspirations, since the proportions of male
and female students planning to go to college increases regularly as the
size of the community increases. Moreover, this increase occurs within each
of three subcategories based on measured intelligence. It is important to
take account of the latter factor because intelligence is also related to educational aspirations. This becomes apparent by reading the table hori-
zontally rather than vertically; within each size-of-place category, more of
the students with higher intelligence plan to go on to college. Social class
position was also taken into account, because it is also related to educational
aspirations. The higher the class standing, the greater is the likelihood that
the student will plan to attend college.

The author—William H. Sewell—has commented on his findings in this way:

> The results of the statistical analysis show that there are sizable differences in the college plans of rural and urban youth which are not artifacts of the sex, intelligence, and socioeconomic [class] composition of the sample. Many factors would probably help to account for this finding. At the most general level, the opportunity structure provided by the more rural communities is clearly very limited both in its educational and occuptional dimensions. . . . Greater access to higher education in urban areas, however, is not the only education factor that encourages the higher aspirations of urban youth. Urban schools generally provide a more academically stimulating climate than rural schools because of their better trained faculties, superior facilities, and more varied and challenging curricula.
>
> Equally obvious is the fact that urban communities offer a much wider and more varied range of occupational opportunities than do rural communities. Many of these occupations require a minimum of college training for entry. While rural high school seniors are probably not completely unaware of either the rewards or the entrance requirements of many of the high-prestige professional, managerial, and technical positions available in urban communities, they are certainly less likely to have had first-hand exposure to most of them.[95]

The community of residence, then, has a measurable impact upon the individual aspirations of youth.

The differential occupational composition of rural and urban communities—regarded by Sewell as an important part of the individual's milieu—has been alleged to play a role in affecting the young person's educational aspirations. The same kind of argument can be made with respect to occupational aspirations *per se*. Where a person is exposed to a wider range of job opportunities, including those that carry high prestige, it might be expected that occupational aspirations will be higher. Sewell has also examined this matter, and some of his results are shown in Table 2.15.

This table has the same basic structure as Table 2.14. The same sample of high school seniors is employed, and they are again subclassified simultaneously according to intelligence and place of residence. The difference is in the choice of the "dependent variable," or the variable to be explained. In the present instance it is occupational aspirations, and the measure is the proportion of each subgroup aspiring to "high" occupational positions (as professional, technical, and kindred workers or as managers, officials, and proprietors).

The results differ somewhat from those shown earlier in the case of educational aspirations. In particular, Table 2.15 reveals some interesting

[95] William H. Sewell, "Community of Residence and College Plans," *American Sociological Review,* **29**, 35 (February, 1964).

Table 2.15   Percentage with High Occupational Choices, by Place of Residence
and Intelligence, for Male and Female Wisconsin High-School Seniors

| Sex and Place of Residence | Intelligence | | | |
|---|---|---|---|---|
| | Low | Middle | High | Total |
| *Males* | | | | |
| Farm | 12.6 | 32.5 | 58.9 | 32.9 |
| Village (under 2500) | 18.2 | 38.5 | 55.4 | 34.7 |
| Small city (2500–25,000) | 20.7 | 41.6 | 69.8 | 45.4 |
| Medium city (25,000–100,000) | 21.7 | 46.2 | 67.2 | 45.7 |
| Large city (100,000 and more) | 34.9 | 51.4 | 74.4 | 57.2 |
| *Females* | | | | |
| Farm | 15.6 | 27.2 | 43.6 | 27.6 |
| Village (under 2500) | 15.0 | 35.8 | 46.7 | 31.1 |
| Small city (2500–25,000) | 19.6 | 36.5 | 60.2 | 38.1 |
| Medium city (25,000–100,000) | 16.5 | 40.7 | 61.6 | 40.8 |
| Large city (100,000 and more) | 17.8 | 37.8 | 65.7 | 41.7 |

*Source.* William H. Sewell and Alan M. Orenstein, "Community of Residence and
Occupational Choice," *American Journal of Sociology,* **70,** 557 (March, 1965),
Table 3.

differences between males and females. As the authors, Sewell and Orenstein, note, "The . . . analysis shows that boys, but not girls, from rural
areas and smaller communities have lower occupational aspirations than
those from larger urban places—independent of intelligence and socioeconomic differences." [96] These authors attempt to account for this sex difference in this manner:

> The occupational alternatives for girls in rural communities are so severely
> limited that those who wish to work, and most of the girls in our sample plan
> on some period of employment before marriage, must look to the urban labor
> market for desirable employment. There the job restrictions generally encountered
> by women force them to consider essentially the same limited set of occupational
> alternatives as urban girls—mainly teaching school, nursing, social work, and a few
> other lower-status professions and white-collar jobs. These occupations are widely
> known, and rural girls, lacking satisfactory rural occupational opportunities, are
> as likely to aspire to them as urban girls of similar intelligence and socio-
> economic status.[97]

[96] William H. Sewell and Alan M. Orenstein, "Community of Residence and Occupational Choice," *American Journal of Sociology,* **70,** 560 (March, 1965).
[97] *Ibid.,* p. 563.

These studies show almost conclusively that the community of residence can be a powerful factor in affecting individual psychology. Persons who come from highly diverse communal backgrounds may be expected to exhibit noteworthy differences in behavior.

## Reprise

The community, like any other multifaceted phenomenon, is subject to analysis from diverse points of view. My perspective is only one of many.[98] In this chapter I have attempted to show the importance of the community as a basic unit of social structure. Beginning with some current views on the significance of the community, I have stated the classical sociological conception, and have reviewed the more recent developments in sociological thinking on the subject, identifying a number of issues that the sizable and rather controversial literature has produced. The net effect of this effort was the construction of a working definition fashioned to serve the main purpose of this chapter: a review of sociological research on the community.

I considered the different kinds of community that can be identified. After reviewing the great diversity of community forms and functions, I examined the various ideal types that have been advanced in the study of the community. I concluded that the matter of urbanization deserves special stress, and that the contemporary metropolitan community warrants particular attention.

Finally, I discussed four main aspects of the community with which sociologists have been concerned—the demographic, the ecological, the structural, and the behavioral aspects. After first identifying these distinctive facets of community life, I systematically reviewed some major *processes* that are currently unfolding over time. Thus, the subjects of urbanization, segregation, bureaucratization, stratification, the rise of voluntary associations, alienation, anomie, and individual aspirations were considered in a community context. In this way, I tried to regard the community from the standpoint of social organization and social change—the main focuses of sociological attention over the years. Whatever "basic social structure" may mean to the student of sociology, I hope that I have given him some idea of the wide range of problems encompassed in the sociological study of the community.

[98] For an alternative treatment that has great merit, see Richard L. Simpson, "Sociology of the Community: Current Status and Prospects," *Rural Sociology*, 30, 127–149 (June, 1965).

# 3

# FORMAL
# ORGANIZATIONS

*Arthur L. Stinchcombe*

# FORMAL
# ORGANIZATIONS

There is a fundamental difference between activities that are systematically planned to achieve some purpose and those that are spontaneous. Generally we call systematically planned, purposeful activities "work," and spontaneous activities "leisure" or "play." Some people have more fun studying than dancing; professors are recruited from this group. But we still call studying "work," and dancing "play" because, unlike studying, dancing is not systematically planned to achieve some purpose. As de Man, a Belgian pioneer of survey research on workers, asserted:

> . . . all work is felt to be coercive. Even the worker who is free in the social sense, the peasant or the handicraftsman, feels this compulsion, were it not only because while he is at work, his activities are dominated and determined by the aim of his work, by the idea of a willed or necessary creation. Work inevitably signifies subordination of the worker to remoter aims, felt to be necessary, and therefore involving a renunciation of the freedoms and enjoyments of the present for the sake of a future advantage.[1]

Sociologists often call work "instrumental activity" and play "expressive activity." [2]

This distinction between planned activities and spontaneous activities is fundamental for sociology for two reasons. First, planning makes it much more likely that the purposes will be achieved. Many things could not be done at all, or not done on a large enough scale, unless the activities for accomplishing them were planned. Building apartment houses, teaching or learning engineering, winning wars, collecting income tax, or protecting and caring for mental patients, all involve planned social activities. People may build apartment houses for fun, but they do not do it without planning.

Second, planned activities lead people to form social relations that are often quite different from the kind they enter into on impulse. The majority of students in an elementary sociology class, if left to their own impulses, would not have chosen to spend 3 hours a week with the professor and about 12 hours more studying the professor's assignments. Furthermore, the professor probably would not have chosen on impulse to associate with 50 or 500 young men and women all at once. Planning, represented in curricula and class schedules, has created social relations between professor and student.

The degree to which activities are planned is, of course, relative. In an automobile assembly plant, the exact place and time for each activity are

[1] Henri de Man, *Joy in Work* (London: Allen and Unwin, 1929), p. 67, as quoted in Robert Blauner, "Work Satisfaction and Industrial Trends in Modern Society," in Walter Galenson and S. M. Lipset, eds., *Labor and Trade Unionism* (New York: Wiley, 1960), pp. 339–360.
[2] Talcott Parsons, *The Social System* (New York: The Free Press of Glencoe, 1951), pp. 145–148, 157–161.

154

planned in great detail. Sometimes even the motions that the worker goes through are planned by industrial engineers. The tools and materials that the worker uses are planned, and his social relations with his foreman and his co-workers are partly planned. A formal dance may have plans for the place, the starting time, and certain people's activities (for instance, the musicians'), but who dances with whom, when, and for what purpose is not planned. A formal dance is thus intermediate. At the opposite extreme from the assembly line is the dormitory bull session, where the place, time, topic, and persons involved are determined by accident—that is, who happens to be where with what on their minds. Planning is almost completely absent.

But the most important distinction for sociology is whether a man *plans his own* activities, or whether his activities are *planned for him*. Most sociology professors very likely study as much, or nearly as much, as their students. But normally the professor plans his own studying of sociology, while the student has the content and amount of his studying planned for him. When one person is in a position to plan a part of the activities of another person for the achievement of some purpose, we say that the first person has *authority* over the second one. Thus, authority and planning of social activities are closely interwined.

Any social arrangement in which the activities of some people are systematically planned by other people (who, therefore, have authority over them) in order to achieve some special purpose is called a *formal organization*. For instance, the university is a formal organization because professors systematically plan the activities of students with the purpose of educating them. An automobile factory is a formal organization because engineers and company officials plan the activities of workers to produce cars. An army is a formal organization because generals plan the activities of their subordinates to defend the country or (in some countries) to interfere in internal politics. But a bull session, a street-corner gang, and a cocktail party are not usually formal organizations.

Mass-production factories involve a great deal of planning. Table 3.1 shows the amount of time that different kinds of white-collar workers spend in planning. A random sample of middle-class people, who were mostly not in factories, spent much less time in either long-range planning or planning daily work than white-collar workers in a steel plant. Top steel executives, especially, spent about one fourth to one third of all of their time in planning. The average white-collar man of the nearby city spent less than one hour a day in planning. The table shows in a very direct way that large complex organizations are devices to allow a few trained and experienced top executives to plan the work of thousands of people.

Just as the degree to which activities themselves are planned is a matter of

**Table 3.1    White-Collar Workers in Steel Plants Spend More of Their Work Time in Planning**

| Group | Average Number of Hours Spent During Last Working Day in: | | | |
|---|---|---|---|---|
| | Long-Range Plans | Planning Own or Others' Work | Total Planning | Number of Interviews |
| Middle-class men of city (random sample) | 0.22 | 0.47 | 0.69 | 64 |
| Low-level steel white-collar | 0.67 | 0.77 | 1.44 | 24 |
| Middle-level steel white-collar | 1.11 | 1.81 | 2.92 | 21 |
| High-level steel executives | 1.76 | 0.69 | 2.45 | 24 |

*Source.* Based on asking samples of Chilean middle-class people what they did during each hour of their last working day. The research was supported by a grant from the Olivetti Foundation to the Joint Center for Urban Studies, and was collected by Rene Marder and Arthur L. Stinchcombe.

more or less, so the degree to which any social arrangement is an organization is also one of more or less. A steel plant is more an organization than a fraternity, and a fraternity is more an organization than a dormitory.

The purpose of this chapter is to analyze the social arrangements by which people's activities are planned to achieve certain purposes. Another way of saying almost the same thing is that this chapter is concerned with the analysis of authority and the relations between superiors and subordinates, because the reason we have authority is so that some people can plan others' activities. Or, finally, still another way of putting it is that this chapter involves the analysis of formal organizations—social arrangements made up of authority relations—that achieve the planning of social activity on a large scale.

## The Elements of Organizations

To plan social activities systematically, three things are usually required: (1) a *theory* of how the activities can be organized to achieve the purpose of the organization; (2) *resources* that can be used in the activities or that can be used to pay or force people to carry out the activities; and (3) an *authority system* by which people are organized and directed in carrying out the activities.

### The Theory

A person plans activities because he thinks there is some way of carrying out these activities that will bring about the desired result. This theory of how to achieve the purpose may be learned from studying books, from experience, or from creative invention. The directors of an organization may be able to tell someone exactly what their theory of its activity is, or their theory may involve empirical intuition, which they have great difficulty in talking about. That is, they may be able to say, "This won't work," or "If we make it that way, it won't sell," or something similar, without being able to put their beliefs into abstract language.

A "theory" is any set of ideas that allows people to make predictions about what will happen if some specified variables are changed. A set of ideas that says that if steel is heated to 2300° F, it can be formed into pipe by pressure applied in a certain manner with certain machines, is a theory. If a pipe does not result from the appropriate activities, the theory is false, and must be corrected. Without predictions, and hence without theories, planning makes no sense. Men create purposive organizations because they are able to theorize.

Modern organizations use many scientific theories developed in laboratories by university research teams. But many theories are much less formal. For instance, the prediction that by issuing more preferred stock, an organization can increase the potential for *both* gain *and* loss of common stock is "proved" only by reading the laws on preferred and common stocks. It is, nevertheless, a prediction based on a set of ideas, and thus a theory. Like a scientific theory, it can be proved false by future circumstances, if the prediction does not turn out to be true.[3]

Whether or not the planners in an organization can tell what theory they base their plans on, the theory must include the following.

*A Technical-Costs Theory.* One part of the theory on which an organization is based must say, in effect, "it is possible to achieve certain purposes by carrying out certain activities, and in order to carry out the activities, we must have such-and-such resources." For instance, universities are based on a theory that if the professor and the students engage in lecture-discussion-homework activities, the students will learn more than they would have

[3] The relation between planning and theorizing, and the implications of this for analyzing organizations, were pointed out by William Starbuck, "Organizational Growth and Development," in James March, ed., *Handbook of Organizations* (Chicago: Rand-McNally, 1965), pp. 451–533, at p. 481.

learned if left to their own devices. This activity involves the costs of find-ing and paying professors who know what they are talking about, since the theory also maintains that people are more likely to learn the truth if the professors know their subject matter. The theory on which Henry Ford developed assembly-line production for cars included a belief that it was more efficient to divide the work into small jobs, and that conveyor belts should be used to bring the work to a place especially designed for doing that work efficiently. That is, every organization is based on an ex-plicit or implicit theory of how to accomplish the purpose of the organiza-tion by using resources and by planning the activities of people.

*A Market Theory.* People do not plan activities unless they think some-one will benefit from the effort and resources put into the activities. Unless someone wants an education in sociology, the best-laid plans for teaching the course are of no use. If someone had not wanted a cheap car, Ford's assembly line would not have made him a millionaire. A theory that the benefits will pay for the costs of the activities is essential before planning and seems worthwhile to anyone.

The "payment" may be in the form of money, votes, prestige, power, or anything that is a motive for the planner. Thus, a state university must bene-fit the students enough to get them to pay the small tuition and devote their time to studying, and must benefit the state as a whole enough to cause legislators to vote the money, land, and autonomy necessary for a university. Indirectly, then, to keep in operation, the state university has to produce sufficient votes for legislators and sufficient opportunities for jobs for stu-dents. The ideas for the particular university activities that will, in fact, produce benefits that students and legislators want is the "market theory" of the university.

*A Theory of the Distribution of the Benefits.* Many noble plans of great benefit to *some* people are never carried out because the people who must pay the costs do not care enough about the benefits to *those* peple. An arrangement by which the planners can predict and control the individuals who get the benefits of the activities is an essential part of any organization. The planner must have a theory of how this distribution of benefits will work before he will invest resources in the organization.

To take a familiar case, the benefits of state support to universities are differentially distributed by making nonresidents of the state pay higher tuition. The benefits of tax-supported education go to the people who pay the taxes. And, of course, if the Fords had not believed that they would get a large share of the profits from producing cars, they probably would not have invested their resources in setting up assembly lines. The predictions of how the benefits will be distributed are usually made secure in modern societies by legal provisions, contracts, elections of boards of directors of corporations, and similar legally enforceable arrangements. The theory of the distribution of benefits is, above all, a theory of how the law will work.

*A Theory of Personnel.* Before we trust people to plan the activities of many other people and to administer large resources, we must believe that they know what they are doing and that they actually will do what they say. We entrust the ultimate management of universities to boards of directors or regents because we have faith that they will not pour the resources of the university into their own pockets, and that they will not run an indoctrination camp for their particular religious or political ideology. The stockholders trust the board of directors with their resources for much the same reasons. The theory that, under specified conditions and arrangements, we can trust certain people or groups of people with large resources so that the use of the resources will be planned effectively is an essential components of all organizations.

The theory on which an organization is based, with its technical, market, distribution, and personnel aspects, is especially apparent at the very beginning of an organization, when it is still a "project." Almost all projects involving substantial investments—government projects, research projects for foundations, prospectuses for new companies—contain explicitly or implicitly a description of the technical-cost theory, a description of the benefits or products and who wants them, a proposed distribution of the benefits (often in a legal document), and a description of the responsible personnel.

Like any other theory, the theory on which an organization is based can be true or false, or some parts of it can be false. It might not be possible, for instance, to mass-produce some product on an assembly line as planned because the parts cannot be standardized sufficiently without additional expense (a false technical theory). Or a new curriculum in a university may fail because not enough students want it (a false market theory). Or a new engineering school in an underdeveloped country may not encourage economic development as planned because the graduates find better opportunities in other countries (a false theory of the distribution of benefits). Or a board of trustees may rent university land at much less than its true market value (a false personnel theory).

Traditionally, most of the theories on which organizations have been based were derived purely from experience. Later, with the development in engineering, cost accounting, and modern personnel practices with psychological testing, the theories began to include not only things learned from experience but also scientific principles learned from investigations outside of the organization. The most modern form of organization is one that attempts to verify the theory on which it is based *before* planning, by special investigation according to scientific procedures.

When this scientific investigation applies mainly to the technical aspects of the activities, it is usually called "research and development." When it applies to other aspects of the theory, it is called "operations research." Scientific research is often a cheaper and more accurate way of finding out the truth or falsity of a theory on which an organization is based than is trial and error with an investment of millions of dollars. It is likely, therefore, that this research tendency will continue to grow in the future. All organizations will eventually become branches or modifications of the university.[4]

### Resources

All social activities need resources, even if the resources consist only of time of people who could have been doing something else. When activities are planned on a large scale—for instance, in a large state university—the time of thousands of students and faculty amounts to a great resource. In addition, activities are usually more efficient if many other resources, such as buildings especially designed for the activity, tools, libraries, and transportation systems, are available. Most of these resources have alternative uses; that is, there are other activities in which the resources also could be employed with benefit.

These resources have to be *created, defended, replenished,* and *administered.* Even after an organization has decided to spend money for a new building, the building must be built, thus *creating* a resource for the organization. Because the resources have alternative uses, people who would benefit from using them in a different way than the one intended try to get control over them. If the resources are to be at the disposal of the organization, other people must be kept from using them for other ends that interfere with the planned activities. Resources must be *defended* from robbery, for instance.

Organizational activities are time-consuming, and this time must be *replenished.* Physical goods wear out—moth and rust do corrupt. Books become obsolete; better tools are invented; the forms filled out yesterday must be replaced with unfilled forms for today's record-keeping; and other things of this kind happen. Thus, organizations are faced with a constant problem of replenishing their resources.

Finally, to make sure that the resources are efficiently used in the planned activities, their use must be scheduled, controlled, cost-accounted, and directed.

---

[4] Oddly enough, the university itself has shown very little initiative in studying, scientifically, the theories on which university education is based.

*Creation of Resources.* When a group of people decide to "invest" in a certain line of activities, they usually cannot just pay the money and forget about it. Instead, the preparation of resources for special purposes is a long process. Special buildings, special machinery, and special public utilities may have to be built. To open a hardware store, for instance, special inventories may have to be accumulated. Good will may have to be developed by special advertising and sales expenditures. Legal obstacles, such as zoning regulations, may have to be overcome. Each of these activities creates a permanent resource for the organization.

The preliminary resource-creating phase of the organization may be relatively short, or it may extend over many years. New steel plants, for instance, rarely are able to develop their resources sufficiently to start making profits until ten or more years after the decision to build a plant. A library for historical research requires centuries of collection.

This building phase of organizations is very different from the operating phase. It is usually less planned in detail—less formally organized. It involves more contractors and outsiders—fewer permanent employees. It involves far greater risks of sizeable losses if done wrong, and potentially great gains if done right. It involves adapting plans rapidly to unforeseen conditions, in order to start getting a return from the investment as soon as possible. Very often the people who do well during the building phase do badly later, and vice versa.[5]

*Defense of Resources.* The fund of resources of an organization consists of different kinds of rights to use a wide variety of things: perhaps ownership of land and buildings; leases of other land and buildings; ownership or leases of machinery; money in cash and in bank accounts; contracts with personnel and with subcontractors, which allow the organization to require the performance of certain activities; the good reputation of the organization; its credit rating; and similar things. The exact composition of this fund of resources is always changing as the organization spends or uses up some of the resources and obtains others. In modern societies, the rights to use these various resources are established in the law, and can be defended from interference or robbery by calling upon the power of the state.

The capacity of an organization to hold and manage its fund of resources and to call upon the government through the courts to defend its rights is the *legal personality aspect* of the organization. Legal personalities may be individuals, families, corporations, or nonprofit institutions, and must usually satisfy certain criteria set up by the government in order to be legally

[5] See Philip Selznick, *Leadership in Administration* (Evanston, Ill.: Row Peterson, 1957), pp. 27–28.

recognized. For instance, individuals must usually be of age, corporations must be chartered, and so on. The conditions under which legal personalities can be created and the powers that they have, once created, differ a great deal among societies. In the Soviet Union, for instance, only agencies of the government can create legal personalities for carrying on larger-scale economic production.

Table 3.2 gives a comparison of the legal personality aspect of factory

**Table 3.2  The Legal Powers of Management of Factory Organizations Differ Greatly in the United States and the Soviet Union**

| Legal Powers | United States | USSR |
|---|---|---|
| Firm management appoints all officials without government intervention | Yes | No |
| Right of eminent domain for firm purposes is automatic | No | Yes |
| Can reinvest all profits in firm | Yes | No |
| Can use firm profits for private consumption | Yes | No |
| Can send profits out of the country | Yes | No |
| Can prevent strikes of workers by government action | No | Yes |
| Political party officials can give some orders accepted as legitimate within the firm | No | Yes |
| Can use government credit to borrow money | No | Yes |
| Waste of resources by lower official can be punished as a crime | No | Yes |
| Can prevent competition by government action | Sometimes | Yes |
| *Salaried full-time managers* | Yes | Yes |

organizations in the United States and the USSR. An American firm can do many things that a Soviet firm cannot; in particular, an American firm can decide what to do with its profits. On the other hand, a Soviet factory administration can do many things that an American factory administration cannot. Soviet factories can use the powers of government for disciplining either striking workers or inefficient lower officials. Soviet factories can also take what land they need where they need it without paying exhorbitant prices to the former owners. They can stop other factories from producing the same goods and underselling them, which American factories can do only if they have patents.

The last entry in Table 3.1, *Salaried full-time managers,* is in no sense a legal power, but was included to suggest that many aspects of administrative practice are not in the least affected by the legal-personality aspects of the organization. A Soviet steel-plant organization is much like an American one, because both have to make steel, even though the legal aspects of organization are different. Both need salaried managers because amateurs would very soon ruin the blast furnaces.

***Replenishment of Resources.*** The fund of rights to control the things that constitute an organization's resources is constantly changing, as resources are used up and new ones come under the control of the organization. It is more difficult to replenish resources than to consume them, as most American children with an allowance learn at an early age.

Organizations replace the resources they have used up or obtain additions to the fund of resources they control by two principal methods. One is by direct sale of the benefits of organizational activities. Businesses depend largely on selling products or services to replenish their fund of resources. Universities get part of their incomes by charging tuition to the people directly benefited, but prisons get practically none of their income from the direct sale of services. The other main device for replenishing resources is "investment," or people putting resources into the control of the organization because they anticipate future benefits.

The distinction between sales and investment is so important because, generally, anyone who invests in an organization has to believe a great part of the theory on which the organization is based. The automobile customer can believe anything he likes about assembly lines as long as he buys Fords—his beliefs make no difference to the Ford company. But the legislators or donors to a university must usually believe that the university will bring benefits in the future. In other words, they must believe that the theory on which the university is based is largely correct. Those who invest a considerable part of United States tax money in military resources and activities must believe that the military will prevent war, or defend cherished values, or otherwise bring future benefits.

To put it another way: investment is almost always an ideological matter—a matter involving politics, visions of the world, and beliefs about the future. Buying and selling is a commercial matter, in which people tend to calculate their immediate costs and benefits and contribute to the organization on that basis.

This ideological or theoretical component in investment causes the organizations whose main source of replenishment of resources is from investments to be much more political, more ideological. Thus there is a far greater difference between "profit" and "nonprofit" enterprises (roughly the same as the distinction between enterprises that replenish resources by selling and enterprises that receive investments) than just a difference in their ledger balances at the end of the year. Profit and nonprofit enterprises depend on fundamentally different kinds of social processes for their continued life and health, since "nonprofit" enterprises must be believed in.

*The Control of Resources.* Resources, because they can be used for things other than planned organizational activity, present a constant temptation. University money can pay for vacations in Europe; university classrooms can be used for political or religious indoctrination; university libraries can serve as a beginning for students' and faculty's personal book collections; and laboratory grain alcohol can be used for other things than chemical experiments. Accountants, library clerks, and administrators of all sorts are partly involved in making sure that the resources of the organization are used in the ways planned.

The defense and replenishment of resources are the main problems that force an organization into relations with the rest of society—relations with the legal system for defense, and relations with customers or contributors for replenishment. Financial control and the scheduling and administration of the use of resources are central parts of the system of internal discipline of organizations.

### The Authority System

Finally, for activities to be planned on a large scale in accordance with a theory about how to achieve some benefits, the activities must be supervised and controlled. One of the principal uses of the resources of most organizations is to motivate people—by payment, force, or moral suasion—to carry out the organizations' activities according to plan. The essential elements of the authority system are (1) *responsibility* for seeing that activities correspond to the plan; (2) *supervision* of the activities of others to direct their activities according to plan; and (3) *discipline* to make sure that people, in fact, do as directed.

*Responsibility.* The concept and measurement of responsibility is one of the most difficult problems in the study of organizations. When we say, for instance, that a particular professor "takes responsibility" for the elementary sociology course, we generally mean that he understands the purposes of the course, the theory of how to teach it, how to distribute the grades, and things of that kind. He is then given broad control over the relevant resources and activities, rewards and punishments, with the expectation that he will try his best to achieve the purposes.

If we criticize him for being "irresponsible," we do not mean that he disobeyed any specific orders, or that he disobeyed general published rules. Instead, we mean that he did not use proper discretion in making use of the resources or in governing the activities of the students. In many (if not most) organizations, delegating and taking responsibility is a more important part of the authority system than giving and taking orders. In a university, for instance, professors may work for weeks or months without ever having been asked or told to do anything.

*Supervision.* By supervision we mean inspecting the activities of people in the organization to determine whether these activities correspond to the theory of how to achieve the purposes of the organization, and indicating in some way to the acting people that their activities are, or are not, up to standard. There are two main kinds of supervision: statistical control and visual supervision.

A familiar example of statistical control is the grading of tests in educational institutions. In testing students, performance is measured and the information on that performance is communicated back to the student. The professor does not watch the student study, nor tell him when to start and stop studying, but, instead, measures the results. A similar device in factories is the graph of delays or "down time" of a production line. This graph is often the chief supervisory device for maintenance departments in factories. By means of the graph, the maintenance department can measure its own performance according to the very simple theory that when the production line is not operating, the organization is not achieving its purposes. This kind of statistical controls encourage people to take responsibility.

Supervision consisting of visual inspection by a superior, who then orders or requests the worker to correct his activity if necessary, corresponds most closely to our common-sense notion of "supervision." But many organizations (such as universities) that plan activities of other people on a large scale use very little visual supervision.

New organizations that have not worked out impersonal statistical controls, or organizations that face rapidly changing new situations (such as armies or construction firms) must rely more heavily on visual supervision. So, also, must organizations in which the members cannot be motivated to assume responsibility (such as prison work gangs). Additionally, industries with a highly unstable or new work force that does not understand the technology and aims of the organization (such as new factories in underdeveloped countries, or some industries like canning) depend heavily on visual supervision.

*Discipline.* The degree of discipline of an organization means the degree to which, once the members understand what they are supposed to do, they do, indeed, do it.[6] In general, the degree of discipline of an organization depends on (1) the degree to which the rewards and punishments that the organization controls are sufficient to motivate the members, and (2) the degree to which these rewards and punishments are tied in a reliable and precise way to the degree of a member's conformity with the theory upon which the organization functions.

One difficulty of discipline is that people are usually strongly motivated by things other than the rewards and punishments that the organization controls. Friendship, love for families, fun at work, the use of organizational money or goods for personal purposes, and similar things are strong motivations. This threatens the *sufficiency* of organizational rewards and punishments as motivations.

Another difficulty is the *inaccuracy* of organizational rewards and punishments; members see "under the sun, that the race is not to the swift, nor the battle to the strong, neither yet bread to the wise, but time and chance happeneth to them all." This inaccuracy means that some men will be rewarded without contributing to the organization, and some will be punished even though they have contributed. Justice is not easy to achieve—either in a society or in an organization.

## Summary of the Elements of Organizations

We see then that, by its very nature, effective planning of the activities of many people for achieving certain purposes confronts organizations with a series of problems. First, the organization is faced with a question of the truth of the theory that guides its planning of action. The theory on which planning of organizational activity is based may be false for various reasons: (1) it might not be technically possible to achieve the purposes of the plan with the resources calculated; (2) no one might want the product badly enough to pay for it; (3) the distribution of the benefits might not be secure enough (or not properly distributed) to motivate people to devote resources to the activity; and (4) the planned personnel might be incompetent, irresponsible, or dishonest.

Second, organizations are confronted with the problem of arranging for scarce resources. This breaks down into the subproblems of (1) creation of special-purpose resources; (2) defending the resources of the organization from robbery or from being put to other uses; (3) replenishing the resources either from sale of benefits or from continuing investment of

[6] Max Weber, *From Max Weber: Essays in Sociology,* translated by H. H. Gerth and C. W. Mills (New York: Oxford University Press, 1946), pp. 253–264.

resources in order to achieve future benefits; and (4) administering the resources in such a way that they are actually used in appropriate activities.

Third, organizations are confronted with a problem of creating an authority system to make sure that the activities actually carried out are those specified in the theory as being the ones that will lead to the achievement of the purposes. This involves (1) the delegation and taking of responsibility by people in the organization, who themselves see to it that activities they control comply, (2) supervision (either statistical or visual), which measures activities that actually take place and communicates faults in the activities to the responsible people, and (3) discipline, which involves the creation and management of rewards and punishments that are sufficient to motivate performance, and that are accurately tied to the actual level of performance.

These inherent problems of planning social activities create similarities in all planned social action on a large scale, and justify treating "organizations" as a special topic in sociological theory. But there are also great differences among organizations.

## Classifications of Organizations

There is as much variation among organizations as among humans' beliefs about how to achieve purposes by planned social activity. To simplify this confusion, sociologists would like to identify the main variables according to which organizations differ. The term "main variable" means a difference among organizations that is an important cause of other differences among the same organizations. All of the basic elements of organizations—the theories on which their planning is based, the way they create, defend, replenish, and administer their resources, and their authority system—have formed the basis of classification systems for organizations.

For instance, there is considerable evidence that the technical-cost basis of organizations—their technology—is a great determinant of their social structure and of the attitudes of people within them.[7] Economists allege great differences among organizations caused by the structure of the markets in which organizations deal, especially whether the markets are com-

---

[7] This was first systematically developed by Karl Marx in *Capital*. Some examples of recent studies in this tradition are Robert Blauner, *Alienation and Freedom: The Factory Worker and His Industry* (Chicago: University of Chicago Press, 1964); Stanley Udy, Jr., "Technical and Institutional Factors in Production Organization," *American Journal of Sociology*, **67**, 247–260 (November, 1961); and Arthur L. Stinchcombe, "Bureaucratic and Craft Administration of Production," *Administrative Science Quarterly* (September, 1959), pp. 168–187.

petitive or monopolistic.[8] Organizations have been classified by the criterion of "who benefits," and great divergencies among them flow from differences in who benefits from an organization's activities.[9] The existence and nature of organizations for carrying out various social functions depend on the availability and type of trustworthy elite personnel.[10]

Thus, each of the main elements of the theories on which organizations are based—technology, market, distribution of benefits, and personnel—have formed a basis for classifying organizations.

The management of resources also forms a basis for classifying organizations. The types of organizations that exist in a society depend intimately on the types of legal personality that exist in the law. If limited-liability corporations did not have legal existence, our economic system would be quite different. Great diversity in other aspects of organizations is associated with different legal forms; corporations are very different from proprietorships, and both are very different from nonprofit, tax-free organizations of various types.[11] Whether private enterprises can form to operate factories or whether, instead, the state creates them is the organizational difference between socialism and capitalism. Finally, organizations are strikingly different if they replenish their resources from the sale of products or services rather than by taxes or donations.[12]

Also, the type of authority system of an organization has been used as a basis for classifying the organization. Current scientific management literature uses the terms, "democratic" and "authoritarian" management mostly to describe differences in systems for distributing responsibility, and "centralized" management is distinguished from "decentralized" management by the degree of delegation of authority.[13] Peter Blau has shown

[8] A classic work is John Maurice Clark's *Studies in the Economics of Overhead Cost* (Chicago: University of Chicago Press, 1923).

[9] Peter Blau and W. Richard Scott, *Formal Organizations* (San Francisco: Chandler, 1962), pp. 42–58.

[10] Edward Banfield, *The Moral Basis of a Backward Society* (New York: The Free Press of Glencoe, 1958), pp. 85–104, who talks about the problem of availability of trustworthy elites; Clark Kerr and others, *Industrialism and Industrial Man* (Cambridge: Harvard University Press, 1960, and New York: Oxford University Press, 1964), who talk about the types of elites.

[11] Max Weber, *Law in Economy and Society,* translated by M. Rheinstein and E. Shils (Cambridge: Harvard University Press, 1954); and John R. Commons, *Legal Foundations of Capitalism* (New York: Macmillan, 1924, and Madison, Wisc.: University of Wisconsin Press, 1957).

[12] Talcott Parsons, " 'Voting' and the Equilibrium of the American Political System," in Eugene Burdick and Arthur J. Brodbeck, eds., *American Voting Behavior* (New York: The Free Press of Glencoe, 1959), pp. 80–120, at p. 88; and John K. Galbraith, *The Affluent Society* (Boston: Houghton Mifflin, 1958), *passim.*

[13] Peter Drucker, *Concept of the Corporation* (New York: John Day, 1946, and New American Library, 1964).

striking differences in the performance of workers, depending on whether they are supervised by statistical controls or by visual supervision.[14] And most likely each one of us received a lecture from a dean during our orientation to college, pointing out that college was remarkably different from high school in its authority system and that we must discipline ourselves. Finally, an extremely fertile classification of organizations is the grouping of them according to whether the main basis of discipline in the organization is payment, force, or moral obligation. This classification was developed by Etzioni.[15]

## Some Main Types of Organizations

Since organizations are strikingly different in other respects when there is variation in their key elements (theory, resource management, and authority system), we know that these elements are actually basic. But this means that any complete description of the main types of organizations would be tremendously complex, since we would have to describe each combination of all the key elements.

It is useful, however, to outline four types of organizations that have played an important role in sociological thinking about organizations since the categories were developed by Max Weber in the first part of this century. These four types are (1) the *charismatic retinue* of followers or disciples of a leader, (2) *feudal administration* of fief-holders, (3) *modern bureaucracies,* such as steel plants or government departments, and (4) *modern professional organizations,* such as universities or hospitals.

The key difference that Weber noted among these organizations is the basis on which the organization decides the truth of the theory on which planning is based. Since this theory is what justifies the exercise of authority and is what makes authority legitimate, Weber called these criteria of truth "principles of legitimacy." [16]

First, he noted that organizations in which the truth of the theory is de-

---

[14] Peter Blau, *Dynamics of Bureaucracy* (Chicago: University of Chicago Press, 1955), pp. 33–48.

[15] Amitai Etzioni, *A Comparative Analysis of Complex Organizations* (New York: The Free Press of Glencoe, 1961).

[16] Weber talked of these types of organizations as "types of authority" or "types of administration," depending on his mood. They were, respectively, "charismatic authority," "patrimonial administration" or "traditional authority," "bureaucratic administration" or "rational-legal authority," and "collegial administration." Weber's discussion of collegial administration is quite confused, and has not been of use to sociologists since Weber's time. See *The Theory of Social and Economic Organization,* translated by A. M. Henderson and Talcott Parsons (New York: The Free Press of Glencoe, 1947).

cided on the basis of *what an inspired leader says* tend to have a distinct form of organization. He called the principle of legitimacy in this case *charisma,* which is a religious word meaning the "gift of grace." If people delegate authority to a man because they think he has an extraordinary gift, genius, or inspiration, we call this "charismatic authority."

We find the charismatic retinue among the followers of inspired religious leaders, among the research assistants at the disposal of a scientist who is thought to be a genius, or among the aides of a President who is thought to represent in his person the wishes of the people. That is, charismatic administration occurs whenever people believe that, in the particular area of organizational activity, "history is the lengthened shadow of a man." In these cases the genius, inspiration, or election makes the sayings of the leader the principal criterion of truth and worth. The organizations, therefore, tend to be created so that the other people serve *to increase the powers* of the genius or inspired leader.

A good example of a charismatic retinue is the group of research assistants of any famous scientist. These assistants do not have defined jobs and responsibilities but, instead, are supposed to do what the famous scientist thinks is worth doing. The financing of the group is usually by irregular and unpredictable contributions from foundations. The foundations donate the money only as long as they believe in the genius of the scientist, which is only as long as he obtains results. This combination is typical of charismatic retinues: subordinates are at the disposal of the chief rather than possessing defined responsibilities or authority of their own, and irregular financing is by contributions from those who believe in the extraordinary qualities of the chief. These same essentials are found in the group of disciples of Jesus Christ, the "Kitchen Cabinets" of the Presidents of the United States, or the street-corner gang following an exceptional gang leader.

In feudal administration (broadly conceived), the basis of truth of the theory on which social activity is planned is tradition. There are several types of traditional administrations, but the most common one is that in which each official in the organization maintains a traditional territory in which he has certain hallowed rights—rights that he administers in his own interest. Combined with his traditional rights, he has traditional duties to the source from which the rights originated. In classical feudalism the source was usually the king or the church. Very similar forms of administration, in the modern world, are dealerships for new cars.

For example, the franchise holder for an automobile company performs a number of functions for the company. He advertises to the community, gives the service provided for in the warranty, stops the development of wildcat discount operators who would cut profit margins, often arranges financing of car sales, and does other things. The automobile manufacturer supposes that the dealer will do these things because of self-interest if he is given more or less complete control of the area. But the dealer has some obligations to the company. For instance, he usually cannot sell his competitors' makes of new cars. This kind of informal administrative system rests on traditional loyalties and obligations, which in modern times are written into a contract. But unlike a charismatic or bureaucratic administration, there is no constant flow of orders from the superior to the subordinate. The subordinate serves the superior because of his own interests and his own sense of honor.

When the organizational theory is based on a mixture of legal principles and rational decisions of a top leadership, a *bureaucracy* tends to develop. Officials hold office for which they draw a salary; the organization as a legal personality holds the resources; and the official, typically, has a career within the organization.

Modern utility companies are perhaps the extreme examples of bureaucratic administration, whether they are governmental (as the Post Office in the United States) or private (as the American Telephone and Telegraph Company). The key cause of extreme bureaucratization in utilities is that they must provide the same service to millions of people—and the same service day after day to those millions. One does not need genius or inspiration today to supply the same electricity to the same people as yesterday. But the electrical system is too interdependent to be parceled out among franchise holders. On the other hand, a good plan decided upon this month for serving a new public or for cheaper electrical production will keep earning the company money day after day for years. In short, routine administration of highly interdependent systems with a steady income produces bureaucracy. Responsibility is finely divided, but each man reports to a superior with wider responsibilities. Men move systematically from positions near the bottom to positions near the top. Unlike the early church, not even being the Son of God would help a person become the head of an electrical utility company at 30 years of age.

When the truth of the theory of organizational activity is certified by specialized knowledge of the trained members of the organization—rather than by a leader-genius, by tradition, or by top management—we tend to get a *professional* type of organization. In this type, people are delegated wide responsibility for planning activities in their sphere of competence, after their competence has been certified by a group of peers. Universities and hospitals are typical examples of this type of organization.

In a university, people are recruited to teach and perform research according to the judgment of the group of professionals in each discipline. The president of the university cannot hope to judge for himself the competence of biophysicists, political scientists, and linguists. Moreover, he cannot direct their work, once they are hired. Consequently, the professionals in each discipline hire people, and usually the person hired decides himself what needs to be done. If he is competent, he alone knows best what to teach and how to perform research in his special field. Extreme decentralization of responsibility to men chosen as competent by their professional peers is distinctive of professional organizations.

The typical ways of dealing with the basic elements of the main kinds organization—that is, charismatic retinue, feudal administrations, bureaucracies, and professional organizations—are outlined in Table 3.3.

## Variations among Societies in Organizational Life

Societies differ not only by having different cultures, beliefs, and values, but also by having different *social arrangements for planning*. We have already noted (see Table 3.2) how socialist economies contrast with capitalist economies in the types of legal personalities that carry on economic production. In this section we point out some further differences among societies in their organizational structure.

First, societies differ in the *degree of predominance of types of organizations*. Second, societies differ in *the number and variety of social functions* that are carried on by organizations. These differences in organizational life are reflected, in turn, in the quality of life in these societies.

### Predominance of Different Kinds of Organizations

In modern societies we entrust most of the important governmental, military, educational, and economic functions to bureaucracies or to professional organizations. This is as true of the Soviet Union as of the United States, as true of Japan as of Great Britain. Feudal and charismatic organizational structures occupy minor parts of social life, parts not yet brought under control of the constant process of rationalization of social life. But in Western Europe during the Middle Ages, government administration was most often carried out along feudal lines. In that era, neither commerce nor production of economic goods was carried out by bureaucracies as it is today.

Furthermore, in many primitive societies, armies, instead of being huge bureaucracies, are organized around charismatic war chiefs. Today, in many Latin American countries, politics is not organized by stable political parties or coalitions that outlive their leaders but, instead, by groups of followers of a political hero, a *caudillo* or "boss." These "parties" are really charismatic retinues.

In general, as "the magic is taken out of the world" in modern societies, social life is organized more and more by abstract legal principles, and each area of social life is governed to a greater extent by planning according to abstract scientific principles that come from books. With this decrease in magic, organizations that are based on magical theories, inspiration of leaders, or sacred traditions become less frequent, and bureaucracies and professional organizations become more frequent.[17]

## *Amount of Organization*

Modern societies have more bureaucracies and professional organizations than they formerly had. Present-day societies are also distinguished by the number of social functions that are carried out by large-scale planned activity. To consider only the extremes, in simple primitive societies: education is carried on in families rather than in schools; there are no paid full-time government officials; economic production is usually carried on in the home or in groups especially organized for short-term activity; war is not a profession in an organization, but an avocation; art works are preserved by individual owners rather than by museums; and recreation is what people do in their free time—it is not a major industry.[18]

## The Effect of Organizations on Daily Life

The theoretical considerations outlined above are of interest in order to understand what happens to human beings under different conditions. Now we turn to some of the differences that organizations make in people's daily lives. These involve the simplest form of scientific proposition: variations in one thing (in our case, number or characteristics of organizations) cause variations in another thing (in our case, in how people live). We

[17] "Taking the magic out of the world" in the theories that people have about how to get things done on a large scale was a main concern in the work of Max Weber. He made extensive studies of rationalization of law, music, religious thought, and economic practices generally. A good summary is Talcott Parsons' *The Structure of Social Action* (New York: The Free Press of Glencoe, 1949), pp. 673–677. An extremely good study of this problem in present-day Indonesia is Clifford Geertz' *The Religion of Java* (New York: The Free Press of Glencoe, 1960).

[18] The best-documented study of the increasing level of organization of American society during the past century is Kenneth Boulding's *The Organizational Revolution* (New York: Harper, 1953).

Table 3.3 **Characteristics of Some Main Types of Organizations**

| Elements of Organizations | Type of Organization and Examples | | | |
|---|---|---|---|---|
| | Charismatic Retinue (Scientist and Research Assistants, President and Aides, Saint and Disciples) | Feudal Administration (Classical Feudalism, Franchise System for New-Car Dealers) | Bureaucracy (Steel Plant, Government Departments) | Professional (University, Hospital) |
| How is truth of theory decided? | Inspired utterances of "genius" chief | Tradition | Rational procedures by top management | Competence of professionals certified by peers |
| Who holds ultimate control of resources (legal personality)? | Leader as person | Official holds permanent grant of income-producing property, which he defends himself | Board of Directors or legislature | Board of Directors, legislature, or the body of professionals as such |
| How are resources replenished? | Irregular contributions depend on evidence of genius of leader | Land or franchise produces steady rents or profits | Varies; sales or investment | Usually a combination of sale of services and investments in future benefits |

| | | | | |
|---|---|---|---|---|
| How are resources managed? | At personal disposition of chief | According to private interests of fief-holder | Formal accounting | Formal accounting |
| How is responsibility divided? | Delegated by chief, usually for limited periods for specific jobs | Permanent delegation of inherited rights; little control | Limited delegation in defined *jurisdictions* of officials, with review by superiors | Wide delegation, almost permanent, based on peers' judgments of competence |
| Who controls supervision? | Personal irregular supervision by chief | Virtually absent | Routine supervision by immediate superior | Rare, except at times of promotion or increase of responsibility—done by peers |
| What rewards produce discipline? | Depends on belief in genius of leader, and on his control of resources for rewards | Depends on sense of traditional obligation, "honor" | Organization controls careers, promotions, and pays salary | Career depends on reputation with peers and clients |

175

are moving from systematic description of planned social activity to scientific propositions concerning what effects variations in the amount and characteristics of planned activity have.

First, we shall give some examples of propositions dealing with the effects of variations in the general level of organizations in societies. Then we shall examine some effects on daily life of specific kinds of organizations. Finally, we shall discuss some of the effects of the variation in peoples' positions within organizations.

### Effects of the General Level of Organization

Modern developed countries conduct many more of their social affairs in formal organizations than underdeveloped countries. Within modern socities, more organizations of greater variety exist in cities than in rural areas. What are the implications of these facts for social life?

1. One extremely important consequence of organizations is that activities planned according to true theories of how to accomplish purposes do, indeed, achieve those purposes. This means that purposes are more efficiently achieved in societies with extensively planned activities. This is most clearly apparent, perhaps, in the increase of national income per capita, which is an approximate measure of the efficiency of social activities.[19] The correlation between per capita income and the number and variety of organizations in a society, or the proportion of the labor force employed by organizations rather than working on their own account, is extremely close. It has been estimated that about 80% of the increase of national income in the United States in the first part of this century resulted from technical change or the application of new theories to the planning of economic activities. And even though it is not reflected in the national income, it is clear also that government services are much more efficient in highly organized societies. These services furnish more benefit for the money spent.

Here, of course, we are mixing up two variables: the *quality* of the theories according to which activities are planned, and the *degree* to which activities are planned. But there is little doubt that generally planned activities yield more output than unplanned activities, if there exists a theory applicable to the activities.

2. One of the immediate consequences of tight planning of some of the

---

[19] Other things besides efficiency influence national income, such as the quantity of natural resources of the country, the foreign trade situation for countries depending on exports, and so on.

activities of a man (his work) is that his time becomes sharply divided between work (when his activities are tightly controlled for him) and leisure (when he controls his own activities). This implies that, during the day, a man moves from one social system (the organization where he works) to other social systems (his family, recreational groups, clubs, and associations) at definite times. The higher degree of planning of social activities in special-purpose organizations implies an accurately scheduled movement from work to play and back to work. This movement is reflected in the high degree of regularity and sharpness of peak traffic loads in cities on a weekday, shown by graphs of traffic counts, in contrast to a much smoother graph in cities on Sunday, or on country roads in agricultural or fishing areas at all times.

The scheduling of cities also is disclosed in some very interesting data on the working time of city and country women in France (Table 3.4).

**Table 3.4   Pressure for Full-Time Work in Cities (Employed Women in Cities Are Much More Likely to Work a Full Day, even if They Have Many Children)** [a]

| | Number of Children | | | |
|---|---|---|---|---|
| | 0 | 1 | 2 | 3+ |
| Residence and Employment | Women Working Eight or More Hours per Day (%) | | | |
| Urban, with occupations | $63_{(159)}$ [b] | $54_{(150)}$ | $37_{(101)}$ | $32_{(70)}$ |
| Rural, with occupations | $48_{(128)}$ | $30_{(89)}$ | $23_{(80)}$ | $15_{(46)}$ |
| Wives of farmers, without occupations | $16_{(146)}$ | $11_{(178)}$ | $12_{(205)}$ | $4_{(219)}$ |

[a] The data are for French women.
[b] The numbers in parentheses indicate the number of interviews on which the percentage is based.
*Source.* Computed from Alain Girard and Henri Bastice, "Le Budget-Temps de la Femme Mariée à la Campagne," *Population* (Paris: April-June, 1959), pp. 254–284, at p. 272.

City women, if they work at all, tend to work full time, even if they have many children. That is, more of the employed city women work eight hours or more. Country women work part-time often, adjusting their working hours to the number of children. The pressure of the highly organized city life requires compliance with the schedule or not working, but scheduling in the country is much more flexible.

3. Another effect of a high level of organization of many different kinds of social functions is that people become specialized in particular activities. Occupations multiply as the number of specialized organizations increases, and as the creation of suborganizations within organizations progresses. This results in thousands of occupational titles, which are listed in the *Dictionary of Occupational Titles*.[20] It also results in the tremendous variety of economic-interest groups that we find in modern society.

4. Finally, the increased level of organization of a society causes a larger percentage of a person's social relations to be the result of the planned social activities. A man must interact with a great many people who are not his friends or relatives. This does not mean that he has fewer friends or relatives or spends less time with them; very likely, the absolute number of social relations of each man is larger in modern societies.[21]

This is important in daily life because the emotional quality of social relations entered into to achieve planned purposes tends to be different from the emotional quality of spontaneous relations. Some of the characteristics that make planned relations different are the following ones.

(*a*) The social relation is important only in a specific area of life (such as in buying shoes) rather than being a relation between whole personalities in all areas of life, such as in friendship. This characteristic of social relations is often called "functional specificity."

(*b*) People's emotions are not greatly involved in the relation. This characteristic is often called "affective neutrality."

(*c*) Since only a few characteristics of people are relevant to their roles in planned activity, people are much more likely to be treated as members of categories, in which only their *relevant* characteristics rather than all of their qualities are taken into account. This is often called the "universalism" of such social relations.

(*d*) The aspects of a person that are relevant to planning are generally his *actions* rather than this *permanent qualities* (for example, his grades on a test instead of his race or sex). Thus, people are judged more by what they do than by what kind of people they are in general. This characteristic is often called the "performance orientation" of a social relation.

These differences in the attitudes that people assume when judging another person in planned social activity are intimately tied to an additional very simple (and obvious) difference: many of the people that we interact with in planned social activity are strangers. The social conditions that

[20] Published by the U.S. Government Printing Office, Washington, D.C.
[21] Largely because there is a decrease of isolated physical work in the fields.

permit us to place enough trust in strangers to carry out complex planned activities with them are extremely complicated.[22]

## *Effects of Specific Kinds of Organizations*

If the general effects of the planning of a large part of social action by some people for others are found in all areas of people's lives, we would expect that the *specific activities* that the planning of others gets people into will also make a big difference. That is, the variations in the kinds of organizations that people participate in cause variations in their social lives.

1. People may have to become resigned to having other people plan their activities, but they do not have to like it. Karl Marx first pointed out the possibility that the greater the extent to which work is *planned for* the person (making him "a mere appendage to the machine"), the more likely he is to hate his work and the capitalists who subjected him to such planning. Marx's conclusion was that "the bourgeois mode of production," especially in its factory form, would take away so much of the planning activity from the worker that he would become alienated and revolutionary. After years of fruitless debate (in which the Marxists claimed as favorable evidence the many revolutions and socialist movements of workers, and the anti-Marxists pinpointed the lack of revolutions and the moderation of workers in many advanced capitalistic societies), the relation between detailed planning of work and alienation has begun to be studied empirically.

Generally, the results of this investigation support Marx's theory. Consequently we find that assembly-line workers in the automobile and food industries really do hate their work; but other workers whose duties are not planned for them in such great detail (such as the craftsmen in the printing industry or the dial-watchers in the chemicals industry) are much more likely to be satisfied with their work (see Table 3.5).

Marx was correct, then, in his theory that detailed planning of a man's work causes alienation from work or hatred for it. However, he was wrong in his prediction that there would be revolution when societies become more highly organized and work is planned for increasing numbers of the population. Even though detailed planning of work creates alienation from

---

[22] As an illustration, very few Americans have had the kind of experience my wife had in a Venezuelan store. She paid for goods with a large bill, and then heard the store clerk ask the boss whether he should give her back her change. The social conditions under which people give back change are not simple, but are quite essential for the organization of large commercial firms.

**Table 3.5   Some Modern Industries, as well as Traditional Crafts, Give Responsibility to Workers and Produce Little Dissatisfaction; Others Give Little Responsibility and Produce Much Dissatisfaction**

| Industry | Percent Who Say Job Is Mostly or Always Dull | Percent Who Say They Can Try Out Own Ideas on Job |
|---|---|---|
| *A traditional craft industry* | | |
| Printing | $4_{(115)}$ [a] | $79_{(112)}$ |
| *Modern industries giving responsibility* | | |
| Chemicals | $11_{(77)}$ | $64_{(75)}$ |
| Oil refining | $20_{(51)}$ | $59_{(49)}$ |
| *Modern industries not giving responsibility* | | |
| Automobiles | $34_{(174)}$ | $47_{(177)}$ |
| Food | $24_{(294)}$ | $48_{(292)}$ |

[a] The numbers in parentheses are the numbers of respondents in a given industry who answered the relevant question.
*Source.* Modified from Robert Blauner, *Alienation and Freedom: The Factory Worker and His Industry* (Chicago and London: University of Chicago Press, 1964), pp. 201 and 204.

it, there is much planning in modern industry that leaves great responsibility for the worker. Thus the worker is not as unhappy as Marx predicted.

2. Bureaucracy as a form of administration is prevalent in certain large-scale industries with a regular, stable market. Thus by comparing these industries with others, we can observe the effects of bureaucratic administration as opposed to other types of administration. One effect is that bureaucratic industries tend to require that all people work about the same number of hours, while less bureaucratic industries permit a wider variation in working hours. (Of course, to compare industries, we must choose people in approximately the same occupations, because people in different occupations work a different number of hours.)

Table 3.6 gives the percentage of members of various occupations who worked more than 60 hours during the census week and the percentage who worked from 1 to 14 hours. Thus, among all engineers, 4% worked more than 60 hours during the week, and 0.6% worked from 1 to 14 hours. Among college professors and instructors, 12.8% worked over 60 hours, while 8.6% worked from 1 to 14 hours. Among college professors, there are many men who work a great deal and men who hardly work at all.

Among engineers, very few work long hours, and very few work short hours. Now, we know that college professors work in professional organizations, while the immense majority of engineers work for great bureaucratically administered business corporations. Thus bureaucratic administration *regularizes schedules,* making all people work about the same number of hours.

Table 3.6   People Who Work in Bureaucratic Organizations Are Less Likely to Work Either Very Long or Very Short Hours [a]

| Occupation | Percentage Who Worked: | |
|---|---|---|
| | More than 60 Hours | 1 to 14 Hours |
| (1) *More bureaucratic* | | |
| Engineers | 4.0 | 0.6 |
| *Less bureaucratic* | | |
| College professors and instructors(NEC) [b] | 12.8 | 8.6 |
| (2) *Most bureaucratic* | | |
| Foremen(NEC), communications, utilities, and sanitary industries | 2.8 | 0.2 |
| *Medium bureaucratic* | | |
| Foremen(NEC), manufacturing | 4.6 | 0.4 |
| *Unbureaucratic* | | |
| Foremen(NEC), construction | 6.6 | 1.1 |
| (3) *More bureaucratic* | | |
| Operatives, manufacturing, meat products | 4.6 | 2.4 |
| *Less bureaucratic* | | |
| Operatives; meat cutters except packinghouse and slaughterhouse | 16.8 | 2.4 |
| (4) *More bureaucratic* | | |
| Policemen and detectives, public | 10.4 | 0.7 |
| *Less bureaucratic* | | |
| Sheriffs and bailiffs | 24.0 | 1.6 |
| Marshals and constables | 30.6 | 6.2 |

[a] The data are for men only.
[b] The notation in parentheses (NEC) means "not elsewhere classified." Thus a foreman classified in some other occupation would not be included among foremen.
*Source.* These data were computed from U.S. Bureau of the Census, "Detailed Occupational Characteristics, 1960," pp. 184–203.

If we look only at foremen (as in the second panel of the table), we notice that in the highly bureaucratic public utilities very few foremen work either very short or very long hours. In the highly unbureaucratic construction industry, nearly three times as many foremen work very long hours, and over five times as many work very short hours. In degree of bureaucratization, the manufacturing industries fall between utilities and construction, and also fall between utilities and construction in the percentage of foremen working either very long or very short hours.

The third panel of the table shows the number of hours worked in the identical occupation, inside and outside of large bureaucratic organizations. About one sixth of the meat cutters who are *not* employed in packing houses or slaughtering houses, worked very long hours, while only about one twentieth of the meat cutters employed as operatives in meat-products firms worked very long hours. About the same percentage of both groups worked very short hours.

The fourth panel shows the same contrast among policemen. There is only a moderate likelihood that police who work for bureaucratically organized public police forces will work very long hours. However, sheriffs and bailiffs, whose archaic titles convey an unbureaucratic image, are more than twice as likely to work very long hours, but also are more than twice as likely to work very short hours. Marshals and constables, also employed in less bureaucratic structures, are even more likely to work very long or very short hours.

In each of these comparisons, we find that the more bureaucratic the administration of the enterprise—that is, the more its administration is carried out by long hierarchies of officials according to rules and routines— the less variation there is in how long people work.

This is also reflected in other suggestive data. Clerical workers—the very typification of bureaucratic administration—are very unlikely to work either very long or very short hours. One of the distinctive earmarks of bureaucracy is the employment of salaried managers, while unbureaucratic administration is often carried out by self-employed managers. If we combine all salaried managers,[23] we find that about one seventh of them (14.6%) work more than 60 hours a week. Among all self-employed managers, proprietors, and officials, the percentage who work such long hours is nearly three times as great (39%). On the other hand, less than 1% (0.9%) of salaried managers had worked from 1 to 14 hours, while nearly 2% (1.9%) of the self-employed managers, proprietors, and officials

[23] Not elsewhere classified. For instance, this excludes all public officials, deans and presidents of colleges, and other managerial posts that have special classifications.

had worked very short hours. Thus, all indications point to bureaucracy as a cause of the regularity of schedules.

3. If bureaucracy is the extreme form of social organization for planning the activity of large numbers of people from a single center of command, we might expect that attitudes toward planning would be closely related to closeness to the top of a bureaucracy.

Table 3.7 gives some data on the attitudes toward planning by middle-

Table 3.7 **The Closer Men Are to the Top of a Large Bureaucracy, the More Favorable They Are Toward Planning; Percentage Who *Disagreed* that "Making Plans only Brings Unhappiness, because Plans Are always Difficult to Realize"**

| Group | Percentage Favorable to Planning | Number of Interviews |
|---|---|---|
| Middle class of city (random sample) | 55 | 66[a] |
| Low-level steel, white-collar | 63 | 24 |
| Middle-level steel, white-collar | 76 | 21 |
| High-level steel executives | 96 | 24 |

[a] Two more people answered this question than provided usable accounts of their last working day. This is why the number of interviews is different in this table from the number in Table 3.1 (p. 156).
*Source.* The same source as Table 3.1.

class men in a Chilean steel town. Barely more than one half of a random sample of middle-class heads of families in the town had favorable attitudes toward planning. Among steel-plant white-collar workers of lower levels, this percentage increases to about five eighths. Among middle-level steel executives, the proportion favorable to planning rises to about three fourths. Practically all of the top executives had a favorable attitude toward planning. The closer a person is to the center of a large highly planned organization, the more favorable he is likely to be toward planning.

4. In an extensive study of the reaction of American social science college professors to the "McCarthy period," [24] Lazarsfeld and Thielens showed that the better a college was, the more strongly its social science faculty defended academic freedom. These authors judged quality by an index combining the size of the library, the number of books per student,

[24] Senator Joseph McCarthy of Wisconsin conducted a campaign against supposed Communists in the State Department and in universities. Many people lost their jobs after accusations of Communist sympathies or past memberships in "Communist" organizations. The main period of pressure was the early 1950's.

the budget per student, the proportion of Ph.D.'s on the faculty, the past record in the production of scholars, and the tuition (the higher, the better). Some of their results are shown in Figure 3.1, reproduced from their book, *The Academic Mind.*

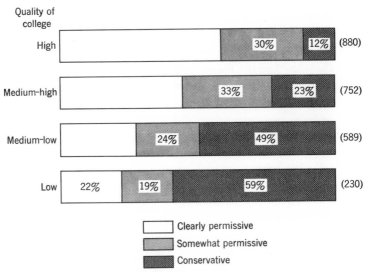

Figure 3.1   The better a college, the more of its social scientists are permissive. [From Paul F. Lazarsfeld and Wagner F. Thielens, *The Academic Mind* (New York: The Free Press of Glencoe, 1958) p. 162.]

The "clearly permissive" teachers agreed either (1) that students should be allowed to form a Young Communist League, or (2) that an admitted Communist teacher should be permitted to remain on the campus. More than one half of these clearly permissive college professors agreed with both. In addition, in order to be classified as "clearly permissive" the professor was required to take a permissive stand on many other free-speech issues. The clearly permissive professor has a rather strong position in favor of academic freedom.

A clear majority of social science professors in top-quality colleges take this strong position. In colleges of medium-high quality the proportion decreases to less than one half. In the low-quality colleges the proportion of clearly permissive professors decreases to less than one fourth.

Why should the quality of the college be so closely related to the attitudes of professors toward academic freedom? There are a number of reasons. First, there is a process of selection. The best social scientists, *as people,* are more permissive than their less-distinguished colleagues.[25] These more-

[25] This is shown in the original study, p. 146.

productive scientists are generally found in the better colleges; because they are more productive they can choose where to work, and they choose the better colleges. This starts a cycle. Once a poor college employs a conservative faculty, a permissive professor may not accept a job there because his job would not be safe. This, in turn, increases the conservatism of the faculty when the next permissive professor considers coming there. Clearly this process has been hurting Southern colleges in their recruitment of good faculty members in recent years.

Another reason why the quality of the college is closely related to its professors' attitudes toward academic freedom is that the administrations of better colleges defend their faculties more strongly.[26] People learn what attitudes they can afford partly from the men who pay their salaries and control their futures. In a superior college these powerful administrators teach "permissiveness." In lower-quality colleges they teach "responsibility."

Once these two processes start working, they determine a *culture* of the organization. If the new professor coming to a leading college had no opinions before, he learns to be permissive from his colleagues. The new professor without opinions at lower-quality colleges learns to be conservative.

5. Ever since Karl Marx observed that the concentration of workers into factories helped their organization into unions and political movements, social observers have repeated the observation. For instance, Leon Trotsky's suggested reason for the socialist revolution having taken place first in Russia was the fact that Russian factories were, on the average, very much larger than factories in Great Britain or the United States.[27] A recent study of printers gives detailed support for this observation of Marx, showing that the level of union activity is generally much higher in larger printing shops than in smaller ones (Figure 3.2).[28]

Thus we see that the specific characteristics of organizations in which people work make a great deal of difference in people's daily lives. These characteristics determine, in a large measure, such things as whether people like their work, how regularly scheduled their work is, how favorably they look upon planning, how strong their belief is in academic freedom, and how active they are in unions.

[26] *Ibid.*, pp. 168–186.
[27] Leon Trotsky, *History of the Russian Revolution* (New York: Simon and Schuster, 1932, or Ann Arbor: University of Michigan Press, manufactured in one volume with the original three-volume pagination), Vol. I, pp. 10–11.
[28] See also James S. Coleman, *Introduction to Mathematical Sociology* (New York: The Free Press of Glencoe, 1964), pp. 283–287, for a treatment of better data in a more solid way. The presentation there is too complex to be reproduced here.

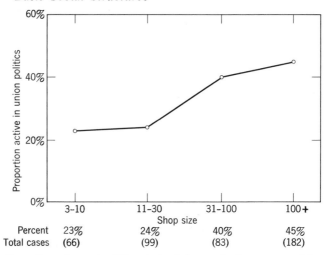

Figure 3.2    Proportion of men in different-sized shops who have engaged in some union political activity recently. *Note.* Political activity includes being a member of a union party, contributing funds, or working for candidates. [From Seymour M. Lipset, Martin A. Trow, and James S. Coleman, *Union Democracy* (New York: The Free Press of Glencoe, 1956) p. 151.]

### Effects of People's Positions in Organizations

The effects of organizations on people's lives depend on the position of the people within the organization. It is especially important whether a person does the planning for others or whether his activities are planned by others.

1. As a general rule, the higher a person's rank is in an organization, the more his relation to the authority system is one of *responsibility* for some set of activities, and the less his role is one of *being supervised.*[29] If people feel a sense of responsibility for some activity, they are likely to *work when work is needed*, rather than *work when they are told.* We would expect that, usually, this will result in their working more. A feeling of moral obligation resulting from responsibility, then, is more likely to motivate long hours of work than is being told to work long hours.

Table 3.8 gives a number of comparisons of the percentage of people working more than 60 hours a week, among occupations that differ according to the amount of responsibility the people have in the enterprise. Foremen have more responsibility than operatives; salaried managers have more responsibility than foremen; and self-employed managers have complete responsibility for the progress of the organization. In all of the

[29] See Elliott Jaques, *The Measurement of Responsibility* (Cambridge: Harvard University Press, 1956), pp. 22–42.

industries for which data are presented in Table 3.8, the more-responsible higher-ranking employees work more than the less-responsible lower-ranking workers.

The last three panels in the table furnish checks on this interpretation. Panel 9 shows that postmasters (as compared with officials and administrators, in general, in federal public administration) worked long hours more often. Postmasters have almost complete charge of an organization, while the average public administrator does not.

Panel 10 shows that public administrators are more likely to work long hours if they are in state and local administration rather than in the federal government. This probably reflects the fact that, at the same level of skill and income, a state or local official is much more likely to be in complete charge of something. Only a few federal administrators are in complete charge of, and responsible for, an organization.

Panel 11 indicates that not only responsibility for an organization, but also responsibility for human life and health, or responsibility to God, can motivate exceptionally long hours. Physicians and clergymen work much longer hours than other professionals, and are even more likely to put in a 60-hour week than farmers and farm managers.

Thus we can point to one strong effect on daily life of positions in organizations: the more responsible a person's position, the more likely he is to work long hours.

2. It has also been established that, generally, people who occupy higher positions are more satisfied with their work. The evidence of this greater satisfaction has been summarized in an article by Blauner,[30] from which Table 3.9 is taken. Blauner states that this may result from the greater prestige of higher positions, the greater control people have over their own work (and other aspects of the job), and the social position of higher-ranking people in organizations.

3. Rank is not the only aspect of people's positions in organizations that affects their social life. Another aspect of great importance is the *number of social contacts* with other workers implied by the job. Walker and Guest have shown that men whose duties isolate them from contact with others during work (for instance, men who work in paint-spray booths in automobile factories) dislike their job more than other assembly-line workers.[31] Also, acute observers of trade unions have noted that maintenance workers, who travel over the entire plant with numerous contacts, are

[30] Robert Blauner, "Work Satisfaction and Industrial Trends in Modern Society" (cited in footnote 1).
[31] Charles R. Walker and Robert H. Guest, *The Man on the Assembly Line* (Cambridge: Harvard University Press, 1952), p. 76.

**Table 3.8  In Various Industries, the Higher the Level of Responsibility of a Man, the More Likely He Is to Work Very Long Hours**

| Occupation | Percentage Who Worked More than 60 Hours |
|---|---|
| (1) Farm laborers | 24.8 |
| Farmers and farm managers | 48.5 |
| (2) Foremen(NEC),[a] construction | 6.6 |
| Salaried managers(NEC), construction | 12.1 |
| Self-employed managers, construction | 18.8 |
| (3) Operatives(NEC), manufacturing | 2.6 |
| Foremen(NEC), manufacturing | 4.6 |
| Salaried managers(NEC), manufacturing | 9.3 |
| Self-employed managers, manufacturing | 22.7 |
| (4) Operatives(NEC), Railway and RR Express | 2.4 |
| Foremen(NEC), Railway and RR Express | 6.4 |
| Operatives(NEC), other transportation | 5.8 |
| Foremen(NEC), other transportation | 9.0 |
| Salaried managers(NEC), transportation [b] | 13.2 |
| Self-employed managers, transportation [b] | 33.4 |
| (5) Operatives(NEC), communications, utilities, and sanitary industries | 2.8 |
| Foremen(NEC), communications, utilities, and sanitary industries | 2.8 |
| Salaried managers(NEC), communications, utilities, and sanitary industries | 6.5 |
| Self-employed managers, communications, utilities, and sanitary industries | 27.3 |
| (6) Operatives(NEC), wholesale and retail trade [b] | 6.6 |
| Sales workers, wholesale trade | 11.2 |
| Salaried managers(NEC), wholesale trade | 12.9 |
| Self-employed managers, wholesale trade | 25.4 |
| Sales workers, retail trade | 16.2 |
| Salaried managers(NEC), retail trade | 25.1 |
| Self-employed managers, retail trade | 51.8 |
| (7) College professors and instructors(NEC) | 12.8 |
| College presidents and deans | 28.1 |

**Table 3.8**    *(Continued)*

| Occupation | Percentage Who Worked More than 60 Hours |
|---|---|
| (8) Officials and administrators(NEC), federal public administration and postal | 2.8 |
| Postmasters | 9.7 |
| (9) Officials and administrators(NEC), public administration | |
| Federal and postal | 2.8 |
| State | 10.2 |
| Local | 9.2 |
| (10) All professional, technical, and kindred occupations | 11.7 |
| Physicians and surgeons | 52.7 |
| Clergymen | 51.5 |

a The notation (NEC) means "not elsewhere classified." For instance, college professors who are also deans would not be included among college professors (NEC), and postmasters would not be included among federal officials (NEC).
b Detailed breakdown not given.
*Source.* Computed from U.S. Bureau of the Census, "Detailed Occupational Characteristics, 1960," pp. 184–203.

much more likely to become union leaders. Thus the planning of social activities places people into quite varying *numbers* of contacts with their fellow workers, even at the same rank, and this affects many aspects of their social life.

## Voluntary Associations

Many legally existing "organizations" that have charters do not satisfy our above criterion for organizations; that is, they do not have extensive systematic planning of some people's activities by other people. In chambers of commerce, trade unions, professional associations, political interest groups, and many Protestant church congregations, there is very little capacity for people to plan the activities of other people. That is, authority, as we defined it above, barely exists. Sociologists generally call these organizations which have very little capacity to discipline the

Table 3.9    A Majority of Professionals, Salesmen, and Managers Would Keep on Working even if They Inherited Enough Money to Live Comfortably, While a Majority of Workers Would Not

| Occupational Group | Percent Who Would Continue Same Kind of Work | Number in Sample |
|---|---|---|
| Professionals | 68 | 28 |
| Sales | 59 | 22 |
| Managers | 55 | 22 |
| Skilled manual | 40 | 86 |
| Service | 33 | 18 |
| Semiskilled operatives | 32 | 80 |
| Unskilled | 16 | 27 |

*Source.* Robert Blauner, "Work Satisfaction and Industrial Trends in Modern Society" (cited in footnote 1), p. 342. This table is one of several. The original data were collected by Nancy C. Morse and Robert S. Weiss, "The Function and Meaning of Work and the Job," *American Sociological Review,* **20,** 191–198 (1955), at p. 197.

participants, "voluntary associations." Without disciplinary capacity, the activities that make up the group are "voluntary" activities by the members.

In such voluntary associations, it is not very useful to classify people by their ranks, since rank is sociologically important only when it implies ability to plan activities of others. Instead, the basic structure of the association is formed by groupings with *different levels of activity.* The core or center of the group consists of highly active people—an executive committee and sometimes a paid staff. These highly active people are sufficiently committed to the group so that, within certain limits, their activities can be systematically planned for the achievement of group purposes.

The surrounding circle of less-active people may be involved in special events (for example, demonstrations in the civil rights movement, or strikes in trades unions), but their activities cannot be systematically planned. Beyond this group comes a circle of members or sympathizers who are generally favorable to the purposes of the organization, but are unlikely to be active except when some particular issue excites them. In the next circle, there is perhaps a group of potential recruits, or potential sympathizers, who adhere to attitudes that might lead them to support the group, but who have no present commitment to the group.

The crucial problem of maintaining a voluntary association is to keep a continuous flow of people from a lower level of activity to a higher level in order to replace those who lose interest. Leaders of voluntary associations formulate these levels of activity in their own language. For an example, Lenin's analysis of the Bolshevik organization is summarized in Figure 3.3.

The basic social cement that holds voluntary associations together is conversation, rather than force or money. In order to keep the association going, the activists must create talk. They do this by inventing news and by publicizing the issues and activities that the group is concerned with, in an attempt to fill the conversations of participants of different levels

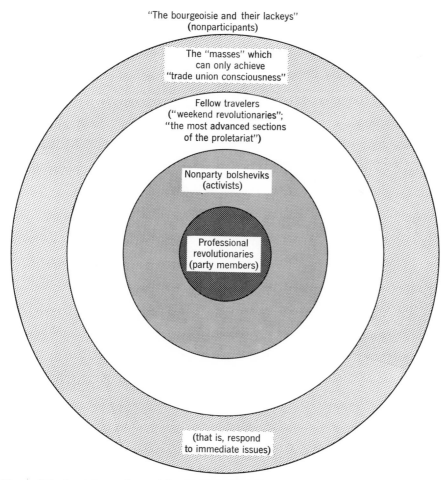

Figure 3.3 Leninist analysis of levels of activity in the Communist movement. Lenin in writing about the Communist movement developed a special language to distinguish different levels of activity in the revolutionary movement.

of activity with topics related to the group. A voluntary association that cannot get into the newspaper is, in modern society, on its way down.

Leadership of voluntary associations, therefore, goes to exceptionally fluent people who manage to create news about the activities of the association. An illustration of the importance of volubility in the leadership of such associations is an experience that Robert Peabody and I had while we were interviewing for a study of a protest movement of property owners against a road-widening proposal. We interviewed ten leaders of the movement, who talked an average of more than one and one half hours each (including one interview not completed). Only one of them talked less than an hour. Seven rank-and-file followers of the movement talked an average of a little less than one hour each, and only two talked more than an hour. Nine interviewees, who lived in the area but were completely inactive, talked an average of three quarters of an hour each.[32]

In addition to creating news (and hence conversation) and to participating volubly in conversations, the active core of the association needs to create activities in which potential activists can be active: visits to public officials, meetings, circulation of petitions, sit-ins, picket lines, parades, bridge tournaments, bingo games, and things of this kind.

By creating news, conversation, and activities in which people can participate, leaders of voluntary associations try to move people to higher levels of activity and thus sustain the core of the organization. In one sense, this does involve "planning" the activities of others—planning that their interest should be aroused by a meeting in which such-and-such a person speaks, or in a bridge tournament, or what not. But most of this planning involves activities that will elicit voluntary participation in the organization, rather than activities that will most rapidly and efficiently achieve the organizational ends.

Thus the fundamental dynamics of voluntary associations revolve around variables and concepts that play a small role in the analysis of organizations based on force or on payment: levels of activity rather than authority, conversations and news rather than organizational resources defended in the law, and activities to elicit interest rather than activities to achieve purposes according to plan. The analysis of voluntary organizations is therefore quite distinct from the analysis of organizations made up of full-time workers, and is rarely done by the same sociologists.

---

[32] The dependence of political machines on conversation is implicit in E. Banfield and J. Q. Wilson's comment on a reason for machine decline: " 'Friendship' is also harder to give [in recent times]. One reason is television. The Precinct Captain who visits in the evening interrupts a television program and must either stay and watch in silence or else excuse himself quickly and move on." *City Politics* (Cambridge: Harvard University Press, 1964), p. 122.

## Elementary Social Processes in Organizations

The plan on which an organization is constructed is never the complete explanation of activities that go on in the organization. In organizations as well as in purely spontaneus activities, people grow older, make friends, fight for their own interests and those of their buddies, or sneak a little cash from the till. That is, the total activity that goes on in an organization is a combined result of planning and spontaneous elementary social processes. In this section we shall consider four of these elementary social processes that go on in organizations and that influence their activities: (1) aging and turnover of personnel, which influences the *demographic structure* of organizations; (2) the formation of *primary groups* of friends in the course of organizational activity; (3) the creation of *vested interests* in certain organizational activities, preventing easy changes of plans; and (4) corruption.

### Demographic Structure

Any set of continuing activities must be carried on by a set of people over a period of time. At any point in time, the organization can be described by the accumulated experience of people in the organization, that is, the amount of time different people have spent in the organization. This demographic structure is the end result of the processes of recruitment and turnover, plus the simple biological process of aging.

Suppose the organization grew rapidly in a few years to a maximum size, and then remained more or less stable in size for a number of years. At first it was probably made up of a large group of young, relatively inexperienced people who had great opportunities because they had no elders to compete for high posts. Later in its history, it will have a very large number of men of middle age with much experience, with relatively few very young and inexperienced and few very old. The young will find fewer opportunities, because now they have to compete with a large group of more experienced elders.

This demographic structure, of course, affects a number of basic elements of organizational structure. Obviously, if the theory on which the organization is based has not greatly changed, the superior experience and knowledge of older men with more years in the organization will likely mean that activities will more closely resemble the plan. But if in the meantime, in the society at large, new important theories are being taught in the universities to young men—theories that older men do not know—the emphasis of the demographic structure of particular organizations on older men may result in slow adaptations to new opportunities. Perhaps part of the rapid progress of aviation and the slow decline of railroads can be explained by their contrasting demographic structures; many more old men run railroads than airlines.

Again, the demographic structure clearly affects the degree to which the organization can use career rewards for encouraging younger men to work hard. A university department with all its allotted full professorships filled by men forty years old does not have a great deal to promise a man with a new Ph.D.

The constrasting demographic structures of different departments in companies may create difficulties in the authority system—for instance when new staff departments are created, populated mainly by young university graduates. If these graduates are supposed to advise much older and more experienced men about how to do their work, great tensions are created.[33] Thus, in many ways, the planning of social action on a large scale is influenced by the demographic structure—the distribution of seniority and age—in the organization.

### Primary Groups

A "primary group" is a small, durable, face-to-face group in which people care about what happens to each other. Primary groups tend to form in any organization that exists for a long time. And people who join do not leave their families or old friends. These primary groups confront organizations with the following problems and opportunities.

*Problem 1.* Because people in primary groups care about each other, they may subvert organizational goals and rules in order to secure the welfare of a group member. Thus, there is a common norm in most primary groups that one does not "squeal on a friend." This increases the *inaccuracy* of the disciplinary system, which we discussed earlier. "Nepotism," or putting the welfare of relatives above the efficiency of the organization, is a particularly important kind of subversion of organizations by primary groups.

OPPORTUNITY. This same feature provides an opportunity for the organization, since if people care about the fate of others they will help others in difficulties. This is especially important in dangerous situations such as combat, mining, or fishing, where organizational success depends

[33] Melville Dalton, *Men Who Manage* (New York: Wiley, 1959), pp. 87–94.

heavily on mutual help. In these cases, the solidity of primary groups can be a great factor in organizational success.[34]

*Problem 2.* Primary groups are very often made up of *peers* in bureaucracies—that is, all members are under the same rules and the same pay scale. Consequently, changes in the rules, such as a change in the amount of a certain kind work that must be performed before premium pay starts, affect all members alike. Since the members communicate easily and have interests in common, and since they can use social pressures on each other, they often form groups that try to manipulate the rules—for example, by restricting production.[35]

OPPORTUNITY. The primary work group can often determine more accurately than superiors just what help a man needs in order to do his work. If this group is motivated to help him, and he to help them, all of the work goes better.[36]

*Problem 3.* When primary groups that include *different ranks* start to form in an organization, they tend to interfere with the objective judgment of the inferior member by the superior member and to cause charges of favoritism. Thus, discipline in the organization may be undermined.

OPPORTUNITY. On the other hand, primary-group attachments between superiors and inferiors may create in the inferiors a desire to help the superior do his job, and hence increase the degree of initiative of inferiors.

*Problem 4.* Primary groups are effective *socializing agents,* that is, they teach people values and norms. Therefore, if a primary group becomes identified with the goals of a *section* of the organization, this group can teach these goals effectively to new members of the section. If the organization wishes to change the goals of the section, it may find that this change is sabotaged or fought against.

OPPORTUNITY. But men work better if they believe in what they are doing; they show more initiative and responsibility. As a result, socializing them into the goals of the section can make the section more effective in achieving organizational goals.

The overall balance of these problems and opportunities depends on the exact conditions and requirements of the organization. Sometimes

[34] Edward A. Shils and Morris Janowitz, "Cohesion and Disintegration in the *Wehrmacht* in World War II," *Public Opinion Quarterly,* **67,** pp. 280–315 (Summer, 1948); Samuel Stouffer and others, *The American Soldier* (Princeton: Princeton University Press, 1949), Vol. II, pp. 172–176.

[35] The classic study of workers restricting production is Fritz J. Roethlisberger and William J. Dickson's, *Management and the Worker* (Cambridge: Harvard University Press, 1939).

[36] See Peter Blau, *Dynamics of Bureaucracy* (Chicago: University of Chicago Press, 1955), pp. 49–67 and 99–179.

dangers of favoritism are more serious than dangers of lack of initiative, and sometimes the reverse is true. It is impossible to make general statements about how primary-group formation influences organizational performance.

### Creation of Vested Interest

The creation of a reward system to motivate and discipline planned activity has the side effect of creating groups of people (1) who are in communication with each other at work, and (2) whose pay is affected in the same way by the fate of the organization and by its rules. People with the same interests, who are in communication with each other, tend to create organizations to defend their interests. Unionism, for instance, is almost an inevitable result of industrialization, or the organization of the economy by large-scale firms.

These organizations then fight to secure and protect their rewards, and to increase them, by the establishment of rules, social arrangements, and collective contracts. Interests that are defended by rules and solid social arrangements are called "vested interests." These vested interests often would not have existed if the organization had not been created. Industrial unions cannot exist until there are factories; but, once the unions exist, they become independent social facts. They can influence the future of the organization by insisting that the jobs of its members must not be destroyed, by urging higher salaries, by striking for fair punishment and promotion systems, or by urging promotion by seniority rather than by merit. Thus the planning of social activity creates other activities, indirectly, by the spontaneous formation of groups to defend collective interests.[37]

### Corruption

The concentration of resources in organizational hands creates a set of temptations that would not exist without the organization. One of the temptations is to divert these resources into private hands. It is particularly strong among men in positions of responsibility. Corruption in governments, businesses, churches, and trade unions has often amounted to millions of

[37] A fine study of the conditions that lead to the formation of unions is David Lockwood's, *The Blackcoated Worker: A Study in Class Consciousness* (London: Allen and Unwin, 1958). The mechanisms of vesting of interests are best described by Philip Selznick, *TVA and the Grass Roots* (Berkeley and Los Angeles: University of California Press, 1949), pp. 259–261, and his *Leadership in Administration* (Evanston, Ill.: Row Peterson, 1957), pp. 91–101, especially pp. 93–96.

dollars; and, occasionally, in great stock scandals or the regimes of dictators, corruption has amounted to hundreds of millions of dollars.

People in organizations keep on growing older, making friends, fighting for their interests, and being tempted. In short, nothing in the plan of the organization can keep them from living. Human life is too tough and resilient to be easily shaped by plans and theories. To get a complete picture of any organization, we must combine knowledge of the *social processes of planning* with the *unplanned social processes* going on at the same time. This chapter deals primarily with planning and organization as social processes. But every spontaneous social process commented upon elsewhere in this book also happens in some organizations. The spontaneous processes discussed here are merely examples.

## Studying Organizations

The object of any kind of scientific investigation is to obtain the necessary information for solving a scientific problem with the least possible work and expense. Research is similar to any planned social activity in this respect. Consequently, when we evaluate ways of studying organizations, we must evaluate the kinds of intellectual problems that a procedure is likely to be able to solve, and the amount of work and expense that will be involved.

Obviously, *information already collected* by other people for other purposes is the cheapest kind. Some of the sources of this cheap information on organizations are listed below, together with the aspects of organizations to which the sources are likely to be most relevant.

1. In order to persuade others to invest resources in an organization, people usually have to explain the theory on which organizational activity will be based. Consequently, the best *time* to collect data on the theory of an organization is generally when it is first starting. Then the arguments and data presented to potential investors (banks, buyers of stocks and bonds, legislators, donors) represent, usually fairly well, the theory on which the organization is based. Good places to get informaiton on organizational theories cheaply are proposals for new research institutes made to foundations by universities, prospectuses of new companies, the speeches of supporters of new governmental organizations in Congressional committees and on the floor of Congress, and newspaper reports on new proposals. The student, guiding himself by the four basic questions that each such theory must answer—technical-costs, market, division of benefits, and

personnel—can often construct quite a complete picture of the theory on which an organization is based.[38]

2. The concrete activities carried out in the organization are fairly well represented by the *occupational composition* of the organization, since an occupational classification is exactly a classification of the main activities that people carry out. A large number of clerks indicates considerable paperwork; a large number of engineers indicates a large amount of technical planning; a large number of skilled maintenance workers indicates activities for maintaining much capital equipment; and so on. These occupational statistics may often be obtained from company records of payrolls and personnel, and may be obtained for groups of organizations (for example, industries) from the censuses of several countries.[39]

3. Another source of information on the activities of organizations is *schedules.* The contrast between a vocational school and a college preparatory school is immediately obvious merely by comparing the number of hours devoted to different kinds of study in the course schedule. These schedules are often printed for use within the organization, which makes them very cheap information.

4. The demographic structure of organizations is very conveniently studied from personnel records, since most important demographic data (age, seniority, sex) are generally included in these records. Rates of quitting and of entry into the organization can often be easily computed from such sources.

5. The budget and financial report is usually formally approved by the board of directors of the organization and hence, quite often, is available in written form. It usually indicates the main elements of the costs of the organization's activities, and gives clues to which of its *professed* purposes it is willing to spend money for. Also it often indicates the main sources of different kinds of income.

6. Organizational charts are quick guides to the authority system. And so also, of course, are relative salary rates of different officials.

At a second level of costs and work in collecting data are *informal field investigations,* in which investigators do not follow rigid procedures but, instead, ask whoever seems likely to be in a position to know. Some of the

[38] An example of the analysis of the original theory on which an organization was based from such published materials is Philip Selznick's, *TVA and the Grass Roots* (Berkeley and Los Angeles: University of California Press, 1949), pp. 3–16, and especially pp. 181–202.

[39] An excellent study based on such data is Mason Haire's, "Biological Models and Empirical Histories of the Growth of Organizations," in Mason Haire, ed., *Modern Organization Theory* (New York: Wiley, 1959), pp. 272–306. Several are summarized by William Starbuck (cited in footnote 3).

informal field procedures that are useful for various research problems include the following ones.

1. The location and number of reserved parking spaces, the size of offices, the number of secretaries, the elegance of the furnishings, and the chain of personnel that one must go through to get to talk to an important person—all are quick shorthand checks on the organizational chart as an index of the authority system.

2. Quite often informal interviews with almost any major official of an organization can clarify the theory on which the organization operates. The questions that one asks, of course, depend on the particular aspect of the organizational theory that is of interest. Questions such as "Who do you mainly sell to?" "What do you think are your main advantages over your competitors in selling to these people?" and others of this kind may get answers that give a quick picture of the market theory of the organization. Different questions may clarify technological theories or other aspects of the organizational view of the world.

3. The history of crucial decisions (such as decisions to invest large amounts of money in a new plant, or to create a new university department) can be traced by going from one person to the others that he mentions as having been involved, and then going from these people to those they mention. This often shows a great deal about both the authority system of the organization and the theories of organizational performance held by different groups of management.

4. Reading court cases and legal documents relating to the chartering of the organization, the distribution of benefits, and the defense of resources (and talking to the lawyers involved) often gives clues to the legal processes mentioned above in connection with the defense and replenishment of resources, and also to the distribution of benefits.

The third level of expense and trouble, which should only be used if satisfactory answers are not elicited by the cheaper methods outlined above, is rigorous scientific procedures for sampling organizational personnel by interviews. Some of the types of measurement that can be carried out by such procedures include the following ones.

1. Interviews asking for approximate distributions of a person's time between different kinds of jobs. The data in Table 3.1 (p. 156), for instance, are based on a series of questions dealing with the interviewees' activities during each hour of their last working day prior to the interview.

2. Attitudes toward work, toward the world in general, toward careers, toward the fairness of the reward and punishment system, and things of this kind can easily be studied by interviews, using attitude questions, as

discussed extensively in any methodology text on sociology. The data in Table 3.5 (p. 180) were taken from such studies.

3. Frequencies of various kinds of activities thought to be influenced by organizational activity, such as frequency of attendance at union meetings, how often the member meets people from the plant outside work, who his friends are, and things of this kind.

4. Detailed information on the work position or position in the authority system not available from organizational charts, such as how often a subordinate must give account of his work to his superior, or with whom, specifically, a staff official has advisory relations, and so forth.

5. Demographic data not included in company records, such as the occupation of the father, the number of courses followed in adult education, the number of children, other sources of income, migration and job histories, and similar things.

The most expensive form of data collection is actual observation and detailed recording of the activities of people. Some of these kinds of data that usually must be collected in this manner include the following.

1. The actual distribution of time, rather than the scheduled distribution published by the company or the (usually somewhat inaccurate) memories of people when asked in interviews.

2. Frequencies of different kinds of interactions: frequencies of giving orders, frequencies of friendly banter, frequencies of offering help to others in their work, or interfering with others' work, and the like.

3. The amount of time that different people talk in meetings.

4. The concrete nature of problems and difficulties confronted by the men in given positions, the things they notice when deciding what to do about these problems, the sequence of problem-solving activities, and so on.

5. The subrosa or unlawful culture of different groups in the organization, which will not be known to top management and may not be expressed even to the very best interviewer. For example, the connection of union stewards with the numbers racket, or informal rules regarding how much a man should produce (and ways of punishing him if he is a rate buster), and matters like this may have to be investigated by direct close observation.

6. Finally, we often use direct detailed observation and informal interviewing when we do not have much of an idea of what is going on. By close observation we can often locate causes or effects of some organizational practice, which we can then study on a large scale with some of the cheaper techniques. Naturalists, such as Charles Darwin, preceded the great growth of laboratory studies of animals and plants. In sociology, we still do not

know enough about what is going on in the social world to dispense with extensive work by naturalists. But, fortunately, most of us have broad experience in naturalistic observation in all of the organizations that we participate in.

## Summary and Conclusions

Organizations have been treated in this book as one of the four basic structures of societies because planned social activities on a large scale are significantly different from spontaneous activities, and because, without the activities of large-scale planned organizations, society as we know it could not exist. Structures for planning systematically the activities of some people by others—or, in other words, organizations—necessarily involve three basic elements: a theory on the basis of which action is planned, resources used in the action, and an authority system so that some people can plan the activities of others.

The theory, in turn, necessarily involves four basic elements: a technical-costs theory of how the purposes can be achieved, a market theory of who will want and pay for the benefits, a theory of who will get the benefits, and a theory of what personnel will be able to carry out the plan.

The resources of the organization must be defended (generally by courts and legal procedures); they must be replenished either by sales of benefits or by investments in future benefits; and they must be administered so that they are used according to plan.

The authority system of the organization usually involves the division of responsibility to make sure that certain activities do, indeed, conform to the plan; it involves supervision to correct the activities when they are not efficient; and it involves discipline to motivate conformity to supervision and to responsibility.

There are as many different types of organizations as there are different ways of creating the basic elements of organizations. Each of the basic elements of an organization and each of the subelements within it have formed the basis of fruitful classifications of organizations. Four especially interesting types of organizations are (1) the charismatic retinue, that is, the followers of a religious or scientific or political genius; (2) the traditionalistic feudal administration in which each man administers his fief and gives traditional services to the king; (3) the bureaucratic administration of salaried career officials arranged in a hierarchy; and (4) the professional organization in which responsibility and resources are distributed according to competence, and very little detailed supervision of the activities of the professional member takes place.

The general level of organization of societies affects the daily lives of people in those societies in these ways: (1) by increasing the efficiency of social activities for achieving social purposes; (2) by increasing the regularity of the scheduling of people's time into work and play (and thus creating traffic problems at peak traffic times); (3) by increasing the diversity of the social body by creating new specialized occupations; and (4) by increasing the proportion of impersonal social relations in social life.

Different kinds of organizations create different effects on daily life. Different industries produce different degrees of hatred of work, depending apparently on the detail of the planning of the worker's activity by others. Bureaucratic organizations, especially, increase the regularity of people's schedules (so that very few people work either very long or very short hours), and appear to encourage a favorable attitude toward planning in general. The quality of a university influences its professors' attitudes on academic freedom. The size of the shop influences its workers' union activity.

In addition to the effects of different kinds of organizations, there are effects of people's positions within organizations. Apparently the more responsible a man's position is, the more likely he is to work long hours. People who hold higher positions generally like their work better than people who hold low positions. Work puts some men in extensive communication with their bosses, and isolates others. It influences attitudes such as whether a man likes his work, and certain activities such as participation in union organizations.

Organizations are affected in carrying out their plans by various spontaneous social processes that go on within them. Especially important are the processes of aging and gaining experience and seniority in organizations, the forming of friendships among co-workers, the creation of vested interests in the rewards of the organization, and corruption. These spontaneous processes make the organization a living social reality, and something more than just an engineering and marketing plan.

*4*

# SOCIAL
# STRATIFICATION

*Leonard Reissman*

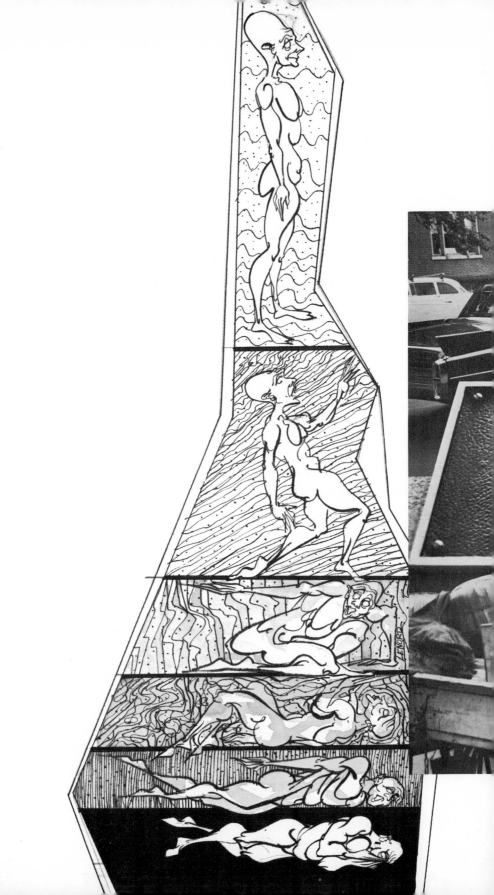

# SOCIAL STRATIFICATION

Systems of social inequity exist in all human societies. This assertion emphasizes two features that are basic for an analysis of social stratification. First, the inequalities—no matter what their origin—appear in a social context. Biological differences, real or presumed, may be used as a basis for social stratification, but biology alone does not make a social difference. For example, biological differences exist between Negroes and whites, but none of these differences is sufficient by itself to explain the patterns of race relations in the United States. It is more likely that biology is invoked as a rationale to support established social inequalities; when social definitions with respect to equality change, so also do the biological justifications that were used. The current shift in Negro-white relations is a clear example of this social flexibility.

Second, the inequalities are systematic. They are organized into patterns that are recognized and accepted by most members of a society. Social differences are interlaced in the dominant values of a society; the inequalities are justified by the very beliefs that regulate a society and give it continuity. Hence, Americans generally would sanction the division between rich and poor as being the outcome of economic competition—a force that they consider necessary, valuable, and desirable. Even though this position has been modified considerably in the last few decades by the acceptance of social welfare programs, and most recently by the antipoverty program, there is more than just a lingering belief that most people get what they deserve in the competitive process.

The above basic features of social stratification may sound simple and mechanical, but they are neither. They invoke a number of questions that put into words the complexity of the subject. Let us consider a few of these questions in order to show the scope of the topic.

Why must societies encourage social inequality by stratifying their members? There are two possible answers. Some sociologists contend that stratification, and its resulting inequalities, is a necessary, functional requirement of all societies. Briefly, they argue that every society must gradate its activities because some are considered more important than others. In other words, a society's activities are ranked according to the core values of the society as being more or less important, more or less desirable. Warfare might be a dominating value in one society, science in another, religion in a third, and so on. It follows, then, that each society encourages only the most talented, skilled, and responsible persons to fill its highly critical functions. As part of this encouragement, a society rewards its successful members with power, prestige, honor, income, or anything else that is considered valuable. Activities—from the most important to the least important—are rewarded according to a standard of social functions. The evaluation of talent or capability is a relative judgment, based upon established criteria and orderly mechanism. In this way, societies become stratified in relation to the core values around which they are organized.

This functional account of stratification is not accepted, at least in its entirety, by all sociologists. Even opponents of functionalism must admit that social inequality is universal and, furthermore, that the basis of social inequality is somehow related to dominant social values. However, these opponents of functionalism draw the line at the proposition that inequality is unavoidable as a functional necessity. They argue that, in reality, as opposed to theory, a system of stratification tends to continue because the members of a society who are in the highest strata want the system to continue unchanged. Power, not functional necessity, is the key to understanding stratification. Chiefs, kings, aristocrats, or the upper class all have the same intent: to secure their position, to discourage outsiders, and thereby to control power relations so completely that they alone determine who can enter their circle. What looks like functional necessity, therefore, is really elite control. What may once have been functionally necessary must become dysfunctional because those in power seek to stay in power.[1]

From a somewhat different direction, M. G. Smith has raised a relevant point. He contends that sociologists should not assert that social inequality is universal. According to his argument, simple inequality is inevitable on the grounds of biological differences and kinship, but these grounds are not by themselves sufficient evidence of stratification. Instead, in Smith's view, sociologists should consider:

The principles by which observable inequalities are institutionalized. . . . Excluding biologically given differences . . . uniformity or inequality in the distributions of access to favoured positions are decisive for societal classification as stratified or not. . . . [S]tratification never consists in the mere existence or occupancy of these positions, but in the principles by which the distribution of access and opportunities is regulated.[2]

There is merit to this argument when one is interested in preindustrial societies, as Smith was. However, the argument is much less cogent when the interest centers on industrial societies.

Yet, Smith's point raises a second question. What social characteristics are used in stratification systems? If the fullest spectrum of societies is con-

[1] For a fuller discussion of these arguments, see (for the functional view) Kingsley Davis and Wilbert Moore, "Some Principles of Stratification," *American Sociological Review*, **10**, 242–249 (April, 1945). For the opposing argument, see Melvin M. Tumin, "Some Principles of Stratification: A Critical Analysis," *American Sociological Review*, **18**, 387–397 (August, 1953).

[2] M. G. Smith, "Pre-Industrial Stratification Systems," N. J. Smelser and S. M. Lipset, eds., in *Social Structure and Mobility In Economic Development* (Chicago: Aldine Press, 1966).

sidered, many criteria must be included. Usually, however, the most common criteria are such biologically grounded factors as: age, sex, race, and kinship; class characteristics such as occupation, wealth, and power; and any number of idiosyncratic characteristics such as talent and personality. By grouping the criteria in this way, I do not mean to imply that they are, indeed, so separated. Actually, my grouping is not a hard and fast one. Political power can be legitimated on a biological basis as in the case of a hereditary monarchy, or kinship can become a basis for class stratification. My point is that all or many of these characteristics are combined in actual situations and, furthermore, can be justified on biological or social grounds. The defense that is given is an important clue to the character of the stratification system.

A pertinent question raised by these considerations of stratification criteria is: How rigid or flexible are the divisions between social strata? Generally, the greater the emphasis upon biological defenses, the more rigid the system is likely to be. Sociologists conveniently pose two extreme situations: one in which social positions are ascribed, the other in which social positions are achieved. In the first case, rigid divisions are the rule, and the separation between strata is unbridgeable so that individuals can do little, if anything, about changing their positions. In the second case, the separation is flexible and social mobility between strata is possible, even encouraged. The class system in America is an example of a situation in which social positions are achieved, while the classical Indian caste system exemplifies a situation in which social positions are ascribed.

Whether a society tends toward one pole or the other depends on the criteria used and upon the values that justify the criteria. Stratification by sex is ascribed. So, too, is stratification by age, race, and kinship. Occupation, on the other hand, can be either ascribed or achieved, depending upon how it is viewed within the social context. Caste position in India, for instance, is very much an occupational matter, but persons are born into their caste and, at least in theory, never escape it. In the United States and elsewhere, occupation is considered a matter of individual achievement, as are wealth and political power. Nevertheless, family inheritance and position can help to boost or to hinder the individual's own advancement. Americans may still like to believe that everyone starts out equally, but they also know that coming from a wealthy or even a middle-class family is an advantage not shared by everyone. Indeed, the current antipoverty program is an explicit effort by the Federal Government to take up some of the slack between real and imagined equality. The poor, by not encouraging education or by not being able to afford it, pass along the unwanted heritage of poverty to their children.

The emphasis upon ascription or achievement criteria depends very much on the whole package of social values. Whether a society tends to stress the concept of ascription or of achievement finally is determined within a social matrix. The emphasis upon achievement in American society, for example, is not isolated but is tightly bound into the emphasis upon individualism, freedom of choice, political democracy, and equality of opportunity. These values harmonize. Some of our cultural heroes have progressed from humble beginnings to the highest positions: Lincoln, Carnegie, and Marian Anderson. More than that, our sacred documents—the Constitution and the Declaration of Independence—proclaim our belief in the need for equal opportunity and present the legal mechanisms whereby those opportunities can be assured. Ideally, then, American stratification has been an open system; that is, one in which talent, character, and a dedication to work generally are to be rewarded. We publicly reject the attempt to allocate those rewards on the basis of ascribed characteristics such as race, color, creed, or national origins.

As can usually be expected, however, the ideal values of a society and its actual practices are frequently at variance. I say this not because of cynicism, but because of the knowledge that all societies function in different ways. The Indian caste system is not so unequivocally rigid as it appears to be, since there are regularized outlets to circumvent caste barriers that are in practice. Nor is the British aristocracy as tightly closed as the stereotype might imply. Similarly, the American class system is not as wide open as our sacred documents affirm. These documents state a hope, not a fact. Indeed, even at this formal, documentary level we have recently recognized that equal opportunity requires more than assertions to make it real. The preamble to the Economic Opportunities Act of 1964 is a revealing statement concerning the change in our estimates of equality in American society. Notice how that preamble recognizes our traditional beliefs while, at the same time, it takes account of current realities.

Although the economic well-being and prosperity of the United States have progressed to a level surpassing any achieved in world history, and although these benefits are widely shared throughout the Nation, poverty continues to be the lot of a substantial number of our people. The United States can achieve its full economic and social potential as a nation only if every individual has the opportunity to contribute to the full extent of his capabilities and to participate in the workings of our society. It is, therefore, the policy of the United States to eliminate the paradox of poverty in the midst of plenty in this Nation by opening to everyone the opportunity to work, and the opportunity to live in decency and dignity.

The concepts of ascription and achievement can also be used to assess social change. The emphasis upon achievement is relatively recent in world history, coming only after centuries of monarchies and aristocracies which depended on ascriptive criteria. In the West, the shift to achievement criteria followed the complex changes associated with the rise of industrialism and all that went with it. Interestingly enough, a similar shift from ascription to achievement is now taking place in the so-called "third-world," the developing nations in Africa and Asia, as well as in the older nations of Latin America. Like the Western nations in earlier times, these developing and older countries are moving away from the traditional, ascriptive forms of stratification and toward achievement. Obviously, not all of these nations will succeed in making the transition. However, it is clear that the shift to achievement is an unavoidable prerequisite for the transition to modernity. At the very least, the older, traditional, aristocratic elite must be replaced by a new ruling elite whose rise is dependent upon and coincides with the creation of a relatively open stratification system. The change is not necessarily democratic, but I shall discuss that matter later.

Until now I have described stratification only as a socially divisive force, a force that separates groups or classes from each other and marks them by differential power, prestige, opportunity, and status. This view of stratification is only half of the picture. If stratification served only a divisive function, how could we explain its universality? Clearly, stratification must also serve as a cohesive social force; otherwise, all societies would be doomed to destruction.

The cohesive element in stratification derives primarily from the social values upon which it depends. In other words, the stratified inequalities that mark all societies are extensions of the societies' core beliefs. Those inequalities, generally, are accepted and justified within the institutional structure of every society. This does not mean that the divisions are accepted by all members or that they are even fair by a given standard. Such potential discontent can be organized into a force for social change; but even so, the change in stratification itself becomes justified by new values.

For example, we believe that Americans who have been trained and educated to qualify for the better occupations deserve the rewards of money and prestige that go with those positions. We generally accept inequalities of this kind as justified and even as fair. In that way, all persons involved in the situation willingly accept their relative positions—those in the lower strata as well as those in the higher strata. Such mutual understandings break down when the arrangement is challenged; for example, as in the case of Negroes today who refuse to accept the inferior position that generally has been allotted them.

The matter is, of course, much more complex than it would seem to be from my description of it. These are not explicitly rational arrangements or even conscious ones. The values and beliefs that I have discussed are seriously and intensely accepted, at least while the values and beliefs are current. Is there any doubt, for example, that a good many Americans accept the class divisions that we have even though these Americans may be unaware of the consequences of class divisions? Is there any doubt that the Southern segregationist intensely believes that the system he is trying to defend and preserve is ordained?

In sum, then, stratification can mean both divisiveness and cohesion. Over a period of time it is possible to observe both forces in operation. I shall describe, later, just how those forces operate and how they affect the structure of societies. But, now, it is necessary to consider some of the major theoretical expositions concerning stratification so that we may have guidelines to evaluate stratification's force.

## Theories of Stratification

There are no unequivocal answers to the questions that have been raised. Instead, there are alternative explanations, each of which brings its own form of order to the complexity of social stratification. These explanations share in common only the acceptance of the ubiquity of stratification and its intimate relation to the core values of society. They differ, however, and sharply so, in what they make of those assumptions.

I call attention to the macrosocial theories that consider stratification an important part of a large social canvas, as exemplified by the writings of Marx, Weber, Parsons, and a very few others. An analysis of these theories serves two important purposes. First, it highlights the relationships between stratification and social structure. In this connection, we must note particularly the ideologies that are expressed more or less explicitly, because stratification is a subject that affects political and social ideologies. Second, an analysis of macrosocial theories provides a basis for evaluating the empirical studies of other aspects of stratification. For example, without a theoretical background, it would be meaningless to consider the numerous studies of occupational prestige, since we would not understand the context in which they belong.

There are, essentially, four distinct theories that can be considered, and each one is identified with a principal author. These four doctrines include most, if not all, of the broad-scale analysis of the subject. The theories that are not included here can easily be encompassed in one of the four that are included. In this way we have before us the widest range of theories of stratification—theories that comment on all of stratification's major features and consequences.

### Marx: Economic Determinism

Usually the work of great social theorists cannot be easily summarized because it follows so many different lines and is so rich in its implications. This generalization is especially applicable to Marx. His work is further complicated because he was as much a politician as a social theorist. As a result, some of his ideas share both political and social motives and, thus, become inseparable. This should not cause any undue intellectual discomfort. However, insofar as is possible, we shall deal with his social theory rather than his politics.

Marx's theory of class dominates all of his work. His views of history, of social process, of economic growth, and of political development are all hinged on the concept of class as an inescapable feature of all societies. The logic of his argument can be conveyed rather simply, even though some of the subtleties will be lost. Marx assumed that all societies were basically an organized means for human survival. This view is generally accepted by social scientists, even today, but Marx insisted on the narrower meaning of biological rather than social survival. The premise that man must live in order for society to exist is a gratuitous assumption that is self-evident but uninformative. It adds nothing to our understanding of social organization or social process. Marx obviously understood this. Consequently, he moved quickly beyond the biological assumption, but not before he had established the primacy of the economic institutions as the means by which societies meet those human biological requirements. Economics, therefore, is designated as the determining cause for all other social factors. In one way or another, all else in society is a reflection of economic organization and of the social relationships that it commands.

In Marx's terms, economic organization was "the system of production," which happens to include much more than just the means for satisfying some indisputable biological needs. For Marx, this was the social core of the whole social structure and of the social dynamics that drive it. The system of production includes at least four distinct elements.

1. It includes the means to satisfy human wants. At minimum, this means bare subsistence, but it also covers the full spectrum of wants that are met by the economy.

2. It includes all the necessary institutional procedures needed to fulfill those wants in an organized manner. This means, even at a bare minimum, some method of exchange, a consensus as to legitimate procedures, an agreement on some standard of economic value, and forms of contractual obligation and the means to satisfy them. In short, these things are in-

cluded in the body of accepted rules by which any economic organization in society is able to function and to continue.

3. It includes the goals of production. In other words, the productive process operates in terms of the values that give meaning to production and make it a more or less desirable activity. Production may be for subsistence, for profit, and even for salvation as in the Calvinist ethical system.

4. Finally, it includes the whole set of interpersonal relationships that are required by the productive system such as producers, consumers, managers, and the full range of specialized roles that are required by modern production. Not only are such roles created, but the relationships between them are set by the nature of the productive mechanisms. It was these relationships that, for Marx, determined the character of a society; under capitalism, the creation of a bourgeoisie and a proletariat; under feudalism, the creation of lord and serf; and in antiquity, the creation of slaveowner and slave.

This last feature of the system of production brings us to the core of Marx's view of stratification. Here is where the stratification system originates, spreading out to color and affect all other social relationships. The individual's class position, then, is the most basic social category that the individual occupies. It is the primary determinant that finally controls what he thinks, what he does, and who he is. He cannot escape, since class determines the socialization of the individual and sets the perspectives from which he sees his society and his place in it. Class, therefore, is not simply a methodological fiction. Class is the primary social category that determines everything for the individual and, by extension, for all of society.

This is a theory of economic determinism. At one level, the individual is controlled by his class position. At a second level, the factors that create classes are also determined by the massive forces of history which evolve to alter and to shape the destinies of society. These are not mystical forces but, instead, are the direct consequences of the tensions created between the classes by any given system of production. Within every system are found the seeds for its own eventual destruction and for the creation of new classes and new relationships. Each new change marks a new historical era from which stratification systems evolve. These new strata or classes, in turn, reorganize the sets of social relationships within society.

For Marx, stratification meant classes. Classes are the inevitable results (as we have seen) of the productive system, appearing generally as a division between the people who own the means of production and the people who do not. In the feudal era, for example, the nobility monopolized the ownership of land, which was the central economic component of that particular system of production. Since land was in limited supply, the monopoly of ownership could be effective and could be limited to a relatively small elite. The feudal serf, on the other hand, owned nothing. In the next era of capitalism, the bourgeoisie owned the means of production, which were now factories and other forms of capital as well as land. The proletariat, by contrast, owned only its labor power. Ownership, then, is one principal dimension of class. The other dimension is the degree of personal freedom allowed during each historical system. The reason for adding this second criterion of class was to separate the several classes that had appeared throughout history. Marx wanted to bring the full force of history to support his predictions for the changes that were to follow capitalism. The slave, at one extreme, and the proletariat at the other—both of them nonowners—had different degrees of freedom. The slave was a form of property, to be bought, sold, or otherwise disposed of by the slaveowner. The proletarian, on the other hand, is not property. He is, at least, free to sell or to withhold his labor, which represents his sole economic asset under capitalism. Even though Marx believed that such freedom was only a relatively slight advance over the position of the slave or the serf, he believed that it was enough to establish the possibility for the proletariat to organize its dissatisfactions into revolutionary action.

To Marx, classes were part of a dynamic historical process. At this point, Marx the theorist merged with Marx the politician, for he was not content simply to describe the characteristics of classes. Instead, he wanted to stress tensions whereby classes were inevitably pitted against one another in an evolutionary process by which each historical period dialectically forged a new synthesis from the class struggles of the preceding historical era. Hence, under capitalism, the very social forces by which the bourgeoisie gained their ascendancy over the feudal nobility would, in turn, assure the ascendancy of the proletariat over the bourgeoisie in the next period. Let us consider more closely this phase of stratification in industrial society.

Marx contended that the bourgeoisie successfully led the countries of Western Europe out of feudalism and into industrial capitalism. The United States might also be included, even though it entered history after feudalism had waned. The bourgeoisie gained control over the new means of production and sources of wealth, while an industrial technology replaced land as the major source of economic power. By virtue of revolution in France, by means of civil war in the United States, and by acquisition in England, the bourgeoisie gained economic power and became the leaders of the societies. Landed aristocrats in each country were replaced by merchants and capitalists who became the ruling class. Economic superiority, in turn, led to political superiority, as groups organized for their own interests. The bourgeoisie, to be successful, had to enlist the support of the masses—the proletariat—and this was accomplished in part by promoting an ideology of political democracy. This ideology not only gained support from the proletariat but, at the same time, justified the actions of the bourgeoisie and released the bourgeoisie from an earlier aristocratic domination. In this way, the bourgeoisie could win the freedom necessary to conduct their own affairs with a high degree of rationality and predictability. The result was an age of liberalism and unequalled political freedom. Even so, Marx contended, the aims of the bourgeoisie were clear; the destiny of this class was set. Its destiny was to use this freedom to amass and concentrate power in its own hands.

Below the bourgeoisie there existed a middle-class stratum, which included the professions, the small entrepreneurs, and independent farmers. Marx believed that this class was doomed eventually because it could not compete successfully with the superior power of the bourgeoisie. Hence, entrepreneurs and farmers would be pushed out of the middle class into the proletariat as they lost out to the bourgeois elite. Similarly, professional persons would become merely the employees of large enterprises, as the independent and free professionals were forced to disappear. These developments had to occur because the economic dynamics of capitalism must lead to economic concentration and monopolization. Competition finally would destroy the weak, in society as in nature.

At the bottom of the stratification hierarchy were the proletariat, numerically the largest class. This group was identified by Marx as the source that would supply political leadership for the next historical phase. In time, the size of this class could only increase, swollen by the unwilling additions from the former middle class as from the former bourgeoisie who had lost out in the competitive struggle. Marx believed that it is an inherent feature of capitalism for a successful few to monopolize and to restrict their numbers. Capitalism as an economic system is especially attuned to maximizing efficiency, to destructive competition, and to a narrowing monopolization over the means of production—all carried out under the banner of free enterprise and the profit motive. The inevitable result of that process would be a society eventually divided into two opposing classes: a small, bourgeois elite who had finally replaced the earlier feudal aristocracy; and the massively large proletariat who were then not much better off than the serfs of the previous epoch.

These two classes are in tension, committed to playing out the roles destined for them by history. The bourgeoisie would be dedicated to seek more and more power at the expense of the proletariat. The proletariat, in its turn, would be forced to face the sharpening inconsistency of its position under capitalism. The proletariat's material condition would worsen.

Furthermore, it would begin to realize that the freedom it had been led to expect was not achieved, as the bourgeoisie monopolized all effective power in society. At first, each person in the proletariat might believe that his inferior position resulted only from personal failure. Later, however, each person would come to realize that the failure was not his own but was society's. At that time, the proletariat would mature into its historic role of revolutionary agent. A third smaller class, the *lumpenproletariat,* played no revolutionary role. It contained the social refuse created by capitalism: drug addicts, habitual criminals, and other social marginals.

The bourgeoisie are powerless to halt this inexorable historical dialectic. They may slow it down temporarily by social welfare measures, but they cannot stop it short of conceding total defeat. In the meantime, the proletariat, led by the intellectuals from the former middle class, gains consciousness of its own strength as a class and of its true destiny. The revolutionary situation is thus produced and society passes into the next historical phase of socialism. After that, classes, as we have known them before, disappear.

Marx moved from the role of social analyst to political organizer, especially in his description of the revolutionary role of the proletariat. Weber, as I shall soon indicate, saw many flaws in that description. Marx seemed to lose his keen analytical insights whenever he projected beyond capitalism and into socialism, thereby committing the inescapable errors of all Utopian thinkers.

Nevertheless, it would be naive to dismiss all of Marx's analysis for that reason. First, any macrosocial analysis of stratification carries with it political overtones of one form or another. As I have already pointed out, the subject of stratification is the study of inequality and of power, both of which terms have inescapable political consequences. Second, Marx's analysis of industrial capitalism was, for his time, brilliant and insightful. Parts of his analysis have worn very well during the past century, including his analysis of monopoly capitalism and the intimate link between political and economic power. Finally, there is merit to Marx's formulation for subsequent stratification analysis. The enormously important role that he assigned to economic causes in industrial society is still valid. It is true, as Weber was to point out, that Marx did not distinguish between the economically *necessary* and the economically *important,* but the power of Marx's analysis still endures. In this connection, notice that much of the recent research on stratification continues to support Marx's contention that class determines a good deal about behavior, attitudes, and values that people hold. However, we must consider briefly the validity of Marx's formulations in the light of current developments.

As previously indicated, Marx's description of social change and its effects on the stratification system stand the test quite well for societies moving into the first phases of industrialization. For example, with some adjustments, Marx's theory provides a fairly accurate framework for considering the development process in the new nations. For mature industrial societies, on the other hand, Marx's theory of stratification, his theory of the class struggle, and his theory of the revolutionary role of the proletariat fall short. The main reason is that capitalism itself has changed since Marx's time. Although we use the same old terms—private property, free enterprise, and even capitalism itself—these terms no longer mean the same things. They have grown to mean something quite different in the past few decades. The greater economic role of government, the rise of the corporation, and the development of labor unions have all served to shift and to alter the relationships that Marx described. We are now living in what Bazelon called "the paper economy," with all of the changes created by that kind of economic shift.[3]

In this period of postcapitalism, in most of the West, the factors that once contributed to the class struggle have been attenuated at the very least and, more probably, have been critically altered. Class differences continue, but not in the monolithic manner that Marx described. They have become tempered into more subtle forms than was the case in 1848 when Marx wrote *The Communist Manifesto*. One of the most concise summaries of these changes and alterations was given by Dahrendorf, and it deserves almost full quotation here.

Thus, what has happened since Marx are in fact changes in the factors that contributed to the intensity and violence of the conflicts of his time. Patterns of conflict regulation emerged in both industry and the state. More and more, the democratic process of decision-making gave both parties a chance to realize their goals. The violence of class conflict was thereby effectively reduced. The institutionalization of social mobility made for a certain degree of openness in both classes. Absolute deprivation on the scales of social stratification gave way, for the proletariat, to relative deprivation, and later, for some, to comparative gratification. Finally, the associations of industry and the state were disassociated to some extent. All these changes served to reduce both the intensity and the violence of class conflict in post-capitalist society, and to make sudden and radical structure changes increasingly improbable.[4]

No one but a politically doctrinaire Marxist would insist upon adhering today to a literal acceptance of Marx's formulations. Even Marx, who once declared that he was not himself a Marxist, probably would agree to signif-

---

[3] For an exciting and imaginative analysis of these changes see David T. Bazelon, *The Paper Economy* (New York: Vintage Books, 1965).

[4] Ralf Dahrendorf, *Class and Class Conflict in Industrial Society* (Stanford: Stanford University Press, 1959), p. 245.

icant alterations of his theory in the light of developments over the past century. I am speaking here of Marx the social theorist rather than of Marx the political tactician.

With respect to our immediate interest in social stratification, attention is called to the following points.

1. As Dahrendorf indicated, the scenes of violence whereby two classes were pitted one against the other have generally disappeared in the advanced nations. Instead of violence, we find conflict, which is controlled, institutionalized, and carried out according to rules accepted by all participants.

2. Society has not been polarized into two classes, except by some absolutely gross generalization. Instead, we see the proliferation of the middle class rather than its disappearance into the proletariat. As much as anything, this has been the result of technological developments and the consequent dependence upon a whole spectrum of technical specialists and professionals to staff the new technology.

3. Living standards have improved for a good many people, although certainly not for everyone even in developed societies, as the preamble to the Economic Opportunities Act recognized. For this we must credit the expanded role of government rather than the gains in economic productivity alone. No matter how vehemently anti-Keynesian modern corporation presidents and chairmen of the boards may proclaim themselves to be, it is evident that increased government expenditures have accounted for the major economic and social gains of advanced nations. Government, not business, has created and nurtured the new middle class in advanced nations, and thereby has set some of the tone for modern class relationships.

To what extent, then, was Marx correct? If we interpret him sympathetically, he was correct in the high priority that he assigned to class as a determinant of behavior. As we shall see later, a person's class position probably tells us more about the person than any other single fact. Consequently, if Marx contributed nothing else, his identification of the pivotal role of class in urban industrial societies is a major contribution to the analysis of stratification systems.

### Weber: Class, Status, and Party

Max Weber (1864–1920), a German sociologist whose contributions to sociological theory are unmatched, effectively modified Marx's theory of stratification and thus fashioned his own unique contribution to the subject. Weber did not object so much to Marx's political analysis of capitalism —part of which Weber shared—but he understood where Marx's political analysis was incomplete as a result of Marx having weakened his analytical posture in favor of a political stance. Hence, Marx's description of the proletariat's rise to power failed to recognize social and political realities. As Weber pointed out, a social movement of such scope does not automatically develop, and certainly not because of a mystical historical need. Organization and leadership are required to convert the proletariat into a class-conscious and revolutionary force.

However, these political aspects are not of primary interest here. Instead, we need to notice carefully the modifications that Weber introduced into Marx's theory of class, as well as his own additions.

Weber began with the situation that Marx identified: social stratification is an organized manifestation of unequal power in society. Although this generalization is universal, Weber (like Marx) focused his interest on industrial societies and capitalism in particular.[5] Power, for Weber, referred principally to institutionalized power; that is, to the effective control over human actions that can be exerted in a legitimate and regular manner. This eliminates from the discussion any illegal force such as a criminal action and piracy, or any abuse of power through overstepping the institutional boundaries.

Institutionally based power can be separated, for analytical purposes, into three spheres of activity: economic, social, and political, and within each sphere power is designated according to class, status, and party. Weber then analyzed the characteristics of power in each sphere as a basis for describing the system of stratification. This kind of analysis was not simply another static classification. Weber, like Marx, considered the tensions between these spheres. This feature of Weber's theory will be considered after we have examined the three analytical units.

1. In Weber's analysis, power in the economic sphere was stratified by a system of classes. All people with similar economic interests and with similar economic power belonged to the same class. This definition was very close to Marx's, and posed the same difficulty of making the definition operational. But let us overlook that aspect. Weber expanded Marx's conception so that stratification consisted of more than two antagonistic economic classes. A number of classes can emerge in the market-place and, furthermore, the economic antagonisms between them are not fatal.

Weber did not accept Marx's simplification of two classes divided into those people who owned the means of production and those people who did

---

[5] One of the best brief comparisons in English is that by N. Birnbaum, "Conflicting Interpretations of the Rise of Capitalism: Marx and Weber," *British Journal of Sociology*, 4, 125–141 (June, 1953). For a good intellectual history of Weber and his period, see H. Stuart Hughes, *Consciousness and Society* (New York: Knopf, 1958).

not. Instead, Weber specified in economic terms the means by which economic power could be gained. For instance, ownership can result in monopoly or control over the sale of economic goods as well as their manufacture. This kind of ownership becomes a form of economic power. Also, ownership can lead to the accumulation of property. Generally, this is what Marx meant when he predicted the trend toward monopolization by the bourgeoisie. Finally, ownership can also mean the ability to take advantage of education to increase one's economic and social standing. Ideally, each of these aspects could be ranked in terms of the power that each conferred, and the class structure of a society could be thus determined.

Actually, of course, these relationships are complex and subtle. But, in analytical terms, Weber's formulation is reasonable and logically consistent. Clearly, economic power is unequally distributed, especially in industrial economies. This kind of power tends to be concentrated in some groups more than in others. Weber's ideas should be taken as guidelines to help determine the power differences rather than as statements of the method to be used. No one doubts, for example, that the managers of large economic corporations command greater economic power than, say, middle-class professionals or factory workers. To be sure, even professionals and workers can exercise power through professional organizations and unions. However, the frequency, regularity, and range of professional organizations and unions cannot compare with the economic effectiveness of the managers of large corporations.

Weber was more pessimistic than Marx concerning the probability of a proletarian triumph over the bourgeoisie. Marx had assumed that the arena of the market place could engender the necessary consensus, consciousness, and organization for a social movement; Weber, on the contrary, contended that it could not. The market place was a social arena characterized by transitory alliances that were dissolved once the immediate economic goal was attained. Economic norms of behavior exist, of course, but they constitute only a set of minimal rules that are insufficient to bind individuals into an effective social group. Classes may find a basis for common action, but not on economic grounds alone. Marx's error, in effect, was to assume that economic forces would more or less automatically be translated into social forces.

2. The second arena of power is social. Weber used the term "status" to mark off by differences the strata in this sphere. All persons who are accorded the same estimations of social honor or prestige and who live according to similar standards generally belong within the same status group. By this definition a person's power in the social sphere derives from the amount and the extent of prestige that he receives from others. Status, unlike class, depends upon a community, since prestige depends upon the judgment made by others. In effect, the individual gains his social power

from other people. Whereas class is a form of impersonal economic place-ment, status is tied to personal evaluations.

Status is judged by standards that are accepted in the community. Usu-ally these norms are realized by some estimate of life styles, of the patterns of taste and consumption. Additionally, levels of education, kinship, and occupation are frequently used as a basis for evaluating the status of per-sons within the community. These several judgments are combined by means of a social arithmetic to arrive at the total status position of the in-dividual. Notice, particularly, that there is wide consensus concerning these judgments as part of the normative structure of the community.

It is clear that part of the status evaluation depends upon economic criteria. Obviously, a standard of living depends upon money and educated tastes. But there are analytical advantages in keeping class and status dis-tinct, since the discrepancy between them can be informative. For example, the *nouveau riche* are those who have become recently wealthy but whose aspirations for high status are not immediately realized. On the other hand, there are the high-status elite who may lack money or economic power, as in the case of faded aristocrats. In other words, although status may depend upon economics, the two dimensions really measure different facets of stratification.

The critical difference between class and status, as Weber defined them, was that status but not class must be set within a community. Status evalua-tions require community consensus as to the standards that are to be used. Most important, status power can derive only from the respect and honor that others are willing to give. Therefore, status has a highly personal quality, quite unlike the impersonal and rational quality that determines classes. In the economic market place, one may never know one's opponents; in the status community, such knowledge is unavoidable.

3. Political power was the last of the three dimensions that Weber identi-fied. He developed this aspect of stratified power least, and it serves mainly as a residual category, including the dimensions of power that do not be-long to either the economic or the social spheres. This intention seems to be implied in Weber's description that position in the political order was to be interpreted as the degree of power the individual could exert to in-fluence "a communal action no matter what its content may be."[6] Gen-erally, political power would be exerted through some form of organized political group. This kind of power is institutionalized and, like status, de-pends upon the existence of a community.

Political power may well reflect social and economic power. In fact, there is a clear tendency for individuals to convert their power in one

---

[6] H. H. Gerth and C. W. Mills, *From Max Weber: Essays in Sociology* (New York: Oxford University Press, 1946), p. 194.

sphere into commensurate power in the other spheres. Men of wealth seek both status and political power. Those in high-status positions seek to exert political influence, and politicians too are interested in status and economic power.

Yet, there are advantages to the analytical separation between these three spheres. As an illustration, let us consider a case where the three spheres exist in tension. During the period of early capitalism, each of the three power spheres was located in a separate sector of the population. The descendants of the earlier feudal aristocracy managed to maintain their status power. In a society in transition when all other traditions were pushed aside, the traditionalism of status seemed to remain. Economic power was concentrated in the new bourgeoisie who had acquired ownership of the new means of production in Marx's terms. Political power was less localized, being shared in some measure between the older aristocracy and the new claimants to power. In the United States, however, political power was concentrated in a group of professional politicians, who monopolized this sector of power. In the transition from feudalism to capitalism, then, power was broken down into its separate components and scattered among different sectors of the population.

As capitalism developed, this separation of power created tensions. For instance, the differentiated institutional areas tended to move closer together; business could not be conducted free of government regulation, and government became a major agent in the economic arena. Therefore, the economic elites had to work more closely with the political elites. Moreover, individuals sought to translate their position in one power hierarchy to a comparable position in another power hierarchy. Hence, the economic and political elites sought to realize a comparable standing in the status hierarchy. In this way, a trend was established toward a merger of the three elite groups.

Later, I shall assess the validity of this description. My purpose here has been to illustrate the richness of Weber's categories compared with Marx's by applying both of them to the same historical situation. I might also point out that this kind of presentation is especially relevant for the analysis of stratification changes in the newly emerging nations as older traditional elites are pushed aside by a new, middle-class, nationalistic leadership. This matter, too, I reserve for a later discussion.

### Warner: Status Reputation

W. Lloyd Warner and his colleagues should be credited with causing American sociologists to take a renewed interest in the subject of stratification. His well-known community study of Yankee City, the first volume of which appeared in 1949, started a sustained interest in stratification, although subsequent research went far beyond Warner's earlier formulations as knowledge developed.

Warner did not mention Weber, but he amplified Weber's status dimension to the general exclusion of the other two dimensions of stratification. Warner's emphasis upon status rather than upon economic classes seemed to strike a responsive chord among American sociologists. His approach was strongly empirical—a clear advantage over other theories of stratification. As Warner described it, his ideas were developed in the field while studying Yankee City; thus it is hard to say whether his theory or his method came first. In any case, his use of income, occupational prestige, and education as the primary measures of status have clear empirical referents. Status, for Warner, was nothing more than a summation of those measures that matched the evaluations made by his respondents.

Another reason for Warner's popularity was that his point of view seemed to fit so well the American scene. His view contained an explanation that reflected our self-image. A person's status depended upon his reputation in his community and upon the judgments made about him by others. In effect, social classes were what the people in a community said they were. This strikes me as being an American attitude; it is democratically located in community consensus.

Warner was concerned with status rather than with class (using those terms as I have been using them here). In fact, his definition is very close to what Weber construed as status. "By class," according to Warner, "is meant two or more orders of people who are believed to be, and are accordingly ranked by the members of the community, in socially superior and inferior positions." [7] The ranking depended upon such criteria as income, source of income, education, occupation, residence, and associates. The residents of a community work out the sum of these several measures by means of an accepted social arithmetic and thus are able to locate everyone in the social hierarchy. In Yankee City and elsewhere, Warner found that the hierarchy was composed of six classes, ranging from the "upper-upper" class to the "lower-lower" class. He claimed that these six classes were real social categories, not simply the results of his own fabrication. The task of the sociologist, therefore, became one of discovering the categories that people used rather than inventing theories of stratification.

Warner described the class categories very much in the terms that

[7] W. Lloyd Warner and Paul S. Lunt, *The Social Life of a Modern Community* (New Haven: Yale University Press, 1941), p. 82.

Yankee City residents would use. The old-time aristocratic residents of Yankee City belonged to the highest class: the upper-upper. The level immediately below—the lower-upper class—included mainly those persons who lacked the aristocratic background but who did have sufficient wealth to qualify. The middle classes were also divided into an upper segment of the well-to-do and independent professionals, and a lower segment of people with less income who worked in clerical and white-collar jobs. The lowest strata included the outcasts at the very bottom and the poor-but-honest people immediately above them. These social categories provided the basis for clique memberships, friendships, voluntary associations, and leisure activities. Hence, upper-class organizations only accepted bona fide "upper-uppers" as members, and other organizations drew their memberships from different class levels. Social stratification thus served not simply as a means for social placement, but as an intervening consideration that extended into all sectors of community life. This description may sound similar to Marx's ideas about the primacy of class, but it really is not. Whereas Marx emphasized the impersonal and objective operation of the stratification system, Warner emphasized the highly personal and subjective elements upon which status really depended.

A number of criticisms of Warner's ideas have centered upon his vague definition of class and upon the errors that he committed in determining classes. Warner contended that class is only what people say it is. But this view is not valid, according to his critics. After all, people can be mistaken because of their own biases or because they are insensitive to class or status differences. Whom are we to believe in cases where sharp discrepancies arise between several informants? Furthermore, if we accept Warner's methods, then we are clearly limited to the study of relatively small communities in which there is a reasonable chance that people know one another fairly well. What are we to do about large cities or the nation? Warner suggested that the national system of social stratification was a summation of all of the smaller community systems, but this assumption cannot be supported in theory or in fact.

Warner's views of stratification moved far away from the broad theories of both Marx and Weber, and also departed from the theories of the functionalists, described in the next section. From the wide perspective of industrial societies, we have been brought to a very narrow community level by Warner's formulation. Instead of the precept that classes exist in a state of tension, which ignites changes, Warner has advanced the view of status groups living together in relative harmony. Instead of a viewpoint of massive social forces engendering class frictions, Warner has substituted the principle of simple personal evaluations.

Yet, there is a certain attraction exerted by Warner's descriptions because they seem to fit our own experience so closely. We can see the differences that Warner described: differences in housing, in the levels of consumption, and in the memberships of exclusive and nonexclusive organizations. But personal experiences and impressions are not enough. We may not "see" either Marx's proletariat or Weber's economic classes, but that does not mean they do not exist. Indeed, to explain the dynamics of stratification and the consequences that they produce, it is necessary to go beyond the sensory level at which Warner stopped, and predicate the more abstract forces and conditions that Marx and Weber hypothesized.

## *Parsons: A Functional Theory*

The fourth and last theory to be considered moves in a direction that is different from the others. No matter how these theories varied, Marx, Weber, and Warner shared an interest in specific, historical stratification systems. The functionalists, however, have moved toward an abstract analysis to develop a theory with universal applicability. This deliberate aim gives the functional theory of stratification an airy quality. It is a theory occupied with definitions and categories that are deliberately designed to apply to all societies—primitive and advanced—and therefore are phrased in general and abstract terms.

Like Marx, the functionalists contend that stratification is a social necessity, but they elaborate this initial assumption quite differently. The functionalists argue that because stratification is found in all societies, it must serve some function vital for social organization. The basis for stratification arises from the need of all societies to develop a division of labor. Even in the most primitive societies not every person does the same thing. Hence, there must be some procedure for allocating different duties and responsibilities.

Once the existence of this social division of labor is recognized, it follows logically that not all of the social activities that are performed are of equal worth or importance, even though all may be necessary. Every society must apply its own standard so that the differences in social activities can be ranked according to the value that each type of activity contributes to the total society. In this way, a system of stratification is developed which is tied directly to the central values of a society because those values provide the standard by which activities are evaluated.

What is it that is ranked? An inadequate answer is that people are ranked—people are evaluated by what they do. But this answer is too general, and Parsons has devoted much attention to specifying the categories of stratification. He has argued that there are three characteristics that are evaluated according to the central or core values of any society:

1. Qualities, which are ascribed to individuals as independent characteristics; for example, lineage or competence.
2. Performances, which are judgments of the activities of individuals relative to the activities of others; for example, in the comparison of occupational differences.
3. Possessions, which are evaluations of the objects that people own or possess, including material goods as well as talent and skill.

These three categories specify what is being evaluated, but they do not indicate just how the evaluation is made. As already stated, the evaluation of these categories is made in terms of the central value standards of a society. Now, we could describe the values that are held in a number of societies in a substantive manner. For instance, religiously oriented societies would prize those activities associated with religion; and the qualities, performances, and possessions of individuals would be appraised in a religious context. Or the main values of American society could be designated as centering on economic competition, and the system of evaluation would be tied to that value or one similar to it. Parsons searched, instead, for a more general classification of central-value patterns as a means of getting away from the substantive content of society values that would vary from one society to another.

To accomplish that goal, Parsons identified four categories of value patterns. Each category has basic features that are characteristic of all societies. The categories correspond to four functional problems that all societies encounter and that must be resolved in some way if societies are to continue. The following description of Parsons' ideas is an abbreviated one because Parsons has devoted a major part of his work to those ideas and to their application to a variety of social aspects.[8]

1. *Adaptation* emphasizes the need of a social system to adjust to the inflexible demands forced on it by reality and, if possible, to master those demands and to control them. The physical environment, for example, imposes a number of these demands that societies must resolve in a regular and organized manner if they are to survive.

2. *Goal attainment* refers to the need of a social system to compel

[8] This description is taken from Talcott Parsons et al., *Working Papers in the Theory of Action* (New York: The Free Press of Glencoe, 1953), Chapter V; also from his essay, "A Revised Analytical Approach to the Theory of Social Stratification," R. Bendix and S. M. Lipset, eds., in *Class, Status, and Power* (New York: The Free Press of Glencoe, 1953).

individuals to restrain any premature gratifications in favor of the final collective goals of the society, whatever the goals may be.

3. *Integration* stresses the need of a society to maintain solidarity so that individuals, social institutions, or other social units are related to each other in a way that reinforces the unity of the total system.

4. *Pattern maintenance* also contributes toward solidarity, but it accomplishes this by maintaining and renewing the cultural patterns that are integral to the system.

Each value pattern tends to elicit or emphasize an appropriate type of activity and motivation. Adaptation, for example, emphasizes an instrumental kind of activity by which individuals seek to manipulate objects. The judgments that are involved are universalistic; "that is, cognizant of the characteristics of the object in relation to other objects or as a member of a class of objects with predictable characteristics." Furthermore, the attitude behind the activity is marked by a specificity of interest in the particular relationships between the object and a given goal. Finally, the attitude is also marked by a tone of affective neutrality rather than by emotional involvement. In a general way, adaptation stresses scientific attitude that typically is characterized by neutrality, specificity, and universalism in Parsons' meaning of that term.

Goal attainment—to illustrate another pattern variable—tends to elicit activity that is also marked by a specificity of interest in the relationship between object and goal. However, goal attainment differs from adaptation in that the attitude is not a neutral one but is suffused with affect. "Similarly, the relation to the object no longer tends to be universalistic, concerned with realistic prediction of later effects or relation to other objects. It gives way to a relation of *particularism* where the object is a goal object, to be possessed, consumed, enjoyed, or appreciated, and its particular relation to the ego is the important thing." Along similar lines, Parsons has described the activities and attitudes appropriate to the remaining two value patterns as well.

Because these patterns are basic, each one can be found in all societies. However, each society tends to emphasize one or another of these patterns in a different sequence of priority, depending in large measure upon the differentiation that is made between institutions. In other words, as societies develop and become more complex, they begin to differentiate between the several social institutions. America and other complex societies accept the separation between (for instance) the economic and the family institutions, but underdeveloped societies do not.

The important point here is that different societies present different profiles of these four value patterns. For example, American society generally stresses adaptation with consequently lesser emphasis upon the other value patterns. We tend to attach greater importance to those activities that maximize control over the inflexible demands of reality; that is, science and associated activities. Underdeveloped societies, on the contrary, are typified by their emphasis upon integration and pattern maintenance in order to maintain their traditional solidarity.

Once the sequence of value patterns has been determined for any particular society, it is logically possible to predict the form and the character of its stratification system. This determination is accomplished by tracing out the different evaluations of performances, qualities, and possessions that are appropriate for each of the four value patterns. For example, in the case of ·adaptation, performances are evaluated in terms of technical efficiency; qualities are evaluated in terms of individual competence; and possessions are evaluated by the ability of the individual to adapt his performance to the norm of efficiency. Similar consequences are developed for each of the remaining categories of value patterns: goal attainment, integration, and pattern maintenance. The result is not only a detailed classification but, more important, an analytical rule that explains the relationship between stratification and other features of the social system. In other words, if adaptation is indeed a dominant value pattern during some phase of society's development, then the emphasis upon efficiency and competence is a necessary consequence; so, too, is the higher prestige and status given to the persons who exhibit efficiency and competence.

The principal basis for this classification is the set of central or core values of a society. These values, according to the functional theory, give form and purpose to the system of stratification. Unlike Marx who assumed that economic factors alone were important, the functionalists seek to broaden the limits for the kinds of values that determine the system of stratification. Evaluation, in other words, must be made in accordance with a standard of functional importance that is more complex than economics alone. These evaluations are then translated into stratification hierarchies so that social positions are ranked by their contribution to the functions considered vital by each society.

This approach to the analysis of stratification has been criticized. Some critics argue that the functional view is essentially too static; that it describes, at best, a system that exists without any indication of how or why the system might change. Indeed, the functional theory does not account for the changes that may take place, although it recognizes that change occurs. Over a period of time, a society will shift from one value hierarchy to another, but the theory does not explain the sequence. At best, the functionalist can only recategorize a society after the change had occurred.

For example, India is in a process of social change, generally moving from a traditionally based caste system into some other form. The functional theory provides no explanation for the change; it only provides for a shift in classification for India from one category to another.

Other critics claim that it is impossible to test the validity of the functional classification and its supporting logic. Parsons, as well as Davis and Moore, who have also written on this subject, conclude with an *ad hoc* description of stratification which sounds plausible enough; but they indicate no way by which the sequence of cause and effect that they have set forth can be tested. For example, Parsons concedes that it is impossible to determine the central value patterns of a society in an independent manner. Instead, we must first determine the relative evaluations made of possessions, qualities, and performances to ascertain which value pattern was paramount. This procedure is the exact opposite of the logic of his classification. Similarly, Davis and Moore concluded that social activities that are highly valued must reflect the central values of a society. This is not very different from saying that societies stratify in the way that they do because that is how they stratify. The argument that patterns of stratification express the basic values of society still remains an untested assumption of functional theory. Yet, it is the very assumption upon which the functional argument rests. This line of argument is an example of "circular reasoning" by which the effect proves the cause, in practice; the cause, in turn, is used to predict the effect, in theory.

## Stratification and Social Structure

The previous discussion has centered exclusively on ideas, concepts, and definitions of social stratification. Now we shift from those abstractions to more substantive matters.

The best way to describe societies is to apply the theoretical background that we have been discussing to actual events. I have selected for that purpose three extremely different societies: the United States, England, and India. A distinguishing feature of the United States is that equality, not stratification, has been a dominant value since the country was founded. Yet, it is evident from the theory of stratification that some kind of social hierarchy must exist in American society. India, at the other extreme, is a country that has maintained a rigid and wondrously complex stratification system for centuries. The caste system extends into every corner of social life and, in theory, determines practically everything that an individual does, or can do, in Indian society. England exhibits some of the characteristics of the other two countries. It has sustained a castelike aristocracy that cuts through British society with an inescapable division of the population. At the same time, much of that situation has been tempered by an insistence upon equality that matches the American situation.

These three examples, therefore, can provide us with an empirical coverage of stratification and social structure. Our treatment of the subject is similar to the one we used in analyzing the four theories of social stratification. It is not complete but it will give us a sense of perspective.

### The United States

Seymour M. Lipset, in the introduction to his study of the United States as *The First New Nation*,[9] noted that two opposing pictures have been drawn of American society in recent years. One view emphasizes the concentration of economic power, the leveling of tastes and opinions effected by the mass media, and the enormous expenditures for enhancing social status. The other view depicts a society marked by affluence, political democracy, equal opportunities, and tolerance.

We can usefully borrow this theme as the basis for describing social stratification, in all of its facets, in America. On all key aspects of social stratification in the United States there is, among social analysts, a recurrent theme of difference and contrast. The source of those differences is in the interpretation given to a particular set of facts about American society. The question is not one of deciding between valid and invalid data, since reliable facts can be marshalled on both sides of the argument. Instead, the question is a matter of trying to decide which interpretation correctly assesses the trends that are developing in American society.

Here, we shall examine the alternative arguments concerning power, income distribution, occupational mobility, and race relations. Then we may be able to assess the points of difference as well as the nature of the difference between the alternative views. There is no other way, if we honestly wish to recognize the dilemma.

*Power.* Essentially, stratification is a condition resulting from the unequal distribution of power. Applying this definition directly, this question is raised: Who holds the power in American society? Two opposing answers have been given: (1) power is concentrated in an elite; (2) power is widely distributed, and no particular group holds a monopoly on the exercise of power.

Those who support the elite view argue that power in the political and economic sectors tends to become concentrated in societies that are at a

---

[9] Seymour M. Lipset, *The First New Nation* (New York: Basic Books, 1936), p. 1.

stage of advanced industrialism. On the political side of the picture, government bureaucracy has developed into a steep pyramid of power so that the people at the apex are able to exert extremely effective control over the entire structure. In addition, government is the largest economic consumer in the nation, which means that government is deeply involved in the national economy. Unlike an earlier period in United States history when the traditional role of government was one of noninterference, the present period is distinguished by the active, decision-making role that the government plays. Along with these developments has come the enormous emphasis placed upon military needs. As the largest consumer of goods, the military establishment has developed its own elite who, in turn, exert political influence.

On the economic side of the picture, a few large corporations have gained monopoly control over major sectors of the economy. The result has been a heavy economic concentration in a few top corporations that, between them, account for the greater part of the wealth that is produced. This kind of concentration of economic power—as of political power—means that those who occupy the relatively few top positions are able to exert more control, over a wider range, than any preceding group in American society. The elite view holds that this kind of power is legal. It is institutionalized and legitimate power because it is exercised through the normative structure of American society, not outside of it.

Changes in American society over the past few decades have tended to bring these two power elites together. The economic elite has become dependent upon the political elite, chiefly because government has become the largest consumer of the goods and services produced by the economy (for example, in the space and defense programs). Involvement in politics, so as to influence governmental action in one's favor, has become sound business practice.

In short order, the political, the military, and the economic elites combine and continue to extend their power. One direction for expansion is to monopolize social power and add it to their political and economic superiority. Thus, the high-status positions also tend to be monopolized by the elite and to be brought into their orbit of control. In this way the elite can determine the qualifications for entry into their circle, and also can establish a continuity to their power by inheritance. The channels for entry into the elite are severely modified to suit the monopolistic purposes of this group. The best universities become dominated by elite members in order to provide an exclusive socializing locale; elite clubs and other voluntary organizations become closed to outsiders; residential areas and resort areas become equally exclusive. The final effect, if attained, is to isolate the elite from all pretenders and to bring all acknowledged members of the group into close and continuous contact with one another —a situation very much like that of the feudal aristocracy.

In this way—according to the theory—American society is developing a power elite. This has been accomplished not by revolution or even by deliberate planning, but instead by the forces inherent within American society itself. Therefore, in spite of our ideals, American society has begun to create an elite power group. C. Wright Mills has succinctly summarized these trends.

> Those who sit in the seats of the high and the mighty are selected and formed by the means of power, the sources of wealth, the mechanics of celebrity, which prevail in their society. They are not men selected and formed by a civil service that is linked with the world of knowledge and sensibility. They are not men shaped by nationally responsible parties that debate openly and clearly the issues this nation now so unintelligently confronts. They are not men held in responsible check by a plurality of voluntary associations which connect debating publics with the pinnacles of decision.[10]

The opposing view about American society denies that a power elite exists or that there is any process toward elite development. Instead, the pluralists argue that American society has been moving toward a social leveling of class differences. At a material level, class differences have been equalized because of the astounding productivity of industry, which has created the affluent American society. The real danger is not from a power elite but from the disadvantages of affluence: mass education, mass housing, and mass tastes that smooth out the valuable differences between social strata and between individuals. It is feared that we are becoming the society of the great, washed, middle class—bought at the cost of individual autonomy and cultural variability.

At the political level, the pluralists see no danger of elite concentration. Instead, they see only a political matrix composed of numerous pressure groups. Political decisions are reached by alliances between those groups, which form and reform into ever-shifting constellations around each political issue. Political competition, not elite domination, is the cardinal point. There are constant antagonisms between groups in the political process so that it is unlikely that any one group could gain and hold unchallenged control. Power, by this conception, is amorphously and widely distributed. "Power in America," writes Riesman, "seems to me situational and mercurial; it resists attempts to locate it the way a molecule, under the Heisenberg principle, resists attempts simultaneously

---

[10] C. Wright Mills, *The Power Elite* (New York: Oxford University Press, 1956), p. 361.

to locate it and time its velocity." [11] According to Riesman, the political arena includes a large number of "veto groups" that can combine to stop decisions that are inimical to the groups' interests. Therefore, power continues to flow irregularly between these veto groups, escaping any attempt that the groups make to contain it and to hold it indefinitely.

Which characterization of American stratification is the more accurate? Are we moving toward the establishment of an industrial aristocracy reminiscent of the feudal aristocracies of Europe, or toward a modern variation of the social and political pluralism that reflects the democratic ethos and intent?

We cannot honestly try to reconcile these opposite concepts. Mills suggested that the pluralistic view can be subsumed under his conception of the power elite, because the veto groups operate only at the middle levels of power and have relatively little effect on major decisions. This is hardly a reconciliation. The plain truth is that there is no valid answer —no valid choice between the alternatives—since we lack the proof necessary to establish the truth of one view and the falsity of the other view. There is insufficient proof even to establish a compromise answer, if indeed such an answer exists.

Meantime, some social scientists have sought an answer by studying the distribution of power in local communities, leaving aside the national level. Obviously, the local community is a more restricted arena for analysis. However, the same division into two views has developed even at this level. Briefly, one doctrine contends that local communities in the United States are controlled by power elites, generally consisting of the business and political leadership. The opposing view contends that local communities, like the nation, exhibit the pluralism inherent in the democratic process.

We might think that studies of power at the community level would allow for substantive data to answer the dilemma. After all, fewer people are involved, and the participants in the process are more accessible to study than people at the national level, where official secrecy and a complex structure make detailed study impossible at the present time. This is a vain hope. The problem is really not just an empirical one to be settled by correct scientific procedure. Instead, it is a problem in which the question that initiates the research determines the kind of answer that is reached. A full discussion of scientific method is beyond the scope of this chapter, but we should recognize that there is an intimate relationship in any science between the questions that are researched and the kinds

[11] David Riesman, "Who Has the Power?" in *Class, Status and Power* (cited in footnote 8), p. 160.

of answers that are produced by that research. I do not fully agree with Polsby in his overeager criticism of the power-elite view. "I have suggested," he writes, "that this approach [the power-elite view] encourages research designs which generate self-fulfilling prophecies, that it leads to the systematic misreporting of facts and to the formulation of vague, ambiguous, unrealistic, and unprovable assertions about community power."[12] A fairer estimate of the difficulty has been given by Anton.

Pluralists quite vigorously deny the permanency of power—or to put it differently, that power is structured in any way. Thus if superficial evidence suggests that no power exists in a particular community, pluralist presuppositions warrant the conclusion that any further examination might well turn out to be a waste of time. . . . Beyond this there is the question of whether persons using pluralist methodology could recognize issues. Issues can be defined either by the observer's commitment to an ideological outlook that defines important problems or by his ability to comprehend fully the issue definitions of the people he studies. The pluralist literature, however, claims no ideology, other than commitment to empirical science—a commitment which emphasizes that which is rather than that which ought to be. And interestingly enough, pluralist ability to get "into the heads" of its subjects appears to be hampered by a similar acceptance of the existing political order.[13]

What both authors are saying is correct: the theoretical or ideological presuppositions that one holds toward the subject affect the questions that are asked and the answers that are obtained. The same is true with respect to the study of power elites and pluralistic veto groups at the national level. The only error that can be made in this connection is to maintain ideological innocence under the mask of scientific disinterest.

I do not intend to sweep the problem under the rug. On the contrary, I intend to illuminate the real issues that are involved in the analysis of power in American society. To me, it seems more ethical for us to recognize that differences exist and to recognize the source of those differences than to blind ourselves to the real problems because of a mistaken idea about the nature of science.

*Income.* There are other, less-encompassing aspects of stratification to be analyzed. Income and occupation are two relevant measures because class (we remember) is a matter of money and how that money is earned. However, neither money nor its use is sufficient to describe the class structure fully. Each provides valuable clues, but each has its limitations:

[12] Nelson W. Polsby, *Community Power and Political Theory* (New Haven: Yale University Press, 1963), p. 112.
[13] Thomas J. Anton, "Power, Pluralism, and Local Politics," *Administrative Science Quarterly*, 7, 454 (March, 1963). For an interesting exchange of views occasioned by this article, see Robert Dahl's letter and Anton's rejoinder in *Administrative Science Quarterly*, 8, 250–268 (September, 1963).

economic power depends on more than wealth alone; and occupation is only a partial index of status.

Income and occupation are related to each other, and both are related to education. The more education an individual attains, the better his occupation is likely to be and the more money he is likely to earn. But let us consider only income and occupation, leaving aside the matter of education.

Conclusions concerning the trend of income distributions in America are as hard to reach as were conclusions concerning power. There is no scarcity of information, but there is some confusion about the various definitions of income and their interpretation. There are rich and poor in the United States, now as previously, but what we wish to know is whether the differences between rich and poor have become greater. Are we developing a form of rigid income stratification? This question has become especially apropos lately because of the emphasis of the federal antipoverty program. We have become aware that poverty exists, but we are still uncertain whether poverty is so ingrained that little can be done about it aside from a few ameliorative measures.

Conflicting conclusions have been reached concerning income trends. Kuznets [14] defends the view that American income distributions have been leveling out, compared to what they once were. The share of the upper-income groups has been "declining substantially," and the gains by the lower-income groups have been rising commensurately. In 1928 the share of the top 1% income group accounted for 15% of all individual income; by 1948 their share had dropped to 8.5%. At the other end of the scale, the 16.4% group, who received less than $1000 a year in 1929, had declined to 9.6% by 1953. Kuznets' reasons for these changes have been the rise in employment, the rise in farm income, the impact of taxation on the rich, and the narrowing gap between the earnings of people in manufacturing as contrasted with the earnings of people in finance, transportation, and communications. According to this view, then, America is taking significant steps toward income equalization.

Kolko has sharply criticized Kuznets' thesis. He believes that opposite trends are occurring. He feels that the United States is far from becoming equalitarian and that it is marked by growing income inequalities. Kolko's analysis of personal income from 1910 to 1959 leads him to the following conclusion.

A radically unequal distribution of income has been characteristic of the American social structure since at least 1910, and, despite minor year-to-year

[14] Simon Kuznets, *Shares of Upper Income Groups in Income and Savings*, National Bureau of Economic Research, Washington, D.C., 1950, Occasional Paper, p. 35.

fluctuations in the shares of the income-tenths, no significant trend toward income equality has appeared.[15]

Miller, an economic statistician, has taken issue with Kolko's interpretation of the income figures, mainly on technical grounds that do not concern us here. What is important in the interchange between Miller and Kolko is that Miller insists that the figures reflect a trend toward growing income equality.[16] Miller contends that, at the very least, income distributions have shown a great deal of statistical stability over approximately the past 20 years. The share of the richest fifth of the population has remained at about 21% since 1944, while the share of the poorest fifth has stayed at about 5%.

These marked differences, like those encountered previously, stem from the interpretations that are given as well as from the type of question that is asked. The variances arise partly from differences in defining income and, as Miller has noted, in "what you do about taxes, undistributed profits, and capital gains; and how much value you place on intangibles such as better health, greater life expectancy, vacations with pay, and many other things." [17]

Putting technicalities aside, the evaluation of the substantive meaning of poverty is a real problem. Poverty is relative, not absolute. It exists only in relation to what others have, and only in relation to some standard of equality. No one would contend that starvation and privation fix the poverty line in American society today, even though 20% of the families in our population earn less than $1000 a year. In a society that rightly boasts of the highest living standard in the world, poverty occurs at a level where individuals are unable to share in the material prosperity available to most Americans; adequate housing, proper diet, opportunities for amusement and self-improvement, and the chance for an education commensurate with one's abilities. The statistics on income do not always reflect this definition of poverty—this accounts for the different interpretations. Nor do the analyses of income always take into account what Myrdal has called "structural" poverty; being poor in America today generally means that people are committed to poverty because there are few, if any, channels open to them to escape it.

We can only conclude that the analysis of income alone does not reveal enough about the nature of stratification in America. Income analysis must always be combined with other information, and it must be used according to an explicit standard of definition.

[15] Gabriel Kolko, *Wealth and Power in America* (New York: Praeger, 1962), p. 13.
[16] Herman P. Miller, *Rich Man Poor Man* (New York: Signet Books, 1965), p. 52.
[17] *Ibid.*, p. xix.

*Occupation.* Occupation is the most-used measure of class. It is some-what more sophisticated than income as a class dimension. Occupation includes not only an income component, but also correlates significantly with education and with community judgments of status. An occupation is more than simply a way of earning money; it is an index and symbol of the style that people live and the level of prestige that is accorded to them by others. The best-known study of occupational prestige was made by North and Hatt [18] in which a nationwide sample of adults was asked to rank the prestige of ninety occupations. From the responses given, a prestige scale of occupations was derived so that occupations could be compared by the relative prestige that they carried. Thus, "physician" was the highest prestige occupation, and "shoeshiner" was the lowest. In between, the professional occupations generally ranked highest, followed by clerical and sales occupations, and skilled workers; unskilled workers were at the very bottom. Numerous replications of the North-Hatt study, in the United States as well as in England, Australia, Germany, and Japan, have produced almost similar results. Clearly, the occupational prestige variable is a valid one.

There is little doubt that occupations are related to social status in advanced industrial societies, in which occupation is at the center of the activities of most persons. People in those societies perceive the prestige differences between occupations, and generally view them along the same dimensions as those described for the United States.

This awareness of occupational prestige is clear, but there is some doubt about its relationship to class or status. Certainly, occupations carry a status component, which was tapped by the North-Hatt study and others. Certainly, occupations show an approximate correlation with class charac-teristics, at least in the middle and lower strata; most professionals are middle class, and most unskilled wage earners are working class or lower class. But these are not clear divisions. Nor does occupation tell us much about the upper class because the measure of occupational prestige comes to an end when we get that high up on the hierarchy. Upper-class people may either have occupations that resemble others (bankers, managers, lawyers) or have no regular occupation at all (oil, investments, inheritance).

Another valid objection has been raised. It has been claimed that an occupation is often insufficient to estimate economic position because there are broad discrepancies even within a single occupation. There are rich and poor salesmen, just as there are rich and poor lawyers. To get

[18] The study is reproduced and discussed in several places, but there are two ac-cessible sources. Albert J. Reiss, Jr., *Occupations and Social Status* (New York: The Free Press of Glencoe, 1961); Leonard Reissman, *Class in American Society* (New York: The Free Press of Glencoe, 1960), especially Chapter III.

around this objection, Nam has devised a method of determining occupational prestige scores that include income and education data from the census.[19] It is a statistical refinement—a multiple rather than a single index—but it still does not clear up the main problem of just what occupation has to do with class. Hatt was aware of this difficulty, and he noted that occupational prestige scores are in the form of a continuum, whereas class is a set of discrete divisions. Neither Hatt nor anyone else has been able to match occupation with class. We continue to use occupation as an approximate index of class simply because there is no alternative.

Even with the restrictions that I have described, how does occupational distribution in the United States reflect on stratification? Is America an open society in which individuals are able to move up as high in the occupational structure as their talents allow? Or, has rigidity set in so that the upper occupational strata are almost closed to outsiders? By now we must have realized that there is no unequivocal answer.

One problem that these questions introduce is this: the occupational structure itself has been changing to reflect the shifting demands of economic organization. The unskilled and farming occupations have decreased while white-collar jobs and professions have increased. We cannot ignore these changes and simply compare the proportions in occupations today with the proportions in occupations previously.

The usual method of assessing occupational mobility is to compare the occupations of sons with the occupations of their fathers. In this way we can gain some estimate of whether the sons' occupations are higher, lower, or at the same level as their fathers' occupations. Several studies have reached the following conclusions.

1. Farmers have a high rate of occupational inheritance; today's farmers are the sons of farmers.

2. There are signs of some occupational inheritance among proprietors and managers at one end, and among skilled and unskilled occupations at the other.

3. The professions and white-collar occupations seem to be the most accessible of all, especially the white-collar occupations. There is more movement into those occupations than into any others. Generally, professionals and white-collar workers seem to have fathers who have been in other occupations. The interpretation of this movement must take into account the expanded demand for professional and white-collar occupations during the past few decades, thereby making more opportunities available now than previously.

[19] U.S. Bureau of the Census, *Methodology and Scores of Socioeconomic Status*, Working Paper No. 15, Government Printing Office, Washington, D.C., 1963.

To answer the question posed earlier regarding how occupational distribution in the United States reflects on stratification, the United States falls somewhere between a condition of open mobility and static rigidity.

However, there is no certainty about the direction of future trends. Some sociologists agree with an interpretation of those trends by Mayer.

America's social structure today and in the proximate future can be perceived as a diamond where the top and bottom are still pretty rigidly fixed, inhabited by upper and lower classes. A working class of the traditional sort also persists but comprises nowadays only a part of the manual workers. Between the extremes, however, classes are disappearing. To be sure prestige, power, and economic differentials persist here, too, of course, and prestige differentials tend even to become accentuated as crude economic differences diminish and lose their visibility. But these differentials are no longer the hallmarks of social classes. In the middle ranges of the various rank orders we are witnessing the beginnings of a classless society in a modern industrial economy.[20]

Mayer is unjustifiably optimistic. Although he might validly argue that there has been a leveling of differences between some occupational strata, he has no basis for extending his interpretation to cover class stratification.

Part of this optimism comes from our earlier belief that all Americans were generally affluent, and part comes from our confidence that poverty can be abolished by having the federal government spend enough money. Both views are, at best, only equivocally true. Many people are affluent, and some poverty can be abolished if enough money is spent to do it. But "the other America"—as Harrington has called the poor—comprise about 20 to 25% of the population. The gains made by the American economy have not filtered down to this group. Even more important these people are likely to be committed to a position of structural poverty. Most of the better-paying jobs are closed to them and to their children because they do not have sufficient education. Without these jobs they must remain in the least stable sector of the labor market: the sector where job security is really nonexistent and where unemployment is frequent. The poor pass along this unwelcome heritage to their children.

To the extent that we have committed so large a proportion of our population to a condition of structural poverty, we have created rigidity in the class structure. There may be some uncertainty about whether America is developing a power elite; some uncertainty about whether there is enough occupational mobility; and some uncertainty about the extent of income equalization that is taking place. However, there is no uncertainty about the future of the people presently committed to the

[20] Kurt B. Mayer, "The Changing Shape of the American Class Structure," *Social Research*, **30**, 468 (Winter, 1963).

lowest stratum: poor people. If the war on poverty is successful, it may well be that in one or two generations we will have decreased the proportion of the poor, but the accomplishment of this goal is as yet uncertain. Alteration of the conditions that create poverty in American society involves major changes in our values and in our institutions. For example, we must learn to accept the idea that everyone who is poor is not lazy; we must learn to accept the idea that poverty is not always the fault of the individual, but results from a failure of society. The success of the antipoverty program, therefore, hinges upon the degree to which Americans are prepared to accept the attitude changes that the program requires.

**Race.** There is no uncertainty about the impact of race as a dominant dimension of American stratification. For years, many Americans seemed to believe that racial stratification—segregation—was confined to the South. It is true that more violence accompanied race differences in the South than race differences in the North. But the Negro's recent militancy in civil rights movements has pointed up the national scope of his segregation. Americans have been forced to become aware of the deep abyss that separates most of the Negro population from active participation in American society, and of the placement of the Negro in the role of a "second-class citizen." The confinement of Negroes to the lowest stratum is clearly a national condition, not simply a Southern one. Because of race alone, the Negro has been kept in the bottom economic class in the bottom status group, and in the most ineffectual power position. For the overwhelming majority of Negroes, this has meant a lasting confinement without any opportunity to escape.

Negroes, unlike many other minority groups in American society, have been prevented from improving their situation by moving upward to a higher social position. As long as the majority of this group stayed in rural Southern communities, the weight of tradition and the institutionalization of prejudice kept them effectively in the social position that they had occupied since slavery, with only a few exceptions. However, since the end of World War II, large numbers of the Negro population have migrated to the cities in and outside of the South. These recent migrants have discovered the realities of segregation throughout the United States—in housing, in education, and in employment. They have encountered what Drake and Cayton have aptly called "the job ceiling."

Despite fifteen years of urbanization during a period of industrial expansion, Negroes had not attained a proportionate share of the skilled and clerical jobs or of the professional and business occupations. They were clinging precariously to the margins of the economy. . . . They had not made the type of rapid progress which white European immigrants had made in an equal period. . . . This was due primarily to the fact that they had not been allowed to compete freely, as *individuals*, for any types of jobs to which they aspired and for which they were qualified.[21]

Inferior or inadequate education, unskilled occupations, unstable employment, and low income are companionable conditions; any one condition tends to produce the others, so that the Negroes were tightly bound into a position of inferiority from which they could not escape. Some sociologists contend that Negroes represent a distinct American caste instead of being a part of a class system. They contend that the Negro, in major particulars, has not really escaped slavery; consequently, race alone determines his social, economic, and political position: ascription, in other words, rather than achievement.

There is some support for this point of view. A form of caste segregation is evident in the restrictions on intermarriage, in education, in housing, and in associational membership. In some states, especially in the South, many of these conditions were or are supported by laws. In other states, the conditions are maintained by less formal social sanctions, which may well amount to the same thing. Furthermore, a social etiquette governing race relations has developed that sets the Negro apart from the whites —an etiquette that has traditional and institutional support. In the South, the attitudes of whites toward Negroes contained many of the elements of the Brahmins' attitudes toward the Untouchables. Negroes were effectively assigned to perform the most menial and demeaning work. They had no equal right under the law. They were denied the right to vote and, generally, were treated more like property than like citizens. This extreme situation was somewhat relieved in other sections of the country, but even there Negroes intimately felt the boundaries of a segregated society.

The major difference that distinguishes the Negro-white situation in the United States from the Indian caste system is that American values do not support caste divisions. This may sound relatively picayune in the light of social realities, but we should remember that the entire civil rights movement today is hinged precisely on the value of equality and equal opportunity. Another distinguishing point is that Negroes share the same values as the ones held by white society; Negroes do not consider themselves inferior in the same way that a low-caste person in Indian society is said to accept his inferiority.

One indication of the similarity of values in both Negro and white society is the enormously important role that has been assigned to educa-

---

[21] St. Clair Drake and Horace Cayton, "The Job Ceiling," P. K. Hatt and A. J. Reiss, Jr., eds., in *Reader in Urban Sociology* (New York: The Free Press of Glencoe, 1951), p. 387.

tional attainment within the Negro community. In a recent study by Glenn,[22] it was reported that education has become the most important single criterion of prestige. The reason is quite clear: high educational attainment can be translated into better occupational and income opportunities. In a segment of American society where advanced education is not widespread, the Negroes who are better educated stand out more sharply. This finding supports the conclusions of many other studies that Negroes seek to apply to themselves the same criteria of prestige that whites use. In other words, success in one community is no different from success in another except for the greater difficulties encountered by Negroes as compared with white persons.

Until the past decade, the situation of the Negro in American society could accurately be described as being castelike. By American standards, the Negro was rigidly confined, but he still was not bound into his position from birth to death as was a low-caste member of Indian society. After all, some Negroes did escape to higher class levels: for example, entertainers and a thin stratum of people who advanced into the middle class. The people who advanced into the middle class—Frazier called them the "black bourgeoisie"—tended to separate themselves from the bulk of the Negro population by moving into better neighborhoods, by sending their children away to better schools, and by building a barrier of exclusive associations between themselves and others. In this way, the Negro middle class behaved exactly like its white counterpart by severing the channels of contact with the lower class.

This decade of effective Negro militancy has begun to alter the situation of the Negro in white society quite markedly, both in the South as elsewhere in the United States. The gains that have been made—supported by a battery of federal legislation and court decisions, and bolstered by the first effective mass leadership that the Negro population has had —have served to alter a situation that goes back more than eight generations. The real effect of these gains has been to break the circle of inferiority to which the Negro had been committed. Integrated educational facilities will eventually mean better educational opportunities for Negroes which, in turn, can result in better-paying, more secure jobs. Equal employment opportunities will give Negroes access to jobs from which they previously were systematically excluded. The increase in Negro voter registration eventually will mean that the Negro can exert greater political influence than he ever could exert before. On all counts, then, the Negro

[22] Norval D. Glenn, "Negro Prestige Criteria: A Case Study in the Bases of Prestige," *American Journal of Sociology,* **68,** 645–657 (May, 1963).

is at the theshhold of full participation in the society of which he is also a member.

Coupled with these structural changes in the Negro's position, there has been a move toward resolving the "American dilemma" among white persons. In one of the best studies of the resolution of this dilemma, Hyman and Sheatsley [23] have confirmed the progress of spreading favorable attitudes toward integration. These writers, in their earlier analysis of national opinion polls in 1956, found that:

A majority of white persons in the North favored racial integration of public schools, believed there should be no racial discrimination in public transportation and said they would have no objection to living near Negroes of their own income and educational status. In the South a majority of whites opposed each of these views.

Eight years later, Hyman and Sheatsley found that there were clear signs of dramatic changes in the support of integration by white communities in the North. In the South there were also signs of a shift in the same favorable direction, especially among young adults. Sufficient changes had occurred by 1964 for Hyman and Sheatsley to conclude as follows.

It appears that the attitudes of white Americans of both the North and the South are continuing to shift toward greater acceptance of integration . . . In the minds and hearts of the majority of Americans the principle of integration seems already to have been won.

Much of what has been described as the castelike situation of the Negro could be applied almost without modification to the positions of other racial and ethnic minorities in the United States. Puerto Ricans in New York, Mexicans in Texas and the Southwest, and Orientals on the West Coast have lived segregated lives not very different from the lives of the Negroes. These other minorities have experienced the same kinds of exclusion and the same kind of social inferiority, although for a shorter period than the 100 years that the Negro has been thus enclosed. Segregation of each of these groups has depended upon the high social visibility of their differences from the majority white society and, to this extent, their inferior position in the hierarchy of stratification has been based upon ascribed qualities rather than upon the results of individual achievements. These matters are, of course, much deeper than our treatment of them would suggest, but other features of stratification must take precedence here. These very brief comments were made to alert the student

[23] Herbert H. Hyman and Paul B. Sheatsley, "Attitudes Toward Desegregation," *Scientific American*, July, 1964, pp. 16–23.

to the similarities between the position of Negroes and the positions of other minority groups in American society.

*Conclusions.* What conclusions, then, can we draw about the condition of social stratification in America? Clearly, America is far from being the open class society that we have formally pronounced it to be. But many Americans must have been aware of the discrepancy. Perhaps the more relevant question is: Are we, or are we not moving toward social equality? Some theorists interpret our history to mean that such a trend has been evident from the beginning. There is evidence of a great deal of upward social mobility in the population and, compared with most other advanced nations, the rate of mobility, indeed, has been astounding. There is also evidence of continued economic growth that has resulted in a higher standard of living for a good many Americans. Again, compared with other nations, our standard of living is far ahead of theirs.

Yet, in spite of these substantial gains, there are contradictory indications. There is evidence of economic concentration, of the increased power of an economic elite, of the military, and of a political elite. An American "establishment" does seem to exist, within which these elites exercise a great deal of power. If American society were to move in this direction, then it would not be long before rigidity would characterize American social structure.

To be realistic, we must admit that American society is far from being at a satisfactory stage of development as long as one quarter of our population continues to live at or near the subsistence level. Who is to speak for the American poor, since they cannot effectively speak for themselves? The poor have become separated from any effective social participation. Economic poverty has come to mean political ineffectiveness and a lack of control over the social environment. The current war on poverty might help the poor, but it is also likely that, at best, programs of this kind will lead out of poverty only those people who are able to walk out themselves, thereby depriving the poor of a potential voice that they might otherwise have had.

## India

The caste system of India illustrates the most rigid and detailed form of stratification in a large, heterogeneous society. No other society, including feudal and ancient ones, has developed so complex a system of stratification nor one covering so large and diverse a population. The Hindu caste system proved its utility by uniting people from diverse backgrounds of color, language, creed, and custom into a viable form of social organization. For the student of social stratification, the caste system provides a rich contrast to the class systems of the West.

What is caste? There are at least four different referents or meanings of caste in India.[24]

1. Caste as *varna* or color. By this definition, there are four major castes in the system: *Brahmans* or priests, *Kshatriya* or warriors, *Vaisyas* or men of commerce, and *Sudras* or workmen. These castes are not exhaustive since some in India do not belong to any of these groups, especially the Untouchables or the depressed caste.

2. Caste categories, which are "aggregates of persons, usually in the same linguistic region, usually with the same traditional occupation and sometimes with the same caste name."

3. Caste associations or groups.

4. Caste as *jati*, which is the main sociological referent for caste. *Jati* refers to about 3000 castes and subcastes throughout India that are designated as social units held together by ritual and kinship, and reinforced by political and economic systems.

Caste, for our purposes, is "a group of families whose members can marry with each other and can eat in each other's company without believing themselves polluted. To this one must add that each of these groups has its place in a hierarchy. It is above, or below, or equal to, every one of the others; and in theory everybody knows where each group comes." [25] The caste system is a complex hierarchy of social categories into which individuals are ascribed at birth and in terms of which a significant part of their activities and attitudes is determined.

The boundaries of castes and subcastes are built and sanctioned by the belief in pollution, undoubtedly one of the main social psychological features of the system because it touches upon so many basic aspects of life. Pollution applies to any physical contact, drinking, eating, and smoking. Obviously, with this restriction of elementary social intercourse, all other forms of social interaction are automatically covered, such as marriage, associational memberships, and informal contacts. In theory, at any rate, the fear of pollution leads to extreme caution in the activities of individuals and to a sharp awareness of caste differences and caste hierarchy. This attitude bears some resemblance to Negro-white relations in the United States, although not to the same extent. Intermarriage, titles of address, eating together, and other forms of race contact seem to be governed by the fear of pollution, but they do not extend with the same force as in the Indian

[24] This summary was adapted from F. G. Bailey, "Closed Social Stratification in India," *Archives Européenes de Sociologie*, 4, 107–124 (1963).

[25] Taya Zinkin, *Caste Today* (London: Oxford University Press, 1963), p. 4.

situation. Let us note two examples. White persons permit Negroes to handle their food and their children, a contamination that would be repellent to the orthodox Hindu. Pollution, in other words, becomes the main motivation for the individual to control his behavior toward those outside of his caste and, at the same time, pollution becomes the means for the individual to create strong bonds within his caste.

As mentioned above, about 3000 castes and subcastes have been identified. This indicates a high degree of specialization, which is principally organized around occupational differences, since occupation is a main social feature of caste divisions. Generally, a caste group that seeks to enhance its status separates itself by specializing its work; then it enforces endogamy (marriage within the group) so that the group can stabilize its separation. A humorous and accurate summary of the process is described by Hutton.

> Modern India, having created a caste of chauffeurs from the menials who tend motor-cars, is almost ripe for a Rolls Royce caste rejecting food or marriage with the Fords. [It should be called] a Rolls Royce subcaste, for at least it would start in that way and, if true to pattern, reject first the giving of daughters to Fords while not hesitating to take wives from among them, secondly, the eating of food with them, and finally, all connection of any kind, discovering a long-forgotten descent, not shared by Fords, from some Brahman or Kshatriya ancestor who drove the fiery chariot of Surya in the misty dawn of mythology.[26]

In this way, the number of castes has proliferated, each with its own distinct characteristics to separate it from all others. To convey some idea of the specificity that is developed around occupational specialization, consider these examples: [27]

> *Jugi,* a caste of rearers of silkworms in Assam; *Ghanchi,* a caste of oil pressers in western India; *Uppiliyan,* a caste of salt workers in Malabar; *Bhangi,* a caste of sweepers and scavengers over all of India except the south; and *Handi Jogi,* a caste of mendicants, pig breeders, quacks, and snake charmers in southern India.

I could give more examples. The point is that each of these castes or subcastes centers around an occupational specialty and, in addition, imposes a rigid set of rituals and rules that govern the behavior of caste members toward others and between themselves.

The caste system depends upon consensus. The participants must accept the hierarchy in at least broad terms. And with it, the participants

---

[26] J. H. Hutton, *Caste in India: Its Nature, Function, and Origin* (London: Oxford University Press, 1951), p. 117.
[27] *Ibid.,* pp. 274–294.

must accept their relative positions within it. There is little doubt that a high level of such consensus has been attained and maintained for some time; otherwise, the system would only stimulate widespread factionalism between caste groups, since each group would refuse to recognize the superior claims of any other group. To the West—with its tradition of individual freedom and emphasis on achievement—the caste system seems mysterious and confining. Yet, to the Hindu, the system has provided a number of gains. Hutton cogently summarizes this aspect.

From the point of view of the individual member of a caste the system provides him from birth with a fixed social milieu from which neither wealth nor poverty, success nor disaster can remove him, unless of course he so violates the standards of behaviour laid down by his caste that it spews him forth—temporarily or permanently. He is provided in this way with a permanent body of associations which control almost all his behaviour and contacts. His caste canalizes his choice in marriage, acts as his trade union, his friendly or benefit society, his slate club and his orphanage; it takes the place for him of health insurance, and if need be provides for his funeral.[28]

Sociological as well as psychological factors help to continue the caste system. Endogamy as well as detailed proscriptions defining the limits of behavior combine to blunt changes that might modify or alter traditional relationships. A good deal of this social control is administered by secular authority through a caste council called a *panchayat.* It is generally a large group, and is a relatively permanent institution with a fairly continuous existence. The powers of the *panchayat* extend to expelling persons from the caste, restoring them to their caste position, and imposing fines and penalties for lesser breaches of caste rituals and rules. In some sections of India, religious leaders have taken over the functions of the *panchayat* with a consequent diminution of secular control. These leaders, whether secular or religious, can exert effective power and direct the behavior of caste members. Individual belief is thereby bolstered by effective agencies of social control.

Yet, India has been experiencing the forces of modernization. In fact, long before India's independence, the caste system has been changing from the neat pattern that has been described. The effects of British colonization forced new ideas into Indian society so that caste relationships and the institutional structure that supported them were already susceptible to alterations. Independence, however, has accelerated those changes and has opened the way for a set of considerable forces to be arrayed against the older caste traditions.

Urbanization and industrialization—the main forces involved—are stimu-

[28] *Ibid.,* p. 111.

lating serious changes in caste. Although neither cities nor industry are new to India, the pace of urbanization and industrialization has quickened in the recent era. Life in the cities is much different from life in the villages, where caste previously had its greatest strength. It is difficult to maintain the traditional caste practices against pollution in the city. Urban densities and the physical and social conditions in cities are not conducive to a good many caste restrictions, except perhaps to endogamy. Similarly, traditional occupational rules are badly adapted to the requirements of an urban industrial society. These rules are irrational in the industrial complex, and they are expensive to maintain. Industry requires more flexibility in its occupational allocations than the caste structure can allow. Quite simply, how would a manager of a factory be able to cope with the problem of ritual pollution on the production line if caste boundaries had to be crossed? To maintain such traditional occupational rules would only increase the cost of production in a country that cannot afford it.

Not only urbanization and industrialization but also the development of modern political attitudes of democracy and freedom may well become forces against the continuation of the caste system. The West has deeply affected the intellectuals and educated classes in India during the decades of British control. Now, the ideas of the intellectuals and educated classes are in process of being extended to other segments of the population in order to build a viable nation.

Even before these recent developments, some students of caste have argued that the system was not so rigid in practice as it seemed to be in theory. Caste groups, especially in the middle range of the hierarchy, have raised their relative positions, although it is hard to determine how frequently this has occurred. Srinivas has noted that, "A low caste was able to rise to a higher position in the hierarchy by adopting vegetarianism and teetotalism, and by sanskritizing its ritual and pantheon. In short, it took over as far as possible, the customs, rites and beliefs of the Brahmins." [29] Other groups converted to Christianity, and after some economic success as Christians attempted to reenter the caste system at a higher position than the one that they occupied when they left.

Some observers who are familiar with the caste system argue that caste will remain for some time. They base their argument upon the fact that so much of social life in India is colored by caste that it would be difficult, if not impossible, to change radically such a basic feature of Indian society. Education, economic commitments, political alignments, and

[29] M. N. Srinivas et al., "Caste: A Trend Report and Bibliography," *Current Sociology*, 8 (3), 139 (1959).

a wide range of social interests are directly affected by caste and by caste relationships. These cannot be altered any more easily, for instance than the informal relationships between Negroes and whites in the rural south.

Although we must recognize the widespread influence of caste through-out the institutional fabric of Indian society, it is difficult to believe that the system will successfully weather the current forces for change. The rate of change may be slowed because of the deep roots of caste. There-fore, changes will be slower in the rural villages than in the cities. How-ever, the process of social modernization will move a significant proportion of the population into the cities and the impact of the cities will sooner or later be felt in the rural areas. The history of Western countries has already shown the enormous force that such trends contain, and it seems unlikely that India will be able to avoid them.

### England

England's stratification system falls between the one in the United States and the one in India. England's system resembles the American sys-tem in its structure of classes, the institutional channels for exercising social power, and the dimensions of stratification that are emphasized. It re-sembles India's system in the tendency for the system to be inflexible, rely-ing upon ascriptive criteria. Yet, England has neither an open class system nor a closed caste system.

The dominating characteristic of British stratification is its history. Eng-land pioneered the West's development out of feudalism and into industrial-ism. Not all feudal elements were swept away. Strong traditions have re-mained that echo feudal stratification: the monarchy, the aristocracy, a landed gentry, and clear-cut status differences throughout British society. It is a country in which a person's accent reflects his class, as Shaw's *Pygmalion* so obviously showed.

But aristocratic features have been tempered by class; class and aristoc-racy have become intertwined. Class in England, unlike the United States is not an open invitation to social mobility—a fact that tends to keep classes relatively closed. England lacks the American stress upon upward mobility as well as America's easier means to realize such mobility. Consequently, classes tend to be more permanent social enclosures in England than we think them to be in the United States. Furthermore, the British are much more class-conscious than the Americans at all levels of British society. As Blondel has put it, "National class differences are the main divisions of society. The British class system may be complex, although it is perhaps no more complex than the class system of other industrial countries. . . . It is at any rate the main line of division between the British people." [30]

The relative inflexibility of the class system stems partly from the fact that the rising bourgeoisie of the 17th and 18th centuries did not destroy the aristocracy. Instead, it would seem from the actions of the bourgeoisie that some of them wanted to gain admittance to the aristocratic structure and then close the door behind them. In this sense, the British bourgeoisie was remarkable, achieving a major social transition without violence. But it did not quite work out so neatly. The area of participation in British society was opened to more than the bourgeoisie alone.

In effect, England has more than one system of stratification, as is true of other countries where aristocracy and class live within the same social framework.

G. D. H. Cole, one of the most perceptive of British social scientists, pointed out the following.

[There are] three separate systems, of which the second and third have been in turn superimposed on the first, in such a way as to leave all three still in existence but with their relative importance greatly changed. These three are, first, an old structure based on relations to the land essentially aristocratic in character; secondly, a predominately plutocratic structure based on the development of modern commerce and industry; and thirdly, a much more diversified structure based on the growth of professional and administrative work, and closely affected by the wider diffusion and considerably differentiated development of the educational system. [31]

Britain is not an open class society. The power once exclusively exercised by a feudal nobility has been assumed by the descendants of the early bourgeoisie who are now members of the upper middle class. Although the upper middle class may mix with the older aristocracy, there has not been, in Cole's words, "a complete fusion." The business and political elites tend to maintain a class, as opposed to an aristocratic outlook, but they rub shoulders generally only with their peers. In effect, the upper middle class acts very much like a ruling elite by limiting membership and by exerting considerable power in British society. Guttsman made some cogent remarks on this point.

There exists today in Britain a "ruling class" if we mean by it a group which provides the majority of those who occupy positions of power, and who,

[30] Jean Blondel, *Voters, Parties, and Leaders: The Social Fabric of British Politics* (London: Pelican Books, 1963), p. 26.

[31] G. D. H. Cole, *Studies in Class Structure* (London: Routledge and Kegan Paul, 1955), pp. 106–107.

in their turn, can materially assist *their* sons to reach similar positions. The character and composition of this class has clearly undergone some changes since the middle of the last century. The members of the aristocratic families form only a minority in the various elite groups. . . . The rest are recruited almost exclusively from the groups of upper-middle-class families.[32]

The elite necessarily comprises a relatively small proportion of the population. Its economic power is considerable. The largest firms have elite representatives on their boards who make the major investment decisions even though the daily operation of the firm is in the hands of managers. The political power of the elite is still felt, although it has been attenuated by the entry of those from middle- and working-class origins. Hence, the Conservative party still reflects the control of a combination of aristocrats and an upper-middle-class group. The Labour party leadership draws from further down the working class. Guttsman's analysis of cabinet members in the Labour Government in 1950 showed this mixture: three members came from aristocratic or upper-middle-class backgrounds; five members came from the middle and lower middle classes; and ten members came from a working-class background.[33]

Class position in Britain is determined largely by education and occupation, with kinship and aristocratic descent being reflected in these two stratifying dimensions. Yet, education in particular is awarded more class significance in Britain than in the United States where it is generally only a means of entry into the higher occupations. In Britain, however, education assumes the kind of exclusiveness that some people have predicted will occur the United States at a later period. As Blondel asserts, "The more one goes up in the social structure, the more education rather than occupation helps to define subtle boundaries between groups and informal connections between individuals." [34]

The role of education in Britain is pivotal for the class structure. The educational system constitutes a major determinant of class position, even though it is not the only one. Certain schools appear to be the main socializing agents for the legitimate heirs of the elite and ruling class, and also the means for mobility for someone from the lower class if he can make the transition. The English public schools, which are comparable to our best and most exclusive private schools, serve to preselect the people

[32] W. L. Guttsman, *The British Political Elite* (London: Macgibbon and Kee, 1963), p. 356.
[33] *Ibid.,* p. 242.
[34] Jean Blondel, *Voters, Parties, and Leaders: The Social Fabric of British Politics* (London: Pelican Books, 1963), p. 38.

who are to move into positions of influence in British society, and the Ox-bridge universities—Oxford and Cambridge—complete the process. More is involved than simply a good education. A broad social experience is needed as a necessary credential for admittance to the elite. The effects of this kind of education are evident in the graduate that is turned out, in his speech, in his dress and in his manners.

Public schools help to create "two nations"; indeed, since State schools are divided into grammar and secondary modern schools, the whole system of education helps create three nations. At the same time, public schools have succeeded in shaping a socially integrated elite. They have helped to perpetuate some of the power and many of the values of the middle and upper classes.[35]

I do not mean to give the impression that England is a tightly closed class society. Several elite groups do share their power. Besides the eco-nomic elite that controls the large firms, there is a trade-union elite that exerts some economic and political force. Yet, in the trade-union elite, even among those from working-class backgrounds, there is a closer resemblance to the middle class than to the lower class. Politics is a profession that tends to transform the individual into a middle-class person at the very least—a process usually started by the educational experience of those individuals. The Labour party leadership, according to Guttsman, has been accepted into and has adjusted to the traditional middle and upper-class environ-ment in which politics are conducted.[36]

However, as this emphasis upon elites is meant to imply, stratification in Britain is distinguished by a relative lack of mobility when compared with the United States. From the available data, it appears that barriers to social mobility are higher in England than in the United States. Miller [37] analyzed the mobility trends for a number of countries, but we shall con-sider only his comparison between England and the United States. He found that in England the movement of persons from manual to nonmanual occupations, as well as in the reverse direction, was relatively high. In the United States, the movement from manual to nonmanual occupations was high. But upward mobility into elite positions in England was low, whether the point of origin was the manual group or the middle class. In the United States, mobility into the highest positions tended to be somewhat more open than in England. These conclusions regarding elite mobility are generally corroborated by Guttsman's analysis of the British elite.

[35] Jean Blondel, *Voters, Parties, and Leaders: The Social Fabric of British Politics* (London: Pelican Books, 1963), pp. 41–42.
[36] W. L. Guttsman, *The British Political Elite* (London: Macgibbon and Kee, 1963), p. 336.
[37] S. M. Miller, "Comparative Social Mobility," *Current Sociology*, 9 (1), (1960).

At present almost half of the traditional middle class—members of the professions, businessmen, managers, Civil Servants and the like—are recruited from men who have grown up in middle class families. Nearly two-thirds of the men in the highest occupational groups, comprising less than 3 per cent of the population, are the sons of men who belonged to the same group . . . In the immediate post-war period, to which the above figures refer, less than one in four of the members of the traditional middle class were the sons of manual workers or those in the routine grades of non-manual workers.[38]

To generalize concerning the stratification system of England over the past few decades, it can be stated that England has opened up the middle segments of the class structure to people previously frozen into lower-class positions. Yet, England has continued to maintain high barriers around its elite groups, which only rarely are pierced by outsiders. Increased educational facilities have helped that process with respect to mobility in the middle and lower strata. Mobility into the ruling elite and into the aristocracy necessarily must remain closed for some time.

## Social Stratification and Behavior

The ultimate reality of stratification is in its effects on behavior. Theory can explain, order, and predict phenomena, but theory must have an empirical referent that shows how stratification alters or modifies what individuals do or believe. Without empirical corroboration, stratification analysis may remain only a set of conceptual categories.

Some sociologists contend that unless individuals are subjectively aware of stratification, stratification does not really exist. The generalization is broadly correct, but only if subjective awareness is broadly defined. People may not be conscious of class, power, or status as such but, at some level and no matter how crudely, they must perceive relative differences between their positions. Each theorist that I have described accepts at least this minimal level of perceptive awareness. For Warner, perception of status differences was an obvious fact of life in Yankee City; for Marx, all individuals were captives of their class and the perception was forced upon them; for Weber and the functionalists, the recognition of existing social values was, at the same time, a recognition of values relevant for stratification. After about two decades of research in this area, it has been firmly established that there are significant behavioral consequences for the different positions in a stratification system.

[38] W. L. Guttsman, *The British Political Elite* (London: Macgibbon and Kee, 1963), p. 330.

### *Class Consciousness and Status Inconsistency*

The effect of class consciousness upon behavior can be considered in two ways. First, class consciousness can be interpreted literally to mean that individuals are more or less conscious of stratification as a system and of their relative place in that system. According to this meaning, the individual is aware of his class and, furthermore, is conscious that his actions are a direct result of his class position. The same applies, of course, to any aspect of stratification including status, power, and race consciousness. In the second interpretation of class consciousness, the individual may lack the conscious awareness of class but his behavior can best be explained in terms of class. In other words, his behavior assumes a pattern that can be explained adequately by assuming that he knows something about where he belongs in the hierarchy regardless of the terms that he may use or the breadth of his conception.

Both interpretations are valid. We are not always aware of the reasons for our behavior (as Freud labored so hard to prove), but this does not keep us from developing a pattern of behavior that is highly predictable. If it can be shown, for instance, that middle-class people buy certain goods or become neurotic or have aspirations that differ from people in other classes, there is a rather solid ground for assuming that a relationship between class and behavior exists whether specific persons are conscious of class or not. On the other hand, according to the first definition of class consciousness, the individual may be aware but incorrectly aware of the reasons for his behavior as measured against the general consensus. For example, he may rate himself higher than anyone else would rate him. This situation requires cautious interpretation, but it is not incorrect; instead, the individual's behavior would have to be analyzed in terms of the discrepancy between his self-conception and that of others. The case of the *nouveau riche* is an excellent example.

In one way or another, interpretations of the effects of stratification on behavior rely upon one of the above two perspectives. Hence, some studies seek to correlate attitudes toward any particular subject or activities with class measures such as occupation, income, education, or race. A high correlation is interpreted to mean that class, status, or race are the independent variables—the cause of the behavior in question—even though the subjects were not directly queried about their consciousness of class. Other studies depend upon the subjects themselves indicating their relative awareness of class by locating their class position. This information is then correlated with other characteristics about individuals.

The latter technique is always open to some doubt because we are never completely sure what the self-identification means. For example, Centers [39] conducted a nationwide survey of American adults in 1945 that asked the respondents to identify themselves as being upper, middle, working, or lower class. Over one half of the respondents replied that they were in the working class; one third of the respondents identified themselves as members of the middle class. Centers then correlated this self-identification with a number of attitude questions and other class measures. His own analysis revealed the difficulty of using the class identifications that people gave of themselves. It was clear from his report that his respondents did not mean the same things by the terms they used, so that some bankers thought of themselves as being in the working class and some semiskilled factory workers identified themselves with the middle class. We would have to probe these deviant cases more deeply in order to get at the different meanings in which the class terms were being used. Americans, especially, are not accustomed to thinking in class terms so that their self-identifications are a mixture of fact, fantasy and misconception.

The confusion is less evident in the case of race than in the case of class, which indicates at least that Americans are much more conscious of race. The high visibility of race, coupled with the emphasis given to it, means that self-awareness is developed in the individual as an integral part of his socialization. Therefore, Negroes develop a race consciousness not simply because of their self-realization alone, but very much because of the responses of white persons toward them. This double relationship builds a set of expectations among both whites and Negroes, which depends upon the shared recognition of racial definitions and their meaning for behavior. In this sense, the aim of current Negro demands can be interpreted as the attempt to alter the content of that definition and, with it, the responses that it evokes. It is not that such demands seek to destroy race consciousness; quite the opposite is true. Instead, certain main features of the racial definition must be changed, first by laws, then by social acceptance.

Something of this quality of race relationships in the United States is present in the class relationships in European societies. In England, for example, the aristocracy and the lower class—at opposite extremes—are each trained to recognize the differences between them and to exhibit the appropriate behavior toward their peers and toward those outside of their class. This experience, taught to consecutive generations, develops and maintains a clear line of class consciousness that is reinforced in daily experience.

American society is distinguished by a formally weak emphasis on class

[39] Richard Centers, *The Psychology of Social Classes: A Study of Class Consciousness* (Princeton: Princeton University Press, 1949).

distinctions. I do not mean that we are totally unaware of classes, but rather that our conceptions about class and what it may mean are often vaguely formulated. This is further reflected in the fact that social structure in America is not so fully integrated around class criteria as it is in European countries. Hence, some Americans are very wealthy, but for one reason or another they lack the social status that should go with wealth. In England, for example, such a person would very likely make the Honour's List and be awarded a title with appropriate letters after his name. In the United States, a person may exert a great deal of economic power but may be prevented from gaining a commensurate level of social or even political power. Economic power, after all, can be exerted impersonally in the market place, but social and political power depend upon consensus, which may not be granted. This discrepancy has been called *status inconsistency,* and has been the subject of several studies.

Status inconsistency, as the term implies, is a situation where an individual's position on one social hierarchy does not match his position on another social hierarchy. An interesting feature of status inconsistency, aside from its consequences for social structure, is the possibility that it develops psychological tensions which, in turn, motivate behavior to relieve those tensions. One direction of status inconsistency is for individuals to try to equalize their positions as between the several stratification hierarchies by raising their lowest position in one sector to a level equal to their highest position in another sector. Consider, for example, a wealthy person who is not given the social deference that he thinks he deserves. He could start spending his money in directed ways that are intended to enhance his social standing as, for instance, Andrew Carnegie or others did by endowing philanthropic foundations. An example in the opposite direction, and one that is more common, involves individuals who earn less than they believe the prestige of their occupation justifies. They, too, are subjected to the tensions of status inconsistency that could lead them to demand more money or to develop attitudes that express their discontent.

The existence of status inconsistency gives rise to a number of attitudes that can be better explained from this perspective than from the perspective of class alone. For example, Goffman found a significant correlation between status consistency and attitudes toward the existing distribution of power in American society.[40] People with the sharpest discrepancies between their relative position regarding income, education, and occupational prestige were also the people who most often wanted to see extensive changes in the distribution of power in America. People who were highly consistent in

[40] Irwin W. Goffman, "Status Consistency and Preference for Change in Power Distribution," *American Sociological Review,* **22,** 275–281 (June, 1957).

their relative standing on those three measures were much less likely to want any redistribution of power. People under tension, in other words, wanted to effect some alteration in the environment that would help resolve the inconsistencies in their own situation.

It is evident that stratification does affect behavior, whether individuals are conscious of it or not. To develop that relationship somewhat, let us describe in more detail several areas where the effects of stratification are substantially documented. These areas represent a varied range of human activities; the effects of stratification can confidently be extrapolated to cover other areas not mentioned.

### Socialization

Class differences begin even in childhood. Through the influences of parents, teachers, and peers, cues and symbols to define the social environment are learned. Apparently, those symbols convey differences that are class related and there is little doubt that the child learns their significance. A number of studies have documented these facts of differential socialization, or the difference that class makes. Middle-class parents tend to be permissive, while lower-class parents are more authoritarian; middle-class parents punish by threatening their love of the child, while lower-class parents punish physically and directly. Of course, there are exceptions in both instances but, in general, the two separate themes seem to apply.

There are also differences in the classroom. Teachers, who are themselves from the middle class, tend to be biased toward the middle-class student— whether consciously so or not. The same bias also appears in the textbooks that the student uses which often assume that everyone shares the same middle-class standard. Although we know less about upper-class mores in these respects, we can surmise that adaptive habits and traits for that class are similarly socialized into the child. The situation could hardly be otherwise.

Very early in life, children learn to establish who they are and what they can do. They learn the differences between being comfortably off and being poor, between being a Negro or being white. The child, from the sum total of his experiences, develops a self-image that has been reflected back to him by others, and it is upon this basis that his actions and aspirations are developed. The process is one of learning, but it is a much more subtle process than the formal learning received in school. The child of a middle-class background learns essentially middle-class social techniques and expectations from the adult society that surrounds him: parents, teachers, and authorities. He learns to compete, not simply for the sake of competiton, but for the sake of the rewards. Society, in general, and his environment in particular, are considered as capable of being altered. He believes that he can do something about his environment to the extent that he is successful in his achievements. The middle-class child seems to learn that his world is not directed by fate, although he may excuse his failures by blaming them on fate.

Lower-class children, on the other hand, are exposed to and live in an entirely different kind of environment. Generally, they are confronted continually with barriers that seem to repel their every effort. Adjustment, for them, means learning to cope with the environment as they find it rather than attacking it or altering it. The environment for the lower-class child can be one of threatening people: parents, teachers, police, and most authorities. A person does not constantly combat this kind of environment but, instead, adjusts to it or tries to outmaneuver it.

The same forces are present in the aspirations and aspiration levels that are held by children and adults in the different classes. Aspirations, after all, are subjective reactions to reality, and they can exhibit one of two general modes. The individual can maintain realistic aspirations; what he hopes to do or to become tends to bear some relationship to reality. Or, on the contrary, the individual's aspirations may be only daydreams— escapes into fantasy from the tensions of reality.

Consider, in this connection, an individual's aspirations for going to college. Several separate studies have established that a high correlation exists between the father's occupation and the probability that his children will attend college. In other words, the parents' class position constitutes an enormously important determinant of the educational prospects of their children. Among children of professionals, it has been found that only 12% will not attend college; while, at the other extreme, 48% and 54% of the children of parents engaged in service and factory work, respectively, will not attend college.[41] Such realities are reflected in the expectations of children so that those from the lower class realistically do not think their chances for going to college are very good. Generally, they are right.

A brief comment must be made on the effects upon the next generation of American children of the federally sponsored plans for the Great Society: increased scholarship and financial aid, the economic opportunities program, the stay-in-school programs, and other social welfare programs designed to improve the situation and the future for the people at the bottom of the hierarchy. The effects of these programs, if successful, will be to move large numbers of the people at the bottom into the middle or lower middle class. The underlying consequence of many of these programs is to produce people with middle-class values. Perhaps it will work for significant

[41] Leonard Reissman, *Class in American Society* (New York: The Free Press of Glencoe, 1960), p. 337.

numbers of those who otherwise would never move upward out of poverty or lower-class origins. For them, in any case, there is likely to be a period of sharp tension because they will be converted into marginal people: no longer a part of the lower class, but then not yet securely members of the middle class.

### Neurosis and Psychosis

The relationship between stratification and mental health is one of the best-documented findings in the literature. Much of that relationship can be surmised from the different social situations that each class encounters and the typical responses made to the situations. On the whole, it appears that serious mental illness is more characteristic of those in the lower class than of those in the middle or upper class.

In part, those in the middle and upper classes are more sensitive to the signs of mental disturbance at an earlier point and, therefore, are more likely to seek medical attention. What is more, they have the income that makes it possible to get psychiatric help. In part, too, those in the middle and upper classes tend to lead socially active lives, building an intricate network of responsibilities to the family, to work, and to friends. Although these responsibilities may induce their own strains, they also provide a kind of psychological insurance against complete psychotic collapse. Those in the lower class, on the other hand, tend to lead lives that are secluded or are limited to immediate family. Although the demands may be less than those encountered by middle- and upper-class persons, the possibility seems greater for the development of severe mental illness.

Class differences have also been discerned in the treatment given to the mentally ill. One of the studies of this aspect of the relationship between stratification and mental illness was the New Haven study by Hollingshead and Redlich. First, they established that in New Haven, and probably elsewhere in the United States: "(1) A definite association exists between class position and being a psychiatric patient. (2) The lower the class, the greater the proportion of patients in the population." [42] Next, they established the differences of mental illness exhibited by those in each class. Regarding the neuroses, they found:

The class V [lower-class] neurotic behaves badly, the class IV neurotic aches physically, the class III patient defends fearfully, and the class I–II [highest classes] patient is dissatisfied with himself.[43]

[42] August B. Hollingshead and Frederick C. Redlich, *Social Class and Mental Illness* (New York: Wiley, 1958), p. 216.
[43] *Ibid.*, p. 240.

Regarding the treatment given, Hollingshead and Redlich found that class differences persisted. The higher the class of the person, the more adequately the individual was treated. Upper-class persons were treated more frequently by private doctors or in private hospitals, which they entered voluntarily. Lower-class persons, on the other hand, were more often committed to hospitals by friends or relatives. Furthermore, those in the higher classes were more likely to receive psychotherapy; that is, psychoanalysis or similar psychiatric treatment of a verbal and intellectual character. Those in the lower classes, however, were most likely to receive organic treatment; that is, drugs or shock therapy, or no treatment at all. Part of this difference comes from the fact that middle- and upper-class persons, even when ill, were still able to talk about themselves and their problems, thus justifying psychotherapy. Part of the difference also comes from the fact that psychiatrists are themselves from the middle class and therefore have somewhat better empathic understanding of their class peers. There is an obvious parallel here to the teacher-student relationship that I described above.

### Social Participation

A number of studies have established that lower-class persons participate less in their society than those in the middle and upper classes. Lower-class persons read less, belong to fewer organizations, are less active in the organizations that they do belong to, and generally are cast into a position of a social underdog.

These findings are not reported simply to show a higher sociability index for the middle and upper classes. The implications are more significant. The main point is that middle- and upper-class persons are able to exert somewhat more control over their environment than can those in the lower class. As mentioned earlier, those in the higher social positions have been socialized to consider their environment as fluid—a complex entity that can be modified through action. Not only does the upper- or middle-class person take this view as axiomatic, but also he knows something of the organizational and bureaucratic channels by which ideas can be translated into action. He questions, considers, and then may act.

The lower-class person is cut off effectively from his environment. He does not know the channels for accomplishing change, or even that change is possible. The environment is threatening, and is best left alone. He seldom takes part in effective organized action, whether it is to get the street paved, the garbage collected, or to elect men to public office that will remain sensitive to his needs. The typical middle- and upper-class person is raised to know and to understand such things. He has been educated into the process, and he continues to remain informed about it. Study after study has underlined the startling differences between classes in how much they read, what they read, what they watch on TV, and their awareness of the usual sources of information in society.

There are other differences in social participation. Lower-class people have fewer and more restricted friendships than people in the upper and middle classes. Lower-class visiting patterns tend to be restricted to the immediate family or immediate neighbors, whereas middle- and upper-class persons range more widely in their choice of friends throughout the community. In Britain, for example, it was found that lower-class persons continue to see "Mom" and usually live near her. Middle-class persons, on the other hand, move far away from Mother and see her much less often. This kind of pattern tends as much to maintain the social isolation of the lower class as it serves to enhance the social participation of those in the middle and upper classes.

Other differences in life styles, health and mortality, migration, and political behavior can be described; but those descriptions would not change the pattern. In sum, our descriptions have conveyed that stratification is not simply an abstract sociological category without reality. On the contrary, the reality of stratification is unavoidable, and there is hardly an aspect of life that is not touched in one way or another by its effects. What is more, these effects tend to be cumulative; that is, the effects of educational differences, of income, and of occupational prestige not only correlate highly with each other, but also extend into every corner of the individual's life. Whether individuals are conscious of class differences or not, the effects of stratification are such that they structure the environment anyway.

## Stratification and Social Change

The social divisions that stratification creates are not static or fixed; they are always under pressure. First, the quality and character of the relationships between the several strata in a society are subject to modification; the upper, middle, and lower classes in American society certainly demand, expect, and get from each other different things today than they got fifty years ago. Second, any changes in society sooner or later bear consequences for stratification. For example, any alteration in opportunities for upward social mobility reflects back upon the structure and the psychological stance toward the structure, perhaps in increased tension for those who find their best efforts blunted.

A series of other changes relevant to stratification can be traced in the severe social transformations that are being experienced by the developing nations. Traditional elite structures have been overthrown or pushed aside to be replaced by new elites. Picking up these two themes, let us consider the changes in stratification that can occur in advanced societies on the one hand, and in the developing nations on the other.

### Change in Developing Nations

The remarkable thing about the process of social development or modernization in the new nations of Africa and Asia, as well as in the older but as yet underdeveloped nations of Latin America, is the resemblance of that process to the one experienced earlier by Western nations.[44] The resemblance is especially striking in the case of social stratification. In general, the process is an alteration in the basis and composition of social divisions, especially at the elite level.

Most of the nations that are included in this category were long typified by a dominant aristocratic elite of one form or another. In India and in most African countries, the elite consisted of colonial rulers who effectively controlled the administration of the colony for the empire. This thin stratum of nabobs directed the colonial society from above, with all other indigenous peoples ranked below them. In Latin America, the elite consisted usually of a feudal, land-owning nobility, leaving a vast gap between themselves and the bulk of society. These structures were rigidly stratified and steeply pyramidal, consisting of a small but powerful elite at the apex, with the rest of society almost committed to the position of a peasantry.

Through a combination of many social forces, the existing arrangements were challenged in many societies, which in turn were altered and greatly modified. The main social agents for the transformation were the nascent middle classes in the countries involved. It should be understood that this middle class was not the type, described throughout much of this chapter, that is found in the developed nations. Instead, it was a middle class that existed much earlier in those countries—the group that Marx had called the bourgeoisie. In the history of the West, this group consisted largely of economic entrepreneurs of one sort or another. As they successfully increased their economic power, they were able to effect political changes that served to make their position more secure.

The middle classes in the newly developing nations today are not entrepreneurs, but are more likely to be lawyers and teachers, political bureau-

---

[44] This thesis is described in Leonard Reissman, *The Urban Process: Cities in Industrial Societies* (New York: The Free Press of Glencoe, 1964), Chapters VI and VII.

crats, military officers, and members of the clergy. The composition of this class differs from that in the West because the international economic scene has changed sharply in the past 200 years. The entrepreneurial role is not so pivotal for the new nations as it was for the West; and other skills, chiefly political and diplomatic, are more important. After all, economic assistance and technical aid are available for the developing countries. The entrepreneurial role is being fulfilled by governments or through government sponsorship rather than by individuals acting independently.

The personnel of the middle class has changed from what it was earlier in the West and what it is presently in the developing nations, but the functions have not. In the West, it was this group of middle-class entrepreneurs who led one of the most important social revolutions in history. Today in the developing nations, this same function is met by what must again be called the middle class.

The reason for this pivotal role of the middle class is that its personnel has the most to win by a successful development from traditionalism to modernism: effective power and control. This group, most of whom have been educated in the West, has learned the historical lesson taught them by the West. They must challenge the existing bases of stratification which support the traditional elites. They must, at the same time, win legitimation for their own claim to power by convincing the large mass of the population—primitives and peasants—that their future is tied to the success of the middle class. The ideology under which this is accomplished is nationalism.

However, before considering the role of nationalism in this process, let me comment briefly about the other strata in a society that is on the verge of change. The traditional ruling elite obviously has no desire for change. They are content with existing social arrangements under which they enjoy almost unlimited power—power that is secured by long traditions. They can respond in one of several ways to the changes that can occur.[45] First, they can resist all changes, which means that if they lose out, they lose everything as enemies of change. Second, they can remain passive, taking the position that nothing will result from the threats to their position. Finally, they can be responsive to some of the changes and go along with them, thereby laying some claim to position after the changes have occurred. Whatever the choice, the traditional ruling elite recognizes changes only when they are occurring or soon before. The elite should not be considered as the initiators of such change.

[45] These alternatives are adapted from Clark Kerr et al., *Industrialism and Industrial Man* (Cambridge: Harvard University Press, 1960).

The peasants or primitives who are at the bottom of the hierarchy cannot be expected to initiate change either. For the most part they are not active participants in the decisions of their society. They hold limited social horizons that do not encompass the possibilities of drastic changes. This group is more likely to stay in traditional paths, as it always has done.

The newly emerging middle class, then, remains as the only significant stratum within developing societies that can foresee the possibilities for the future and for their own position within it. As I mentioned above, the ideology or explanations by which such classes have mobilized the necessary sentiment of the peasants and others behind them has been nationalism. By nationalism I mean the idea that the nation-state commands the primary loyalty of the individual above such lesser loyalties as those of region, race, religion, or language. The nation becomes the viable social category which serves to command loyalties and to legitimate social action. Such was the course of changes by the bourgeoisie earlier in the West, the historical point at which nationalism first emerged. Again, today, nationalism has emerged as the principal ideology within which the changes in stratification are taking place.

Nationalism is not a negative term that refers only to dictatorship or antidemocratic political beliefs. In the context in which the term is used to refer to political ideology in the development process, it is most often a sign of democratic influence. Certainly this was the case in the history of the West where nationalism provided a justification for an essentially democratic movement. Thus, today, Emerson (among others) has argued for the same positive force of nationalism.

Nationalism is peculiarly a product of the distinctive forces which have gone into the shaping of the modern world. Those forces are inherently and inevitably "democratic" in the sense that they mobilize formerly submerged elements and classes of society into new social roles, eat away at traditional relationships, and work toward the building of a new great society into which, in principle, all men are actively drawn. Obviously what is involved here is by no means necessarily a democratic constitutional structure nor even an immediate approximation of a society striving toward egalitarianism, although both of these are likely to be present at least as active aspirations. Far more, it is the general conception, derived from the changing social scene, that the people, the mass of ordinary human beings, are of consequence, that they are achieving a sense both of their own worth and of their right and ability to do something about it, and that the leaders must speak in their name.[46]

[46] Rupert Emerson, *From Empire to Nation* (Cambridge: Harvard University Press, 1960), p. 215.

The current developments in the new nations, as I have tried to point out, are especially relevant in an analysis of social stratification. Behind the considerable economic, political, and social problems that these new countries face, an enormous social revolution is occurring. Not only are there radical changes in the distribution of power, but also there are changes in the values around which the new countries are organized. The traditions that maintained the status quo are giving way to new values which have been familiar to the West: the emphasis upon education, upon increased opportunities for social mobility, and the shift from ascription to achievement as a basis for social classification.

### Changes in Developed Nations

As suggested in the introduction to this section, stratification is a dynamic process. It does not stand still in the developed nations any more than it does in the newly developing nations. With respect to the developed nations, however, we are considering the effects of a mature class structure and how it responds to social changes.

In our discussion and argument regarding the direction in which the developed nations are moving, we mentioned that there is no unanimity among social scientists concerning those trends. One group contends that a new ruling class is emerging or has emerged from the complex vectors of change in the institutional structures of advanced societies. An opposing group argues that the channels for social mobility are as open as ever, and that the continual conflicts between pressure groups destroy any opportunity for an elite to form and to gain total control.

There is a lower level, however, at which change can be described. No one disputes that important changes have been taking place in the stratification systems of advanced societies. Even those who contend that no ruling class exists would accept the view that the system is not so open as it was once believed to be. However, these social scientists tend to be optimistic about the future; to see new functions performed by a nonruling elite—an elite that is not so stifling as a true ruling elite must be in order to maintain its power. Keller, for example, in a recent book, argues that the notion of a ruling class is outmoded. Instead, she sees the development of what she calls "strategic elites" which, unlike the ruling elite,[47] are distinguished by their sensitivity to social responsibilities. Keller's argument is far from convincing. A somewhat better argument is advanced by Young. He contends that the new type of society emerging in the advanced countries (such as England and the United States) is

[47] Suzanne Keller, *Beyond the Ruling Class* (New York: Random House, 1963).

one in which the experts are elevated into elite positions as part of the new "meritocracy." He describes the situation as it might look by the next century.

Under the new dispensation the division between the classes has been sharper than it used to be under the old, the status of the upper classes higher, and that of the lower classes lower. . . . Any historian knows that class conflict was endemic throughout pre-merit times, and, in the light of past experience, might perhaps expect that any rapid diminution in the status of one class would necessarily aggravate such conflict. . . . Why has society been so stable in spite of the widening gulf between the bottom and the top? The cardinal reason is that stratification has been in accord with a principle of merit, generally accepted at all levels of society. In the new conditions the lower classes no longer have a distinctive ideology in conflict with the ethos of society, any more than the lower orders used to in the heyday of feudalism. Since bottom agrees with top that merit should reign, they can only cavil at the means by which the choice has been made, not at the standard which all alike espouse.[48]

Perhaps this prognosis is correct. It is one logical extrapolation of current trends and their emphasis upon achievement and merit. However, short of that, there are other trends of change, initiated by the conflict between ideal values and social realities. This assumption forms the basis of an interesting analysis of political behavior by Hofstadter.[49] He sees two general types of political motivations. One is "interest politics," which is the "clash of material aims and needs" among various political groups. The other is "status politics," which is the "clash of various projective rationalizations arising from status aspirations and other personal motives." Hofstadter maintains that during periods of economic stress or depression there is a tendency for interest politics to predominate. During periods of affluence, which are enjoyed by a large section of American society today, there is a tendency for status politics to predominate. Hofstadter then uses these kinds of politics to explain the "pseudoconservative" in politics today. A pseudoconservative is an individual with strong status aspirations who expects the structure to remain as it once was, so that he can realize his status ambitions: the just reward to those who are economically successful. But the structure has changed, and the pseudoconservative's economic success has not produced the status rewards that he had expected. The status acceptance that he seeks is needed to ensure his own feelings of respectability. Frustrated in the attainment of

[48] Michael Young, *The Rise of the Meritocracy, 1870–2033* (London: Penguin Books, 1961), pp. 123–124.
[49] Richard Hofstadter, "The Pseudo-Conservative Revolt," Daniel Bell, ed., in *The Radical Right* (New York: Doubleday, 1963).

this status respectability, the pseudoconservative has turned to the far political right. This extreme political expression and movement to the far right are attempts to turn back the clock, to return to an earlier era when status supposedly was the rightful reward for those who had succeeded in other sectors. Consequently, the force of the political right is directed against progressives who want to change the structure and against the status elite who deny the conservatives the position that they so desperately desire.

The logic of this argument rests, in part, on the sound sociological principle that the values supporting stratification change more slowly than do the realities. However, the matter is not simply a question of having continuous access to mobility opportunities, even in American society. As Lipset and Bendix have pointed out, even that view might be dated.

The argument that increased social mobility will create a healthy society is part of the nineteenth-century intellectual tradition. Its rationale was strongest when the theory of increasing misery appeared most reasonable; that is, during the initial phases of the industrialization process, when it appeared to be true that "the rich got richer, and the poor got poorer." . . . But it appears hazardous to base future studies of social mobility on the intellectual legacies of a nineteenth-century political argument. If it is true, as we have tried to show, that all developed industrial societies are characterized by a high rate of social mobility, it becomes questionable whether further studies of this phenomenon should be based on the implicit simple assumption that more mobility is a good thing. Is it? To assume as much is to ignore the abundant evidence of the social and psychic cost of a high degree of social mobility.[50]

Perhaps too much mobility is not a good thing. However, the final judgment really depends upon the level of expectations held by a majority, in conjunction with the real possibilities for fulfilling those expectations. I believe that Lipset and Bendix have overstated the case concerning the amount of social mobility that is, in fact, available. Certainly, in the case of the Negro in American society, their generalization does not hold true. The expectation far exceeds the possible realization. The Negro's protest today is heavily based on the demand for greater mobility opportunities that for so long have been denied him. Perhaps other groups may find reasons for making similar claims in the future. Perhaps the working class as well as the lower middle class will become dissatisfied, or more dissatisfied, with their present position and their current rewards. The main point is that there is no absolute standard of how much social

---

[50] Seymour M. Lipset and Reinhard Bendix, *Social Mobility in Industrial Society* (Berkeley: University of California Press, 1959), pp. 284–285.

mobility is enough; there are only relative levels of expectations that people maintain.

Nevertheless, it is clear that stratification is not a static social condition but a changing one. This requires that we remain alert to change. It also requires that we view stratification not solely through the categories of an earlier history, not solely through the perspectives of a political ideology, but that we view it with the most objective awareness we can muster in order to realize that we are studying the very core of social organization in process.

# II

# SOCIAL
# INSTITUTIONS

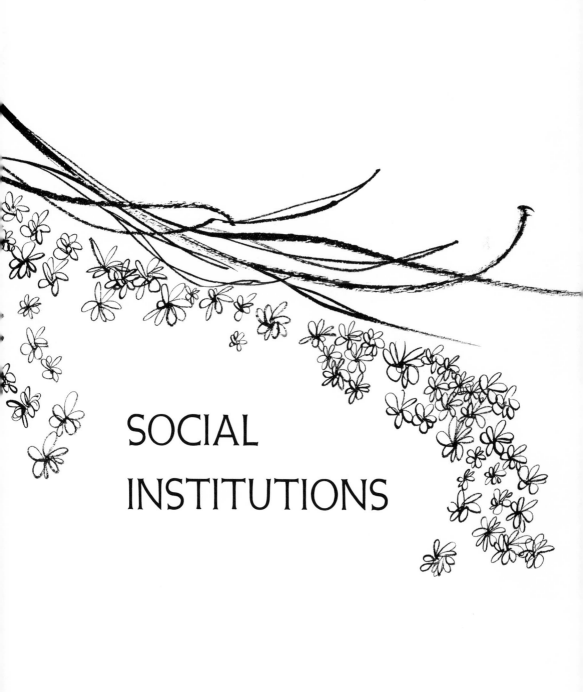

# SOCIAL
# INSTITUTIONS

*5*

# ECONOMIC AND PROFESSIONAL INSTITUTIONS

*Wilbert E. Moore*

# ECONOMIC AND PROFESSIONAL INSTITUTIONS

Economic production is so vital to the organization and plans of contemporary societies that we may be tempted into an uncritical acceptance of the supremacy of economic matters in human concerns. The view that economic activities are primary commands a durable allegiance, whether it be expressed in naïve motivational terms of the hedonic quest for material comfort, or in the sophisticated structural terms of the Marxian theory of historical materialism. Ironically, the notion of economic primacy is superficially more tenable now than, for example, early in the twentieth century. One element of unity in a generally disorderly contemporary world is a considerable—and explicit—preoccupation with economic stability and growth. And this is especially the situation in formerly colonial and other non-Western areas that were earlier cited by anthropologists and sociologists as holding values and complying with rules and practices that minimized the importance of the mere production of goods.

The critics of economic primacy were not wrong, however, except here and there in emphasis and interpretation. Many of the values that men live by and the ways in which they regulate their relations with others still differ in time and place. These differences include modes of economic organization and, importantly, the uses or goals to which productive activities are directed. What has changed has been an increased emphasis and reliance on the *instrumental* use of economic production for such common goals as health and longevity or such diverse ones as national power or religious philanthropy.

## Identifying Economic Elements

The question of the relative importance of the economic aspects of social organization cannot be sensibly answered without some definitions and distinctions. A few illustrations will indicate that the problem of identification is not simply fustian and pedantic.

Consider, first, the large American manufacturing or financial corporation. This appears to be an excellent example of a specialized economic organization. Its avowed purpose is to produce goods or render services for sale in an impersonal market in the hope of yielding a profit on its operations for distribution to its investors. But a closer view casts doubt on the simple identification of the corporation as purely economic in its character. As an *organization*, the tasks of individuals and their relations to other individuals may be affected by the labor market—the possibility of selling one's services elsewhere if one is dissatisfied—but there are distinctly legal, political, and customary elements in the role structure. Indeed, the non-

276

economic elements are such a prominent component of business corporations that corporations constitute one of the major examples of bureaucratic structures (discussed in Chapter 3).

Consider, next, a small tribal society in which nearly all production of food or textiles or building materials is for the use of the family that is the producing unit. If there is some specialization among producing units—for instance, perhaps, in making utensils or tools or weapons—there will be some mode of exchange. Yet the way exchange takes place will probably be *particularistic,* that is, dependent on who is involved rather than on an impersonal financial transaction based on ability to pay. If the exchange takes place almost entirely as a part of the role specifications for various members of a kinship system, we are dealing with a situation in which there is no specialized economic organization at all. Yet we should scarcely be justified in concluding that economic considerations are irrelevant in such societies.

Or, consider as a third illustration the congregationally organized religious denomination, wherein the members and officials of the local church manage their collective affairs. Although it may be expected that their concerns will primarily relate to the religious welfare of members and the broader community, these organizations are not exempt from mundane matters such as construction and maintenance of buildings and equipment, payments for heat and utilities, and provision for the support of clergymen and perhaps other specialized officials.

The important inferences to be drawn from these illustrations are obvious on the surface and a little more subtle on closer inspection. An obvious moral is that the apparent function or mission of an organization may be partially deceiving, in that other elements are involved. If we carry this inference one step further, we can conclude that organizational specialization, or the lack of it, does not evade the pervasive aspects of social relationships. Virtually all patterned relationships involve political aspects (problems of power and responsibility), educational aspects (transmission of relevant knowledge and attitudes), and economic aspects (allocation of scarce goods and services). Thus, even in a highly specialized and pluralistic society where there are many predominantly economic organizations, the economy is an *analytic structure* rather than a concrete one.[1] One may properly ask to which family an individual belongs, which church, which voluntary association, perhaps which social "class." But one cannot ask if he is a member of the economy. If he is alive, he is.

[1] See Marion J. Levy, Jr., *The Structure of Society* (Princeton, N.J.: Princeton University Press, 1952), pp. 88–100.

### Defining the Economic [2]

The quest for the economic aspects of social relations or social structures is challenging because of the diversity of the concrete situations that we confront. We seek what is common among nonliterate societies without a monetary medium of exchange; among capitalist systems with their emphasis on rational self-interest and impersonal transactions; among communist systems with most decisions on production and distribution made by political authorities; or among mixed systems such as those of the United States and Western Europe with large and small profit-seeking enterprises, nonprofit organizations, and various levels of government engaged in producing and exchanging goods and services that have monetary value. One simple expedient in definition is too simple: namely, to view economic activity in terms of material products. Economic activity would then consist of human effort devoted to gathering, growing, or transforming material things (animate and inanimate) for human use and consumption. This definition has a certain appeal, for it identifies a basic and universal category of human behavior. And this conception of what is "the economic" was basic in Marxian theory; until well after World War II the category of intellectual workers, whose efforts had no effect on physical products, was distinctly embarrassing to the Soviet political and statistical system. Policemen, lawyers, teachers, and many of the governing bureaucrats themselves were technically not doing productive tasks. That example reveals the fatal flaw in equating economic activity with physical production, since in modern economies a large and growing portion of all production that has a monetary value comprises *services* rather than *goods*. Protective, educational, legal, medical, and various personal benefits require no storage shelves when acquired by consumers. They do generally require financial remuneration by the consumer or by someone else acting in his behalf. Even if some services are free to the consumer as such, they may be supported by the taxpayer or the employer or the donor to a charitable organization. Thus we must deal with services, but we shall see presently that this is not an altogether easy matter.

There is another way of getting around the differences in social systems in identifying what is economic activity, and this method has some merit.

---

[2] The general conceptualization of economic processes and controls presented in this chapter owes much to three sources: Talcott Parsons and Neil J. Smelser, *Economy and Society* (Glencoe, Ill.: Free Press, 1956); Neil J. Smelser, *The Sociology of Economic Life* (Englewood Cliffs, N.J.: Prentice-Hall, 1963); and my own small volume, *Economy and Society* (New York: Random House, 1955). The approach and emphasis in the present discussion is sufficiently different, however, that these sources are not extensively cited hereafter.

Under the assumption that men's *wants* (for instance, for goods and services) exceed their capacity to fulfill all of them, individually or collectively, most goods and services have some degree of *scarcity*. Economic activity, then, involves the production and allocation of scarce goods and services.

This will serve as a preliminary approximation for identifying our subject, but a cautionary note is in order here. There are universal scarcities in the human condition that are difficult to compare and evaluate in the same context as goods such as food or clothing. Time is such a scarcity, and it is only partially subject to either "production" or "allocation." As expressed elsewhere, "man being mortal, the ultimate scarcity is time." Yet it is noteworthy that in modern market-based or bureaucratically organized economic systems, the scale of pay for labor is most commonly expressed in temporal units, implying correctly that at least some time is subject to allocation—allocation to one activity *at the expense of another.* For now we see that economic scarcity involves *costs*—the sacrifice of some benefits for the sake of others—since all benefits cannot be attained.

Still another scarcity is that of affection or loyalty. The person who "loves everybody" scarcely does so with equal force and vigor. It is a mere prejudice of our particular scheme of values that heterosexual affection must always be singular, but it is unlikely to be extremely plural. The important point about this scarcity is that it has very little comparability with scarce goods. Although an individual may display affection by giving things of value, it is universally assumed that he is not thereby buying affection in return. Indeed, the person whose loyalty is "for sale" is presumed not to have had genuine loyalty in the first place. The existence of affection, despite its scarcity, reminds us that human behavior is emotional and moral as well as merely calculating and acquisitive.

There is still a further alternative approach to the identification of economic activity, and this too has some merit. Its merit is that it works rather well when it works at all. This alternative is to define economic activity as any activity that yields a good or service that has a monetary value in a market. All of "classical" theory in the discipline of economics and much of contemporary theory also rest upon this conception of economic matters. The assumptions underlying the market-based economy (and thus the "principles" of its operation) need not be fully explained here, for they will appear under appropriate topics later in the chapter. The most fundamental assumptions are these: a plurality of producers and consumers (of sellers and buyers) is caught up in a system of impersonal competition, each person attempting to maximize his well-being as measured in monetary terms. Thus the system requires money as a generalized medium of exchange. All goods and services are subject to valuation in a monetary *price* determined by the intersection of supply and demand, and are subject to transfer at the market price.

Our ordinary language of economic affairs derives from a system that approximates these assumptions. Concepts of capital, labor, rent, interest, and wages are meaningful only in a monetary market system. For example, without the "market test" it is impossible to distinguish between *labor* and other presumably useful activities. With the market test we have an *operational* definition of labor as any activity that has a market value. The utility of this conception of "the economic" is of course greatly enhanced by the fact that it comprises the principal subject matter of the highly developed social-science discipline of economics.

The principal liability involved in defining economic matters in terms of monetary markets is that it "prices us out"—to use a play on words—of historical and near-contemporary societies lacking this structural and institutional mechanism. Since the spread of the market system is rapid and increasingly pervasive in the contemporary world, the limitation will be less severe in the future for first-hand observation. Yet in the sociological quest for broader generalizations in time and space, the restrictions imposed by the market-based conception of economic matters is a severe handicap.

It is proper to add here that even where markets are highly elaborated, where there is some approximate validity to the disenchanted view that "everything has its price," and, perhaps, "everyone has his," some goods and many services do not move through the market. Some of these are hardy survivals of presumably simpler times: the services "produced" and "consumed" within the family; those "exchanged" among kinsmen and neighbors on the basis of traditional reciprocities with little implication of market valuation. Other services derive from charitable organizations, or from the tax-supported activities of the state. These commonly involve financial transactions, but to attribute a real or putative market value to goods and services that rest on *administered* prices may be rather arbitrary.

Note, too, that standard economic concepts are difficult to apply in socialist and communist regimes. For the producer, fulfillment of plan is the criterion of success, not profits (which, technically, do not exist). For the consumer, the prices paid for goods and services are determined by administrative agencies of the government, and in principle those prices have no relevance to current supply or demand. Yet it is also noteworthy that no complex industrialized economy has been able to dispense with monetary transactions, financial budgets, or some consumer discretion in the use of money as a means of acquiring many of the goods and services that the system affords.

We have, then, two alternative ways of identifying the economic aspects of human behavior caught up in social systems. We shall use them both, since they serve somewhat different analytic functions. By the first and most general definition, *the economy comprises the structures and processes of producing and distributing scarce goods and of those services that are amenable to allocation and exchange.* (The qualifying clause is necessary, it will be recalled, because of the possible ambiguity of the term "services" and the existence of scarcities such as loyalty that do not lend themselves to either production or distribution.)

By the second definition, *the economy comprises the structures and processes of producing and distributing scarce goods and services amenable to evaluation in a monetary market.* With the change of only a few words, the applicability of the definition has been restricted in time and place but, correlatively, we have gained in conceptual and analytical clarity where it is permissible to use the market test.

### Variable and Common Characteristics

The difficulties encountered in identifying "the economic" resulted from substantial differences in time and place in the way that goods and services are produced and distributed. We may now identify the sources and types of variability in economic behavior somewhat more systematically than was done in the examples noted thus far.

*Size and Efficiency.* The natural resources that man has found use for, including cultivable land, are distributed quite unevenly over the earth's surface. Since we have not achieved a world common market, to say nothing of world political unity, the share of resources commanded by nations or empires is unequal. This is clearly one important factor in the size of economic output, and in the difference between rich countries and poor countries. But resources are always relative to technology and other elements in the variable efficiency of economic organization. A country relatively poor in resources may still prosper through international trade if it specializes in technical and administrative skills. Switzerland imports cocoa beans, mixes them with domestically produced milk, and exports milk chocolate. Various metals are imported, "mixed with" highly specialized technical labor, and exported as watches and other precision instruments. Perhaps even more importantly, Switzerland produces banking and other commercial services for export as well as for the domestic market. England's economic leadership rested not only on importing raw materials and exporting manufactured products, thus capitalizing on skilled human resources, but also on rendering important services in banking, insurance, and marine shipping. Japan, too, has followed the trading pattern, but the "services" that Japan sought to export were primarily military and political, which led it into a disastrous conflict and defeat.

Some countries that are rich in natural resources have lacked other essential ingredients for economic growth, such as political stability. Argentina and Brazil remain mainly "primary producers," that is, producers of agricultural products and minerals, processing being done elsewhere. In the contemporary world economic growth (as measured by per capita income) requires not only improved efficiency in agriculture but the diversion of capital and labor into manufacturing and services. The supposed exceptions of Denmark and New Zealand as well-to-do agricultural countries are illusory. Very much less than one half of the labor force in these countries is engaged in agriculture; the others are engaged in manufacturing and various services.[3] Industrialization is the principal key to economic success, a point well understood by the leaders of new nations and other underdeveloped areas that are seeking to join the modern world. And that brings us back to technology.

Technology is often confused with its partial embodiment in tools and machines. More properly, technology comprises the compendium of principles and practices useful for the transformation of the environment to suit human goals. Thus the selective breeding of plants and animals to increase the quality and quantity of agricultural products is as surely technological as is the new alloy of steel, the new automatic machine tool, or the new chemical compound. And the same is true of techniques of accounting, administration, or education. To think of technology as materialistic is to indulge confusion, a confusion that has beset social theory at least since the time of Marx. Technology is mostly carried in the heads of individuals, or in the linguistic and other symbols that they have set down on paper. It is a major source of variability in the magnitude and efficiency of economic production.

Resources may be squandered, of course, and human talent and energy may be applied wastefully in economic production and distribution. The concept of *efficiency* has various meanings, but in the present context can be considered as the *economizing* of scarce inputs to yield useful outputs. Any of the meanings of efficiency imply the notion of *rationality*, that is, the use of the best available verified knowledge and logical inference to suit means to ends or to predict situations and events not directly observed. There are many sources of inefficiency in economic systems, but no matter

[3] See Wilbert E. Moore, "Changes in Occupational Structures," in Neil J. Smelser and Seymour Martin Lipset, eds., *Social Structure, Mobility, and Economic Growth* (Chicago: Aldine Press, 1966).

how justifiable in other respects, they may be expected to impair the magnitude of goods and services available for distribution.

*Forms of Economic Organization.* We have noted that it is never proper to regard the economy as a concrete organization comprised of people set apart for certain tasks, while other people belong to the educational, religious, or political segments of societies. Where an occupationally specialized labor force exists the distinction may have a sensible meaning as the source of livelihood, but fundamentally the distinction comprises aspects of individual life organization or the operation of social systems rather than mutually exclusive segments of societies. The degree of structural specialization is highly variable, however. One does somewhat less damage to analytical clarity by referring to the economy of modern, complex societies than in the use of the concept in a nonliterate or predominantly agrarian society. Comparison of economic functions across systems with radically different degrees of specialization is difficult or meaningless. The peasant cultivator is likely to be also an artisan and trader, whereas the American farmer commonly buys his tools and often even his seed, and sells his produce to a jobber or other middleman rather than displaying it in a market for sale or barter. As the monetary market system spreads to areas previously engaged in "subsistence production," specialization will inevitably follow in its wake. Thus the future should bring a reduction in the qualitative differences among economies and make comparisons more feasible.

*Specialization necessarily requires coordination*—among complementary producers, such as the suppliers of parts for an elaborate machine, and between partial producers and general consumers. One form of coordination is provided by a system of exchange. This was the form of integration assumed in "classical" economic theory: specialized producers offering wares for sale to selective consumers, producers also perforce being consumers of the products of others. But this model assumes that production will be carried out by individuals (or, at most, households). Where larger capital in the form of factory buildings and machinery and many and varied skills are required to turn out a product, another type of coordination is essential: political or administrative coordination. All complex, modern economies use a mixture of these principles. The free-enterprise or capitalist systems place greater emphasis on the market as coordinator, but still organize much of manufacturing through vast bureaucratic organizations that secure internal coordination by administrative decisions. These systems also increasingly rely on the state both for various types of production and for controls on the market and private administration in the volume, types, and conditions of production. Communist and other state-controlled systems of production place greater emphasis on officialdom as the coordinator, but still find it necessary to use a kind of market in transferring raw materials and com-

ponents among manufacturing producers, and a more extensive market in
the exercise of consumer discretion.

Some degree of specialized and therefore coordinated economic activity
is likely to occur in even the most seemingly simple, household-oriented
productive systems. There are, we shall see, many alternatives to the
atomistic, impersonal market of producers and consumers. Both traditional
and carefully calculated cooperative ventures abound in the production
and distribution of goods and services. Even in modern, complex economies
the "mom and pop store" and the simple partnership without employees
coexist with the giant financial or manufacturing corporation; these, in
turn, coexist with publicly owned enterprises, service producers whose
rates are regulated by public commissions, and with insurance companies
"owned" by their policyholders and banks "owned" by their depositors.
But this is not yet the end. Scarce goods and services are distributed directly to consumers by tax-supported agencies and by private philanthropic
organizations.

All of this is in the context of a "pluralistic economy." The situation is
only slightly simpler in modern communist states, for simplicity and centralization are difficult to maintain along with elaborate specialization of
functions. Political authorities commonly lack both the knowledge and the
power requisite to a completely bureaucratized economic system. This may
be diversity by default, but diversity it is for all that.

***The Social Setting of Economic Activity.*** The economy being always
an aspect of the organization of societies rather than something concretely
set apart, the interplay between economic activities and others is somewhat
more complex and difficult to grasp than, for example, the relations between preclusive groups such as doctors and nurses, or corporate management and labor unions, or white and Negro residents in a neighborhood.
The relations between "business" and "government" in a pluralistic society
are complicated by the circumstances that businessmen are commonly
citizens, voters, taxpayers, and subjects of police and other public administrative organizations, and by the further circumstances that public officials depend upon private manufacturing and distribution in both their
private and public positions.

But let us assume that we may deal with the economy as a kind of sub-
system within a larger social framework, as we are certainly permitted to
do for analytic purposes. It then becomes clear that the scope and kind of
economic activity cannot be expected to be purely autonomous, that is,
independent of environing conditions. Economic activity is always instrumental toward individual ends or subservient to collective values. It serves
to preserve or enhance health, longevity, creature comforts—and, in a
complex market economy, the enjoyment of experiences, esthetic tastes, phil-

anthropic orientations, and (with dubious efficacy) eternal salvation. From an aggregative or collective point of view, we may examine the influence on the economy of values such as national prestige or "building the socialist fatherland"; of beliefs such as other-worldly Buddhism, or seemingly this-worldly communism, or the "worldly asceticism" of Protestant Calvinism; and of social theories such as the efficacy of socialist concentration or capitalist dispersion. Ironically, the crude Marxist views of economic primacy are belied by the fact that communist *doctrine* has had a wider acceptability than the economic conditions that presumably produced it.

*Ideology* thus is an important variable in accounting for differences in economic organization. Ideology gets translated into particular structures (the profit-seeking firm or the communist central planning bureau) and particular actions (the quest for status mobility or worldly immortality through good works or good donations).

The form and direction of economic activity are correspondingly influenced by the way *power* is exercised in the selection among alternative courses of action. Who makes the decisions? The so-called "liberal" economic order—the model of which was essentially atomistic—relied on *consumer sovereignty*. But no modern economy relies solely on consumer discretion. The taxing power of the state is used to support production for collective, public purposes—for example, highways, schools, and national defense—and also to support various welfare benefits and income redistribution to rectify the inequities in the operation of the market.

The state is only the most conspicuous among the structures affecting the economy. The economy is also affected, for example, by the rate at which new families are formed and the rate at which they produce children, by the quantity and quality of the products of schools, and even by the policies and practices of religious bodies.

These and other aspects of the social environment are, of course, subject to change over time as well as to differences among societies at any given time. Their effects on the size and shape of the economy lead by still another route to the rejection of the theory of economic autonomy.

*Common Features.* Despite the diversity in the organization of economic activity, it remains true that any society that survives must provide for the material support of its inhabitants, and must do so through rules for producing and allocating scarce goods and services. It is particularly in the production of goods, and most particularly in the production of the necessities for physical survival, that the common problems of the human condition emerge most clearly. To reduce economic activity to such an elementary common denominator is, of course, to lose the rich variety that we have been illustrating, but the common elements still deserve attention. We can carry the identification of uniformity across time and space one step further. Economic activity provides a major link between man and his nonhuman environment. And although man may populate his environment with religious and magical beings and forces, he will not survive unless he also adopts a rational, technical stance of adaptation and actual manipulation. The actual state of knowledge and of technical skill has been highly variable among societies, but we are now moving toward a common "world pool of technology." Even where the techniques of production have been "primitive" indeed, man has used what skill he has in his never-ending quest for mastery of the environment for his own purposes.

### Plan of the Chapter

A prospectus on the organization of this chapter is perhaps a little tardy at this point, but it has been deferred pending necessary conceptual clarification and the identification of elements and variables. The next principal sections will be devoted, respectively, to production, distribution, and consumption as the three categories of economic activities. Throughout these sections, our attention will be selective. First, negatively, we shall not be much concerned with the organizational characteristics of the contemporary corporation, since those have received attention in Chapter 3, nor will we give much attention to the processes of modernization of underdeveloped countries, as that is a matter for Chapter 12 on social change. Second, positively, each of the major sections ends with a uniform subheading on institutions. This focus is for the deliberate reason that the rules of conduct, ideal and actual, are the main elements of order and therefore predictability in social action, social patterns, and social systems.

The institutional emphasis is also carried into the final section of the chapter, which comprises an "extended illustration" on the professions. The professions exemplify the complex intersection of economic and noneconomic elements in the supply and distribution of very specialized services.

## Production

The wondrous abundance and variety of goods available to consumers in the stores and shops of the Western world testify to the productive capacity of industrialized economies, as well as (incidentally) to the frequent frivolity of consumer tastes. The goods made available to the ordinary consumer, if he can afford them, represent only a part of economic output. The economy also turns out tools and machines used to fabricate consumer goods; ships, trains, trucks, planes, and buses to carry people and things;

equipment to deliver news and entertainment via the radio and television, communication via the telephone, light and energy via the electrical system; laboratory and other research equipment for the furtherance of man's knowledge; office buildings, legislative halls, museums, and monuments; and weapons of fearsome complexity and destructiveness. Yet much of the "production" of modern economic systems has scant or no physical manifestation: services ranging from professional and technical through the entertaining and esthetic to the maintenance of cleanliness and good grooming.

### The Factors of Production

Traditional or "classical" economics identified three components in the productive process (which was usually, although usually implicitly, limited to the output of goods). These *factors of production* were land, labor, and capital. *Land* comprised not only agricultural surfaces but also mineral and other resources. *Labor* was often considered as additive, interchangeable units of human effort, although attention to specialization impaired the notion of equality of the units. *Capital* comprised the tools and equipment used in production, and also the financial resources available for investment in such tools and equipment.

Each of the factors of production was conceived as yielding a distinct form of income: land yielded *rent*, labor a *wage*, and capital either *interest* or *profit*, the latter being presumably proportional to the risk undertaken by the investor.

Later economic theorists suggested the addition of a fourth productive factor, necessary to put the others together: either *organization* or *entrepreneurship*. Schumpeter, especially, emphasized the role of the entrepreneur, not primarily as a coordinator or even as a risk-taker, but as an innovator.[4]

Now, leaving aside for the moment the factor of land, it can be readily seen that the "factor mix" can be altered within wide limits according to the relative prices of the two remaining factors, capital and labor. If capital is scarce and therefore expensive and labor abundant and therefore cheap, production is likely to be *labor-intensive*. Under contrary circumstances the production is likely to be *capital-intensive*. If two manufacturing firms are operating under approximately equivalent conditions of capital and labor, one firm may have a competitive advantage because of the superior skill of its management and the superior form of its productive organization.

---

[4] Joseph A. Schumpeter, *Capitalism, Socialism, and Democracy*, 3rd ed. (New York: Harper and Row, 1950).

Industrialization in the strict sense entails the substitution of inanimate sources of power (thus, capital) for some human sources of power (thus, labor). Yet there is an increased demand for workers with skills not previously needed, and for higher levels of skills. Since this labor, and perhaps less-skilled labor also, tends to be persistently scarce relative to demand, rising wages encourage profit-seeking employers to attempt ever-new ways of substituting capital for labor.

However, this way of conceptualizing the components of production has substantial defects. There is little sensible basis for dististinguishing between land and capital, since land has economic significance either as a good for producing other goods or else as mere space for the location of economic activity. And management or entrepreneurship is surely nothing else than a specialized kind of labor. That confusion rested on a deeper one: the failure to appreciate the importance of the *quality* of labor, as represented by skill levels and distributions, as distinct from mere quantity. (This basic theoretical error of classical economics led to more than a century of tendentious arguments over the "general level of wages," which is an essentially meaningless concept in a diversified labor force, other than as a statistical average having virtually no labor-market significance.)

The failure to identify *technology* as an extremely important factor of production was more justifiable in strictly conceptual terms. For technology represents either a qualitative dimension of labor inputs, or else, when embodied in machine tools or productive processes, capital. But technological change is a principal dynamic factor in productive systems, and its neglect, no matter how conceptualized, is intolerable.

### The Marxist Reformulation

The tremendous importance of Marxism as the theoretical or ideological foundation for vast and powerful nations would alone commend Marxist theory to our attention. Our concern here, however, is not to trace the course of Marxism as a political ideology, but the much narrower one of examining the theory of productive processes. Although many believers in Marxist ideology would argue that the conspicuous political success of the ideology verifies the economic theory that is its alleged base, we do not have to accept this assertion in order to justify examining Marx's attempted revision of the factors of production.

For Marx,[5] the shape and size of an economic system was the consequence of the interplay of three components: the *conditions of production*—ap-

---

[5] Karl Marx, *Capital: A Critique of Political Economy* (Chicago: Charles H. Kerr, 1909), Volume 1. See also Karl Marx, *A Contribution to the Critique of Political Economy* (New York: International Library Publishing Co., 1904).

proximately equivalent to resources and population; the *forces of production*—approximately equivalent to technology; and the *relationships of production*—approximately equivalent to the relations between the control of property and the allocation of labor.

Since Marx was interested in developing a dynamic view of productive systems, and (as he argued) of changes in societies as a whole as a consequence of economic transformations, he was led to emphasize technological change. Indeed at times he almost appears to be a technological determinist. But he actually concentrated his attention on productive *relationships*, that is, on what we may call the organization of productive enterprises. Those relationships, on analysis, prove to be determined not solely by technology but more importantly by the way that *power* is allocated in a system and, especially, by the power implications of differential property rights in productive equipment. (Thus, although Marx insisted that his social theory was materialistic, his "economic factor" included major political and normative elements.)

Marx's major work was entitled *Capital*,[6] yet capital does not figure as a factor of production in his economic theory, except rather implicitly and even surreptitiously in his attention to property ownership. Why? First, *Capital* was an analysis and critique of capitalist economic systems, which he thought were doomed to be overthrown because capital ownership was being used by a minority to exploit a majority comprised of workers "who owned only their own labor." Second, Marx espoused a "labor theory of value," whereby any good, whether for consumption or production, was no more than "embodied labor." Capital, then, had no independent standing as a factor of production. However, in Marxist theory capital does enter the economic system by way of technology, "the means and instruments of production." In that form, capital is viewed as one determinant of the size and growth of the economy.

### The Problem of Capital Formation

The Marxist theory of production points to a problem that is common to all modern economic systems, and indeed to all systems except the most primitive forms of hunting and food gathering. The problem might be expressed in the aphorism, "You can't have your cake and eat it too," although that does not quite catch the critical issue. The issue is the allocation between goods produced in order to produce more goods and those available for current consumption. At the simplest level this problem is evident in the case of the farmer who grows edible grains or such legumes as peas and beans. If he consumes, barters, or sells his entire crop, he must have

[6] Karl Marx, *Capital: A Critique of Political Economy, op. cit.*

some means for getting part of it back as seed for his next planting. A factory cannot long maintain even its current level of output, to say nothing of expansion, unless part of the product is converted into savings to replace outworn equipment.

The problem increases, of course, when growth in the quantity of output is made the goal. Marx considered a system iniquitous that permitted part of current output to be "withheld" as profits; by the labor theory of value, this constituted *exploitation* of labor. Yet in a capitalist economy, profits constitute a principal source of investment for expanded production. In any socialist economy where economic growth is sought by those exercising political power, the "exploitation" of workers in the Marxist sense must also occur. Indeed, if the political regime is essentially totalitarian and severe, the exploitation of labor may be substantially greater than in a "free enterprise" system, for workers will not be permitted to bargain for a larger share of the product.

In a "pure" capitalist system, which of course has never existed, capital would be accumulated only through the individual decisions of income receivers who save some portion of their income (wages, interest, profits) and seek to invest it in some economic activity that will yield a further income. In a "pure" socialist system, which also has never existed, all capital would be collectively owned, and it would be expanded only by the political decision of central planning agencies, by allocating some portion of the current product—or its monetary equivalent—to upkeep and expansion of productive facilities. In fact, all capitalist countries have also used the taxing power of the state at least for such public capital expenditures as highways and schools, and often for a great variety of other purposes besides. And even in Soviet-type economies, the individual is permitted some discretion in the sense that he may invest his savings, but theoretically only in government bonds, thus adding to the public resources that are allocated by others, while the saver receives interest as a reward for deferring the expenditure of some of his income.

Savings constitute a source of capital only if they are put to productive use. Even relatively impoverished tribal or agrarian societies may have substantial "frozen" savings in the form of jewelry or even coins of precious metals. But these yield no income to their owners nor investment resources for the economy.

One of the most important inventions in the long, slow course of "modernizing" the economic regimes of the Western world was the *bank*. Apparently an invention of Italian traders of the renaissance, a bank provided for pooling and relatively safekeeping of the funds of depositors. Since, normally, all depositors do not want to withdraw funds simultaneously, the banker can invest some portion of the funds for commercial investments.

Banks came to be supplemented by joint stock companies, from which emerged such modern economic structures as the corporation with its equity shares and the mutual insurance company which is "owned" by its policy-holders.

Banks, corporations, and mutual companies provide ways of pooling small funds and of investing them by persons presumably having unusual competence in business and financial affairs. But now the individual investor is not making the major investment decisions. He is not quite as powerless as is the taxpayer who helps support the economic activities of the modern state, for he is free to withdraw his participation, and may have some kind of a vote in the selection of corporate directors or even in setting major policies. Yet, unless his resources are very large, his influence is likely to be small.

It is important to highlight these forms of capital formation, for they are the major source of private capital for the productive systems of modern "capitalist"—or, more properly, "mixed"—economies. And the outstanding feature of these mechanisms is that the individual investor places his *trust* in the managers of his funds, and thus those managers have a *fiduciary* relationship to the beneficiaries. Private, profit-oriented businesses share with the trustees of university endowments or philanthropic foundations—additional forms of capital management—this essentially normative or institutional position. We have come a long way from the model of the atomistic, self-regulating economic order comprised of individual risk-takers.

The problem of capital accumulation is acute in the underdeveloped countries of Asia, Africa, and Latin America. The leaders of these countries, but also a major portion of the general populace, desire sharp increases in material well-being. Although some improvements in output can be achieved simply by more efficient practices within existing types of production (mainly agricultural in most such countries), substantial improvement requires greatly expanded capital investments: in power plants, roads, factories, and, not least, schools. It is scarcely possible simultaneously to improve current consumption and to secure the capital for further, future improvements. Even with substantial foreign capital the modernization of such economies will be very difficult.

The difficulty is worsened by rapid population growth, the outcome of reduction in death rates with little decline in birth rates. In the classic formulation of the "population problem" by Malthus [7] the pessimistic view

---

[7] T. R. Malthus, *An Essay on the Principle of Population* . . . (Homewood, Ill.: Richard D. Irwin, 1963); first published in 1798; second edition (and only important alteration), 1803. See David Glass, ed., *Introduction to Malthus* (New York: Wiley, 1953).

was expressed that the biological reproductivity of man would always exceed man's capacity to expand production. In view of the historic course of concurrent population growth and improved levels of living in the older industrial countries, the Malthusian thesis was far too simple. It remains true, however, that there may be a basic conflict between production of people and production of economic goods and services.

### The Inputs of Labor

The pace of mechanization and automation of production in the most advanced economic systems has not yet made man obsolete as a producer. It could scarcely do so, despite fanciful notions of machines that not only reproduce themselves, in a chaste, asexual way, but also invent their improved replacements. It is man who invents the machine, supervises its production, installs it, maintains it, and repairs it, and still "mans" its operations in major ways. The automatic factory or the automatic inventory and billing process still require highly skilled human intervention. Although machines will go on replacing people in a number of occupations, the demand for skilled and highly specialized activities increases at least proportionately. In general, the occupations most readily replaced by machines are those that already have been routinized to a degree that individual decisional elements have been reduced to the point of virtual elimination.

But let us back up. Labor is a major factor of the productive process in all of the world's economic systems, historical and contemporary. Man has always wrestled with nature, with his material environment and animate competitors, to extract his livelihood. Through much of man's earthly existence as an emergent biological species, his survival, individual and collective, has been precarious. But with the gift of intelligence, and therefore a calculating and innovative rather than simple passive and adaptive capacity, he has used his environment to his own ends.

There are a few human habitats in which the challenges to man's survival are not very severe. In warm and relatively constant climates, with an abundance of edible botanical foodstuffs simply available for gathering, productive activity may be minor. But it is easy to exaggerate the idyllic quality of the islands of the South Seas (where's that?). Man's natural proclivity to reproduce beyond the carrying-capacity of his environment, together with attacks by such unseen enemies as microbes, bacteria, and viruses, means that either scarcity will prevail or that the idyllic life turns out to be disease-ridden and short.

No, man is a struggling animal, and seeks not only environmental adaptation (in a perceptive and not simply passive way) but also environmental mastery. In the course of his history he has invented all sorts of devices that would reduce his input of sheer physical exertion and improve both the quality and quantity of the output of goods available for consumption.

Tools for cultivating, planting, and harvesting increase the productivity of labor in agriculture, as does the use of natural and artifical fertilizers. Weapons for killing game remain important only in very primitive economies; the domestication of animals for milk, meat, and hides provided a surer source at less effort than the chances of the chase.

The *productivity* of labor always represents a combination of human skill and energy, on the one hand, and the use of tools, techniques, and non-human power, on the other. Although technology is commonly viewed as "labor-saving"—possibly threatening the livelihood of some workers in a labor-market system—its more general effect is that of labor-enhancing in productive processes. A major component of the high productivity of labor in industrial systems is the extensive use of *motorized power*—driven by steam, internal combustion, or electricity.

There are two additional factors in labor productivity, however: *specialization* and *organization*. These are interactive with given types of technology, to be sure, but they are not determined by technology acting as a sovereign, independent variable.

Some degree of specialization is to be found in all economic systems, if for no other reason than the biological characteristics of the human species. At the minimum, sex and age are clearly relevant for productive capacity. A sexual division of labor is universal. That its form is not exactly biologically determined is evident from the fact that the exact definition of suitable male and female roles is highly variable in space and time. Yet biological relevance is apparent in the usual association of women with tasks of the household and its environs, which is consistent with the primary female function of child-bearing and child-rearing. Women rarely go on hunting expeditions or war parties or engage in exceptionally heavy physical labor. In tropical Africa,[8] for example, some tribes have practiced a form of cultivation often encountered in rain forests. Patches of ground are cleared and burned, permitting cultivation of foodstuffs. But as the fertility leaches away, a new area must be cleared. It is the men who clear and burn, and the women who plant and tend the crops.

The descriptive literature on productive practices in nonliterate societies offers ample evidence of social variability, however. Many of the normal expectations concerning sexual distinctions—normal in a statistical view of the world's societies—have exceptions. And most systems offer types of

[8] See Wilbert E. Moore, "The Adaptation of African Labor Systems to Social Change," in Melville J. Herskovits and Mitchell Harwitz, eds., *Economic Transition in Africa* (Evanston, Ill.: Northwestern University Press, 1964), Chapter 13.

situations in which there is scant specialization. The transplanting and harvesting of paddy rice, for example, seems to call for all available labor, exempting only infants, the infirm aged, and the acutely ill or handicapped.

Industrial productive systems tend to blur sexual distinctions in productive roles, particularly where sheer physical strength is not demanded. Hiring whole families was not unknown in early British and American textile mills. However, industrialism—or, rather, the wage system strongly associated with it—introduces a distinction between labor and other useful activities. Its general effect in early stages has been to reduce the economic role of married women, at least as measured in financial terms. The separation of work from the household makes it inconsistent with female familial duties, until such time as the practice of birth limitation partially restores women to some potential participation in the economy.

Age, too, is clearly a basis of role specialization. At the very least, infants and the senescent must be exempted from participation in production. In some nonliterate societies, little further distinction is evident; in others, age-grading of roles is elaborate and the stages of the life cycle are clearly marked off. In modern industrial societies, the significance of age is almost entirely institutional. That is, economic participation is governed by minimum age laws, compulsory education, and rules relating to formal retirement. Within the economically active population, or the labor force, age has its significance in less direct ways: seniority practices in employment security and promotions, the new skills brought to the labor market by younger workers, and the dangers of economic obsolescence among older workers.

In nonindustrial societies, kinship position is likely to provide additional bases of specialization. Older sons may have different rights and duties than younger sons—an illustration of the importance of relative age rather than absolute age. The patriarch of a clan may enjoy his authority primarily in kinship terms rather than for reasons of age alone. And to the degree that social distinctions are hereditary, as is commonly true in nonindustrial societies, the accident of birth determines the child's adult social position. In industrial societies, family and kinship operate primarily in their effect on individual life-chances in a competitive occupational system rather than in determining precise productive roles.

Note that specialization based on sex, age, or kinship is arbitrary in the sense that the individual has little choice in what he does, and also in the sense that virtually no account is taken of individual variations in talent, skills, or effort. It seems highly unlikely that in any society no account has been taken of individual variability, at least by way of protecting the system against patent incompetents, and probably by permitting—if not encouraging—special abilities. Udy found that workers performing such skill-requiring (and commonly cooperative) tasks as sea fishing and house construction were recruited on grounds of competence rather than arbitrary social position.[9]

It is precisely when the division of labor is based upon criteria of competence that it has clear implications for productivity. The advantages of the division of labor noted by Adam Smith [10] rested upon the subdivision of tasks, so that the performance of each could be at a higher level of proficiency than could be expected over all of the operations required for a finished product. Assuming that the product had previously been made by single artisans, this kind of specialization involves *dilution of skills*. Most of the social criticism of industrialism—including some Marxist criticism—has been in terms of the degradation of labor and the worker's subservience to technologists through the instrumentality of managerial authority and of work-pacing machines.

This clearly has been part of the continuing process of specialization associated with industrialism. Yet to concentrate on skill dilution alone is misleading and tendentious. A vast majority of the products of a modern industrial system were simply not made prior to industrialization. Hence, their introduction into the productive system has required *new* skills, even if those skills may have needed rather brief training. More important, the process of industrialization has produced a tremendous *diversification* of labor, much of it requiring a high level of training.

Over the long term, the major trend in the skill distribution of occupations has been that of *upgrading*. This has come about, negatively, by the radical reduction of the demand for relatively unskilled labor. Skill dilution, in effect, has been an intermediate stage in the process of changes in organizational and machine technology. When the worker's task has been reduced to short-cycle and decisionless routine, a machine may be deliberately invented to perform the operation. But upgrading has also come about, positively, by greatly increased complexity of management and technology, diversity of product mix, expansion of sales and distribution and, especially, in the production of technical and professional services that have little to do with manufacturing.

Specialization so permeates the structure of a modern economic system that it goes to extremes far beyond the ken of the ordinary citizen—whose own job may carry a title and duties not readily understood by his family, friends, and neighbors. The last, and not very recent, edition of the *Dic-*

[9] Stanley H. Udy, Jr., *Organization of Work: A Comparative Analysis of Production Among Nonindustrial Peoples* (New Haven: HRAF Press, 1959).
[10] Adam Smith, *Inquiry into the Nature and Causes of the Wealth of Nations* (New York: Modern Library, 1937), first published in 1776.

*tionary of Occupational Titles* [11] contained about 22,000 legitimate occupations in the United States—pimps, prostitutes, and pushers were excluded—in addition to several thousand occupations that were essentially the same but were called by different names.

With the steady expansion of knowledge and useful technique characteristic of modernized economic systems, it is scarcely conceivable that the process of specialization should come to a halt. That could only occur after a world-wide plague or nuclear holocaust when the person of somewhat general skills would stand out from his specialized, but therefore terribly dependent, fellow survivors.

Specialization has reached epidemic, or rather pandemic, scale in university teaching and in engineering. It has even invaded such long-established professions as law and medicine. There the common elements of professional identity are elementary indeed, and beyond that specialists have difficulty in mutual communication, to say nothing of making common cause with their clients.

The machine has not made man obsolete, but it has made automatons obsolete. And that raises serious questions concerning the future social and economic position of persons of meager genetic intelligence and poor adaptibility to changing demands of the productive system.

Specialization occurs on the grand scale as well as the fine. Industrial, financial, and commercial organizations exist in complex complementarity. If these are all established by a central planning bureau in a communist state, it is quite unlikely that the ratio of successes to failures will be appreciably higher than occurs in a free-enterprise system. In either, it is difficult to chart the exact level and type of production that will bring materials through various stages of processing in exactly the proper quantity and quality, and at the proper time. The communist state's contempt for the consumer as an element in this process may be a very slight advantage. Administrative wisdom and control may not be markedly superior to the play of profit-seeking market forces in responding to a perceived demand for particular goods and services. Either alternative is certain to produce unanticipated delays, shortages, and overages in a complex economic network.

Specialization on the grand scale also has a temporal dimension. Labor is specialized not only by specific occupation (with all that implies in terms of education and acquired skill) but by major "sectors" of the productive system. In the course of economic modernization, labor is *always* shifted out of agricultural production into manufacturing and services. Historically, the pattern of relative growth in the "industrial" distribution of the labor force

[11] United States Department of Labor, *Dictionary of Occupational Titles*, 2nd ed. (Washington, D.C.: U.S. Government Printing Office, 1949), Volume 1.

was first an expansion of manufacturing employment, and then a relative expansion in services of all types. This is consistent with Colin Clark's [12] thesis concerning the relative expansion of primary, secondary, and tertiary production. The situation in contemporary developing areas does not follow the historic pattern.[13] The quest for new economic opportunities has led to a rate of urbanization far in excess of the expansion of industrial employment. The result has been an expansion of services, *faute de mieux*, which may be highly specialized but not really very productive.

Specialization *between* major sectors of a complex economic system is quite consistent with specialization *within* each sector. The productivity of labor has always been increased by relative decreases in amount and increases in quality. This has occurred in both agriculture and manufacturing. But beyond services there is no place to go. This raises the question as to whether specialization, on the grand scale and the small, does indeed have limits. Even without catastrophe, generalists may once more command a premium—as they do already in business management—as compared to the person who knows a lot about little, or the organization or sector of the economy that is highly dependent on a given (but precarious) state of complementarity with other parts of the system. The quest of many American corporations for product diversification may be viewed as an attempt to reduce the risks attendant on extreme specialization.

*Specialization without coordination is chaos.* The notion of the entirely self-reliant individual is mostly nonsense, and could not fit the survival requirements of the human species. (The aged and infirm might be allowed to perish, but to adopt this practice with infants would quickly erase human habitation of the earth.) The devices for securing coordination in nonliterate societies became centered, in the course of social evolution, on the family and kinship system. But we have noted that the kinship expedient will not take care of all situations. The greater man's achievement of rational control over his environment, the less he can rely on merely arbitrary bases of role allocation and the exercise of decisional authority.

We thus come to the question of the *organization* of labor—not initially in the sense of interest-oriented and calculated combinations of workers into unions. Labor is organized by any patterned form of allocation of duties, even if those duties are incidental to sex, age-grade, and kinship position. More clearly differentiated forms of organized, cooperative activities for foodgetting or construction are rather common, as already noted. Where clear-cut specialization of functions, presumably allocated according

[12] Colin Clark, *The Conditions of Economic Progress,* 2nd ed. (London: Macmillan, 1951), pp. 395–439.
[13] See Wilbert E. Moore, *The Impact of Industry* (Englewood Cliffs, N.J.: Prentice-Hall, 1965), pp. 70–72.

to ability, is combined with a clear-cut source of authoritative coordination, we have a form of organization that is essentially *bureaucratic*. The term should not concern us as much here as the particular combination of social processes.

The rational legitimacy of a bureaucratic order rests on its outcome: the authoritative coordination produces cooperative results that could not have been achieved so well by alternative ways of doing things. (The ultimate basis for the authority of the coordinator is rarely rational in pure form. The authentication of his position is likely to rest upon property rights, or some nonrational belief in political ultimacy, such as the hereditary divine right of rulers, the doctrine of apostolic succession in the Catholic Church, or the view that a popular vote lends credence to administrative wisdom.)

There are alternatives to the presumably legitimate authority of bureaucratic organization. At the one extreme is the atomistic, self-regulating system of producers and consumers, governed by impersonal market forces. It was an interesting notion concocted by the classical economists. It had fatal defects, only a few of which will be noted here. First, the theorists failed to note that unregulated competition is, in a dynamic sense, a contradiction in terms. The end product of such a system would be, inevitably, a monopoly, or total chaos. Second, the psychological assumption of the purely self-seeking individual would work only within very narrow limits. Man is not "naturally" much of anything in motivational terms. And if he, a fully matured adult without childhood socialization, were to appear solely as a rational calculator, he could neither countenance children except in an exploitative way nor attempt in any way to improve their lot.

An economic system that is uncalculated in the gross, although closely calculated in the fine, has a certain appeal. Its appeal is especially strong in self-acting, democratic political systems. But the notion has a third fatal defect, and that is the failure to recognize the fact that *organized* production, with attendant specialization, has competitive advantages over individual production. Actually, classical economic theorists did recognize this fact. They simply had no way of incorporating it into theory, for their models of the economy—like most economic models since—had very little resemblance to observed practices and events.

There is another, and radically different form of organizing labor, and that is to make the authority of managers absolute through slavery. Slavery has a hardy survival power in the contemporary world, although its incidence is now chiefly confined to the supply of girls to the overprivileged rulers of obscure Islamic kingdoms in the Arabian peninsula. Over the course of human history, the most general rule regarding slaves has been the assumption—backed by power—on the part of slaveholders of their natural (ethnic, genetic) superiority over slaves. Wherever this assumption broke down to some degree, slavery became more nominal and less burdensome.

Slavery as an incident of political conquest was self-confirmatory of the superiority of the conquerors. And the tables could turn.

Enduring and elaborate systems of slavery—the Roman Empire, the Ottoman Empire, and the American South—came to depend upon slave labor for skilled and administrative tasks. And in every case, the nominal slaves who performed more than menial and unskilled tasks lost some of the burdensome accoutrements of slavery. In the American South some slaves were permitted to purchase their freedom, out of independent earnings, which makes no sense at all in a system of absolute slavery. The essential point here is that the purely coercive organization of labor—and many more indirect forms have been invented under contemporary totalitarian regimes—has little chance of producing exceptional and talented performance.

In modern industrial societies the most typical form of organizing work is bureaucratic, at least in the most elementary sense of that term. That is, the worker sells his services to an employer. This is a market transaction, but part of the bargain entails submission to the functionally specific authority of the employer, and to the rules that have been propounded for assigning tasks and regulating performance. In a communist regime, all workers are technically employees of one or another agency of the state. In the mixed systems prevalent in other economically advanced countries, the employer may be an individual, a private collectivity such as a corporation or nonprofit organization, or some branch of the government.

In nominally capitalist countries there has been a long-term decline in self-employment: the individual farmer or business man, the independent artisan, and the professional in private practice. We may identify this trend as the growing *bureaucratization* of the labor force.[14]

The term bureaucracy is being used here in a very elementary sense. The actual organizations that produce goods and services vary in size, in technology and therefore the relation of men to machines, in the occupational mix of employees, and indeed in the theories and philosophies of administration. These differences will not be dealt with here, although they would need to be taken into account in any close analysis of the social determinants of economic productivity.

The discussion of the way that productive labor is organized cannot be dropped without some brief comments on labor unions. The two principal bases for representing the common interests of employees in negotiations

[14] See Wilbert E. Moore, "Changes in Occupational Structures" (cited in footnote 3).

with employers are *occupational* interests and *status* interests.[15] In the United States the former principle leads to *craft unions* and the latter to *industrial unions.* Neither principle is exclusive of the other, however. Thus craft unions may make common cause with others when their like interests as employees are at stake; the coalition becomes in effect a temporary industrial union. Industrial unions frequently must face the divergent interests of particular occupations or occupational groups that they encompass; their political problems of cohesion may be rather severe, resting, in effect, on a coalition.

Nor do these sources of common interest exclude interests that employees share with their employers: the viability and prosperity of the firm or agency, and even the relative position of an industrial sector or type of service. All of these interests are concurrent, although sometimes inconsistent. I have argued elsewhere [16] that, contrary to the American experience, the industrial union—relying on common status interests—is more typical of *early* industrialization. Persistent specialization and upgrading make occupational interests the most salient, although, to repeat, the alternative identifications do not disappear.

Outside of the United States, unions are commonly very political in orientation, unless they have been actually "captured" by the government in totalitarian regimes. This is an interesting subject for comparative sociological analysis, but not directly relevant to our interest here in economic production.

## Values and Power

In nominally capitalist economies, a considerable part of production remains responsive to consumer demand. The "sovereignty" of the consumer is impaired, however, not only by a great deal of production for capital expansion and various public purposes but also by rules and practices that range from the protective to the manipulative.

Rules relating to food purity or the distribution of drugs are designed to protect the consumer from his own ignorance or folly. The cultivation of consumer demand through advertising or the determination of women's clothing fashions by a small number of designers may restrict the independent choice of consumers.

In Soviet-type economies, even consumer goods are predominantly produced according to a decision on consumer needs by planning officials

[15] See Wilbert E. Moore, "Notes for a General Theory of Labor Organization," *Industrial and Labor Relations Review*, **13,** 387–397 (April, 1960).
[16] *Ibid.*

rather than as an attempt to satisfy consumer demand in an impersonal, competitive market.

It is a little too simple to say that what an economy produces, and in what quantity, will reflect the values of the particular society. If values have any authenticity at all, they are bound to be significant. But there may be a diversity of interests and thus a considerable lack of value consensus. And since all goals may not be simultaneously achieved, some decisions are necessary about priorities. These may be made by consumers voting with their money, but also may be made by corporate executives and by political officials. To the degree that modern nations are not only welfare states but also—with some exaggeration—garrison states, the exercise of political power over the economy may well continue to grow.

### Institutions

Institutions, as normative complexes relating to major social functions, provide the framework for nearly all orderly and patterned human activity. In modern complex societies, norms of conduct are often embodied in law, rather than entrusted to informal and conventional social controls. But informally sanctioned norms, and various bodies of private law such as the regulations that abound in business bureaucracies, also persist, and new ones appear.

Here it is useful to distinguish two sets of norms that are, perforce, universal in their relevance to productive systems, and two that are especially relevant to contemporary industrial systems. The universal institutions of special relevance to productive processes are *property* and the *division of labor*. Of the institutions that have peculiar relevance to industrial systems, the first is *contract;* the second has no conventional designation, but we shall use the convenient designation, *trust*.

Property—rules defining rights in scarce values—is crucial for the allocation of decisional responsibility in economic production. The simple declaration that all property is held is common—by a nonliterate tribe or a modern communist state—is always evasive and inaccurate. How productive resources will be used always involves decisions that do not include all living inhabitants. The decisions may be made by a familial patriarch or a commissar, by a corporate captain or an elective official of the state; but neither in participation nor results will everyone share equally.

Property is best viewed as a "bundle" of rights in scarce values, but there is no reason to suppose that the bundle is tightly tied. The conception of private property allots "all" rights to a tight bundle: use, advantageous or slovenly nonuse, appropriation of increase, sale, gift, testamentary transfer, and so on. But all property rights are subject to restriction in the public interest—for example, requirements that a plot of land not be used for or become a public nuisance, or restrictions on the use of weapons that could endanger the legitimate rights of others.

The American heritage in law and social philosophy shows a marked preference for freely transferable private property, and that is consistent with the philosophy of the atomistic, impersonal market. But the property rules relevant to the modern business corporation are much closer to feudalism than to private property: different people have different rights in the same aggregate of resources.

The notion that property consists of rights of men in *things* will not stand close scrutiny. The scarce values of contemporary society include patents and copyrights, business good will, a protected professional reputation, and even freedom of the individual from false allegations of misconduct.

Property rules are crucial in economic production, since they relate both to rights of access to the factors of production and rights of decision in the way production is organized and carried out.

Household tools and utensils, furniture, clothing, and other consumer items that have little significance for the continued productivity of an economic system are mostly controlled by individuals or family units in all societies. Productive resources, on the other hand, are usually subject to much more public scrutiny, if not outright communal control. It would be difficult to say, across the whole breadth of the human historical and contemporary experience, whether private or public control had predominated. Certainly contemporary societies present complex mixtures of these principles. Yet economic scarcity is such an intrinsic feature of the human condition—even in seemingly affluent societies—that conspicuous nonuse or waste of productive resources is always likely to lead to communal intervention, including possibly revolutionary changes in the forms and rules of proprietary rights.

The ways by which labor is allocated to productive tasks are also hedged by a multitude of rules. In preceding paragraphs we examined some of the alternatives, and in doing so we were dealing with institutions somewhat surreptitiously. The *division of labor* is a kind of special, succinct phrase for role allocations. Since all social roles are presumably useful, by some standard of value, we have had to adopt rather different stances with respect to economic systems that have no monetary system of exchange and economic systems that do. In the former, productive labor tends to be determined by such arbitrary criteria as sex, age, and kinship position. But we found that somewhat more rational practices were likely to appear where talent was critical. And the arbitrary bases of labor allocation do not disappear in contemporary, rationally oriented economic systems; they are played down, and made to be conditional rather than precisely definitive elements.

In modernized societies, economic role allocation takes place through the mechanism of the *labor market*. Access to the market and exit from it involve age rules for participation, some sex rules for participation, and a great variety of formal training and educational qualifications.

It would be a mistake to view a modern economy—or, for all we know, a premodern one—as governed by a kind of mindless process in the allocation of labor. Formal rules of qualification for positions—a combination of education and experience—probably originated in public civil service systems. The rules were designed to discount nepotism, patronage, and other nefarious practices that prejudiced the efficiency of operations.

The rules of competence in labor allocation had rough going in private employment practices, for there they encountered the proprietary right of owners to assign powers to familial heirs without regard to talent. Many hateful, and some justifiable, complaints have been voiced about the practices of contemporary business corporations that have wide public participation in stock ownership; but in the recruitment of people to positions of responsibility, the corporations increasingly follow the civil-service norm and not the hereditary, familial, and proprietary norms.

The communist and other totalitarian economies often substitute one set of irrationalities for another: for hereditary privilege they substitute ideological purity. Neither offers any assurance that proper people will be put in proper places.

The rules for the allocation of labor are much more extensive than those that we have examined. Every bureaucratic system—now in a moderately full sense of the term—maps out job specifications and corresponding qualifications of potential claimants on positions. These specifications are, in effect, rules for placement and performance. Note, too, that part of the role differentiation is in terms of relative *authority*—power delimited by rule to the appropriate context of managerial decision and coordination.

An exact correspondence between differentiated skill demands and differentiated skill supplies *will not occur*. Job specifications always turn out to be ideal; the availability of people will not match.

The message to be drawn from this disharmony is not uniformly disheartening. Individual talents often exceed those role specifications set out by organizational planners or by the operation of mindless traditional systems. Although the rules of competence tend to discourage creative innovation, the talented misfit may be able to change the system for its own good.

Two other institutional complexes are of special importance in highly industrialized economic system: rules of *contract*, and rules of *trust*. These principles are almost antithetical, but in practice they tend to be complementary.

Let us first examine the rationale behind rules of contract.[17] The elements involved in production, such as financial resources, raw materials, manufactured components, and labor, must be somehow assembled. This often involves not only transportation but anticipatory requests for future delivery at an agreed time. Moreover, at least the nonhuman elements may be subject to different property owners (or their socialist equivalent, different administrative officials). Without some confidence in the reliability of agreements, it would be impossible to plan production schedules or to continue orderly operations. Contracts formalize these agreements, and are made enforceable by appeal to governmental administrative agencies or courts. As the justly famous French sociologist Durkheim noted, late in the nineteenth century, the "noncontractual elements in contract" include the backing of a political and institutional order.[18]

Not all agreements are so formal. Some transactions allow little time for drawing up agreements. Although our knowledge of the operation of some economic transactions is not very precise, it seems quite clear that the system depends to a considerable degree on *trust*.

Trust plays a much more conspicuous role in centralized economic decision making. Managers of business and industrial corporations and governmental officials operate with "other people's money." Although democratic governments afford a kind of "contractual" ratification through elections, as do corporations through votes of stockholders, wide discretionary authority rests with the decision makers. The nominal owners of corporations and the beneficiaries of public investments thus *entrust* their interests to others, who stand as *fiduciaries*. In the management of endowments and even current funds for educational or charitable purposes, the concept of *trusteeship* has been formally and legally institutionalized, but the powers and duties of trustees remain widely discretionary.[19]

When the presumption of honorable and disinterested conduct by trustees and other fiduciaries proves unwarranted, or a businessman's word is no longer "his bond," remedies are likely to be found either in formal contract or in formal administrative supervision. But the latter is, in effect, simply a

[17] Talcott Parsons and Neil J. Smelser (cited in footnote 2; pp. 104–113) refer to contract as "the central economic institution." Their view of the economy, however, is mainly delimited to the kinds of activities and transactions that are the focus of economic theory, and therefore to a system based on an impersonal market.

[18] Émile Durkheim, *The Division of Labor in Society*, translated by George Simpson (Glencoe, Ill.: Free Press, 1949), Book I, Chapter 7.

[19] See Marion R. Fremont-Smith, *Foundations and Government* (New York: Russell Sage Foundation, 1965), Chapters III and IV.

substitution of one fiduciary mechanism for another. We have come a long way from the presumption of individual self-help in the regulation of economic processes.

## Distribution

Through much of the history of humanity, a large share of the goods and services produced has been consumed by the producing unit. Nomadic hunters and gatherers engage in little exchange, nor do those people whose livelihood rests upon subsistence agriculture. Yet even in such situations there is a sort of microdistribution system. The producing unit is normally the family, not the individual. Not only does man not live by bread alone; normally man does not live alone. Distribution within the family is likely to be relatively independent of the contributions of each to the productive process. This principle is universal. Even in complex monetary market systems, the market stops at the household door. Thereafter, distribution is according to kinship position and need, not according to "merit."

Any degree of specialization among producing units implies some mode of exchange, but the forms and mechanisms of the transactions may bear slight resemblance to monetary markets.

### *Traditional Exchange and Modern Markets* [20]

Although many subtler distinctions may properly be made for some analytical purposes, the forms of exchange can be conveniently classified into three types: (1) ceremonial exchanges and gifts, (2) direct barter, and (3) true markets with money as a generalized medium of exchange. True markets, when introduced, *tend* to supersede other forms of exchange, but do not do so completely, as we shall see. In fact, all of these alternatives may and commonly do coexist, and there is no clear evolutionary sequence in their appearance.

One of the more famous of the exotic forms of exchange is the *kula* pattern of the Trobriand Islands in the South Pacific, extensively recorded by Malinowski.[21] Here articles of solely decorative use—necklaces and arm-

[20] See Cyril S. Belshaw, *Traditional Exchange and Modern Markets* (Englewood Cliffs, N.J.: Prentice-Hall, 1965). I have partly followed Belshaw's organization in this section. See also Bert F. Hoselitz, "The Market Matrix," in Wilbert E. Moore and Arnold S. Feldman, eds., *Labor Commitment and Social Change in Developing Areas* (New York: Social Science Research Council, 1960), Chapter 12.
[21] See Bronislaw Malinowski, *Argonauts of the Western Pacific* (London: Routledge and Kegan Paul, 1932).

bands made of shells—were traded in an elaborate clockwise and counter-clockwise pattern around an archipelago. Other, more consumable products were traded also, but ideally this was incidental to the ceremonial exchange. The exchange partners were not necessarily kinsmen, although other forms of distribution in the Islands followed kinship rules regarding duties for economic support.

Perhaps equally famous was the *potlach* of the Kwakiutl Indians of the Pacific Coast of Canada.[22] Giving away of blankets was competitive and aggressive, designed to assert the superiority of the giver, but setting up the expectation of a countermeasure by the economically fortunate but socially demeaned recipient.

In an excellent recounting of these and other ceremonial exchanges from the original ethnographic sources, Belshaw [23] has added his own comparative interpretation. He argues that such ceremonial gift-giving confers power on the giver, and always implies some form of reciprocity. And, so that all this will not seem simply the irrationality of untutored savages, he reminds his readers of both the competitiveness and the implied reciprocity of Christmas gifts and donations to bridal couples. To emphasize the expected reciprocity, Belshaw uses the term *prestation* for ceremonial gifts—viewing them as something like a loan.

Ceremonial distribution, such as wedding or funerary feasts or for stately occasions in religious calendars, does serve as a form of income redistribution. Although the poorer guests may not be able to compete with their wealthy hosts when it comes their turn, their status embarrassment is at least partially compensated by the fact that they have had a feast. And it is not uncommon to carry food away for later consumption, making less sharp the contrast with the normal fare.

The reciprocity need not be exactly balanced between donor and recipient. Indeed, in the operation of kinship systems, the support of parents or other adult kinsmen for children may not involve directly reciprocal expectations. Particularly in the contemporary Western family, the obligations of children toward ill or indigent parents are institutionally vague and minimal. Thus something different from true reciprocity prevails. It is, to some extent, a kind of *serial service*—pass it on, rather than pass it back.[24]

We come closer to the true market in the practice of barter, althoug Bel-

---

[22] The basic ethnographic source is Franz Boas, "The Social Organization and the Secret Societies of the Kwakiutl Indians," in *Annual Report of the Smithsonian Institution for 1895* (Washington, D.C.: U.S. Government Printing Office, 1897).

[23] Cyril S. Belshaw (cited in footnote 20), pp. 46–52.

[24] See Wilbert E. Moore, "Aging and the Social System," in John C. McKinney and Frank T. de Vyver, eds., *Aging and Social Policy* (New York: Appleton-Century-Crofts, 1966).

shaw notes the presence of rational calculus and even haggling in ceremonial exchanges.[25] Barter typically involves exchange of foodstuffs among
specialized producers, as well as trading food for handicraft products.
Again, although some haggling takes place, an enduring barter system is
likely to develop conventional terms of trade that are fairly immune to
short-term changes in supply and demand.

As recently as 1949 in a provincial market in Mexico I found direct barter
according to traditional terms of trade going on side by side with cash
transactions.[26] (In fact, there was an intermediate form, a kind of money-
mediated barter. Each product was valued in monetary terms, which thus
determined the appropriate quantities to seal the bargain, but no money
changed hands. However, payments "in kind"—more properly, in goods—
are not rare in highly commercialized economies where money is scarce.)
Only five years later, on a revisit to the Mexican market, I found no trace
of barter. What had happened meanwhile was that the region and its market were no longer self-contained. Commercial buyers of foodstuffs, flowers,
and handicrafts for resale in other cities competed with local purchasers,
and merchants offered manufactured goods from outside the region, competing with vendors of their own products for the pesos of market participants.

The social functions of traditional markets, as distinct from mere trade,
have often been noted by observers. But again, if one recalls the aisle-
blocking, gossipy groups in a modern supermarket, or the alcoholically gay
businessman's lunch, the contrast between the traditional market and
nominally impersonal transactions seems exaggerated.

It would be virtually impossible to operate an industrial system without
a monetary market. Apart from the necessity of a rational accounting system in the calculus of costs in production and distribution, the chief utility
of money is that it permits the specialized producer to become a generalized
consumer. Imagine the complications if factory workers were simply paid
a portion of the week's products! And, for heavy capital goods, that alternative is simply impossible.

The market, of course, need not be pure in the sense of operating only
in terms of supply and demand. Public officials may introduce price controls
or rationing—commonly using coupons or tokens as a kind of secondary
currency. Indeed, at one period in the Soviet Union different classes of consumers were charged different prices for identical goods or services. But
that, too, is not radically different from special discounts (for instance, to

[25] Cyril S. Belshaw (cited in footnote 20), pp. 11, 47–49.
[26] Wilbert E. Moore, *Industrialization and Labor* (Ithaca, N.Y.: Cornell University
Press, 1951), pp. 226–228. I was wiser than I knew when, on page 240, I identified
markets as agencies of change.

teachers and clergymen), special prices to kinsmen, or employees' discounts.

A modern mixed economy offers a wondrous variety of markets. Trading in corporate stocks and bonds is essentially a capital market, and has more to do with productive processes than with distribution as such. The same is paradoxically true of the never-never land of "commodity markets," where rights are bought and sold in "futures," that is, in crops not yet harvested. No goods are moved.

Goods are moved, however, in ways additional to the chain of distribution from manufacturer through one or more levels of wholesaling to the retailer and eventually to the consumer. Commodities ranging from race horses and tobacco to paintings and postage stamps for collectors often move through auction markets, and household goods are often so redistributed. The auction market normally puts only one intermediary—the auctioneer—between seller and buyer, and often serves as a way of identifying a specialized clientele for goods that might otherwise have a slow turnover and thus require a high markup by a retailer.

The simple flow of goods from producers to consumers, through a series of sales and purchases, is much more complex when viewed in its totality. Two organized networks of services stand out, and others exist less prominently. *Banks* serve not only to provide capital to investors, but also as accounting and not infrequently as credit agencies for consumers. We shall return to credit later, for it forms an important ingredient in an open-market system. Bank checks serve as an alternative to official currency in financial transactions but, unlike "bearer" notes, checks require identification and their negotiability implies, once more, trust.

The other network is that of *advertising*. In its simplest form, advertising entails a mere announcement of where specified goods and services are available, usually with a stipulation of price. But in competitive distributional systems, the producer, wholesaler, and retailer are aided by advertising agencies. Such agencies (and their counterparts in the actual distributive chain) appeal to any consumer interest or irrational motivation that will lead to a sale. This is an area of "applied" sociology and psychology that clearly does affect sales. In the United States, advertising provides the principal support for newspapers, magazines, radio, and television. For the American, the radio or TV "commercial" is a kind of inescapable fact of life. Yet the question of whether advertising genuinely expands markets—and thus pays for itself by making possible mass production for mass markets—or only reallocates consumer expenditure, often temporarily, cannot be definitively answered. Clearly, if there is a relatively fixed market for a given product, advertising by one competitive producer or distributor is essentially a blackmail tactic, leading to increased advertising expenditures by others as a defensive measure, with no net social welfare benefits except for the salaries of advertising agents and the profits of the mass media, at the expense of consumers. This is, incidentally, one example of the tremendous expansion of services in modern competitive economies, where the net consequence may be of little or no use.

Any attempt at an exhaustive list of distributive mechanisms would almost certainly turn out to be incomplete. We should note in passing, however, two types of organization that are linked to credit: bill-collecting agencies, and credit reference bureaus. Additionally, "Better Business Bureaus" attempt a sort of private policing of the morals of merchants, and all sorts of "trade associations" attempt to identify the common interests of competitors without incurring the official wrath of public administrative agencies and the courts by suppressing competition.

Things are apparently simpler in communist regimes, where there is no competitive market. Yet official agencies proliferate, "representing" producers, distributors, and consumers. Competition in effect persists; the fiduciary component increases, and the arena of competition shifts from the market to the bureaucracy. The large American corporation consolidates the same divergent interests, with no more nor no less assurance that these interests are in fact accurately and adequately representative.[27]

The market for services, which now comprises over one half of the national product and the labor force in the United States, presents some special features in distribution. With minor exceptions, services cannot be transported or stored. (The exceptions chiefly involve electronic data storage and retrieval systems.) Many of the useful activities that comprise services are closely linked to a complex economic network: transportation, communication, investment analysis and sales, banking, insurance, and distribution—as examples of economic functions—and secretaries, receptionists, statistical clerks, computer programmers, filing clerks, and accountants—as examples of types of occupations. But other services are less closely linked to the production and distribution of goods: sports and entertainment, personal care, household duties, and a great variety of professional activities.

The expansion of services in contemporary complex economies is partly real, partly artifactual. The "real" components are comprised of services necessary to the operation of a complex economic system, and of those that add genuinely new knowledge and skills to the social system. The "artifactual" components are those that involve the simple process of moving services "into the market," although the activities were previously per-

---

[27] See Wilbert E. Moore, *The Conduct of the Corporation* (New York: Random House, 1962), especially Chapter XIII on the way that the corporation's clienteles are represented in management.

formed by the consuming unit (laundry, bread-baking, clothes-making) or on the basis of mutual aid among kinsmen and neighbors (residential and farm construction, care of the young during the temporary absence of parents, emergency labor).

Many transactions for services are quite straightforward and impersonal: dealing with a trash service, newspaper delivery man, or appliance repairman. Others involve special norms. The conventions for the payment for professional services are highly variable. Some involve a kind of bargaining, or at least an understanding, in advance of the service. In other situations, such as many physician-patient relations, any mention of money may be positively *gauche*. The service is sought, performed, bill rendered, and paid, as if the whole dirty, commercial transaction were unworthy of notice. Physicians prosper that way; patients often do not.

### The Market and Its Competitors

No society has entrusted the distribution of services solely to an impersonal market mechanism. Even the ideal, mechanistic models of the classical economists accorded a kind of grudging acceptance to the state as a rule maker, rule enforcer, and arbiter among discordant interests. The role of the state in providing postal communications, at least part of the means of transportation, to say nothing of national defense, scarcely entered the economic calculus; it did enter into the way societies organized themselves for public as well as private services.

The alternative mechanisms for economic distribution, particularly as depicted in the polemical social criticism of the last century or more, have been supposed to be the market and the state. The market alternative left the consumer with sovereignty, his actual power dependent on his financial resources—these, too, presumably dependent on his merit and skills in the labor market and other factor markets. (Hereditary privilege has always been embarrassing in Western institutional systems. It provides a clear collision between traditional kinship principles and the norms of fair competition. All nominally capitalist countries have temporized with the institutional conflict by imposing inheritance taxes, gift taxes, graduated income taxes, and by attempting to alleviate inequities among the young through free public education.)

The essence of the political alternative to the market is caught by the socialist slogan, "From each according to his abilities, to each according to his needs." Soviet-type systems have by no means dispensed with a merit system of economic rewards—indeed they have carried the principle to unusual lengths. However, those states, and other economically advanced states in varying measure, have extended the social services that are supported by taxation and "free" provision rather than through a market transaction.[28] In mixed economies many of these welfare benefits are complementary to the market. They involve "transfers" from taxpayers to benefit-receivers in the form of income maintenance. This leaves the recipient discretion on market expenditures. But many "services," from national defense to art museums, from police protection to education, and from pollution controls to medical clinics, are provided directly. These services are not without economic cost and often provide substantial distributions to private manufacturers and to public and private workers, but they are distributed by exercise of the *fisc* rather than the consumer market.

Money and direct services are also distributed in several other ways, which are largely neglected in the long and tedious arguments between advocates of capitalism and socialism. Traditional forms of kinship duties and informal reciprocities have a hardy survival power in the seemingly harsh, impersonal, urbanized world. Self-help, familial cooperation, and neighborly mutual aid provide mechanisms for the allocation of some goods and many services. Great varieties of voluntary associations exist, some of them serving only very narrow and special interests of their members, others rendering all sorts of unpaid volunteer services. These shade over into a very important economic resource, particularly in the United States: the private philanthropic organization, whether dependent on current funds or administering an endowment.

None of these alternatives to the market as an agency of distribution is totally immune to market forces, since a kind of imputed "price" is likely to be implicit in the most informal of unilateral or reciprocal services. Yet the market is warmed by human emotion and transformed into acts of humanity—qualities that are alien to the coldly calculating transaction.

## Institutions

As the discussion of the market's competitors as agencies of distribution has demonstrated, normative principles pervade all aspects of the distributive process.

Let us examine first the extreme case of the impersonal, competitive market, which appears about as emotionally neutral a situation as can be examined.[29] Yet not only is any competitive system dependent upon effective rules for its actual survival, but the behavior of participants is under

[28] Such "redistributive" patterns were by no means unknown in traditional economic systems. See Karl Polanyi, Conrad Arensberg, and Harry Pearson, eds., *Trade and Markets in the Early Empires* (Glencoe, Ill.: Free Press, 1957).

[29] For a somewhat differently oriented discussion of market norms, see Arnold S. Feldman and Wilbert E. Moore, "The Market," in Wilbert E. Moore and Arnold S. Feldman, eds., *Labor Commitment and Social Change in Developing Areas* (cited in footnote 20), Chapter 3.

a further constraint: the presumption of *rationality*. Whatever the deep, devious, and possibly dirty motives that prompt a consumer's choice, he is expected to behave *as if* he were acting rationally. The principle of *caveat emptor*—let the buyer beware—is hedged about by public regulation, private ethical codes, and the special responsibilities of professionals. But the sharp, apprehensive view of human relations is no more "natural" than an attitude of trust, of dependence, of status-enhancement (a powerful incentive in buying shoddy, overpriced, but prestigious merchandise), or the sheer indulgence of whim. Rationality is a norm, even though its sanctions are mainly informal and occasionally ineffectual.

Apparently at the opposite extreme from the rule of rationality is the rule of charity. Although the Rotary Club motto asserts that "He profits most who serves best" and fund-raisers may try to convince potential business contributors that community welfare services are really good for business, the basis for much of philanthropy is clearly nonrational and, in that precise sense, religious. Some donors may seek to assuage their guilt for unmerited prosperity, and others may seek, through named endowments or buildings that are at the same time monuments, to achieve a kind of worldly immortality. Yet charitable endowments, for the benefit of generations yet unborn, scarcely come within the norms of reciprocity. This alternative to the rule of rationality deserves closer examination than it has received.

The norms of reciprocity in traditional forms of exchange appear to mix a strictly economic calculus—poorly calibrated for want of a monetary metric —with rather altruistic forms of kinship duties and rather self-interested status-enhancement. Indeed, modern as well as tribal societies permit great varieties of "mixed currencies": gifts may not be reciprocated in kind, but by the according of deference. A curious kind of balance occurs when the unreciprocated gift is given to a person of unusual prestige, who may be improvident or, in the vagaries of the market, has not been well rewarded. Has he been patronized or exalted?

The importance of *credit* in modern markets was noted previously. Credit, in effect, once more combines the conflicting principles of contract and trust. The credit rating of an individual or a firm includes some estimates of assets that might be liquidated to satisfy the claims of the creditor if the promised payment is not forthcoming, but also commonly involves such behavioral indexes of "character" as promptness in paying bills and, in simpler times, such indicators of sturdy virtue as sobriety and church attendance.

A final normative complex affecting distribution may be called the *standards of distributive justice*. In the calculating and mechanistic view of distribution espoused in classical economic doctrine, the market was a quite adequate mechanism for just distribution, since individuals were rewarded according to the merit of their economic contributions. One trouble with this doctrine was that economists forgot that they once were children, that they might become dependent in their old age, or that they might suffer an incapacitating illness or accident for which they were in no way culpable.

The realistic normative problem—a problem to which the answers vary in time and place—may be posed: What are the common rights of man (or citizens or inhabitants) as compared with differential rights based on the accident of birth or the somewhat chancy operation of competitive economic systems? All major traditional religious systems have countenanced or endorsed inequality in economic benefits rationalized one way or another. (If comunism is viewed as a religious ideology, which is perfectly proper, then it does espouse equality; it is a distant and, one would suppose, unrealizable ideal in actual communist regimes.) Yet, in the modern secular state, there is a strong tendency to expand the common and equal benefits, while not at all eliminating all sorts of differential benefits that are accorded by various criteria of competitive merit.

## Consumption

A principal measure of the relative success of an economic system is the volume of goods and services available to the ordinary household consumer, along with public and private organizations. Of course another measure of economic success is military power, which may be achieved at the expense of the supply of ordinary consumer goods—guns versus butter. Still another measure of success is the rate of economic growth, since that indicates a sufficient level of prosperity (or a sufficient level of exploitative terror) to permit the use of part of the gross product for expanding the economic base through new capital and new productive technology.

### Types of Consumers

We have seen that the flow of goods and services in a modern, mixed economy is very complex. And the "end of the line" is not necessarily the individual household. It is convenient to distinguish four categories of consumers, although each could be divided further in terms of such variables as type and volume of purchases: (1) the private household; (2) agencies of the government at national, state and local levels; (3) manufacturing and business establishments; and (4) various nonprofit organizations such as voluntary associations, private schools and hospitals, churches, and charitable organizations.

Our attention will turn presently to familial consumption patterns. Here we shall comment briefly on the nonhousehold consumer.

Part of the activities of the state involve simple transfers from taxpayers to public beneficiaries of one kind or another, and others involve services delivered directly, as we have previously noted. But the state exercises a near-monopoly on the purchase of weapons—the principal exceptions being the firearms owned by sportsmen, nervous householders, and professional criminals. Food and clothing are bought for members of the armed services, automobiles for public officials and, of course, paper in vast quantities for official reports and interoffice memoranda. It is indeed difficult to imagine any type of goods purchased by a family that is not also bought by some agency of government: building equipment, furniture, garden equipment, or home-workshop tools. Some of these purchases are on behalf of "institutional" populations such as military forces, prisoners, and hospital patients—for those, in other words, who temporarily or permanently have little discretion in what they consume.

The business or industrial purchaser gets us involved in a conceptual problem. Tools, machines, raw materials, and semifinished products are clearly "producers' goods" rather than "consumers' goods," and the same should be true of buildings, rail sidings, trucks and other equipment for moving materials. But what of typewriters and filing cabinets, billing machines and postage meters, furniture and light bulbs? Since these expenditures are viewed by accountants as costs of doing business, they may be considered as capital expenditures. Yet they comprise important markets for *other* producers. The question gets really sticky in the case of such purchases as paintings for reception rooms or executive offices, dining and bar equipment for the comfort of the staff, or carpeting somewhat more luxurious than the executive can afford in his own home.

Any resolution in this issue is likely to be arbitrary, but we can derive a couple of lessons from the exercise: (1) the "private business community" is one of its own best customers, and (2) the significance of an economic product is not in its form but in its use.

The goods and services consumed by nonprofit organizations involve comparable conceptual problems, for even though the services that such organizations distribute or the goods (for example, books or clothing for the poor) that they sell or give away are not supposed to yield a net profit, some of their purchases are in fact directly consumed and others are converted or passed along to other consumers.

In communist regimes there are presumably only two categories of consumers: the state and the private household. The household consumer has considerably less discretion in his consumption than his counterpart in competitive markets, at equivalent income levels, partly because of centralized planning of production and the reluctance of the state to compete with itself in vying for the consumer's income. Major errors in estimating effective demand have occurred in the Soviet Union, however. Greater attention to consumer preferences not only concedes some small measure of "consumer sovereignty," but also may reduce the waste involved in unsold goods.

### Rich Countries, Poor Countries

World-wide comparisons of consumption levels reveal the dramatic differences between economically modernized countries and those that remain "underdeveloped." Calculations showing annual per capita incomes of less than $100 in countries of Africa or South Asia [30] cannot be taken too literally, since clearly no one could survive in the United States on such an income. Yet such data do underscore the abject poverty of a considerable majority of the world's population. If we take account of health and longevity as well as such current consumption as food, clothing, and shelter, the general poverty in these areas is greater than that of the lowest income groups in the United States. Virtually no one is permitted literally to starve in the United States or the advanced countries of Western Europe although, for some, malnutrition may be a kind of slow starvation.

We have earlier examined the sources of difference in the output of productive systems. Viewed in terms of consumption, the consequences of low production are represented in high death rates, high morbidity rates, and general malnutrition. The poor of the world spend the largest proportion of their incomes (or income equivalents) on food, thus confirming "Engel's law" to the effect that food expenditure is inversely related to income.[31] Yet of course the absolute amount spent for food by the average consumer is far higher in prosperous countries. Thus, although Engel's law was stated in terms of cross-sectional income differentials, it appears that the principle can also be stated sequentially: as general income levels rise through time, smaller proportions will be spent for food. Indeed, the principle can be extended to the traditional triad of "necessities": food, clothing, and shelter, and possibly to material goods generally. The latter inference derives from the steadily growing importance of "services" in consumer budgets in the economically advanced countries.

[30] See Simon Kuznets, "Consumption, Urbanization, and Industrialization," in Bert F. Hoselitz and Wilbert E. Moore, eds., *Industrialization and Society* (Paris and The Hague: UNESCO and Mouton, 1963), pp. 99–115. Kuznets does not exaggerate the accuracy of national income data.

[31] For reference to the classic work of Ernst Engel, see Carle C. Zimmerman, *Consumption and Standards of Living* (New York: Van Nostrand, 1936), pp. 22–41.

Average income and consumption data may of course conceal radical income inequalities. Absolute income inequalities—as measured, for instance, by the income ratio of the highest one tenth of income earners to the lowest one tenth—are not as high in strictly agrarian economies as in commercial and industrial economies, or sectors of economic systems.[32] Most countries have afforded an "old elite" of wealth, however, and many now have a "new elite" based upon modern commercial and industrial ventures. The wealth of this new elite may lead to the appearance of substantial growth in income per capita, with little or no practical effect on the vast majority of the population.

Income inequality is in fact greatest at early stages of economic modernization, and precisely in the modernizing sectors. Mainly this is because new commercial or industrial recruits are relatively unskilled, and their incomes may be little better than those of their rural kinsmen. Owners and managers, meanwhile, may fare very well indeed. This was the situation correctly observed by Marx midway in the nineteenth century. His mistake was to predict increasing polarization. Precisely the opposite has happened, with the bulk of the labor force shifting into middle-range positions in skills and earnings.[33] Another way of putting this is that poor countries have a tiny "middle class," whereas rich countries are predominantly middle-class, the designation thereby losing much of its meaning.

### Income Distribution and Styles of Life

Naturally, levels and types of consumption vary with income levels. But the relationship of income to expenditure is not entirely simple. The poor will spend higher proportions of their income on necessities and the rich on luxuries, but the poor also contribute disproportionately to religious and charitable organizations.[34]

The counterpart of the bewildering variety of goods and services available in an economically advanced country is the circumstance that for a substantial proportion of consumers some portion of their expenditures is *discretionary*. This discretion involves not simply brand preferences, or one kind of diet or clothing style or residential design instead of another. It extends to the whole concept of *style of life*. Some families will be cautious and thrifty, saving for their own future and that of their heirs; others will

[32] See Simon Kuznets, *Quantitative Aspects of the Economic Growth of Nations: VIII. Distribution of Income by Size,* Supplement to *Economic Development and Cultural Change,* Vol. 9, No. 2 (January, 1963).

[33] See Wilbert E. Moore, "Changes in Occupational Structures" (cited in footnote 3).

[34] See F. Emerson Andrews, *Philanthropic Giving* (New York: Russell Sage Foundation, 1950), Chapter 4.

live beyond their means, hoping for future solvency. Some families will keep on acquiring things—additional automobiles, home workshops, swimming pools, and summer homes—and others will acquire experiences—attendance at operas, plays, and concerts, participation in amateur sports, or travel. Veblen's concept of "conspicuous consumption" [35] is no less valid now than at the turn of the century, but it is no longer confined to "the leisure class." Many more people can now play the game, but the rules are highly variable. What's "in" and what's "out" differs from one group to another, as well as being, for some groups, subject to volatile change.

The central point here is that for this discretionary expenditure, income is a poor predictor of behavior. Educational levels, occupation, residence, and ethnic identity are likely to be the major determinants of life styles. This approach to consumer behavior in terms of social structural variables rather than strictly economic variables is overdue as an area of careful empirical inquiry.

## Institutions

The norms appropriate to the market place have been discussed already with respect to the distributive system. Here we should note two additional and somewhat inconsistent sets of expectations. The one is, once more, the rule of *rationality*. Both the collective consumer and the decision makers in private household are supposed to operate on the basis of correct information on the quantity and quality of goods and services, to make purchases in terms of clear needs or goals, and to seek the best bargain available.

The rule of rationality encounters the norms of *status symbolism* (to say nothing of buying on sheer impulse). Indeed, the term status symbolism tends to have too restrictive a connotation. The household consumer (but business firms and other organizations are not entirely exempt) is not only expected to acquire the goods and services appropriate to his relative station in life in a "vertical" order, but also to perform according to the canons of his particular subset of the social system, which may be very different from the styles of another subset without being reliably ratable as higher or lower. One notes the stultifying conformity in hair styles and clothing of teenage nonconformists, the required conservatism of dress for business executives and the required casualness of (equally expensive) attire for college professors, the rumpled tweediness of housewives in wealthy Eastern suburbs, the uncomfortable sports cars that superseded comfortable Cadillacs, and similar things. The poor people buy ties, the

[35] Thorstein Veblen, *Theory of the Leisure Class* (New York: Modern Library, 1934; original edition, New York: Macmillan, 1899).

well-to-do buy cravats or neckwear. Professionals read books or at least buy them, executives buy country-club memberships, and successful entertainers buy art. The individual with multiple memberships, or who is mobile in one of the several senses of the term, is expected to pick up the cues quickly and react accordingly. Since the rules are informal and not well codified, compliance is not always easy.

Conformity with the norms of appropriate symbolism is made more difficult particularly with respect to status symbols in the full, invidious sense. In a competitive market system, *all status symbols are subject to degradation,* and quickly so. This keeps the "in" consumer active, but also perhaps slightly anxious.

## An Extended Illustration: The Professions

Professional practice provides an exceptionally good illustration of the ways in which economic transactions intersect with strongly normative elements that specify positive duties and prohibited behavior.

### Criteria of Professionalism [36]

The occupations that we shall be concerned with here are the so-called "learned" professions, to the exclusion of such quasiprofessional groups as artists, performers, and entertainers. Even so, however, there are degrees of professionalism, and it seems preferable to recognize the variability rather than to insist on a more or less arbitrary dividing line. Although a clear-cut scale of professionalism has not been fully verified empirically, the following points along a scale can be suggested.

1. The professional possesses esoteric knowledge, based on specialized training of exceptional duration. The knowledge is useful according to values held in the particular society.

2. The professional is set apart from the laity by various signs and symbols, but by the same token is identified with his peers—often in formal organization.

3. In the use of his exceptional knowledge, the professional proceeds

---

[36] The literature on defining the professions is very large, and definitions are by no means uniform. For three examples, see Talcott Parsons, "The Professions and Social Structure," *Social Forces,* **17,** 457–467, reprinted in Parsons, *Essays in Sociological Theory, Pure and Applied* (Glencoe, Ill.: Free Press, 1949), Chapter VIII; Everett C. Hughes, "Professions," in Kenneth S. Lynn, ed., *The Professions in America* (Boston: Houghton Mifflin, 1965), pp. 1–14; and Bernard Barber, "Some Problems in the Sociology of the Professions," in *ibid.,* pp. 15–34.

by his own judgment and authority, and thus enjoys autonomy, restrained by responsibility.

These three criteria can be summarized as *education, organization,* and *autonomy.*

Two other characteristics of professionalism have been urged by students of the subject, and these, too, have merit. One is an orientation to *service,* in that the professional is expected to put the client's interests above his own if necessary. A correlative principle is dedication or *commitment* to the occupation as a *calling,* with all the connotative flavor of that concept of identification with the highest technical and ethnical standards that underlie and surround the use of skills. The scale of professionalism suggested above rests on structural or behavioral dimensions of occupations. The service orientation and commitment to a calling are essentially normative in character, and we shall return to them in the consideration of institutions.

By these criteria, nurses do not qualify for full professional standing, as all except a limited number of public-health nurses lack autonomy with regard to physicians and surgeons. Pharmacists appear to have slipped in professional standing under the dual pressures of the growing use of prescriptions by physicians and the precompounding and even prepackaging of pharmaceuticals by drug manufacturers. Laboratory technicians in hospitals or assistants in commercial laboratories fail both on education and on autonomy.

These defining criteria do not answer all problems of identification: What of the salaried law clerk, the untrained clergyman who has a divine "call" to preach, the self-taught expert consultant on the authenticity of art objects who has no professional organization to authenticate his standing? These problems are not considered here, but they do add to the difficulty of dealing with the professions as a homogeneous segment of occupations.

Professional practice may be one of the most ancient (or primitive) forms of the market for services. The tribal shaman, witch doctor, or other curer normally received some material reward for their services, as did the physicians and priest doctors in ancient civilizations.

The essence of professional service is the provision of solutions (or at least attempted solutions) to life's problems that are beyond the capacity of the ordinary, socialized person. Thus problems of health and of life itself, almost universally, have required specialized services. The combination of rational technique (within the knowledge available) with magic and religion has been understandably common. Lawyers appear only when statutes and practice achieve a technical complexity beyond the ken of the citizen or subject, and the whole range of technologists—from metallurgists to agronomists—appears only when the rational manipulation of the environment is conceived as being not only desirable but technically possible.

Even if we adopt a rather rigorous definition of professionals, they comprise the most rapidly growing occupational category in highly modernized societies, and often in newly developing areas.[37] The number of professional occupations is also increasing, and the older professions are subject to ever greater internal specialization. This growth can be traced to several interrelated sources: (1) the explosive expansion of knowledge; (2) the multiplication of "problems" in a complex and interdependent social system: for example, accounting, investment analysis, personality disorders, and marital strain; and (3) the extension of secular rationality, a view of both nature and the social order as operating by principles that can be understood and controlled.

Professional services are normally rendered for *clients*, individually or collectively. We shall see that it is not essential that the client also be the employer, as he is in fee-for-service, private professional practice. Whether the service for a client excludes "pure" scientists or the non-teaching humanistic scholar is another detail that is not discussed here.[38]

### Professional Roles and Their Strains

Some role relationships are fairly standard for professionals, and others affect only part of the universe of practitioners. With the minor exceptions just noted, the professional has *clients* and *peers*. Salaried professionals may have *employers* different from their clients, and some have administrative *subordinates*. We shall discuss each of these relationships briefly, with selective emphasis on the interplay between the norms of the market and the norms of service.

*The Professional and His Clients.* Private practice is often viewed as the pure case of professional-client relations. It certainly has a long history, particularly in the "established" professions of law and medicine. Yet other old professions, notably university professors and the clergy, have been normally salaried for centuries. However, let us examine the situation where the client is the employer.

The individual client seeks from the professional some technical service and advice beyond his own competence. Note that if the client has discretion in seeking help, we may expect variable *thresholds* of client

---

[37] See Wilbert E. Moore, "Changes in Occupational Structures" (cited in footnote 3).
[38] Wilensky argues that pure scientists are not strictly professionals. See Harold L. Wilensky, "The Professionalization of Everyone?" *American Journal of Sociology,* **70,** 137–158 (September, 1964).

behavior, according to the salience of the type of need, the relative seriousness of the particular problem and, possibly, according to prospective ability to pay. In most advanced countries the threshold for seeking medical services is relatively low—often aided by prepayment plans or publicly supplied services. Lawyers, on the other hand, are probably seen rarely if ever by the great majority of the population. Architects and marital counselors are a long way from being "taken for granted" as being persons who are normally to be consulted by the ordinary adult.

The client presents a complaint, problem, or challenge. He is presumably free to select his advisor, and to determine the limits of his involvement. However, the professional may refuse to accept the case or assignment unless his judgment supersedes that of the client. The client's nominal freedom of action is of course subject to various restrictions. For the particular service that the client needs, the professional may have no competitors; the client may not be able to afford the reputedly best advice; and through the cohesion of professional peers, the client is definitely discouraged from "shopping around," particularly with respect to price.

The economic nexus is indeed a curious one in private practice. Again we find an intersection of conflicting principles. The one principle sets fees according to the quantity and quality of service rendered. The other principle sets fees in terms of the client's ability to pay, ranging from the "charity case" to the man of wealth. A general rule in law and medicine appears to be the relatively standardized fee for "normal" (or even routine) services, but graduated fees for exceptional services—for instance, brain surgery or setting up a complex trust fund. Since most of a lawyer's work—all of it in civil practice—involves financial transactions such as damage suits or property transfers, there is a strong tendency to grade the fee according to the size of the sum involved. Indeed, although part of the legal profession frowns on the practice, it is still common for plaintiffs' attorneys in civil liability suits to take the case on a "contingent-fee" basis: a proportion of the settlement if the client wins, and nothing if the client loses.

Strictly individual professional practice is of course increasingly rare, as increasing specialization leads to the banding together of complementary specialists in law firms, medical clinics, or firms of engineering consultants. If the young professional joins an established group he may benefit in building clientele from the reputation of his senior colleagues; his first clients may very likely come by referral from a successful and therefore overworked practitioner. The sole practitioner may face more severe difficulties. The self-imposed restraints on "commercialism" in established professions prohibit all but the most subdued advertising: listing in the telephone directory, a "business card" in the local newspaper, a modest "shingle" in front of his office. Clients chiefly come from "connections," and these are made by joining clubs and possibly a church, volunteering for civic duties, and accepting invitations to parties. Through all of this the sole practitioner must also appear to be busy, and not simply waiting for someone to walk through his office door for instantaneous attention.

For the dubious admonition to the ordinary consumer in a competitive market, *caveat emptor*, professional practice substitutes the admonition, *credat emptor*—let the buyer *trust*. The *authority* of the professional is, in fact, entirely based on the client's confidence. Actually it is not strictly authority, since the professional has no real sanctions for noncompliance; the professional supplies *advice*, which the client neglects at his own peril.

For the trust accorded the professional, the professional owes various duties, including competence and wise judgment, and protection of the clients' interests. This is sometimes expressed as the duty of *loyalty*. Lawyers, particularly, are supposed to avoid representing actually or possibly adverse interests in any transaction or litigation. But this restraint does not apply to the real estate broker, who is subject to an examination and licensing in many jurisdictions, but represents both buyers and sellers in transactions.

The concept of "privileged communication" is rather uniformly followed in professional practice, but only physicians, lawyers, and clergymen have a firm legal basis for refusing to divulge "guilty information," or information that could at least be embarrassing to the client.

There is also some lack of clarity in the professional's duty to refer clients to other sources of help when he uncovers problems beyond his own competence. Abuses exist at either extreme: needless referral to high-priced specialists on the part of physicians, possibly with a fee-splitting kickback, and simply closing the eyes to physical, psychological, economic, or social problems of the client disclosed in professional consultation, on grounds that "it is outside my jurisdiction."

The client dealing with a salaried professional has even less control over the adviser. Many such services are in the form of "fringe benefits" from employers, and some of them—such as free advice from corporate attorneys or accountants—may be more nearly a matter of courtesy than of right. Even when the clients as a collectivity are the principal support of the professional—as in congregationally organized churches and some private schools—the salaried professional is under direct client influence only at the extremes of popularity or unpopularity. But note also that in some situations the salaried professional's authority may exceed advice. By delegation of power from executive superiors, the professional's instructions may, indeed, constitute orders: the teacher's instructions, the house counsel's insistence on deletion of a paragraph from an essay or a speech, or the company physician's restrictions on work assignments.

***The Professional and His Peers.*** The professional's relations with his fellows are again many-faceted, and we shall have to be radically restrictive in our focus. We shall only deal with self-regulation through organizationally backed codes of conduct, and problems of jurisdiction among specialists.

The fundamental rationale for codes of competence and ethical performance adopted by professional associations is to insure *responsibility* in return for the *trust* of the client. In the nature of the role relationships, the client cannot judge the details of competence or performance; he can only judge results. And since superior knowledge does indeed carry power, the client needs to be protected from exploitative misuse of the asymmetrical power distribution.

It should not surprise us by now that practices may serve more than one purpose, although in the present instance there is no intrinsic conflict in the ideal case. Ideally, the professional group will seek to control standards of competence for admission to practice, standards of competence for continuation of practice, and ethical standards with respect to both clients and peers. These controls, in turn, are ideally designed to protect the client against the unqualified and unscrupulous practitioner, and to protect the qualified and scrupulous practitioner against unfair competition.

One side effect of this set of self-controls is, of course, the attempt to monopolize the skill (just as craft unions do) and, not infrequently, to restrict access so as to enhance the earning power of those already in the club.

Self-regulation is only minimally impaired when private professional associations seek the aid of government to reduce or eliminate the competition of the "unqualified." State licensing nominally transfers the regulation from a private to a public agency, but in effect examining and licensing boards are comprised of professionals, authenticated by some state authority, and gaining thereby the authority of the police and courts in controls that are, hopefully, beneficial to both clients and practitioners.

Regulation also affects problems of *jurisdiction* among specialists, but here the situation is much more complex. The extremely rapid growth of knowledge and demand for technical advice has resulted in fractionation of well-established fields, development of disputed territory between established fields, and the settlement of pioneers in previously unclaimed territory.

None of the older professions has been immune to internal specialization. Even within the clergy, which has had to contend with no great burst of new information, the size of congregations and denominational organizations permits the demarcations of theologian, administrator, preacher, and pastor. Lawyers in the United States have valiantly resisted specialization. In private practice, specialization goes on surreptitiously in law firms by reliance on salaried specialists who supply the attorney of record with requisite information and advice to be passed on to the client. Yet the legal guild grudgingly admits that there are judges; public prosecutors; criminal lawyers for defendants; tax, patent, and maritime lawyers; divorce lawyers; and ambulance-chasing liability lawyers. And then there are labor lawyers and house counsel for corporations, not to mention the derogated members of the fraternity who sit in legislatures and draft laws.

The medical profession has faced up to specialization. Only a few decades ago an American doctor could decide to specialize in any branch of medicine, and if he killed too many patients, he could simply shift to a less hazardous specialty. No longer. Specialists now extend their medical training with internships, residencies, and special examinations. (All of this represents a substantial capital investment, with relatively high subsequent returns.)

The medical men, however, have not agreed on a uniform classification of their arts. The result is that patients are divided into parts and treated by opthamologists, dermatologists, urologists, cardiologists, gynecologists; into age groups, and treated by obstetricians, pediatricians, geriatricians; and the skills of doctors are divided by technique—surgeons, anesthetists, radiologists, psychiatrists. Fortunately, in place of the general practitioner there is now the internist, who serves as a kind of holding company and referral agency for other specialists.

We cannot abandon this exotic terrain without noting that the university—the "mother" of professions, although occasionally and unwed one—is so rife with professional specializations that nominal colleagues in the same department or discipline find nothing interesting to say to one another, even though each can identify real peers on other campuses. It is by no means clear in the college or university that there is an equivalent of the internist who considers the student-client in somewhat more integrated terms.

The query "Who's in charge here?" is difficult enough within occupations that provide some modicum of common training and tradition. Between professions, relations may become a little more bitter, and especially where a new specialty challenges a seemingly established sovereignty. Who owns man's emotional problems—medically trained psychiatrists, clinical psychologists, clergymen, or psychiatric social workers? Who owns man's tax difficulties—lawyers or accountants? Who owns marital status—lawyers, clergymen, or marital counselors?

Note that law is such a ubiquitous feature of human relations in complex societies that lawyers have border disputes on countless fronts: with labor arbitrators, management consultants, social workers, fiscal policy economists, investment advisors, real estate brokers, private investigators and, seemingly, anyone in sight. Well, the lawyer is trained to be combative, or at least litigious, but he can scarcely claim to be in charge of social relations generally.

It would be improper to view jurisdictional disputes among professionals as solely crass and materialistic. Time-honored authority and prestige are challenged. The appearance of new bodies of knowledge and technique may prompt rather anxious defensive maneuvers, including an attempt to derogate what one does not comprehend. (Sociology remained for decades in the status of the unproved and pretentious newcomer in colleges and universities. The present favorable market position of sociology may prompt its practitioners to a kind of vindictive cruelty to classicists —a reaction no more rational than the classicists' original attempt to retain ownership of man.)

*The Professional and His Employer.* Here we must be brief indeed. The important dimensions of role relationships to be added are two, and both involve problems of role strain. The first is the question of the primary identification of the salaried professional as between his employers and his peers; the second, closely related, is the conflict between responsibility to the employer and to clients where the two are not the same.

The problem of organizational loyalty as compared with professional loyalty is endemic wherever professionals are employed in bureaucracies or administrative organizations.[39] The problem is acute in colleges and universities where the preponderance of the staff is professional. The professor's prestige, and indeed his market value, depends far more on the favorable judgment of his colleagues across the country and perhaps around the world than it depends upon the good will of an administrative officer. The professor may certainly choose a strictly local acceptability, but that makes him far more dependent on the good will of his administrative superiors than if he is an eminently marketable intellectual commodity. Similar strains appear in corporations and governmental agencies. The increased reliance of organizations other than universities on professional employees as suppliers of information and advice has had the unintended effect of forcing marked changes in administrative theory and practice, since the professional's organizational loyalty (and subservience) is likely to be inversely proportional to his competence.

The employer-client dilemma arises in both conspicuous and subtle ways. Let us take a few examples that are quite overt. A teacher's union strikes

[39] See, for example, William Kornhauser, *Scientists in Industry: Conflict and Accommodation* (Berkeley: University of California Press, 1962).

in behalf of its demands for a better economic bargain with the school board, but the clients (students) miss classes. A union of social workers strikes, also as a bargaining maneuver, against public or private welfare agencies, but the welfare clients do not get their accustomed checks or personal counseling. Similar strikes have been called by hospital attendants. For a reverse twist, physicians in Belgium and Saskatchewan went on strike to resist bureaucratization under publicly supported health-service schemes, but may have hoped to get clients' political support by this maneuver.

All of these cases present clear-cut ambivalence in loyalties, yet all present certain additional ambiguities. Public school teachers, welfare workers (doubtfully fully qualified social workers), and hospital attendants, would scarcely meet all of the rigorous tests of full professional position. The recognized professional is more likely to leave his position, perhaps unjustly and, on his part, cravenly, than to withdraw his service or to appear to be a mere trade unionist.

A somewhat more subtle problem arises in our final example. A young *pater familias* has been talked into a life-insurance policy, and has been told to report to a local physician for a medical examination. Now this young man has had a family physician, and is not disturbed by dealing with this unfamiliar local professional. In most instances no problem arises, the young man gets his standard or preferred-risk policy, and he lives to pay all of the premiums. But what is normally unclear about this situation is that the examining physician is working for another client, the insurance company, and not for the man who came to be examined in his office. The physician is not obliged to tell his nonclient anything; the nonclient has, in effect, waived all of his rights of privileged communication, and it is entirely left to the discretion of the examiner whether he informs the subject if he uncovers a medical problem warranting attention. Being a professional, the examiner normally will inform the subject. But once again the role relationships are ambiguous.

*The Professional as Administrator.* We shall bypass here the moot question of whether there is a profession of administration. Instead, our attention will be directed only at that occupational career path that leads from the practice of a profession to the administration of practitioners. The oustanding examples are found in university administration, in hospitals, and in the supervision of research laboratories and institutes. The curious feature of this situation is that the administrator *must have been* a professional, but his administrative authority is clouded by two circumstances: (1) by the act of becoming an administrator he has in some degree "gone over to the enemy," since he now represents organizational interests, which are possibly adverse to strictly professional interests; (2) given the rapid changes in knowledge and state of the arts, the administrative professional loses his professional authentication. Since administrators are commonly (although not always) paid more than their expert sub-ordinates, two more doubts arise, and they are not mutually exclusive. Did the administrator sell out? Or did he choose an alternative path to success that he was not going to achieve on strictly professional grounds?

The sweet, gentle, service-oriented life of the professional—all of which, incidentally, is mostly genuine—is thus not immune to competitive orientations and ambivalence.

## Institutions

A recapitulation here of the institutions surrounding the professions would only appear redundant, for of all occupational positions in modern economic systems, the professions seem most affected by explicit normative criteria.

By way of review, let us note three constellations of professional norms. The first relates to *competence*. It is not enough for the professional to have been minimally competent at some youthful time. That may still serve in a few retrograde fields of intellectual specialization, but competence in most professional fields requires continuous learning and, not uncommonly, increased specialization. The sanctions are both exalted and severe, for prestige more commonly runs to exceptional competence than to exceptional morality, and poor performance brings both social and economic penalties.

The second group of norms relates to professional *identification*—a sense of calling—which not only submits to but also shares in individual and collective discipline and control.[40] The code of career officers in modern military organizations perhaps catches this set of norms more precisely than do other professional groups, but it is evident in all of them.

Since the professions are not only prestigious but influential in public and private affairs, we should note a third institutional configuration: the rules of *honorable authority*. Knowledge, if at all useful, does indeed have power. The norms of professional practice, the inculcation in young professionals of ideals and high duties, emphasize *service*—the wise and somewhat disinterested dedication of knowledge to the welfare of others.

In this chapter we have observed how the economy relates man to his nonhuman environment, and the ways by which that nonhuman environment is manipulated for human sustenance and survival. We have also

[40] See William J. Goode, "Community Within a Community: The Professions," *American Sociological Review,* **22,** 194–200 (April, 1957).

observed that this rational, mechanical, and manipulative view of economic activity is unduly limiting on two counts: (1) both in the production and in the distribution of the hard-won fruits of labor, man is an inescapably social animal, necessarily cooperative and charitable as well as calculating and self-interested; (2) much of what we must consider to be economic activity has little to do with nature, and has much to do with the flow of services within the interaction patterns of human beings with each other. On both counts the observed behavior patterns exemplify the interplay between the rational calculus and the demands of shared values and shared rules of conduct. In production, distribution, and consumption we have examined the mechanistic models of purely self-interested and unregulated economic transactions—models favored by economists. Despite their undoubted utility where some of the institutional presuppositions prevail, these models have been shown to be inadequate for understanding—which means predicting—economic behavior across the spectrum of social experience. The analysis of professional practice underscored the inadequacies even in contemporary, market-oriented economies. Thus the institutional emphasis recurrent in our deliberations has been partly polemical, by way of redressing improper restrictions in conventional views of economic affairs, and mainly positive because it is right.

# 6

# RELIGIOUS INSTITUTIONS

*Peter L. Berger*

## Religion—"What Everybody Knows"

Sociology has frequently been accused by its critics of being a string of pretentiously presented platitudes. The sociologist supposedly wastes his and other people's time by hammering away at what everybody already knows. On occasion, admittedly, sociologists have not been quite innocent of this charge. Most of the time, however, the problem lies elsewhere. It is true that sociology deals mainly with matters that concern many people in their everyday lives and about which they have all sorts of preconceived ideas—precisely the ideas that add up to "what everybody knows." It is also true that "what everybody knows" is generally somewhat unclear and often downright false. For example, "everybody knows" that there are classes in our society, but actually this "knowledge" is very vague as to just what these classes are and how they work. In many groups in our society, even today, "everybody knows" that there are superior and inferior races, and people act with strong conviction on this "knowledge" that has no basis in reality at all. Sociological analysis is useful just because it clarifies and corrects the "platitudes" operating in everyday life.

The charge that sociology tells people only what they already know seems particularly plausible when it deals with social phenomena of considerable prominence. Religion is certainly such a phenomenon, especially in contemporary America. Religious institutions are steadily in the public eye and a large part of the population is actively involved in them. Although it is recognized, of course, that there are different varieties of religious belief and also varying degrees of unbelief, there is no great problem in defining the phenomenon. "Everybody knows" what religion is all about, what claims are made in its name, and what the institutions that are concerned with it are supposed to do.

But are these common notions about religion adequate as a basis for permitting sociological reflection on the subject to proceed? Or perhaps is such reflection unnecessary in the first place? A few years ago a study of a group of American college students revealed some interesting findings on their notions about religion.[1] Of the students interviewed, 80% expressed a "need for religious faith." But only 47% felt that "acceptance of the Deity is a highly important component of a religious or ethical system." In other words, more than one half of these students were apparently capable of conceiving something that could be called "religion" and that would not include a belief in God. At the very least, we must suspect that there is some ambiguity here in the way in which the term religion is commonly

[1] Rose Goldsen et al., *What College Students Think* (Princeton: Van Nostrand, 1960), pp. 153 ff.

understood. Another interesting finding concerned the characteristics regarded by the students as essential for an "ideal religious or ethical system." The four formulations that received the highest percentages of positive responses were: "a focus for personal adjustment and development,"
"intellectual clarity about the fundamental problems of living," "a strong
community feeling of closeness with your fellow men," and "an anchor for
family life, children." If these views are considered typical of "what everybody knows" about religion, can we in good intellectual conscience let the
matter rest there?

We could make a good case for saying that these views are very revealing
of what religion is like in contemporary America. The authors of the above
study discussed this rather unique religious situation under the apt heading
"secular religion." Even in our particular society, however, popular opinions
of this kind cannot provide a comprehensive picture of the nature and activity of the religious institutions in the entire society. Popular opinions
can be of even less help if we want to understand religion in other societies
or in other periods of history. Thus the students' mixed response to the
question of whether God is a necessary part of religion may serve as a good
illustration of the difficulty of defining religion by its believed contents.
The students who responded negatively are in very good and large company. Buddhism, which is generally regarded as one of the great world
religions, has been agnostic on the question of God in some of its major
historical branches. The students' views on the essential characteristics of
an "ideal religious or ethical system" are not very helpful either, since they
are highly relative to the social and cultural milieu of modern middle-class
America out of which they come. Religion is intended to foster "personal
adjustment," yet the founder of the world religion to which most of these
students at least nominally belong was executed as a dangerous criminal.
Religion is intended to be conducive to "intellectual clarity," yet religious
history has produced some of the most violently irrational conduct that men
are capable of. The notion that religion produces "community feeling" is
the only one of the four propositions that is empirically viable, but the
further notion about the payoff for family life and children can be retained
only if we ignore that whole area of asceticism in all of its forms that has
occupied such a prominent place in the history of religion.

Perhaps the point has been made now that "what everybody knows"
about religion is not satisfactory as the basis for a clear intellectual grasp
of the phenomenon. It would be easy to make the further point that there
is even less of a basis here for an understanding of the multiple ways in
which religion has been intertwined with social structures. In the present
area, as in other areas of social life that the sociologist investigates, he will
do well to follow the advice of his great French predecessor Emile Durk-

heim, who insisted that sociology should always approach its subject matter as being, in principle, unknown. Here then, as elsewhere, there is ample space for sociological analysis.

It is very important to stress that the sociologist who approaches religion as a legitimate area for his investigations does so within specific limitations. While these limitations are similar to the ones that determine sociological work on other subjects, they are particularly important in the present context because religion involves such profound human passions and aspirations, Sociological analysis is, above all, a scientific undertaking. This means that it has the same limitation that scientific work has whenever it touches on questions of ultimate truth or value, namely, that it cannot make statements on their intrinsic validity. Max Weber, the classical German sociologist, has expressed this limitation in his concept of sociology as a "value-free" science, that is, as a discipline which can (and, indeed, must) study human values but which cannot decide whether these values are in themselves true or false, good or bad.

The sociologist studies religion as one of many socially significant phenomena. This study will often lead him to analyze in detail religious propositions, insofar as they are relevant to the social situation, and will try to understand their social causes and consequences, and the manner in which they relate to the institutional fabric of society. None of this will ever enable him to judge these propositions on their own merits. Thus, the sociologist (to return to the previous illustration) may ask how religions that include a belief in a personal God differ in their social manifestations from religions that do not. He may not (that is, not as a sociologist) decide which of these two options is finally true. This fundamental limitation, rooted in the character of sociology as a scientific enterprise, may either comfort or disappoint the individual with a personal stake in the religious propositions in question. Such an individual can be comforted if he is worried that sociology will destroy his faith, but he will be disappointed if he looks to sociology for any sort of intellectual support for this faith. Correctly understood, sociology can do neither.

Another limitation of the sociological approach to religion is that it constitutes only one of several possible scientific approaches to the subject. There are also, for example, the approaches of history, cultural anthropology, and psychology (all of which, incidentally, operate under the same overall limitation previously discussed). Even within the scientific frame of reference, the sociological approach is only one particular focus. It would be a mistake to expect from it some sort of total scientific explanation of the phenomenon. However, it is important for the sociologist constantly to relate his own work to that of other scientists, especially in a field with such enormous ramifications as that of religion. Thus, in the considerations that follow, it will be necessary to examine contributions that come from outside of the proper scope of sociology. In other words, the sociology of religion is part of a general scientific study of religion.

With such limitations in mind, is the study worth the effort? This question can be fairly answered only if we have gained an idea of just what insights about religion that sociology has to offer. In the end, we shall have to say what the lady at a dinner party said to the specialist on the study of insects who had finished explaining his researches to her: "This is very interesting, if you're interested in it."

## Religion as a Phenomenon

A first essential step in any effort of scientific understanding is a clear definition of the subject of study. As I have already indicated, this is by no means easy in the case of religion. The scholarly literature is full of widely differing definitions. Some definitions are very broad indeed. Therefore, we could define religion so as to include everything that men in a particular society consider to be the highest good. In American society we could make a good case for saying that economic success and sexual fulfillment are considered to be the highest good, at least by large numbers of people. The sociology of religion, to stay true to such a broad definition, would then have to investigate such areas of social life as occupational aspiration and courtship patterns. Probably this is not a very helpful idea. We could also define religion in very narrow terms, for example, as belief in God. But, as we have seen, this definition would not only exclude such interesting types as Buddhist monks, as well as Confucian scholars and assorted primitive witch doctors, but would even disagree with the conception of religion held by many contemporary American college students. It is useful now to examine briefly the way that this problem has been dealt with in the general scientific study of religion.[2]

During the nineteenth century there was a tendency to define religion in terms of its supposed origins.[3] Since no one could really know what

[2] The term "general scientific study of religion" is a somewhat awkward translation of what in other countries has become a recognized scientific discipline. In Germany, where it originated, it is called *Religionswissenschaft* and is taught as such in the universities. It is close to the history of religion and to comparative religion, but is more systematic than historical in its approach. There are some signs that this discipline might develop in the United States, in which case somebody will probably think of a better English name for it.

[3] For an idea of what some of these explanations were like, see William Lessa and Evon Vogt, eds., *Reader in Comparative Religion* (Evanston, Ill.: Row, Peterson and Co., 1958), pp. 9 ff.

these origins were, this tendency caused a great deal of disagreement, which could not be settled by empirical evidence. An important step toward a less speculative definition of religion came at the end of the century, when the idea of *mana* was discovered in Melanesia. Similar phenomena were then found in many other parts of the world, but the Melanesian name was kept as a generic term. It was not easy then, and still is not easy, to convey this idea to modern Westerners. Perhaps the best way of translating the idea is to say that something that has mana is "religiously charged." This conveys something of the impersonal and ethically indifferent character of mana. It can be attached to almost anything—a rock, an event, or a person. It may be connected with a conception of supernatural beings, but this is not necessary. Mana also is quite neutral; it is neither ethically "good" nor "bad." Its main quality is power—mysterious power—which is always dangerous to man and which he can only approach with great caution.

While the idea of mana was discovered in the context of primitive religion, it is to be found in more or less refined forms in so-called civilized religions. The Biblical account of the death of Uzzah, who inadvertently touched the ark of the covenant and was instantly destroyed by "the anger of the Lord" (Samuel 2:6), is a case in point. Indeed, Latin scholars claim that our own word "religion" comes from the verb *relegere*, which means "to observe" or "to be careful." The discovery of mana was important because it suggested that there might be something like a fundamental religious category of crosscultural scope.[4] This suggestion was worked out with great force and with a wealth of illustrative material by the German scholar, Rudolf Otto.[5] His book on the nature of the sacred, which was first published in 1917, is probably the most important single work in the scientific study of religion published in this century. Much of the discussion in the field since then has revolved around modifications of Otto's original statement.

Otto sought to clarify the phenomenon of religion by explaining it not from the outside (as in the attempts to determine the origins of religion) but from within, that is, by explaining the major themes to be found in actual religious experience, as reported by those claiming to have had such experience. Although Otto was not the first scholar who attempted this (William James, the principal founder of the psychology of religion, had similar ideas), his results were unusually concise and convincing. The themes that Otto stressed as essential to the experience of the sacred (or, we might say, of religious experience generally) were otherness, mystery and tremendousness. The sacred refers to a reality that is quite different from

---

[4] *Ibid.*, pp. 203 ff.

[5] Rudolf Otto, *The Idea of the Holy* (London: Oxford University Press, 1923).

human reality—a reality that is incomprehensible to rational thought, and that overwhelms man by its majesty. The typical human reaction to this reality is awe, or dread, a peculiar emotion similar to fear—and often becoming fear—but different from fear because of its ambivalence. The sacred not only terrifies man but fascinates him; it repels and attracts him at the same time. Otto cites evidence for this ambivalence from a wide variety of religions, for example, from the Old Testament (the famous vision of the throne of God by the prophet Isaiah, in Isaiah, Chapter 6) and from the religious literature of India (the hair-raising vision of the divine form of Krishna, as recounted in the *Bhagavad Gita*). An essential element in all of this is the quality of religion as a reality (that is, a believed reality), totally transcending the normal dimensions of human existence.

Gerardus van der Leeuw, a Dutch scholar who founded the so-called phenomenological school in the scientific study of religion, developed Otto's key concept into an elaborate system for the analysis of religion.[6] He traced the development of the idea of religious power from its early impersonal form to the construction of complicated pantheons and finally to the various religious theories, in which the entire universe is explained as an ultimate order within which human life receives its definitive meaning.

This conception of religion as an all-embracing, meaning-bestowing order is most prominent in the work of Mircea Eliade, another European scholar, who is now teaching in this country.[7] For Eliade, the key dichotomy in religion is that between cosmos and chaos. Cosmos is always that territory in which, by means of the manifestations of the sacred, the levels between gods and men have been and can again be breached. In this way, human life is ever again restored to its essential connection with the ultimate order of the universe. Eliade coined the curious term "cosmization" to refer to all those religious practices by means of which everything that was previously chaos is incorporated or reincorporated into the cosmos. What is especially important for the sociologist here is the constant relationship between cosmic and human order. Human order, including all that we now call society or social institutions, is "right" only insofar as it continues to be in accordance with the ultimately "right" order of the universe. Often this relationship is expressed linguistically. For instance, in ancient Iranian the word for the ultimate, sacred order of the world is *arta*. A just man is called *artavan* (one who lives in accordance with this order), and a judge is called *ratu* (one who restores the order where it has been disturbed).

[6] Gerardus van der Leeuw, *Religion in Essence and Manifestation* (London: George Allen and Unwin, 1938).
[7] See Mircea Eliade, *Cosmos and History* (New York: Harper, 1959).

Our own use, in an ethical sense, of words such as "right," "just," or "correct" is reminiscent of this age-old conception.

Certainly, all definitions are risky. But, now, a definition of religion can be suggested that will at least be adequate for our considerations: religion is the human attitude toward a sacred order that includes within it all being —human or otherwise. In other words, religion is the belief in a cosmos, the meaning of which both transcends and includes man. With this definition in mind, we can now return to the sociological question proper—the question of the place of religion in human society.

## Social Functions of Religion

It should now be clear that when we ask about the social functions of religion, we are asking a question that is limited in scope. The question concerns the social effects of religion; it asks what it is that religion does in and perhaps for society. Not only, as we have seen, is this approach unable to lead to statements about the intrinsic worth of religion, but even in the sphere of what can be empirically investigated, the approach does not exhaust the phenomenon. For example, it is quite possible that religion may have psychological functions that are not readily translatable into social functions. In other words, religion may do something for the individual that is quite different from what religion does for society at large.

Sociologists, especially in the United States, have the tendency to look for positive social functions—positive not in the sense of a phenomenon being regarded as a fine thing, but in the sense of contributing to the continued existence and effective operation of society as a whole or an institution in society. This is quite alright, as long as we keep in mind that some phenomena cannot be interpreted in this way. In the case of religion we shall also look mainly for its positive social functions, in the above sense. However, there are some religious phenomena that have no particular social functions, except perhaps for a very small number of people. For example, a small colony of hermits, living somewhere in the wilderness and going quietly about the pursuit of mystical illumination, need not have wider social functions at all. A sociologist might be interested in how such a colony functions as a miniature social system within itself but, especially if the colony is an isolated phenomenon and is not in connection with similar ventures elsewhere, there may be no reason to think that any larger effects on society are involved. There are also religious phenomena that are not only functionally indifferent but are downright dysfunctional. For instance, the Aztecs, who ruled large parts of Mexico before the Spanish conquest, had the disconcerting habit of sacrificing large numbers of human beings to their gods. Understandably, they tended to recruit these victims from the other indigenous peoples of Mexico rather than from among their own numbers. It is hard to imagine a religion less functional for the continued existence of the Aztec empire and, indeed, the Aztecs' sacrificial practices were probably one of the important reasons why the Spanish conquerors found willing allies among the subject peoples of Mexico. In this case the dysfunction was unintended. There are also cases where a religious movement quite intentionally sets out to disrupt the continued existence of the prevailing social system. An important example of this in Western history is the Anabaptist movement of the sixteenth century, in which religious radicalism and social revolution went hand in hand.

This brings us to another important point. When sociologists say that something has a certain social function, this does not necessarily imply that the people involved desire or are even aware of this function. The contemporary American sociologist Robert Merton has coined the terms "manifest" and "latent" functions to distinguish intended, conscious functions from the unintended, unconscious ones. Thus the Aztecs, of course, did not think up their bloodthirsty god Quetzalcoatl *in order to* set in motion processes that would end in the destruction of their empire. As for the Anabaptists, although they certainly wanted to destroy the feudal system, they neither desired nor were able to foresee the post-feudal society which their rebellions probably helped to bring about.

### Symbolic Integration

If, with these reservations in mind, we turn now to our question of the place of religion in human society, we come first to one social function of religion that is so crucial that it almost includes all of the others. This is the function of symbolic integration. This function is at the heart of the sociology of religion as it was understood by Émile Durkheim (he and Max Weber are the two most important figures in the development of the sociology of religion). Durkheim's entire sociological work culminates in the interpretation of religion as the great integrative power in human society.[8]

Every society is a precarious organization of different—often conflicting—human interests, aspirations, and perspectives on the world. The fundamental question that troubled Durkheim throughout his work as a sociologist was how it was possible that something like a cohesive order could emerge

[8] See Émile Durkheim, *The Elementary Forms of the Religious Life* (New York: Collier Books, 1961). This book, first published in French in 1912, is one of the classics of the sociology of religion. For a very simplified but useful introduction to it, see Maurice Halbwachs, *Sources of Religious Sentiment* (New York: Free Press, 1962).

in society at all. How was society ultimately held together? How did human beings develop a feeling of mutual belonging (he called it "solidarity") in which they could transcend their narrow personal and factional interests? Durkheim's sociology of religion was his final answer—a rediscovery in new terms of the insight of Francis Bacon that of all the bonds that tie men to each other, religious bonds are the strongest.

Why should this be true? If we reflect upon our previous definition of religion, the Durkheimian view is not so surprising. Religion is, above all, an ordering principle in human life. It organizes the indivdual's experence in terms of ultimate meanings that include but also transcend the individual. If many people share such an ordering principle, it becomes possible for them not only to deal with each other within the framework of meaning thus given, but to transcend themselves and their various egotisms, sometimes even to the point of self-sacrifice. At least the major social acts (for instance, in marriage, in work, or in war) are given a significance that is far greater than the individual who must perform them. The particular way in which these acts have come to be institutionalized in a society are thus imbued with solid meanings that ultimately relate them to the sacred order of the universe. To marry becomes a sacrament, to work becomes a duty pleasing to the gods, and to die in war, perhaps, becomes a passport to a happier afterlife.

All human social interaction is dependent on symbols (Durkheim called them "collective representations") of one sort or another. Religion supplies the ultimate symbols, the overarching ones, the ones beneath which all of the others make sense. Religion is a symbolic canopy stretched out over the network of social institutions, giving them an appearance of stability and "rightness" that they would otherwise lack. In this manner, religion functions maintain and perpetuate social institutions.

The symbolic-integrative function of religion is most easily apparent in cases of ritual. Here, visibly and publicly, the vital concerns of society are symbolically lifted up toward the realm of the sacred. For example, in the great New Year festival in the countries of the ancient Near East the ritual reenacted the entire drama of the creation of the world and the establishment of the "right" human order. The present was linked with the past and the future—all parts of the grand design of the cosmos—and each individual's humble present was thus reaffirmed as having its own place in that design. Significantly, the most important ritual acts of the New Year festival were performed by the king, in whom the divine order of the society was symbolized *par excellence*. Similar ritual symbolizations of the ultimate meanings of life, both individual and collective, can be found in all archaic and primitive societies. Although (as will be discussed later) modern society has become too differentiated for religion to function in quite the same way, and other symbolic forms have taken over some of the old religious functions, it would be a mistake to think that close analogies to the great solidarity-generating religious ceremonies of the past cannot be found even today. The American anthropologist Lloyd Warner has given us a perceptive analysis of Memorial Day ceremonies in a New England community in which religion still operates in a way best formulated in Durkheimian terms.[9]

## Social Control

Another very important function of religion is that of social control, that is, of helping to keep people in line with the norms of society. We may distinguish here between external and internal controls: those that coerce the individual from outside and those that do so from within his own consciousness. Religion has historic connections with both types of social control.

With respect to external controls, religion operates by way of what Max Weber called "legitimation"; this means that religion justifies, "explains," and "rationalizes" (in the psychological sense) the exercise of power in society. Weber saw very clearly that human beings not only want power and privilege but also the feeling that these things belong to them as a matter of right. Religion, from earliest times, has provided rationales that thus served the needs of the powerful. These rationales sometimes take the form of elaborate theories—the mythologies that make the establishment of the sociopolitical system in question an act of gods or demigods; the so-called "royal ideologies" that imbue the institution of ancient kingship with divinity; the theory of the divine right of kings in the modern absolute state; and even the very recent conceptions of democracy as being rooted in God-given natural rights. The legitimating function of religion, however, is already given whenever obedience to the agencies of social control is interpreted as religious duty, and disobedience is interpreted as religious sin. Religion sustains the effective operation of social control by converting the *de facto* powers of this world into manifestations of the *a priori* right order of the universe.

This legitimation of power (that is, of the specific agencies exercising social control) becomes especially important when fundamentally indispensable social arrangements are involved or when certain situations demand extreme sacrifices from individuals. Root institutions in society, such as marriage and property, must be protected by extremely powerful so-

[9] Lloyd Warner, *American Life—Dream and Reality* (Chicago: University of Chicago Press, 1953).

cial controls, sustained in turn by correspondingly powerful religious legitimations. Even in our own highly "secularized" society, marriage and property are regarded as sacred institutions—marriage almost universally so. A look at the material amassed by cultural anthropologists on the savage religious sanctions surrounding the incest taboo—probably the most ancient social control of all—gives us a good idea of the importance of religious legitimation for the earliest and most basic institutions of human society. Religious legitimations are also crucial when individuals are called upon to engage in extreme efforts: to kill, or to risk being killed. For this reason, religious symbolism (again, even in our own times) is particularly prominent on the occasions of official violence, when men solemnly march out to war or when a member of society is to be ceremoniously deprived of his life. There is an important sociological connection between the formulas "for God and country" and "may the Lord have mercy on your soul." In both cases the religious symbolization of the events assuages their horror and places them in a context of ultimately "right" order.

Social control, however, not only constrains the individual from the outside, but also is "internalized" within his own consciousness and operates there in the form of what is commonly called "conscience." Indeed, external social control is unlikely to be effective unless there has been a great deal of internalization of its norms. It is easy to see how religion is involved in this process. The function of religion in shaping conscience in such a way that people are restrained from socially disapproved conduct is actually one of the most "manifest," generally desired, and proclaimed social effects of religion. There is no doubt that the specific contents of the religiously shaped conscience are relative in time and space. A medieval person may have felt the same religious guilt if a witch were *not* burned that we would free if she were. A traditional white Southerner may feel religious guilt about miscegenation or even its possibility, just as his progressive, northern fellow-Christian may feel religious guilt about the traditional means employed to prevent miscegenation.

The obvious fact that the social relativity of conscience raises inconvenient questions for any system of ethics cannot be pursued here. But we see again in connection with social control what was said above on the possibility of dysfunctional religion. The functions described are in the nature of tendencies—very strong tendencies, to be sure, so much so that we can make confident statements about what religion has done throughout most of its history. However, there are also cases of religion legitimating, or for that matter initiating, challenges to the prevailing controls. It was pointed out that marriage and property, even in our society, are credited with sacred status. Yet, coming from the same religious context, there have been attacks on both marriage and property in the name of religion. The

Oneida Community provides a curious combination of both attacks in nineteenth-century America, in which there are also other instances of Christian antifamilism and Christian communism. If we emphasize the religious legitimations of violence, it is well also to keep in mind religiously based pacifism and opposition to capital punishment. As previously stated, the search for the social functions of religion is always in danger of over-simplification. Nevertheless, valid generalizations can be made if the historical evidence is viewed in its entire scope.

### Social Structuration

A third social function of religion that must be mentioned, although it is less general than the two previous ones, is that of social structuration. Very often religion serves to legitimate social structures that clearly have profane origins. Sometimes, however, religion actually provides the principles of structuration, so that the significant differentiating categories of society can only be put in religious terms. An outstanding case in point is the traditional caste system of India—that unique and terribly complex structure which, although it resulted in great advantage to the political rulers, was almost certainly the creation of the Brahman priesthood.[10] In our own society, as some sociologists have recently claimed, there are indications that the three major religious groups are developing into cohesive communities that may eventually become more important in determining an individual's status than the old criteria of class and ethnic background.[11] Although we can also analyze such cases in terms of legitimation, they are interesting in showing the possibility of religion not only supplying the legitimating ideas but also the differentiating criteria for social structures. These cases become more frequent the farther back we go in history. When we get to archaic and primitive societies, in most instances the functions of structuration and legitimation appear to merge.

If we look only for the positive social functions of religion, we are in danger of thinking of society as always being the independent variable and religion the dependent one in all situations. This danger also exists in an uncritical application of the Durkheimian approach (Durkheim himself avoided it). The sociology of religion of Max Weber is particularly useful as a corrective against this one-sidedness.[12] While Weber by no means

[10] See Max Weber, *The Religion of India* (Glencoe, Ill.: Free Press, 1958).
[11] See Will Herberg, *Protestant—Catholic—Jew* (Garden City, N.Y.: Doubleday, 1955); and Gerhard Lenski, *The Religious Factor* (Garden City, N.Y.: Doubleday, 1961).
[12] For Weber's general approach to religion, see Max Weber, *The Sociology of Religion* (Boston: Beacon Press, 1963). For a useful overview of Weber's opus, including his sociology of religion, see Reinhard Bendix, *Max Weber—An Intellectual Portrait* (Garden City, N.Y.: Doubleday-Anchor, 1962).

proposed an "idealist" inversion of the above scheme (where religion would evolve as the great motor force of history and society), he insisted on the possibility that purely religious phenomena, even elements of theological thought, could sometimes have important consequences far beyond the area of religion itself. The most famous instance of this is Weber's theory of the relationship between Protestantism and what he called the "spirit of capitalism." [13] Penetrating into the most abstract spheres of Protestant (especially Calvinist) theology, Weber found certain themes (specifically, the complex of attitudes toward the world that he called "inner-worldly asceticism"—a historically unique configuration of disciplined self-denial applied to rational economic activity) that, in a manner totally unintended by their original creators, became an essential factor in the development of the capitalist economic ethos.

More generally, Weber understood the relationship between religion and society as being one of mutual influence (he used the term of "elective affinity"). Certain social processes and certain religious developments, in a way, "seek each other out" in history. Once this has happened, it is quite possible to analyze religious phenomena as "functions" of the social situation (although Weber would not employ this concept). It is important, however, not to make the mistake of confusing functions and causes. Religion is not merely a sociological by-product. It has its own logic and, sometimes, its own potency in influencing the course of human events.

## Religion in Premodern Societies

Looking at the contemporary religious scene, many of the sociological problems that suggest themselves are of the "and" variety—religion *and* culture, church *and* state, religion *and* the family, and similar problems. This makes sense if our aim is to understand the present situation. It presupposes, however, that religion has become sufficiently localized in special institutions so that these, in turn, can be compared with other institutions in society. In other words, it presupposes that there is something that can be called a specifically religious institution. This presupposition is not valid for most of human history. It is, of course, valid for our own society, in which the institutional specificity of religion was sharpened to a unique degree by the Christian conception of the church and then, as we shall see, carried even further by the process known as secularization. How-

---

[13] Max Weber, *The Protestant Ethic and the Spirit of Capitalism* (London: George Allen and Unwin, 1930). This essay, first published in German in 1904–1905, is probably the most famous work in the sociology of religion. It aroused a controversy among historians and social scientists that still continues today.

ever, if we want to understand the place of religion in premodern societies, we must free ourselves of this presupposition.

The prevailing pattern in premodern societies, especially those outside of the Judaeo-Christian orbit, was that religion was *not* institutionally specified or specialized, but was embedded in the general institutional system of the society. All human activity was permeated directly or indirectly by religious symbols and practices. Although from very early times there were individuals who specialized in religious services, there was no set-aside "field of religion," as we put it today. All of society was the "field of religion." This lack of institutional differentiation is not peculiar to religion; as cultural anthropologists have shown, the social fabric of primitive societies is very undifferentiated institutionally as compared with ours. Possibly the only real institution is kinship, which structures and controls nearly everything that goes on in the society. Kinship, however, is permeated with religious meaning, and the terrible prohibition that is the foundation of all kinship—the incest taboo—is in its essence a religious phenomenon. But kinship embraces not only what we would now call religious institutions, but also what we would regard today as political, economic, or educational institutions, to name only a few. If we move on in history toward the societies that we think of as ancient civilizations, the institutions become more differentiated and complex. Yet religion particularly lags behind in this process of differentiation. It continues to extend into the other institutional spheres rather than to be localized in its own "field."

Even in times as relatively close to ours as those of ancient Rome, the family continued to be in itself a religious entity. The family was constituted by those (whether they were "blood relatives" or not) who worshipped at the family shrine. The awesome powers of the Roman father were religious powers, for he was the presiding priest of the family cult. When a Roman woman married, she shifted her religious allegiance from the shrine of her own family to that of her husband's family—an act almost comparable to conversion from one denomination to another in contemporary America. The city of Rome itself, like the Greek *polis* before it, was also a religious entity. To be a citizen meant first to be religiously subject to the city's gods. Through much of the ancient Mediterranean world the question "What are your gods?" addressed to a stranger had the same meaning as our contemporary question "Where do you come from?" This is why exile was such a terrible punishment. Under Athenian law it was customary to give a condemned citizen a choice between death and exile. The more common choice was death. This only becomes meaningful when the religious significance of exile is understood—separation from one's gods. In Christian terms we could say, "separation from the means of grace"—this would amount to full excommunication to a believing Catholic. Even the empire built by the Romans continued to have the religious meaning that originally appertained to the city. One of the titles of the Roman emperor, later taken over by the popes of Rome, was that of supreme pontiff, that is, a priestly title referring to the emperor's function as chief celebrant of the imperial cult which had its center in the worship of the Capoline Jupiter.[14] This, incidentally, was the reason for all the unpleasantness between the Roman government and the early Christians. It was not because of the Christians' far-out religious beliefs, but because of their "uncivic" refusal to participate in the imperial cult.

The typical ancient pattern is one in which (as Eliade puts it) the society relates to the ultimate religious order of the universe as microcosm to macrocosm. Everything that happens "here below" is an analogue of what forever occurs "up above." Human sexuality is analogous to divine creativity. Human labor imitates the work of the gods. Human power is a reflection of cosmic power. Thus the entire social order exists only by virtue of its religious significance. Consequently, every "social problem" is always a religious problem, and vice versa. If there is a lack of rainfall or if there are natural catastrophes of some kind, this indicates that something is amiss in the proper relationship between microcosms and macrocosm. But the same is true if the peasants are restless or if the army has met with defeat. All of these events are indicative of disturbances in the "right order" of things (which the Iranians called *arta*, the Indians *rta*, the Chinese *tao*, and the Egyptians *ma'at*). The "solution" to such problems, then, was also primarily religious. The ceremonies must now be performed with greater care, or some ritual impurity must be removed, or some special religious means must be employed to cope with the emergency. It would be a mistake to think of these notions as "magical." Instead they are rooted in the fundamental archaic understanding of society as constituted by divine manifestations.[15]

If we ask what this meant for the individual in his everyday life, we can recollect once more the probable etymology of the world "religion" as caution, care, careful observance. Each stage in the individual's biography was circumscribed by religious rituals and duties to ensure his remaining in harmony with the "right" order. The most important of these were what cultural anthropologists call the "rites of passage," the religious ceremonies

[14] See Fustel de Coulanges, *The Ancient City* (Garden City, N.Y.: Doubleday-Anchor, 1955). This work by a nineteenth-century French historian is not only a classic statement of the religious character of Graeco-Roman society, but is of interest for the history of sociology, since its author was Durkheim's teacher and exerted a strong influence on his student's thinking on religion.
[15] The Chinese variety of this pattern is well brought out in Max Weber, *The Religion of China* (Glencoe, Ill.: Free Press, 1951).

marking the great turning point in life—birth, puberty, marriage, and death. But these were only the most important of countless religious occasions throughout life. If the individual "watched himself," that is, if he were truly "religious," his life would remain safely embedded in the overall order of things. If he slipped up somewhere, there were usually religious repair services available, so that he could make things "right" again—as we say, "straighten himself out." It is apparent that religion functioning in this way is not conducive to innovation or radical experiments. The religious laws of ancient India frequently emphasized that it is better to do one's own duty (*dharma*) poorly than to do someone else's duty well. If, viewed from our perspective, such a world seems narrow, it is well to remember that it was also more secure.

While religion extended throughout the social fabric, there was one focus of special concentration—the political. This particular "affinity" between the religious and the political (which, in modified forms, has continued into modern times) is not difficult to understand in light of the preceding considerations. If we accept Van der Leeuw's conception of power as the key element in religious experience, and if we recall the common definition of politics as the exercise of power, then we can say that the political in premodern societies is the actualization of cosmic power in the affairs of men. The "dread majesty" of the symbols of political power is only a reflection of the terrible might of the gods, and the individual's reaction to the religious and the political is similar—the same complex of awe, fascination, and (finally) readiness for self-immolation that Otto described in his analysis of sacred experience. The sacred makes men tremble because it manifests ultimate power—ultimate danger. The political, in turn, has always been represented by the symbols of violence —the sword, the lion, the eagle. Indeed, as Macchiavelli (the father of modern political science) saw very clearly, the political is unthinkable without force, that is, the power to move and control others, which is ultimately expressed in the power over life and death. The gods create and kill. The king has the final decision over the killing of men. It is important to understand that men's submission to both powers is not just because of fear alone but because of the profound desire to be "in order," even if this order is guarded by terrifying violence.

This does not mean that the close linkage between the political and the religious always took the same form. Premodern societies vary in the degree to which political power is identified with the religious power that is its prototype. The closest identification in civilized societies is found in the institution of divine kingship, in which the king himself was venerated as a god. Ancient Egypt is the ideal example of such a religious-political symbiosis remaining intact over many centuries. In Elizabethan England, on the threshold of the modern period, we find the theory of the king's two bodies developed by the crown's lawyers—the "body natural," which referred to the king's own person, and the "body politic," which was the ineffable incarnation of royalty in that person, mysteriously potent and free of any weaknesses belonging to the mere physical being. A pale reflection of the sacred potency of the political remains even in our own highly secularized, democratically legitimated society in both the legal theories and the popular notions that attach to the highest political offices. The inauguration ceremonial of an American president offers ample empirical evidence on this.

If the political is the area generally closest to the religious, the economic is the one generally furthest removed. In premodern societies, of course, this does not mean that economic matters are secularized in the contemporary sense, but they are relatively prone to developing a logic of their own that is apart from the religious symbols proper. This difference between the political and the economic can probably be explained rather simply. The foremost political problem is how to convince people that the authorities have the right to exercise power. The problems of the economic area, however, are less centered on people than on things, thus necessitating various rational procedures (for example, technological improvements) for which legitimation is only secondary. Religion can be of immense help, for instance, to a primitive chief who wants to keep his tribe permanently impressed with his own awesome qualities and privileges. Religion will be of only limited help if the chief faces the problem of transporting food-stuffs from the territory where they grow to the territory in which they are to be eaten. On the other hand, religion will continue to be relevant to the transportation problem in terms of motivating people to carry on or perhaps improve the economic and technological measures employed. The very nature of economics as a "worldly" activity makes it all the more interesting to see how religion relates to it, either directly or indirectly.

Weber's principal interest in religion was in how religion defined the "world" (that is, all of those activities that were not directly part of the sacred) and what the economic consequences of the various definitions were.[16] Having satisfied himself that there was an important connection between Protestantism and the extreme "rationalization" of modern capitalism, Weber tried to discover why other religious traditions led to different results. The term "rationalization" is not to be understood in the current psychological sense. Instead, it means the process of making more rational the economic and technological procedures of society.

---

[16] See H. H. Gerth and C. Wright Mills, eds., *From Max Weber* (New York: Oxford University Press, 1959), pp. 267 ff., as well as, Max Weber, *The Sociology of Religion* (cited in footnote 12).

Although it is impossible to summarize here the immense work of historical research and sociological analysis involved, we can conclude that its main result was negative, in the sense that throughout most of religious history the rationalizing influences were weak. The important question is not whether economic activity is given *some* religious meaning, since this can be found almost everywhere, but rather whether and to what extent economic activity was interpreted as directly conducive to the attainment of salvation or other religious benefits. The tendency of the great religions of Asia is to depreciate the significance of the "world" altogether (Hinduism and Buddhism), thus making economic activity religiously second-class, or to emphasize "wordly" activities other than the economic, such as political (Confucianism) or military (Islam) activities. Only in the religious history of the Jews is it possible to find the roots of that rationalization of the "world," which in its Christian and particularly in its Protestant developments became such an important factor in the birth of the modern West.[17]

Weber's concept of "elective affinity" is most clearly apparent in his discussion of the way in which different strata of society relate to religion.[18] It is a remarkable sociological fact about religious history that different strata (classes or other social groupings) have reacted to religious ideas in quite different ways. For instance, the peasantry and the aristocracy have tended toward religious conservatism, while the lower-middle strata (*not*, it must be stressed, the lowest strata) have always been most hospitable to innovating ideas in religion. These patterns are not to be interpreted in terms of a simple social determination of religious ideas, but instead in the affinity to some of the religious ideas that induced specific strata to become their "carriers." Therefore, it is very helpful for an understanding of the great religions if we observe which social groups were instrumental in "carrying" them, especially in their early phases, or to put it differently, in which social strata these religions were originally "localized." For Confucianism, we must look to the literary class that served as the bureaucracy of traditional China, for Hinduism to the priestly caste of the Brahmans, for Buddhism to the wandering communities of monks, for Islam to a warrior elite, for rabbinical Judaism to an urban merchant class, and for early Christianity to the itinerant artisans of which Paul is the most famous example.

I hope I have indicated that it would be a mistake to think of religion, even in premodern societies and even in those where the microcosm macrocosm scheme held most strongly, as only a static or passive phenom-

---

[17] See Max Weber, *Ancient Judaism* (Glencoe, Ill.: Free Press, 1952).
[18] See Max Weber, *The Sociology of Religion* (cited in footnote 12), pp. 80 ff.

enon in society. Even in Egypt (the ideal illustration for such a society), there was the so-called Amarna Revolution in the fourteenth century B.C. when, under the leadership of the strange Pharaoh Akhenaton, the complete religious system was overturned during a brief period of incredible spiritual turmoil. Indeed, one of the great revolutionary forces of history, recurring over and over again, often in the most unexpected places, is essentially a religious phenomenon—the phenomenon that Weber called charisma.[19] Weber's theory of charisma is one of the most important theoretical formulations in the sociology of religion, and some attention must be given to it here, although it will be impossible to give an adequate idea of its scope and implications in various areas of sociological analysis.

Charisma (the word comes from the Greek New Testament, where it means a "gift of grace") is defined by Weber as a form of authority that its legitimated, not by tradition, law, or other rational considerations, but by the extraordinary character of the person or persons claiming this authority. Sociologically speaking, it does not matter what the actual psychology of the charismatic leader may be. Charisma is present when there are those who believe it to be present. It is extraordinary in the sense that it breaks through all of the conventions that previously structured everyday life in society. It is in essence radical, innovating, and irrational. The charismatic leader is surrounded by an aura of power and mystery. His followers respond to him as one responds to the sacred in its immediate manifestations—with fascination, dread, and the readiness to obey blindly and, if necessary, to sacrifice oneself. The revolutionary quality of charisma is well brought out in the reiterated statement of Jesus, "You have heard that it was said. . . . but I say to you," and the totality of its claim to men's allegiance in Jesus' saying, "He who is not with me is against me." Charisma erupts in society like a natural catastrophe, exploding traditional structures and radically challenging traditional assumptions about the world. People who do not fall under its sway will naturally look upon it as a monstrous derangement and upon its promulgators as dangerous madmen.

The study of charismatic movements is one of the most exciting in the sociology of religion because of the passionate violence with which the movements are accompanied and the cataclysmic consequences that they sometimes engender. Perhaps the most astounding example of the cataclysmic consequences in religious history is the appearance of Muhammad in seventh-century Arabia, who within a brief period of years united the Arab tribes that had fought each other for millennia and whose followers, within a hundred years of his death, created an empire that

---

[19] See H. H. Gerth and C. Wright Mills (cited in footnote 16), pp. 245 ff.

stretched from the Atlantic Ocean to India. On a less grandiose world-historical scale we may recall such amazing civilizing feats as the creation by Buddhist monks of a viable society in the inhospitable, lonely plateaus of Tibet or, closer to home, the settlement of Utah by the Mormon pioneers.[20] To some extent, at least, the fascination of charisma may be felt whenever sociologists or others study the turbulent sectarian movements that exist on the fringes of "respectable" religion.[21]

A good many observations have been made about the social structure of charismatic movements which cannot be discussed here. However, the most important observation was made by Weber, namely, that charisma does not last. This idea is expressed in Weber's theory of charisma by the concept of "routinization." Indeed, it is possible to make an approximate prediction when the process of routinization will set in—usually, when the first generation of followers of the charismatic leader has died. Routinization is the loss of the extraordinary quality that defines the charismatic phenomenon in the first place. Now, a new generation takes over to whom the unheard-of novelties of the first followers have become often-heard, taken-for-granted aspects of their normal lives. The extraordinary becomes ordinary again; the original passions are domesticated by the routines of everyday life; and the tremendous wonder gives way to the normal social problems of any on-going group; the most important of which are usually the economic and political ones. To solve these problems, the early, typically loose and informal organization of the movement will no longer suffice. Stronger, more stable forms of organization must be adopted, and in this "hardening" of the movement, not surprisingly, some of the traditional patterns that were thrown out in the heat of revolutionizing fervor make their reappearance. There are two directions that the routinization of charisma may then take. It may be traditionalized, often in ways identical to those that preceded it in the society. This happens, for example if the charisma is reinterpreted as a quality that can be inherited and a religious dynasty may claim it by virtue of descent from the original leader. An instance of this type of routinization is the veneration of the descendants of 'Ali in Shi'ite Islam. Or charisma may be rationalized, attached not to a person but to an office. The development of the episcopate and the papacy in Roman Catholic Christianity is the best illustration of this type.

[20] For an illuminating study of the Mormon case by a sociologist, see Thomas O'Dea, *The Mormons* (Chicago: University of Chicago Press, 1957).
[21] For a sociological study of sectarianism that has by now almost become a classic in the sociology of American religion, see Liston Pope, *Millhands and Preachers* (New Haven: Yale University Press, 1942). Also see a more recent work by a British sociologist, Bryan Wilson, *Sects and Society* (Berkeley: University of California Press, 1961).

Routinization does not mean, of course, that nothing remains of the original transformations brought about by charisma. It acts, however, as a constant and highly predictable brake on the innovating force of religious revolutions (and, incidentally, also on the political ones). This is why the ancient revolutionary force of charisma, despite its frequent recurrences in history, so often ended in an at least partial reversal to the old, pre-charismatic ways. The other great revolutionary force in history, according to Weber, is rationalization—less abrupt and spectacular in its initial appearances than charisma, yet for this very reason more pervasive and long-lasting. Like charisma, rationalization has religious roots and is capable of secularization. If we turn to religion in modern societies, although we shall continue to find charismatic phenomena, it is rationalization that is by far the most important fact. Under the impact of rationalization, both the wider social functions and the inner social structures of religion have been radically transformed. The sociological meaning of these transformations will concern us in the following discussion.

## Transformation of Functions

Rationalization, in the sense that Weber understood this term, is the leading motif of modern history.[22] It is the initially slow but nonetheless revolutionary force by which the traditional structures and conventions of society have been transformed, one by one, to give way to patterns of conduct in which means and ends are conjoined with rational consistency. The original location of this process was almost certainly in the economic and technological areas of society. It was economic activities, specifically those of early capitalism, and the technological procedures employed both for economic and noneconomic (for instance, military) ends that were first rationalized. To carry through such rationalization, however, all of the social formations within which these activities and procedures were carried on had to be rationally restructured. The most important consequence of this restructuring of institutions has been bureaucracy, both in the political area and then, increasingly, in every other conceivable area of the social system as well. The overall effect of rationalization on the modern West has thus been as complete a metamorphosis of society as may be found in human history. It does not require too much sociological sophistication to suspect that this would also have far-reaching consequences for the values and the world view of the society in question.

[22] The discussion throughout this section is essentially based on Weber's sociology of religion. Since Weber's major works have already been cited in previous footnotes, I have refrained from giving further references to these at each point of the argument.

The consequences of rationalization for religion are, of course, of great importance for our present considerations. Before examining these consequences, however, let us look at the other end of the process, figuratively speaking. One of the most interesting aspects of Weber's discussion of rationalization is his proposition that the rationalization process not only has religious consequences (which we would expect) but that it also has religious roots (which flies in the face of everything that we would expect).

On the level of the individual's everyday life, rationalization implies above all discipline, that is, the systematic, self-denying, and calculating marshalling of all available energy for the envisaged goal (no matter now what that particular goal may be—not necessarily an economic one). Now, discipline as such is not a new or even recent historical phenomenon. For example, even primitive or archaic societies impose disciplines for military purposes; some of these are rational (such as disciplines of physical fitness), while others are more magical in character (such as sexual or dietary taboos for times of war). The most interesting cases of discipline for our present considerations, however, are those in which the individual's marshalling of forces is geared to a religious end. This type of discipline is commonly called asceticism. Into this generally used concept Weber introduced a very useful distinction—the distinction between asceticism directed toward goals in another world beyond this one (which he called other-worldly asceticism) and asceticism directed toward goals *in* this world (inner-worldly asceticism). Even military disciplines can be differentiated in this way. Most men in war probably deny themselves for the strictly inner-worldly purpose of achieving victory over the enemy, but there are also holy wars (as in Islam) in which the military discipline is directly geared to the achievement of salvation in the next life.

The great bulk of religious asceticism in history has been oriented toward other-worldly goals. Especially in the great salvation doctrines of Asia (in Hinduism, Buddhism, and Taoism) the strenuous efforts of self-discipline were always motivated by the desire to achieve liberation from the sufferings and the finitude of worldly existence. Generally, the same has been true of mysticism wherever it appeared (also in the religious traditions that derive from the Bible). As a result, the activities of "mere" worldly existence (including economic activities, as we have seen previously) are depreciated to the level of the religiously or even the ethically indifferent. Inner-worldly asceticism, on the other hand, seeks to discipline *all* of the activities engaged in by the individual and to structure them in accordance with the religious ideal in question. Therefore, inner-worldly asceticism tends to have much more far-reaching consequences in terms of society. It does not limit its disciplining rigor to a set-apart religious sphere, but makes it encompass the totality of social life.

Although Weber believed that the inner-worldly asceticism of Protestantism had the strongest influence on the rationalization of the modern West, he sought its historical roots all the way back in the religion of ancient Israel. He particularly emphasized the importance of the Israelite prophets in preparing the way for the overall rationalization of life and, although more recent Old Testament scholarship necessitates certain modifications of Weber's understanding of this development, his basic argument remains very convincing. One of the leading motifs of the prophets' teaching was the insistence on a thoroughly ethical conduct in *all* activities of life instead of a mere reliance on the correct performance of ritual obligations. What was required of man was, in the words of Micah, "to do justice, and to love kindness, and to walk humbly with your God." This emphasis on ethics was rationalizing in its consequences because it kept reiterating the demand that *all* of Israelite society be "overhauled" to conform to the commandments of God. In other words, there was implicit in the prophetic movement from the beginning a radical, even revolutionary approach to the social structures of the time.

This implicit antitraditionalism became vitally important after Israel lost its political sovereignty, first after the destruction of Jerusalem by the Babylonians and in the period of the Babylonian exile, and later in the general dispersion of the Jews from Palestine. The rigid organization of every aspect of social life in conformance with the divine law that became the principal characteristic of rabbinical Judaism in the Diaspora may be understood as a logical development of the ethical radicalism of the prophetic movement. However, in view of the increasingly segregated character of the Jews in the centuries that followed the dispersion, the peculiarly Jewish rationalization of life had much less world-historical influence than its Christian derivatives. In this connection, incidentally, Weber disputed other scholars who credited the Jews with a major contribution to the development of modern capitalism.

In the Christian Middle Ages the rationalizing energy of asceticism was largely "localized" in the monastic orders. In its fundamental religious motivation this monastic asceticism remained other-worldly, although it had strong inner-worldly components (as in the Benedictine ideal of "prayer and work"). Monasticism impressed upon Catholic Christianity the "double standard" of the "religious life" of the monk or the nun (the term is still employed in this sense in modern Catholic usage) as compared to the "life in the world" of the ordinary laity. It was precisely the vigorous rejection of this "double standard" by Protestantism that made Protestantism such a potent rationalizing influence. This becomes most apparent by considering the shift of meaning in the term "vocation." In medieval usage (retained by Catholics to this day), the term refers only to the "calling" of priests and monastics. Luther rejected this limited meaning, stressed that any lawful occupation engaged in by a Christian was a "vocation" in the full sense of the word; that is, an activity that ought to be structured so as to conform fully to the will of God. In other words, secular work was now endowed with religious dignity. In Lutheranism, however, the notion of "vocation" remained relatively conservative, implying the religiously faithful performance of the duties imposed on a person by his particular station in life (a complex of attitudes almost certainly at the roots of the much-praised German sense of workmanship).

Calvinism further radicalized the notion by including in it a religiously motivated duty "to better oneself," "to prove oneself," (a motivational pattern that Weber related to the Calvinist doctrine of predestination and to the urge that it engendered "to prove" one's status as a member of the elect). In this way Protestantism released into the world the tremendous energies of ascetic discipline that had been shut away behind the walls of the monasteries, turning them from other-worldly preoccupations to the systematic reshaping of the social structures. This Protestant inner-worldly asceticism thus became one of the mainsprings of the tradition-shattering rationalization that finally gave birth to the two modern dynamisms of capitalism and industrialism.

The unique intensity and scope of rationalization in modern Western society, then, may be related to the peculiar religious development of this society. There is probably an even deeper relationship between Western rationalization and Western religion. In discussing the contrast between the Protestant and the medieval views of the world, Weber applied the suggestive term "disenchantment." Protestantism helped to "disenchant" the world by divesting it of the mystery, the miracles, and even the magic of medieval Catholicism. The mysterious ritual of the mass was transformed into the fairly sober, matter-of-fact practice of the communion service. Indeed, the entire sacramental apparatus of Catholic Christianity—that continuous communication link between men and the divine—was not only shrunk quantitatively (the number of sacraments was reduced from seven to two) but was stripped of much of its awesome character. Miracles, even if still admitted in theory, were no longer seriously expected to take place in contemporary life. The religious "underground" of superstitions and magical beliefs, widely tolerated within the Catholic orbit if only as a concession to human weakness, was violently driven out of the Protestant churches. In Calvinism, particularly, there occurred a radical polarization in the religious imagination, with an inscrutable God addressing sinful man through the one narrow channel of the revealed Word, with all of the mediating instrumentalities (the Virgin, the saints, the angels, the grace-dispensing sacraments, and the forever anticipated eruption of the supernatural through the miracles) harshly eliminated from the Christian universe of discourse. The world, both the natural one and that world that is incorporated in human institutions, then became "disenchanted"—and, by the same token, it became amenable to rational interpretation and manipulation by man himself. To put this a little differently, Protestantism divested the world of almost all traces of divinity—and thus opened it up to secularization both in theory and in practice.

It would be an exaggeration to say that modern secularization has only religious roots. There is at least one other historical factor: the influence of Greek rational thought on the development of Western culture. But it is possible to conclude that secularization cannot be understood apart from certain religious themes already found in the Old Testament. The peculiarity of the religion of ancient Israel was precisely the radical transcendentalization of its concept of God, that is, the divorce between God and all the "natural" processes of this world. The Israelite God was, from the earliest records that we possess, a divinity hostile to and unamenable to magic, a divinity other than and separate from the rhythms of nature worship in all of its forms (for example, his passionate opposition to sacred sexuality as institutionalized throughout the ancient Near East in temple prostitution and religious orgies) and against the divinization of human beings (for example, the Israelites' refusal to acknowledge the divinity of kingship) developed from this conviction of the "otherness" of the God who had made a covenant with Israel. This "unnatural" conception of God, which of course was extended in Christianity, may be considered as the ultimate *religious* source of what much later became that complete desacralization of the world we know as secularization. Certainly, there is a profound irony in this historical development from the most grandiose conception of divine sovereignty possible to human thought to a world view in which no place is left for God at all. Yet human history is made of such ironies.[23]

At the end of this chapter we shall give a general picture of the overall effect of secularization on contemporary religion. But it should be clear now that the process of rationalization would have to have had far-reaching consequences for the social functions of religion discussed a little earlier. We can begin to see this by looking at the Durkheimian function *par excellence:* the function of symbolic integration. This function,

[23] For a recent interpretation of the radical reinterpretation of the world in Israelite religion, see Eric Voegelin, *Israel and Revelation* (Baton Rouge: Louisiana State University Press, 1958).

it will be recalled, involves the fundamental capacity of religion to hold human beings together in a social system (as Durkheim would say, "to engender and preserve solidarity"). Now, one of the main presuppositions for this function is that religion must really be the one, great, all-embracing symbolism of the society in question. Religion fulfills the function of symbolic integration by supplying values and cognitive interpretations that form a sort of overarching canopy for *all* of the institutions. In this way, wherever men are and whatever they do, religion bestows meaning on their social position and the activities springing from this position.

This function is radically transformed as modern society emerges. Religion becomes less and less capable of furnishing overarching symbols for the full range of social institutions. Quite apart from the deeper reasons, which are already given in the process of secularization itself, this change of functionality is a logical consequence of the immense institutional differentiation of modern society. The old religious symbols can no longer be made to stretch, so to speak, to encompass the new range of institutions. Different institutional areas develop their own autonomous symbolisms, most of them having little or no relationship to the traditional religious ones. This shrinkage in the integrative power of religion is commonly deplored by religious spokesmen, and in recent times a good deal of energy in the churches has been used up in trying to reverse this trend. Typically, this has taken the form of various projects that seek to make religion "more relevant to modern life," to erect "bridges between church and world," or simply to bring religion "up to date." The term *aggiornamento* (Italian for "bringing up to date"), coined by Pope John XXIII and now so important in the reform movement in the Catholic church, is an expression of this trend.

While the theological issues involved in these modifications of tradition do not, of course, concern us here, it is easy to see that the institutional structure of modern society is not favorable to the realization of such projects. In the realm of politics there are frequent protests against the notion that modern society is or should be any less "Christian" than it had been in the past. Conservative political movements on both sides of the Atlantic have had the habit of embellishing their programs with a call to a religious renascence in all areas of social life. Frequently such appeals for a "Christian Occident" (a favorite slogan of Catholic-inspired "Christian Democratic" parties in Western Europe) or for a "Christian America" (consider, for instance, the outcry against the Supreme Court decision on prayer in the public schools) are mainly rhetorical in character. Where the attempt to restore a traditional relationship between religion and society achieved a measure of apparent success (as in fascist Spain), the further modernization of society (especially through growing indus-trialization) seems to imperil the continued maintenance of this restoration.[24]

We would be hasty, however, to conclude from the above that con-temporary religion has lost all integrative power. A better description of the actual social situation is that religion has moved from overall integra-tion of society to specific integrations of specific social groupings. For example, religion can only integrate American society as a whole rhetori-cally, but it continues as an important integrative force in the insti-tution of the family. Or, for another case, the political process as a whole is integrated by religion in rhetorics only, but specific political movements may be religiously integrated in a more than rhetorical way. The fact that such movements may use similar religious symbols for opposite political goals (so that in a Southern community both the leader of the Ku Klux Klan and the leader of CORE may be Baptist ministers, both using very similar religious vocabularies to legitimate their respective activities) need not occupy us here. The pertinent point is that religion may still serve symbolically to integrate distinct social groups (in the example, the conservative whites and the rebelling Negroes), providing each with intense solidarity that may be dysfunctional for the overall society but highly functional for the interests of each group. We shall consider later the general implications of the fragmentation of integrative symbolisms in contemporary society.

The other social functions of religion have undergone similar transforma-tions. Religion continues to function as an agency of social control, both external and internal, but once more in an institutionally differentiated way. For instance, religion may continue to possess external sanctions (such as economic pressure or social ostracism) in certain sectors of the society such as ethnic communities or underdeveloped rural areas, but may completely fail to do so in other sectors such as the highly anonymous worlds of the metropolis. The individual's religiously shaped conscience may control him strongly in, for example, his marital life or in the raising of his children, but may fail to exercise any control over him in his business activities. The same man who might be overcome with a terrible sense of sin if he commits adultery may not feel the slightest twinge of conscience in economic activities that, in terms of traditional religious morality, may be tantamount to theft. Again, contemporary religious literature is filled with denunciations of this kind of "hypocrisy," but what is generally not

[24] For a discussion of the general relationship between institutional differentiation and the social functionality of religion in America, see Talcott Parsons, *Structure and Process in Modern Societies* (Glencoe, Ill.: Free Press, 1960), pp. 295 ff. For a different inter-pretation, see Peter Berger, *The Noise of Solemn Assemblies* (Garden City, N.Y.: Doubleday, 1961), Chapters 1–6.

recognized is that the structure of modern institutions makes such ethical "specialization" almost inevitable. The control function of religion, just like its integrative function, appears today in highly fragmented forms.

As we would expect from the above discussion, the capacity of religion to serve as an agent of social structuration in modern society has largely disappeared. Stated differently, religion is mainly a passive or reactive factor (in scientific parlance, it acts as a "dependent variable") in the structuring processes of modern society. The religious institutions are vitally affected by what occurs in the wider society. The reverse is rarely the case. But this does not mean that religion, even in this passive role, has *no* relationship to social structuration. For example, religion in American society continues to function as a symbol of status. Religious affiliation continues to be an indicator of class, especially within Protestantism, and also serves as a useful label to locate an individual in the social structure as a whole.[25]

The functional transformation just outlined is closely related to the development of the two most important modern institutions: the political and the economic. An autonomization of both of these institutions is possible. The autonomization of the political as against the religious, already foreshadowed in the struggle between emperors and popes during the Middle Ages (when, however, this struggle took place within the frame of reference of "Christendom" common to both antagonists), is the consequence of the emergence of the modern state. On the level of institutions, this brought about the peculiarly modern problem of "church and state." Typically, this problem manifests itself no longer as a defense of political interests against the universal claims of the church but, on the contrary, as resistance to the encroachments of state authority upon the shrinking domain of religion. In democratic societies, where the state concedes the independence of the religious domain (although there may still be "jurisdictional disputes"; for example, in education or the legal regulation of marriage), the problem is frequently one of different religious groups vying with each other for various political benefits (consider for instance, the current question of government support for religiously sponsored education in this country). On the level of ideas, the problem is manifested in the emergence of so-called *raison d'état*, that is, the notion that the state must follow a logic of its own that cannot be bound by religio-ethical norms. Macchiavelli was the early "prophet" of this kind of political thinking, but it is important to notice that even where political figures indignantly

---

[25] For discussions of this, see the works by Will Herberg and Gerhard Lenski (cited in footnote 11), and by Peter Berger (cited in footnote 24). For documentation on the place of religion in contemporary American society generally, see David Moberg, *The Church as a Social Institution* (Englewood Cliffs, N.J.: Prentice-Hall, 1962).

disavow the alleged moral cynicism of Macchiavellianism, their *de facto* conduct tends to follow the prescriptions of the gloomy Florentine.[26]

While there continue to be cases in the contemporary world of "theocracy" (the attempt to subject the state to the church) and "caesaro-papism" (the subjection of the church to the state), the global trend is toward the separation of church and state. "Theocratic" projects (like those of the Spanish church or the ultra-orthodox groups in modern Israel) and "caesaropapistic" ones (like the efforts of totalitarian regimes to control all aspects of the churches' life) appear to fail precisely to the degree in which the societies in question approach economic maturity in the sense of full industrialization. At that point the separation model begins to be realized. How potent the social forces contributing to separation are today can be seen by the successful exportation of this ideal to the non-Western world. India and Japan are good illustrations. The case of Pakistan is perhaps even more instructive. Although Pakistan was founded in 1947 as an Islamic state and was consciously opposed to the secular conception of neighboring India, it has had endless difficulties in its attempts to formulate a constitution—precisely because it has been very hard to figure out just what the term "an Islamic state" might mean for modern society.

The autonomization of the economic area of social life has already been touched upon in our previous discussion of rationalization. On the institutional level, the economic area now organized itself in sharp differentiation from the political institutions on the one hand and the family on the other. The feudal continuum between these three institutional spheres is decisively shattered. Just as the modern state developed its own logic separate from that of the church, so did the modern economic system (specifically, capitalism and industrialism) develop its autonomous rationales as against the state. Economic laws began to be envisaged as a new form of "iron necessity," even less amenable to religio-ethical modification than *raison d'état*, and economics achieved the distinction of becoming "the dismal science" because it sought to explicate these laws. On the other hand, the requirements of modern production separated the economy from the family, with enormous consequences for that institution, which became a nonproductive and consumptive agency economically, thereby losing much of its previous importance in the wider society. Needless to add, the autonomization of the economic entailed as much secularization, or even more, than that of the political. Religion, both as institution and as symbolism, is generally regarded today as being

---

[26] The definitive historical work on church and state relations in this country is Anson Phelps Stokes, *Church and State in the United States* (New York: Harper, 1950).

out of place in the economic sphere. Management and labor, no matter what else they may disagree upon, generally agree that religion must be checked at the entrance to factory or office (although this agreement may be a tacit one in societies, such as the American one, where people can still get some political mileage out of the rhetorical invocation of religious values). Naturally, religious thinkers have deplored this separation of religion from the economic as much as they have deplored the separation of religion from the political. Nevertheless, efforts for a religious penetration of the economy have been even less promising then those directed toward the state. "Relevance" of the churches to economic life has meant, chiefly, an adaptation of religio-ethical norms to the functional requirements of the capitalist industrial system, rather than the reverse.[27]

The overall effect of the rationalization of society in the modern West has been the segregation of religion, both as institution and as symbolism, within specific social sectors. The segregation has been, above all, within that peculiarly modern domain commonly known as "private life." It is in this private sphere, separated from both the political and the economic driving forces of society, that religion has found itself in close neighborhood with another institution that has undergone a similar shrinkage in functions: the family. Later, we shall get some understanding of what this new social "location" of religion means. Now, however, we must briefly examine the transformation in the inner social structure of religious institutions that has accompanied the functional transformation just discussed.

## Transformation of Structures

If we reason sociologically, we shall promptly suspect that a transformation of functions as far-reaching as the one just discussed will also entail at least some change in the inner social structures of the institutions involved. This does not imply that there must always be some sort of rational connection between social structures and social functions with respect to means and ends. Society is not that rational an operation. Not only is there often a gap between traditional forms and present

---

[27] The classic statements of this in American sociology were made by Thorstein Veblen. They are still instructive, despite their polemic bias and their datedness in detail. See Max Lerner, ed., *The Portable Veblen* (New York: Viking Press, 1948), pp. 480 ff. For a discussion of the relationship of organized religion to the (predominantly business-oriented) decision-making groups in contemporary American communities, see Floyd Hunter, *Community Power Structure* (Chapel Hill: University of North Carolina Press, 1953).

tasks that social scientists call "cultural lag" (for example, witch doctors participating in a modern public health program), but often there is a puzzling lack of logical connection between forms and tasks even in new social phenomena (for instance, an innovating public health program itself being organized along lines so unpractical that the attainment of the program's goals are improbable). Nevertheless, there tends to be some nexus between what men do and how they gather themselves in groups to do it, if only because men are *also* rational. In the case of religion there has, indeed, been a structural transformation in the religious institutions to conform to the transformation of functions, although (and this is quite important) much of this has been unintended and even unrecognized.

Christian theologians and churchmen of both major confessions are much concerned today with questions of "polity," that is, of ecclesiastical structure. For instance, what is to be the relationship between the pope and the bishops? Are bishops necessary to the essence of the church? Is the independence of the local congregation an essential principle of church structure? Behind the theological arguments, however, there is an interesting empirical presupposition that the theologians largely share with the man in the street—namely, that the *actual* organization of the religious bodies is in accordance with the theological formulations of their organization. Now to some extent this presupposition is obviously valid. We know, after all, that the Catholics have a pope with great powers, that the Episcopalians have bishops who do things that the top officers of other denominations do not do, and that the Baptists have local congregations with a fierce pride in their self-government. But if we probe a little further, the presupposition begins to be somewhat less plausible. We then find that each religious organization faces certain problems in our society that are similar. Consequently, the forms of religious organizations must be geared to the solution of these problems. Next we find that various positions in the structures of religious bodies resemble each other even if they are called by different names and are given different theological justifications. Thus a Methodist bishop may do more or less the same things as a Presbyterian "stated clerk" or a Lutheran "synod president." And the problems faced by a Catholic parish priest who wants to generate financial support among his laity for some expensive new project are very similar to the problems faced by his Protestant or Jewish colleagues. These common patterns in the social structure of contemporary religious institutions may be divided, for purposes of sociological analysis, into simple headings—the patterns of organization, on the level of denominational bodies, and the patterns of association, on the level of lay participation. The key sociological category under the first heading is bureaucracy; under the second, voluntarism. To put all of this succinctly: Almost all religious institutions in our society (with the exception of the smaller groups, especially those with a nonmiddle-class clientele) are bureaucratically organized. The religio-bureaucratic organizations deal with a population that is free to choose its religious affiliation out of a variety of possibilities.

The fundamental sociological observation concerning the structure of contemporary religious institutions is that bureaucratic forms make their appearance without regard to "polity" or the theological legitimations of "polity." [28] This does not mean that theological formulations have no socio-logical importance at all, but their influence is probably to be conceived as one of modification of social patterns with essentially mundane roots. While bureaucracy by itself is a meaningful category for sociological analysis, it is possible to distinguish between different bureaucratic models. In much of Europe, for example, where both Catholic and Protestant churches have long traditions of establishment by the state, the religio-bureaucratic forms have tended to be modeled after the political bureaucracies with which they have had such intimate historical contact. In the United States, on the other hand, where there is no tradition of state churches, the bureaucratic model adopted by the churches is largely one derived from economic organizations. There are reasons to believe that recent developments in Europe, specifically those tending toward greater "pluralism" and separation of church from state, also lead to this economic model of bureaucracy. The hoary and highly complex bureaucracy of the Vatican is a special case, which we cannot discuss here.

On the whole, it makes sense to assume that the choice between an essentially political and an essentially economic model of bureaucracy will be determined by the major practical problems faced by religious bodies. Where there are still strong vestiges of the political establishment of religion, the organization of the religious bodies must facilitate the on-going and often delicate political negotiations with various branches of government. Where, on the other hand, the state has adopted a hands-off policy with regard to religion, the main worries of the church bureaucrats are very similar to those of other "organization men" charged with keeping a big operation going on the basis of free consumer patronage. At the risk of some oversimplification, we may argue that the decisive question is where the money comes from. If it comes chiefly from the public treasury, a political model of bureaucracy is the more functional one. If the money comes, *and must be kept coming*, out of the contributions of a voluntary membership, an economic model is almost inevitable. To put this a little

[28] The best sociological study to date of an American religio-bureaucratic organization, of the American Baptist Convention, is Paul Harrison, *Authority and Power in the Free Church Tradition* (Princeton: Princeton University Press, 1959). Also, see Marshall Sklare, *Conservative Judaism* (Glencoe, Ill.: Free Press, 1955).

differently, in a social situation such as the American one, religion finds itself in a free, competitive market, financially dependent on the continuing goodwill of lay consumers. Despite all obvious differences, then, religion has the *economic* character of a consumer commodity; it must be marketed as such; and, therefore, it must organize itself in such a way that it (or, rather, any specific religious "firm") can stay in the market. Consequently, we should not be surprised that religious bodies strongly resemble other organizations that market less-spiritual commodities.

In the United States, bureaucratization has reached the point where every part of the large religious bodies "above" the level of the local congregation is organized bureaucratically. The local congregation itself, depending upon its size and class character, may be administered by a bureaucratic apparatus of some complexity. The religio-bureaucratic organizations not only resemble their secular equivalents in their *modus operandi* but often even in their nomenclature and in the physical paraphernalia employed. Protestant denominations have hired professional efficiency experts to evaluate their operations, and the advice heeded has sometimes even included the amount of office space allocated to different persons in the bureaucratic hierarchy. Additionally, at least in the American milieu, the prestige symbolism of the business executive and of his typical appurtenances is as important a motivating factor here as the rational functionality of such bureaucratic "streamlining."

The consequences of bureaucratization in religious institutions are far-reaching. Possibly the most important is the centralization of power in a professional staff of "religious managers." This power may or may not be theologically legitimated, and it may or may not be camouflaged by the retention of older noncentralized forms of organization. In any case, it is this managerial staff that controls the organization, administers its finances, and is in a position to dominate its more "representative" gatherings. In this respect, incidentally, the religious bodies are very similar to other voluntary organizations in our society, such as political parties and labor unions, not to speak of the economic corporations proper. Notice particularly that such centralization of power is not the result of some sinister conspiracy by power-hungry manipulators (although it may be assumed that religious institutions have their fair share of this human specimen). It is, instead, an almost "natural" consequence of the bureaucratic situation, as has been shown by the various sociologists who have analyzed this situation. In the case of religious bureaucrats, who commonly are "soft" when it comes to the logic of power and who may sincerely believe in the rarefied theological "explanations" of their positions, the process may be altogether an unconscious one and may even be overtly denied. Centralization of power does not mean that there is a center of absolute power in the organization. Instead, there appears to be a system of checks and balances within the organization, of power positions and power vacuums, of good and bad channels of power-relevant communication. The successful bureaucrat, here as in other bureaucratic settings, is the individual who has a "nose" for these things, recognizes them, and knows how to manipulate them.

There is a multitude of problems of "human relations" in such an organization. But when it comes to the overall policy-making process, it is economic motives above any other that are determinative. It could not be otherwise. The logic of the primacy of economic motives is given in the conditions under which such an organization must operate. Sometimes the influence of economic motives is indirect, as in the nervousness of religious bureaucrats concerning the "public image" of their organization —a phenomenon reflected in the adage that the only thing more nervous than a million dollars is two million dollars. Once the organization is established, it must guarantee the steady influx of funds into its treasury. The logic of this, of course, can always be justified in terms of the professed spiritual goals to which the organization is sincerely dedicated. There is some evidence to indicate that this may change somewhat as an increasing portion of religio-bureaucratic funds (at least in the United States) is derived from investments, the dividends from which, of course, are dependent on the goodwill of nobody. However, as long as the main portion of ecclesiastical income continues to come from ongoing voluntary contributions, the cultivation of "public relations" and "public image" in the interests of economic viability will continue to be major concerns. This necessarily entails a conservative approach to spending. Risky expenditures must be avoided as "unsound," even if there might be theological or ethical rationales for them. Cases in point in the United States are the overwhelming concentration of "church extension" activities on the affluent middle-class areas and the reluctance of ecclesiastically controlled treasuries to invest in such fiscally adventurous enterprises as interracial housing. The economic imperative of keeping the contributing membership "loyal" to the organization entails the invention of ever-new promotional gambits and, more important, the avoidance of overly "controversial" stands that might alienate a sizable group of members. The tendency of the religio-bureaucratic staff is toward conservative, middle-of-the-road, "safe" positions, both on theological and nontheological questions.

Inevitably, there are certain types of persons who are drawn to and who are successful in these positions of bureaucratic power. Thus there has arisen a new breed of "religious managers," similar to other executive types in their social-psychological traits and often appalling to their more traditionalistic coreligionists. The horror of a "superchurch," as the alleged ultimate result of the ecumenical movement, felt by many religious conservatives is very probably related to this social-psychological constellation. The relationships of these religious managers to various categories of other religious functionaries (the "troops" of the clergy, the theological intellectuals, the experts in publicity and fund-raising, the "leading laymen," and others) are very complex and often rather funny. What is sociologically essential is that all of these relationships tend to perpetuate the same men in the central positions of bureaucratic power. The religious managers (who are similar to each other as human types and in the problems that face them) in the different parallel religio-bureaucratic organizations have an understandable way of dealing with each other in a rational manner when it comes to matters of possible common interest. These religious bureaucrats, rarely intellectuals themselves, will tend toward a "practical" orientation in their conduct of church affairs. While the managers cannot dispense with the theologians altogether (who, after all, are the ones who can supply the most plausible legitimation of the whole enterprise), the managers are frequently irritated with the "impractical" and often obscure difficulties concocted by the theologians. This interdenominational and even interfaith affinity of bureaucratic types trying to solve bureaucratic problems is a rarely acknowledged but nevertheless potent factor in the improved climate of relations between religious bodies.

As already mentioned, bureaucratic forms are strongest in the large religious bodies with a predominantly middle-class clientele. That is, bureaucratic forms are strongest in the organizations that have to administer large sums of money and deal with large masses of people under the conditions of free competition for consumer preference. Since bureaucratization is the principal structural consequence of rationalization in general, this is tantamount to saying that it is in these religious bodies that rationalization has gone furthest. We shall examine later the question of the degree to which this rationalization of social form may be accompanied by a rationalization of religious contents. An interesting point here, however, is the effect of bureaucratization and rationalization on the age-old phenomenon of the routinization of charisma. As we have seen, charisma may be routinized in both traditional and rational forms. Under the conditions of modern society, the first possibility becomes more and more improbable. Routinization today almost invariably means rationalization, with the charisma of office being absorbed into patterns of bureaucratic organization. A favorite example in the sociology of religion of the routinization of charisma has been the tendency of small, enthusiastic, loosely organized sects to develop into large, sedate, strongly structured churches.[29] Sects still develop into churches, especially on the American religious scene. What this means today, however, is primarily the sprouting by sects of the typical trappings of bureaucratic organization and the entrance by sects into the cooperative procedures through which the already bureaucratized bodies deal with each other. Furthermore, the virtual identification of routinization with bureaucratization brings about an acceleration of the process. Contemporary sects with a measure of success on the "religious market" may develop bureaucratic forms, with all of the other characteristics of routinization, even before the first generation has passed from the scene. Thus even "prophets" today may surround themselves with a bureaucratic machine designed to "mass-communicate" the charismatic message, a procedure tending toward the demise of the charisma before its "natural" time (if only because of the built-in obsolescence of all the contents of mass communications).

The associational aspect of contemporary church structure, as suggested by the term itself, is rooted in the voluntary character of church adherence. As a result, the local congregation is comparable sociologically to other groupings in which people gather together out of free choice for some common interest.[30] The sociological study of local congregations, much of which has taken place under ecclesiastical auspices and for very pragmatic reasons of "religious management," reveals a multiplicity of subgroups and factions, some utilizable by the clergy for the avowed purposes of the organization, and others not. Also, research on these matters shows, as we would expect, that there are considerable differences in patterns of association depending on the class composition of the membership. In all of these matters, the religious association is very similar to other voluntary groups, and it would not be very interesting to discuss its "group dynamics" here. The typical "problem" from the viewpoint of "management" is the relationship of organizational aims and associational interests. The two do not always tally.

One area in which discrepancy has been especially well documented, at least for Catholics, is the area of religious belief itself.[31] The membership,

[29] The classic sociological statement of the development of sects is by Max Weber, for which see H. H. Gerth and C. Wright Mills (cited in footnote 16), pp. 302 ff. For a richly documented discussion of the routinization of sects, see Joachim Wach, *Sociology of Religion* (Chicago: University of Chicago Press, 1944), pp. 196 ff.
[30] The best-known American sociological work on the local congregation is that of Joseph Fichter on Catholic parishes. See Joseph Fichter, *Social Relations in the Urban Parish* (Chicago: University of Chicago Press, 1954). For sociological analyses of local religious situations generally, see Kenneth Underwood, *Protestant and Catholic* (Boston: Beacon Press, 1957), and Arthur Vidich and Joseph Bensman, *Small Town in Mass Society* (Princeton: Princeton University Press, 1958), pp. 227 ff.
[31] See Joseph Fichter (cited in footnote 30).

even in as dogmatically firm group as the Catholic, deviates to an astonishing measure from the theological and ethical norms for which the religious institution in question officially stands. Sometimes this deviation is some sort of conscious heterodoxy, but more commonly it is simple ignorance of and indifference to the traditional norms. The reasons for church adherence of the membership often have little to do with the official rationale of the organization. Such purely secular motives as status symbolism, conformity to the conduct of friends and neighbors, a general moral and social conservatism (especially as related to the raising of children), and a vague desire to find some sort of "fellowship" free from the competitive pressures of business relationships play an important part in the members' (that is, the "unofficial") rationale for belonging to the church. The organization must adapt itself in varying degrees to these lay expectations if it is to retain its membership. Generally, the relations between organization and association are marked by an ongoing mutual accommodation, in which the association wields the economic stick, while the organization must rely on moral suasion as mediated through its clergy and other communication channels.

The clergy occupies an interesting position in this situation.[32] On the one hand, the clergyman appears as the local representative of the organization (as though he were its principal "retail man"). On the other hand, he is very much dependent on the goodwill of his lay members and, in most Protestant and all Jewish cases, he is actually *employed* by the lay members insofar as the economic base of his existence is concerned. It is easy to understand how this in-between position is bound to lead to conflicts of all kinds. The conflicts tend to be centered on the definitions of the actual role of the clergyman. The theological definition of this role (which, at least in the beginning of his career, tends to be identical with the clergyman's self-definition) may not agree with either the organizational or the associational expectations concerning the role. The clergyman thus finds himself being pulled at by at least three different sets of expectations, sometimes in diametrically opposite directions. There is good evidence, certainly in the Protestant case and very likely in the Jewish one, that the expectations of the lay members (who constitute the clergyman's most continuous social "reference group," in addition to being his source of finances) have the strongest pull in the long run.[33]

The impact of rationalization on the associational aspects of contemporary

[32] For a summary of studies of the clergy, see David Moberg (cited in footnote 25), pp. 481 ff.
[33] For a sociological study of this phenomenon in a situation of social conflict (the 1957 school integration crisis of Little Rock), see Ernest Campbell and Thomas Pettigrew, *Christians in Racial Crisis* (Washington, D.C.: Public Affairs Press, 1959).

religious institutions is less immediately apparent than that on the organizational aspects. However, it is important to keep in mind that the very existence of the contemporary pattern of voluntary religious associationism results from the overall rationalization of society, which deprived the religious institutions of their access to the political and economic control mechanism, forcing them (whether this was theologically congenial to them or not) into a catering relationship vis-à-vis an uncoerced and increasingly choosy clientele of religious consumers. All religious bodies have had to adapt to this situation. The Protestant groups with a free-church tradition have adapted easily and even with a measure of enthusiasm (although the free-church ideology has served as an obfuscation of the real character of contemporary voluntarism as compared to, for example, the "covenant" of early New England Puritanism). Other groups have adapted much more reluctantly. None can avoid adaptation indefinitely and even the Catholic church has been forced to take steps in this direction. The widespread theological discussion of the "problem of the laity," which is prominent today in both of the two major Christian camps, is essentially a theoretical reflection of much more practical problems. The social roots of the more practical problems are in the demands of the religious market situation that we have briefly described. The theological reformulations may be understood as rationalizations in both the Weberian and the psychological sense—that is, as ways to make more rational the institutional response to the situation and, at the same time, as *ex post facto* justifications of actions that had to be explained away.

## The Contemporary Situation

Sociological analysis cannot always be counted on to have timely, practical applicability. However, if the preceding considerations have merit, it is reasonable to hope that they can help us in getting a better picture of the situation of religion and religious institutions in our own society. Before we conclude this chapter, then, we shall sketch an overall picture of the contemporary situation.[34]

A very significant consequence of the emergence of industrial society is the emergence of the so-called private sphere, that is, of a domain of social

[34] The following argument is strongly indebted to Arnold Gehlen's theory of institutional change in industrial society, and to the applications of this theory to the case of religion made by Helmut Schelsky and Thomas Luckmann. To date, the main sources for these recent contributions are only available in German, but see Thomas Luckmann, "On Religion in Modern Society," *Journal for the Scientific Study of Religion* (spring, 1963), pp. 147 ff.

life, segregated from the major economic and political institutions, in which the individual is expected to fulfill himself as a person in a variety of voluntary relationships. As already indicated, the phenomenon of the private sphere has both structural and social-psychological implications. Structurally, it is a domain in which social controls are at least relatively relaxed and in which the individual is allowed considerable latitude in shaping his life. In the social-psychological context, the private sphere has been defined culturally as the place *par excellence* for self-realization and personal satisfaction, and for a majority of individuals in our society it is probably just that. Thus, the individual who is subjected to quite rigid controls on his job and who (as is typical in the lower and middle echelons of the occupational hierarchy) considers his job as a means rather than an end in itself will invest considerable ingenuity in choosing voluntary relationships (ranging from his marital partner to his hobby club) in such a way that he can be, or perhaps can become, his "real self." In other words, the private sphere is then defined as somehow more "real" for the person than the highly constrained, anonymous, and fragmented relationships of the great public institutions (among which, through work, the economy is by far the most important for most individuals).

As an arena of voluntary associations, the private sphere is relatively "underinstitutionalized," that is, it is full of activities that have not been strongly structured, that are sustained more by consensus than by sanctions, and that are weak in unambiguous norms.[35] For example, methods of child-rearing are left to individual preferences to a remarkable degree, are only minimally limited by law (as in legal provisions for compulsory schooling or against parental neglect), and are notoriously influenced by shifting fashions of "expert" opinion. Other private activities, such as "culture" and entertainment, are even more free of sanctions and of binding norms. This does not mean, however, that the private sphere has no institutions at all. It has generated some institutions itself (for instance, institutions regulating sports), but these do not interest us here directly. Also, however, institutions that previously had great public (for example, political or economic) significance have come to be relegated to the private sphere where they continue to function as institutions, even though in a greatly redefined way. It is this second case, which may be called the process of privatization, that is relevant to our present discussion. The most important institution to have been privatized is the family. Religious institutions have gone through a very similar process.

We have discussed the manner in which the overall force of secularization has driven religious institutions and symbolisms out of social areas

---

[35] The term "underinstitutionalized" is derived from Gehlen.

where they were previously important or even predominant. This is the negative side of the social process which, positively, may be described as the privatization of religion. For while religion has lost importance in the great public institutions of society, it continues to be highly relevant in the private sphere. Indeed, if we keep in mind that there are exceptions to this (as, for instance, the current involvement of American churches in the civil rights struggle), contemporary religion can be adequately described in most of its manifestations as a private institution. This institutional "localization" of religion has far-reaching implications.

First, the understanding of religious institutions as private ones brings into sharper relief the transformation of functions and structures that interested us previously. As an institution of the private sphere, religion is inherently deprived of efficacy in the public domain of political and economic events. As an institution of the private sphere, religion is forced to organize itself in social forms that are appropriate to this sphere. We have considered in some detail what this means. It is now possible to understand more clearly what this weakening of institutional sanctions and norms entails for the religious individual in his everyday life. It is inherent in the nature of the democratic rhetoric, at least in America and for easily understood historical reasons, that the individual may have various misconceptions about the applicability of traditional religious norms to political processes. These misconceptions become political facts simply because they are held by significant numbers of people and can serve as ideological ammunition for political figures as far apart as, for instance, Barry Goldwater and Martin Luther King. This, however, cannot change the autonomy of the political sphere once that autonomy has become a structural fact, and even the sincerely religious politician will have to act "realistically" (that is, in accordance with *political* rationales) if he is to achieve any of his goals. In any case, politics is not a significant element of everyday life for most individuals in our society.

The economy is significant by virtue of the simple fact that almost everybody works or is dependent on someone else's work for livelihood itself. The autonomy of the economic sphere thus enters into everyday experience in a much more massive way, and is considerably more difficult to deny ideologically. The religious individual, then, finds himself strongly pressured by his own everyday experience to acknowledge the predominantly irrelevant relationship of his religion to what is, after all, a substantial segment of his life. Whether he admits this happily or unhappily, loudly or tacitly, is another question. However, to the degree that he finds that "religion and business won't mix," he is all the more motivated to find other areas of his life in which "religion *can* make a difference." The area in which this is generally plausible is that of private relationships.

The religious symbols thus become especially relevant for the individual in his life away from work, away from the great public institutions. To put it a little crudely, religion is most relevant as a "leisure-time activity." The religious individual finds that he has considerable latitude in shaping his private life in accordance with his religious beliefs. Not only is he free to join "the church of his choice," but he can be careful "to marry within his faith," take various steps to ensure the religious education of his children, involve himself to the extent that his leisure time allows in the pursuit of his "religious interests" and—if he so wishes and can get his immediate family to go along with this—he can make religion the principal criterion in all of his private activities, associations, and friendships. At least in middle-class America, he will find that choices of this kind meet with general approval and are even conducive to his status in the community. If he makes these choices (and let us bear in mind the cultural expectations concerning the private sphere), the individual will make of religion a vehicle for the purposes of self-realization and self-discovery that are central to the private sphere. Notice that these goals are not only to be attained in the private sphere but also that they are highly private in themselves. The "self" to be realized or discovered is pre-eminently a private self. It is that portion of the total person that can "express itself," "be creative," and "become mature" through the media of private relationships—in the neighborhood community and the circle of friends and, above all, within the family. Characteristically, this private understanding of what is most important about the "self" has found its strong affinity with modern psychology, especially of the psychoanalytically influenced variety.[36] Indeed, there has been a pronounced tendency to understand religion as such in terms of its supposed utility in the attainment of psychological happiness.[37]

The religious institutions have adapted themselves to this situation in their overall program. They have emphasized strongly the same values that serve as general guideposts in the private sphere for both the religious and the nonreligious individual—family, children, neighborhood, as social values; and maturity, mental health, personal happiness, as individual values. Middle-class American churches and synagogues have become community centers, family-oriented and child-centered to the same degree that middle-class culture is generally.[38] Age, sex, and marital status are the

[36] For a recent sociological inquiry into the institutional consequences of this affinity, see Samuel Klausner, *Psychiatry and Religion* (New York: Free Press, 1964).

[37] For an illuminating discussion of this in terms of religious literature, see Louis Schneider and Sanford Dornbusch, *Popular Religion* (Chicago: University of Chicago Press, 1958).

[38] For a community study bringing out these values, also with respect to religion, see John Seeley et al., *Crestwood Heights* (New York: Wiley, 1963).

general differentiating criteria of local church programs. Religious education absorbs a large amount of local church budgets and requires the employment of substantial personnel. The local church, sealed off from the public institutions, seeks to relate itself to the neighborhood of private residence and sometimes becomes a symbol of it. Preaching, pastoral care, educational activities, and even ecclesiastically sponsored programs of psychotherapy seek to meet the "needs" of the individual—needs that upon investigation turn out to be almost exclusively private ones. To some extent this adaptation of the religious institutions to the requirements of the private sphere has been unreflected—an almost automatic response to changed social expectations. Sometimes religious institutions have been reluctant to adapt, refusing to make a virtue out of necessity (as, for instance, in more conservative religious bodies). However, there has also been a large-scale enterprise of legitimating the privatization of religion theoretically and even theologically. Popular religious literature, books for clergymen on preaching and pastoral care, the literature of religious education and religiously oriented psychotherapy, and even purely theoretical books on religion have served this legitimating function. The slogans, "The family that prays together, stays together," "A church-going community is a better community," and "Go to the church of your choice this week—you will feel the better for it," are popular slogans of religious promotion that aptly sum up the adaptation of the churches to the ideological demands of the private sphere.

As we might expect from the similar fate undergone by the institutions of religion and family in industrial society, religion has found itself in a state of social "proximity" to the family in the private sphere. The family is the institutional area in which traditional religious symbols continue to have the most relevance in actual everyday living. In turn, the family has become for the religious institutions the main "target area" for their social strategy. This affinity between the two institutions—both "victims" of the process of privatization—has expressed itself clearly in an emergent ideological configuration common to both: the ideology of familism. Broadly speaking, this is a set of both cognitive and normative assertions that interpret the family as *the* crucial social institution, both for the individual and for society as a whole. Ideas largely derived from the psychoanalytic movement are employed to assert (1) the primacy of the family for the individual, (2) his parental family as the crucial influence of his earlier years, and (3) the family that he may then found as an adult by his own mariage as the crucial "testing" area for his existence as a person. The family is, then, also asserted to be the most important institution in society as such, the implication being that it is "basic" and that all other institutions are influenced by it as a result. While the notion that the family is basic has some empirical validity simply because of the contemporary definition of the significance of the family, the assertion that all other institutions are influenced by the family is quite distortive of the real institutional relationships of industrial society. The ideology, no matter how illusionary in its social perspective, is very functional as a legitimating device for the religious institutions, simply because it credits with great importance precisely the area to which these institutions have been *de facto* relegated. If the churches believe in the primacy and "basic" character of the family, then they have a perfect justification for concentrating on the family in their program (for instance, along the lines of the slogan "Christian homes make a Christian nation").

The contemporary situation of religion is determined not only by the process of privatization but by another ultimately related process: the process of demonopolization. Through a great part of human history, even after the reformation of the sixteenth century, religious institutions occupied monopoly positions in terms of supplying the fundamental integrative symbols for the societies in question. The typical case today, however, is that different religious and secular *Weltanschauung* are in competition with each other. In America, for well-known historical reasons, this state of affairs is described by the term "pluralism." There is a great number of religious institutions in the society, and not one of them can hope for (most would not even want) a monopoly position. Although the history of European immigration to the United States explains the particular form taken by this demonopolization in this country (that is, the system of denominations, none of which is "established" by the government and each of which must come to terms with the presence of the others), it is important to notice that the demonopolization of religion is not a uniquely American phenomenon. Indeed, it can be argued that "pluralism" of some kind is endemic to the secularization process as such. The autonomized economic institutions no longer require an ongoing religious legitimation. The autonomized political institutions may still employ religious rhetorics for legitimating purposes, but they are pushed by the social forces of the modern situation toward a "separation" relationship with the religious institutions. In other words, even in societies in which the great majority of the population belongs to one religious group (for instance, in modern France), the religious institution (in this instance, the Catholic church) can no longer count on the state to provide it with the means to enforce the old religious monopoly. Thus there emerges a "pluralistic" situation in which the old dominant group has to compete—if not with properly religious rivals, then with a variety of secular world views and ideologies, or with plain indifference. The basic social consequences of demonopolization are not that different whether, for example, the Catholic church in a particular society has to find ways to get along tolerably with Protestants and Jews, or has to face the competition of Communism or some other political ideology with quasi-religious characteristics, or must simply recognize the fact that the old social pressures to make people go to mass are no longer effective. The traditional monopoly is impaired in all of these cases.

Competition entails the emergence of a market. To put it bluntly, while monopolistic religion could be imposed on people, demonopolized religion must be "sold." The market character of the contemporary religious situation has consequences both for the social form and the ideational content of the religious institutions. We have already considered in some detail the consequence for the social form. To sum up this discussion concisely: the religious institutions must organize themselves in such a way that their "selling" job can be effectively carried out. As we have seen, this implies, above all, their bureaucratization. But it is not only in their inner social structure that the religious institutions must be revamped; there must also occur a change in their relationships with each other. In some strata of society, particularly in the lower ones, unrestricted competition along the lines of classical free enterprise is still possible. In the more genteel middle-class regions, which constitute the main reservoir of members and funds for the major religious bodies, such competition has become increasingly impractical. A sophisticated clientele of religious consumers is resistant to "hard-sell" techniques. Furthermore, religious programs (especially the building of new churches) have become so expensive that they must be planned in a rational manner. Rationality dictates that this planning take place in cooperation with the other "firms" in the field. The consequence of this rational imperative has been the immense growth of inter-denominational cooperation. While it would be foolish to maintain that this is the only factor behind the contemporary ecumenical movement, it is very probably the most important *social-structural* factor. To stay within the economic analogy of competition on a free market, contemporary ecumenicity can be interpreted as a process of "cartelization," that is, of mutual accommodation of a number of large, rationally operating competitors.[39]

Demonopolization also affects religious contents. Again, putting it in a somewhat oversimplified way, the "product" of the religious institutions must be "salable." It is one thing to threaten a captive audience of medieval peasants with hellfire and damnation. It is quite another thing to market a doctrine of this sort in a population of suburban commuters and housewives. In other words, the "needs" of the consumer clientele must now be taken into consideration. Naturally, this is not easy

[39] For a more detailed discussion of this, see Peter Berger, "A Market Model for the Analysis of Ecumenicity," *Social Research* (spring, 1963), pp. 77 ff.

to do for an institution that claims for its "product" a divine source. The process of doctrinal modification has, therefore, been largely unavowed or even unrecognized. But at least in the liberal Protestant and Jewish groups, there has developed a theological rationale that serves to legitimate the doctrinal erosion necessary for survival under modern conditions. In its most common American form, again heavily equipped with ideas derived from psychoanalytic thought, this entails a theory of "religious needs." The function of the religious institutions is then redefined as the satisfaction of these "needs." Insofar as the "religious needs" of the consumer clientele have become homogenized, the religious "products" have gone through economically understandable processes of "standardization" and "marginal differentiation." There has been a lessening of the sharpest doctrinal contradictions between the major groups. At the same time, there has had to be a re-emphasis on the peculiar features of each. The first process is dictated by the necessity to keep one's consumers interested at all, and the second by the equally compelling necessity to convince them that one's own "product" is significantly and interestingly different from the others available on the market.

One of the commonplaces of social psychology is that changes in the social structure and changes in the psychological makeup of groups are interrelated. Insofar as religion is also a psychological phenomenon, it is to be expected that the change in the social location of religion will be related to some change of its location in individual consciousness. While there is as yet a sparsity of data on this question, it is probable that the change of the location of religion in individual consciousness can be described as a process of "subjectivization." [40] To put the same thing negatively, the change has been a loss of "objectivity" with regard to religious content. To develop fully what is meant in this connection by "subjective" and "objective" would involve us in a longer excursion into theory than is possible here. Stated simply, what is meant by these terms is the degree to which any particular interpretation of the world appears plausible or real (that is, "objectively real") to individuals. For example, we consider the proposition that the earth is round as "objectively real," which means that it is round whether we like it or not, and that there is nothing we can do in our minds (that is, "subjectively") to change this. For the people of traditional China, however, it was just as "objectively real" that the earth is a flat disc with their own country in the middle. Now, while probably most of us would believe that in an argument between one of us and a traditional Chinese the weight of evidence would favor our view, the important point is that very few of us could actually present this evidence

[40] This concept is also taken from Gehlen. See Thomas Luckmann (cited in footnote 24).

and, in any event, the manner in which we came to hold our view did not result from any consideration of evidence at all. We arrived at our conviction in the same way that the Chinese arrived at his—by the fact that everyone around us has always assumed that this particular view represents the way things are and that all the relevant intellectual authorities (from schoolteachers to travel agents to authors of geography books) have assured us that this is the only possible view. In other words, the conviction that something is "objectively real" is produced and, once there, is sustained by social confirmation, that is, by other people who continuously, consistently, and in a matter-of-course way confirm that this is true. Furthermore, this social fabrication of "objectivity" occurs not only with regard to nature but also with regard to the cultural and social worlds made by men themselves. We are convinced through the same social means that little boys do not want to play with dolls and that grownups should not steal automobiles. In those cases, however, in which social confirmation becomes weak, divided, or intermittent, that which is confirmed begins to seem less than "objectively real." It becomes a matter on which different views can be held; that is, it becomes "subjectivized." [41]

Now, most of our preceding considerations have tended to show that the social processes that traditionally maintained the "objective reality" of the religious interpretations of the world have become weak, divided, and intermittent. The religious institutions have been deprived of their age-old prerogative of being in charge of the ultimate, overarching symbols of social life. The individual now spends much of his life in areas where religious symbolism is absent or greatly reduced. As a result of "pluralism," moreover, he is confronted with different and often mutually incompatible religious viewpoints. Religion is no longer the massive, "self-evident" reality it once was for the entire society. The very fact of the choice that is now possible serves to deprive religion of its character as "objective reality." No such choice, it should be noted, exists with regard to other interpretations of our world. It hardly makes sense to say that we have the choice of believing that the earth is round or that it is flat. If we actually chose to believe that the earth is flat, this would be a self-certification that we were incredibly ignorant or, more likely, downright mad. We are quite free, on the other hand, to have a "religious preference," as the highly apt American phrase puts it. On the basis of essentially individual decisions (that is, of a "subjective" process) we may prefer one Christian denomination over another, or we may even prefer to take a crack at Zen Buddhism, or we may

---

[41] The broad implications of what has been sketched here are the concern of the so-called sociology of knowledge. Obviously these questions cannot be pursued here, but enough may have been said to indicate that they are of considerable interest both for the sociology and the psychology of religion.

take the option of not stating any preference at all and remain sitting on the fence of more or less mild agnosticism. And we can get away with any of these choices because the religious institutions have lost their monopolistic power to define officially "what's what" for everyone in the society.

Religious views held as "preference," "interest," or "opinion" occupy a different place in consciousness from religion that is held as taken-for-granted reality. Traditionally, religion was anchored in those levels of consciousness containing the things that could never be doubted this side of insanity. Today, religion has become psychologically kindred to many other propositions on which reasonable men may differ. If we want to stay with the picture of consciousness having different levels, we can say that religion has "percolated up" from the deeper to the more superficial levels of consciousness. That is, religion has become "subjectivized." This process, which I hope is now clear, is not attributable to some mystery of the soul of modern man, nor can it be adequately explained by the influence of nonreligious or antireligious ideas (for instance, the influence of modern science or of various atheistic ideologies). The process can only be understood if it is related to the transformation of social structure and to the consequent shift in the social place of religion. That is, the "subjectivization" of religion is the psychological concomitant of its privatized and demonopolized position in society. Once more, a lot of contemporary religious thought (for example, that of Paul Tillich, which is quite popular among American intellectuals today) begins to make better sense when we understand it as an *ex post facto* legitimation of something that happened for very nontheological reasons—the social *and* psychological metamorphosis of religion in modern society, with the concomitant decline in the plausibility of traditional religious doctrines.

## Summary and Conclusions

Having almost reached the end of our considerations, we can look once more at the views on religion of American college students with which we began. We found there a conception of religion as meeting specific "needs." We found great confusion as to just what beliefs would have to be incorporated in religion capable of satisfying these "needs." We also found a strong association of religion with personal and social adjustment. It was clear from the beginning that such notions would not be very helpful for a scientific understanding of the religious phenomenon. We may now say, however, that they are quite helpful as data on the character of religion in our own society. These data took these forms: religion geared to the expectations of a sophisticated clientele on consumers, religion that has become doctrinally eroded and vague, religion as a therapeutic device for personal psychological problems, religion as integrative symbolism for the private worlds of family and neighborhood—these were the key themes found in the responses of the students. We can now place these same themes in a comprehensive sociological interpretation of the phenomenon. The intellectual (as distinct from the practical) utility of such a sociological interpretation may be tested by the degree to which it thus illuminates the world of everyday life in which we all exist.

There is one final question that we must touch upon, which is in the realm of sociology. We have tried to give a picture of the importance of religion in human society and of the profound change that religion has undergone in recent times. It is logical to ask whether sociology is in a position to make any predictions about the future course of religion. It is certainly possible that, provided our analysis has merit, we may expect the same overall forces to continue having similar overall results. For example, in view of the structure of modern society it is improbable that the processes of secularization and privatization will be dramatically reversed in the foreseeable future. But there is the further question, recently raised by quite a few thinkers within the religious world itself, of whether perhaps religion is not approaching the end of its long human history, whether perhaps we are not already living in a "post-Christian" or "postreligious" era. Recently an Italian Catholic sociologist, after carefully documenting the decline of religion in various domains of modern society, asked poignantly whether perhaps we have not arrived at the "end of the sacred." [42] To answer this question reliably probably exceeds the powers of sociological prediction. But we can venture a guess. We have seen early in our considerations how the idea of the sacred has always expressed man's hope for an order that would embrace all of reality and give ultimate meaning to his own life. Religion, whatever else it has been, has always been man's quest to define the universe in terms that will ultimately, and hopefully, make sense. It is unlikely that this quest will vanish from human experience and from the social structures that embody this experience.

[42] Sabino Acquaviva, whose work in the sociology of religion is to date not available in English.

7

# THE SOCIOLOGY
# OF EDUCATION

*A. H. Halsey*

Crisis

# THE
# SOCIOLOGY
# OF
# EDUCATION

In this chapter we attempt a sociological analysis of education in all societies. But let us begin with some relevant facts about the contemporary United States. The population is moving toward 200 million. Between 1950 and 1970, 60 million will have been added to the population, an increase of 40% in less time than it takes for a child to go from birth to the commencement ceremony of a university. Forty million babies will have been born in the 1960's.

These people are being born into, and must be educated for, an urban industrial society. In 1960, 70% of Americans were classified by the census as living in urban communities. The farming population is less than 1 in 10 of the whole population, and is in absolute as well as proportionate decline. Moreover, this predominantly urban population is engaged increasingly in white-collar employment. Since 1955, white-collar workers have outnumbered those in manual jobs, and professional and technical occupations are the fastest-growing in the labor force. In 1960 nearly 7.5 million people were in professional and technical employment; by 1970 the number will be 10.7 million.

The educational implications of these facts are profound: more people need or want more education for more skilled and specialized jobs in an urban industrial civilization. High-school enrollments, which went up by 40% in the 1950's, will rise by another 50% in the 1960's until, by 1970, 92% of all persons between 6 and 18 years old will be attending school. College enrollments is also rising—by 40% in the 1950's and 70% in the 1960's. By 1975 there will be more than 8.5 million students enrolled full-time at colleges that offer degree-credit courses.

Why this enormous expansion? Is it the same in other countries? What are the economic, social, and political causes and consequences? These are the kinds of questions that we hope to answer in a study of the sociology of education.

The plan of this chapter follows the same logic of sociological analysis that is used in the study of any social institution or organization. This means that we must ask about the institution's functions, its structure, and its relation to the wider society in which it is placed. Therefore, the chapter falls into three parts. First, we deal with the functions of education—its task of passing on culture from one generation to the next, its role in fitting individuals into society, and its contribution to social integration. Second, we describe how education is organized to perform these functions in different societies, and this involves a comparison of different systems of primary, secondary, and higher education as well as an analysis of the role of the teacher and his relationships to his students and colleagues. Finally, we relate education to society by considering education's place in the structure of class, status, and power and the part that it plays in distributing opportunities between individuals and groups.

## Functions of Education

Every society is a unique product of its own history and its relation to other societies. Nevertheless, societies, in spite of their bewildering variety, also have common characteristics. They are social systems, and consequently require the performance of certain universal functions if they are to continue to exist. Education is a process concerned with some of these universal functions. This is true about education in all societies. In other words, it is possible to identify the universal functions of education. There are two major ones.

1. All societies maintain themselves by the exploitation of a culture, that is, a set of beliefs and skills that are not carried in the genetic constitution of individuals but must be learned. This social heritage must be transmitted through social organizations. Education has this function of *cultural transmission* in all societies.

2. Individuals must have personalities fashioned in ways that fit into the culture. Education, everywhere, has the function of *the formation of social personalities.* By transmitting the culture through appropriate molding of social personalities, education contributes to the integration of society as a mechanism that enables men to adapt themselves to their environment, to survive, and to reproduce themselves.

Our task is to describe and explain the variations between societies in the ways in which educational systems perform these two major functions. As a first step, we shall sketch two ideal types of society: the primitive and the technological.

### *Primitive and Technological Societies*

Our model of primitive society is the nearest human approximation to a system of adaptation to the environment through genetic inheritance. In primitive society the social inheritance is minimal and unchanging. Life is based on a simple technology, and there is a correspondingly simple division of labor with roles ascribed according to age and sex. Learning is closely tied to childhood and ends with puberty, and the transition to adult status is often socially emphasized by the ceremonials known as *rites de passage.*[1] Apart from puberty rites there are no specialized educational organizations: the culture is transmitted by kinship. Similarly, there are no "specialists" although, in reality, the shaman or witch doctor represents the

---

[1] See, for example, Audrey Richards, *Chisunga: A Girl's Initiation Ceremony among the Bemba of Northern Rhodesia* (London: Faber and Faber, 1956).

prototype of the scholar or professional man. The content of education is identical with the culture—a general education in all the elements of the social heritage, moral and esthetic as well as technological and utilitarian. The simplicity of the culture and the absence of specialization imply that the individual is microcosmic of the total culture and that education is egalitarian. In other words, two of the characteristic problems of education in industrial society—its specialization and its social distribution—are absent from primitive society.

Our model of technological society represents the opposite conditions. The social inheritance is elaborate and, because research is institutionalized, is self-transforming. Life is based on a complex technology with a correspondingly complex division of labor. Learning continues into adult life through specialized formal educational organizations in which the cognitive rather than the moral elements of the culture are stressed. Education beyond the primary stage is aimed at the production of specialists, and society depends on coordinating the work of individuals who possess competence in only a tiny part of the total culture. Through training of specialists in a technological society, education becomes the central selective agency for the social distribution of life chances.

These two directly contrasted ideal types are useful for analyzing the variable functions of education. But two warnings must be given against their misuse. First, ideal types are valuable as guides, but nonetheless they are fictions. In the present case we have outlined an "anthropological" and a "sociological" fiction: the primitive society is a tribal group without history or cultural contact; the technological society is a sociological sketch of future possibilities for the scientific age. Neither society has existed in reality; both are bench marks for, not descriptions of, actual societies. The second warning is against a less obvious danger. The two models suggest an evolutionary trend in social development from the simple to the complex. World history, in fact, roughly corresponds to such a trend, from relatively simple and unchanging cultures with small-scale organization toward "one world" sharing a complex culture in large-scale and elaborately differentiated organization. But these trends are neither inevitable nor irreversible, and no given society follows any predetermined sequence of historical stages. The polar opposites are useful only if they are taken as a yardstick, enabling us to gauge variations in the educational systems of actual societies.

Our starting point, then, is that no general theory of society is conceivable without reference to education. The educational process transforms biological organisms into social personalities and carries the culture of a society from one generation to the next. But this question immediately arises: May we treat these functions either as psychological or historical problems? By considering these alternatives, we can clarify what is meant by a sociological conception of education and decide what kind of theory and method can be contributed by the sociologist to phenomena which, on the one hand, involve both the psychological and organizational structure of society and, on the other hand, involve the unique configurations of history in particular societies.

In his description of education among the Tallensi, the British anthropologist Meyer Fortes states that "the problem presented [to the social analyst] by this [educational] function of society is of an entirely different order from that presented by the religious or economic or political system of a people. The former is primarily a problem of genetic psychology, the latter of cultural or sociological analysis." [2] This view is valid in the most general sense that all socialization involves a modification and development of the human personality and therefore may be treated as a psychological process. It also makes sense when it is applied to societies in which the organizational structure is simple and the culture unchanging.

But insofar as social organization is differentiated so that socialization is a function shared between independent or partially independent institutions, or where there is change either in the organization of society or in the culture that is transmitted, then new problems are generated that fall unequivocally within the province of sociological analysis. In changing and complex societies, educational tasks are undertaken by specialized agencies, which operate as independent variables in the functioning of the social system, promoting or impeding change, and producing unintended as well as intended dysfunctional and functional consequences. The formation of social personalities is elaborated by the requirements of a more complex role structure in society; the relation between individual socialization and social consensus (that is, the Durkheimian problem of "organic solidarity") emerges and, along with it, the function of selection as well as differentiation in upbringing. Education therefore may be the focus of political conflict as new or dissident groups claim right of entry to established institutions or the right to institute new forms of schooling. Conflict may emerge between different social organizations carrying distinctive interests in socialization— for example, churches, ethnic groups, or associations of parents with common social aims. These conditions are characteristic of industrial societies. They justify the analysis of educational organization in the same terms as any other kind of social institution—economic, religious, or political.

Yet all of this still leaves the question of whether what is left in the study of education from "genetic psychology" is not adequately subsumed under

[2] Meyer Fortes, *Social and Psychological Aspects of Education in Taliland* (London: Oxford University Press), p. 6.

the history of educational systems in particular countries or periods. This question hinges on the distinction between the aims of sociology and history. At the extremes of generality, sociology and history are plainly distinct. Propositions that are true of all social systems interest only the sociologist. We began with two such propositions: (1) that all human societies must contain processes for individual socialization, and (2) that all societies must contain processes for cultural transmission. Generalizations of this kind are important but uninteresting truths. The establishment of concepts with universal application is necessary, but is only a beginning to social analysis. Universal functions are the first term in the differentiation of variable functions, which raise the interesting problems of classifying types of social systems. Classification ultimately leads to enumeration of unique cases. Both the sociologist and the historian may be interested in problems at any point in this chain. What distinguishes them is the focus of interest. The sociologist aims at the general problem. He therefore tends to look at an individual case in order to induce a generalization from it or to test a general hypothesis. The historian does not deny the possibility in principle of a general theory of behavior. Indeed, any description of concrete action implies such a theory. The historian's theory is, however, typically unstated, and his focus of attention is empirical and concentrated on the explanation of a particular sequence of events. Both focuses of attention are legitimate, necessary, and useful in the study and explanation of educational systems. The sociological and the historical approaches are not opposed, but are complementary. When they are divorced, both suffer; when they are juxtaposed, they bear fruit. This is illustrated in Bernard Bailyn's use of a sociological perspective to review the history of education in America from colonial times [3] which, among other things, points to the unexploited possibilities of sociological study of the family system as throwing light upon the distinctive development of formal educational organizations in colonial America as contrasted with Europe.

### Education and Cultural Transmission

If we classify societies according to the kind of culture that underlies their system of production—in a classification that corresponds broadly to primitive, agrarian, and industrial societies—we arrive at an approximate continuum of increasing complexity or differentiation. Along this continuum the function of cultural transmission changes its character from a function

---

[3] Bernard Bailyn, *Education in the Formation of the American Character* (New York: Random House, Vintage Books, 1960).

of simple *preservation* to a function of increasingly complex *dissemination* and *innovation.*

A primitive hunting-and-gathering tribe approximates the extreme of cultural preservation. Education is socially organized in the institutions of kinship and age levels. Where innovation occurs, it is accidental or idiosyncratic rather than systematic or the product of deliberate allocation of resources to research and discovery. The cultural life of such a society may be considered as a repetitive cycle of generations. At the other extreme is the advanced industrial society, in which large resources are devoted to purposive cultural change, especially in the application of science to productive processes.

Within the educational system this means that the frontiers of knowledge are continuously changing; that research is an increasingly important function of higher education; and that strains develop between the research and the teaching function. Cultural change rather than stability becomes the norm, and the educational emphasis is on innovation and dissemination of new knowledge. The preservation of culture is not, of course, eliminated but old ways of adaptation are constantly subjected to the rationalizing forces of a science-dominated culture. In the intermediate range of societies, the balance between preservation and innovation is constantly shifting. In the contemporary world this is dramatically exemplified in the so-called underdeveloped countries where a rapid absorption of some of the elements of the technological culture of the Western industrial countries is taking place. These countries consequently exhibit marked contrasts of "traditional" and "modern" culture, accompanied by efforts on the part of the state to transform their educational systems in order to equip their populations with the learning necessary to exploit the new culture that is being imported from Europe and America.

Again, it is only in the modern world that the implications of culture have been fully realized as a self-sustaining dynamic force, capable of unending transformation of the society that created it. The rise of science as a social institution, in effect, has become a guarantee of continuous social change with unprecedented consequences for each new generation. This is the impressive aspect of modern society from the point of view of the sociologist of education. It transcends the national, political, and religious boundaries of human society, and is rapidly sweeping the whole world into the orbit of the industrial system.

Social change is becoming more and more institutionalized through educational systems. Schools and universities no longer confine themselves to the preservation of a traditional culture. They are increasingly concerned with cultural innovation through research and with cultural dissemination to new classes and new nations through educational expansion.

*Education and the Formation of Social Personalities*

As was true with cultural transmission, it is also true with respect to the formation of social personalities that contemporary educational systems may be considered as a range of intermediary types between the extremes of the primitive and the technological, with a broad tendency of movement from the primitive to the technological. The process changes from a common upbringing for all in a primitive society toward selection and training for the highly diversified occupations of industrial society. Meanwhile, the socializing and educative functions traditionally performed by family, neighborhood, class, caste, and tribe are attenuated, and formal institutions of education come to occupy a strategic position as agents of socialization, mediating between the *Gemeinschaft* world of the child and his fate as an adult member of *Gesellschaft* society. Over a wide range of intermediate societies, there is socialization into the style of life of particular strata. Here, education has been closely linked to religious organization and to social stratification.

Formal education, at least beyond the primary stage, usually has been aimed at the training of a priesthood or the preparation of young men for places in the upper strata of hierarchically ordered societies. It is only with advanced industrialism that mass secondary and higher education become both possible and necessary in order to prepare individuals for an ever-widening variety of specialized occupations and professions in a growingly wealthy economy.

The problems of specialization and social distribution of education in advanced industrial societies connect the sociology of education to the study of the maintenance of order and the containment of conflict in society. We shall examine the American primary school from this point of view in more detail later. Meanwhile, notice that although the problem of order and conflict is universal to human society, its form in an advanced industrial society is complicated by unprecedented rates of change in the requirements of the division of labor, the consequent rewards to be allocated, and the mechanisms through which consent is maintained. When we say, as we do, that educational institutions are central to advanced industrialism, we mean the following things. First, education in industrial societies is closely concerned with the placement of persons in roles in a changing division of labor: occupational selection takes place through education. Second, education plays a role in determining the size and nature of the values to be distributed: education is investment in the productive capacities of men, it carries a status claim, and it ensures cultural change. Third, education contributes to social integration by socializing individuals into both the common value system and into the changing structure of specialized roles.

The newly independent nations provide a graphic illustration of the relation between education and social integration under conditions of rapid cultural change. Although most of these nations are politically very new, they are highly traditional in their culture and social structure. The position of an individual in these societies is determined mainly by ascription. In other words social placement is a function of kin membership and, in some countries, of caste and linguistic grouping. These factors, together with their economic base of agrarian poverty, constrict social participation and loyalties and tend to separate the mass of the population from the national, metropolitan elite. At the same time, there is in the new nations an ardent desire to become modern industrialized societies. The educated elite are usually the proponents of this aspiration, but they often disagree on the value to be placed on traditional indigenous culture. The trend toward industrial modernity creates new demands for skilled scientists and professional people, demands for rising standards of life, for opportunities for mobility, and for a wide range of political, economic, and social opportunities. These demands press hard on new and inexperienced governments.

Among the characteristic conditions of new and developing countries, and at once both cause and effect of ubiquitous poverty, is the intractable combination of mass illiteracy and scarce education resources. Usually higher education is either withheld altogether from the native population of these predominantly colonial or formerly colonial territories or is confined to a tiny minority of the wealthy and fortunate class. The social composition of the educated classes is therefore highly selective and dissimilar from the general populations, which are characteristically rural, ill-educated, and poor.

The man who has had a Western education, whether in his native country or in Europe or America, is inevitably separated from the uneducated man in outlook and mode of life. Western education introduces him to new styles of dress, speech, behavior, and opinion; it teaches him the value of Western culture and, by implication, the worthlessness of tribal life and primitive custom. His reference group tends to become not his kin and people of his native region, but the community of the educated by whose standards he has been taught to live. He tends to be cut off also from indigenous religious and intellectual traditions, to be critical of traditional sources of authority, and to become oriented to the secular industrial, urban, and international culture of the West.

Under these circumstances, political integration of the new nations along democratic lines is problematical. Research surveyed and summarized by

S. M. Lipset has shown that democracy is closely related to the level of economic development of a country: "The more well-to-do a nation, the greater the chances that it will sustain democracy." [4] Thus, by comparing European, English-speaking and Latin American countries in four groups, according to the degree of democracy exhibited by their recent political history, Lipset shows that indices of wealth are consistently correlated with the stability of democratic institutions. In his table (shown here as Table 7.1), education is also related to the likelihood of democratic politics.

**Table 7.1    Democracy, Economic Development, and Education**

|  | Per Capita Income (United States Dollars) | Percentage Literate | Postprimary Enrollment per 1000 Persons |
|---|---|---|---|
| 1. European and English-speaking stable democracies [a] | 695 | 96 | 44 |
| 2. European and English-speaking unstable democracies and dictatorships [b] | 308 | 85 | 22 |
| 3. Latin American democracies and unstable dictatorships [c] | 171 | 74 | 13 |
| 4. Latin American stable dictatorships [d] | 119 | 46 | 8 |

[a] A group of 13 countries including the United States, the United Kingdom, Norway, and Australia.
[b] A group of 17 countries including the USSR, Spain, France, Poland, and Greece.
[c] A group of 17 countries including Argentina, Mexico, Brazil, and Chile.
[d] A group of 13 countries including Bolivia, Ecuador, Panama, and Peru.
*Source.* S. M. Lipset, *Political Man* (cited in footnote 4), Table II, pp. 41 and 53.

Lipset's group of stable democratic European countries (Group 1) are almost entirely literate; whereas his group of unstable democratic countries in Europe (Group 2) has an average literacy rate of 85%. The figure falls to 74% for the group of Latin American countries classified as unstable dictatorships (Group 3), and further to 46% for the stable dictatorships (Group 4).

The significance of these comparisons may be gauged from a survey of the world's current literacy rates. Literacy is much less common in Asia and

[4] Seymour Martin Lipset, *Political Man* (New York: Free Press, 1959), p. 49.

Africa (where the newly independent states are concentrated) than it is in Latin America. Usually not more than 10 to 15% of the native population of African states can read or write, although these rates have been rising rapidly over the past decade in many parts of Africa. Nevertheless, the comparisons given in Table 7.2 give us an approximate geographical dis-

Table 7.2    The Distribution of Literacy

|  | Total Population (in Millions) | Percentage of Adult Literates |
|---|---|---|
| Africa | 198 | 15–20 |
| Asia | 1376 | 35–40 |
| South and Central America | 162 | 56–60 |
| Oceania | 13 | 89–90 |
| Europe | 393 | 91–93 |
| USSR | 186 | Over 90 |
| North America | 168 | 96–97 |
| World total | 2496 | 55–58 |

*Source.* Adapted from UNESCO, *Basic Facts and Figures 1959*, Paris, 1960, p. 25.

tribution of the viability of democracy as a political doctrine. The table suggests that the training of leaders committed to democratic politics through exposure to Western higher education is much weakened in the absence of the appropriate social bases. Lipset argues that "if we cannot say that a 'high' level of education is a *sufficient* condition of democracy, the available evidence suggests that it comes close to being a necessary one."[5] Investment in education, then, regardless of its specific content and within a wide range of cultural and economic contexts, is an investment in political development toward democracy. Mass literacy is an essential prerequisite for identification with and political participation in a national as opposed to a local or kinship culture. Education in the new nations will exercise a powerful influence over the type of political and social integration that will emerge in the future.

### Social Integration in Industrial Societies

Another approach to the problem of education and social integration is to examine the manner in which schools, by their organization and curriculum, fashion social personalities in ways that "fit" the requirements of

[5] *Ibid.,* p. 57.

the social structure. The "aims of education," in this sense, are often formally stated. An important example among the industrial countries is the USSR where "education is primarily a political tool for the construction of a communist society." [6] In 1959 the Russian Minister of Higher Education, V. P. Yelyutin, made it explicit that "the role of Soviet education is to assist in the building of a communist society, in shaping the materialist world outlook of the students, equipping them with a good grounding in the different fields of knowledge and preparing them for socially useful work." [6]

These statements of manifest aims tell us something about the formation of social personalities. But the organization of schooling also involves latent functions, which must be discovered by sociological analysis. Talcott Parsons has provided this kind of analysis of the American primary school.[7] We are dealing here with an advanced industrial society, in which primary schooling is universal and in which the problem of social integration is linked to the preparation of individuals for specialized roles in a complex division of labor. Thus, Parsons begins by identifying the dual functions of the American school: *socialization* (that is, "the development in individuals of the commitments and capacities which are essential prerequisites of their future role performance"), and *selection* (or "allocation of human resources within the role structure of the adult society"). Commitments and capacities are further subdivided. Commitments are of two kinds: commitment to the common values of society, and commitment to the performance of a specialized role (usually, of course, an occupation). Similarly, capacities are considered (1) as skills necessary to perform a role and (2) as "role responsibility" or the capacity to meet the expectations of others with respect to responsible interpersonal behavior appropriate to a role. The second distinction is between the "technical" and the "social" skills demanded by an occupation.

In order to follow Parsons' analysis of the socializing role of formal education, it is necessary to examine part of his scheme for classifying different kinds of roles. Roles are distinguished in terms of "pattern variables," which are pairs of alternatives relating to aspects of role-playing. The following four pattern variables are relevant here.

1. Ascription versus achievement.
2. Particularism versus universalism.

[6] Nigel Grant, *Soviet Education* (London: Penguin Books, 1964), p. 23.
[7] Talcott Parsons, "The School Class as a Social System: Some of Its Functions in American Society," in A. H. Halsey, Jean Floud, and C. A. Anderson, eds., *Education, Economy and Society* (New York: Free Press, 1961), pp. 434–455.

3. Diffuseness versus specificity.
4. Affectivity versus affective neutrality.

These terms can be explained by examples that are specially relevant in the present context. We can contrast an occupational role that arises in an elaborate division of labor, such as the role of a research chemist or of a professor of sociology, with a kinship role such as mother, wife, or daughter. In a complex economy, the incumbents of roles will behave in *specific* rather than diffuse ways toward their correlatives; high *achievement* will be expected of them; and their personal qualities (except insofar as they affect performance) will be relatively unimportant. Incumbents will be treated as members of a *universal* class of incumbents of the specialized role, and will not expect special treatment because of any particular relationship to particular persons. They will be expected to control their individual likes and dislikes in pursuing the aims of the specialized role; that is, they will be expected to be *affectively neutral*.

Familial roles are defined by the opposite alternatives. For example, the mother role is *ascribed*: it is a personal quality or attribute. The mother cares first and foremost who the *particular* child is rather than whether he is a member of the universal class of children. Her obligations to her child are diffuse, and *affectivity* is expected: by definition, a mother loves her child. Parsons' analysis of the school is focused on the process whereby the child is taught to accept and to play roles defined in terms of the right-hand alternatives rather than the left-hand ones listed in his pattern variables. Socialization of this kind is essential if children are to move successfully from the first experience of their family situation to the secondary organizations of a complex industrial society. In the wider society, both the common-value system and the placing of persons in specialized roles are dominated by the criterion of *achievement*. The inculcation of these common values and, above all, commitment to a system of differential evaluation in terms of achievement are viewed as the major functions of the primary stage of education. In this stage of education, the moral and the cognitive aspects of socialization are not sharply distinguished. Both goodness and intelligence are rewarded. This is the first and most vital step in the upbringing of a child so that his personality will fit the requirements of adult—and especially occupational—roles in an advanced industrial society.

Notice that Parsons, in describing the school class as a social system adapted to the exercise of these functions, assumes a high degree of homogeneity of family and class background among the pupils—a condition that is assured in American primary schools by the residential segregation of classes and ethnic groups. He then emphasizes the equal status of children in the classroom and their universalistic rather than particularistic treatment by the teacher. This is a new social situation for the child, which contrasts with his ascribed status and particularistic relationships at home. Through adaptation to the school situation, supported by the pattern of relationships typical in peer groups, the child begins to learn to live in the adult world, in which roles are defined in terms of achievement rather than ascription. The secondary stage of education is then interpreted as focusing mainly on the selective function—channelling pupils (again, principally according to achievement criteria) toward specialized occupations, which are divided approximately evenly in contemporary America between pupils who will go on to college and those for whom secondary education is terminal.[8]

Parsons' analysis is valuable in showing how children are brought to accept the common-value system of their society. We can carry the analysis further, however, by relating the process of character formation to the power-and-authority system of society. Such an analysis was attempted by Max Weber in outline form, and was illustrated in his discussion of charisma and bureaucracy and their application to the social roles of the Chinese literati.[9] Weber distinguished three types of social personality: the charismatic personality, the cultivated man, and the expert. These three types of personality correspond to three kinds of power and authority in society. In the first kind of power and authority, the autocratic personal authority of the religious, military, or political leader is magically or divinely inspired and is expressed as charisma. In the second type of power and authority, the customarily or traditionally sanctioned authority of a status group is expressed educationally in a wide cultivation of the humanistic aspects of the culture. Weber uses as an example the education of the Chinese literati; other examples are the upbringing of the English upper classes in the public schools and ancient colleges in the eighteenth and nineteenth centuries or the education of the full citizen in an ancient Greek city state. The third kind of power and authority is characteristic of advanced industrial societies with their rational and bureaucratic forms of authority and their educational expression in the specialized expertise of the scientist and the professional man.

Weber's typology is, of course, concerned with the formation of social personalities for the elite strata of society. Parsons' analysis of the American primary school deals with the first step in this process as it appears in a mass system of education. The link between the two analyses is supplied

---

[8] Talcott Parsons (cited in footnote 7).
[9] H. Gerth and C. Wright Mills, *Essays from Max Weber* (London: Routledge and Kegan Paul, 1947), pp. 416–444.

partly by Parsons' description of the selection process in secondary schools
and partly by a consideration of the way in which power in society
determines the distribution of material facilities. This means that we must
look not only at the values that govern the internal operation of the school
as a social system but also at the differences between types of school that
derive from unequal social class distributions of educational opportunity.
We shall deal with this question later. Here, however, it should be noted
that forces other than those of status differentiation are emphasized in
recent analyses of socialization in American schools.

For Parsons, the school is a specialized and independent organization
acting positively in the socialization and selection processes although,
of course, the school is influenced by the wider social structure of family,
neighborhood, peer groups, and similar things. Social class is one influence
of this kind, but it does not dominate. Selection is "not simply a way
of affirming a previously determined ascriptive status." Thus, for example,
the failure of a minority to attain moral integration into the common-
value system is not viewed primarily as a failure of assimilation of working-
class children into middle-class schools, nor as a class-typed "alientation"
from cultural and intellectual values. Parsons stresses, instead, the growing importance of the selection processes and the upgrading of educational
standards in each new generation. Intergenerational rather than class
conflict is emphasized as the consequence of social change. For instance,
the anti-intellectual side of the American "Youth Culture" is, in Parson's
opinion, partly a protest against adults. Of course, the characteristically
rising standards demanded in education bear most heavily on children
with low ability from low-status homes, and lead to rebellion against
the dominant achievement value through truancy and delinquency. For
the high ability–low status group, Parsons draws a parallel with cross-
pressured voters to explain the relatively high incidence of "indifference"
to school performance among them. "Those pupils who are exposed to
contradictory pressures are likely to be ambivalent: at the same time
the personal stakes for them are higher than for the others because what
happens in school may make much more of a difference for their futures
than for the others, in whom ability and family status point to the same
expectations for the future." [10]

Stress on intergenerational conflict is an even more prominent characteristic of James Coleman's *Adolescent Society*,[11] and leads to the recognition of a feature of advanced industrialism—the separation of a distinctive
adolescent culture or "society within society"—which Coleman places at

[10] Talcott Parsons (cited in footnote 7), p. 447.
[11] James Coleman, *Adolescent Society* (New York: Free Press, 1961).

the center of his analysis of the socialization process in secondary schools. It is significant that Coleman's analysis includes the "Elmtown" studied by Warner, Hollingshead, and their associates in the depression years in the United States before World War II. Hollingshead's study [12] placed major emphasis on the role of the school as a mechanism reinforcing the class structure. Coleman's findings, less than 20 years later, suggest a dramatic reduction of the impact of class on the life of the Elmtown High School. He summarizes the position as follows.

As long as meaningful social rewards could be directly supplied by adults there was little need to be explicit about them in educational theory for they were naturally provided by the very process of interaction between parent and child or student and teacher. To be sure these rewards were often distributed in ways that reinforced the stratification system and took away the lower class child's meagre chance for equality; as some authors have shown very well, the middle class background of teachers often made them unable to hold out reasonable rewards for reasonable achievement to lower class children. The situation, however, was fundamentally simpler than it is today, because teachers and parents had direct control over the levers they could apply to motivate children. Now the levers are other children themselves acting as a small society.[13]

Adolescent culture in parts of North America is a phenomenon that cuts across social class lines, and its significance is likely to increase in the future. Where stratification was the major source of both integration and conflict, the function of the school and of the university was to differentiate different levels of aspiration, attainment, and styles of life for the various strata. The nineteenth century British public-school boy was taught leadership, and the elementary-school boy was taught follower-ship. Conflict was channeled through politics and industry. But a dominantly selective system of education based on equality of opportunity denies the relevance of class in education while satisfying the requirements of a complex division of labor. Thus we may no longer have a working-class education to "gentle the masses" but a selective education to tame the individual. As Bernstein puts it:

. . . as a result of the close relation between education and occupation a situation may soon be reached where the educational institutions legitimise social inequality by individualising failure. Democratisation of the means of education, together with the internalisation of the achievement ethic by members of the working class strata, may lead to an individualising of failure, to

[12] A. B. Hollingshead, *Elmtown's Youth* (New York: Wiley, 1949).
[13] James Coleman, *op. cit.*, p. 11.

a loss of self-respect, which in turn modifies an individual's attitude both to his group and to the demands made upon him by society.[14]

Social control of this kind probably operates more efficiently through the American type of educational system (with its relative openness and absence of clearly recognizable selection points) than in the English tripartite system or similar European types with sharply defined segregation at an early age. The American system reduces revolt among the unsuccessful by delaying clear recognition of the realities of the situation until the individual is thoroughly committed. For example, the American "open-door" junior college permits entry to higher education by people with very little chance of successfully completing a degree course and, as Burton Clark expresses it, "cools them out" by individual choice under guidance rather than by authoritative external decision.[15] Ralph Turner [16] notices that where this type of control system operates effectively, the kind of organized or gang deviancy that develops is more likely to take the form of an attack on the conventional or moral order than on the class system itself. The United States has its beatniks and criminal gangs, but it has very few active revolutionaries. Nevertheless, the pace of change in America is so rapid that the sociologist of education there is already able to look at the school in terms that are applicable to a closer approximation to our ideal type of technological society.

## The Structure of Education

The development of education in modern society involves adding innovation and dissemination to the traditional process of preservation as culture is transmitted from generation to generation. The major force for change has been the pressure in industrial society to incorporate a scientific culture into the organization of study and research. Consequently, despite wide variations in the social and political structure of industrial countries, there is a basic trend in educational structure toward increasing the scale, specialization, and bureaucratic administration of schools and colleges. Since 1850, educational systems have expanded in numbers of students, in range of teaching, and in provision for research until education now has become a major industry that usually claims more than 5% of a country's productive resources.

[14] B. Bernstein, "Social Class and Linguistic Development: A Theory of Social Learning," in A. H. Halsey et al. (cited in footnote 7), p. 308.
[15] Burton Clark, *The Open Door College* (New York: McGraw-Hill, 1960).
[16] Ralph Turner, "Sponsored and Contest Mobility and the School System," *American Sociological Review*, **25** (**5**), 855–867 (1960).

This trend dominates every aspect of educational organization—that is, who teaches, what is taught, and to whom. First, we shall examine the trend in relation to the role of the teacher. Next, we shall examine it in relation to the structure of primary and secondary education. And, finally, we shall consider in more detail the trend's impact on the organization of higher education.

### The Role of the Teacher

In our model of the primitive society, culture is transmitted from father to son. Teaching as a set of specialized professions arises only in societies that approximate the model of technological society. Bryan Wilson comments as follows.

> Certainly in traditional societies there is often a distinctive intellectual elite but they are not so much teachers as guardians of knowledge, and knowledge is esoteric, sacred, aristocratic. It is frequently the knowledge of the gods, revealed to inspired seers; its guardians are priests or literati: . . . The literati do not transmit new ideas, but rather keep pure old dogmas: they are not teachers and disseminators, but custodians of the sacred. Their intellectual institutions are closed—segregated seminaries set in remote places, preserving a shrine-like quality of apartness.[17]

On the other hand, in industrial societies knowledge becomes secular rather than sacred; new knowledge is actively sought instead of being closely controlled in the interests of received belief; and education is extended, in impersonal instruction to the masses, instead of being restricted to the few: the student replaces the novitiate. This change in the process of cultural transmission implies that the teacher becomes a specialist, a professional, a researcher, and a kind of secular missionary.[18] The production and distribution of knowledge becomes an industry that extends beyond the boundaries of formal educational organizations and includes research and development in such fields as business enterprises, governmental departments, the mass media, information service, and information machines. Using this broad definition, the "knowledge industry" employs almost one third of the labor force in modern America.[19] In 1960, the elementary and secondary schools in the United States employed 1.75 million teachers and other staff members. An additional 200,000 were

[17] Bryan Wilson, "The Teacher's Role—A Sociological Analysis," *British Journal of Sociology,* **13** (1), 15 (March, 1962).
[18] See Jean Floud, "Teaching in the Affluent Society," *British Journal of Sociology,* **13** (4), 299–308 (December, 1962).
[19] See F. Machlup, *The Production and Distribution of Knowledge in the United States* (Princeton, N.J.: Princeton University Press, 1962).

employed in higher education. Cultural innovation through research has also generated sizable "Ph.D. communities" outside of the schools and colleges. For example, scientists and engineers working in research and development laboratories totaled 425,000 in 1962. But, in 1920, there were less than 10,000.

An increase in the scale of the modern educational labor force is also accompanied by differentiation into a hierarchy of specialized occupations. The hierarchy ranges from the highly paid professor of international repute at (and frequently absent from) a major university to the young woman teaching "the three R's" in a local primary school. Teaching is not a unified profession but, more and more, has become a loosely connected series of professional and would-be professional occupations. Unity becomes increasingly difficult not only because of the trend toward specialization but also because of the very different levels of prestige and status attached to different schools in the expanded modern systems of education and because there is a tendency for teaching and research to become divorced. Thus, recruitment to higher education is now separated from recruitment to secondary schools. This is true even in countries like France where, traditionally, service in a lycée was the normal first step in a university teaching career, but now the young graduate is likely to enter higher education through a research post given by the Centre National de Recherche Scientifique.

Expansion of educational systems usually produces a lengthening of the occupational hierarchy. In the United States, for example, there is a chronic concern that either the quantity or the quality of teaching will be made inadequate by the expansion of higher education, research, and competing claims for the services of educated people.[20] The conflict between teaching and research is obvious under these conditions. Research funds tend to go to university graduate schools rather than to undergraduate liberal arts colleges where teaching is relatively highly valued and emphasized. Consequently, the more ambitious and gifted scholars seek careers at graduate schools rather than undergraduate institutions because they are able to find lighter teaching duties, higher salaries, more prestige, and better opportunities for academic recognition and promotion. The result is a widening gap between the research frontier and the undergraduate classroom and a corresponding distribution of talent and reward between research and teaching.

Differentiation of professional status and income at the lower levels of education is further conditioned by the nature of the teaching career and

[20] See Organization for Economic Cooperation and Development, *Higher Education and the Demand for Scientific Manpower in the United States,* Paris, 1963.

the function and location of different kinds of schools. Teaching as a career in secondary and especially in primary schools is strongly influenced by the preponderance of women teachers. They constitute 85% of the teachers in American primary schools and one half of the staff of secondary schools. Thus, although school teaching is an attractive occupation for women, it is thereby made relatively unattractive for men: "feminization" reduces both salaries and status. Burton Clark makes this pertinent comment:

> For men the anticipated career in education is up or out, rather than in or out. They go into teaching hoping to advance up the school ladder into administration, or permanently leave education to take employment in another field. Among beginning men teachers, over one-half hope for a non-teaching post in education, and an additional one-fifth expect to move to another occupation, leaving only 3 out of 10 who plan at the outset to teach until retirement.[21]

### Primary and Secondary Schools

The culture of industrialism and its characteristic demand for experts are such that education must be organized in a complex of schools and colleges with more or less specialized aims in relation to education, training, and research. Quite apart from the need to ensure in all societies—industrial or preindustrial—the handing down of some kind of common-value system, the economic functions of education require that secondary and higher forms of schooling be based on universal or near-universal primary schooling. Thus, all advanced industrial countries have universal compulsory schooling at the primary stage, beginning at the age of 5, 6, or 7, with curricula designed to equip the whole population with a basic knowledge of letters and numbers.

However, the tendency toward expansion does not stop here. Both an economic demand for trained scientists and professional people and a political demand for educational opportunity and a higher educational "standard of living" carry this primary expansion into what can be considered as a second and a third stage. In the second stage, universal secondary education emerges and modifies the secondary school's previously specialized role. The United States reached this second stage of educational development by World War II and, since then, has entered a third stage, in which some form of higher education becomes a universal

[21] Burton R. Clark, "Sociology of Education," in Robert E. L. Faris, ed., *Handbook of Modern Sociology* (Chicago: Rand McNally, 1964). See also W. Mason, *The Beginning Teacher: Status and Career Orientations,* U.S. Office of Education, Washington, D.C., 1961.

goal. Each stage of development is obviously dependent on prior expansion of the earlier stages of education. The figures for enrollment in higher education in the United States reflect this necessity. By the end of the nineteenth century, while a system of universal primary schooling was being built up, the proportion of 18-year-olds to 21-year-olds in full-time enrollment was 4%. Then, during the second stage of developing universal secondary education, the percentage enrollment in higher education doubled every 20 years to 8% in 1920 and 16% in 1940. With the second stage complete, the period since World War II has witnessed steady advance into the third stage of mass higher education. The majority of young Americans now plan to go to college, and the ratio of students enrolled in degree-credit courses to the 18- to 21-year-old population has been estimated for 1970 at 47.6%.[22]

Expansion in the same direction is evident all over the industrial world. For example, in Britain full-time enrollment in higher education was 8% in 1961 and is planned to rise to 18% in 1980. But the different systems vary enormously. In post-revolutionary Russia, schooling has been centrally organized to meet estimated demands for labor through selective technical education, and has incorporated both political indoctrination and a fusing of school and work at the secondary stage in order to foster loyalty to Soviet society and its political and social ideology. It is significant for both of these aims of Russian education that plans have been announced for secondary boarding schools to be established for 80% of the pupils by 1980. In Western Europe the organization of education still preserves its traditional form as a reflection of the demand of a class society for schooling according to social origin and as preparation for a particular social position. Secondary schools are differentiated, and a minority of them offer curricula that prepare pupils for entry to higher education. In most European countries, entry to skilled trades is by some form of apprenticeship or learnership organized wthin industry, although the trend is toward transferring industrial training to technical schools and colleges along either American or Russian lines.

Outside of the United States, where secondary schooling developed from a movement to "Americanize" large numbers of immigrants and to raise the educational and social level of new and growing communities, there generally has been opposition to the integrated extension of compulsory common schooling. The problem in Europe and in many of its Asian and African colonial or former colonial territories is to develop comprehensive types of secondary education out of a system of separate

[22] Martin Trow, "The Second Transformation of American Secondary Education," *International Journal of Comparative Sociology*, **2**, 144–166 (1961).

schools with unequal social prestige designed historically for different social classes. Attempts in this direction have met with varying success. In Czechoslovakia, Yugoslavia, and elsewhere in Eastern Europe, the break with tradition has been sharp. There are also strong comprehensive school movements in Scandinavia (especially Sweden),[23] and weaker ones in France [24] and Britain.[25]

The state, partly as the main source of finance, exercises a large measure of control over the educational system in all industrial countries. The degree to which religious and private control is permitted varies, and private education may be of crucial social significance as in the case of the British "public" schools. The degree of centralization also varies, and this determines the level at which religious bodies, political parties, teachers' unions, and parents' associations exert pressure in favor of their particular interests. Centralized government may be combined with centralized administration (as in France), or with decentralized administration (as in Sweden), or both may be decentralized (as in the United States). But decentralization does not guarantee the autonomy of individual schools. There is, for example, a marked contrast between Britain and the United States in the degree of insulation of the British school from outside influence and the freedom of the classroom teacher to determine his own methods of teaching and choice of textbooks.

The American classroom teacher in primary and secondary schools is much more open to external pressure from parents and from the governing lay boards through the school superintendent than is the British teacher. In England the teacher is relatively more protected from these influences by the centralized national organization of schools, the relatively weak development of parent-teacher associations, and the stronger traditions of professional autonomy.

### Higher Education in Industrial Societies [26]

Universities have assumed a special place in the modern world, which reflects the emergence of a new relation between higher education and the requirements of advanced industrial society. Learning and research,

---

[23] T. Husen and S. Henrysson, eds., *Differentiation and Guidance in the Comprehensive School—Report on the Sigtuna Conference 1958, Stockholm* (Stockholm: Almquist and Wiksell, 1959).

[24] W. R. Fraser, *Education and Society in Modern France* (London: Routledge and Kegan Paul, 1963).

[25] R. Pedley, *The Comprehensive School* (London: Penguin, 1963).

[26] In this section, I have drawn heavily on my "The Changing Function of Universities in Advanced Industrial Societies," *Harvard Educational Review*, spring, 1960, pp. 119–127, and "British Universities," *European Journal of Sociology*, **3** (**1**), 85–101 (1962).

as we have argued, have become crucial to the maintenance of contemporary economic and social life and, in the twentieth century, to its further development. Educational aspirations are part and parcel of both popular hopes for the future and of national plans for the economic development of states.

The European university is an institution with an eventful but unbroken history, dating from medieval origins in Bologna and Paris. In the medieval and preindustrial periods, the history of the universities in relation to the economy was, by and large, one of imperfect and usually belated adaptation to the occupational demands of a culture that was gradually increasing in complexity. There are other, more ancient, traditions of higher learning in the Islamic world, in China, and in India, but "the remarkable fact is that among all the lines of descent of higher learning one, and only one, has adapted itself to modern civilization, and by a process of natural selection among social institutions has displaced other lines of descent." [27] The biological analogy is apt. The notion of descent with modifications, the challenge of continuity and change, of preservation and innovation, must lie at the center of a sociology of higher education, and the adaptability of the university to the social environment of industrialism is its crucial contemporary problem in all countries—developed or underdeveloped.

Higher education is a specialized agency, charged with the conservation of some of the most highly prized beliefs and intellectual skills in the cultural tradition. Accordingly, organizations of higher education must be regarded as partially independent of, and functioning in relation to, other aspects of social structure such as government, the economy, and religious and military organizations. The existence of higher learning presupposes certain social conditions, notably a level of economic and political development that affords the possibility of "idleness" for a scholarly class. Indeed, universities always play a role in social stratification for this reason: since they control access to highly valued cultural elements, they are intrinsically inegalitarian. As Durkheim pointed out, "to find an absolutely homogeneous and egalitarian education, it would be necessary to go back to prehistoric societies in the structure of which there is no differentiation." [28]

Thus, universities touch on all aspects of life and must be considered in terms of multiple attachments to social organization. But today the key to understanding the idea of a university is in its new and developing link to the economic organization of society. This is the crucial connection

---

[27] Sir Eric Ashby, *Patterns of Universities in Non-European Societies* (London: School of Oriental and African Studies, 1961), p. 3.
[28] E. Durkheim, *Education and Sociology*, translated by S. D. Fox (Glencoe, Ill.: Free Press, 1956), p. 69.

between education and society in the modern world. It defines the functions
of the modern university. Although the university traditionally has been
conservative in its functions (that is, "a place of teaching universal knowledge rather than the advancement of knowledge" [29]), it is now one of the
organizations through which the content of the culture is changed by
research. Higher education has become an essential part of the apparatus
through which the inevitability of future social change is built into present
social structure. Therefore the university, which has always played the
uneasy role of both guardian and critic, preserver and destroyer of the
existing state of knowledge, becomes a sharp focal point of the conflict
between continuity and change.

In the long history of the universities these struggles have been expressed in a gradual secularization of learning. Today, universities are
concerned above all with the rise of science. The explosion of scientific
knowledge in the twentieth century has dramatically shifted the balance
between teaching and research. Over the past century the number of
publications has increased at an exponential rate. The universal scholar
is now unthinkable. Knowledge is elaborately differentiated in its structure.
Universities that once were small communities of teachers and students
grouped around a library and set apart from the world now tend to
become "multiversities" [30] with specialized departments, laboratories, and
research centers. New specialties in the natural and social sciences constantly
clamor for a place in the organization of learning and, as universities
grow in size and numbers, the proportionate place of traditional classical
learning within them shrinks. In short, the modern university is the center
of cultural innovation.

### Universities and the Emergence of Industrialism

Today, the university is directly and obviously linked to the economy in
an industrial society through the market for professional manpower and
through research activities in the applied sciences. This was not always true.
Richard Hofstadter has contrasted the present situation with the period
before the American Civil War: "In the middle of the twentieth century,
the American student of the history of higher education will find it hard
to understand why college teaching responded so slowly to social change
unless he realizes that the old time colleges were not organically knit

[29] Cardinal Newman, *The Idea of a University* (New York: Doubleday, book edition,
1959; first published in 1853), preface.
[30] Clark Kerr, *The Uses of the University* (Cambridge, Mass.: Harvard University
Press, 1963).

into the fabric of economic life." [31] The medieval European universities were an organic part of religious rather than economic life. This was also true even of the much later American institutions where, until the early years of the eighteenth century, the majority of graduates became clergymen. Today, a negligible proportion of the alumni of Western universities enters the ministry.

However, the transition of universities from their earlier functional emphasis was not simply a matter of extending secular professional training in response to the demands of developing industrialism. On the contrary, there was an overlapping phase in which universities were dominated by their function as preserves of the aristocratic and gentry classes. Indeed, the nineteenth-century history of European and American universities is one of more or less successful resistance to the pressures generated by economic change. Max Weber's view of education as a differentiating agency, which socializes individuals into the total style of life of the strata for which they are destined, must be interpreted as being applied to an aristocratic "structure of domination" prior to World War II. In this sense, higher education has been essentially a phenomenon of status rather than class—a process directed "against the market."

Traditionally, the university has rightly been considered as being primarily devoted to the education—moral and physical, as well as intellectual—of the "cultivated man," [32] with its emphasis on "character," "service," and the rounded personality of the gentlemen. For the lower strata, the educational equivalent in Europe was a simple literacy heavily imbued with ideas of docility, piety, and nationalism.

Vocationalism was resisted in the European universities long after the religious domination of curricula had been overcome and long after secular universities had been founded on state and industrial patronage. Thus, the creation of the University of Berlin in the early years of the nineteenth century, which set the tone for much of the subsequent modernization of universities in Europe and America, "was intended primarily to develop knowledge, secondarily and perhaps as a concession, to train the professional and the official classes.[33] In America the land-

---

[31] R. Hofstadter and C. P. Hardy, *The Development and Scope of Higher Education in the United States* (New York: Columbia University Press, 1952), p. 21.

[32] Weber points out that " 'the cultivated man,' rather than the 'specialist' has been the end sought by education and has formed the basis of social esteem in such various systems as the feudal theocratic and patrimonial structures of domination: in the English notable administration, in the old Chinese patrimonial bureaucracy as well as under the rule of demagogues in so-called Hellenic democracy." H. Gerth and C. Wright Mills (cited in footnote 9), p. 242.

[33] A. Flexner, *Universities: American, English, German* (New York: Oxford University Press, 1930), p. 312.

grant colleges (created after the Morrill Act of 1862) failed, despite the lead given by Wisconsin [34] to create a comprehensive link between higher education and agriculture, through either research or teaching, until after World War I. In England the great champion of the modern universities, T. H. Huxley, asserted before the Cowper Commission of 1892 that "the primary business of the universities is with pure knowledge and pure art—independent of all application to practice; with progress in culture not with increase in wealth." [35]

Although the emergence of modern British universities as undergraduate professional schools began with the foundation of the University of London, it is largely a twentieth-century phenomenon and, even then, is explicable primarily in terms of the continued command held by Oxford and Cambridge over the avenues of entry into the national elites. Even in America, where the absence of an indigenous aristocracy made professional and technological training more acceptable, this training was absorbed into the universities more by their extension into graduate schools than by revision of undergraduate curricula.

The aristocratic domination of universities that was typical of Europe in the eighteenth century (with its American equivalent: the education of ministers and lawyers as community leaders) continued, despite the shifting class basis of power in the nineteenth and early twentieth century. However, this did not preclude the more limited function of higher education as an agent of social mobility, of assimilation into elite groups, and of "resocialization" for a selected minority of able boys from the lower strata. The nineteenth-century American colleges and the German universities both recruited from the middle and lower classes. And in England with the beginning of expansion of professional and administrative employment in the second half of the century, "the old and the new middle classes needed avenues of employment which would provide both prestige and relatively high income for their sons." [36] But the working classes were scarcely touched by these developments.

Nevertheless, as Hofstadter says of the American college, "Education was for gentlemen, it was designed to create among them a core of central knowledge that would make of them a community of the educated." [37] And even Veblen's bitter classic, although directed against "the conduct of universities by businessmen" and the perversion of scholarly

---

[34] See C. McCarty, *The Wisconsin Idea* (New York: Macmillan, 1912).
[35] Quoted in C. Bibby, "T. H. Huxley's Idea of a University," *Universities Quarterly*, **10**, 383 (August, 1956).
[36] D. V. Glass, "Education," in M. Ginsberg, ed., *Law and Opinion in the Twentieth Century* (London: Stevens, 1959), p. 326.
[37] R. Hofstadter and C. P. Hardy (cited in footnote 31), p. 11.

values by the predatory ethics of business, describes an example of the ideal university man as one striving for "lifelike imitation of a country gentleman." [38]

A new relationship is now discernible. Generally, whereas both Weber and Veblen considered the university as a corporate structure in process of adaptation (Veblen thought betrayal) to industrial society, W. H. Whyte, writing 40 years later, viewed it as an integral part of the organization of a technological society.[39] Development in this direction originated in the nineteenth-century application of science to industrial processes—"the invention of invention"—and the slow subsequent development of technological professions in agriculture, chemistry, metallurgy, mechanical and electrical engineering, and similar fields. However, the new relationship is discernible as a direct connection of economic organization to the higher learning only with escape from the economic depressions of the 1930's and the search for national economic growth and international military strength of the war and postwar years. During this period, institutions of higher education, both as research organizations and as training establishments, have been drawn more closely into the economy either directly or through the state. The exchange of ideas, of people, and of contracts between university departments and research institutes and their counterparts in private industry and government agencies serves to merge these organizations and to assimilate the life styles of their staffs. Basically, the new functions reflect a new stage in the development of the means of production in which, as Drucker puts it "the highly educated man has become the central resource of today's society, the supply of such men the true measure of its economic, military and even its political potential." [40]

However, these developments in the nature of the scientific culture and their social consequences need not, and in most countries do not, elicit a total response from the universities. Institutions may adapt themselves to cultural and social change by becoming more specialized. Therefore, teaching and research may develop in separate organizations. Advanced teaching and research may be segregated into quarternary institutions as in the great American graduate schools. Research may be concentrated in government or industrial institutes. Training for particular professions, for example, school teaching in England or engineering in Russia may be obtained in a nonuniversity institution. The Russian institutes are a clear example of differentiated organizations that provide education in a single specialized field. In Britain or America this specialization of function has usually been

[38] T. Veblen, *The Higher Learning in America* (New York: B. W. Huebsch, 1918), p. 164.
[39] W. H. Whyte, *The Organization Man* (London: Jonathan Cape Ltd., 1957).
[40] P. F. Drucker, *The Landmarks of Tomorrow* (London: Heinemann, 1959), p. 87.

limited to the separation of departments and faculties (such as medicine or engineering) within the university, whereas the Soviet institutes are entirely separated from the universities.[41] To a greater or lesser extent the rise of higher learning in industrial countries has resulted in the emergence of the university as a specialized organization within a larger complex of institutions of advanced education.

Educational adaptation to modern scientific culture varies from country to country in both form and rapidity. At different times since the Enlightenment, various countries including France, Scotland, Germany, and England have led movements for university reform. But the contemporary "models" for future development increasingly tend to be sought outside of Western Europe—in North America and the Soviet Union. Although British conceptions of the university still exercise considerable sway over the former colonial territories in Africa and the Caribbean,[42] and British intellectual traditions retain extraordinary dominance over the educated Indian,[43] the United States and the Soviet Union now receive rather than send the would-be planner of new universities. A Royal Commission on Oxford and Cambridge in 1922 said that "the two senior Universities of the Empire have also now the chance of becoming to a much greater extent than formerly centres of research, and of graduate study for the whole Empire and for American and foreign guests." [44] A generation later, David Riesman, surveying American universities, asserted that "we can no longer look abroad for our models of cultural and educational advance. . . . Europeans and Japanese, West Africans and Burmese now come here to look for models or invite American professors to visit and bring with them the 'American Way' in higher education." [45]

Russia is like America in the sense that higher education is geared closely to the economy but, unlike America, enrollment and curricula are controlled centrally in the interests of maximizing economic growth. At first glance the Soviet Union appears to be educationally underdeveloped. At the end of the 1950's, it had proportionately only one half as many secondary-school graduates as the United States and only 16 of each 1000 of its people had had higher education, compared with the American figure

---

[41] See N. De Witt, *Education and Professional Employment in the U.S.S.R.* (Washington, D.C.: National Science Foundation, 1961), pp. 216–220.

[42] For a recent account, see A. M. Carr-Saunders, *New Universities Overseas* (London: George Allen and Unwin, 1961).

[43] See Edward Shils, "The Intellectual Between Tradition and Modernity: The Indian Situation," *Comparative Studies in Society and History,* Supplement I, 1961, pp. 8–87. "India was, and remains, an intellectual province of London, Oxford and Cambridge."

[44] Report of the Royal Commission on Oxford and Cambridge 1922, paragraph 33.

[45] David Riesman, in A. H. Halsey et al., *Education, Economy and Society* (cited in footnote 7), p. 481.

of 44 of each 1000.[46] But the essential factor with respect to Russia is that the Revolution resulted in the development of a system of higher education adjusted directly to manpower demand. Therefore, in the supply of professional and scientific workers in such fields as agriculture, medicine, engineering, and the like, the Russian system is as far advanced as the American system. For example, in engineering and science, the number of graduates for each 1000 of the population is 9 in the Soviet Union and 10 in the United States.

The different stages reached by these two countries in their advancement toward the technological society are indicated by the fact that in Russia 55% of all graduates are science and engineering students, whereas in America the corresponding percentage is 21. This certainly does not mean that higher learning in America either already is or is becoming less closely geared to the economy. On the contrary, there is a strong tendency for business to increase its influence over the content of American higher education, as is indicated by the proportionate decline of the fundamental disciplines and the rise of applied subjects, especially subjects connected with business administration and commerce. The "extra" output of American graduates in the humanities and social sciences mainly reflects the professionalization of the tertiary sector of American industry, and may be viewed as an adornment of the affluent society, which Russia has yet to become.

### The English Idea of a University

There is a distinctive English idea of a university, which Cardinal Newman was acutely aware of when, in 1852, he wrote that "some persons may be tempted to complain that I have servilely followed the English idea of a university to the disparagement of that knowledge which I profess to be so strenuously upholding; and they may anticipate that an academical system, formed upon my model, will result in nothing better or higher than in the production of that antiquated variety of human nature and remnant of feudalism, as they consider it, called 'a gentleman.' " [47]

Behind this traditional English conception there lies the conflict between the cultivated man and the specialist, which Max Weber identified as fundamental to educational theory. As already mentioned, Weber distinguished two opposite polar types of educational system: one designed "to

---

[46] For these and subsequent figures, see N. de Witt, "Basic Comparative Data on Soviet and American Education," *Comparative Education Review,* **2,** 9 (June, 1958), and also De Witt's *Soviet Professional Manpower,* 1961, where a comparison is made of the supply of professional manpower in the USSR and the United States.

[47] Cardinal Newman (cited in footnote 29), p. 7.

awaken charisma" and the other "to impart specialized expert training." [48]
He observed that, in modern Western, rational bureaucratized society, educational systems tend toward the type that imparts specialized expert
training. But between the two opposites he recognized many educational
systems that aim at cultivating the student for a "conduct of life," that is,
the style of life appropriate to the status group for which he is destined.
Elements of training for an expertise as well as education for participation
in the culture of a status group are present in all educational systems. However, the modern Western type of industrial society maximizes the training
for an expertise and minimizes the education for participation in the culture
of a status group. The traditional status-differentiating functions of education have been heavily modified by the requirements of selection and of socialization into particular professional groups. "The modern development of
full bureaucratization brings the system of rational, specialized, and expert
examinations irresistibly to the fore." [49] Educational qualifications are, as
Weber emphasized, a status claim—a substitute for birth or ascriptive claims
to a style of life.

But in a country like Britain, which has a past "structure of domination"
other than the modern bureaucratic one, the expert examination meets resistance. The great period of the English universities as schools for the
aristocracy and the gentry is represented by Oxford and Cambridge in the
century and a half before the reforms initiated by the Royal Commissions
in 1850—a point that marks the beginning of the ascendancy of the examination principle in English public life. In this period the universities were
"seats in which the youth of the country could acquire a modicum of
classical learning; they gave an intellectual sanction to the domination of
the gentry and brought up the young men to be gentlemen, accepting and
exemplifying the ideals of a class." [50]

Industrialism has changed the face of Britain since that time: certainly
the primary and secondary school systems were started much later, and
two thirds of British university students now attend institutions founded in
the Victorian or post-Victorian era. Nevertheless, "the English idea" has
manifested a stubborn resilience. It expresses itself partly in the conspicu-
ousness of Oxford and Cambridge and partly in the vagueness bordering on
invisibility, the placelessness of "Redbrick" University. Oxford and Cambridge, in the public mind, still stand for the older social and educational
ideals of the cultivated, well-rounded member of an elite rather than the

[48] H. Gerth and C. Wright Mills, *Essays from Max Weber* (London: Routledge and
Kegan Paul, 1947), p. 426.
[49] *Ibid.*, p. 241.
[50] W. Dibelius, *England,* translated by M. A. Hamilton (London: Jonathan Cape, Ltd.,
1930), pp. 2, 569.

highly trained professional expert. The ideal model of a university in England is, therefore, either Oxford or Cambridge or a successful imitation of them.

In the fourteenth century, Oxford and Cambridge, backed by royal power, established themselves as national institutions with a monopoly of higher learning. The monopoly was challenged frequently but unsuccessfully until the rise of universities in the great industrial cities of the nineteenth century and, even then, monopoly gave way only to pre-eminence. The challenge of industrialism and nonconformity was met partly by reform and expansion of the ancient foundations, partly by assimilation of the sons of successful businessmen through the colleges and the "public schools" that supplied them, and partly by sending staff members to the newly created universities.

One illustration of the effect of the traditional English idea of a university should be noted. Britain, compared with other advanced industrial countries, has an exceptionally low intake of students. Nevertheless, the meaning of comparative statistics becomes clearer if data for degrees granted are compared with those for enrollment. According to the enrollment figures shown in Table 7.3, the United Kingdom ranks below not only

Table 7.3    Proportion of 19-Year-Olds Enrolled in Institutions of Higher Education and Proportions Obtaining First Degrees—1957 and 1958

|  | First Enrollments as Proportion of Population Aged 19 (%) | First Degrees as Proportion of Population of the Median Age of Graduation (%) |
|---|---|---|
| United States | 33.03 | 16.65 |
| Canada | 14.08 | 7.57 |
| France | 7.19 | 2.55 |
| Sweden | 6.40 | 2.23 |
| United Kingdom | 2.98 | 2.92 |

*Source.* A. H. Halsey, ed., *Ability and Educational Opportunity* (Paris: Organization of Economic Cooperation and Development, 1961), pp. 191–192.

the United States (which had a comparable enrollment proportion in 1900) and Canada but also below several European countries, including France and Sweden. But when the numbers of degrees granted are compared, the United Kingdom shows a higher enrollment proportion than either France or Sweden. What lies behind and explains the discrepancy is the distinctive

English idea of restricted entry to a basically residential university which has low student-staff ratios, making up a community of older and younger scholars and guaranteeing for the younger scholars a low drop-out rate. In France and Sweden, both enrollment and drop-out rates are high. Many state colleges and universities in America have an open door to high school graduates, and in the system as a whole less than two thirds of college entrants graduate even when all delays and transfers are taken into account. By contrast, in Oxford or Cambridge 97 or 98% graduate. In Britain, generally, the straight and narrow path to a degree for the highly selected minority in full-time attendance is paralleled and shadowed by other routes to the same destination—part-time courses in technical and commercial colleges, and correspondence courses offering preparation for an external degree of the University of London. The London external degree acts as a safety valve against pressure for university education that cannot be satisfied in the "normal" way, that is, where the conditions of the English idea of a university cannot be met.

Consequently, taken as a whole, the emerging structure of the British system of higher education constitutes a response to the pressures of the scientific culture. However, it is so dominated by its history that it forms a "pyramid of prestige" [51] of institutions fixed in the hierarchy according to their distance from the pure model of the English university, which Oxford and Cambridge, in practice, most closely resemble in their aims and organization.

## Education and Society

### Education and Stratification

Education has always been closely related to class, status, and power; but this relationship has radically changed in character since World War I. Education has become part of the economic foundations of modern society—a major avenue of social mobility, a central agency of social distribution and, consequently, an object of political debate and social policy as urgent and as important as poverty, sickness, or unemployment.

Society may be considered as an apparatus of controlled allocation of rewards and facilities. Of course, social control of the distribution of life, liberty, and happiness is neither absolute in fact nor completely possible in principle. Nowhere do men exercise complete control over the means of

[51] See my "A Pyramid of Prestige," *Universities Quarterly*, September, 1961, pp. 341–345.

satisfaction, nor do they always even understand the consequences of voluntary social action designed to promote their own welfare. Partial control over social distribution is, however, essential to the idea of civil society. The problem of social consensus arises directly out of the necessity of this kind of control.

There are many principles in terms of which allocations can be made. One is the principle of equality. It is an increasingly powerful idea, deeply rooted in the history of politics and religion, and a ubiquitous point of moral reference in human affairs. Yet its meaning is imprecise, and its application is resisted by complex forces of will and circumstance. No known society has ever been unequivocally egalitarian by any reasonable definition: the concept in relation to social structures is a relative one—a yardstick by which to gauge variations in inequality. At least two distinguishable kinds of egalitarianism have been important in political movements. One is primarily concerned with rewards, the other with opportunities. The first is focused on the ultimate results of social distribution: it seeks equality directly in restriction of the range of distribution in income, wealth, health, and power. The second is "liberal," concentrating not on the ultimate structure of rewards, but on the rules of competition for them: it seeks equality of opportunity irrespective of whether this implies facilities for men to become the same or different from one another. In short, egalitarianism may be directed primarily to rewards or to opportunities.

Education is significant for equality in both senses, although most discussions and nearly all proposals for educational reform have hinged on the principle of educational equality of opportunity. In fact, education is part of both structures of distribution. It is a consumption as well as a production good: indeed, in all but advanced industrial societies it is a part of a more or less ascribed style of life rather than an opportunity to achieve a new social position; and even in an advanced industrial society, education is often considered as a mechanism whereby an ascribed status deriving from family, class, or race is converted into an achieved status in the occupational sphere. In other words, while the response to educational opportunity is largely a function of family and class position, the rewards of one generation are readily converted into the opportunities of the next generation. Moreover, in education, as in other mechanisms of social distribution, change in the structure of opportunity causes change in the structure of rewards, and vice versa. For example, where primary education is rapidly expanded (as has recently been the case in many new African states), literacy declines in marketable value and, more generally, where educational opportunities are widened, differential income between skilled and unskilled work is reduced. Conversely, where incomes rise (as in the industrial countries of Europe and America), there is generated a demand for higher educational standards of living.

Therefore, in order to decide the significance of education for equality, it is necessary to examine three broad aspects of social stratification. First, the structure of rewards: What and how much is socially distributed? Second, the structure of opportunities: How are life chances distributed? Third, the distributive role of education: To what extent and in what manner are rewards and opportunities allocated through education?

The notion of socially distributed rewards is as complex as the myriad satisfactions sought by men in society through their economic, political, religious, familial, and cultural relationships. Comprehensive measurement is certainly beyond the compass of social science. It involves a total evaluation of the quality of human life and implies ultimately a definition of what constitutes a good society. In practice, measurement must be partial and simplistic—that is, confined to such measures as capital, income, life expectancy, political enfranchisement, social mobility, freedom of religious affiliation, and the like. This kind of crude and imperfect measurement sets close limits to evaluate inferences concerning the human value of one society or period as against another. Nevertheless, if due regard is paid to these limitations, economic and social indices of wealth, health, and freedom can offer some guidance both in the ordering of our conception of society and in the framing of social policy. Certainly the limitations are not totally misleading, in that most men in most countries prefer to have more rather than less wealth, health, leisure, and choice of association. Moreover, the use of only a small number or even only one of the possible indices of socially distributed rewards does not necessarily mean that the others are wholly ignored. This is especially true of the economic indices. Wealth, in fact, is within broad limits translatable into a wide range of physical, political, and cultural satisfactions.

Nevertheless, the amount of economic wealth created by a society clearly affects the significance of the degree of inequality of its distribution. About two thirds of the world's population enjoy less than one third of the world's income and live in about one hundred countries in which no possible internal redistribution could alter the characteristic life chances of the average individual.[52] The immediate prospect for the ordinary human being is one of poverty, ill health, and illiteracy or semiliteracy.

---

[52] See Adam Curle, *Educational Strategy for Developing Societies* (London: Tavistock Publications, 1963), p. 39. "In the decade ending 1959 per capita income in the approximately 100 under-developed nations of the world increased by around $10 from about $90 to slightly over $100, but this has to be set against an increase in Holland of over $300, in United Kingdom, Western Germany and Switzerland of $400 and in United States and Canada of more than $500."

The countries that are escaping or have recently escaped from these conditions are also the ones that have mass secondary education and expanding systems of higher education. International inequalities of wealth are correlated with educational inequalities. However, to state the correlation is not to postulate that education is either the cause of international inequality or the necessary and sufficient means toward international equality. Actually, the causal relation between education and national economic growth is an intricate one, varying with the stage of development and the types of economy on the other hand, and the structure of educational systems on the other.

However, two sociological generalizations can be made concerning this relationship. The first hinges on the meaning of the word "ability" and the traditional assumption in education that ability is considered as the property of individuals which, once measured, indicates an appropriate form of education. Modern psychological research tends to redefine ability, not as a unitary concept or capacity, but as a whole range of human skills and excellences—literate, numerate, and manual. Thus, refinement or differentiation of the measures used, a widening of the curriculum of schools, or indeed any change in the demand that the society puts on its members will reveal new abilities among them.[53] In fact, not one ability but many abilities must be sought in a program designed to educate talent. In other words, intelligence and other human capacities must be considered less as the qualities of individuals and more as social or cultural products. Consequently, investment in education as a means of satisfying the manpower requirement of economic growth is not a simple one-way process. Increased resources make it possible to mobilize new reserves of talent. We are therefore led to the conclusion that the higher the national income per head enjoyed by a country, the greater is the amount of human ability that can, in practice, be made available for mobilization.

The second generalization is that within societies, whether as cause or effect of other social forces, educational inequality is greater in poor countries than in rich ones. As we noted earlier, the educational elite of the new nations tend to form a tiny minority of the privileged and powerful, cut off from the mass of illiterate peasants and workers, and having more in common with their Western contemporaries than with their fellow nationals. In the underdeveloped countries, education can only be considered as an inegalitarian force separating small elites from large masses.

In Western industrial countries the relation between equality and educa-

---

[53] See A. H. Halsey, ed., *Ability and Educational Opportunity* (Paris: Organization for Economic Cooperation and Development, 1961), p. 24.

tion is less clear. First, these societies are rich—they generate rewards on an unprecedented scale. Second, compared with the poor countries, both rewards and opportunities are more equally distributed within them. Literacy is almost universal and therefore of no market significance. Poverty within them is of a qualitatively different kind, and is confined to minorities.[54] On the other hand, because the rich countries depend upon complicated industrial and technical processes that demand skilled and competent workers, the lack of education involves a severe penalty. Thus, in the United States, unemployment is heavily concentrated among persons who have not completed secondary schooling: occupations that require a college education have the lowest rates of unemployment. A rising minimum of educational qualification is required for membership in the affluent economy.

At the same time, the pressure toward educational expansion is strongly reinforced by claims to equality of access on the part of the traditionally underprivileged. The claim is partly moral—the right of the individual to be afforded opportunity for the attainment of his full human stature. It is also associated with the tendency of industrial societies to legitimize social positions by tests of competence or qualification as opposed to ascribed or traditional or inherited right. The principle of formal equality of educational opportunity is now universally regarded as a moral right in the advanced industrial countries. This emerging educational revolution in the social policies of industrial countries is linked historically with earlier efforts in other fields of social welfare. In the second half of the nineteenth century there was a change in the outlook of many European countries concerning the problem of material poverty. When economic advance brought about the possibility of the abolition of material poverty, it was gradually redefined as a moral evil to be eliminated by enlightened public action. Today, with the further advance of affluence and the gradual development of knowledge about the determinants of educability, education is beginning to occupy a position as the object of social policy which is analogous to the position once held by poverty, sickness, unemployment, and the other social ills of industrial society. For example, education plays a prominent role in modern political programs in the United States that are directed toward ensuring equal citizenship for Negroes and toward eradicating the disabilities of other "culturally deprived" groups.

Meanwhile, as social policy has been directed toward the educational status of the powerless, the changing relation of education to stratification has also transformed the nature of elites.

[54] See Margaret Gordon, ed., *Poverty in America* (San Francisco: Chandler Publishing Co., 1965).

## Education and Power

For traditional elites in European society, educational institutes such as the German law faculties, the French *grandes écoles,* or the English public schools and ancient universities, have played a characteristic role for the rising generation of established privilege groups. These institutions have been vehicles for the preservation, transmission, and renewal of the styles of life, lines of communication, intermarriage, and social freemasonry of the elevated strata *"dont on parle."*

But the twentieth century has witnessed fundamental changes in the formation and function of elites. These changes have not occurred so much through the expansion of the function of schools and universities as promoters of mobility for the gifted sons of the masses, thereby giving them a legitimate status claim to assimilation into the elite; this, after all, was a function—if a minor one—of advanced education wherever it has existed. The changes are more a question of the differentiation and expansion of elite groups, less closely knit in their familial and educational origins and connections, with specialized economic and social functions deriving from the increasingly complex technological basis of society. From the point of view of the individual, education tends to become mastery of an expertise, and *scientia est potestas.* Thus, for example, during the course of the century, an organized community of scientists and technologists has emerged in the industrial countries and, mainly through military and economic planning, has been drawn into government and into the direction of large-scale industrial enterprise. These "new men" of knowledge are drawn increasingly into decision making in contemporary society. Whether or not a "power-elite" thesis is accepted concerning the politics of the modern state, there can be no doubt that science and technology have become not merely the instrument but also an important object of social policy, and with this development new elements are created among the elite strata.

This does not mean, however, that advanced industrialism necessarily generates technocracy and far less a generalized meritocracy. The historical conditioning of the distribution of power in particular countries results in one or another kind of accommodation between established and emergent elites. In Russia the accommodation seems to take the form of control by the political elite over bureaucratic industrial and military organizations. In France the technocratic traditions instituted by Napoleon in the *grandes écoles* are closely assimilated to the metropolitan and governmental elite. In England the amateur and classical traditions of Oxford and Cambridge have largely contained the expansion of science and technology and have subordinated the "expert" to a relatively subservient role among higher officialdom and large-scale industrial enterprise.

The role of education in the formation of new elites in the new or under-developed countries is especially dramatic. Not only is education a force that separates the new rich and powerful from an illiterate mass, but the modernizing elite is heavily recruited from those with educational experience in European and American schools and universities. Consequently, the problems that all new nations face in establishing acceptable forms of government are exacerbated by wide cultural differences between the people in power and their supporters in popular political movements. Correspondingly, within the elite groups, there is an enormous emphasis on the importance of education; and there is considerable tension between a desire, on the one hand, to incorporate elements of the traditional culture in the educational systems of these new countries and, on the other hand, the concern of governments to emulate and incorporate the scientific and technological culture of the Western countries as a means to modernization.

## Equality of Educational Opportunity

The goal of educational equality of opportunity is practically universal in the industrial countries, and may be thought of in terms of establishing a natural order of inequality based only on differences of innate capacity. This definition, however, can be no more than a touchstone. In reality, an infant enters the social world with an ascribed position, which forms the basis for his subsequent achievements. The process of selection through education must be viewed as a cumulative interplay of ascription and achievement—including even the achievement of that common measure of innate capacity, the intelligence quotient. Thus the retrospective right of adults to have been educated up to the limits of their capacity can mean very different things, according to the degree to which social class enters into the process of defining capacity and educational performance.

In considering the distinction between ascription and achievement, it is important first to recognize that the legitimation of role allocation in advanced industrial societies is more and more in terms of achievement, but that the actual processes of role allocation are weighted heavily toward preserving stability of status level between different generations of the same family. We have referred to Parsons' emphasis on the role of the school in America as an agent for the indoctrination of achievement values,[55] but

[55] Talcott Parsons (cited in footnote 7), p. 436. This part of the article deserves quoting here:

The evidence also is that the selective process is genuinely assortative as in virtually all comparable processes ascriptive as well as achieved factors influence the outcome. In this case the ascriptive factor is the socio-economic status of the child's family and the factor underlying his opportunity for achievement in his individual ability.

The essential points here seem to be that there is a relatively uniform criterion of

judging by the results of social selection and allocation in the system as a whole, the fundamental question appears to be why, despite this role (which Parsons analyzes convincingly in his treatment of the school class), there should continue to be such a close relation between filial and parental status.

To explain the relationship, that is, to explain why educational systems, although legitimized in terms of equality of opportunity, actually act as the agents for the perpetuation of inequality, it is necessary to examine the social determinants of both opportunity and performance.

### Social Determinants of Educability

First, the principle of formal equality of opportunity is not universally applied. There are legally segregated schools, for example, in South Africa. Second, there are many social influences that distribute educational resources in favor of the higher strata of society. Private fee-paying establishments such as the English public schools favor the rich against the poor. Residential segregation results in school segregation between whites and Negroes in many American communities. Urban and rural inequalities of school provision have similar effects in many countries.

Forces of this kind are obvious and unsubtle. The more subtle influences are those that operate within a framework of formal equality of opportunity. These influences appear as cumulative determinants of educability, and arise out of the learning experience of the child not only in school but in his family and neighborhood. Their effect is to produce a close link between the educational performance of parents and children, and persistent differences between social class and racial groups. They include various cultural ingredients of the differences between social classes, such as the role of language in the development of capacity to use abstractions, the social distance between teacher and pupil, the level of educational aspiration, the definition of roles in the school, and the nature of peer groups in childhood and adolescence.

One way to approach the problem of educability is to think of education as establishing new kinds of communication over unfamiliar social differ-

selection operating to differentiate between the college and the non-college contingents and that for a very important part of the cohort the operation of this criterion is not a "put up" job—it is not simply a way of affirming a previously determined ascriptive status to be sure the high status, high ability boy is very likely indeed to go to college and the low status, low ability boy is very unlikely to go, but the "cross pressured" group for whom these two factors do not coincide is of considerable importance. Consideration like these lead me to conclude that the main process of differentiation, which from another point of view is selection, that occurs during elementary school takes place on a single main axis of achievement. Broadly, moreover, the differentiation leads up through higher school to a bi-vocation of college-goers and non-college-goers.

ences. These distances are created in the modern world by parochial mentality, limited class horizons, poor motivation, and noneducational aims. For example, the educational and vocational aspirations of a Negro-slum child are limited from the child's point of view by the remoteness of edutional stimulation in his daily life and neighborhood. Similarly, rural backwardness in education is more instructively viewed as a problem of social rather than geographical distance. Social distance again hinders parents' understanding of the educational purposes of a secondary school or college if their children are the first generation to attend such an institution.

But the key variable in social determination of educational success is social class. Much of the relatively poor performance of Negro children can be accounted for in class terms. Children from materially and culturally impoverished backgrounds are ill equipped to take advantage of what the school can offer. For example, Bernstein has shown that linguistic capacity is retarded by the culture of working-class community and family life through the use of what he calls a "public" as distinct from a "formal" language. A public language uses a simple grammar and syntax to express emotions and injunctions; a formal language is a more elaborate language adapted to individual conceptualization and exploration of the social world. In groups of working-class children, scores on verbal tests are relatively lower than scores at the higher level of nonverbal tests.[56] Another study has shown that intelligence-test scores at successive ages increase for middle-class children and decrease for working-class children.[57] It seems that the very nature of the child's ability is profoundly influenced by his social environment.

Moreover, the interaction between family and school is structured along social class lines to reinforce class differences of educational achievement. In this connection, Jean Floud comments as follows.

Teachers may take for granted and find it reasonable to demand of all children the social equipment with which the average middle-class child tends to come to school; a certain capacity to assume responsibility, a relative independence of mind and breadth of interests. They may demand assumptions about life on the part of their pupils which are in fact "middle-class" assumptions; such as that life is one long progress towards ever deferred gratifications; that the present is always at a discount and the future at a premium; that one must have always a career rather than a job; that the popular pleasures purveyed by the mass-media are at best worthless and at worst sinful.

Schools, in fact, make all sorts of tacit social and cultural demands on children to which they are not all equipped to respond, and it is worth making the point that the tendency for the gap between the demands and assumptions

[56] B. Bernstein (cited in footnote 14).
[57] J. W. B. Douglas, *The Home and The School* (London: MacGibbon and Kee, 1964).

of the school and the skills and assumptions that the children bring with them is widening. This is partly because the social composition of our secondary schools is becoming increasingly representative of the population at large and they contain a substantial minority, in some areas a majority, of pupils from working-class homes. It is also because the effect of current competitive pressures is to load examination syllabi and push minimum standards of acceptable performance ever higher. Every year the dice are loaded more and more heavily against children from under-privileged homes and in favour of those who come with an initial set of cultural advantages in the shape of parental supports and pressures, which are in the same direction as those which the school expects them to be. The children from culturally impoverished homes can spend to-day less and less time on the pursuits which might conceivably mitigate the effects of their impoverished background, and the schools have at least two jobs to do in present circumstances. They have not merely to instruct their pupils up to an ever rising standard of competence; they have also to tackle for an increasing proportion of their pupils all sorts of educational tasks formally undertaken in a middle-class home by parents with at least some degree of education analogous to, or comparable with, that to which the child aspires or is entitled by virtue of his ability.[58]

## Measurement of Equality of Opportunity

For the purposes of measurement, social classes may be classified in terms of paternal occupation, and ability levels may be defined in terms of measured intelligence and/or previous academic performance. At a specified level of ability, social classes may then be compared in their rates of success at crucial points in the process of selection through the school system. Thus, European studies usually focus on the entry to selective secondary education,[59] and American studies focus on the entry to college.[60] By referring rates of entry to the size of the relevant age group in each social class, comparisons of "class chances" may be made between different periods and different countries.

Natalia Rogoff has distinguished three basic patterns of class chances: [61] "radical," "moderate," and "conservative." The radical and conservative patterns are extremes. In the radical pattern, ability alone determines access to

[58] Jean Floud in A. H. Halsey, ed., *Ability and Educational Opportunity* (Paris: Organization of Economic Cooperation and Development, 1961), pp. 34–35.

[59] See, for example, J. E. Floud, A. H. Halsey and F. M. Martin, *Social Class and Educational Opportunity* (London: Heinemann, 1956); and Alain Girard et al., "Enquete Nationale sur L'Entree en Sixieme et la Democratisation de L'Enseignement," *Population*, No. 1, 1963, p. 46.

[60] See Dael Wolfle, *America's Resources of Specialized Talent* (New York: Harper, 1954).

[61] Natalia Rogoff, "Public Schools and Equality of Opportunity," *Journal of Educational Sociology*, February, 1960, pp. 252–259.

higher education, irrespective of social class. In the conservative pattern, social class determines access to higher education, irrespective of ability. Neither of the extremes is ever found in practice: there is no totally "ascriptive" or totally "achievement" society; even the meritocracy is based on IQ *plus effort*. In the moderate pattern, both forces operate so that ability has an effect greater than or equal to social class in determining the probability of entry of an individual into higher education. The moderate pattern, represents a range of possibilities and actual circumstances tending from one extreme to the other. However, notice again that in fact all measures of ability, whether defined in terms of intelligence or attainment, are to some degree measures of social experience and therefore to some extent reflect the operation of ascriptive forces. Even so, the typical tendency, even in advanced industrial societies, is toward the conservative pole.

Two examples illustrate the tendency of the moderate pattern. In a study of the United States, Rogoff measured the relative influence of social class and ability and produced the results shown in Table 7.4. The numbers in the table are percentages of high school seniors who plan to attend college. The rows show that at each level of scholastic ability there is a reduction in the percentage of would-be college students at successively lower levels of family social status. Similarly the columns show that for any social-status level the less scholastically able are less inclined to go to college. Both family status and scholastic ability play a part in determining whether the individual will obtain education beyond high school. Previous studies had varied in the relative importance attributed to these two factors. This study, based on a nationwide sample, suggests that family status and scholastic ability have approximately equal weight.

Similarly, the British Robbins Report [62] contains evidence that at descending levels of social class, children of equal ability have reduced chances of entering higher education. The data are shown in Table 7.5. Column 1 shows that among children with intelligence quotients of 130 or more, the children of nonmanual workers have better than twice the chance of attending a full-time university-degree course compared with the children of manual workers. And the differential class chance is greater at the lower levels of intelligence. Again the pattern is moderate—both low-class origins and low intelligence reduce educational chances.

A comparison of the educational chances of Americans and Britons at specified levels of ability is not possible on the basis of these statistics. Neither the social-class classifications nor the measures of ability are the same. Moreover, it should be noted that both the class composition and the overall chances of higher education are different in the two countries.

[62] Her Majesty's Stationery Office, Cmnd. 2154, Appendix I, p. 43, Table 5.

Table 7.4  Percent of High-School Seniors Planning to Attend College, According to Scholastic Ability (in Quartiles) and Socio-educational Status of the Family [a]

| Scholastic-Ability Quartile | Family-Status Quintile | | | | | | |
| --- | --- | --- | --- | --- | --- | --- | --- |
| | (Top) 5 | 4 | 3 | 2 | (Bottom) 1 | All Quintiles | Number of Cases |
| (Top) 4 | 83 | 66 | 53 | 44 | 43 | 61 | (8647) |
| 3 | 70 | 53 | 37 | 29 | 29 | 44 | (8709) |
| 2 | 65 | 41 | 31 | 20 | 21 | 33 | (8696) |
| 1 | 53 | 30 | 22 | 16 | 18 | 24 | (8509) |
| All quartiles | 72 | 47 | 35 | 26 | 24 | 40 | |
| Number of cases | (6520) | (6647) | (6465) | (8116) | (6811) | | (34,561) |

[a] Students are classified according to their scholastic-aptitude quartile in their own high school. Family status position, however, is constant for all students coming from a given family background, no matter what the social composition of their high school. The number of cases on which each of the percentages is based ranges from 963 to 2505.
*Source.* A. H. Halsey, J. E. Floud, and C. A. Anderson, eds., *Education, Economy and Society* (New York: Free Press, 1961), p. 246.

**Table 7.5  Academic Achievement of Children at Maintained Grammar Schools: by IQ at 11 Plus and Father's Occupation; England and Wales; Children Born in 1940 and 1941**

| | Degree-Level Course (1) [a] | At Least Two "Advanced" Levels (2) [b] | At Least Five "Ordinary" Levels (3) [b] | Percentage | |
| --- | --- | --- | --- | --- | --- |
| | | | | Weighted Sample Numbers (= 100%) | Unweighted Sample Numbers |
| **IQ** | | | | | |
| **130 and over** | | | | | |
| *Father's Occupation* | | | | | |
| A. Nonmanual | 37 | 43 | 73 | 67 | 50 |
| B. Manual | 18 | 30 | 75 | 60 | 63 |
| A divided by B | 2.06 | 1.43 | 0.97 | | |
| **115–129** | | | | | |
| A. Nonmanual | 17 | 23 | 56 | 201 | 151 |
| B. Manual | 8 | 14 | 45 | 403 | 237 |
| A divided by B | 2.12 | 1.64 | 1.24 | | |
| **100–114** | | | | | |
| A. Nonmanual | 6 | 9 | 37 | 130 | 80 |
| B. Manual | 2 | 6 | 22 | 236 | 124 |
| A divided by B | 3.00 | 1.50 | 1.68 | | |

[a] The figures in column 1 relate to Great Britain, since the corresponding tabulation was not made for England and Wales alone. The weighted sample numbers on which this column is based are thus somewhat higher than those shown. Column 1 relates to those entering courses of degree level.

[b] Columns 2 and 3 relate to passes obtained at school. All those with 1 or more Advanced levels have been treated as having 5 or more Ordinary levels. Ordinary-level examinations are taken at 15 or 16 years and Advanced-level examinations at 17 or 18 years.

*Source.* Survey of 21-year-olds.

America has a considerably more "middle-class" population and a more expanded system of education. However, leaving aside the question of intelligence, an estimate of the distribution of class chances in the two countries is as shown in Table 7.6. The expanded American system appears to

**Table 7.6   Social Class Chances of Higher Education**

| Great Britain: Children Born in 1940 and 1941 [a] | | United States: Percentage of Each Group Entering College [b] | |
|---|---|---|---|
| | (%) | (%) | |
| Higher professional | 62 | 67 | Professional and semi-professional |
| Managerial and other professional | 25 | 50 | Managerial |
| Clerical | 13 | 48 | Sales, clerical, and service |
| Skilled manual | 7 | 26 | Manual |
| Semiskilled and unskilled manual | 4 | 24 | Farm |
| All children | 11 | | |

[a] *Source.* Robbins Report, Appendix I, p. 20, Table 2.
[b] *Source.* D. Wolfle in *Education, Economy and Society* (New York: Free Press, 1961), p. 230, Table 6.

offer considerably greater educational opportunities to the lower middle- and working-class population.

### Trends in Class Chances

In industrial societies, education traditionally has differentiated children along social class lines for entry into advantageous social positions. But both the economic and political pressures to which we have referred have resulted in a gradual expansion of educational provision from primary through secondary to higher education. Thus, the expansion of secondary education in the first half of the twentieth century transformed the primary schools into common schools accessible to all social classes. After World War I in America and after World War II in Europe, a similar movement began in the relation between secondary and higher education. Secondary schooling is now nearly universal in the United States. In Europe the same process has begun, but it is still sharply modified by distinctions in the quality of provision between schools leading to university entrance and terminal schools within the secondary system as a whole.

In an inquiry into education and social selection in England in 1952,[63] it was appropriate to consider entry to grammar schools as opposed to secondary modern schools as the crucial point of educational opportunity. Using entry to grammar schools as the measure of opportunity in the early 1950's, class chances decreased from nearly 1 to 1 for the children of the professional and business-owning and managing classes through 1 to 2 or 1 to 3 for the children of white-collar workers to 1 to 6 for skilled workers and to 1 to 10 for unskilled workers. During the subsequent decade, a slow modification of the English secondary system has taken place with slight increase in the provision of grammar school-type courses, either in grammar schools or comprehensive schools, and through the extension of secondary modern school courses to enable children to take General Certificate of Education (G.C.E.) qualification examinations, which have two levels, "Ordinary" and "Advanced," given at different ages. Thus the proportion of the 17-year-old age group in school rose from 6.6% in 1950 to 7.9% in 1954 and to 12% in 1962. The proportion attaining five or more "Ordinary" level passes in G.C.E. rose from 10.7% in 1954 to 15.3% in 1961. There are no data on the changes in class chances in secondary education but, in discussing this issue, the authors of the Robbins Report have concluded that "if there were data on the educational attainment of school children in each social class in, say, 1950 and in 1960, this would probably now show a great narrowing of social class differences." [64]

Evidence relating to developments in France during the 1950's show a somewhat different picture (Table 7.7). In 1953 a national survey of France showed that class chances of secondary education varied systematically with social status, from 87% of the children of professionals to 13% of the children of agricultural laborers. The 1959 reform of the structure of secondary education included the development of long courses in *collèges d'enseignement général* from which transfer can be made to the lycées at a later stage. If the C.E.G. courses are added to those at the traditional lycées, then it appears that between 1953 and 1962 the proportion of all children entering secondary courses (*entrée en sixième*) rose from 30 [65] to 55%. The expansion was accompanied by marked reduction in differential class chances of secondary education. Thus, comparing the professional and unskilled groups, in 1953 the chances of children in the professional

[63] J. E. Floud et al. (cited in footnote 59).

[64] Robbins Report, Appendix I, Cmnd. 2154-I, p. 52. See also A. Little and J. Westergaard, "The Trend of Class Differentials in Educational Opportunity in England and Wales," *British Journal of Sociology*, 15 (4), 301–316 (December, 1964).

[65] The earlier inquiry excluded the Department of the Seine and the children attending the *Sixième* in public and private secondary schools. It is estimated that correction for these omissions would raise the figure for the whole age group to 35%, but would not alter the distribution of class chances.

Table 7.7    Social Class Chances of Entry to Secondary Education in France in 1953 and 1962 (Percent)

| | | September, 1962 | | |
| Father's Occupation | October, 1953 (1) | C.E.G. (2) | Lycées (3) | Total |
|---|---|---|---|---|
| Agricultural laborers | 13 | 21 | 11 | 32 |
| Farmers | 16 | 24 | 16 | 40 |
| Unskilled workers | 21 | 29 | 16 | 45 |
| Tradesmen, artisans | 39 | 34 | 32 | 66 |
| Clerks | 45 | 34 | 33 | 67 |
| Lower-grade officials | 81 | 29 | 55 | 84 |
| Industrialists | 68 | 28 | 57 | 85 |
| Professionals | 87 | 18 | 75 | 93 |
| Senior officials | 86 | 19 | 75 | 94 |
| All | 30 | 28 | 27 | 55 |

*Source.* Alain Girard et al., "Enquête Nationale sur L'Entrée en Sixième et la Democratisation de l'Enseignement," *Population,* 1963, No. 1, p. 46.

group were four times better than the chances of children in the unskilled group, and in 1962 these chances were reduced to twice as good, although if only the lycées are considered there was an increase in the differential from four times to nearly five times.

In Britain the trend in differential class chances of entry to full-time higher education in the period 1928 to 1960 again shows a static picture (Table 7.8). The proportion of boys aged 18 entering universities in the

Table 7.8    Percentage of Boys Aged 18 in 1928 to 1947 and 1960, Entering a University in Britain: By Social Class

| | Boys Aged 18 in: | |
| Social Class | 1928–1947 | 1960 |
|---|---|---|
| | (%) | (%) |
| A. Nonmanual | 8.9 | 16.8 |
| B. Manual | 1.4 | 2.6 |
| C. All boys | 3.7 | 5.8 |
| A divided by B | 6.4 | 6.5 |

*Source. Robbins Report,* Appendix I, Cmnd. 2154-I, p. 54.

period 1928 to 1947 was 3.7% and had increased by 1960 to 5.8%. The chances of entry for boys of all classes had roughly doubled, leaving the situation in 1960 as it was earlier: one in which the child of a nonmanual worker had six and one half times the chance of entry to a university of that of a boy from the manual working class.

Estimates by Havighurst for the United States during the period from 1920 to 1960 indicate that a trend a little more like the trend in French secondary education in the 1950's had been taking place in American higher education (Table 7.9). Havighurst distinguishes four strata; com-

Table 7.9    **Percentage of a Given Social Class Who Enter College in the United States**

| Social Class | 1920 | 1940 | 1960 Male | 1960 Female |
|---|---|---|---|---|
| Upper and upper-middle | 40 | 80 | 85 | 70 |
| Lower-middle | 10 | 20 | 55 | 35 |
| Upper-lower | 2 | 5 | 25 | 18 |
| Lower-lower | — | — | 10 | 5 |

*Source.* R. J. Havighurst, *American Higher Education in the 1960's* (Columbus: Ohio State University Press, 1960), p. 35.

paring boys in the upper-middle and upper-lower strata, the differential chances in 1920 were 20 to 1; for the upper and upper-middle class the differential chances more than doubled in the case of boys by 1960, and the differential chances between this class and the upper-lower class in the same year had been reduced to a little more than 3 to 1. These estimates are only approximate ones, and do not take into account either the differences in average quality of higher education in Britain and America, nor of the very much higher drop-out rates in the American system. Nevertheless, other studies have shown that there is very little relation between social class and probability of drop-out from college, when allowance is made for measured intelligence. All in all, then, we can conclude with some confidence that during the past generation, in a much more expanded system of higher education, there has been a much greater reduction in differential class chances in America than in Britain.

In summary, we can conclude that the principle of equality has a powerful and persistent appeal. It forms a ready expression of the aspirations of the powerless individuals, and a moral threat to those who exercise privilege. Its influence is reinforced in advanced industrial society by the impersonal demands of the economy for efficiency, for a fluid labor force, and for rational allocation of jobs by tests of fitness to fill them. No matter what the actual processes are through which men find their way into an occupation, men's fortune or misfortune increasingly tends to be legitimized by external criteria of competence. Hence the emergence of education as a central agency of social distribution, and hence its prominence in political as well as economic discussion. Education in modern society carries the burdens both of creating and maintaining an efficient labor force and of justifying the selective process in order to ensure consensus on the distribution of unequal life chances.

In view of these economic and political circumstances, the tendencies toward equality of opportunity, which reveal themselves in modern empirical studies of the relation between education and stratification, are not in the least surprising. What is sociologically interesting in the statistics is not so much the strength of the economic and political pressure toward equality but the power of other social and biological factors to contain these tendencies. The range of theoretically possible social systems extends from pure caste conditions, in which roles are allocated by ascription and intergenerational mobility is zero, to the opposite pole where all social positions are open and mobility is "perfect" in the sense of a random relation between parental and filial status. In the real world an approximation to pure caste has existed in societies living by a simple and static preindustrial technology. But the pressure of advanced industrialism toward the limit of perfect mobility is very much weaker and, despite the legitimation of role allocation by "achievement," a strong association between parental and filial status persists. Certainly the patterns of opportunity in the industrial countries are, in Natalia Rogoff's terms, "moderate" but they usually tend toward the "conservative" model.

The possibility of further movement toward the "radical" extreme clearly exists. There are obvious substantive barriers to equality of opportunity everywhere, which are in principle removable, although they imply additional incursions into the autonomy of the family. But the more these tendencies develop, the more urgent becomes the issue of what equality implies for the ordering of social relationships. And, particularly, these tendencies raise the questions (1) of the degree to which occupational status is necessarily generalized into social status (that is, the connection between posts and persons), and (2) of the supremacy of *merit* for the sake of economic efficiency as compared with *need* for the satisfaction of citizenship claims. In other words, the issue finally narrows down to the meaning of the notion of a classless society. In turn, for education, the question hinges on the compatibility of playing the dual role of differentiating a specialized labor force and, at the same time, integrating a common culture.

These questions have been faced by Michael Young in a brilliant essay on the rise of the meritocracy.[66] Young attacks the political principle of equality of opportunity, and advances the case for direct equality, and he does this by an ingenious elaboration of the consequences of pursuing the principle of equality of opportunity in a modern technological society. He assumes that psychometric measurement of intelligence and attainment can be translated directly into position in the hierarchy of social stratification. The short-term results are an increased social mobility toward a more random relation between parental and filial status, the decline of gerentocracy, and an increase in the efficiency of education as a training apparatus for a modern economy. But the long-run results are the creation of genetically different social strata through educational selection and the genetic basis of measured intelligence, together with assortative mating according to intelligence. Social mobility, of course, is left in the system through the operation of the regression phenomenon and the variability of inheritance. The weakness of the thesis is that it begs an important question in its assumption that intelligence can be measured and translated into social positions. As Young says:

This vicious circle—the vagueness of merit leading to its rejection—was only broken when the means of selection employed in the schools were adapted for use in the economy. Intelligence tests and aptitude tests were objective, and a good deal more reliable than the older forms of examination which they supplemented. The first stage, as we have seen, was for the level of performance achieved in the tests (when taken together with the level of education with which the test results were correlated) to determine the level of entry into industry. Once people were ready, it was then but a step to extend the sway of the tests until the markings controlled promotion as well as selection.[67]

In fact, while a genetic base to individual differences in intelligence is reasonably well established, there is also a powerful set of social forces determining measured intelligence which, in large measure, accounts for the differences between social groupings, and if this is true for IQ, it is even more true for effort. The sociological problem is precisely to unravel the complex effects of social structure on educational performance.

On the other hand, the strength of Young's essay is that it points directly to the dangers for consensus that are implicit in a society which overemphasizes the selective role of education for the economy despite, or even because of, the application of the principle of equality of opportunity, and underemphasizes the integrative role of education with its principle

[66] M. Young, *The Rise of the Meritocracy 1870–2033* (London: Thames and Hudson, 1958).
[67] *Ibid.*, p. 73.

of equality not only of opportunity but also directly of reward. Attempts to solve this problem will occupy an important place in the future both of the sociology of education and of social policy.

## Summary and Conclusions

Education has two basic functions: it transmits culture between generations and socializes individuals into particular cultures. In performing these two functions, education contributes to social integration, but its role in this respect varies according to the type of society and the rate of social change. In static societies with a simple culture, education is a conservative agent. But in complex societies undergoing change or development, education may give rise to division or conflict; and, in the advanced industrial societies, education becomes a source of cultural and therefore of social change. This means that cultural transmission is a process that differentiates in complex societies so as to include not simply preservation of a traditional culture but the systematic invention of new culture and its dissemination to a wider range of social groups. In its ultimate development, cultural innovation (especially in science) becomes, in effect, an apparatus of self-transformation. In this way, education becomes a vital institution of modern society.

In primitive societies, education is not formally organized, but is carried on by kinship. The teaching of skills and values remains an important function of the family in all societies and, even where formal educational organization develops, education often assumes a quasifamilial form (for example, in apprenticeship). However, as culture becomes more complex, educational organization becomes more formalized, more large-scale in nature, and more specialized. Moreover, in the industrial societies, cultural innovation becomes institutionalized on a large scale in higher education and in the research and development organizations of industry and government.

The culture of industrialism is of such nature that education must be extended to wider sections of the population. In nonindustrial societies, higher education is a luxury afforded to a privileged minority of the upper strata or to an intellectual elite of priests or literati. In advanced industrial societies, education takes on the characteristics of a production good: it becomes a necessary investment in the training of individuals as members of the labor force of a modern economy. Thus, in industrial society, the educational and economic systems are comprehensively linked with education organized to produce both new technology through research and professional and scientific manpower through training.

This connection between education and a modern complex economy further implies that the task of occupational and therefore social selection is increasingly centered on the school. The modern school distributes life chances. Therefore, it is not surprising that educational opportunity becomes an object of wide political concern in industrial and industrializing countries. And the economic forces that demand higher educational standards also make possible the realization of political aspirations that lead to a higher educational standard of living. These two forces, together, underlie the characteristic tendency in industrial countries toward expansion of educational systems.

The Western European and North American countries, which led the industrialization movement, are consequently passing through three broad stages of educational development. In the first stage, which began in the second half of the nineteenth century, universal primary schooling was established. In the second stage, which ended in the United States by World War II, universal secondary schooling was developed. And, finally, a third stage of advancement toward universal higher education appears to be underway in contemporary America.

Clearly, educational expansion eases the strains of educational selection, but it does not eliminate them. The problem of "who shall be educated" remains. Analysis of this problem reveals two important facts about modern society. First, the idea of equality of educational opportunity has become firmly rooted in both public opinion and government policy. But, second, the strength of social forces from both outside and inside of the educational system is sufficient to ensure a high level of stability in the relative educational status of fathers and sons. The background of an individual in family, neighborhood, ethnic group, and social class remains as important as the school in determining educational achievement. Removal of barriers such as segregation and fee-paying does not eliminate educational inequalities. Instead, barriers of opportunity become differences of educability with substantially similar social distribution. The trend in most countries is toward more public control over the destinies of children and away from the autonomy and continuity of the family. It is a trend from "ascription" to "achievement," a trend in the direction of meritocracy, guided by the tightening link of education to the economy.

Much of the energy of sociologists of education is now directed toward understanding the social influences on learning. With understanding comes the possibility of control. But there are still questions that are to be answered. How will control be used? What kind of society will be aimed at as knowledge accumulates? These questions take us beyond the province of the sociologist.

# 8

# POLITICAL SOCIOLOGY

*Seymour Martin Lipset*

# POLITICAL SOCIOLOGY

E ver since the term sociology was first applied, the analysis of political processes and institutions has been one of its most important concerns. Sociologists argue and many political scientists agree that it is difficult to study political processes except as special cases of more general psychological and sociological relationships. In recent years many political scientists elaborated and tested many politically relevant aspects of social science theory. The term political sociology has come to be accepted both within sociology and political science as encompassing the overlap between the two parental disciplines.

Within political science, such work is often described as the behavioral or social science approach, but political sociology is of fairly recent vintage as a major subfield within sociology; there were few courses or books that used the term before World War II. Yet the linkage and overlap between sociology and political science date back, in fact, to the formal origins of both disciplines in the late nineteenth century. In Europe, the work of Weber, Michels, Mosca, Pareto, and Siegfried was relevant to the emerging concerns of what eventually became two fields and, in the United States, it is debatable whether various scholars were sociologists or political scientists. Thus, one review contends that the major sociologists in the late nineteenth century "were, for the most part, political sociologists, or, it may even be said, sociological political scientists." [1] It calls attention to the fact that William Graham Sumner's chair at Yale was called "political and social science," and that Lester Ward, the first President of the American Sociological Society, wrote much on politics and urged that "government . . . had to be equated with society." [2] Franklin Giddings had been a professor of politics before holding the first chair of sociology at Columbia University (1894), a career pattern that was somewhat similar to that followed by another "father" of American sociology, Edward A. Ross. Albion Small came close to being a "pure sociologist," but he had taught constitutional history at Johns Hopkins for many years before creating at Chicago the first independent sociology department in the United States. After publishing his *General Sociology* (1905) he wrote a detailed study of the rise of European bureaucracies, *The Cameralists* (1909).

Conversely, a number of men who formulated basic concepts and methods in political science were closely identified with sociology during their academic careers. Arthur Bentley, whose classic work *The Process of Government* played a major role in introducing the concepts of interest

[1] Albert Lepawsky, "The Politics of Epistemology," *Proceedings of the Western Political Science Association* (supplement to *The Western Political Quarterly*, September 17, 1964), p. 32.
[2] *Ibid.*, p. 33.

group and process into political science, received his basic training in sociology, and his only academic appointment was as a member of the sociology department of the University of Chicago.[3] Stuart Rice, who received his doctorate in sociology under Giddings at Columbia, wrote a doctoral thesis that was the first to apply correlation techniques to the ecological analyses of voting, completed the first panel (repeat interview with the same people) election survey in 1924, made the first statistical studies of the behavior of American legislators, and co-related changes in party support over periods of time with fluctuations in the business cycle.

It is indicative also of the close relationship between sociology and political science in their early periods that sociology first appeared in the title of an American university department because the department had been forbidden to use its preferred terms, politics or political science. Frank Blackmar, the founder of the new social science department at the University of Kansas in 1889, called the department "History and Sociology," after the regents of the University had turned down "History and Politics" and "History and Political Science" on the grounds that there was enough politics in Kansas!

In the emergence of political sociology, one of the chief intellectual issues that had to be resolved was the conflict over the analytic primacy of *society* or the *state*. This controversy stemmed originally from the breakdown of the religious consensus of the Middle Ages, which had contained both political and social institutions within the same fabric. The church was supreme over all institutions, political or not. The rise of the bourgeoisie, the absolutist state, and the national church produced a crisis over the differentiation and the legitimacy of the state. Various social philosophers sought a secular basis for the legitimacy of state authority, which they found in Bodin's principle of sovereignty, while others questioned it entirely, arguing that the interests of society, of citizens, were superior to those of the state, that the state must serve rather than control man, and that it should be weakened rather than strengthened. In nineteenth-century Europe, men like Saint-Simon, Proudhon, and Marx took the side of society; for them it was the fabric that had to be strengthened and reinforced, while the state had to be limited and controlled by society. On the other side were Hegel and his followers, Lorenz von Stein and others, who believed that the solution lay in the subordination of society's disparate elements to the sovereignty of the state.

In the early period of American sociology and political science before

[3] Lepawsky points out that these concepts first appeared in the work of Albion Small, *ibid.*, p. 34. See Albion Small, *General Sociology* (Chicago: University of Chicago Press, 1905), pp. 209 ff.

World War I, leaders of both disciplines were concerned with this conflict, which arose from the fact that the two concepts, state and society, both were all encompassing. That is, political scientists pointed to the fact that the state has sovereignty—legitimate authority over all persons and institutions within its boundaries. And the notion of society was equally grandiose: all that came within the province of society, or a society, was part of it. To many early political scientists, much of what concerned the sociologist seemed to be a part of political science, while the sociologists took the opposite position. It was, in fact, the imperialistic claims of both fields that encouraged the overlap in the substantive concerns of men who placed themselves in one or the other discipline.

This controversy seems to have been outgrown, at least on an analytical level. The solution was to declare that the question had been asked in the wrong way. The error lay in dealing with the state and society as two potentially independent organisms, and in asking which was the more important. Social scientists increasingly agree that their concern is to study all of man's practices and institutions, and that while jurisdiction is divided, all fields still deal with behavior within the social system. Thus the political scientist is primarily concerned with the dimension of power and the factors affecting its distribution. Within different institutions, particularly the state, certain positions have a monopoly of legitimate power. The state has the most power and is, as Max Weber stressed, the one institution with the right to use force legitimately. The sociologist, on the other hand, is more concerned with social control, with the way in which the values and norms of a society pattern relationships among different units of the larger system. His emphasis is on social ties, rather than on formal structures and legal definitions.

Political sociology can be defined as the study of the interrelationship between society and polity, between social structures and political institutions. It is important to note that this definition does not assign causal priority to society over polity; political sociology is not solely the study of the social factors that condition the political order. Indeed, political institutions are themselves social structures, and hence are often the independent (that is, causal) factors that affect nonpolitical social structures. For example, there is a considerable body of literature that seeks to demonstrate that the way in which nations elect their executives and parliaments in large measure determines the number of parties and often the kind of parties that nations have. This, in turn, may affect the sense of group identification among diverse strata. That is, some writers suggest that nations that use a system of proportional representation (in which parties send the same percentage of members to parliament as they secure among the national electorate), rather than single-member districts as the United States or Britain uses, are likely to have a multiparty system. Under proportional representation, for example, a party that is supported by only 10% of the population will elect a noticeable number of representatives.[4] In the American system, however, it is always obvious that any new or small party cannot hope to elect a president or governor, and hence that a vote for the party is "wasted." This has made it difficult for "third parties" to get going in the United States, and consequently efforts to form parties based on class, religious, ethnic, or sectional interests, such as exist in many European countries, have always failed here.[5] If such groupings could elect significant numbers of candidates, they would become major sources of group identification; parties would maintain a "consciousness of kind," of common interest among their potential supporters. These political-identity groups are elements in the wider social structure. The formal institutions of the polity, therefore, do affect social structure.

The polity may be viewed as that part of the social system which is responsible for allocating the resources and facilities of the society. Obviously the various subgroups within society are concerned with the way such resources were allocated. Decisions made by those in control of the state necessarily bear unequally on groups and individuals. Consequently, there must be some mechanisms that lead individuals to accept the propriety of the decision-making system, that make them obey and carry out even decisions that they do not like. At the same time, since the various subgroups in the system disagree about the policies to be followed, polities must formulate mechanisms through which such groups can maximize their position, and through which they can bring pressure to bear on the decision-making structure. These two requirements of a polity—consensus about the propriety of the rules of the game, and ways of handling diverse interests and values—have been dealt with in sociology under the headings of legitimacy and cleavage. In this chapter, I shall report on some of the theoretical ideas and empirical research bearing on these two aspects.

The problem of legitimacy contains several issues. What are the different ways in which a polity can obtain legitimacy—"a built-in title to rule?" What are some of the various consequences of diverse forms of legitimacy,

[4] On proportional representation, see Karl Braunias, *Das parliamentarische Wahlrecht* (Berlin: Gruyter, 1932); F. A. Hermens, *Democracy or Anarchy?* (Notre Dame: University of Notre Dame Press, 1941); and Maurice Duverger, *L'influence des systèmes électoraux sur la vie politique* (Paris: Armand Colin, 1950).

[5] See E. E. Schattschneider, *Party Government* (New York: Rinehart, 1942), pp. 65–98.

of regimes having much or little of it? What are the ways in which a new polity or postrevolutionary political system can gain legitimacy? The next section deals first with different types of legitimacy, and then discusses the principal way in which the legitimacy of a regime can be strengthened: prolonged effectiveness. That section is followed by an analysis of the major institutional process through which democratic systems resolve the problems of cleavage: party systems and elections. Since a single chapter cannot adequately deal with all of the work bearing on this question, I have limited my discussion to a major factor connected with structural cleavage—class—and one linked to value differentiation—religion. The analysis of parties and elections raises the issue of the adequacy of representation: To what extent and in what ways are parties and blocs representative of the interests and values of their members or supporters? A considerable amount of sociological research has been devoted to analyzing this issue, some of which is reported on in the final section of this chapter.

## Legitimacy and Effectiveness

The stability of any given polity—its long-term ability to make decisions and secure adherence to them without the use of naked force—depends in large measure upon the legitimacy and effectiveness of its political system. Legitimacy involves the capacity of the system to engender and maintain the belief that the existing political institutions are the most appropriate ones for the society; effectiveness means actual performance, the extent to which the system satisfies the basic functions of government as most of the population and key powerful groups within it (such as the army and those who control the basic economic institutions) see them. While effectiveness is primarily instrumental, legitimacy is evaluative, linked to values.

There are basically three ways through which an authority may gain legitimacy, that is, an accepted "title to rule."

1. It may gain legitimacy through *tradition*, that is, through "always" having possessed it. The title held by monarchical societies is essentially of this type.

2. *Rational-legal* authority exists when those in power are obeyed because of a general acceptance of the appropriateness of the system of laws under which they have won and held office.

3. *Charismatic* authority rests upon faith in a leader who is believed to be endowed with great personal worth: this may come from God, as in

the case of a religious prophet, or may simply arise from the display of extraordinary talents.[6]

The contemporary world has witnessed many societies in which legitimacy is weak. A crisis of legitimacy is essentially a crisis of change. Crises of legitimacy have occurred in societies that are undergoing a transition to a new social structure; for example, from feudal agrarianism to capitalism, or from capitalism to some form of socialist, welfare, or planning state. New nations and postrevolutionary regimes, like those of France in 1789 or Russia in 1917, obviously all lack any claim to traditional legitimacy. Legal-rational legitimacy is weak in most such nations since the law had been identified with the interests of a foreign or domestic exploiter to much of the population.

Severe crises flowing from the weak sense of legitimate political authority are likely to occur in such polities if (1) the *status* of major traditional important groups is threatened during a period of structural change, and (2) if not all of the major groups in the society have access to the political system in the transitional period, or at least as soon as they develop political demands. To develop legitimacy, the new system must sustain the expectations of major groups (on the grounds of "effectiveness") for a long period, so that they may gain confidence in, and accept the propriety of, the "rules of the game" under which the new system operates.

Clearly the best way to avoid political tensions is to incorporate basic structural changes, while maintaining traditional legitimacy in political institutions. Notice that if we classify democratic states as stable or unstable according to the criteria of whether they have had the uninterrupted continuation of political democracy since World War I *and* whether there has been the absence in them during the past thirty years of a major political movement opposed to the democratic "rules of the game" (that is, no major fascist or communist parties), then we come up with the curious fact that ten out of the twelve or thirteen stable democracies in the world (those that fulfill these two requirements) are monarchies. Great Britain, Sweden, Norway, Denmark, The Netherlands, Belgium, Luxembourg, Australia, Canada, and New Zealand are kingdoms, or dominions of a monarch, while the only republics that meet the conditions of stable democracy are the United States, Switzerland, and possibly Uruguay.

[6] These are essentially the distinctions drawn by Max Weber. See H. H. Gerth and C. W. Mills, eds., *From Max Weber: Essays in Sociology* (New York: Oxford University Press, 1946), pp. 78 ff. I have discussed these ideas in my books *The First New Nation* (New York: Basic Books, 1963), pp. 16–17, and *Political Man* (New York: Doubleday Anchor Books, 1963), pp. 414–415.

In the first group, the preservation of the monarchy during the transition to a modern industrial society apparently retained for these polities the loyalty of the aristocratic, traditionalist, and clerical sectors of the population, even though these groups resented and resisted increased democratization and equalitarianism. In countries where monarchy was overthrown by revolution, and orderly succession was broken, the republican successor regimes have not been able to win legitimacy from all important sectors down to the fifth postrevolutionary generation or more.

The second general source of loss of legitimacy during periods of drastic social change arises from the ways in which different societies handle the "entry-into-politics" crisis—the decision as to when new social groups will obtain access to the political process. Whenever new groups become politically active (for example, when the workers first sought access to economic and political power), easy access to the *legitimate* political institutions has tended to win the loyalty of such new groups to the political system, and they, in turn, have permitted the old dominating institutions or strata (such as the monarchy or aristocracy) to maintain their *status*.

Political systems that deny new strata access to power except by drastic pressure or revolution also threaten legitimacy by introducing millennial (utopian or unattainable) hopes into the political arena. Groups that have to push their way into the body politic by force are apt to exaggerate the possibilities that political participation affords. Consequently, regimes born under such stress not only face the difficulty of being regarded as illegitimate by groups loyal to the *ancien regime* but may also be rejected by those whose millennial hopes are not fulfilled by the change. Today many of the newly independent states of Asia and Africa face the thorny problem of winning the loyalties of the masses to states that can do little to meet the utopian objectives set by nationalist movements during the period of colonialism and the transitional struggle of independence.

Given the legitimacy problems facing new nations and postrevolutionary societies, it is not surprising that many of them seem to find charismatic authority suited to their needs. Charisma (the cult of the leaders' personality), as a source of authority, is highly flexible and requires neither a long time to accrue nor a rational set of accepted rules. A charismatic leader is primarily the hero of the nation, who symbolizes in his person its values and aspirations. But more than this, he legitimates the new secular government by endowing it with his "gift of grace." [7] Charismatic authority, as exhibited in the leadership cults erected around

[7] See Richard M. Morse, "Political Theory and the Caudillo," in Hugh M. Hamill, Jr., ed., *Dictatorship in Latin America* (New York: Alfred A. Knopf, 1965), pp. 62–67.

Lenin and Stalin in the Soviet Union, Touré in West Africa, Nasser and Bourguiba in North Africa, Castro in Cuba, and Mao in China, can be seen as a mechanism of transition, an interim measure, which gets people to observe the requirements of the nation out of affection for the leader until they eventually learn to do it out of loyalty to the collectivity.

In my book, *The First New Nation*, I have argued that the early American Republic, like many of the contemporary new nations, was legitimized by *charisma*, although it also retained strong elements of rational-legal legitimacy carried over from the prerevolutionary provincial governments. We tend to forget nowadays that George Washington was idolized as much as many of the leaders of the new states of today. Unlike most of these leaders, however, he resisted the pressure from those close to him to become an autocrat. However, he deliberately took on an aspect of a constitutional monarch, recognizing that his most important contribution to the new state was to give it time to establish a government of men under law, which we now call a rational-legal system of authority. He permitted the members of his cabinet to form hostile factions under the leadership of Hamilton and Jefferson, even though he personally disliked the views of the Jeffersonians. Washington refused to take full advantage of his charisma, even withdrawing from the presidency voluntarily and seemingly in good health; in so doing, he pushed the American polity faster toward a legal-rational system of authority than would have developed if he had taken over the charismatic role *in toto*. The almost unique, half charismatic–half rational-legal leadership had a critical stabilizing effect on the society's evolution.

In new states or postrevolutionary regimes, legitimacy must be won through demonstrated effectiveness. Loyalty to the system must be attained through developing in the various groups a conviction that the new government is the best way—or at least an excellent way—to accomplish their objectives. The populace subjects even charismatic claims to a highly pragmatic test—that is, what is the payoff? For most such regimes today, demonstrating effectiveness means one thing: economic development. In view of the "revolution of rising expectations," the need for payoff in terms of economic goods and living standards is more important than ever. Payoff, however, need not be defined only in economic terms.

The polity may win general acceptance through enhancing national prestige. Thus, the French regime of the Fifth Republic has won considerable acceptance among left-wing intellectuals because DeGaulle's emphasis on France's position as a major nation and his insistence on the supremacy of French language and culture strongly appeal to the educated strata. Various foreign observers have testified to the extent to which Red China's defeat of the United States in the Korean War has appealed to the emotions of anti-communist Chinese, who rejoiced to see once-humble China humiliate a major white power.

During its first half-century of rapid economic growth and territorial expansion, the United States gradually acquired legitimacy as a result of being *effective*. There was no question that the new nation worked, that its economy had "taken off." Henry Adams, in his great history of the early years of the republic, considered the economic growth of the years 1800 to 1816 as crucial in guaranteeing the survival of the country. It "set at rest the natural doubts that had attended the nation's birth." [8]

In any attempt to analyze a nation's political stability in a crisis of effectiveness, knowledge of its level of legitimacy is decisive. The relationship between different degrees of legitimacy and effectiveness in specific political systems may be presented in the form of a fourfold table, with examples of countries characterizing each type:

|  | Effectiveness | |
|---|---|---|
|  | + | − |
| Legitimacy  +  | A | B |
| Legitimacy  −  | C | D |

Societies in Box A, which are high on both legitimacy and effectiveness, have stable political systems, as have the United States, Sweden, and Britain. Ineffective and illegitimate regimes, which fall in Box D, are unstable and liable to break down, unless they are dictatorships maintained by force, such as some of the governments of Eastern Europe, whose authority rests on the actual or latent presence of the Russian army. [9]

The political experience of different countries may illustrate the effect of various combinations. During the Great Depression of the 1930's those nations that were high on legitimacy could withstand a considerable decline in effectiveness. This was particularly true of the United States, which in relative terms was more severely affected economically by the depression than any other major country with the possible exception of Germany. In Europe, after World War I, Germany and Austria had political systems that were widely regarded as illegitimate but that were stable as long as they were reasonably effective economically. In terms

[8] Henry Adams, *History of the United States during the Administration of James Madison* (New York: Albert and Charles Boni, 1930), Book IX, pp. 172–173.
[9] Much of this discussion is taken from Chapter 3 of my book, *Political Man* (cited in footnote 6).

of the above table, they were in Box C. When the effectiveness of various governments broke down in the 1930's those European polities that were high in legitimacy remained democratic, while countries such as Germany, Austria, and Spain lost their freedom, and France narrowly escaped a similar fate. Or, to put the changes in terms of the table, countries that shifted from A to B remained democratic, while those that shifted from C to D broke down. The military defeat of 1940 underlined French democracy's low position on the scale of legitimacy. It was the sole defeated democracy that furnished large-scale support for a Quisling regime. And, more recently, the postwar Fourth Republic's ineffective handling of the Algerian problem resulted in the only successful military *coup d'état* in postwar Europe.

Various analysts have attributed the recurrent breakdowns in Latin America to the fact that few of their regimes have acquired legitimacy since their break with Spain and Portugal a century and a half ago. Lacking economic or symbolic effectiveness, these regimes have failed to achieve legitimacy, and hence are unable to withstand crises.[10] The various military coups in 1965 and 1966 in East Asia, the Arab areas, and Africa south of the Sahara also indicate the problems inherent in polities low in legitimacy that repeatedly face effectiveness crises. The political stability of those few Afro-Asian nations with traditional legitimacy, such as Ethiopia and Thailand, stands out in sharp contrast to the situation in nearby former colonial territories.

As recent history has demonstrated, the political behavior of the military poses a special problem for nations weak in legitimacy. Only the military have the internal organization, the sense of group loyalty, the authority and, most important, the means to overturn the government quickly whenever they find its acts repugnant. The strength of the norms governing civil-military relations are, therefore, of crucial importance in any consideration of the factors making for political stability. We may compare the need of the polity for powerful norms prescribing civilian control over the military to the need of the family for the incest taboo. Sociologists seeking to account for the universality of this taboo, for the great repugnance felt everywhere against incest (sexual relations among close relatives), have suggested that this ban is a vital requisite for a human society. They point out that within a family the older members are more powerful than the younger ones, and that the more powerful members —parents and older siblings—could take younger members as sexual partners. Since this is true, and the sex drive is also extremely strong, the

[10] See Martin C. Needler, *Latin American Politics in Perspective* (Princeton: Van Nostrand, 1963).

only way to avoid the threat to the stability of the family posed by the possibility of incest is the existence of a norm more powerful than all others, which fills people with a sense of horror, of great sin or evil, if it is violated. And in a comparable vein, we may suggest that the military can overturn regimes at will, and hence destroy the possibility of stable government. Polities, therefore, require a strong norm, which the military have absorbed, that insists on the separation of the political and military areas, no matter how much the military dislike the given policies of the government.

Inherent in the concept of legitimacy is military acceptance of civil authority. Hence, where legitimacy is weak, the taboo against military intervention in politics will also be weak, and we would expect to find the military taking part whenever the polity violates their concepts of right and wrong. Given this possibility, societies establish particularly strong norms which insist that officers must not violate their oath to obey the government. A considerable amount of symbolism and ritual is attached to the oath, the pledge of allegiance, of loyalty. The idea is drummed into the heads of professional soldiers that there is no higher virtue than obedience. (The emphasis on obedience, of course, is also linked to the need to make certain that men will obey their military superior in times of actual combat.) And reports of the deliberations of officers who have considered or been involved in coups indicate that they have often long delayed such actions because of their feeling that by violating their oath they were committing a heinous crime, that they were repudiating the honor of the military. Many German officers, who despised Hitler and the Nazis, and who were morally incensed at the crimes committed by the Nazis in murdering millions of Jews and others, still could not bring themselves to violate their oath.

Where legitimacy is weak, where armies do not have a tradition of accepting the authority of civilians, where they have shifted allegiance from one regime to another in the recent past as a result of the nation's gaining independence or a revolution, the commitment to the oath will be weak. And if such regimes are not only low in legitimacy but are relatively ineffective in handling domestic problems or in dealing with foreign powers, we may expect to find (as we have already noted) recurrent military coups. Recognition of this fact points to the need to consider the relationship between political systems and effectiveness. In contemporary society, effectiveness has most commonly been perceived in material terms in the level of economic development. Let us now consider the relationship between economic effectiveness and political systems.

## Economic Development and Political Systems

Instrumental effectiveness and legitimacy are much more decisive for democracies than for autocracies, since democracy rests on consensus. Democracy involves the highest degree of access to the decision-making structure by various groups and individuals in the polity. And in complex social systems, as Max Weber and Joseph Schumpeter stressed, the distinctive way in which such access is made possible is through the formation of the political elite (the office holders) in the competitive struggles for the votes of the electorate. In large-scale societies, democracy means an institutionalized competitive party system; in the absence of such a system, hardly anything limits the power of the political elite to ignore the desires of large segments of the population, or to use repressive methods.

Since democracy requires popular endorsement, it will also require prolonged effectiveness; that is, it must satisfy most of the people most of the time. Consequently, it is not surprising that the most common generalization linking political systems to other aspects of society has been that democracy is related to the state of economic development. The more well-to-do a nation is, the greater are the chances that it will sustain democracy. From Aristotle to the present, men have argued that only in a wealthy society with relatively few really impoverished citizens could the mass of the population intelligently participate in politics and develop the self-restraint necessary to resist irresponsible demagogues. A society divided between a large impoverished mass and a small favored elite results either in oligarchy (dictatorial rule of the small upper stratum) or in tyranny (popular-based dictatorship). To give these two political forms modern labels, tyranny's face today is Communism; oligarchy appears in the traditionalist dictatorships found in countries like Paraguay, Haiti, Thailand, Spain, or Portugal.

A number of different scholars have pointed to the statistical relationship between level of economic development, democracy, and the existence of democratic polities. These studies show that the more economically developed and literate a country is, the more likely it is to have a competitive party system.[11]

[11] See S. M. Lipset, *Political Man* (cited in footnote 9), pp. 48–67; James S. Coleman, "The Political Systems of the Developing Areas," in Gabriel Almond and James S. Coleman, eds., *The Politics of the Developing Areas* (Princeton: Princeton University Press, 1960), pp. 538–544; Everett Hagen, "A Framework for Analyzing Economic and Political Change," in Robert Asher, ed., *Development of Emerging Nations* (Washington: Brookings Institute, 1962), pp. 1–8; and Charles Wolf, Jr., *The Political Effects of*

Increased economic development and education may affect the nature of the polity in various ways. Following Aristotle's assumptions, notice that increased wealth will affect the shape of the stratification structure. In a poor underdeveloped country, the class structure may be pictured as an elongated pyramid with a very large lower-class base, a quite small middle class, and a tiny wealthy group. Economic growth will increase the size of the middle and upper strata and change the shape of the social hierarchy to a pyramid; while a highly developed technological society such as exists in the United States will have a class structure that resembles a diamond, that is, large in the middle and smaller both at the bottom and top. These images are pictured in Figure 8.1. A large middle-

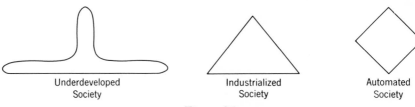

| Underdeveloped Society | Industrialized Society | Automated Society |

Figure 8.1

class tempers the character of internal conflict by rewarding moderate and democratic parties and penalizing extremist groups.

The character of national politics is not simply affected by the size of the middle class relative to the upper and lower strata; the political styles of these two broad groupings will also be determined directly by the wealth of the society. Economic development, producing increased income, greater economic security, and widespread education, permits those in the lower classes to develop a complex and gradualist view of politics. A belief in reformist gradualism can be the ideology of only a relatively well-to-do lower class. Thus, extremist, large-scale, lower class–based parties (Communist and others) are found largely among the poorer countries of Europe and in a number of underdeveloped countries.

This does not mean that economic hardship or poverty *per se* is the main cause of radicalism. There is much evidence to sustain the argument that stable poverty, in a situation in which individuals are not exposed to the possibilities of change, breeds (if anything) conservatism.[12] Individuals whose experience limits their significant communications and inter-

*Economic Programs* (Santa Monica: The Rand Corporation, RM-3901-1SA, February, 1964), pp. 19–34; and Daniel Lerner, *The Passing of Traditional Society* (Glencoe: The Free Press, 1958), p. 63.

[12] See Émile Durkheim, *Suicide: A Study in Sociology* (Glencoe: The Free Press, 1951), pp. 253–254; see also Daniel Bell, "The Theory of Mass Society," *Commentary*, **22**, 80 (1956).

action to others on the same level as themselves, other conditions being equal, will be more conservative than people who may be better off but who have been exposed to the possibilities of securing a better way of life.[13] The dynamic in the situation would seem to be exposure to the possibility of a better way of life rather than poverty as such. As Karl Marx put it in a perceptive passage: "A house may be large or small, as long as the surrounding houses are equally small it satisfies all social demands for a dwelling. But if a palace arises beside the little house, the little house shrinks into a hut." [14]

Since position in a stratification system is always relative and gratification or deprivation is experienced in terms of being better off or worse off than other people, it is not surprising that the lower classes in all countries, regardless of the wealth of the country, resent the existing distribution of rewards and support political parties that advocate some form of redistribution. These political parties tend to assume a more extreme and radical form in poorer countries than in wealthier ones, more probably as a result of the greater degree of inequality in poorer countries than because their poor are actually poorer in absolute terms. A comparative study of wealth distribution by the United Nations "suggest[s] that the richest fraction of the population [the richest tenth, fifth, and so on] generally receive[s] a greater proportion of the total income in the less-developed than in the more developed countries." [15] The gap between the income of professional and semiprofessional personnel on the one hand and ordinary workers on the other is much wider in the poorer than in the wealthier countries. Among the manual workers, "there seems to be a greater wage discrepancy between skilled and unskilled workers in the less developed countries. In contrast the leveling process, in several of the developed countries at least, has been facilitated by the overall increase of national income . . . not so much by reduction of the income of the relatively rich as by the faster growth of the incomes of the relatively poor." [16]

[13] There is also a considerable body of evidence which indicates that those occupations which are economically vulnerable and those workers who have experienced unemployment are prone to be more leftist in their outlook.

[14] Karl Marx, "Wage-Labor and Capital," in *Selected Works*, Vol. 1 (New York: International Publishers, 1933), pp. 268–269. "Social tensions are an expression of unfulfilled expectations," Daniel Bell (cited in footnote 12), p. 80.

[15] *United Nations: Preliminary Report on the World Social Situation* (New York: 1952), pp. 132–133. Gunnar Myrdal, the Swedish economist, has pointed out: "It is, indeed, a regular occurrence endowed almost with the dignity of an economic law that the poorer the country, the greater the difference between poor and rich." *An International Economy* (New York: Harper, 1956), p. 133.

[16] *United Nations: Preliminary Report on the World Social Situation, op. cit.* (see also Table 11). A comparison of income distribution in the United States and a number of Western European countries concludes that "there has not been any great difference"

The distribution of consumption goods also tends to become more equitable as the size of national income increases. The wealthier a country is, the larger is the proportion of its population that owns automobiles, telephones, bathtubs, refrigerating equipment, and things of this kind, and the more equitable can be the distribution. For example, the number of people who can afford good facilities, or who can afford to have their children complete high school still represents only a minority of the population in many European countries. The great national wealth of the United States or Canada, or even to a lesser extent that of the Australasian Dominions or Sweden, reduces the distance between the standards of living of adjacent social classes; even classes that are far apart in the social structure will enjoy more nearly similar consumption patterns than will comparable classes in southern Europe. Within the "underdeveloped" countries, social stratification is characterized by even greater distinctions in ways of life, with little overlap in the goods that the various strata own or can afford to purchase. It may be suggested, therefore, that the wealthier a country, the less is status inferiority experienced as a major source of deprivation.

Marx believed that the proletariat was a revolutionary force because it had nothing to lose but its chains, and could win the whole world. But Tocqueville, analyzing the reasons why the lower strata in America supported the system, paraphrased and transposed Marx before Marx ever made his analysis by pointing out that "only those who have nothing to lose ever revolt." [17]

The political values of the upper class, too, are related to national income. The poorer a country is, and the lower the absolute standard of living of the lower classes, the greater is the pressure on the upper strata to treat the lower strata as a vulgar, innately inferior, lower caste, beyond the pale of human society. The sharp difference in the style of living between people at the top and people at the bottom makes this psychologically necessary. Consequently, the upper strata in such a situation tend to

in patterns of income distribution among these countries. These findings of Robert Solow appear to contradict those reported above from the U.N. Statistics Office, although the latter are dealing primarily with differences between industrialized and underdeveloped nations. In any case, it should be noted that Solow agrees that the relative position of the lower strata in a poor as compared with a wealthy country is quite different. As he states, "in comparing Europe and America, one may ask whether it makes sense to talk about relative income equality independently of the absolute level of income. An income four times another income has different content according as the lower income means malnutrition on the one hand or provides some surplus on the other." Robert M. Solow, *A Survey of Income Inequality Since the War* (Stanford: Center for Advanced Study in the Behavioral Sciences, 1958, mimeographed), pp. 41–44, 78.

[17] Alexis de Tocqueville, *Democracy in America*, Vol. 1 (New York: Alfred A. Knopf, Vintage edition, 1945), p. 258.

regard political rights for the lower strata, particularly the right to share power, as essentially absurd and immoral. The upper strata not only resist democracy themselves, but their often arrogant political behavior serves to intensify extremist reactions on the part of the lower classes.

The general income level of a nation affects its receptivity to democratic norms. If there is enough wealth in the country so that it does not make too much difference to the elite whether some redistribution takes place, it is easier to accept the idea that it does not matter greatly which side is in power. But if loss of office means serious losses for major power groups, these groups will seek to retain or secure office by any means available.

A certain amount of national wealth is also necessary to ensure a competent civil service. The poorer the country, the greater the emphasis on nepotism—support of kin and friends. And this, in turn, reduces the opportunity to develop the efficient bureaucracy that a modern democratic state requires.

Intermediary organizations, which act as sources of countervailing power, seem to be similarly associated with national wealth. Tocqueville and other exponents of what has come to be known as the theory of the "mass society" have argued that a country without a multitude of organizations relatively independent of the central state power has a high dictatorial as well as revolutionary potential.[18] These organizations serve a number of functions: they inhibit the state or any single source of private power from dominating all political resources; they are a source of new opinions; they can be the means of communicating ideas—particularly opposition ideas—to a large section of the citizenry; and they train men in political skills and thus help to increase the level of interest and participation in politics. Although there are no reliable data on the relationship between national patterns of voluntary organization and national political systems, evidence from studies of individual behavior demonstrates that, regardless of other factors, men who belong to associations are more likely than others to give the democratic answer to questions concerning tolerance and party systems, to vote, or to participate actively in politics. Since the more well-to-do and better educated a man is, the more likely he is to belong to voluntary organizations, the propensity to form such groups seems to be a function of level of income and opportunities for leisure within given nations.[19]

[18] See Emil Lederer, *The State of the Masses* (New York: Norton, 1940); Hannah Arendt, *Origins of Totalitarianism* (New York: Harcourt, Brace, 1951); Max Horkheimer, *Eclipse of Reason* (New York: Oxford University Press, 1947); Karl Mannheim, *Man and Society in an Age of Reconstruction* (New York: Harcourt, Brace, 1940); Philip Selznick, *The Organizational Weapon* (New York: McGraw-Hill, 1952); José Ortega y Gasset, *The Revolt of the Masses* (New York: Norton, 1932); and William Kornhauser, *The Politics of Mass Society* (Glencoe, Ill.: The Free Press, 1959).
[19] See Edward Banfield, *The Moral Basis of a Backward Society* (Glencoe, Ill.: The

The relationship between education and democracy deserves a separate discussion, since an entire philosophy of government has viewed increased education as a basic requirement of democracy.[20] As James Bryce wrote, with special reference to South America, "education, if it does not make men good citizens, makes it at least easier for them to become so." [21] Education presumably broadens man's outlook, enables him to understand the need for norms of tolerance, restrains him from adhering to extremist doctrines, and increases his capacity to make rational electoral choices.

The evidence on the contribution of education to democracy is even more direct and strong on the level of individual behavior within countries than it is in cross-national correlations. Public opinion data from different countries about people's beliefs on tolerance for the opposition, their attitudes toward ethnic or racial minorities, and their feelings for multiparty as against one-party systems have shown that the higher a person's education, the more likely he is to believe in democratic values and to support democratic practices. Many studies indicate that education is the most important factor, more significant than either income or occupation.[22]

These results should lead us to anticipate a far higher correlation between national levels of education and political practice than we actually find. Germany and France have been among the best educated nations of Europe, but this by itself did not stabilize their democracies. It may be, however, that their educational level has served to encourage as much democracy as has existed.

If we cannot say that a high level of education is a *sufficient* condition for democracy, the available evidence suggests that it comes close to being a *necessary* one. In Latin America, where illiteracy is still widespread, none of the nations in which more than one half of the population is illiterate have had continuous democratic institutions since World War II.

Lebanon, the one member of the Arab League that has maintained democratic institutions since World War II, is also by far the best educated (over 80% literacy). East of the Arab world, only two states (the Philippines and Japan) have maintained democratic regimes since 1945 without

Free Press, 1958), for an excellent description of the way in which abysmal poverty serves to reduce community organization in southern Italy.
[20] See John Dewey, *Democracy and Education* (New York: Macmillan, 1916).
[21] James Bryce, *South America: Observations and Impressions* (New York: Macmillan, 1912), p. 546.
[22] See G. H. Smith, "Liberalism and Level of Information," *Journal of Educational Psychology*, 39, 65–82 (1948); Martin A. Trow, *Right Wing Radicalism and Political Intolerance* (Ph.D. thesis, Department of Sociology, Columbia University, 1957), p. 17; Samuel A. Stouffer, *Communism, Conformity, and Civil Liberties* (New York: Doubleday, 1955); and Kotaro Kido and Masataka Sugi, "A Report of Research on Social Stratification and Mobility in Tokyo" (III), *Japanese Sociological Review*, 4, 74–100 (1954).

the presence of large antidemocratic parties. And these two countries, although lower than most European states in per capita income, are among the world's leaders in educational attainment. The Philippines actually rank second to the United States in the proportion of people attending universities, and Japan has a higher educational level than any European nation.

The available evidence indicates that all of the various aspects of economic development—industrialization, urbanization, wealth, and education —are so closely interrelated as to form one major factor that correlates with democracy. Daniel Lerner found a close connection among urbanization, literacy, voting rates, media consumption and production, and education. Simple and multiple correlations among four basic variables were computed for all countries for which United Nations statistics were available (in this case, 54) with the following results.[23]

| *Dependent Variables* | *Multiple Correlation Coefficient* |
|---|---|
| Urbanization | 0.61 |
| Literacy | 0.91 |
| Media participation | 0.84 |
| Political participation | 0.82 |

Lerner suggests that these key variables in the modernization process may be viewed as historical phases in which democracy is one of the later developments—the "crowning institution of the participant society" (one of his terms for a modern industrial society). His conception of these variables as stages merits quoting at some length.

The secular evolution of a participant society appears to involve a regular sequence of three phases. Urbanization comes first, for cities alone have developed the complex of skills and resources which characterize the modern industrial economy. Within this urban matrix develop both of the attributes which distinguish the next two phases—literacy and media growth. There is close reciprocal relationship between these, for the literate develop the media which in turn spread literacy. But, literacy performs the key function in the second phase. The capacity to read, at first acquired by relatively few people, equips them to perform the varied tasks required in the modernizing society. Not until the third phase, when the elaborate technology of industrial development is fairly well advanced, does a society begin to produce newspapers, radio networks, and motion pictures on a massive scale. This, in turn, accelerates the spread of literacy.

[23] The study is reported in Daniel Lerner's *The Passing of Traditional Society* (Glencoe, Ill.: The Free Press, 1958), p. 63. These correlations are derived from census data; the main sections of the survey dealt with reactions to and opinions about the mass media, with inferences as to the personality types appropriate to modern and to traditional society.

Out of this interaction develop those institutions of participation (e.g. voting) which we find in all advanced modern societies.[24]

Let us now examine the key institution of participation: voting.

## Parties and Voting

Perhaps the largest single field of inquiry in political sociology has been the study of voting behavior partly because it is more easily researchable. Statistical data bearing on elections are available for many countries for long periods of time, and samples of the electorate may be easily interviewed by using conventional opinion survey techniques. Concentration on electoral behavior is valuable for analysis, since voting is both a key mechanism of consensus in democratic societies and a major means of institutionalizing the conflicts among different groups. Students of elections have been primarily concerned with the relationship between political parties and such types of cleavage as class, occupation, religion, ethnic group, and region, more as factors that generate political strife than political consensus.

The study of the integrative aspects of electoral behavior, although still inadequately treated, is important for the understanding of the way in which democratic polities hold together with a minimum reliance on force.

Political parties, parliaments, and elections may be considered as part of the structure of organized tension; they may also be viewed as institutions that prevent serious internecine battles among the contending forces of any given society. The advocates of revolutionary change do, in fact, recognize that the sheer existence of parliamentary democracy serves to hamper their own growth. In looking at political behavior, it is clear that

---

[24] Daniel Lerner, *op. cit.*, p. 60. Lerner also focuses upon certain personality requirements of a "modern" society, which may also be related to the personality requirements of democracy. According to him, the physical and social mobility of modern society requires a mobile personality, capable of adaption to rapid change. Development of a "mobile sensibility so adaptive to change that rearrangement of the self-system is its distinctive mode" has been the work of the twentieth century. Its main feature is *empathy*, denoting the "general capacity to see oneself in the other fellow's situation, whether favorably or unfavorably." (See pp. 49 ff.)

Whether this psychological characteristic results in a predisposition toward democracy (implying a willingness to accept the viewpoint of others) or is rather associated with the antidemocratic tendencies of a "mass society" type of personality (implying the lack of any solid personal values rooted in rewarding participation) is an open question. Possibly empathy (a more or less "cosmopolitan" outlook) is a general personality characteristic of modern societies, with other special conditions determining whether or not it has the social consequence of tolerance and democratic attitudes, or rootlessness and anomie.

we may analyze the same processes in a very different light, depending on whether we are studying sources of conflict or of integration. Thus, voters who deviate from the predominant tendency of their major social-group affiliation are often dealt with in voting studies that emphasize conflict as "deviant cases." The problem is to explain why some workers back conservative parties, or to show why some wealthy people support the socialists, when there is a strong correlation between class position and party vote in most countries. Church-going Catholics who back historically anti-clerical parties are an anomaly for the voting analyst, as are the atheists who vote for the Christian Democrats. But the student of integration perceives such "deviants" as fulfilling a necessary condition for stable democracy. Deviant behavior may be looked on as fulfilling part of the basic requirements for the maintenance of a democratic political system.

A stable democracy requires a situation in which all of the major political parties include supporters from many segments of the population. Where different parties correspond too closely to basic social divisions, a state of conflict is so intense and clear-cut that it makes democratic compromise difficult. Where parties are cut off from gaining support within a major stratum, they lose an essential reason for compromise. It is also important that parties have leaders from diverse backgrounds, so as to represent symbolically their concern with many groups, even if the parties have little support from some of the groups. The fact that Republicans have nominated Negroes and Jews, even though most members of these groups in recent years have voted Democratic, has undoubtedly had a unifying effect, and has reduced the chance that party division along racial or religious lines could become permanent.

Agreement on issues across group lines and party cleavages is also important. Cross-pressures resulting from multiple-group affiliations or loyalties account for much of the deviation from the dominant voting pattern of a given group. Individuals who are subject to pressures driving them in different political directions must either deviate or "escape into apathy." Multiple-group identification has the effect of reducing the emotion in political choices. In the United States and Great Britain, manual workers who vote Republican or Conservative are less liberal on economic issues than workers who support the Democratic or Labor parties, but are more liberal than middle-class supporters of their own party.[25] The fact many voters of each major party identify with the values of other parties forces the leaders of each party to make concessions when they are in power, and offers them hope for support when they are in opposition.

[25] Bernard Berelson, Paul F. Lazarsfeld, and William McPhee, *Voting* (Chicago: University of Chicago Press, 1954), p. 27; M. Benney, A. P. Gray, and R. H. Pear, *How People Vote* (London: Routledge and Kegan Paul, 1956), p. 194.

In contemporary democratic countries the greatest stability of party support comes from two kinds of cleavage: factors related to stratification and factors related to cultural values. There are relatively permanent party alignments between higher and lower orders in status, income and power, and also between specific groups that differ greatly in their views about the good society. The prototype of the first kind of cleavage is the class party, and of the second is the religious party. Differences rooted in stratification are preponderant in economically developed, stable polities in which the "politics of collective bargaining" is customary—fights over the division of the total economic pie, over the extent of the welfare and planning state, and the like.

Cultural or deeply rooted value conflicts are much more characteristic of developing countries with unstable polities. In addition to conflicts rooted in class controversy, there remain divisions of opinion based on institutions rooted in the premodern era, and on institutions that are endemic in the processes of social and economic development. We see examples of cultural conflicts in the effects to sustain the traditional position of historic religion, to maintain the status and privileges of higher social strata such as the nobility whose position is a function of a preindustrial society, and to protect the family pattern of a static rural society from the demands of a more universalistic system. Many of the variables that are associated with positions in a *Kulturkampf* (culture conflict) are not linked to stratification, but to involvement in traditional or modern institutions (for example, poor religious peasants may be conservatives, while well-to-do young professionals may be radical), and to generational experiences—the young and better-educated persons versus the older and the less-educated persons. Sex, too, may provide a base for diversity where such issues are significant, since in most societies women's roles are more implicated in religious institutions, less in modern economic ones. Women are also less educated on the average than men. Consequently, women tend to be more supportive of traditionalist parties than of modernizing ones.

In all developed countries there is a correlation between the leftism or conservatism of political parties and variables that can be ranked in stratification terms. The more liberal or left-wing parties are disproportionately supported by persons with low income, by workers, by poorer farmers, by the less educated, and by members of low-status religious, racial, or ethnic groups.

This pattern is most clearly apparent in the five English-speaking democracies. In all of these countries, lower-class status, Catholic religious affiliation, and recent immigrant background are associated with support for the

Democrats or for Labor and Liberal (Canada) politics.[26] The size of the correlation varies among these nations, but it seems clear that such status-defining variables as occupation, income, religion, and ethnicity account for much of the variation in party support.

The picture is somewhat more complicated in the various multiparty systems of the nations of continental Europe. These countries, in spite of the variations among them, do have a number of elements in common. First, the nineteenth-century cleavage between liberal and conservative or religious parties, which antedated socialism, has been maintained in most of them. There is a continuation of strong liberal and conservative parties in Scandinavia, and of Christian-Democratic parties and liberal or other anticlerical bourgeois parties in Catholic Europe and Germany. All of these countries have strong working class–oriented parties, but they differ greatly as to whether there is one dominant Social-Democratic party opposed by a small Communist party (as in most of Northern Europe), or whether there is a mass Communist party, which is larger than the Socialists—as in France, Italy, and Finland. In addition to these parties, a number of these countries have agrarian or peasant parties.

Class and religion are the preponderant sources of difference among the European parties. Where there are large Communist and Socialist parties, the Socialist parties generally derive more support from the skilled and educated workers. Communists, too, draw disproportionate support among the socially uprooted, in rapidly changing areas, and among people who have been unemployed in the past. The religious parties include rich and poor and are relatively stronger among farm people and women.[27] The urban religious manual workers often adhere to Christian trade unions, which work closely with socialist unions. The liberal parties tend to be small and to be based on the anticlerical bourgeois and professional groups. The Swedish Liberal Party is supported both by the irreligious bourgeoisie and the very religious sectarian opponents of the Conservatives who, in turn, tend to be the party of the more well-to-do, and of persons involved in the traditional church.

The European party system is most complex in the Catholic countries where a cleavage structure has developed that cannot be readily fitted into a broad two-party coalition. The sources of cleavage are numerous—a lower level of economic development, less legitimate political institutions, and the superimposition of the nineteenth-century fights concerning the status of the old privileged classes, the position of the church, and the eco-

---

[26] Robert Alford, *Party and Society* (Chicago: Rand McNally, 1963).
[27] See S. M. Lipset, *Political Man* (cited in footnote 6), pp. 257–260.

nomic class struggle. The continuity in traditional issues is strikingly evident in the name of the party that represents the views of the Dutch orthodox Calvinists, the Anti-Revolutionary party. The Revolution that this party is against is the French Revolution of 1789. Broadly speaking, the "normal" division in these nations is a three-party one: a large multiclass Catholic party (based disproportionately on the rural population) opposed by a large Socialist party (rooted in the urban working class), with a much smaller middle class–oriented, anticlerical Liberal party (which holds the balance of power). In France and Italy, both the clerical and anticlerical sectors of the nation have been greatly divided, so that each has a six-party structure.

The pattern of politics that has emerged in the nations of the "third world" varies somewhat from the pattern of Europe and the English-speaking countries. In Latin America, early party divisions resembled those in Western Europe. That is, the first conflicts were largely between proclerical and rural upper-class dominated conservative parties and anticlerical and bourgeois controlled Liberal parties. Socialist and anarcho-syndicalist movements arose on the working-class left before World War I in a number of countries, but secured relatively little strength.

During the interwar period, and since World War II, however, political movements have emerged that have expressed ideologically diverse forms of nationalist, anti-imperialist doctrines, opposing foreign domination of the economy, and seeking through state control or ownership of the economy to foster rapid economic development. Some of these movements, such as the supporters of Peron in the Argentine and Vargas in Brazil, resembled Fascism or Nazism, except that they were genuinely based on the working-class or poor rural population.[28] Other movements were aligned to the Communists, especially in Chile and Brazil. And still others, such as the Aprista of Haya de la Torre in Peru, the Acción Democratica of Betancourt in Venezuela, and the National Liberation Movement of Figueres in Costa Rica, may best be described as nationalist Social Democrats comparable to the Indian Congress party. In some of the Latin American nations, Christian-Democratic parties have arisen recently, which tend to be relatively left-wing, supporting land reform, economic planning, and state intervention to foster economic development—reform movements similar to those that exist elsewhere in the underdeveloped world.

The pattern characteristic of the emerging nations (the few which retain

[28] George Blanksten, "The Politics of Latin America," in Gabriel Almond and James S. Coleman (cited in footnote 11), pp. 455–531; Donald Dozer, *Latin America: An Interpretive History* (New York: McGraw-Hill, 1962), pp. 369–414.

some democratic politics) is a division between modernizing and traditionalist elements, which overlaps with and largely supercedes the left-right
stratification fight of the older and more stable polities. Socialism and Communism, to a considerable extent, are associated symbolically with independence, rapid economic development, social modernization, and ultimate
equality. Capitalism is seen as aligned to foreign influences, traditionalism,
and slow growth. Hence, support for enhanced leftism is not only based on
segments of the working class, but also secures considerable backing from
the better educated who favor modernization. This pattern is clearest in
Japan.[29]

Japan, although more developed than any other country outside of
Europe or the English-speaking nations, resembles the other emerging nations in its politics. Education, rather than lower class position, is the major
correlate of modernism and leftism. University students and university
graduates disproportionately back variants of socialism. On the other hand,
many less educated poor workers and peasants who are still tied into traditional social structures support the conservative party. And in many other
nations in Asia, Latin America, and Africa, the better educated are often
the most significant backers of the more aggressively leftist tendencies.

The significant factor that differentiates supporters at the left and right
in emerging nations is the extent to which groups or individuals are in the
modernizing or the traditional part of the society. This division cuts sharply
across stratification lines.

I am not saying that stratification does not continue to differentiate left
and right in the developing nations. It certainly does. The mass Com-

[29] A study based on interviews with a sample of 3000 Japanese reports that the most
radical segment is "the employed professional specialists. They are more in favor of
denuclearized neutrality than laborers or blue-collar workers. They lend as much support
to political strikes called by labor unions as do the laborers themselves. Most of the
white-collar stratum favors and gives support to the socialist parties." Research Society
on Japanese Social Structure, "Special Traits of White-Collar Workers in Large Urban
Areas," *Journal of Social and Political Ideas in Japan*, 1, 78 (August, 1963). A 1958
national sample reported heavy socialist support among professionals and managerial
groups. See Z. Suetuna, H. Aoyama, C. Hyashi, and K. Matusita, "A Study of Japanese
National Character, Part II," *Annals of the Institute of Statistical Mathematics* (Tokyo),
Supplement II, (1961), p. 54; see also Joji Watanuki, "White-Collar Workers and the
Pattern of Politics in Present-Day Japan," in S. M. Lipset and Stein Rokkan, eds.,
*Party Systems and Voter Alignments* (New York: The Free Press, 1967); Robert A.
Scalapino and Junnosuke Masumi, *Parties and Politics in Contemporary Japan* (Berkeley:
University of California Press, 1962), p. 177; Douglas Mendel, *The Japanese People
and Foreign Policy* (Berkeley: University of California Press, 1961), pp. 44–45, 47.
A comprehensive report on many Japanese opinion surveys is Allan Cole and Naomichi
Nakanishi, *Japanese Opinion Polls with Socio-Political Significance 1947–1957*, Vol. 1,
*Political Support and Preference* (Medford: Fletcher School of Law and Diplomacy,
Tufts University, 1960), *passim*.

munist or left Socialist parties in some of these countries are composed of workers or impoverished sectors of the rural population. Although the Castro movement originated among university students, and drew much of its initial support from middle-class "modernizing" elements, after Castro came to power the proportion of those who backed him increased with lower status and education.[30] However, it is important to note that the modernizing-traditionalist division brings to the left heavy support from the better-educated and more privileged individuals—students, military officers, civil servants, and executives—who associate leftism or socialism with rapid modernization.[31]

## The Dilemma of the Conservatives

If class is one of the main sources of party division, and if the lower strata back parties that advocate greater equality—parties that oppose the privileged elites—how can conservative parties compete in democratic elections? Concern with this problem led conservatives the world over to oppose universal suffrage in the nineteenth century. Many explicitly argued that the extension of the suffrage would result in the end of private property rights. As T. H. Marshall and others have pointed out, these conservatives were, to a certain extent, correct. There has been an inherent bias in favor

---

[30] That Castro's initial following was largely based on young well-educated middle-class Cubans has been documented by Theodore Draper. He points out that of Castro's 18 cabinet members in 1960, everyone was a university graduate, that they were of middle- or upper-class background, and professionals or intellectuals occupationally. Theodore Draper, *Castro's Revolution, Myths and Realities* (New York: Praeger, 1962) pp. 42–43. Draper also points out that the list of Cuban defenders of Castroism who were interviewed by C. Wright Mills in his effort to present the authentic voice of the Cuban Revolution for his book *Listen Yankee* did not include a single worker or peasant. "Without exception, his informants were middle-class intellectuals and professionals," p. 21. For data on mass attitudes, see Maurice Zeitlin, "Economic Insecurity and the Political Attitudes of Cuban Workers," *American Sociological Review*, 31, 35–51 (1966).

[31] The appeal of left-wing ideologies to the intellectuals and other sections of the university-trained intelligentsia in the underdeveloped nations has been analyzed in some detail. See Morris Watnick, "The Appeal of Communism to the Peoples of Underdeveloped Areas," in R. Bendix and S. M. Lipset, eds., *Class, Status and Power* (Glencoe, Ill.: The Free Press, 1953), pp. 651–662; Hugh Seton-Watson, "Twentieth Century Revolutions," *The Political Quarterly*, 22, 251–265 (1951); John H. Kautsky, "An Essay on the Politics of Development," in Kautsky, ed., *Political Change in Underdeveloped Countries* (New York: Wiley, 1962), pp. 44–49; 106–113; Edward Shils, "The Intellectual Between Tradition and Modernity: The Indian Situation," *Comparative Studies in Society and History*, Supplement I, pp. 94–108 (1961). Perhaps the most comprehensive treatment of the subject is Edward Shils, "The Intellectuals in the Political Development of the New States," in John H. Kautsky, ed., *op. cit.*, pp. 195–234.

of the extension of equality in all democratic societies. Parties dominated by the privileged classes have had to make constant concessions to equalize opportunity and reward. Measures that a previous generation of conservatives objected to as radical or socialist are accepted by the next one.[32]

However, even though democratic societies do move to the left, there still remains the question of how conservatives retain enough strength to compete successfully with leftists; the leftists should be able to draw upon the majority of "poor" workers or rural groups that exist in almost every nation. A number of answers have been suggested to account for the ability of conservative political groupings to win significant lower-class support. This support is a requirement for political stability. For the legitimacy of a democratic polity rests on the opportunity for all significant actors to have access to power. If the conservatives are deprived of such opportunities, they would eventually lose their commitment to the democratic "rules of the game." No one wants to keep playing in a game that he can never hope to win.

Some possible explanations are the following ones.

1. The normative system inherent in all stratified societies reduces the political effectiveness of the lower strata. To a very high degree, lower classes throughout history have acceded to the societal values that define them as being, in various respects, inferior to those of higher status. This has been true even in modern industrial societies, despite the influence of Marxism and the wide diffusion of egalitarian values. Implicit in the very concept of a stratification order is the assumption that people in lower-status positions are oriented upward; that is, that most of them would like to move up in the social structure, whereas people in higher positions are rarely motivated to move down. Insofar as individuals in lower-class positions use people in higher position as a reference group toward which they aspire or whose approval they desire to win, we would expect them to take over the values of the higher-status group. People in high positions will be unlikely to adopt political attitudes that are associated with people of low status, but some lower-class people will be proud to take over reactions associated with the higher classes.

Conservative parties and policies, which reflect upper-class values, have by and large been surrounded by a halo of high prestige and status, while left parties have been "tainted" by association with the lower classes.

2. The lower classes, by virtue of their inferior position in the structure and the fact that the dominant legitimate norms of culture are middle- and upper-class ones, are necessarily exposed to conflicting normative pressures

[32] T. H. Marshall, *Class, Citizenship and Social Development* (Garden City, N.Y.: Doubleday, 1964), pp. 65–122.

as they become politically class-conscious or leftist in their orientations. Politically, they tend to develop or accept values that are functionally related to their needs as underprivileged groups, but as individuals they are faced with the problem of reconciling lower-class norms with a conflicting set of values that are functional for the political and social position of the upper class. In large measure, the values transmitted by a culture tend to reinforce conservative predispositions and to challenge left-wing ones. Consequently, again we might expect this factor to create more deviation from the modal-class pattern among lower-class people than among middle- and upper-class persons.

3. Lower-class individuals are more exposed to conservative values transmitted through the schools, media of mass communication, and other powerful agencies of persuasion than are well-to-do, middle-class people faced with propaganda or media favoring liberal or leftist politics. For example, in the area of newspaper reading, the large majority of the population in every Western country reads newspapers that support the conservatives politically. This means that voters predisposed to back conservatives will have this predisposition reinforced by the press and the magazines that they read, whereas voters disposed to support leftist parties will have this predisposition contradicted by the mass media.[33] This pattern of exposure is intrinsic to a stratified society and will normally result in greater deviations from the modal-class political pattern within the lower strata than among the middle and upper strata.

4. The political advocates of changes in the existing society must mobilize support from individuals and groups who adhere to the old institutional order. Normally, it is much harder to get people to *change* their opinions or political allegiances than it is to get them to *retain* the ones they have. Since the factors that operate to induce individuals or groups to recognize the need for change will necessarily not affect all persons in the stratum that is changing equally, it may be expected that political tendencies advocating major changes will only secure a portion of the potential support from the social base to which the changes appeal; the party with links to the historic *status quo*, on the other hand, may expect to retain most of its support from the privileged strata.

Those lower-class groups, which are isolated from the pressures that are pressing their strata toward new reform politics, will continue to adhere to the conservative tradition. Thus, it has been pointed out frequently that workers who are socially isolated from other workers but who are in close contact with persons in the middle class (such as personal servants, and

---

[33] See Stein Rokkan and Per Torsvik, "The Voter, the Reader and the Party Press," *Koelner Zeitschrift für Soziologie und Sozial-Psychologie*, **12**, 278–302 (1960).

workers in very small companies or stores) will continue to be conservative, although their pay and status may be low. Lower-class housewives, more isolated from political information than men, tend to be more conservative and traditionalistic in their political outlook than men.

5. The lesser deviation of upper- than of lower-class individuals from modal-class behavior patterns may be a result of the more homogeneous political environment of the higher-status persons. In all countries, persons in the middle class are more likely to belong to many voluntary organizations than are lower-class individuals. Most of these associations tend to be homogeneous in class terms. The more privileged strata tend to travel and move around among people like themselves, in jet planes, in leading hotels, and the like. Studies of poltical interest and participation indicate that the higher the position individuals occupy in the social structure, the greater their interest and activity in politics. Consequently, middle- and upper-class individuals are more likely than those in less-privileged positions to be continuously exposed to political information and propaganda, that reinforce their inherent class-based political predispositions.

Conversely, lower-class individuals, who are less prone to belong to formal organizations or to interact with individuals who are informed and opinionated about politics, are consequently less likely to secure information that points up the need for class political action.

6. The structure of interclass communication will increase the deviance from the modal-class response more among lower-class than middle-class individuals. Interaction between individuals who belong to different social strata is much more likely to result in the lower-status individual being affected by the opinions of those in the higher class than vice versa. (This is based on the earlier assumption that most lower-class individuals concur in the general evaluation system of any given complex society.) Social interaction between social strata should increase the deviation among the lower-status groups but should not greatly increase the frequency of deviation among members of the higher group.

7. Individuals with higher status in contemporary society are inherently more sophisticated about the relevance of political action to self-interest. This assumption flows from the facts that: (a) higher status is associated with higher education, and greater education is conducive to increased political sophistication; (b) the more transparent the relationship is between governmental policies and the welfare of a group to which a person belongs, the more likely he is to understand the need for political action. In an industrial society, as Max Weber pointed out, the relationship between government action and consequences is much clearer for the self-employed person and for people involved in directing businesses or associations of various kinds than it is for lowly employed persons. Lowly em-

ployed individuals are more likely to view, as personally relevant, power within the *plant* rather than within the *polity;* and (c), as already noted, higher status is associated with greater personal exposure of an individual to politically knowledgeable and active persons of the same background as himself.

These mechanisms (inherent in social stratification), by strengthening conservative parties and weakening left parties, help balance the left and right in stable societies where the attributes associated with high status have not changed. In many of the former colonial and so-called emerging nations, however, this assumption of relative stability and general acceptance of the attributes of high status does not hold true. In these nations, certain varieties of high status are associated with hated foreign imperialisms and with social institutions that are felt to perpetuate national inferiority. Thus, conservative parties backed by businessmen and/or the rural elite in underdeveloped nations do not necessarily have the advantage of traditional legitimacy and identification with the summits of the status system. Leftism and nationalism are often identified with the nation and the national elite. The lower strata, insofar as they are politically conscious, have been won to the side of leftism around the symbols of national independence.

In colonial situations, the native elites derive their status, or are protected in it, by virtue of their connection with the status and power of the foreign ruler. And with independence, the values of hierarchy, aristocracy, privilege, primogeniture, and (more recently) capitalism, all associated with the foreign imperialist power, are easily rejected.[34]

In a context in which a large section of the elite supports leftist ideological goals, and in which the large majority live in poverty, the chances for conservative parties representing the traditional elite to remain viable electoral alternatives to the predominant leftists are quite rare. Quite commonly, one dominant mass-based "leftist" party controls.

But let us return to the democracies of Europe and the English-speaking world. In these nations, regardless of whether conservatism is strengthened by being linked to the national tradition (as it is in Britain) or is not strengthened (as in the United States), conservative politicians know that they must find ways of securing considerable lower-class support. They cannot win without it. Conservative parties must attempt to reduce the saliency of class as the principal basis of party division by sponsoring nonclass issues, while leftist parties will seek to emphasize their anti-elitist objectives. The first of these efforts of conservatives is illustrated by the responses of both

---

[34] S. M. Lipset, *The First New Nation: The United States in Historical and Comparative Perspective* (cited in footnote 6), pp. 76–77.

the pre-Civil War American (conservative) Whig party and later the post-Civil War Republicans to the anti-elitist Democratic party. The Whig party emphasized national-interest issues and symbols—patriotism, defense of traditional religious morality, and the use of military leaders as political leaders. The only two Whig presidential candidates who were elected against the Jacksonian Democrats were military hero generals. After the Civil War the Republican party successfully emphasized its role as the savior of the Union, and nominated a number of Civil War generals. Most recently, the one successful Republican presidential nominee in the past forty years has been the hero of World War II, Dwight Eisenhower.

A second conservative tactic in some countries has been to attempt to introduce some sort of pseudoleftist (anti-elitist) issues. For example, in late nineteenth-century Germany, some conservative leaders attempted to counter the growing support for socialism among the workers by the formation of workers' associations, which tried to deflect the working-class antagonism to capitalism and the upper classes onto the Jews.[35] The support given to the anti-elitist Fascists and Nazis in post-World War I Europe by businessmen and conservatives was probably motivated by similar reasons.

To sum up: conservative parties in a political democracy usually seek to reduce the saliency of class as a basis of party controversy in order to win more lower-class votes. These efforts may take the form of (1) introducing national patriotic issues and nominating military heroes as candidates; (2) stressing noneconomic bases of cleavage such as religious or ethnic differences, or issues of morality; (3) the fostering of Tory socialism, that is, legislation designed to benefit the socioeconomic position of the lower strata; and (4) using a variant of pseudosocialism and anti-elitism, a surrogate-exploiting scapegoat which will absorb the antagonism to the societal elite.

The behavior of conservative parties, of course, will vary greatly with the number of competing parties. Where multiparty systems exist, there are a number of non-left-wing political forces such as religious, liberal, conservative, regional, and agrarian parties, which do not seek an electoral majority, but instead try to maximize the support of the social base predisposed to them (for example, all coreligionists for a religious party, all farmers for an agrarian party, and all businessmen and professionals for a liberal party). In multiparty systems, the most successful non-left party is usually the religious party. Issues affecting the place of religion in education and other areas of life have kept many working-class Europeans voting Christian Democratic rather than Social Democratic or Communist. Like secular conservative parties, the religious political groups deny the saliency

---

[35] See Paul Massing, *Rehearsal for Destruction* (New York: Harper, 1949).

of class, insisting that transclass moral values and allegiances should be the most important differentiating factors in politics.

Leftist parties around the world have continued to use anti-elitist symbolism and class interest to mobilize the support of the lower classes against the conservative parties.

The rise of the "white-collar workers," or the "new middle class," has affected the tactics of both right and left. This increasing stratum, which in some countries already challenges the blue-collar workers for numerical supremacy, resembles the old manual proletariat in being in a dependent employed relationship, but differs sharply from the manual stratum in its sense of higher social status, its superior education, its style of life (consumption patterns) which resembles that of the old middle class, and in its greater opportunities to mount the ladder of achievement within the bureaucracies of business or government.

The superior status and advantages of the employed white collar technicians and professionals predispose them to reject the proletarian class appeal of the left, particularly traditionally Marxist parties, while the insecurity inherent in being employees leads them to favor economic planning to avoid unemployment, and to support welfare-state measures. As their careers will be spent within bureaucracies, not among the self-employed, members of this stratum also are less concerned than other segments of the middle class about the issue of private ownership or public ownership. The left-wing parties must appeal to this new employed middle class, and increasingly they have done so by dropping class symbolism and claiming to represent the people instead of the workers or the poor. These parties also seek out special issues that concern the nonmanual employees. Conversely, the main conservative or non-leftist parties find that they are no longer bourgeois parties, that the self-employed are a dwindling part of their mass base. As a result, many non-leftist parties have become the parties of employed nonmanual workers, and endorse the welfare state and the mixed economy. These developments have reduced the policy disagreements between socialist and "conservative" or "Christian" parties in well-to-do democracies and have contributed to the widely noted "decline of ideology." [36]

## Class and Politics: A Multidimensional Problem

In accounting for deviations from the correlation between class position and party choice, I have pointed to the modification of such choices by

[36] Otto Kirchheimer, "The Waning of Opposition in Parliamentary Regimes," *Social Research*, **24**, 148 (1957).

strengthening both the influence of traditional dominant strata, and the significance of bases of cleavage not linked to class. To a considerable extent, however, the weakness of the correlation is a consequence of the pluralistic character of modern stratification. Stratification is multidimensional, but much of political analysis has treated it as if it were unidimensional. There are many diverse ways of obtaining rewards and power and these affect political relations differently.

The assumption of the unitary nature of stratification, or perhaps more accurately the tendency to use only one indicator to locate an individual's class position, has had unfortunate effects on political and sociological research. As Max Weber argued perceptively, men may have a variety of stratification positions: "Only persons who are completely unskilled, without property and dependent on employment without regular occupation, are in a strictly identical class status." [37] He pointed out that "class statuses . . . are different with each variation and combination" of items that locate individuals in the social structure.[38]

A number of concepts have been suggested to account for variation in political behavior as the consequence of varying combinations of social positions. Listing even a few of them will indicate the complexity of this analysis, and some of the reasons why any unidimensional treatment of class and party must report a considerable degree of variance from the general relationships. Many of these stratification concepts have, in fact, been used as explicit bases of political appeals by different parties.

1. Income—the poorer versus the wealthier.
2. Sources of income—employees versus employers.
3. Occupational position hierarchy—unskilled, skilled, white-collar, professional, and so on.
4. Property—owners versus nonowners; landlords versus tenants.
5. Creditor-debtor status.
6. Accorded social status—honorific deference or prestige hierarchy, as determined in part by economic attributes, ethnic or religious background, duration of residence in community, and duration of possession of status-ascribing attributes (old wealth versus new, parental background, and the like).[39]
7. Power rankings—those that involve subordination on one side and superordination on the other. Labor leaders (possibly relatively low in status

[37] Max Weber, *The Theory of Social and Economic Organization* (New York: Oxford University Press, 1947), p. 425.
[38] *Ibid.*, p. 424.
[39] This is the factor described as "social class" by W. L. Warner in his *Yankee City* series of books.

and income but with considerable power), civil servants and elected officers, and heads of organizations whose members are lowly, all present examples of positions that convey much less income and status than they do power. Conversely, men may have considerable status and/or income but may feel that they have very little influence on decisions that concern them, and hence react as political out-groups.

8. Subjective stratification reactions: in all of the above dimensions the individual's position is determined by objective attributes, or the status that he or his possessions are accorded by others. Individuals, however, may perceive their position in the stratification system in ways that diverge from the normal pattern. When asked what class they are in (upper, middle, working, or lower), many manual workers and poor people in all countries say "middle class," while a smaller proportion of those who are in non-manual or well-paid occupations report themselves as "working class." [40] The self-placement of the actors is usually described as *subjective class*. The concept *reference class* refers to the status group toward whose modal behavior an individual is oriented. Various aspects of a person's behavior may not correspond to his status, but instead to the prescriptions of another status. If a manual worker adopts the style of clothing or housing typical of people in higher occupations or seeks a level of education for his children similar to theirs, we may say that he has a middle-class reference group.

Knowledge of an individual's subjective or reference class will increase the ability to predict his political behavior. Workers who report themselves as "middle class," or who adopt middle-class consumption styles, are more likely to support conservative politics than those who identify with the working class.

However, these various dimensions of stratification are not all independent hierarchies, but are intercorrelated. Subjective class and reference class are closely interwoven. A man's subjective class is a fair indicator of his reference class. Changes in power positions are likely to affect reference-class outlooks. For example, those who attain low-level political-party or union posts are much more likely to exhibit a middle-class frame of reference than are rank-and-file workers.

The most interesting political aspect of the diverse stratification dimensions is the way in which incompatible stratification attributes subject individuals to contradictory political pressures. Thus professors may be much higher in occupational status than they are in income; members of ethnic minority groups may more easily move up in economic position than in community prestige (social status); labor leaders may be high in power

[40] Richard Centers, *The Psychology of Social Classes* (Princeton: Princeton University Press, 1949).

and low in occupational or community status; and the like. Variations such as these have been conceptualized in sociological analysis by Gerhard Lenski as the problem of status crystallization (in which statuses are congruent) or status discrepancies.[41]

On the most general level, of course, status discrepancies may be regarded as a special example of cross-pressures operating on individuals or groups. As the earlier discussion of cross-pressures suggested, those involved in politically relevant status discrepancies should exhibit a lower level of interest and activity. On the other hand, much of the literature has pointed out that extremist forms of political behavior have often been caused by the strains of status discrepancies. Seeming contradictory propositions of this kind may be compatible, if we assume that people under cross-pressures may attempt to reduce the strains either by retreating into apathy, saying that they do not care which position triumphs, or by adopting a position that will reduce the strains in a more extreme manner and in a more committed fashion than persons not faced with the need to resolve cross-pressures. Which reaction occurs will depend on other factors specific to the situation.

The types of extreme political behavior explained by reactions to status discrepancies are also quite diverse.

Thus it has been suggested that the *nouveaux riches* (newly wealthy) have responded frequently to the experience of having wealth without the corresponding high status by giving support to leftist or egalitarian movements that challenge the legitimacy of the traditional basis of social status. This thesis has been advanced to account for the behavior of the bourgeoisie in the French Revolution, and for the leftism of relatively well-to-do Jews in various countries. Similarly it has been argued that groups whose social class position is higher than their occupational-economic class—the "decayed aristocracy"—are frequently ultrareactionary, defensive of traditional values and institutions. But it should be noted that these two examples of discrepancies have also been used to explain quite opposite political reactions. Analysts of the "radical right" in the United States have suggested that some American *nouveaux riches* react to the strains inherent in their position by becoming even more conservative than the old rich, that they seek to adapt to the value and behavior patterns that seem common in the status group above them.[42] It has been suggested also that old but economically declining upper classes are sometimes relatively liberal. Thus the emergence before

[41] Gerhard Lenski, "Status Crystallization: A Non-Vertical Dimension of Social Status," *American Sociological Review*, **19**, 405–413 (1954).
[42] See the various essays in Daniel Bell, ed., *The Radical Right* (Garden City, N.Y.: Doubleday, 1963).

World War I of Tory Socialism in England and Progressive Republicanism in America has been explained as a consequence of the felt hostility of declining old wealth to the rising *nouveaux riches*—industrialists and capitalists—who had outstripped them economically. These speculations and historical interpretations indicate the limits of comparative political analysis. Similar status discrepancies have been used to account for arch-conservative behavior and liberal action. To differentiate the conditions under which one or the other occurs calls for specific analysis on a case-study basis.

It is difficult also to be precise about the effect of variations in power position. For example, the pure logic of stratification analysis, which urges that high position results in greater conservatism, would suggest that those who hold greater power as a result of leading the lowly will be more "conservative" than their followers. Presumably becoming a union leader or a Labor Member of Parliament heightens interaction with those high in the social structure, and affects the reference class of those in such position. These assumptions have been advanced to explain the presumed shift to the right of leaders of unions and left-wing parties. On the other hand, such leaders, while high in power and often high in income as well, are in a relatively low position in terms of social-status position. Daniel Bell has suggested that American labor leaders are more liberal than their followers, partly because of the strains in their stratification position. Many labor leaders resent being outranked in prestige by business leaders, and may react to this self-discrepancy by supporting liberal or radical political movements through which they can gain more power and status recognition and by attacking those groups that deny respect to their power positions. This analysis, of course, suggests that trade-union and other leaders of low-status groups, far from being conservative influences on the policies of their organizations, are in fact often more radical than their rank-and-file members, since they feel more status-deprived.

When men occupy incongruous social positions, some aspects of their stratification rankings may predispose them to be conservative, while other aspects operate to favor a liberal political outlook. Moreover the contribution of two discrepant statuses may produce responses that are different from the effects of either discrepant status taken by itself; for example, it may make for a more extremist reaction.

It may be suggested that, on the whole, conflicting and overlapping stratification rankings tend to contribute more to the support of the right than of the left. It seems natural that individuals should attempt to order their perception of the environment so as to maximize their claim to as high a status as possible. The man who achieves high occupational position, for example, is likely to drop his memberships in organizations that are lowly in status, to move to a higher-statused neighborhood, perhaps even to leave his low-ranking church for one whose members are higher in position, and in general to try to take over the behavior pattern of higher social classes. Politically, this implies a pressure to become more conservative. This is another example of the conservative bias inherent in stratification that we referred to earlier.

It should be clear, however, that this "conservative bias" is only one factor among many, and is countered by others. Thus the worker who has moved to the suburbs may still receive left-wing stimuli from his shopmates, his union leader, and his conflicts with authority in the plant, all of which may override any pressures to conform to the more conservative values of his neighborhood. Or, as has been indicated above, many persons with a claim to higher status in one dimension find that they experience social rebuffs when they attempt to translate that claim to social status in another dimension and, as a result, become even more leftist than they might have been if their statuses were congruent.

## Religion and Party

Religion, next to factors directly inherent in the stratification systems, has been, perhaps, the most influential source of political diversity in electoral democracies. As a value-generating institution, religion must affect the nature of political discourse seriously. Religion explains much of the variation in such nonpolitical aspects of behavior as work habits, achievement aspirations, and parent-child-relations.[43] A religious denomination is an important reference group for a member, from which he takes his standards of judgment in many matters. Different religious groups exhibit varying political identities, and one of the tasks of political sociology is to account for these variations. The most explicit form of religious participation in politics is, of course, the religious political party such as the Christian Democrats of various European nations. However, many countries that do not have explicitly religious parties are still politically greatly affected by religion. In discussing the subject, therefore, I suggest, first, some hypotheses concerning the impact of religion on political choice and then examine the factors related to the presence of clerical political parties.

There are at least three kinds of variation among religious groups that bear on their political differentiation. These are discussed below.

[43] Melville Dalton, "Worker Response and Social Background," *Journal of Political Economy*, **55**, 323–332 (1947). Gerhard Lenski, *The Religious Factor* (Garden City, N.Y.: Doubleday, 1961), pp. 75–119.

**1. Different Social Characteristics.** Church groupings differ in socio-economic and ethnic composition as well as in geographical concentration, and the interests of predominant sections of a denomination may become identified with given political tendencies. Churches composed of the more well-to-do, or the high-status ethnic strata, are often politically conservative. Thus Catholics and Jews in the various English-speaking nations are much less likely to be Conservatives or Republicans than are Protestants, and the association is not solely a result of stratification positions; Catholics or Jews are much more likely to back the more liberal party than are Episcopalians (Anglicans) at the same socioeconomic levels.

**2. Different Historical Experiences.** When past events have structured a relationship between a denomination and a political tendency, the relationship may continue indefinitely. For example, in Europe churches that are, or have been, state churches (established) tend to be associated with conservative parties, while churches that have faced discrimination from the state tend to have links to the "out-group" parties—parties that oppose both the religious and secular establishments. In Britain, which still has a state church, the out group "nonconformist" (Baptist and Methodist, for example) sects and Catholics supported the Liberals in the past, and back the Labor party today. In France, well-to-do Protestants and Jews, as well as anticlerical voters of Catholic ancestry, tend to vote for the more left-wing parties, as compared to committed Catholics of comparable economic position.

Consequently, the policies of different parties may be linked to the secular interests of a religious group. Thus, in much of Catholic Europe, parties differ with respect to the issue of state support for religious education. In the United States, the Democrats have always been less willing than their opponents to impose immigration restrictions (an issue of greater relevance to Catholics and Jews than to Protestants), have been more supportive of the Catholic position on public education, and have been more receptive to giving public posts and nominations for elective office to persons who are not of Anglo-Saxon Protestant background.

**3. Different Religious Values.** Religious groups differ theologically in spheres of public morality as well as social welfare. These differences may affect political behavior when theological formulations carry with them political directives, as in the case of papal encyclicals. The papal encyclicals, on the one hand, have endorsed many "welfare-state" policies and, on the other, have condemned atheistic and materialistic socialism and communism. Religious values may indirectly predispose individuals to accept certain congruent secular political ideologies. Thus many observers have called attention to Protestantism's contribution to an emphasis on individualism, on self-reliance, on feelings of personal responsibility for success and failure, and on the interpretation of social evils as a result of moral turpitude. Catholicism, on the other hand, tends to be more accepting of human and societal weakness; it gives the Church authority to relieve the individual of some sense of responsibility, and emphasizes communal responsibility.

Similar differences between churches and sects affect their reaction to public morality. Groups such as the Anglicans, Lutherans, Greek Orthodox, and Roman Catholics, are or have been established churches. Membership in a *church*, in the sociological sense of this world, comes with birth. In the pure case, national citizenship and church membership go together—for instance, almost all Scandinavians are Lutherans; most Englishmen are formally at least Anglicans; and Latin Europeans are baptized as Catholics. Given a socially diverse laity, a tolerant attitude toward the possibility of "sinning" must emerge if continued loyalty to the church is to be assured. Acceptance of human fraility and the assumption that the faithful will not all be saints are natural consequences of legal establishment—the coincidence of church membership and citizenship. On the other hand, many Protestant groups that were once nonconformist sects rather than birthright churches still retain their evangelical sectarian character. New converts to these organizations, and birthright adherents on reaching adulthood, are expected to have joined as a result of a conscious voluntary decision; in some organizations a violent conversion experience has been required as a sign of sincere faith. Good standing in these groups has been contingent on righteous living according to precepts that are sometimes very concrete.

The variations between American Protestants and Catholics in their reaction to the welfare state may flow from a more or less conscious rejection of reliance on policies of community help where individual responsibility should be dominant. A study of the 1952 American elections indicated that within the same party Protestants were more opposed to social-welfare measures than were Catholics.[44] Another study, which indicates a relationship between religious ethos, work orientation, and party choice, reported that Protestant and Republican workers in the same shop had higher rates of productivity than Catholics and Democrats. The author of the study, suggests that these relationships are a consequence of a greater emphasis on individualism among Protestants.[45]

Religious values, of course, have directly affected politics insofar as morality issues (such as prohibition, gambling, divorce, or birth control) become salient. In a number of countries the parties that have drawn

[44] Angus Campbell et al., "Political Issues and the Vote, November 1952," *American Political Science Review*, **47**, 374–375 (1953).
[45] Melville Dalton (cited in footnote 43), 323–332.

support from the more ascetic wings of Protestantism have tended to support measures seeking to inhibit or limit alcoholic beverages. This has been true of the American Republicans and the British and Scandinavian Liberals.

**4. *Religious and Political Dissent.*** It has been suggested that sects serve as a functional alternative for, or pave the way for political discontent. New sectarian splits from dominant religions often seem to express the resentment of depressed strata with their inferior position. This is most manifest in transvaluational beliefs (reversing present values), which emphasize the identification between poverty and virtue, and stress that only the poor but honest will be rewarded in the afterlife. Given the combination of transvaluational elements and hostility to worldly matters often found together in such sects, these groups may reduce the predispositions of poorer groups to back radical political protest. During the Great Depression in the United States, when left-wing protest was minor, such sects grew rapidly. In India, Islam and later Christianity's greatest successes have been in region largely inhabited by Hindu outcastes.

On the other hand, religious protest, by severing sectors of the population from loyalty to the religious establishment may serve to weaken their traditional political allegiances in the process. Many of the leaders and early supporters of the British Labor party came from the "nonconformist" or "dissenting" sects.[46] In Czarist Russia, Leon Trotsky consciously recognized the political implications of religious dissent. In 1897, he deliberately sought his first working-class recruits from among the members of "the religious sects opposed to the Orthodox Church." [47] And studies in a variety of countries have pointed to direct connections between the social roots of religious and political extremism.[48]

**5. *The Religious Political Party.*** The most explicit form of religious participation in politics is, of course, the religious political party. These parties exist in a large number of Catholic, Calvinist, and Moslem countries, but less frequently in non-Calvinist Protestant nations, and in India, Israel, and the various Buddhist states. It is difficult to differentiate between the religions that participate explicitly in politics from the ones that do not, since so many factors vary with national systems and historic experiences. The following generalizations have, however, been suggested.

---

[46] See Robert F. Wearmouth, *Methodism and the Working-Class Movements of England, 1800–1850* (London: Epsworth Press, 1937); A. D. Belden, *George Whitefield the Awakener* (London: S. Low, Marston and Co., 1930), pp. 247 ff.; and Franz Linden, *Sozialismus und Religion* (Leipzig: Tauchnitz, 1932).

[47] Isaac Deutscher, *The Prophet Armed, Trotsky, 1879–1921* (London: Oxford University Press, 1954), pp. 30–31.

[48] See S. M. Lipset, *Political Man* (cited in footnote 6), pp. 106–108, for a summary and discussion of a number of these studies.

(*a*) The more a church conceives of itself as God-ordained and has an ecclesiastical constitution that is completely separated from state power, the more likely is it to be interested in government action. In the West, the Catholic best fits these conditions. As a church in the sociological sense, it assumes that it is God-ordained, and it claims authority over all persons born within it, rather than (as with Protestant denominations, which have sectarian origins) over those who voluntarily give it allegiance. Unlike other Christian *churches* (the Lutheran, the Anglican, and the Greek Orthodox), it is genuinely supranational, accepting an authority outside of the nation: the pope. The other state-supported churches have been closely linked to those who hold power in their state, and their tie to state power prevents them from playing an independent political role. The politics of the three Baltic states before their absorption by Russia in 1939 illustrates decisively that Catholicism and Lutheranism respond differently even when all other circumstances are comparable. Catholic Lithuania was dominated throughout its democratic history by the Christian Democrats, who secured between 35 and 45% of the vote in a multiparty system. In Estonia—as Lutheran as Lithuania is Catholic (over 80%)—a Lutheran Christian-Democratic party never secured more than 7%. And in Latvia with a Lutheran majority and a large Catholic minority, the Lutheran party secured less than 5%, while the Catholic party secured a majority of the votes from the predominantly Catholic section of the country. Similarly in Germany, today, a much larger proportion of Catholics vote for the nominally nonsectarian Christian Democrats than do Lutherans, although the leaders of both churches back the party. And among people who adhere to the predominantly Lutheran Evangelical Church, a large ratio of those who stem from the small Calvinist wing of the Church support the religious party, than do those of Lutheran background. Seemingly Calvinism, where it retains its ancient strong faith, retains more of the attributes of the God-ordained universalistic church than any other Protestant group. In The Netherlands, there are two strong Calvinist parties.

(*b*) Where a cultural community is threatened by outside values, and there is a close identity between the community and a given religion, religious parties are more likely to emerge. This proposition applies particularly to the situation of various colonial peoples.[49] In Indonesia, Pakistan, Morocco, Egypt, and other nations, the Mohammedan religion served as a major basis around which to organize a nationalist movement. As religion is a sphere in which rulers find it difficult to interfere, it is often the least suppressed base of local autonomy. As in the case of lower class-based

[49] George M. Kahin, *Nationalism and Revolution in Indonesia* (Ithaca, N.Y.: Cornell University Press, 1952), p. 38.

movements, latent nationalist movements have first taken the form of religiously oriented organizations, which prepare the way for a political movement.

In many of the postcolonial new states, religion has appeared as a basis of party formation, which is fostered by conservative strata. National identity and left-wing values are often intertwined; the purpose of independence is seen as the creation of a new and radical social order; and the leftist parties are, therefore, identified with the accepted national goals. Consequently, religion is the one institution with popular support around which an opposition to socialism may be based. And the leftist nationalists often perceive religion as one of their obstacles on the road to modernization, and hence initiate a *Kulturkampf* against religious practices. This effort to use religion to strengthen conservatism in radically oriented new strata is not new, the early American conservatives tried similar tactics in their efforts to defeat the Jeffersonian Democrats.[50]

Religious parties vary considerably from country to country, and from period to period, in their social base, program, and position on various issues. In the nineteenth century, European churches that had been established belonged on the "right." They described themselves as "antirevolutionary." In contemporary times, however, the strong conservative commitment of most religious parties which stem from historic established churches, has declined, partly because of the growing weakness of total ideologies in European politics generally. Basically, however, the centrist character of most religious parties results from the fact that they must appeal to the lower strata, while retaining the support of deeply religious conservatives. A religious party that is far over to the right (or to the left) would risk the possibility of alienating important sectors of the population from the church. The ultrarightist activities of the Austrian Catholic party in the 1920's actually led many Catholics to leave the Church.[51]

The factors that determine the presence or absence of a major religious party have been of particular importance in affecting the possibilities for socialist electoral victories in industrially developed nations. The countries that do not have religious parties are essentially divided along class lines politically, and the socialist parties have held majority political power in some of them—a condition that has not occurred in the others. Essentially, as we have seen, there are three kinds of parties in contemporary Europe: working-class (socialist and communist); middle-class (liberals or conservatives, and occasionally agrarians); and religious (Catholic and

[50] S. M. Lipset, *The First New Nation* (cited in footnote 34), pp. 81–88.
[51] Charles Gulick, *Austria from Hapsburg to Hitler* (Berkeley: University of California Press, 1948).

Calvinist). The religious parties are in a deciding balance-of-power position in a number of countries. Their heterogeneous social base produces considerable internal factionalism, which enables these parties to be all things to all men. The right wing can appeal to the traditional conservative forces, while the left wing and the religious trade unions can appeal to the workers. Thus, any strain between the secular affiliations and interests of supporters of religious parties and the policies of governments dominated by them may be eased by identifying with a given wing of the party, or a functional organization linked to it such as a trade union or peasant league.

The social factors that are associated with support of religious parties, not surprisingly, are those that correlate with faithful adherence to religion as such. This is particularly noteworthy with respect to sex differences. In all nations, women are much more religious than men; and, consequently, in countries with religious parties, voters for secular (particularly left, anticlerical, or liberal) parties are disproportionately male, while a large majority of the electorate of the religious parties are usually women. Rural groups are customarily among the more religious part of the population, and also disproportionately give their support to religious parties.

It is obviously important but difficult to distinguish between the impact of religious beliefs on politics and the relationships between religious and political institutions. For example, the hypothesis advanced by Erich Fromm and others that the *Autorität Glaube* (faith in authority) of Lutheranism was congruent with Nazi ideology and facilitated its hold on power is compatible with the evidence of opposition to Hitler by some Protestant leaders. In the first case, Fromm was talking about predisposition to accept certain political ideologies flowing from religious tenets, while the second case involved a power conflict between leaders of an organized church and the state's efforts to deny its traditional rights.

It is not easy for sociologists to formulate propositions about religion and politics that appear valid outside of specific contexts. For, as Max Weber noted, one of the chief determinants of the precise political role of religion in any given polity largely depends on historical circumstances, and therefore, it is difficult to generalize easily about relationships. While general statements may be made about the functions of religion on the whole, the variation in denominational structure and values limit propositions to highly specific complex contexts. Factors such as the following ones will affect the reality in any given nation: the number of different groups existing in one society; the pattern of ecological distribution of a denomination; the relationship of different religious groups to other structural sources of difference; the relative majority or minority position of a group; the extent to which a given electoral system encourages or discourages special interest parties; and many more. But complexity does not mean inability to generalize, and with value-generating institutions as with varying systems and orders of stratification, the political sociologist is obligated to look for functional relationships.

## The Interplay of Class and Religion in Recent American Politics

Public opinion polls have provided political sociologists with a reliable method of studying the nature of the electoral choice. This method has been employed since the United States presidential election of 1936. Reanalyzing some of the data collected over the past 30 years permits us to examine the way in which the two variables discussed here—class and religion—have affected the results of various national elections. To do this, I have followed a method (Table 8.1) first used by Robert Alford, in which urban voters are divided between those in manual and nonmanual occupations, and these groups plus rural voters are divided between Protestants and Catholics.[52] Obviously, different kinds of social circumstances might affect the operation of these social forces. For example, if a depression (which would ordinarily increase class voting) and a Catholic candidate for President (which would increase religious voting) occurred simultaneously, the two indices would not increase as much as they would if either event were to take place without the other. Thus, there is no absolute standard; the effects of religion and class should be compared over time and in light of auxiliary knowledge.

Southerners and Negroes have been excluded from Table 8.1 because of the relations that we are concerned with are different among them. Negroes, although predominantly Protestants, have voted overwhelmingly Democratic since 1936. White Southerners, ironically, continue their post-Civil War pattern of voting Democratic even though this traditional loyalty has greatly declined in presidential contests.

Comparing the internal variations within the Protestant and Catholic groups, it seems evident that religious differences have remained important. Class factors consistently differentiate among Protestants. That is, the middle-class Protestants have always been much more likely to back the Republican than manual workers with similar religious loyalties. Among Catholics, however, class differences in party support, while present, are somewhat less powerful. Alford, who reports similar findings in his analysis of survey data from 1944 to 1960 (including Negroes and Southerners), comments that the lesser strength of the class-party relationship among

[52] Robert Alford (cited in footnote 26), pp. 241–248.

Catholics is "consistent with the presumed ethnic and minority sentiments among Catholics which override class sentiments as a basis for political loyalties." [53] As "out-group" minorities, Catholics, Jews, and Negroes are much more likely to respond politically in terms of their ethnic-religious group identification than is the majority white-Protestant population. Other bases of diversity affect Protestant reactions more than they do the others.

Both class and religious voting were extremely high in 1936. There was a difference of 52 percentage points between the Democratic vote of Catholic manual workers (86) and middle-class Protestants (34). Four years later, the differences were practically as great, although the Democrats lost part of their national majority. The difference in party support linked to religious voting dropped considerably from 1940 to 1944, then remained fairly steady for both presidential and congressional elections until the election of 1960. The change from 1940 to 1944 suggests that the issue of America's policy toward Communism may have affected Catholics even before the war ended. Class differences, as measured by the gross indicator of manual versus nonmanual divisions, also declined during this period, although the drop was smaller and less consistent than that of religion.

Although the indicators of class and religious voting are gross, it appears that the Catholic-Protestant difference has been somewhat more important than the manual versus nonmanual cleavage from 1936 to 1960. However, this result is in some measure a consequence of the fact that the two factors have been dichotomized. When the impact of class is estimated, for example, by dividing the population into more than two classes, or in terms of a number of occupational strata, the variations linked to class become much greater than the variation between Catholic and Protestant groups. Well-to-do businessmen often vote from 80 to 90% Republican. These differences are clearly larger than the variations between Catholics and Protestants. Similarly, the impact of religious affiliations on voting varies with degree of involvement in religious activities, although the correlation between voting and religion is not intensified as consistently or to the degree that occurs with the increased specification of class. Some estimation of the effect of these factors may be seen in the statistics reported in Table 8.2, which were drawn from an analysis of a 1954 opinion survey with a sample of 9852 interviews in 11 states outside of the South.

As examination of Table 8.2 suggests that there is somewhat more variations within each religious group between the highest and lowest class than between Protestants and Catholics in the same class. Thus Catholics vary between 36% Democratic in sympathies among "upper-class" non-manuals to 69% within the lower manual stratum, or a difference of 33%.

---

[53] Robert Alford (cited in footnote 26), pp. 243–244.

Table 8.1 Percent Voting Democratic among Protestants and Catholics Within Farm, Manual, and Nonmanual Occupations (Non-Southern Whites Only)

| Occupations | Total | Catholics | Protestants | Religious Voting (Difference between Catholics and Protestants) |
|---|---|---|---|---|
| | | *1936* | | |
| Farm | 53 (330) | 56 (32) | 46 (190) | Plus 10 |
| Manual | 71 (556) | 86 (138) | 63 (243) | Plus 23 |
| Nonmanual | 47 (732) | 71 (122) | 34 (401) | Plus 37 |
| Class voting (Difference between manual and non-manual) | Plus 24 | Plus 15 | Plus 29 | |
| Total | | 76 (292) | 45 (834) | Plus 31 |
| | | *1940* | | |
| Farm | 47 (363) | 56 (34) | 47 (213) | Plus 9 |
| Manual | 67 (692) | 85 (178) | 53 (295) | Plus 32 |
| Nonmanual | 44 (990) | 62 (174) | 32 (523) | Plus 30 |
| Class voting | Plus 23 | Plus 23 | Plus 21 | |
| Total | | 72 (386) | 41 (1031) | Plus 31 |
| | | *1944* | | |
| Farm | 39 (158) | 61 (18) | 36 (95) | Plus 25 |
| Manual | 63 (458) | 74 (111) | 55 (178) | Plus 19 |
| Nonmanual | 43 (398) | 60 (70) | 31 (217) | Plus 29 |
| Class voting | Plus 20 | Plus 14 | Plus 24 | |
| Total | | 68 (199) | 41 (490) | Plus 27 |
| | | *1948* | | |
| Farm | 48 (138) | 62 (13) | 47 (123) | Plus 15 |
| Manual | 64 (306) | 75 (77) | 57 (205) | Plus 18 |
| Nonmanual | 46 (448) | 59 (107) | 35 (291) | Plus 24 |
| Class voting | Plus 18 | Plus 16 | Plus 22 | |
| Total | | 65 (197) | 45 (619) | Plus 20 |

*continued*

**Table 8.1** (*continued*)   Percent Voting Democratic among Protestants and Catholics Within Farm, Manual, and Nonmanual Occupations (Non-Southern Whites Only)

| Occupations | Total | | Catholics | | Protestants | | Religious Voting (Difference between Catholics and Protestants) |
|---|---|---|---|---|---|---|---|
| | | | *1952* | | | | |
| Farm | 32 | (90) | 36 | (14) | 31 | (75) | Plus 5 |
| Manual | 52 | (370) | 63 | (150) | 43 | (202) | Plus 20 |
| Nonmanual | 28 | (336) | 35 | (85) | 18 | (211) | Plus 17 |
| Class voting | Plus 24 | | Plus 28 | | Plus 25 | | |
| Total | | | 52 | (249) | 30 | (488) | Plus 22 |
| | | | *1954* | | | | |
| Farm | 38 | (69) | 33 | (12) | 38 | (56) | Less 5 |
| Manual | 62 | (265) | 74 | (89) | 54 | (167) | Plus 20 |
| Nonmanual | 45 | (236) | 57 | (65) | 36 | (148) | Plus 21 |
| Class voting | Plus 17 | | Plus 17 | | Plus 18 | | |
| Total | | | 64 | (166) | 44 | (371) | Plus 20 |
| | | | *1956* | | | | |
| Farm | 45 | (62) | 78 | (9) | 39 | (52) | Plus 39 |
| Manual | 50 | (294) | 60 | (101) | 44 | (185) | Plus 16 |
| Nonmanual | 33 | (210) | 49 | (61) | 21 | (124) | Plus 28 |
| Class voting | Plus 17 | | Plus 11 | | Plus 23 | | |
| Total | | | 57 | (171) | 35 | (361) | Plus 22 |
| | | | *1958* | | | | |
| Farm | 55 | (53) | 67 | (6) | 53 | (45) | Plus 14 |
| Manual | 66 | (282) | 81 | (95) | 57 | (178) | Plus 24 |
| Nonmanual | 48 | (271) | 59 | (81) | 35 | (156) | Plus 24 |
| Class voting | Plus 18 | | Plus 22 | | Plus 22 | | |
| Total | | | 71 | (182) | 47 | (379) | Plus 24 |
| | | | *1960* | | | | |
| Farm | 36 | (120) | 69 | (13) | 32 | (106) | Plus 37 |
| Manual | 58 | (719) | 84 | (240) | 43 | (438) | Plus 41 |
| Nonmanual | 40 | (565) | 78 | (159) | 19 | (336) | Plus 59 |
| Class voting | Plus 18 | | Plus 6 | | Plus 24 | | |
| Total | | | 81 | (412) | 33 | (880) | Plus 48 |

*Source.* S. M. Lipset, "Religion and Politics in the American Past and Present," in Robert Lee and Martin Marty, eds., *Religion and Social Conflict* (New York: Oxford University Press, 1964), pp. 92–94.

Table 8.2   Relationship between Socioeconomic Status and Traditional Party Preference for the Three Major Religious Groupings; Percent Democratic and Republican—1954 (White Respondents Only)

| Stratum | Protestant | | | Catholic | | | Jews | | |
|---|---|---|---|---|---|---|---|---|---|
| | Democratic | Republican | (N) | Democratic | Republican | (N) | Democratic | Republican | (N) |
| Nonmanual | | | | | | | | | |
| Upper | 14 | 61 | (169) | 36 | 39 | (39) | 31 | 0 | (13) |
| Upper-middle | 24 | 49 | (714) | 36 | 27 | (232) | 55 | 10 | (58) |
| Lower-middle | 25 | 44 | (910) | 50 | 18 | (406) | 63 | 5 | (79) |
| Lower | 45 | 40 | (62) | 64 | 7 | (28) | — | — | |
| Manual | | | | | | | | | |
| Upper-middle | 36 | 37 | (300) | 49 | 10 | (144) | — | — | |
| Lower-middle | 40 | 30 | (1696) | 63 | 11 | (945) | 66 | 2 | (44) |
| Lower | 50 | 24 | (361) | 69 | 10 | (267) | — | — | |
| Farm | | | | | | | | | |
| Upper | 24 | 41 | (34) | — | — | | — | — | |
| Upper-middle | 29 | 44 | (168) | 38 | 44 | (16) | — | — | |
| Lower-middle | 32 | 43 | (402) | 58 | 20 | (96) | — | — | |
| Lower | 34 | 41 | (129) | 44 | 12 | (25) | — | — | |

*Source.* Computed from the data of a survey conducted in eleven states by International Research Associates in 1954. The states are California, Michigan, Minnesota, Massachusetts, Iowa, New Mexico, Illinois, Ohio, Oregon, Pennsylvania, and New Jersey. Independents are included in the base. They are the difference between the two-party totals and 100%. See S. M. Lipset, "Religion and Politics in the American Past and Present" (cited under Table 8.1), p. 97.

The corresponding difference among Protestants between the highest and the lowest group is 36%. Within any one stratum, the largest variation in the percent Democratic between Catholics and Protestants is 25%, but more intraclass differences are less. A comparable analysis (not reported here) for actual vote in the 1952 election resulted in differences of comparable magnitude.

The usual concentration on the Protestant-Catholic-Jewish trichotomy serves to conceal variations among the Protestant denominations. When these are separated, the available survey evidence would suggest that the average socioeconomic status of the members of a given denomination is an important determinant of the relative position of the denomination with respect to support of the two major parties. However, there is some evidence that Protestant denominational differences do exist that are independent of class position. A large national sample of the electorate interviewed in the spring of 1952 was asked which party the respondents most often have favored between 1936 and 1952. When this sample was differentiated among those in manual and nonmanual occupations, the data indicated that the two "lowest-status" and most fundamentalist groups "contained the smaller proportion of Republicans within the manual and the nonmanual strata, while the denominations of the more well-to-do, the Episcopalians, the Presbyterians, and the Congregationalists, contributed heavily to Republican support." A substantial majority of the manual workers who adhered to the latter groups indicated they had voted Republican most of the time.

To a considerable extent, the data reported in Table 8.3 would seem to confirm the assumption that the general political set of a Protestant denomination is determined largely by the average socioeconomic status of its adherents. When segregated by denomination and occupational status, every Protestant group is more disposed to back the Republicans than are Catholics or Jews. The differences between all of the Protestant denominations and the Catholic and Jewish groups are greatest among the white-collar strata. However, intra-Protestant variation is greater within the manual groups than in the middle classes.

These findings would suggest that worker members of predominantly high-status churches are greatly affected by the modal opinion of the group or, perhaps, that the workers who adhere to these denominations do so in part because they are "upward mobile," that they seek to identify with the more privileged classes. Conversely, working-class members of the three lowest-status (in terms of average socioeconomic position) churches (the Baptists, the Methodists, and the Lutherans) are much more likely to be Democrats. The poorest denomination, the Baptists, is the most Democratic of all the major sects.

**Table 8.3  Predominant Past Voting Behavior, Religion and Occupation—1952 (Non-Southern Whites) Percent Two-Party Vote**

| Denomination | Blue-Collar | | | White-Collar | | |
|---|---|---|---|---|---|---|
| | Democratic | Republican | | Democratic | Republican | |
| Baptist | 61 | 39 | (31) | 35 | 65 | (23) |
| Lutheran | 51 | 49 | (29) | 18 | 82 | (45) |
| Methodist | 48 | 52 | (52) | 32 | 68 | (62) |
| Episcopal | 40 | 60 | (15) | 24 | 76 | (41) |
| Presbyterian | 33 | 67 | (28) | 28 | 72 | (39) |
| Congregational | 27 | 73 | (11) | 21 | 79 | (28) |
| Other Protestant | 65 | 35 | (39) | 27 | 73 | (56) |
| Total Protestant | 50 | 50 | (215) | 26 | 73 | (294) |
| Catholic | 81 | 19 | (170) | 53 | 47 | (106) |
| Jewish | 83 | 17 | (6) | 74 | 26 | (43) |

*Source.* Data for analysis are from a 1952 survey by Elmo Roper Associates, see S. M. Lipset, "Religion and Politics in the American Past and Present" (cited beneath Table 8.1), p. 98.

There clearly are significant differences among Protestants in comparable class positions which are associated with denominational affiliations. It would appear, however, that these differences are not a function of variation in theological beliefs, of the difference between ascetic and nonascetic, or religious liberal and conservative doctrines. Groups like the Baptists or fundamentalists who have stressed ascetic morality and anti-Catholicism —doctrines that should dispose them to favor Republicans—are, in fact, seemingly more inclined to support the Democrats.

Benton Johnson offers an explanation of the apparent paradox that the more fundamentalist and ascetic Protestant groups are disproportionately Democratic.[54] He first points to another paradox, that the churches of the more well-to-do have also been more liberal not only in their theology but in their social and economic pronouncements. The liberal National Council of Churches, although representing the wealthier Protestant denominations, has given considerable support to the Social Gospel movement. The clergy of the highest-status church in the United States, the Episcopal church, are very liberal in their political views. On the other hand, the churches of the poorer Protestants, predominantly the fundamentalist groups, have on the whole opposed the Social Gospel, and have taken conservative positions on economic and political issues.

Johnson argues that the political position of the poorer-Protestant groups is congruent with historic theological elements in ascetic Protestantism. The liberalism of the churches of the more well-to-do derives from the fact that their ministers are often men "who have received their training from the more influential and prestigeful seminaries . . . many of which are close to large universities, and have participated in the trend toward liberal humanitarianism that has been going on in intellectual circles for many years." [55] The churches of the poor, on the other hand, prefer a simple unintellectual theology. Both parishioners and clergy tend to be low in educational attainments, and the seminaries of these groups are often deliberately removed from contact with secular university life.

The general correlation between the average socioeconomic status of the members of different denominations and the religious and political liberalism of their clergy and official church bodies suggest the hypothesis that the more integrated an individual is in the religious life of the liberal high-status churches, the more liberal he should be in his outlook, holding other factors constant; conversely, the opposite pattern should occur among the adherents of the low-status and more fundamentalist sects.

An analysis of interviews from Eugene, Oregon, sustains these assumptions.

---

[54] Benton Johnson, "Ascetic Protestantism and Political Preference," *Public Opinion Quarterly*, **26**, 38–40 (1962).

[55] *Ibid.*, p. 39.

Members of low-status churches are more likely to be Democrats than those adhering to the high-status ones. These tendencies hold true within classes as well. However, when the supporters of the liberal churches are divided on the basis of church attendance, frequent churchgoers show a lower Republican propensity than do those who go rarely. Among the fundamentalist groups, the exact opposite occurs: frequent attenders are more likely to vote Republican, while those who are rarely seen in church retain a strong Democratic allegiance. This relationship holds true even when class position is held constant.

The data presented in Table 8.4 clearly suggest that religious practice

**Table 8.4   Percentage of Two-Party Vote of Liberal and Fundamentalist by Frequency of Church Attendance and Class Position**

| Occupational Class and Frequency of Attendance | Party Identification (Percent Republican) | | Voting Behavior (Percent Republican) | |
|---|---|---|---|---|
| Liberal: | | | | |
| White-collar | | | | |
| Attend frequently | 54 | (29) | 62 | (26) |
| Attend seldom | 63 | (16) | 93 | (14) |
| Blue-collar | | | | |
| Attend frequently | 44 | (9) | 38 | (8) |
| Attend seldom | 56 | (9) | 63 | (8) |
| Total Liberal: | | | | |
| Attend frequently | 51 | (37) | 56 | (34) |
| Attend seldom | 60 | (25) | 82 | (22) |
| Fundamentalist: | | | | |
| White-collar | | | | |
| Attend frequently | 65 | (17) | 71 | (17) |
| Attend seldom | 44 | (16) | 55 | (11) |
| Blue-collar | | | | |
| Attend frequently | 48 | (27) | 53 | (17) |
| Attend seldom | 27 | (11) | 33 | (6) |
| Total Fundamentalist: | | | | |
| Attend frequently | 55 | (44) | 62 | (34) |
| Attend seldom | 37 | (27) | 47 | (17) |

*Source.* Benton Johnson, "Ascetic Protestantism and Political Preference," *Public Opinion Quarterly,* **26**, 43–44 (1962). Voting behavior is based on a scale derived from reported votes in four elections between 1952 and 1958.

and class position operate independently to affect partisan choice. As Johnson points out, the varying Protestant religious beliefs serve to reduce the relation between class and party among church attenders.

The finding presented earlier that adherents of different denominations are disposed to follow the predominant political choice of the denomination may be shaped mainly by those who identify with, but are not involved in, the religious life of a given church. To be a nonpracticing Episcopalian or Congregationalist means to have a public high-status attribute; nominal church affiliation affects a person's self-conception and public image, but apparently it does not much affect his values. Hence nonpracticing supporters of these churches are among the most Republican of individuals with comparable socioeconomic traits. Conversely, to remain identified with a low-status church means to retain a status-ascribing characteristic that lowers a person's general social status. An individual who so defines himself is presumably less oriented toward upward mobility, toward the values of the higher-status groups. Consequently, people of this kind are among the most prone to vote Democratic within their stratum.

Religion, therefore, would seem to affect political choice in the United States in two independent ways: as a source of beliefs and as a determinant of status. Active membership in a liberal high-status church pulls a person toward political liberalism; nominal adherence primarily serves as a source of status and hence strengthens the political conservatism associated with high position. And the opposite pattern operates among the inactive and active adherents of the more fundamentalist low-status groupings.

Class and religious differences then remain as the two most significant correlates of party support. An examination of the survey data from 1936 to 1958 reported in Table 8.1 suggests that there was little change in the relationship of these two variables and party support during this period, although the parties varied in strength. Thus, in the 1950's Eisenhower gained among all groups—Catholics and Protestants and those in manual and white-collar occupations. As Philip Converse concludes from a national survey of a panel of voters conducted by the University of Michigan's Survey Research Center in 1956, 1958, and 1960:

Of those citizens considering themselves to be Democrats and thereby voting Democratic unless they perceived compelling reasons to do otherwise, over one-quarter had defected to vote for Eisenhower in 1952 and 1956. Two facts stand out about this massive defection. First, it was a defection and in no sense a conversion. Democrats voting for Eisenhower continued to think of themselves as Democrats, and continued to vote Democratic at other levels of office, particularly when Eisenhower was not on the ticket. Our subsequent data since 1956 have made it clear that Eisenhower's appeal was rather completely disassociated from the Republican Party: even among Democrats most attracted to him, it is hard to find evidence of any change induced in personal loyalties.

Second, and most important for our purposes here, the Democratic defections of the Eisenhower interlude seem to have occurred quite independent of religious background. That is, rates of defection were essentially the same for Protestant and Catholic alike. By sample estimates, Catholic defections were slightly less frequent than Protestant defections in 1952, and slightly more frequent in 1956. However, neither difference exceeds sampling error. More generally, it may be shown that the Democratic rates of defection to Eisenhower were remarkably similar across all the commonly studied social groupings: he enjoyed an "across-the-board" appeal which paid no visible respect to the major social boundaries.[56]

However, the data presented in Table 8.1 do suggest that among Catholics there was a somewhat greater return to the Democrats in 1958 than there had been in 1954, particularly among Catholic manual workers, possibly because of the eclipse of McCarthyism.

The 1960 election produced a major convulsion in the previously stable level of religious voting. The measures of religious differences in voting in Table 8.1 among both manual and nonmanual workers are far higher than in any other of the elections recorded. Contrasted with the "normal" pattern of 1954 and 1958 we can see that both Catholic groups moved toward the Democrats (although the shift among manual workers was a small one), and that both Protestant groups moved toward the Republicans. Using results of a panel study interviewed in 1956, 1958, and 1960, Converse reaches a similar verdict:

> Instead of concluding that political choices of Catholics were profoundly affected by the candidacy of a Catholic while Protestants were left unaffected, we must conclude that the impact on the two religious groupings was rather more equal, although opposite in direction.[57]

Let us attempt to account for the Catholic shift toward the Democrats. Kennedy was our first President not only of a minority religion, but also of a minority group, although a highly acculturated one. Converse reports that there is only a "mild sign that Irish Catholics were more affected by the Kennedy candidacy than were non-Irish Catholics." Italians and other

[56] Philip Converse, "Religion and Politics: The 1960 Elections" (unpublished dittoed paper: Survey Research Center, University of Michigan, 1962), pp. 4–5. An analysis of the effects of moving to the suburbs by Catholics based on a survey in metropolitan St. Louis in 1956 reports that even in this Eisenhower year: "In voting, both central city and suburban Catholics remain heavily Democratic. When we control country of origin, generation since migration, and education, only in the suburbs and in the most extreme classes, do we find small Republican pluralities among Catholics—those with northern and western European backgrounds, those who are third generation, those with college educations. And these are far less Republican than their counterparts among the non-Catholics." Scott Greer, "Catholic Voters and the Democratic Party," *Public Opinion Quarterly,* **25,** 623 (1961).

[57] Philip Converse, *op. cit.,* p. 9.

non-Irish Catholics voted overwhelmingly for him, as they had for Al Smith in 1928. Converse concludes, therefore:

> While it is plausible to suppose from these data, then that the ethnic factor contributed some extra "push" to Catholics in 1960, there is of course no question but that its role was entirely eclipsed, like an eddy in a torrent, by movement along broader religious lines.[58]

The unique pattern of Catholic voting in 1960, which is apparently not explicable in terms of class differences (which, of course, are controlled in Table 8.1) or ethnic loyalties, presumably can be accounted for only in terms of some more narrowly religious-linked factors. In 1958, Converse found no consistent relationship between political party preference and church attendance, or between party preference and "identification with the Catholic community." However, in examining the *deviation* of the 1960 vote from the 1958 party preferences, Converse reports that both church attendance and community involvement were related to Kennedy voting. He suggests that when an election is relevant to the interests or values of a group, conformity to its political norms will be related to involvement in the group, but if direct political relevance is low, this relationship is reduced. Thus, in 1960, the nomination of a Catholic gave the group tie increased relevance, and the relationship between conformity to political norms and involvement in the group was intensified.

The intensity of Protestant reaction against Kennedy was striking. Despite the decline of anti-Catholicism, the rapid rise of Catholics into a position of social prominence and power seems to have set off a new wave of uneasiness.

In a survey administered during the 1960 campaign, direct references to Kennedy's religion were avoided, yet almost one half of the white Protestant respondents spontaneously mentioned the matter. More than three quarters of those who did mention it were coded as "unequivocally negative." Negative references to Kennedy's religion were given most frequently by unskilled workers, but least often from persons in the middle of the occupational scale, clerical and sales workers. The anti-Catholic reaction of the upper-middle-class occupations is, at first glance, surprising. In Southern areas anti-Catholicism was related to low status and Protestant religious involvement, but "where Catholics reside in large numbers and have come to compete for some of the forms of secular power, the reaction of the anti-Catholics fell much less clearly along lines of religious involvement in the narrow sense. This was particularly true of the upper middle class in the non-Southern metropolis, where the Catholic encroachment has been most notable. Here, despite its high education level, the Protestant business

[58] *Ibid.*, p. 29.

and professional community responded in a manner which suggests a threat along a broad front, not simply a challenge to religious orthodoxy." [59]

Apparently there were two types of anti-Catholicism in 1960. The lower-class nonurban kind is the religious anti-Catholicism of American history, tied to a lack of education, strong commitment to one's own Protestant church, and little direct contact with the targets of one's feelings. Presumably, this attitude has been declining in importance in recent years and, with the spread of education and urbanization, will continue to weaken.

Anti-Catholic sentiment among higher-status persons may be a different matter. Probably this is the response of Protestants to their "growing minority consciousness" discussed by Will Herberg. The same forces that cause the old nativist anti-Catholicism to decline help the new form to flourish; the outdated stereotype of the Catholic immigrant as a drunk and a bum fades away, but a new picture emerges of a community which is fully American, yet not Protestant, in which the Catholic and the Jew continue to increase their visible importance.

## Representation, Oligarchy, and Democracy

I have previously defined democracy in this chapter, following Max Weber and Joseph Schumpeter,[60] as the process by means of which the elite is formed through the competitive struggle for support from a mainly passive electorate. Talcott Parsons [61] sees the political system as providing leadership for the larger social system in setting and attaining collective goals. The various interested social groups support the leadership in the expectation of the approval of their special-interest measures. For example, trade unions and workers tend to endorse the Democratic or Labor parties because these parties generally back the interests of the workers and the unions. Various social groups initiate and advocate particular policies which are taken up by public officials who enact them as government policy.

---

[59] Philip Converse (cited in footnote 56), pp. 50–51.
[60] See J. Schumpeter, *Capitalism, Socialism, and Democracy* (New York: Harper, 1947), p. 269: *From Max Weber: Essays in Sociology* (cited in footnote 6), p. 226. I have discussed and used this approach to democracy in my work. See "Party Systems and the Representation of Social Groups," *European Journal of Sociology,* 1, 50–53 (1960); *Political Man* (cited in footnote 9), pp. 45–46; and S. M. Lipset, Martin Trow, and J. S. Coleman, *Union Democracy* (Garden City, N.Y.: Doubleday, Anchor Books), pp. 405–412.
[61] See Talcott Parsons, "Voting and the Equilibrium of the American Political Systems," in E. Burdick and A. Brodbeck, eds., *American Voting Behavior* (Glencoe, Ill.: The Free Press, 1959), pp. 80–120.

The successful Negro struggle for civil rights legislation is an example of this phenomenon. Negroes, by giving votes to those politicians who helped them, have been able to secure legislation which, at times, has been opposed by a majority of the electorate.

The competitive struggle within the political elite (the leaders of the various parties who hold or seek office) for generalized as well as for specific support gives those outside of the authority structure access to political power if a section of the political elite must consider how a given group will react to a given policy, even if their participation is limited to voting. That is, if politicians worry how the farmers, the Negroes, and southerners will vote if a measure is passed, the group has access.

This interchange between leadership and support takes place through the system of representation. Various institutional practices found in democratic society—party systems and interest organizations—serve to facilitate the interchange between authority and the spontaneous groupings of society which have specific interests. The representation system links authority (legislative, executive, and judicial) with a variety of subgroups such as classes, religions, ethnic groups, occupations, and regions.

The general notion that the representation system permits access by groups outside of government to political power has been challenged by the so-called "elite" theorists, Robert Michels, George Sorel, Gaetano Mosca, and others, who have pointed out that the organization of diverse-interest groupings establishes a bureaucratic structure which inherently gives power to the officers at the top. Michels noted that most groups of this kind have an oligarchical internal polity, that leaders can stay in office indefinitely, can choose their own successors, and can control the communication within the organization, so that most members only know the officials' interpretation of what is good for the organization.[62] The leaders possess many advantages over the members in formulating the decisions of the group. These include (1) superior knowledge—for example, they are privy to much information that can be used to secure assent for their programme; (2) control over the formal means of communication with the members—for example, they dominate the press; they may travel about presenting their case at the organization's expense, and can command an audience; and (3) skill in the art of politics—for example, they are far more adept than nonprofessionals in making speeches, writing articles, and organizing group activities. The rank-and-file members have much less opportunity to be active and knowledgeable about the organization's activities. The pulls of work, family, personal leisure activities, and the like, severely limit the amount of time

[62] Robert Michels, *Political Parties* (New York: Free Press Paperback, 1965). This book was first published in 1911.

and psychic energy which the average person may invest in membership groups.

Since this pattern of internal politics is typical of large-scale organizations, the question has been posed as to whether we must not reject the assumption that leadership in democracies is representative. Michels did reject it, and attempted to demonstrate that those who become officials of interest groups, political parties, or government, even when they have been placed there by the lower strata "whilst belonging by social position to the class of the ruled, have in fact come to form part of the ruling oligarchy." [63] That is to say, even the leaders of the masses are part of the "power elite," and derive perspectives and interests from their position among the more privileged elements of the society. Consequently, the idea of representativeness breaks down, since the policies of mass organizations do not reflect the will or interests of their members or supporters but the will or interests of their leaders. And various social scientists have documented the existence of one-party oligarchy in a variety of such "private governments." [64]

This approach has been criticized for being overdeterministic; that is, for seeing only the restrictive side of bureaucracy and failing to see it also as a means through which groups may achieve desired objectives. Thus, many of the recent analyses by social scientists have been concerned not only with the self-interested aspect of bureaucratization but also with the factors that make some organizations more successful than others and factors that make organizations vary in their behavior. And among the variables noted are the nature of goals, the ways in which goals and methods are absorbed into the *modus operandi*, the way in which the multifunctions of organizations affect behavior, and the extent to which different kinds of

[63] *Ibid.*

[64] Clark Kerr, *Unions and Union Leaders of Their Own Choosing* (New York: The Fund for the Republic, 1957), p. 12.

The evidence sustaining the oligarchic tendencies of these groups has been summarized in various works. The sociologist, Bernard Barber, reports: "No matter what interest any particular organization represents, we find the existence of an active minority in control." "Participation and Mass Apathy in Associations," in Alvin W. Gouldner, ed., *Studies in Leadership* (New York: Harper, 1950), p. 584. Barber points out the way oligarchy operates in various groups. "The American Legion was founded in 1919 by a small group and is run by a self-perpetuating oligarchy . . . ," and he cites evidence concerning similar patterns in fraternal organizations, Consumers' Cooperatives, and other groups. For discussion of similar points elaborating and citing evidence concerning oligarchy in many groups such as the National Association of Manufacturers and the American Medical Association, see David Trumen, *The Governmental Process* (New York: Alfred A. Knopf, 1958), especially pp. 129–210.

See also Peter M. Blau, *Bureaucracy in Modern Society* (New York: Random House, 1956); Paul M. Harrison, *Authority and Power in the Free Church Tradition* (Princeton: Princeton University Press, 1959); and Douglas V. Verney, *The Analysis of Political Systems* (London: Routledge and Kegan Paul, 1959), pp. 155–156.

members or clients modify the actions of leaders. Maurice Duverger, Sigmund Neumann, and Robert McKenzie, and others have shown that Michels was overdeterministic in his analysis of party behavior.[65] Political parties differ in organizational structure. For example, the two major parties in the United States vary greatly from the Michels model, in that they lack central control at the national level and exhibit comparatively little centralization even at the state level. Moreover, factionalism is replete in American parties, and turnover in party control is more common than in most European parties. This is partly the result of the two-party pattern in America which, in turn, is largely a consequence of constitutional forms that virtually require conflicting interests throughout the country to unite into two large electoral coalitions. (The primary executive power is determined by the election of a single man, the president or governor, rather than members of parliament.) Diverse groups, which in multiparty nations have independent parties with relatively little internal changes in leadership, form the bases for factions in two-party political systems.

Leaving the problem of oligarchy aside, there still remains the question of representativeness. Some analysts who acknowledge that almost all unions are controlled by an entrenched administration argue that these unions still fulfill their primary function: protecting their members' interests. Thus V. L. Allen states in answer to Michels that "the end of trade union activity is to protect and improve the general standards of its members and not to provide workers with an exercise in self-government." He suggests, however, that this end will be fostered only when "the penalty [to union leaders] for inefficiency, the misuse of resources, or the abuse of power is severe . . . . The voluntary nature of trade unions provides such a penalty. A trade union leader who is in continual fear of losing his members will inevitably take steps to satisfy their wants. . . . A failing membership is a much greater stimulant than a strongly worded resolution." [66]

Alvin Gouldner argues that in all organizations there is "a need that consent of the governed be given—at least in some measure—to their governors. . . . And if all organizations must adjust to such a need for consent, is there not built into the very marrow of organization a large element of what we mean by democracy? This would appear to be an organizational constraint that makes oligarchies, and all separation of leaders from those led, no less inherently unstable than democratic organizations." [67]

Furthermore, the problem of representativeness within organizations is

[65] Maurice Duverger, *Political Parties* (London: Methuen, 1954); Robert McKenzie, *British Political Parties* (London: Heinemann, 1963).
[66] *Power in Trade Unions* (London: Longmans, Green, 1954), pp. 15, 63.
[67] "Metaphysical Pathos and the Theory of Bureaucracy," in S. M. Lipset and Neil Smelser, eds., *Sociology: The Progress of a Decade* (Englewood Cliffs, N.J.: Prentice-Hall, 1961), p. 88.

confused by the absence of any organized opposition group in most unions and other private associations which prevents the members from choosing a leader who shares their views. It is difficult to believe, for example, that the differences in the behavior of the two predominantly Jewish garment unions in the 1930's and 1940's represented variations in the sentiment of their members. The Amalgamated Clothing Workers' Union under Sidney Hillman was a pillar of the CIO and cooperated with the Communists in New York's American Labor party. The International Ladies Garment Workers' Union under David Dubinsky rejoined the American Federation of Labor, and formed the vigorously anti-Communist Liberal party. John L. Lewis, the head of the United Mine Workers, endorsed the Republican candidate for United States President in 1940, while the large majority of his coal miner members were obviously for Franklin Roosevelt. A survey conducted of the membership of the British Medical Association at a time in which the leaders of the association were strongly fighting all proposals for state medicine showed that a majority of the members of the B. M. A. agreed with the government on most issues rather than with their officials.[68]

It is difficult to determine when there is actually a serious cleavage between the interests and conscious objectives of members and those of their leaders. Michels argued that the shift to the "right" prior to World War I of the German trade unions and the Social-Democratic party demonstrated the way in which the inherent bureaucratic conservatism of leaders deflects organizations from their goals and the benefits of their members. However, Rose Laub Coser suggests that the goals and beliefs of the members changed first. She points out that the rapid improvement in the social and economic position of the German working class in the two decades prior to World War I produced a relatively conservative, contented, lower stratum, to whom the revolutionary and internationalist ideology of the party leadership up to 1914 had little appeal. In the United States, the International Longshoremen's Association, expelled from the AFL-CIO as corrupt, racket-ridden, and dictatorial, won three secret-ballot elections conducted by the government against an AFL-CIO backed rival. Similarly, the Teamsters' Union led by Jimmy Hoffa, although also expelled from the AFL-CIO as corrupt, and denounced by government agencies as dictatorial, has been one of the most rapidly growing unions in the United States. This paradox of trade-union membership support for oligarchy, corruption, Communism, Republican politics, or other policies that are clearly at variance with their sentiments and/or interests may be explained by assumption that unions are perceived by the members primarily as instruments of collective bar-

[68] Harry Eckstein, "The Politics of the British Medical Association," *The Political Quarterly,* **26,** 345–359 (1955).

gaining. Leaders are permitted considerable leeway in areas viewed as less salient than that of collective bargaining.

Although organizations must in some general sense "represent" their members, the basic assumption of Michels regarding the effect of the division of labor within organizations remains valid. This division, as he said, results in the delegation of power to leaders who are usually able to remain in power indefinitely. These leadership groups often develop aims that are at variance with the original objectives of the organizations and the interests and attitudes of their members.

Michels and his followers have clearly demonstrated that democracy in the sense of active participation by all members in the decision-making process is inherently impossible. Michels showed the technical impossibility of ending the separation between rulers and ruled within a complex society. Elites always have special group interests that are somewhat at variance with those of the people they represent. But even if we accept all of these points as valid, they do not mean that democracy is impossible; instead, they suggest the need for a more realistic understanding of the democratic potential in a complex society.

Michels' view of power assumes that all dominant minorities follow a logic of self-interest, of exploiting the masses to maintain or extend their own privilege and power. This view of political life assumes, as Talcott Parsons has suggested, "that it is only power which 'really' determines what happens in society." [69] Against this, he points out that power is only one of several cognate factors in the determination of social events. The power of any organized minority is circumscribed by the internal and external social setting of the polity which it leads. Clearly, mass organizations and political parties have been responsible for many changes that have increased the effective freedom of the mass of the population (freedom of speech, of movement, guarantees of job security, and so forth) and have equalized opportunity and income. Workers in Scandinavia, Britain, and the United States have more government welfare today because the political parties they support have been elected to office. The American Medical Association and the unions within the AFL-CIO are dominated by self-perpetuating oligarchies, but the heads of these bodies take sharply conflicting stands on the question of medical care guaranteed by the government. To win the support of the mass electorate, the Republicans in the United States and the Conservatives in Great Britain maintained most of the extensions of the welfare state enacted by their predecessors. Power may be viewed as the "capacity to mobilize the resources of the society [or an organization] for the attainment of goals for which a general 'public' commitment has

[69] *Structure and Process in Modern Societies* (Glencoe, Ill.: The Free Press, 1960), p. 22.

been made, or may be made." [70] A primary emphasis on the oligarchic or "power elite" aspects of organizational or political life is clearly inadequate. It results in ignoring the sources and positive consequences of controversy. Michels was forced to deny that conflicts among factions within the socialist movement or other parties represented anything but struggles for the spoils of office and, in fact, he hardly alluded to such controversies in his book. Similarly, the most recent exponent of elite theory, C. Wright Mills, almost completely ignored the existence of political parties in the American power struggle. [71]

Democracy in modern society involves the conflict of organized groups competing for support. Since many organized groups are always out of office or out of favor with those in office, they have an interest in institutionalizing safeguards for democratic rights of speech, press, assembly, and so on. This image of democracy as conflict of organized groups and of access by the ruled to their rulers may be far from the ideal of the Greek city-state or of small Swiss cantons, but in operation as a system it is far better than any other political system that has been devised to reduce the potential exploitation of man by man. Only by conflict and public commitment to explicit goals, can egoistic misuse of power be limited.

While most private governments, unions, professional societies, veterans' organizations, and political parties will remain one-party systems, since they do not possess the basis for sustained internal conflict, oligarchic organizations often help to sustain political democracy in the larger society and to protect the interests of their members. Democracy rests on the fact that no single group is able to secure such power and command over the majority as to effectively suppress its opponents. The labor movement, with its ideal of equality, has played a major role in fostering institutions of political democracy. In all of the political democracies, workers today can speak out with much less fear of jeopardizing their livelihood than they could even three decades ago. There are a few unions that have as much potential over their members as employers once had over their workers. (Unfortunately there are some.)

The concern with the consequences for the larger polity of the internal structure of private governments is, of course, not the sole interest of the political sociologist in such organizations. As a social scientist, he primarily seeks to study institutions to account for variations in their behavior in terms of propositions linked to a larger system of social theory. And in order to do this, there has been a considerable body of research following up Michels' analysis which seems to account for differences from the ideal-type model of oligarchic rule. There are many exceptions to the "iron law of

---

[70] *Ibid.*
[71] C. Wright Mills, *The Power Elite* (New York: Oxford University Press, 1956).

oligarchy" within the realm of private governments, including trade unions and political parties. Some trade unions have regular opposition parties, or irregular factions, which do vote out incumbent administrations from time to time. American and other political parties certainly have frequent internal battles for control of the party and nominations for public office, which give the registered supporters of the parties an opportunity to choose among varying tendencies. A detailed discussion of the factors that appear to affect the propensities for less rather than more authoritarian rule within these groups is not within the scope of this chapter, but I do not want to end it without at least indicating that such research and considerations exist.

## Conclusion

In conclusion, I must mention that the topics that have been discussed here do not exhaust the interests of political sociologists.[72] These interests go far beyond the limited considerations of the conditions affecting legitimacy, political stability, consensus and cleavage, the analysis of voting behavior, or the discussion of the problems of representation as related to the analysis of the oligarchic structure of voluntary groups. There is a considerable literature devoted to the study of political participation at various levels. Many scholars have concerned themselves with the analysis of the conditions that foster the emergence of new social movements; this analysis has involved special concern with the background of extremist political tendencies of both the left and the right. Students of public opinion have investigated the correlates of different varieties of attitudes, for example, internationalism, ethnic and racial prejudice, beliefs in civil liberties and democratic rights for "deviant" minorities, orientations toward the welfare state, and the like. Many sociologists have been interested in the phenomenon of bureaucratization, seeking to specify the relationship between the formal structure of large social organizations and other aspects of the social system. Most recently, political sociology, like most other branches of the field, has become increasingly comparative in its methodology. A growing body of work seeks to systematically relate varying aspects of national politics to differences in the overall social systems of which they are a part, such as their basic value orientations or class structures. To report on all of these would have required a book, and consequently, this chapter has been limited to a few illustrations of the concerns and findings of political sociology.

[72] For a detailed effort to deal with much of the data on parties and voting presented here on a more rigorous theoretical level, see the introductory essay by the editors in S. M. Lipset and S. Rukkan, eds., *Party Systems and Voter Alignments* (New York: The Free Press, 1967).

# III

# SOCIALIZATION
# PROCESS

# SOCIALIZATION
PROCESS

*9*

# FAMILY
# AND KINSHIP

*William N. Stephens*

# FAMILY AND KINSHIP

In trying to comprehend kinship, we might start with a familiar biological fact: people have sexual intercourse and, as a result, women bear children. Next we might consider a second fact: given the nature of human memory and language, blood ties are held in mind and are signified by special terms of relationship: mother, child, grandmother, mother's brother, and others. Beyond this stage, biology appears to have little to do with kinship. Each culture has begun from this starting point, and has set up an elaborate system of rules. These rules are the customs of kinship. Here are a few examples.

- A person should not address an older-generation relative by the personal name. He should say "Father" or "Mother"—not "Charlie" or "Elizabeth." He should say "Grandfather" or "Grampa"—not "Jake" or "Ernest." And the same holds true for grandmothers, uncles, and aunts.
  - A mother must be married.
  - A man may not help his wife with the cooking.
  - A brother and sister, after puberty, may not touch each other.

The rules of kinship accomplish two major tasks. First, they create groups: special groupings of kin. Thus the social invention of marriage assigns each mother a husband, and makes her children his children, thereby creating a special group of father, mother, and children, which we are in the habit of calling a "family." By use of additional rules and social conventions, larger kin groups are created: extended families, lineages, clans, and moieties.

The second major function of kinship rules is to govern the role relationships between kin; that is, how one kinsman should behave in a particular kinsman's presence, or what one kinsman owes to another. Some kinship rules specify the rights and duties of membership in particular kin groups. Other rules pertain to diadic relationships between kin: the manner in which a person should behave, for instance, with his mother's brother, his father's father, or his daughter.

Kinship provides a sort of social grid. People in a society are joined to each other by genealogical ties and by common kin-group membership. They are "placed" in relation to each other: "my sister's daughter"; "my mother's father"; "my clansman." Kinship assigns guidelines for interactions between persons in these social niches. It defines proper, acceptable role relationships between father and daughter, between brother and sister, between young husband and mother-in-law, and between fellow lineage members and clansmen. As a result, kinship acts as a regularizer of social life. Within a particular society, a given kin relationship—for example, the relationship between a woman and her father-in-law—assumes some de-

508

gree of uniformity, both in space (from one village to the next) and in time (from generation to generation).

The term "patterned kin behavior" is used here to describe the rules governing the relationship between a pair of kinsmen. Certain kin relationships in some societies are so highly "patterned" that little leeway is allowed for spontaneity or individual differences; interaction between the pair of kin becomes an elaborate ritual. Other kin relationships have little obvious "patterning," and therefore leave much room for individualized behavior. Similarly, in some societies, patterned kin behavior is highly developed; in others it is undeveloped. Our own society has the absolute minimum of patterned kin behavior. If roles were assigned on the basis of kinship only, our society would be as near-chaotic as any. However, other bases for role assignment exist, of course, such as age and sex, occupations, and situationally determined bases like the roles of grocery-store customer, motorist, and patient.

The importance of kinship as a regularizer of social life depends on three things: (1) the extent to which a person is surrounded by kinsmen; (2) the degree of development of patterned kin behavior; and (3) the degree of development of alternative bases for assigning people to roles, such as occupational specialties.

When working, going to school, shopping, or driving, our own behavior is not channeled by kinship rules since, ordinarily, we are not interacting with kinsmen. This situation is in marked contrast to the usual peasant village, tribal hamlet, or band where practically everyone in the community is related to each other and, consequently, nearly everything that a person does is in the presence of kin. In some small societies, everyone is kin to everyone else. (". . . in Tikopia . . . every person of ordinary competency can ultimately trace connection with every other person in the community of over twelve hundred souls. As it is said, 'The whole land is a single body of kinsfolk.'"[1]) In such a community of kin, if patterned kin behavior is highly developed, and if alternative bases for assigning roles are undeveloped, then kinship takes on an overweening importance. An anthropologist can record a significant portion of the rules and regularities of social life by merely tracing the kinship roles. He takes each kin relationship, one by one: first, mother to son perhaps, then mother to daughter, then father to son, father to daughter, brother to brother, sister to sister, husband to wife, a male Ego to father's brother, and so on down the list of possible kin ties. For each relationship, he will give the kin terms that are used, and

[1] Raymond Firth, *We, the Tikopia* (New York: The American Book Company, New York, 1936), p. 234.

then describe the rules that govern the kin relationship. When he has finished, he will have described a large portion of the social structure.

Patterned kin behavior might be divided into the following two categories.

1. Rules governing rights and obligations.
2. Rules of comportment or "manners."

Let us consider the first category—rules governing rights and obligations. These rules apply where one kinsman owes another certain services, or duties, or privileges. For example, a generalized hospitality ethic often prevails among kin. If a relative decides that he wants to come to visit, he may have a right to expect free meals, a place to sleep, and other tokens of hospitality—these are defined as rightfully his because he is a kinsman. Another example is rules of inheritance. They may dictate that a deceased father's estate descends to his eldest son (primogeniture), or that it descends to his wife, or that it is to be divided among the children, or that is to revert to the father's clan. A further example is the manifold obligations that accompany parenthood: obligations to feed and shelter one's child, to train him properly, perhaps to provide him with the price of a bride, and things of this kind. A final illustration is the complex of rules defining the proper division of labor, responsibilities, and privileges between husband and wife: for instance, who should go for the firewood, who empties the garbage, who decides how the fields will be planted, and who has control over the family capital.

Within some kin relationships, rights and obligations are balanced fairly equally. Within other relationships they are quite unbalanced: one party gives, the other receives; one kinsman has rights, the other has obligations. This state of affairs characterizes the parent-child relationship in our own society. We are unusual in this regard. In most societies a child, when he reaches working age (which might be eight or ten years old), assumes heavy return obligations toward his parents, which he continues to shoulder until the parents die.

The second category of kinship rules—those dictating comportment or "manners"—might be further divided into three subcategories: rules of deference, avoidance, and joking.

1. *Deference* customs are a ritual expression of social inequality. A lower-status person gives deference to a higher-status person. Deference customs typically develop within power hierarchies. The person in command—the major, the boss, the white plantation owner, the raja—tends to receive deference from his underlings. Thus our armed services have rituals of subservience: the salute, the honorific terms of address for superior officers ("Sir"), and rules regulating body posture (standing at attention).

Within other hierarchical organizations in our society such as businesses, deference is shown one's superior in more subtle and less formalized ways. In a courtroom, the judge receives deference. Kings, customarily, got very elaborate deference from their subjects. In the old kingdoms, the nobility received marked deference from commoners.

The deference customs, ritually expressing unequal relationships, are themselves unequal. The inferior person bows, kneels, doffs his cap, says "Sir" to the superior person, but the superior person does not reciprocate. The plantation worker may address his white boss with some honorific term such as "Captain," "Sir," or "Boss," but the boss calls him "Boy," or "Billy," or "You."

In some societies, deference patterns according to age-sex roles. All people who are markedly older than Ego [2]—or perhaps only all older men—are due a certain amount of deference. This is partially true of our own society; there is some expectation that children give adults some mild degree of deference. Superimposed on the age-sex roles are the kinship roles which, generally, are powerful determinants of the direction and degree of deference.

In many societies—especially in those that are (or were until recently) within the territories of the old kingdoms [3]—a person owes extreme deference to his father. The details of the deference customs differ, of course, from one locality to the next. Below are some common types of deference customs.

*Honorific terms of address and special respectful language.* The personal-name taboo; addressing one's father by terms equivalent to "Sir," "Excellency," "My Lord"; various other "respectful" modes of speech. The child might be expected to speak in a low voice in his father's presence, and not to laugh or joke.

*Body-placement rules.* In some societies the child is not supposed to be physically higher than his father. If the father sits on a stool, the child sits on the ground. In other societies the rule is reversed, and the child must stand when his father comes into view and, perhaps, must remain standing while father is seated. Various rules may govern where father and child sit in relation to each other: possibly not on the same bench, or not face to face. Usually, at dinner time, the father has a special, honorific seat at the

---

[2] In speaking of kin relationships, the term "Ego" is often substituted for the term "a person." Thus, we might speak of the relationship between "Ego and his father," meaning the relationship between "a person and his father"; or "Ego and her mother-in-law," meaning "a person and her mother-in-law."

[3] China, Japan, India, most of Southeast Asia, the Moslem Middle East, the kingdoms of Black Africa, Eastern Europe, Spain and Portugal, and the better part of Latin America.

table. When father and child are walking together, the father frequently is supposed to walk ahead of his child.

*Greetings.* The child may have to bow, kiss his father's hand, tug his forelock, kneel, or utter some stereotyped honorific greeting.

There are many more miscellaneous deference rules, which often are idiosyncratic to particular cultures or culture areas. Thus a child may not be allowed to smoke in his father's presence, or to chew betel in his father's presence.

Many societies manifest an extreme development of child-to-father deference. Others do not. In our own society there is only the personal-name taboo, plus a modest, informal expectation of a certain amount of generalized "respect." Ordinarily, a fairly young child is bound by deference rules, and he must adhere to them until his father dies. Where extreme deference is given to father, it is also given to other older male relatives: usually to father's brother and to father's father, sometimes to elder brother, and sometimes to all older male consanguineal kin. A substantial number of the world's societies exhibit many extreme deference relationships: Ego to father and to various other older male relatives, and (since many of these are societies within the old kingdoms) commoner to nobleman.

On the other hand, female kin—mothers, aunts, grandmother—rarely receive more than the mildest of deference, if even that. Men, generally, are "respected," and women are not. Also, deference to *junior* relatives is practically unknown. Older male kin are the ones who receive deference, in those societies with pronounced deference customs. They receive it from their juniors and from their women. A final kin relationship that is frequently characterized by extreme deference is the wife-to-husband relationship. The wife gives deference to her husband (it is rarely the reverse).

Deference customs apparently reflect existing power relationships. More often than not, where father is treated as an Exalted Being by his children and his wife, he is a bona fide patriarch with considerable power over his family. In societies where he gets little noticeable deference (as in our own society), his power is usually considerably less. In some societies (like our own), family relations are relatively "democratic" and nonrespectful; in others, they are relatively autocratic and deference-ridden. Interestingly enough, family power relations seem to mirror the political structure. If the state has been autocratic for a long time (if it is a kingdom), family relations also will be autocratic, benefiting the husband-father. If the society has цо state government at all (which has been the case in many primitive societies), family relations are usually fairly equalitarian; the husband-father is not a hallowed patriarch; and little deference is given to him. If the state has been democratic for a considerable time, family relations also tend strongly toward relative equalitarianism and nonrespect. (This is true of the United States, of the mature democracies of the British Commonwealth and, to a lesser extent perhaps, of the democracies of northern Europe.)

2. *Avoidance*, the second class of comportment rules, has less to do with subservience and "respect" than with curtailment of intimacy—a keeping of one's distance. Avoidance rules usually apply to cross-sex relationships, and seem to have much to do with sex and avoidance of sexual intimacy. In our society as in many others, some of the milder avoidance rules apply between all men and women (except husbands and wives). A certain amount of modesty must be maintained in dress (not letting the opposite sex see genitalia and, perhaps, other body parts), speech (not talking about sex in mixed company), gait and gesture, and, ultimately, the sex act itself (except relationships where intercourse is permitted).

Added to this minimum of avoidance between men and women are more extreme avoidance customs which, in some societies, characterize certain kin relationships. First, most societies expect a certain amount of public avoidance between husband and wife. In many societies, spouses are not supposed to touch each other or show affection when others are present. The personal-name taboo may apply between them, perhaps the wife calling her husband "Husband," and the husband calling his wife "Mother-of-My-Children." Public avoidance between husband and wife usually is a little more pronounced than the minimal avoidance or "modesty" rules that pertain, generally, to relations between the sexes. However, it is mild compared with avoidance within other kin relationships.

There are three classic and common avoidance relationships: brother and sister, a man and his mother-in-law, and a woman and her father-in-law. These extreme avoidance relationships are also "focal," because they appear to determine other and less common avoidance relationships. If a man avoids his sister, he often will avoid various female cousins. If a man must avoid his mother-in-law, he usually avoids other relatives of his wife—most typically the mother-in-law's sisters and mother, and perhaps the wife's father or sisters. Similarly, if a bride must avoid her father-in-law, she will often avoid her father-in-law's brothers-and father. Finally, the three focal avoidances tend to be associated with each other. As a result, the world's societies polarize toward two extremes: (1) avoiding societies, with many extreme avoidance relationships, and (2) nonavoiding societies (such as our own), with little if any avoidance beyond the bare minimum of "modesty" between the sexes and, perhaps, some extra public decorum demanded of husband and wife. The avoiding societies are most numerous.

Some of the more extreme avoidance rules are these: the parties cannot touch each other; they cannot eat together; they can converse only from a distance; they cannot look at each other, eye to eye; they cannot see or talk with each other at all; they cannot mention each other's name or hear the other's name mentioned. Two of the less extreme avoidance rules are: the parties cannot sleep in the same house; and they must not both be present when sexual matters are discussed. Whereas "respect" is the generalized attitude that accompanies deference, the attitudes of shyness, embarrassment, and "shame" are the hallmarks of avoidance.

Extreme avoidances appear to be a burden to the people who must observe them. When an individual is surrounded by many relatives who must be avoided, considerable diligence and social dexterity is required. He must be prepared to watch what he says, be careful where his eyes go, and perhaps hide his face or run away if the wrong person enters a gathering. Also, a generally circumspect manner is seldom appropriate, since avoiding societies are often also joking societies; some kin relationships require avoidance, while others call for ritualized joking.

Extreme avoidance, in addition to being bizarre in appearance, is also mysterious with respect to its origins. Nothing is really known about the causes of these rules of decorum, or why they pattern as they do within particular kin relationships. To my knowledge, there are three competing explanations for kin avoidances. Two of them are functionalist explanations; both take the view that although avoidance might be a great bother, it actually exists because it serves to forestall further and more serious trouble. According to the anthropologist, Fred Eggan,[4] avoidance heads off potentially disruptive conflict; it springs up between relatives who are especially prone to fight with one another (such as a man and his mother-in-law). The second functionalist explanation, which was advanced by several early anthropologists and more recently, in modified form, by G. P. Murdock, takes the view that avoidances exist because they reinforce incest taboos; they tend to prevent sexual intercourse or marriage between persons who are sexually taboo to each other (such as brother and sister). According to Murdock,[5] if sufficient self-control is instilled during the socialization process, then the extreme avoidances are unnecessary. In societies whose members tend to lack the necessary internalized inhibitions, the avoidances arise as an added safeguard against incest.

The final explanation for avoidances is a Freudian one: the extreme avoidances represent a sort of institutionalized neurotic symptom. They express the people's fear of their own desires to commit incest. To my knowledge, this is the only one of the three explanations that has any real

---

[4] Fred Eggan, "The Cheyenne and Arapaho Kinship System," in Fred Eggan, ed., *Social Anthropology of North American Tribes* (Chicago: University of Chicago Press, 1937), pp. 77–81.

[5] George Peter Murdock, *Social Structure* (New York: Macmillan, 1949), pp. 273–286.

evidence to support it,[6] and even this evidence is considerably short of proof. The Freudian explanation is also incomplete. It does not account for the peculiar patterning of avoidance relationships: the fact that mothers-in-law, daughters-in-law, and sisters are frequently avoided, but daughters rarely are, and mothers never.

3. *Joking* is the third and final category of comportment rules. The "jokes" in a joking relationship are sexual or derogatory. The nearest that our society comes to the joking relationship is in certain "stag" social milieux, such as in army barracks and on some jobs, where profanity is so common that it goes virtually unnoticed, references to sex are constant and irreverent, and "dirty jokes" combine with defamatory "kidding." All of this behavior tends to be ritualized, in the sense that a very limited number of "dirty words," obscene references and gestures are repeated over and over.

A kin relationship characterized by "joking" often approaches this barracks-room mood. However, there are important differences. The kin relationship is frequently a cross-sex one; many joking relationships are between a man and his aunt, cousin, niece, sister-in-law, grandmother, or granddaughter.

A joking relationship is not a kin relationship within which the parties *may* joke; it is a relationship in which they *must* joke. Joking assumes the nature of obedience to rules, similar to giving deference or observing avoidance rules. The specific nature of the "joking rules" and the degree to which they permit individual deviations and lapses into occasional sobriety vary from society to society, and from one joking relationship to the next. Some ethnographers paint a picture of extremely strereotyped behavior within a joking relationship. In other societies the joking seems to be less ritualized, more individualized, and perhaps occasionally even fun.

From our cultural vantage point, joking relationships seem as bizarre as extreme avoidances. It is hard to empathize with a man who is bound by custom to insult his old uncles, tell dirty stories to his little nieces, and indulge in extravagant mock flirtation with his brother's wife. The origins and causes of joking relationships are utterly obscure. With the exception of a few vague references to the possibility that these relationships might, somehow, minimize social conflict by permitting a sort of "safety valve" for hostility (but what of the sexual component?), no one, to my knowledge, has hazarded an explanation for them.[7]

Joking societies also tend to have extreme avoidance relationships. Therefore, there are three main types of highly kinship-structured societies:

[6] William N. Stephens. *The Oedipus Complex: Cross-Cultural Evidence* (New York: The Free Press (1962), pp. 124–150.
[7] Fred Eggan (cited in footnote 4); and George Peter Murdock (cited in footnote 5), pp. 272–276.

(1) joking-avoiding societies, (2) societies with extreme deference relation-ships, and (3) societies with extreme deference, *and* avoidance, *and* joking. (That is, a person gives or receives deference within some kin relationships, avoids other kinsmen, and jokes with still other kinsmen.) There are, of course, a few societies with extreme avoidances and no joking, and vice versa. Also, there are a few societies that have none of the more extreme rules of patterned comportment but, nevertheless, have a good many rules regarding rights and obligations between kin; if the settlement pattern is such that Ego is surrounded by many relatives, these societies might also be termed "highly kinship-structure."

The rules that dictate patterned comportment among relatives—defer-ence, avoidance, and joking—act, to some extent, to standardize the relations between kinsmen. Additional rules, prescribing rights and obligations be-tween kin, act to give added structure to social life. These rules, too, lend some predictability to social interchanges within various kin relationships. Also, they create and define social ties; they pull people together, and make them interdependent. People who are "tied" to each other by reciprocal rights and obligations co-occupy kin groups.

## Forms of the Family

The smaller kin groups are based on residence. A group of kin lives to-gether in one house or in a cluster of houses forming a compound or homestead. Usually, this small residential kin group is a single economic unit. All of the members, except the very young and, perhaps, the very old, work for the common good, either at subsistence work ("breadwinning") or domestic work ("housekeeping"). All members share in the rewards of this work. There is a more or less formalized division of labor. The women (or woman) take charge of the domestic work. Perhaps the men (or man) are the breadwinners (although the women are customarily important breadwinners too). This unit is also a "political" group of sorts. The vesting of authority may be pluralistic and relatively "democratic," with various persons having separate spheres of influence and with some joint decision making; or it may be fairly autocratic, with a single patriarch (or, rarely, a matriarch) ruling supreme. We usually call this small residential kin group a "family."

Murdock [8] distinguishes three types of families. First, there is the *nuclear family,* composed of husband, wife, and children. When this unit com-prises a residential kin group in its own right, it is called a *nuclear-family*

[8] George Peter Murdock (cited in footnote 5).

*household.* Nuclear families sometimes combine—as Murdock says, "like atoms in a molecule"—to form larger residential kin groups. There are two types of these: polygynous families, and extended families.

A *polygynous* family is made up of one husband, two or more co-wives, and the children. (The other theoretical possibility—a polyandrous family with one wife and two or more co-husbands—is rare.) All family members either live in a single house, or each co-wife occupies a separate house or hut of her own, and the huts are clustered together within a family compound or homestead. Most societies do permit polygyny, and have a mixture of polygynous and monagamous families. (About 80% of the societies in Murdock's World Ethnographic Sample [9] show a mixture of polygyny and monogamy.) A polygynous family can be considered as a merger of several nuclear families, with the husband being a member of each.

*Extended families,* too, can be viewed as a merger of several nuclear families. Thus a small extended family (a "stem" family) might include an old man and his wife, their son, the son's wife, and the son's children—two nuclear families, the son being a member of both. A large extended family might include the old man and his five wives, their unmarried children and married sons, and the sons' wives (each son having one wife or several) along with their unmarried children. An extended family may be crammed into a single house, or it may occupy a cluster of houses or huts within an extended-family compound, or the houses may be more widely dispersed than this.

Extended families are of various forms. They may be big or small; they may or may not incorporate polygynous families; they may be patrilocal— where the married sons remain on the family homestead, and married daughters move away to join their husbands on other homesteads; or they may be matrilocal, where the reverse takes place, and the married daughters remain and married sons move out. Occasionally an extended family may show a mixture of patrilocality and matrilocality. Other rules of residence occur also; for example, avunculocal residence, where the newly married couple joins an extended family presided over by a maternal uncle of the groom.

In the United States (and in Europe) in the recent past, when most people lived on farms, small extended-family homesteads were common. But with the shift to urban living, extended families have been supplanted by nuclear-family households.

The extended-family arrangement has a number of important structural consequences. I shall mention two of these. First, an extended family is

[9] George Peter Murdock, "World Ethnographic Sample," *American Anthropologist,* Vol. 59, No. 4, 1957.

continuous, while a nuclear family is not. If a person belongs to an extended family, he is a member of a residential kin group which has probably persisted for many generations, perhaps on the same site (the old homestead). When the patriarch dies, an elder son is promoted to the office and the family continues. Wives are brought in (if patrilocality is the rule) and bear children, who in turn grow up, marry, and bring in new wives, who bear more children. The generations roll by, the members come and go, but the group continues. In contrast, a nuclear family "lives" only until one of the parents dies.

A second structural consequence involves authority. A nuclear-family household is, to some degree, a separate and independent unit, which can be run by husband, wife, or both jointly. An extended family is usually run by the patriarch (or, occasionally, by a council of several of the elders). The patriarch may demand much deference or little deference. His grip on power may be tight or loose. He may grant to the constituent nuclear families a relatively large or small margin for independent decision making regarding their own nuclear-family affairs. The fact remains that when a nuclear family merges into an extended family, it is in some measure subservient to the extended-family head.

When a young American couple marry, move away from home, and set up housekeeping, they are on their own. This is not true when a person marries and stays within an extended family. If it is a patrilocal extended family, the son marries and brings his wife into the homestead. He will probably have a status, relative to the elders in the family, analogous to that of an American teenager. Being a physically mature adult, he is capable of a full day's work for the family homestead, but he is still subservient to the head of the homestead. He is a married child. His bride becomes the wife of a married child—also to some extent subservient to the elders in her husband's homestead. Full "emancipation," which an American may achieve when he gets married or even before marriage, must be postponed until the elders die and the son becomes an elder in his own right.

## The Larger Kin Groups

A person customarily lives within a residential kin group—a "family" of some sort—and simultaneously maintains ties with other kin who live elsewhere. Various aunts, uncles, cousins, nieces and nephews, perhaps grandparents or grandchildren or in-laws—one may have many such "relatives," or only a few. (If a person could only trace all of his genealogical ties, he would find that he has thousands of potential relatives.) In other words, one also belongs to a more dispersed kin group, which includes these other relatives. In the United States, with our geographic mobility and our disregard for genealogy, we tend not to have so many relatives. We are deviant. A person living in another country (particularly a non-European country), and especially in a nonurban setting, would almost certainly have scores of relatives. (As with the previous quotation from Firth: if one were a Tikopian, he would have about 1200 relatives.) In short, each person simultaneously occupies a place in a small, residential kin group (a family) and a place in a larger, dispersed, nonresidential kin group. What is the larger kin group? What are its boundaries? Who is in it? These things are, to some extent, matters of choice.

One way to delineate the larger kin group is to trace genealogical ties. Then the size of the group is limited by little more than the fidelity of memory. An alternative is to exclude numerous genealogical ties as not constituting "real" kinship. In this manner, a person might rule out potential kin whom he has never met, or potential kin who are so distant, genealogically, that they do not constitute "real" kin. A mother's father's father's sister's son's wife's sister's husband's brother might be an example of this. Finally, a person might want to differentiate between consanguineal kin ("blood relatives") and affinal kin (relatives only by marriage); perhaps, he feels, blood kin are more truly his relatives than are in-laws.

It does seem that a basic distinction is customarily made between blood kin and in-laws. The larger kin group to which a person feels that he belongs tends to be consanguineal, that is, a certain group of blood relatives. In-laws are recognized as "kin" too, of course; one may be obliged to maintain patterned kin behavior with them. Some ties with affinal kin are close; especially with people who belong to one's residential kin group— one's spouse, plus other in-laws who might co-reside in an extended family. However, blood kin are generally considered a separate and distinct group. Anthropologists call this group the *bilaterally reckoned kindred.*

Kindreds are not especially viable groups. They are ill-suited for group action and group policy making. The boundaries of a kindred tend to be hazy. Which kin are so distant—genealogically or geographically—that they do not belong to one's kindred? Also, no two persons, excepting siblings, belong to the same kindred. For example, a person's mother's blood kin are part of his kindred, but they are not part of his father's kindred. They are his father's in-laws. As Murdock points out, kindreds "interlace and overlap." With each of our blood kin, we share a certain number of common consanguineal relatives but, with respect to each of these (except siblings), some persons are our consanguineal relatives but are not the consanguineal relatives of our blood kin (or vice versa).

To create viable, unitary consanguineal kin groups, the kindred must be cut in two. This option has been taken and formalized into custom by most of the world's societies. There are various ways in which this can be done but, in practice, one of two methods is nearly always chosen: patrilineal descent or matrilineal descent.

With *patrilineal descent* an individual joins, at birth, a special group of consanguineal kin—on the father's side of the family. The patrilineal kin group includes siblings, father, father's siblings, father's father, his siblings, father's brothers' children, and father's father's brothers' children—relatives in the "male line." Mother and her kin are excluded from this special group, as are sister's children, father's sisters' children, and children of other men who (by virtue of incest taboos) belong to other patrilineal kin groups. (We have a small trace of patrilineal descent in our assignment of surnames. A person gets his family name from his father, who got it from his father. However, with fully developed patrilineal descent, wives do not change kin groups when they marry. If a Smith girl marries a Jones boy, she would continue to belong to the Smith unilineal kin group and call herself "a Smith.")

With *matrilineal descent* the reverse rule is followed. At birth, a person becomes a member of his mother's matrilineal kin group. The group includes his brothers and sisters, mother, her brothers and sisters, his maternal grandmother and her brothers and sisters, along with mother's sisters' children, maternal grandmother's sister's children, and her daughters' children—relatives in the "female line." Relatives in the male line—father, paternal grandfather, father's brothers and their children, and so on—belong to other matrilineal kin groups. They are all children of women who, by virtue of incest taboos, belong to matrilineal kin groups different from Ego's mother's. In Murdock's World Ethnographic Sample, 238 societies are designated as patrilineal, 77 are matrilineal, and 30 have *double descent*. In these, everyone belongs to two unilineal kin groups: a patrilineal group (his father's), and a matrilineal group (his mother's).

*Unilineal kin groups*, as opposed to kindreds, do not "interlace and overlap." There is no ambiguity about the boundaries of a person's unilineal group, about which group he belongs to, or about who his (unilineal) kinsmen are. Unilineal descent divides society into discrete, separate segments, similar to a primary school with its separate grades, a town with its separate households, or the National League with its ten teams. These groups, in contrast to kindreds, *can* function well as corporate entities. In many places they are as well developed, important, and laden with functions as is the family. Below are some common attributes of unilineal kin groups.

1. Unilateral kin groups often own property. In many places they own all of the land, or at least all of the farmland. A farmer may hold his fields in trust. The crops are his. The land is his to use; but he cannot sell it,

since it is owned by his clan, say, and it will revert to the clan when he dies. Perhaps, then, it will be "returned" to his son, or perhaps it will be given to some other member(s) of the clan. [Anthropologists have given various names to unilineal kin groups. The smaller, more localized, and more function-laden unilineal groups are often called *lineages*. The terms *clan* or *sib* sometimes also refer to relatively small, important (to its members) unilineal groups; but sometimes these terms describe larger, more geographically dispersed, near-functionless unilineal groups. Other terms for the larger, more scattered, and usually relatively unimportant groups are *phratry* and *moiety*.] Unilineal kin groups frequently own other kinds of property also: houses and house sites, money, temples, servants or slaves, or more exotic items such as songs.

2. As a property-holding unit, a unilineal kin group often may be, to some extent, a unit for corporate enterprise. Some communal work may have to be performed for the benefit of the kin group. Or a man may have a special right for help from clansmen at harvest time, or during planting, or when building a house, or for other sorts of aid. In other words, there may be many kinship rules dictating rights and obligations between unilineal kin. Some unilineal kin groups are rather highly developed mutual aid societies; hospitality may be expected from fellow clansmen, as well as help of various kinds, and property or wealth may be borrowed (or simply taken) from them.

3. When a unilineal kin group is a property-holding group, and a mutual-aid group, it usually must have some machinery for group decision making and group discipline; in other words, it must be "governed," as a family must be "governed." Thus there may be a clan headman or a clan council.

4. Often a unilineal group is a military unit as well. It fights some other kin groups within the same society. These fights seldom develop into large-scale pitched battles or campaigns. They are usually feuds, that is, long-standing states of enmity between certain unilineal groups, fed by traditions of past wrongs and obligations of blood vengeance, that break out in occasional small-scale violence, skirmishes, or ambushes.

5. A unilineal kin group frequently has its own religion. "Ancestor workship" is ordinarily a unilineal kin group affair. The kinsmen are further tied to each other by their mutual obligations to common ancestral spirits. (Ancestor worship might be viewed as an extension of the unilineal kin group—with its rules of patterned rights and obligations—to include non-living members.) Sometimes the ancestral spirits are human, but often this is not the case. Many unilineal groups are totemic. They recognize one or several primal, nonhuman ancestors; these ancestors are usually animals, birds, or reptiles, but they may be plants or inorganic natural

phenomena. The individual maintains a quasi-kinship tie with the species to which his totem ancestor belonged. This means, for one thing, that ordinarily he does not kill or eat them; if a person is a member of the Bear Clan, for instance, he would not eat bear meat.

6. Unilineal groups are often named; for example, the Fire Clan, the Tiger Phratry, the Tree-Rat Sib, the Cuckatoo People, the Red Clay Clan. (The name may designate a totem ancestor, as in the case of the Bear Clan, or it may not.) Names are handy for keeping clear the boundaries of the kin group. If a person who is a Bear meets a stranger and asks, "Are you a Bear?" and the stranger answers, "Yes," then the person knows that they are kinsmen. Names are easier to remember than distant genealogical ties. Indeed, in the larger unilineal groups, some members often cannot trace genealogical ties with each other; but since they belong to the same unilineal group (they answer to the same kin-group name), they "know" that they are kin.

7. Finally, nearly all unilineal kin groups are exogamous; that is, their members marry outside of the group. Incest taboos are extended to include all unilineal kin. If a person is a Bear, then he cannot marry a Bear, and he probably would face a stiff penalty if he were caught dallying with a Bear girl.

As a result of exogamy, unilineal groups tend to crosscut communities and to tie communities to each other with bonds of kinship. No community can ever be homogenous with respect to unilineal-group membership, since no family can be. Because of exogamy the husband belongs to one unilineal group, and the wife belongs to another. Since unilineal groups must necessarily exchange women they are, in effect, exchanging hostages. To the extent that ties of marriages bind two unilineal groups, friction and hostilities between the two groups are held in check. (This appears usually to be the case, but there are some exceptions: groups that feud and intermarry simultaneously.)

In many societies the community, being fairly small, is itself exogamous. There is absolutely no woman nearby whom a man can marry (unless a kinsman dies, and he inherits his kinsman's wife). All of the women are either kin or the wives of kin. If the rule of residence is patrilocal, a man's bride will be brought in from another community. If the rule of residence is matrilocal, the man will move to his bride's community. In such a situation, communities as well as unilineal groups are exchanging hostages. The scattered communities within the society will each embrace members of two or more unilineal kin groups, and each unilineal group will have its members scattered about in a number of communities. A system of crosscutting allegiance is created—to the unilineal group, on the one hand, and to spouse and community, on the other. The balancing allegiances may conflict, at times, producing various stresses and strains; but the crosscutting system does tend to integrate a fairly large group of people, to resist centrifugal pressures, and to tie village to village, family to family, and locality to locality.

In other societies the strain toward community exogamy is weaker, and an individual has a better chance of finding a marriageable girl (of a different kin group) in his community. In such a case there will be less crosscutting of kin group with community.

Of course, pressure toward community exogamy, which links neighboring communities by bonds of kinship, can be strong even in the absence of unilineal groups (although unilineal groups seem to facilitate greatly such a situation). Kindreds can do this job also, especially when the community is small—leading a man to search for a bride in neighboring communities—and when the kinship feeling is strong, leading to continuing ties and obligations among distantly residing kindred.

Extended kin groups, then, whether unilineal groups, or kindreds, or both combined, tend to integrate society, to knit together a scattered population and prevent fissionings into smaller subgroups.

Many a primitive society, more or less uniform in language and culture, has occupied a fairly large territory in the absence of any sort of territorial government or state. One reason that such a unitary culture can spread over a large area, in the absence of a state, seems to be the kinship bonds linking the scattered localities. Each community has ties of marriage with its neighbors, and the large kin groups spread their members throughout many communities. Because of community exogamy, the population is continually "mixing," and the communities exchange some of their members. Thus the area is characterized by one culture, not twenty or fifty, and by one language instead of many.

The United States, of course, does not require such a mode of territorial integration. Other pressures (aside from wife-hunting) drive us to geographic mobility and population-mixing. Newly emergent phenomena, such as the mass media, press for cultural uniformity. Finally, territorial integration is provided by our nation-state with its boundaries, laws, and coercive powers.

However, there was a time when mankind knew no nation-state; when there was merely family, community, and kinfolk; when a man's "countrymen" or "people" were those who shared a common language and culture and who resided in his village and in other villages tied to it by kinship.

## Marriage, Incest Taboos, and the Spreading of Kin Ties

In cross-cultural perspective, kinship rules show some sameness and much variation. Many kinship customs are peculiar to single cultures or culture areas. An example of this is the Western European custom of "chivalrous" manners of husbands toward wives. Other customs are widely scattered, although some cultures have them and some do not: for instance, the more extreme rules of deference, avoidance, and joking. Finally, some kinship customs are found almost everywhere. Among these are customs that we ordinarily associate with "marriage," and incest taboos or exogamous rules.

Almost every society demands that a mother be married. Her husband lives with her or near her. The two have sexual rights to each other (during nontaboo periods). Ordinarily they have work and economic obligations: the woman cooks for the man, perhaps keeps house for him, and mends and makes his clothes; the man gives the woman economic "support" (and, frequently, vice versa); the two share and, possibly, co-own property. They call each other "husband" and "wife" (or the local equivalents). The special relationship between them begins with a public announcement which is, in most societies, elaborated into one or more ceremonials. In other words, they begin the relationship by "getting married." If it is the woman's first marriage, she probably has not become a mother before she "got married." Finally, any children subsequently born to the woman are socially recognized as "his" as well as "hers." The children become the father's kin as well as the mother's. (The resulting small kin group of mother, father, and their children is, of course, the nuclear family.) The woman's children trace a genealogical tie to the woman's husband; they call him "my father" (or the local equivalent); he calls them "my son" and "my daughter." Also, father's consanguineal kin (his father, mother, grandfathers, grandmothers, uncles, aunts, cousins, nephews, nieces) become the childrens' kin too. By this social arrangement of marriage and fatherhood, a person's genealogical ties are multiplied; they are about double what they would be if the person only had a mother (but no father) through whom he could trace his genealogy.

The reason that marriages so greatly expand the child's genealogical ties is that the father and mother, themselves, are not close blood relatives. They are either distantly related (the closest possible relationship, permitted in some societies, is first cousins), or they are not related at all (as far as anyone can tell). They, themselves, are never brother and sister, or father and daughter, or mother and son.

Nuclear families cannot be self-perpetuating because of incest taboos. They must give up their members (their marriageable children) for the formation of new nuclear families. At each new marriage, at least one spouse must leave home. Either wife joins husband (patrilocal residence), or husband joins wife (matrilocal), or they move to the extended family of some other kinsmen (as in the case of avunculocal residence), or they set up a new menage of their own (neolocal residence).

The effect of the combination of marriage and incest taboos is that it multiplies kin ties, and forces interchange between residential kin groups, thus setting in motion the process that leads to a crosscutting and overlapping of local with kin allegiances. People are "pushed out of" relatively small, self-contained groups, and are forced to take up ties in larger, more ramified groups.

The process is accelerated to the point of community exogamy—intermarriage and kinship ties between neighboring villages—by the extension of incest taboos. A great many kin are always covered by incest taboos. The coverage is often rather irregular, in the sense that some relatively close kin are not taboo (usually some type of cross-cousin) while many distant kin are taboo. If the society is unilineal, Ego cannot (with rare exceptions) marry anyone in his unilineal group. If he is a member of the Bear Clan, he cannot marry a Bear Clan woman (even if a genealogical tie cannot be traced). If the society is divided into exogamous moieties, more than one half of the persons in the entire society are "kin" to Ego and are covered by the incest taboo. Thus, a great many persons are always nonmarriageable for Ego because of the incest taboo. They may number in the dozens, or even in the hundreds. Therefore, there is pressure on a man—especially if his community is small and stable—to leave home to look for a bride, to venture out from his residential group and establish ties with others. (Actually, the potential groom's parents or other kin usually do this "looking" and choosing for him.)

In light of the extreme degree of cultural variability the world over, it would seem that somewhere there should be a society where mothers were not expected to be married, where anything recognizable as "marriage" would not exist, and at least one society without incest taboos as well. This is not the case. No society that lacked incest taboos has ever been found. There are a few near-exceptions concerning marriage. Some societies have a certain percentage of unwed mothers, who may mate casually and serially without ever becoming officially "married"; however, all of these societies also have bona fide marriage customs, which are observed by some mothers and, usually, by most mothers. The old-time "marriage" customs of the Nayars, a caste group in southern India, approached nonmarriage. At puberty a girl had a quasi-marriage ceremony performed for her; but, after that, she usually had nothing more to do with her "husband." She lived and raised her children in a household of matrilineal kin, having a series of casual lovers who apparently did not recognize kin ties with her children.[10]

It is easy to imagine the form that a nonmarriage society would take. It would resemble the just-mentioned arrangement of the Nayars. A woman lives in a house, perhaps with other kin such as her mother, brothers and sisters, and perhaps other matrilineal relatives. She has one or more lovers and, in time, has one or more children. The lovers are not considered as "husbands"; they do not live with her, and they are not regarded as "fathers" to her children. The children grow up in the household of their mother and her relatives, and recognize their mother's kin as their kin. They never have a father or a grandfather, although they have uncles —the brothers of mother and of mother's mother. Some maternal uncle may live with them and play a patriarchal, fatherlike role in the household. Their kin are solely matrilineal; they have no ties on the father's side of the family, since there are no fathers. There are no in-laws, since there is no marriage. When a girl grows up she can keep right on living at home if she wishes. She can start receiving lovers of her own, and can eventually have children and make her own addition to the matrifamily. When a boy grows up he can also keep on living at home, making nightly excursions, but living in, and working for his mother's household. If other factors do not intervene (such as a food shortage, a job shortage, or a lover shortage, which might cause some of the men to wander) this matrifamily can persist indefinitely throughout the generations, self-perpetuating and self-contained. Offhand this seems like a simple and viable arrangement, and it is remarkable that no other known society has ever adopted it. Of course, there would be fewer kin ties. Also, there would be few ties between households and communities. The marriage arrangements and heavy marriage payments, which burden and complicate the lives of so many primitive peoples, would be unnecessary.

A society without incest taboos would also be easy to imagine. Mother could marry son, and father could marry daughter, although most marriages would doubtless be between siblings and close cousins. New and fascinating forms of the family would be found: two or more siblings, married to each other; father, mother, son, and daughter, with marriage ties between father and mother, mother and son, father and daughter, and son and daughter—the latter marriages producing children of their own. The tracing of genealogy would certainly be complicated. A woman might be,

[10] E. Kathleen Gough, "The Nayars and the Definition of Marriage," *Journal of the Royal Anthropological Institute of Great Britain and Ireland,* Vol. 89, Part 1, 1959.

simultaneously, Ego's mother, wife, and (given plural marriage) sister-in-law. If plural marriage (or simply polyandry) were ruled out, there would be less of a genealogical tangle, with fewer marriages within the same "nuclear family." Without incest taboos, families could be self-contained and self-perpetuating, so long as there were sons and daughters, and to the extent that family members felt like marrying other family members. Marriage would not "push" people away from home. In the absence of some other pressure for population-mixing (such as job-hunting), communities also could be self-contained. They need not give up some of their members to other communities for the sake of marriage, or bring in new members from the outside. No one would have to confront the interpersonal strains and adjustments that go with outmarrying. Also, marriage payments (bride-price and dowry) and the resulting debts and financial hardships would be unnecessary. This, too, seems in some ways to be a simple and efficient arrangement. Of course, ties of kinship between families and communities would be minimal.

The simplest arrangement would be *neither* marriage *nor* incest taboos. People could have love affairs as they wished, and the women would have children. If the community were small, memories of enchanted nights and possibilities of paternity ("Doesn't the child look like me?") might be expected to create a pan-community family feeling, with the men taking an avuncular interest in their past lovers' children. The community should be a tight-knit group, with strong solidarity and cohesion. (It might be argued: "No. It would be torn by sexual jealousies." Perhaps. But some people seem able to share their mates with no apparent jealousy. This appears to be especially true of co-spouses who are also siblings or close relatives, as these people in our imaginary society would tend to be.[11]) Again, this would be a self-contained community, with no need to seek women, give women, or otherwise establish kin ties with other groups.

Perhaps, sometime in the history of early man, these arrangements were tried out. If so, they did not survive to be recorded by anthropologists. No matter what form a particular society takes, it seems that some sort of social imperative *demands* the presence of marriage and incest taboos. Why is it that marriage and incest taboos are so inevitable and, apparently, so necessary? We do not know. A good many theories have been advanced to account for the universality of incest taboos. (Curiously, writers

[11] William N. Stephens, *The Family in Cross-Cultural Perspective* (New York: Holt, Rinehart and Winston, 1963), Chapters 2 and 5; George Peter Murdock and John W. M. Whiting, "Cultural Determination of Parental Attitudes: the Relationship Between the Social Structure, Particularly the Family Structure, and Parental Behavior," in Milton J. E. Senn, ed., *Problems of Infancy and Childhood* (Josiah Macy, Jr. Foundation, 1951).

apparently have not felt a similar need to explain the universality of marriage.)

Below are eight separate explanations for the universality of incest taboos. (The list is not exhaustive. Certain of the more complex explanations—such as those advanced by G. P. Murdock, Émile Durkheim, and Albert Ellis—are not cited.)

1. A number of early writers speculated that "early man" (the forefathers of all known societies) recognized that close inbreeding has adverse biological effects, and therefore instituted incest taboos.

2. Lowie,[12] at one time, believed that humans have an instinctive aversion to incest.

3. Westermarck [13] speculated that persons who grow up together, in close contact (such as brother and sister), tend to lose sexual interest in each other by the time they reach maturity. (Even if this were true, it would hardly explain the necessity of rules to prevent people from committing incest.)

4. According to the psychoanalytic explanation, family members *do* have incestuous wishes (even if unconscious) toward each other, which for various reasons are frightening. The incest taboos represent a rejection of sexual desire directed at parents and siblings. In other words: men bear within them sexual yearnings toward their mothers and sisters; similarly, women have dimly recognized, perhaps completely repressed, sexual designs on their fathers and brothers. For some reason, these incestuous wishes arouse guilt and anxiety. Incest-fear may seldom be experienced directly; however, it may express itself indirectly, as a generalized and vague concern about the general issue of incest. *Ergo*, so the theory goes, from this diffuse discomfort spring the incest rules.

The following four functionalist explanations account for incest taboos on the basis of some service that they perform for society.

5. Incest taboos do, of course, greatly curtail any possible sexual rivalry between family members. Father and son may not share the same sex partners, nor (ordinarily) may mother and daughter. Kluckhohn,[14] among others, felt that such a curtailment is, probably, universally necessary; otherwise, the resulting jealousy would breed intolerable conflict within the family and the larger kin group. This rationale for the universality of incest taboos does collide with two awkward facts. First, it

[12] Robert H. Lowie, *Primitive Society* (New York: Horace Liveright, 1915), p. 105.

[13] Edvard A. Westermarck, *The History of Human Marriage* (The Allerton Book Company, 1915).

[14] Clyde Kluckhohn, "Variations in the Human Family," in Norman Bell and Ezra Vogel, eds., *A Modern Introduction to the Family* (New York: The Free Press, 1960), p. 46.

appears that many persons are able to share their sex partners without apparent jealousy. Second, some societies permit polygyny. With polygyny, co-wives are in a position of potential sexual rivalry. Often the resulting jealousy and conflict is widespread and intense. Yet polygyny endures.

6. Davis[15] has pointed out that if there *were* no incest taboos, kin relationships would degenerate into a stupendous muddle. If a man could marry his mother, for example, then this woman could be both his mother and his wife; his sister would be both his sibling and his own daughter; his father would also be his co-husband; his brother would also be his son; his maternal grandmother would also be his mother-in-law; and so forth. Such multiple kin relationships (between a given pair of close kin) would, among other things, pose innumerable conflicts and ambiguities about patterned kin relationships. Hence, says Davis, for a clearly ordered grid of patterned kin relations, incest taboos are necessary.

7. Tylor,[16] writing in the late nineteenth century when such interpretations were popular, proposed a sort of Darwinian explanation for the universality of incest taboos. In the early days of mankind people must have lived in small hunting bands. Quite possibly, some of these small, mobile communities were without incest taboos; brother could cohabit with sister, father with daughter, maybe even mother with son. Such a small incestuous band would probably be a single body of kinfolk. In the absence of incest taboos, the band would be sexually self-sufficient. There would be no need to establish ties with other bands in order to make nonincestuous marriages; the group would not have to trade members with other bands. Such an isolated and self-sufficient group would be expected to develop its own distinctive culture over time. However, eventually the little band would disappear. War, or famine, or drought, or disease would, sooner or later, wipe out this little "society." When that happened, its culture would disappear too.

A hunting band *with* incest taboos, on the other hand, is practically forced to exchange members with other bands. The incest taboos force some neighboring bands to establish ties of kinship with each other. Such a process of population-mixing would be expected to lead to cultural diffusion as well, so that the intermarrying bands would be similar, possibly identical, in culture. When one of these bands did disappear, perhaps as a result of famine or disease, its culture (including the incest taboos) would be carried on by its surviving neighbors.

[15] Kingsley Davis, *Human Society* (New York: Macmillan, 1949), pp. 399–405.
[16] Sir Edward B. Tylor, "On a Method of Investigating the Development of Institutions: Applied to Laws of Marriage and Descent," *Journal of the Royal Anthropological Institute of Great Britain and Ireland*, Vol. 18, 1889.

Hence, so the argument goes, cultures embracing incest taboos were "selected out" and cultures without them eventually disappeared.

8. Finally, Slater's [17] social regression theory asserts that a society, to survive, must generate various mechanisms which force people to reach out beyond their small primary groups and establish ties so as to create larger, more ramified groups. Incest taboos represent one such mechanism.

Why, really, did incest taboos originate, and why do they represent a cultural universal? This will probably remain one of nature's better-kept secrets. Many of these explanations are plausible, and perhaps one or several of them grope toward the truth. However, none of them can be tested. This appears to be one of those situations in which the number of possible explanations is limited by little more than the inventiveness of the theories.

## Husbands and Wives

Husband and wife begin by "getting married." Their mateship is announced publicly, and is usually celebrated in one or several marriage ceremonies. In most societies a person's first marriage occurs, by our standards, at a very early age. A boy and girl may be betrothed to each other when they are little children; sometimes they are betrothed before they are born. Full marriage usually occurs around puberty; sometimes shortly afterward, sometimes before. Very early marriage is especially apt to be the fate of girls.

Our society and a few others permit people to choose their own spouses. Nearly everywhere, parents' permission is needed as an absolute minimum requirement, and in many societies the parents (or other kin) do the choosing. A child is "married off" by his or her family. Sometimes the potential spouse may be able to exercise a certain amount of veto power over his or her parents' choice; often this is not the case. In societies with arranged marriage, a minority of people usually do choose for themselves. Older men, who have already married at least once, can often choose their subsequent wives. Also, there may be a few couples who are sufficiently strong-willed to resist family pressure and who elope. Women generally have less to say about whom they will marry than have men. Even an older woman whose husband dies will, in many societies, be "married off" again; if the custom of the levirate prevails, someone will simply inherit her.

[17] Philip E. Slater, "On Social Regression," *American Sociological Review*, Vol. 28, No. 3, 1963.

Arranged marriage seems to follow from a high development of kinship. The few societies that allow, as the general rule, love matches and marriage by free choice tend to be those without unilineal groups, without substantial extended family groups, with a high percentage of neolocal residence, and with a general attenuation of extended kinship ties and obligations.[18] Where the larger kin groups are highly developed, marriage tends to be considered as an alliance between kin groups, not merely as an alliance between two individuals. Thus, it seems, Ego may seldom choose for himself; the choice is made by parents or by other kin.

When kin groups ally themselves through a marriage, capital is customarily exchanged. In most societies brides must be paid for, often at a heavy price. Unless it is an older man who is choosing his own wife, the groom's parents customarily foot the bill, frequently taking contributions from other relatives. Sometimes there is a series of payments, perhaps starting when the couple are betrothed in childhood, and occasionally lasting for years after the marriage has been consummated. As a result, the groom and/or his kin may be in debt to the wife's people for years. The indebtedness usually ramifies. The groom may be debtor to whichever kin raised his original bride price. His parents may owe return favors to kinsmen from whom they raised contributions. Bride price is sometimes supplemented (or even replaced) by bride service; the groom owes work or other services to the bride's people. Also, many societies have reciprocal marriage payments: the groom's people pay bride price to the bride's people, and the bride's people reciprocate with dowry payments. A marriage, in most societies, sets in motion a complicated series of financial transactions: pledges, the taking of contributions, payments given and received, distribution (to other kin) of marriage gifts and payments, and the creating and paying of favors and debts. As a result, financial and legal obligations spring up among members of a kin group, and between kin groups of bride and groom. Since marriages occur continuously, they form part of the social cement (as well as sources of contention) between kin and kin groups.

Once married, a husband and wife customarily start living together. Usually they live in the same house. Sometimes they reside in adjoining huts in a family compound. Perhaps they set up a new and separate household of their own; but, if they are not Americans, the chances are that they would not. Instead, the newly created nuclear family merges with several other nuclear families in a larger residential kin group, such as a polygynous or an extended family.

And husband and wife start having intercourse (assuming that they

[18] William N. Stephens, *The Family in Cross-Cultural Perspective,* p. 199.

have not begun already). In our own society, the transition with respect to sexual rights is drastic. Prior to marriage, sexual activity is taboo, and, if undertaken, is illict and ordinarily surrounded by secrecy. Marriage creates a legitimate, openly recognized sex relationship; spouses may have intercourse with each other any time they wish. Also, they are each other's private sexual property; neither can have another spouse, nor is either supposed to philander or "cheat." In most other societies marriage does not involve such a drastic transition.

Most societies freely permit premarital intercourse. Within Murdock's 1949 sample, in 70% of his societies premarital sex was permitted for both sexes, and in many of the remaining 30%, some attempt was made to keep unmarried girls chaste, although boys were free to philander where they could.[19] Also, for many societies with formal premarital sex restrictions, the ethnographer suspects the rule is ineffective. (This applies to the rules against adultery also.) [20] No known society, however, gives absolutely free reign to sexual urges. First, incest taboos, which seem generally to be taken seriously, can severely limit the range of possible sex partners. Further limitations can stem from occasional sex taboos. Finally, some societies try to channel premarital sex within one or several specific kin relationships—male Ego to father's sister's daughter, or to mother's brother's daughter, or to brother's wife—so as to limit sex to relationships that may eventually end in marriage anyway. In any event, in the majority of the world's societies, people go into marriage with previous sexual experience. (This is somewhat more apt to be true for grooms than for brides.) This prevails even when the couple marries when quite young.

After marriage, in nearly all societies (except our own), husband and wife may *not* have intercourse with each other whenever they wish. If a woman marries into a polygynous family, then, more often than not, an equal-time arrangement has been worked out among the several co-wives. Also, there are the occasional sex taboos. Most common of the occasional sex taboos is the menstrual taboo; the wife may not have intercourse while menstruating. Not quite so common are the long periods of sexual abstinence before and after a mother gives birth; the pregnancy sex taboo and postpartum sex taboo, combined, frequently last several years, thus making mothers sexually continent during many of their child-bearing years. Also, many societies have (or had) a variety of sex taboos in honor of special occasions: for example, harvests, war parties, ceremonies, and special holy days.

Most societies resemble ours in one respect: a wife is supposed to be

[19] George Peter Murdock, *Social Structure* (cited in footnote 5), p. 265.
[20] William N. Stephens, *The Family in Cross-Cultural Perspective* (cited in footnote 11), pp. 245–257.

her husband's private sexual property. About 80% of the societies in Murdock's 1949 sample had a rule against adultery, as did 61% of the societies in Ford and Beach's [21] cross-cultural sample. But, as Murdock comments, in a good many of these societies the rule is "more honored in the breach than in the observance." [22] Again, women seem more tightly restricted than men. The possibilities seem to be these: (1) an apparently effective adultery rule applies to both sexes; (2) women are fairly effectively kept from adultery, while men break the rule more easily and frequently; (3) men are formally permitted to commit adultery, while women are formally prohibited (in some places effectively, it seems, and in other places not); and (4) both sexes are allowed to commit adultery.

Where adultery is permitted it is, of course, subject to incest taboos and occasional sex taboos, and it may be limited to specific times (ceremonial license) and/or to specific categories of persons, such as in special permissive sex relationships with selected relatives.

A man, on the other hand, is seldom bound to be faithful to one woman. First, adultery rules are less apt to be effectively binding for men. Second, most societies are polygynous. In these societies, a man—if he wishes, and if he can raise the capital, and if he is not deterred by domestic objections—can add more wives.

Along with the ties created by love-making and parenthood, man and wife are bound by other, quasi-economic ties that develop from living together. Each contributes to an establishment—a household, to which each owes certain duties from which the other benefits. They both care for the children. (The husband is rarely exempted from this.) The wife cooks, keeps house, goes for fuel and water, sometimes with some help from the husband, but often alone. Usually both bring in food. If it is a hunting-and-gathering society, the husband usually hunts animals and the wife gathers vegetable foods. If they are farmers, then both work in the fields. Sometimes the husband does the bulk of the farm work, sometimes the wife. At other times both divide the work fairly equally. If there is a commercial economy, then the husband, wife, or both may go into it to sell, barter, trade, lend, or work for wages. In nearly all societies, wives work hard for their households; husbands often work hard too, although their contribution (even in the subsistence realm) is usually less than that of their wives.[23] The children also are put to work as soon as possible in nearly all societies.

[21] Clellan Ford and Frank A. Beach, *Patterns of Sexual Behavior* (New York: Harper, 1951).
[22] George Peter Murdock, *Social Structure* (cited in footnote 5), p. 265.
[23] William N. Stephens, *The Family in Cross-Cultural Perspective* (cited in footnote 11), pp. 56–59; George Murdock and John W. M. Whiting (cited in footnote 11), pp. 20–21.

Perhaps every society has a somewhat formalized sex division of labor: some jobs are defined as women's work, others as men's work, with the remaining tasks being performed by either men or women. Thus a fair degree of uniformity prevails, from one family to the next in a given society, with respect to who does what. The sex division of labor may be meticulous, detailed, and—for many tasks—may have the nature of rules that people are ashamed to break (what real man would agree to bake cookies?). Or the division of labor may be less clear and more lax. Our society, in accordance with its general tendency toward cross-cultural deviance, "freedom," and dearth of clear rules, appears to have an extremely lax and vague sexual division of labor. Thus, each American couple must decide for themselves who changes the diapers, who takes clothes to the laundromat, who empties the trash, buys the groceries, pays the monthly bills, washes the dishes, earns an income, and other things of this kind.

Along with a division of labor, there must also be a division of power and privilege. Who does what for whom? Who decides? Who gets his or her way on various issues and decisions? The cross-cultural trend strongly favors the husbands. The wife, generally, contributes most and gets least in return. There are, of course, great intercultural variations, as well as marked differences from one family to the next within a given society. Each family power struggle is, to some extent, a separate war of its own, which may be won by the husband, the wife, or neither—depending partly on the personalities involved. Often, however, society stacks the cards in the husband's favor. The formal expectation is that he is to be more powerful and privileged. Sometimes woman's wiles and power drive can subvert the formal expectation, sometimes not. (This seems easiest to manage with neolocal residence and isolated nuclear-family households, in which the countervailing pressures of public opinion and, especially, kin-group opinion, should be weaker.)

In many societies, as mentioned previously, women owe their husbands tokens of deference: bows and curtsies; honorific terms of address; and precedence when walking, sitting, or talking. (Usually, the man walks ahead, and his wife humbly follows. If there is a horse or donkey to ride, the husband gets it; the wife walks behind. If there is a burden to carry, the wife will often bear it. When sitting, she may have to arise when he approaches; he will often have an honorific place to sit, for example, at the head of the table, or a special place by the fire, or the only stool. When speaking, the common rule is that, when others are present, the husband does the talking and wife hovers in the background; she speaks at his bidding and generally shows "respect"—until she gets him alone at any rate.) The husband may have precedence in eating (he may eat first

while the wife serves him, or he may eat alone, or he may get the best food);
and the wife may perform various little personal services which are not
reciprocated—massages, foot-washing, and similar services. Some of the
deference customs are themselves privileges, and would seem to signify
a cultural expectation that the husband should get the best of it. In some
societies wife-to-husband deference is highly developed; in other societies
it is not. The reverse—husband-to-wife deference—is (to my knowledge)
limited to one Berber group and to the "chivalrous" customs (if these could
be termed "deference") practiced by some Western Europeans.

As far as privilege is concerned, then: if there is deference to be given,
the husband gets it. His sexual freedom is equal to or greater than his
wife's. His wife customarily works as hard or harder than he does; and
she serves him as cook and housewife.

Power, on the other hand, presents more intracultural variation and,
in general, is hard to obtain information about. My guess is that, if a
family power average could be calculated for each society, and if societies
were placed on a family power scale, it would look something like this.
The scale would range from extreme husband-dominance through
successively milder degrees of husband-dominance through husband-wife
equality to wife-dominance. At the top of the scale would be most of the
societies with highly developed deference customs—with a few exceptions,
the old kingdoms. (The peasant grovels before his lord, and his wife
grovels before him.) The societies without many deference customs would,
I imagine, mostly be more mildly husband-dominant. A minority of these
would come to rest at the point of husband-wife equality. Finally, a
scattering of rare, exceptional cases might be found in the wife-dominant
half of the scale. From my ethnographic readings, I know of four or five
cases that appear as if they might be, generally, "matriarchal." (These
include Tchambuli, a New Guinea tribe; the Modjokuto region of Central
Java; the Jivaro, a head-hunting tribe of the Amazon basin; possibly the
Nama Hottentot, an extinct culture of South Africa; and a Berber group
in North Africa.)

## The American Family

American family customs, viewed in cross-cultural perspective, are
characterized by considerable freedom. Our kinship rules are so blurred
and attenuated that they give much freedom of choice, and much latitude
for variation between families in the division of family chores, rights,
and obligations. The American family is unusually equalitarian; the power
of father over mother and grown children is relatively weak. Moreover,

most of our nuclear families are "free" in the sense that they are fairly autonomous vis-à-vis any larger kin group; they are not subsidiary units of extended families or clans.

Our system of mate-choice is "free"; we belong to that minority of societies in which arranged marriage is not the rule. Of course, the freedom of American mate-choice is, in part, illusory; a suitor's choice of a bride is indirectly influenced by social pressures. For one thing, we tend strongly to obey the rule of homogamy. Two people who marry are very likely to be of the same race, of the same religion, and of the same broad social class group. They will also probably be similar in age, level of education, and IQ.[24] Some set of social influences presses us to choose mates who are similar to ourselves with respect to range of social characteristics. The method of choosing a spouse—the sequence through which one moves on the way to the altar—is also culturally shaped. The sequence starts with dating, which develops into "going steady" or being "pinned" or "engaged" to one or several persons, and ends with an engagement that culminates in marriage. Ordinarily one begins to date within the context of an adolescent peer group, which to some extent regulates dating behavior and shapes one's view of heterosexual relations. The peer group may actually require a certain amount of dating in return for a modicum of peer-group acceptance and prestige. It may influence whom a person dates (as in the case of fraternities that date with only certain sororities). It may have much to say about how a person dates (thus, one adolescent peer group will interdict "going steady"; another will approve it). Finally, what a person *wants* from dating and—eventually—from marriage is largely a product of social influence. In our society, the suitor's expectations are "romantic"; they are shaped by the ideology of love. A person "falls in love" and marries; love is the reward of marriage. This, too, is in large part a product of cultural conditioning; and, too, our society is highly unusual in this emphasis on "falling in love" as the rationale for getting married.

Whereas the ideology of love "fits" in a system of free mate-choice, needless to say it certainly does not "fit" with an arranged marriage system. Where parents do the choosing, the criteria for a good bride (or groom) are typically "practical" rather than "romantic." "Son, that girl will make you a good wife because . . . we know her family and they have a good reputation . . . She is a strong healthy girl . . . a hard worker . . . a good weaver. Her brothers are powerful persons, and they can help you greatly . . . She brings you a fine farm and six cows. . . ." In contrast to such "practical" expectations from marriage (which are typically concrete,

[24] William J. Goode, *The Family* (Englewood Cliffs, N.J.: Prentice-Hall, 1964), pp. 32–40; Robert F. Winch, *Mate-Selection* (New York: Harper, 1958), pp. 5–7, 14.

clear, and limited from an emotional standpoint), when American lovers marry their expectations are, presumably, less clear and, from an emotional standpoint, are practically unlimited. If a person marries for love, he expects love in marriage. Perhaps, if he gets married in the grip of a powerful mutual infatuation, he expects, however hazily, that the state of infatuation will continue more or less indefinitely. On the other hand, just what he expects his new spouse to *do*—once the new household has been set up and the children have come—may not be at all clear.

After marriage, the roles of husband and wife must be gradually shaped and clarified, as issues arise that call for "decisions" about the division of chores, duties, rights, and spheres of authority—that is, what, precisely, each must do for the household, and what each spouse has a right to expect from the other. This process was begun, of course, during the dating period; it will continue as changes in the family's situation—for example, a move from an apartment to a house with a yard, or the arrival of children—necessitate new allocations of tasks and added agreements about decision-making prerogatives. Many of these decisions and agreements are made automatically and implicitly, and never even have to be discussed. Others create conflicts, some of which may never be fully resolved. Even after a grudging division of duties has been made, and bickering has subsided, one or both spouses may feel that the other spouse really ought to do more.

Viewed in this light, our great freedom of choice with respect to division of labor and more general role expectations between husband and wife is a mixed blessing. It is a burden and a source of strain; especially so, perhaps, during the early days of a marriage. By contrast, in the typical peasant village or primitive society the bones of contention are much fewer. Cultural rules prescribe, in meticulous detail, the traditionally proper division of chores, duties, and privileges between husband and wife. Thus, the scope for conflicting role expectations is much less. When a person enters marriage, he has a clear notion of what he must do, give, and receive, and what his spouse will do, give, and expect.

While the formalized and detailed blueprint for family roles, which is found in many other societies, does have its attractive aspect, it has its darker side too. These clear rules often look suspiciously like they were drawn up by a group of men—giving a disproportionate share of power and privilege to the father, at the expense of the wife and children. Our society, in contrast, along with its variability of family roles and vagueness of kinship rules, has a high degree of equalitarianism in its family relationships. First, our women do very well vis-à-vis power and privilege. They do not owe their husbands deference; if anything, the reverse is true. The work that wives are expected to do is less in our society than in most others. Perhaps American wives still work harder than their husbands, merely caring for children, but most of them have been removed from subsistence work. Finally, if a sexual double standard still prevails in America, it is certainly less pronounced than in most other lands; polygyny is outlawed, and the formal sanctions on extramarital sex relations are equal for both sexes.

Young children are, of course, under the authority of their parents; but they are largely free of parental control by the time they "leave home," and when they marry they are, in most cases, completely independent of their parents.

Because of our high frequency of neolocal residence and our inherited lack of unilineal descent, the American family is, relatively speaking, rather isolated from any larger kin group and from other kin. Extended kinship still exists in this country, of course; a small minority of Americans continue to live in extended family households. Most Americans still maintain ties with distantly residing parents, children, cousins, and uncles and aunts. Mutual aid and visits are still exchanged.[25] Extended kinship in our society is simply unimportant, as compared with the situation in most other societies.

The attenuation of extended kinship has major consequences, one of which is "freedom" in various respects. The nuclear family is free with respect to any other kin group; it is not subsidiary to an extended family, or subservient to an extended-family patriarch. House, land, and other property are not a temporary loan from a clan or lineage, nor are work and other contributions owed to a larger kin group. Another possible consequence of the weakening of extended kinship is the husband-father's loss of power over wife and children. The trend toward intrafamily equalitarianism and democracy may possibly be facilitated by isolation from other kin. Finally, it is possible that the atrophy and blurring and kinship rules, the widening nargin of free choice about comportment and obligations between family members, follows from the isolation of the nuclear-family household.

With this freedom, however, go burdens—burdens customarily carried by the larger kin group which, in its absence, must be borne by the nuclear family (and by the state).

Large kin groups, where they are highly developed, are customarily agencies of social security, caring for widows and orphans, the aged, the disabled, and providing for the scattered remnants of any disaster-struck nuclear family. In such a situation, a person's "family" numbers countless

[25] Eugene Litwak, "Occupational Mobility and Extended Family Cohesion," *American Sociological Review*, Vol. 25, February 1960; Marvin B. Sussman, "The Help Pattern in the Middle Class Family," *American Sociological Review*, Vol. 18, February 1953.

people, who can be called on in time of need. This ever-waiting reservoir of rightfully due help and support is only partially replaced, in our society, by Social Security, Aid to Dependent Children, alimony laws, and community agencies. Old people seem most hurt by the trend to isolated nuclear families. With extended kinship the aged often have much of the power. They own the property or are ranking trustees for the kin group. They need not be "taken care of" by their children; instead, the elders most likely "take care of" their juniors, in the sense of having power to decide, give, and withhold. Likewise, in the presence of large kin groups, Aid to Dependent Children and alimony laws are unnecessary. If a woman loses her husband her economic security is not threatened. His kin will care for her and the children, typically through the mechanism of the levirate, where she marries one of her husband's kinsmen; lacking this, she can live with her own kin. (In a cross-cultural survey, I found only three other societies that had alimony laws; all were characterized by neolocal residence.)

Along with social security, large kin groups doubtless provide emotional security. If there are many strong and significant kin ties then, no doubt, affectional relations tend to diffuse. The isolated nuclear family is a tiny island of kin, clinging to each other in the midst of non-kin. Affectional ties are few and are loaded with importance: one wife, one husband, one father, one mother. Much depends on intrafamily harmony. If disapproval is received from one or two family members, where can one turn for approval and support? If, on the other hand, a child is surrounded by many kin, then he may have numerous surrogate—but significant—fathers and mothers, while adults may have numerous close and available kin in addition to their spouses. When there are many "family" relationships, any one relationship is less significant, and hostility or alienation from one or two family members would be expected to be less threatening and demoralizing.[26]

Perhaps the key term to describe the American family is *autonomy*. It gives considerable freedom to its members; and the family itself is relatively autonomous in that it is so loosely integrated into the larger society. Cultural guidelines, in the form of kinship rules, are scanty and vague. The nuclear family is not imbedded in a larger kin group, and hence it is cut loose from the manifold supports and restraints which can be offered by a clan or an extended family.

The American family, to a considerable degree, has also been stripped of its functions. Seldom, nowadays, does our urban family function as an economic unit or work group. Other agencies have taken increasing responsibil-

[26] Talcott Parsons, *Essays in Sociological Theory: Pure and Applied* (New York: The Free Press, 1949), pp. 256–258.

ity for functions that were in former times, and still are in many other countries, largely the job of the family and the larger kin group: education, food-gathering, food-processing, manufacturing, and social control. Parsons has commented that this "loss of functions" should not be construed as a sign that the family is "withering away": rather, it is simply becoming more specialized in a particular direction.[27] Whereas some functions have certainly been "lost" or greatly attenuated, with respect to two others the modern family carries an unusually heavy load. These are: the care and socialization of young children, and the giving of emotional support and love. With the "withering away" of extended kin groups, the nuclear family is left as practically the sole source of nurturance, love, and care.

The burden appears to be heavy. In the past fifty years, our divorce rate has increased threefold; between one third and one fourth of modern marriages end in divorce.[28] (This is evidence, but not "proof," of an intensification of intrafamily strains and marital dissatisfaction. Conceivably, the rising divorce rate could be merely a result of weakening sanctions against divorce. Probably, as our family life has changed its character over the past fifty years, the major sources of pathology within the family have changed their character, too. For example, it may be that the decline of Puritanical sex mores and the trend toward more lenient and flexible child-rearing practices [29] have been forces for familial and individual "health," whereas other aspects of life in the modern family have been increasingly productive of familial disharmony.) Another possible index of familial strains is our substantial rate of mental illness; some families "break," and some individuals "break" too.

The nature and relative importance of intrafamilial strains, as well as the mechanisms through which they work, are largely matters of speculation. We can, with confidence, point to the unusual features of American life; to the extent that they are productive of strains, they signify trouble-spots that are unusual and rather distinctively American. Perhaps the most distinctive feature of the modern American family is its high degree of isolation from extended kin, and the consequent emotional burden that it must bear. Parsons reasons that such a small, ingrown, "tight" interaction unit, with minimal diffusion of nurturance, lacking alternative objects of love and dependency, should tend to make family members very mutually involved and mutually dependent and, perhaps, less emotionally secure than

[27] Talcott Parsons and Robert Freed Bales, *Family, Socialization and Interaction Process* (New York: The Free Press, 1955).

[28] William J. Goode (cited in footnote 24), p. 94.

[29] Urie Bronfenbrenner, "Socialization and Social Class Through Time and Space," in Eleanor Maccoby, Theodore Newcomb, and Eugene Hartley, eds., *Readings in Social Psychology*, 3rd ed. (New York: Holt, Rinehart and Winston, 1958).

the members of a larger extended family. This may be one of the distinctive sources of pathology in American family life.

The previous review of American marriage suggests other possible sources of strain. Because marriage occurs when bride and groom are "in love" (ideally, at any rate), their expectations of emotional gratification within marriage must often be rather extravagant. If, after marriage, the relationship descends somewhat from its high pinnacle of mutual infatuation, we would expect this to lead to a certain amount of disillusionment. In contrast, a marriage which is not a love match (that is, an arranged marriage) seems less in danger of any such letdown.

Also, as we have seen, our expectations of marriage are relatively vague. Each couple must determine for itself the division of tasks, chores, prerogatives, services, and spheres of authority for man and wife. This, too, must be a source of discord and stress. In one sense, the Hindu child bride, who is married to her husband before she even meets him, knows her husband better than does the American bride who marries after a long and intimate courtship. The child bride knows her husband as a social individual. She is provided a blueprint of the proper husband role and wife role. With respect to many specific details of the relationship, she knows what is "right" for her to expect.

Turning to the role of the child in the American family, two distinctive features might be mentioned. First, we are in a period of rapid social change. The world that our children grow up in is different, in many respects, from the world that their parents knew when they were children. As the formative experiences of the parents occurred in a social milieu that no longer exists, parents are apt to be "old fashioned"; standards of conduct that they aspire to, in behalf of their children, tend to clash with disparate values that children learn from other socializing agents. This cultural gap between the generations has been pointed to, by some writers, as a source of parent-youth conflict.[30] Where social change is less rapid, the cultural gap should be less and, presumably, this possible source of strain in the parent-child relationship should be less marked. (Of course, our society has no monopoly on this particular problem; in many parts of the world, at present, social change is more rapid and revolutionary than it is here.)

Finally, the position of the child in our society is unusual in that he must remain in the child role for so long. Induction into the adult role is extraordinarily delayed. We marry late. (The median age at marriage is about 20 for women, in our society, and about 22 for men.)[31] Our children do little

[30] Kingsley Davis, "The Sociology of Parent-Youth Conflict," *American Sociological Review,* Vol. 5, August 1940.
[31] William J. Goode (cited in footnote 24), p. 34.

productive work; they have little chance to practice adult occupational and parental roles. In a previous cross-cultural survey, I found only two other societies that appeared to give their children so little practice in parenthood.[32] Nearly everywhere, children take on heavy child-care duties themselves. Girls, especially, are put to work early as surrogate mothers. The responsibility placed on the child-nurse is usually heavy; her ward is often an infant or toddler who needs a good deal of protection and special care. The hours spent are frequently long. Sometimes the child-nurse spends more time in charge of the baby than does the mother herself; the mother is away working.

Especially when people live by farming, herding, or hunting and gathering, children also do subsistence work. They help with the farming, or help care for the livestock. In a hunting-and-gathering society, children help gather plants for food, and the boys play at hunting. In addition, they do household maintenance tasks, such as fuel- and water-fetching, and various odd jobs. In nearly all societies, children are working hard by the age of ten; work usually begins between the ages of three and six. This is not mere "work"; it is induction into adult occupational roles. A little girl follows her mother and older female kin about, sees the work they do, learns from them, starts doing simpler tasks herself, and gradually acquires increasing skill, responsibility, and work-load. Boys do the same, usually in the company and tutelage of older boys, their fathers or other male kin. Some children's tasks have little carry-over to adult work—running errands, for example. The bulk of the work, however, is of the same type that adults do. Within the sphere of work, the children "grow up" quickly. In some respects they are functioning as adults by the time of puberty. From an early age, they make valuable work contributions to their families.

In our society we have compulsory education and child-labor laws. Instead of education in the course of work—direct role practice—schools offer "education" which is *not* a direct practice of adult occupational roles, and which is of no intrinsic economic value. Children spend their time at "useless" school work, on jobs which are not what adults do, and are not what the children will do as adults. Occupational adulthood is achieved only after school is finished: at sixteen, eighteen, twenty-one, thirty, or later.

The postponement of sociological adulthood produces a social status which is filled, somewhat uncertainly, by millions of our society's members. This is adolescence: the state of being physically mature but not working, sexually mature but not married, "grown-up" but still dependent on parents. It is probably unavoidable. The thrust of our technological development

[32] William N. Stephens, *The Family in Cross-Cultural Perspective* (New York: Holt, Rinehart and Winston, 1963), p. 367.

demands protracted schooling for the great mass of our society's members, and the need for extended school presses for relatively late marriage and delayed assumption of adult occupational roles.

The consequences of this long period of adolescence—for the adolescent, for the persons who must live with him, and for the adult he will become— are, no doubt, both varied and profound. The process of social maturation in our society has less the appearance of orderly and solid development than it does in primitive and peasant societies, where children begin adult work early in life, and grow early and naturally into the adult role with no adolescence, as we know it, at all. We, on the other hand, become parents with little previous practice at child care. Our young men get married with little if any previous experience in the role of breadwinner, and often before they have even stepped into their ultimate occupations. Also, writers have remarked that our adolescent period represents a discontinuity in social maturation, in that the various localized "cultures" of adolescent peer groups inculcate values and shape life-styles for adolescents which— rather than being a preparation for adulthood—actually stand in opposition to the values and practices of the adult world.[33] In other words, attitudes learned in adolescence must be unlearned in adulthood. And specific be- haviors and work-skills that will be demanded of the adult are not being learned during adolescence. The twenty-year-old in a more traditional society must, to a great extent, "see himself" as an adult, since he has had much practice in doing what adults do. This must be less true of most twenty-year-olds in our own society.

In many respects, the American family is unusual. As time goes by, how- ever, I suspect that many of the characteristics of the American family will spread to other parts of the world. Our family and kinship customs must surely be heavily influenced by the fact that ours is a highly industrialized society. As industrial development accelerates in other countries, it should bring urbanization, geographic mobility, rapid culture change, and pro- tracted schooling for the masses—which, in turn, may be expected to lead toward American-style family customs: a progressive "isolation" of the nuclear family from the larger kin group; a blurring of cultural guide lines for family roles; love matches in lieu of arranged marriage; greater egali- tarianism within the family; loss of the family's economic functions; and— with mass education and urbanization—the emergence of adolescence.

[33] Talcott Parsons, *Essays in Sociological Theory: Pure and Applied* (New York: The Free Press, 1949).

*10*

# SOCIAL BASES
# OF PERSONALITY

*Philip E. Slater*

# SOCIAL BASES
# OF PERSONALITY

. . . we must consider what estate all men are naturally in, and that is, a state of perfect freedom to order their actions, and dispose of their possessions and persons as they think fit. . . .

Men being . . . by nature all free, equal, and independent, no one can be . . . subjected to the political power of another without his own consent, which is done by agreeing with other men, to join and unite into a community. . . .

John Locke, *Of Civil Government*

. . . the two processes of individual and of cultural development must stand in hostile opposition to each other and mutually dispute the ground.

Sigmund Freud, *Civilization and Its Discontents*

There is no proper antagonism between the role of society and that of the individual. One of the most misleading misconceptions due to this nineteenth-century dualism was the idea that what was subtracted from society was added to the individual and what was subtracted from the individual was added to society.

Most people are shaped to the form of their culture because of the enormous malleability of their original endowment. They are plastic to the moulding force of the society into which they are born.

Ruth Benedict, *Patterns of Culture*

All men are socialized in the [sense of acquiring uniquely human attributes], but this does not mean that they have been completely molded by the particular norms and values of their culture. All cultures . . . do violence to man's socialized bodily drives. . . .

Dennis Wrong, "The Oversocialized Conception of Man in Modern Sociology"

## Society and the Individual

The opening quotations suggest but by no means exhaust the range of possible visions of the relation between society and the individual. We could, indeed, perform here the familiar rite of showing that the issue is sharply joined in Plato, or even before, and certainly it continues unabated in present Western thought. Nor does this debate result solely from the notorious capacity of the academic mind for creating and maintaining specious controversies. There is an inherent difficulty in defining the relation between two structures when one is almost entirely contained within the other—temporally as well as spatially. Yet to approach an understand-

548

ing of the social bases of personality we must in some way come to terms with the society-individual relationship.

## Locke's "State of Nature" Theory

Let us begin with a brief analysis of Locke's image of the individual in society, for although it dates from the seventeenth century it probably still epitomizes the layman's view. Locke envisions society as an artifact, consciously and deliberately constructed by individuals for their own welfare, and then superimposed upon a "natural" state of personal freedom. This "state of nature," however, is found nowhere in nature, except as a fantasy of human beings—more correctly, as a fantasy of human beings who have reached a state of urbanity in which self-awareness is highly developed, a stage that paradoxically is found primarily in large complex societies.

The "state of nature" fantasy, which was so popular in the seventeenth and eighteenth centuries, was probably stimulated in part by the voyages of discovery and the encounters with nonliterate societies in various parts of the world—some of these societies being far more primitive than Europeans. Europeans, in their ignorance of the language and customs of these tribes, imagined them to be "freer" than themselves. Subsequent anthropological investigations, however, have shown us the extraordinary social complexity of many such "primitive" societies, and the manifold rules of comportment with which their inhabitants are afflicted.

But only a few contemporary nonliterate societies can be considered truly "primitive." They have, after all, been evolving for hundreds of thousands of years; and, by almost any criterion, many of them are far more advanced than the European tribes of two millennia ago (a mere moment in time), when Western Europe housed the hopelessly ignorant and "innately" backward savages against which the bright Mediterranean civilizations were silhouetted. Could not Locke's view apply to men of 500,000 years ago?

Against this possibility two sets of data can be arrayed. The first consists of studies of isolated or "feral" children—children who, because of parental neglect, rejection, or abandonment, have somehow managed to survive with a minimum of human contact. Kingsley Davis has studied a number of such cases, some at first hand, with an eye to discovering "what an unsocialized mind (and body) is like after developing beyond the point at which normal minds have been socially molded." [1]

---

[1] K. Davis, *Human Society* (New York: Macmillan, 1949), p. 204. See also W. F. Ogburn, "Wolf Boy of Agra," *American Journal of Sociology*, **64**, 449–454 (1959); B. Bettelheim, "Feral Children and Autistic Children," *American Journal of Sociology*, **64**, 455–467 (1959).

Davis points out that under these conditions it becomes extremely difficult to find a behavioral criterion by which isolated or feral children would be objectively classified as human, since their cognitive development is so deficient. He concludes that "most of the mental traits we thinks of as constituting the human mind are not present unless put there by communicative contact with others." [2]

Spitz has shown that when such social isolation occurs in early infancy, life itself becomes precarious. In an unimpeachably hygienic foundling home in which the infants were well cared for physically but received almost no social stimulation, one fourth of the children under the age of two and a half died in a measles epidemic, despite the best medical care. All of the children showed, "from the third month on, extreme susceptibility to infection and illness of any kind," and were severely retarded, both in motor skills and in intellectual development, despite initially normal developmental quotients. [3] An analogous crippling can occur even with monkeys. [4]

These studies demonstrate rather clearly the impossibility of discussing the human individual outside of a social context. Although mere social contact cannot in itself be equated with the existence of a society, there must be some kind of social organization if the infant is to be guaranteed regular social contact. A human being can no more exist without a society than a human society can exist without individuals.

The second body of data which has undermined the "state of nature" notion comes from the study of the social behavior of animals—a field that has expanded impressively in the past thirty years. These studies show, among other things, that the "freedom" to which Locke refers cannot be found even among the lower mammals. The much-bandied dependence of animals upon instinct now appears to have been greatly overestimated, and we find increasingly that animals cannot survive without considerable socialization and an even greater degree of social organization. [5]

Of particular interest is the way in which aggression is controlled among animals. Hobbes, whose use of the "state of nature" fantasy antedates Locke (although he was intelligent enough to realize that such a state was "never generally so"—that is, not a historical reality) viewed it as a "warre of every man against every man" [6] and this is the popular view of

[2] K. Davis, *op. cit.,* p. 208.

[3] R. A. Spitz, "Hospitalism," *Psychoanalytic Study of the Child,* 1, 53–74 (1945).

[4] H. F. Harlow and Margaret K. Harlow, "Social Deprivation in Monkeys," *Scientific American,* November, 1962.

[5] J. P. Scott, *Animal Behavior* (Chicago: University of Chicago Press, 1958).

[6] Thomas Hobbes, *Leviathan* (Oxford, England: James Thornton, 1881), p. 95.

life in the animal kingdom. Yet as Lorenz and others have pointed out, "war" among animals is essentially a matter of interspecific hunting rather than intraspecific quarreling—fights between animals of the same species in the wild are largely bluff and bluster, highly ritualized interactions that are rarely lethal. Aggressiveness is mollified by a variety of cues, such as the "surrender" gesture, which consists of an animal offering to his opponent the most vulnerable part of the body—the part that is most carefully protected during the early part of the fight: the neck of the wolf, the top of the head for many bird species.[7] Aggression is also kept on a harmless level through signals with which one animal "tells" another that the behavior, indistinguishable to a human from serious aggression, is actually only play.[8] Equally surprising to humans is the rigid territoriality of many mammals, birds, fishes, and even insects.[9] A bird will angrily attack another bird who invades its territory until the fleeing opponent has crossed back over into his own, at which point the pursuer will gradually lose interest, while the pursued will suddenly turn and attack his attacker, apparently emboldened by the fact that he is now defending *his* territory.[10]

In many species, aggression is controlled by dominance orders. Scott describes what happens when two strange hens are put together:

> They usually fight vigorously, flapping and pecking. Soon one of the hens gives up and runs away. At the next encounter there is a short repetition of the fight, with the same animal tending to come out on top. In successive meetings there is less and less fighting until finally the dominant hen has only to threaten to peck the subordinate one to make it get out of the way.
>
> At this point the two hens get along together with a minimum of fighting. A flock organized into a dominance order eats more and lays more eggs than a group of strangers. Thus a dominance order may be thought of as an adaptation for reducing destructive fighting within a group.[11]

Among primates the dominance order is often complicated by the existence of coalitions, so that a single dominant animal will retreat when threatened by several subordinate ones who support each other.[12] Social

---

[7] K. Z. Lorenz, *King Solomon's Ring* (New York: Crowell, 1961), pp. 185–194.

[8] G. Bateson, "The Message 'This is Play,'" in B. Schaffner, ed., *Group Processes: 1955 Conference* (New York: Macy Foundation, 1956).

[9] J. P. Scott (cited in footnote 5), p. 213.

[10] I. Eibl-Eibesfeldt, "The Fighting Behavior of Animals," *Scientific American,* December, 1961.

[11] J. P. Scott (cited in footnote 5), p. 159.

[12] S. L. Washburn and I. DeVore, "The Social Life of Baboons," *Scientific American,* June, 1961. Dominance is not necessarily based on size or strength, nor is it in any way related to leadership behavior in animals. J. P. Scott (cited in footnote 5), p. 172.

organization among primates is, in any case, far more complex than the dominance order. Infants are more helpless, and there is far more care-giving behavior by the mother. The young animals are often the focus of social activity, even for males. Furthermore, instead of a brief period of sexual excitability, we find in primates the phenomenon of menstruation and, concomitantly, a more or less permanent sexual receptivity in the female. This means that "sexual behavior is no longer altogether concerned with fertilization but is an important part of social organization which tends to produce a more permanent relationship between adult males and females."[13]

If we define societal existence (as opposed to the "state of nature") as living permanently within a definable group that is sharply distinguished from other similar groups, under conditions such that (1) survival outside of the group is impossible, (2) disruption of the normal socialization process will prevent the attainment of fully adult behavior, and (3) everyday adult behavior is limited, controlled, and shaped by other members of the group, then we must admit that most primates live in societies and not in a "state of nature."[14]

Thus the social sciences seem to have demolished Locke's notion of the free state of nature. What is most interesting about Locke's idea is precisely its blithe ignorance of man's total dependence upon his society for the way he thinks, sees, and feels—for the definition of his desires and sometimes the desires themselves, and for the way in which he frames possible solutions for those desires.

### Language and Perception

The best illustration of man's dependence on society is found in language. During the past few decades, linguists, led by Benjamin Lee Whorf, have become increasingly aware of the extent to which language determines our ways of thinking and perceiving. Whorf effectively punctured the common-sense notion that "different languages are essentially parallel methods for expressing" the same thought, by pointing out that different cultures used totally different systems of classifying the world and experience, and that these systems were compelled by language:

We cut nature up, organize it into concepts, and ascribe significances as we do, largely because we are parties to an agreement to organize it in this way. . . . The agreement is, of course, an implicit and unstated one, *but its terms are ab-*

[13] J. P. Scott (cited in footnote 5), p. 170.
[14] See, for example, S. L. Washburn and I. DeVore (cited in footnote 12) and A. Kortlandt, "Chimpanzees in the Wild," *Scientific American,* May, 1962.

*solutely obligatory;* we cannot talk at all except by subscribing to the organization and classification of data which the agreement decrees.

. . . no individual is free to describe nature with absolute impartiality but is constrained to certain modes of interpretation even while he thinks himself most free.[15]

Only familiarity with a number of different linguistic systems would enable one even to approach such freedom.

Whorf notes, for example, that the English language divides nature into two classes of events, which we call respectively nouns and verbs, and which seem superficially to be differentiated by a time dimension: nouns being relatively permanent events, and verbs being relatively temporary ones. He shows that in fact there is no logic whatever to this classification—that it corresponds to no polarization in nature. The Hopi language, on the other hand, makes the noun-verb division *solely* on the basis of duration, whereas the language of the Nootka Indians in the Pacific Northwest makes no such division at all—to say "a house" a Nootka says, in effect, "a house occurs" or "it houses," just as we would say "a flame occurs" or "it burns." The Hopi have a single word for anything that flies except a bird. We, on the other hand, have only a single word for snow whether it is falling, lying, packed, slushy, or driven, which are all different words for the Eskimo. Hopi verbs have no tenses nor any concept of velocity, and Whorf shows how a totally different but equally effective mathematics and physics could emerge from such a linguistic system.[16]

But language is not merely a filter through which passes an experience common to all. As Hall points out, experience itself is a function of culture. An American cannot experience Navaho time, nor Balinese space, and can transcend only with great difficulty his own habitual assumptions about time and space. Most Americans, for example, are aware that our concepts of time are unusual in the world, but regard those of other cultures as simply irrational or backward. The ideas of quantified time units, fixed schedules, and urgency are too fundamental to our entire technological existence to be questioned closely. Yet Hall also notes other time-oriented characteristics peculiar to us which are not tied to this system in the same way and which have no inherent utilitarian value: the fact that "permanent" means five or ten years (an assumption which eliminates the possibility of strategic retreat in our foreign policy) and that century-long projects are never undertaken; or that fifteen minutes after an appointed hour is late for a morning appointment, early for a cocktail party, and on time

[15] B. L. Whorf, "Science and Linguistics," in E. E. Maccoby, T. M. Newcomb, and E L. Hartley, eds., *Readings in Social Psychology* (New York: Holt), pp. 1, 5.

[16] *Ibid.,* pp. 6–8; also B. L. Whorf, *Language, Thought, and Reality* (New York: Wiley, 1956).

for a dinner party. A planned one-hour meeting can be concluded before that time only with great difficulty, even if the business could be finished in five minutes—a pattern that would be hard to justify as more rational than the nonquantitative systems of many other cultures, in which a matter is dealt with until the participants are finished or interrupted. Hall's discussion of how Americans use space is also worth examining.[17]

We tend to make an artificial (and often convenient) distinction between perception and interpretation, but if we did not lump disparate things together and ignore other things completely, we would not "see" anything. "Life would be a stream of unique, never-recurring events."[18] An untrained person looking through a microscope or at an X-ray film "sees" or "experiences" very little, because he has such limited categories for organizing his perceptions—for knowing what to look *at*—what to group, what to ignore. The trained person sees more because he has a more elaborate theory for looking. But both the trained and untrained person receives the theory (whether sophisticated or based on common sense) from his culture.

We may be able to get physically outside of our society, but we can never really escape its culture. Even if we wish to rebel against society, the very terms in which we define that rebellion are derived from its culture; consequently, we can oppose it in its own terms, but we cannot act *independently* of it. Our culture even imposes upon us the ways that we choose to express our negation. This is why social change is so often dependent upon some contact with alien cultures; we often cannot imagine alternative ways of behaving, no matter how inconvenient and distressful the present ways may be. Recognition of the existence of alternatives is always the first step in the development of change, although the alternative may be at first disdained. The best we can usually do is to exchange part of our society's culture for part of another society's culture. The state of nature is forever beyond our grasp.

Freud once said that mankind had suffered three blows to his *amour-propre* from the researches of science: the first from Copernicus, who finally shattered the notion that the earth was the center of the universe; the second from Darwin, who destroyed the fantasy that man was a special being unrelated to animals; and the third from psychoanalysis, which pointed out that the conscious ego was "not master in its own house," but frequently dominated by impulses of which it was unaware.[19] To

[17] E. T. Hall, *The Silent Language* (Garden City, N.Y.: Doubleday, 1959), pp. 145, 165–210.

[18] R. W. Brown and E. H. Lenneberg, "Studies in Linguistic Relativity," in E. E. Maccoby et al., *Readings in Social Psychology* (New York: Holt), pp. 9–18.

[19] Sigmund Freud, "One of the Difficulties of Psychoanalysis" (1917) in *Collected Papers* (London: Hogarth, 1953), Vol. IV, pp. 347–356.

these we might well add the researches of sociology, social psychology, and anthropology, which have undermined the fantasy of man as an autonomous being, capable of behaving independently of the society in which he lives.

## Wholes and Parts

Locke's notion of the relation between individual and society is based on a common error—the tendency to view a whole as developing historically from its parts. A complex structure, however, arises not from its current constituents but from a simpler structure. The human organism was not created by a union of cells, but through an evolution from a simpler structure of cells. An even more cogent example may be taken from American history: Americans have always been attracted to the social-contract theory because it seems to describe the way our own nation was formed, but this also is a misconception. The thirteen colonies were not diverse and isolated entities, but already represented a whole—a common language, common customs, common problems, and a prior total structure. The union they created was not so much a unification as an improvement and elaboration of their existing structure.

At the same time, however, historical priority must be distinguished from formal or virtual priority. A whole *may* be dissolved into its parts, and in this sense the parts bear a formal priority to the whole.[20] Once this distinction is recognized, we must admit that we have been somewhat unfair in our treatment of social-contract theorizing. What men like Hobbes, Locke, and Rousseau were concerned about, after all, was not so much the historical origins of societal existence, but rather the nature of the bonds that currently held men together in societies. All were preoccupied with discovering viable principles of unity and conformity during times of change, although Hobbes viewed nonsocietal man as brutal, while Rousseau saw him as noble.

Hobbes usually receives credit for stating the problem, which has come to be referred to as "the Hobbesian problem of order"—a usage initiated

[20] The argument is sometimes stated that the human individual is "prior" by virtue of being more highly integrated or "organic" than his society. This, however, is very difficult to assess. There is no clear line between an organism and a colony of organisms even at the cellular level and interdependence is not easy to measure. J. T. Bonner, *Cells and Societies* (Princeton, N.J.: Princeton University Press, 1955). If the heart stops pumping blood a majority of the body's cells will "die" in a measurable period of time and will not be replaced. But by the same token, if all of the planes, trains, boats, and motor vehicles in the United States were suddenly deprived of fuel, most of our population would starve in a matter of months and not be replaced. Are these comparable degrees of interdependence?

by Talcott Parsons.[21] Parsons summarizes Hobbes' formulation as follows.

> Hobbes considered the "passions" of the individual to be the ultimate determinants of his action, and he specifically denied that there could be any "common measure" between the passions of different individuals. . . . Hobbes was principally concerned with the implications of this independence of one individual's passions from those of another . . . through the fundamental insight that other individuals are important as obstacles or aids to one individual in his gaining ends dictated by his passions, Hobbes came to his famous proposition: each individual's unregulated attempts to gain his ends would, through individuals' mutual attempts to "subdue or destroy one another," result in the war of all against all.[22]

Given such a set of assumptions, how is it possible that social order is achieved, and that "man becomes tractable to social discipline?" [23]

It would seem from our discussion thus far, however, that Hobbes' problem is an unreal one. If, as Benedict argues in the passage quoted at the beginning of the chapter, the individual is simply malleable clay molded by his society, and if man has never existed outside of a social context, then "social discipline" will never be experienced as such. The "passions" that Hobbes talks about will be common rather than independent because they are shaped *and even instilled* by a common force—the society in which men live. There is no "Hobbesian problem of order," because the order is given right from the start.

For many sociologists this answer has been sufficient. "To a modern sociologist imbued with the conception that action follows institutionalized patterns, opposition of individual and common interests has only a very limited relevance or is thoroughly unsound." [24] The neo-Freudian school has echoed this position for dynamic psychology: "Although there are certain needs, such as hunger, thirst, sex, which are common to man, those drives which make for the *differences* in men's characters, like love and hatred, the lust for power and the yearning for submission, the enjoyment of sensuous pleasure and the fear of it, are all products of the social process. . . . Man's nature, his passions, and anxieties are a cultural product. . . ." [25] Fromm explicitly rejects the idea of a conflict between a regulatory society and a biologically driven man.

---

[21] Talcott Parsons, *The Structure of Social Action* (New York: McGraw-Hill, 1937), pp. 89–94.

[22] Talcott Parsons, E. Shils, K. D. Naegele, and J. R. Pitts, *Theories of Society* (New York: Free Press, 1961), p. 87.

[23] D. H. Wrong, "The Oversocialized Conception of Man in Modern Sociology," *American Sociological Review, 26*, 184 (1961).

[24] Quoted by D. H. Wrong, *ibid.*, p. 186, from F. X. Sutton et al., *The American Business Creed* (Cambridge, Mass.: Harvard University Press, 1956), p. 304.

[25] Erich Fromm, *Escape from Freedom* (New York: Rinehart, 1941), pp. 12–13.

Other sociologists, whose position has been most tellingly expressed by Dennis Wrong, feel that this "oversocialized view of man" leads only to an avoidance of rather than a solution to Hobbes' question. If the "over-integrated" view is correct, Wrong asks, "How is it that violence, conflict, revolution, and the individual's sense of coercion by society manage to exist at all?" [26] We might add the specific query: How did Hobbes, a well-socialized member of his society, ever happen to conceive of a state of nature and a war of all against all?

The most often-discussed flaw in the "overintegrated view of society"— one which is really a simple matter of emphasis—is its tendency to ignore those "passions" for which society is *not* responsible: the so-called biological drives. Most of the sociologists criticized by Wrong do at least pay lip-service to the idea that the body plays some role in socal life, even in America, but in the development of social theory we must agree with him that it is relegated to a very minor position.

More important, however, are two assumptions that seem to have emerged somewhat inappropriately from the insight that society does in fact mold and even on occasion create desires in men. The first assumption is that the desires thus molded or created are necessarily compatible with that society. Connotations often trick us into absurd conclusions, and the use of words like "mold" and "create" implies a wise and foresighted demiurge rather than the blind mechanism that society must be considered to be. In fact, the Hobbesian problem would logically remain, even if there were no biological drives whatever, but only bland social passions.

The second false assumption is that because desires are created or molded by society, they can be sated without conflict between individuals. Once the possibility is admitted that two men can badly want something which only one can have, Hobbes' problem is entirely reinstated. We need only discard the notion that the war of all against all is confined to an imaginary state of nature. We can instead regard it as a perpetual virtuality *within* every social system. As Wrong says, ". . . the war of all against all is not simply effaced with the creation of political authority: it remains an ever-present potentiality in human society." [27] It is thus not so much the *origin* of society which is the focus of concern here, but the nature of the force that prevents this virtuality from becoming an actuality. To ignore this problem would be as foolish as to ignore those forces maintaining the integrity of the human body. Between any dynamic structure and its component parts there is potential conflict as well as substantial identity

[26] D. H. Wrong (cited in footnote 23), p. 186.
[27] *Ibid.*, p. 185.

of goals. Otherwise, all structures would be tension-free and permanent, and exchange of components would never occur.

## Freud

The most complete statement of the nature of this conflict appears in Freud's *Civilization and Its Discontents*. Unlike the social-contract theorists, Freud does not argue from an imaginary state of nature but from history itself:

> . . . men are . . . creatures among whose instinctual endowments is to be reckoned a powerful share of aggressiveness. As a result, their neighbour is for them not only a potential helper or sexual object, but also someone who tempts them to satisfy their aggressiveness on him, to exploit his capacity for work without compensation, to use him sexually without his consent, to seize his possessions, to humiliate him, to cause him pain, to torture and to kill him. *Homo homini lupus* [man is a wolf to man]. Who, in the face of all his experience of life and history, will have the courage to dispute this assertion? [28]

Freud argues that this aggression is normally held in check by "counterforces," but emerges in full force when these counterforces are removed, as in wartime, and in particular during mass migrations and invasions, when social controls are weakened. He points out that even under optimum conditions it is possible to unite large numbers of people only if there is some outside group they can hate in common.[29]

But what are these counterforces? Freud suggests that, through a complicated process which need not be outlined here, a part of sexual energy is transformed in such a way as to neutralize aggressiveness, at least in part. He maintains that this same transformed energy also provides the raw material for the technological and artistic achievements of civilization. He raises doubts, however, as to the value of this mechanism, since only "the crudest excesses of brutal violence" are prevented by a very high expenditure of energy, and the security provided by civilized social life is bought at the expense of happiness.[30]

The problem posed by Freud still remains as one of the largest items of unfinished business on the agenda of sociology. His formulation cannot be criticized for its assumptions about "human nature" in the abstract, since it is based upon observations about man-in-society. Nor can we very well argue that man has become somehow less aggressive since Freud's time. His remark that men have gained such control over nature that they

[28] Sigmund Freud, *Civilization and Its Discontents* (New York: Norton, 1961), p. 58.
[29] *Ibid.*, pp. 59–61.
[30] *Ibid.*, p. 62.

"would have no difficulty in exterminating one another to the last man" [31] may have seemed exaggerated when it was written, but is a commonplace of our lives today. The chronicity of war and violence might alone convince us, and we are becoming increasingly aware that the potentiality for such violence resides in all of us, and that no nation, region, class, or category is immune to it. Nor is idealism any solution, as can be seen from the hatred which splintered peace organizations express toward each other.

Finally, one cannot object that Freud's theory ignores the role of society in molding human desires since, as Wrong points out, it is this very plasticity of instinct upon which Freud's theory is based. [32]

We can ask, however, whether all of the aggression that we see in humans springs full-blown from man's instinctual repertory, and is merely softened or intensified by social norms; or whether some of it may not be derived from the social transformation of other impulses. There is evidence, both historical and crosscultural, favoring Freud's theory that cultural development depends heavily on social restriction of sexual expression, [33] but there is very little evidence that this process has contributed anything to the inhibition of aggression. On the contrary, some students of the problem have argued—and from psychoanalytic premises—that sexual repression, far from neutralizing aggressive tendencies, actually increases them: that blocked sexuality expresses itself in sadism and violence. Taylor makes a particularly good case for this argument in the instance of medieval and modern European trends. [34] On the face of it, furthermore, it would certainly appear that the most peaceable groups to be found in the world are small tribes with negligible cultures and permissive sexual norms. [35] If this is true, instead of viewing sexual repression as the price of curbing aggression, increased aggressiveness would be the price of repressing sexuality which, in turn, would be the price of civilization. This formulation, of course, augments rather than decreases the notion of an opposition between society and the individual, and certainly does

---

[31] *Ibid.*, p. 92.

[32] D. H. Wrong (cited in footnote 23), p. 192.

[33] J. D. Unwin, *Sex and Culture* (London: Oxford University Press, 1934); G. P. Murdock, "The Regulation of Premarital Sex Behavior," in R. A. Manners, ed., *Process and Pattern in Culture* (Chicago, Ill.: Aldine, 1964), pp. 399–410.

[34] G. R. Taylor, *Sex in History* (New York: Vanguard, 1954). See also Grace Stuart, *Narcissus* (New York: Macmillan, 1955).

[35] Not all "primitive" societies are sexually permissive—many that would seem highly primitive to us have far more stringent regulations than our own. The relationship seems to hold only one way: a *lack* of literacy and other perquisites of a high cultural development does not guarantee sexual permissiveness; but no civilization that we know of has ever emerged in a society that did not place profound restrictions on sexual expression.

nothing whatever to modify Freud's doubt whether civilization is worth all the trouble it causes.[36]

Parenthetically, this view articulates well with Weber's interpretation of the relationship between Protestantism and the rise of capitalism.[37] Weber tried to explain how an ascetic, world-rejecting ideology could give rise to a system of wealth accumulation and more complex social organization. At another level, we can see how an ideology that virulently attacked all pleasurable sensation and stressed the unimportance of all social bonds [38] might have the dual effect of releasing energy for cultural development and increasing aggressiveness (in the form of competitiveness, ambition, and the like). One of the advantages of substitute gratifications, from a social viewpoint, is that they are never quite satisfying. Hence the individual, like an addict, continually seeks more, so that his energies may be continually fixed on and poured into culture-building activities. Normal hunger, thirst, and sexual desire are readily extinguished, but the desire for wealth, power, or fame (listed in order of decreasing possibility of satiation and increasing perversion of the desire for pleasure) cannot easily be laid to rest. Gratification is delayed and circuitous, and requires constant application of energy (the same is true, of course, of sexual perversions, which seem to increase along with these more acceptable transformations). An individual cannot, like the deculturated Siriono tribe of Bolivia, simply lie in his hammock until hunger or sexual desire become so insistent as to impel action.[39]

The negative aspect of this energy tapping, obviously, is the destructiveness that accompanies such a combination of aggressiveness and insatiability. If our theory is correct, we might question whether less crude and wasteful social methods for tapping human energies might not be available, now that we have achieved a level of cultural development at which the rate of change is faster than most humans can tolerate.

### Durkheim

Although in general Freud and Durkheim have little in common, both agree that cultural development does not bring individual happiness.

---

[36] For critical discussion and suggested revisions of Freud's theory, see H. Marcuse, *Eros and Civilization* (Boston: Beacon Press, 1955); and N. O. Brown, *Life Against Death* (New York: Vintage, 1959).

[37] M. Weber, *The Protestant Ethic and The Spirit of Capitalism* (New York: Scribner, 1930). See, in particular, Chapter IV.

[38] *Ibid.*, pp. 105–110, 156–159.

[39] A. R. Holmberg, *Nomads of the Long Bow,* U.S. Government Printing Office, Washington, D.C., 1950.

In support of his view, Durkheim points to the high correlation between cultural complexity and the suicide rate, but seems to shrink from drawing the obvious conclusion that individual happiness actually *decreases* with the progress of civilization.[40]

The reasons given by the two men for this failure of culture, however, are totally disparate. For Freud, it occurs because cultural evolution—the formation of ever-larger and more complex social entities—necessitates ever-increasing embezzlements of instinctual energy, and hence gratification becomes constantly more circuitous, blocked, and indirect for the individual. For Durkheim, individual unhappiness is also based upon the increased size of the collective unit, but reflects the *decreasing* control of the group over the individual. The collectivity is viewed as having diluted its impact on the individual through overextension.[41]

What seems like a complete opposition, however, disappears when we examine it more closely. The crucial point is that while both men are pitting a unitary concept of society against a binary view of the individual, they are slicing the individual in unrelated ways. For Durkheim, the individual is split in terms of that portion which is personal and particular to him, and that which is common to all men in a given group.[42] For Freud, the individual is split in terms of pleasure-seeking impulses and a control apparatus.[43] This control apparatus is sometimes identified with social restraints and sometimes placed in direct opposition to them. According to some psychoanalytic theorists, the blocking of pleasurable bodily sensation leads to tendencies toward self-aggrandizement (usually referred to as "narcissism"), normally at the expense of others. Grace Stuart summarizes this position somewhat polemically by arguing that "a culture which has so long feared the virtues of pleasure and the physical has thus robbed itself of that very love of neighbour for which it has so necessitously cried out." [44] If this view is correct, then Freud and Durkheim are pointing to two aspects of the same process: the expansion of social units to larger and more complex forms is achieved by "borrowing" from the libidinal economy

[40] Émile Durkheim, *The Division of Labor in Society* (Glencoe, Ill.: Free Press, 1933), pp. 241–250.
[41] Émile Durkheim, *Suicide* (Glencoe, Ill.: Free Press, 1951), pp. 373, 388–389.
[42] Émile Durkheim, *The Division of Labor in Society* (cited in footnote 40), p. 105. Durkheim remarks, and it should be emphasized here, that talking of the individual in relation to society as a whole is just a convenient simplification; actually, since the individual belongs to many groups, he has many "collective consciences."
[43] This is a gross oversimplification, but it is impossible even to attempt to summarize in a few sentences the many changes in Freud's instinct theory and the complex assumptions underlying each version.
[44] Grace Stuart (cited in footnote 34), p. 41.

of the individual—he then behaves more egoistically, which is facilitated by the more diluted control exercised by the larger social unit.

Despite this possible synthesis, however, it might be profitable to examine the different assumptions upon which the two positions are based. For although Freud was aware of the extreme cohesiveness of many contemporary primitive societies, some of his sociological writing can be placed with very little distortion into the social-contract genre, in the sense that he at times seems to be assuming some sort of primeval individualism, or at least an individualism tempered only by despotism.

Durkheim's awareness of the lack of what we would call individualism in primitive societies is much more explicit.[45] Rousseau's notion that man was "born free" seems ludicrous to us today, knowing as we do the infinitesimal effect of any individual on the culture that molds him, determines his life course, and unconcernedly buries him. But it took almost a million years for men to achieve a clear awareness of their existence as individuals, and it is not too surprising that a few additional centuries should be required for them to realize that it was not always thus, and to be able to achieve an empathic understanding of what it meant to be without that awareness. Not until the latter part of the nineteenth century was there any general recognition that individualism is a modern rather than a primeval phenomenon.

Durkheim was, in any case, well aware of it: ". . . the place of the individual in society, of no account in its origins, becomes greater with civilization."[46] Furthermore, this lack of individuality was not because of artificial repression—it simply did not exist. There was no concept of the self separated from society. Durkheim thus, in a sense, inverts Hobbes'

[45] A caution is in order here. The long-delayed recognition that "primitives" were not the free spirits imagined by social-contract theorists tended to create an equally absurd reaction. As Malinowski notes: "When it became plain that hypertrophy of rules rather than lawlessness is characteristic of primitive life, scientific opinion veered round to the opposite point . . . ," seeing the primitive man as having an "automatic submission" to tradition and custom, as if deviant behavior occurred only under civilized conditions. B. Malinowski, *Crime and Custom in Savage Society* (Paterson, N.J.: Littlefield, Adams, 1959), pp. 9–10. This is the "oversocialized" man in the "overintegrated" society of which Wrong complains, and it must be confessed that it characterizes a sizable fraction of the ethnographic literature. It could be considered almost as absurd as Thomas Hobbes' belief (cited in footnote 6), p. 95, that the American Indians had "no government at all." Hobbes' remark, however, contains a special irony: the patterns of cooperation developed by these same Indians, such as work-bees and confederations (usually accompanied by intertribal athletic competitions), were borrowed by the English settlers, and formed a model for such institutions as the American confederation and federacy, and through them, the League of Nations and the United Nations—the principal bulwark against the "war of all against all" in the world today. R. Linton, *The Tree of Culture* (New York: Knopf, 1959), pp. 601–603.

[46] Émile Durkheim, *The Division of Labor in Society* (cited in footnote 40), p. 193.

problem of order. Instead of asking why societies do not fall into anarchy, he asks how individuality comes to arise at all; and instead of asking how men refrain from killing one another, he asks why society bothers itself about murder at all: "What is one man less to society? What does one lost cell matter to the organism?" [47] Yet this does not really involve a different question, for Durkheim, like Hobbes, is concerned with the nature of those bonds that hold men together in groups. The important point is simply that Durkheim's awareness of the permanence and pervasiveness of society's control over the individual enabled him to offer what is perhaps the first sophisticated treatment of the relationship between individual and society, despite a hopelessly naive and inadequate psychology. Let us consider some of his more specific ideas in terms of the light they throw on the various questions we have raised.

Durkheim's fame rests in no small part on his empirical study of suicide rates and the theoretical conclusions that he drew from it. Suicide has always fascinated social scientists, partly because its occurrence refutes common-sense psychological ideas about the motive of self-preservation, and partly because the extensive elaboration of laws and customs surrounding it refute the common-sense modern idea that a man's life is his own affair. On the basis of variations in suicide rates by such demographic variables as sex, marital status, religion, and occupation, Durkheim arrived at what he felt were three distinguishable types of suicide: egoistic, altruistic, and anomic. Egoistic and anomic suicide seem to belong under the same heading, since they "both spring from society's insufficient presence in individuals," although they are expressed in ways which Durkheim felt it was important to distinguish.[48] In egoistic suicide, society failed to provide collective activity and thus deprived life of meaning; in anomic suicide, society failed to limit individual aspirations and desires. Thus Durkheim gives us both of the models of society which appear in arguments over the individual-society relationship: the positive, cultural model of society as the molder of man, and the negative, Hobbesian model of society as the regulator of man.

Of special interest to us is the altruistic type of suicide. Durkheim suggests that if "excessive individuation leads to suicide, insufficient individuation has the same effects." In Durkheim's view, altruistic suicide occurs primarily in primitive societies, among religious fanatics, and in the more archaic segments of modern societies, such as the military. The act is defined as either obligatory, highly honorable, heroic, or holy, and hence is carried out in acceptance of social norms.

[47] *Ibid.*, p. 72.
[48] Émile Durkheim, *Suicide* (cited in footnote 41), p. 258.

Some of these acts—the obligatory suicide of widows or bereaved servants, for example—present no problem, since they are "altruistic" in the popular as well as the technical sense. But the man who kills himself to achieve personal salvation under a religious conviction, or simply because he is insulted and wishes to express his anger or contempt toward his enemy, presents a problem. For what, after all, could be more "egoistic," in the popular sense, than the man who leaves a family destitute to further his own immortal well being? or the man whose pride is so egregious that the most trivial snub will cause him to take his own life? This problem was of no interest to Durkheim, for whom "altruism" in this instance meant simply that (1) suicide was made either obligatory or prestigious by the society, and that the individual, by committing the act, was behaving in accordance with rather than in opposition to social norms; and (2) that little value was placed on the life of the individual by either himself or the group. Personality and subjective motivation are explicitly disregarded by Durkheim, who considers only the raw behavior in its social context. After all, "our very egoism is in large part a product of society." [49]

This remark leaves us somewhat unsatisfied, however, since we could well argue that the very individualism which detaches a person from collective life in modern society and causes him to contravene social norms which proscribe suicide is *also* a product of the society, if only in a negative sense. The mere fact that an individual lacks meaningful collective activity does not mean that he is any the less molded by his society. Are we then forced back to Ruth Benedict's position that the whole question of opposition between individual and society is absurd?

### Competing Structures Within the Individual and Society

The solution lies in the fact that the norms of any society form an inconsistent and contradictory hodgepodge (particularly in a large, complex society), so that if an individual violates one norm he stands a good chance of simultaneously conforming to another. This reaches its ultimate development in our own society, where even if an individual should find a way to conform to all other norms, he would, by so doing, violate the cultural norm against "conformity."

From this viewpoint, not only opposition between individual and society but also concord between them becomes meaningless. There is always some sense in which there is agreement, and another in which there is conflict. The controversy about the nature of this relation has raged largely on the basis of positing a unitary concept of society, or of the individual, or both.

[49] *Ibid.*, p. 360.

In abandoning such a position, however, we need not abandon the issue, which is still an important one. What we must abandon is the notion that conflict between the individual and society revolves around specific social norms. It is not when an individual violates a norm that he is in opposition to society, but when he shifts his interest and involvement (or, in Freudian terms, transfers his libido) from the group to himself. His personal goals and the group's goals may, in fact, be identical with regard to any specific issue—indeed, one of the group's (contradictory) norms may be of such nature as to encourage his withdrawal. In India, for example, under certain conditions, such a withdrawal would be considered a desirable ideal,[50] and our own society approves and rewards invidiousness, personal avarice, and uncooperativeness in many areas of life (as well as their antitheses). The transfer of interest nevertheless creates a conflict between the two structures (individual and society), since they compete (as do all social entities) for the limited [51] resources of time, energy, and emotional commitment. No two social entities—no matter how much they share interests, or overlap, or even if one is entirely contained within the other—can share these resources without conflict.

Consider, for example, the much-belabored case of state and federal competition within our own society—it does not cease to exist simply because the federal constitution itself includes a number of provisions guaranteeing certain autonomy to the states. Nor would anyone imagine that subdivisions of the federal government itself, such as the State Department and the CIA, which are dependent for all of their power and personnel on that totality, never compete with the government as a whole. It is often said that the central goal of any bureau is to increase itself, which is merely another way of stating this inherent competition.

To return to altruistic suicide, then, we must conclude that Durkheim's category system, while helpful as a technique for grouping the empirical data in a memorable way, does not pertain (as it would seem on the surface) to the degree of conflict or congruence between individual and society. For the category of altruistic suicide includes extremes of both orientations. What is important about Durkheim's framework, however, is that instead of merely taking a fixed stance regarding the relationship

[50] It would not be explicitly *defined* as self-involvement, of course, but quite the opposite. From an objective standpoint, however, any form of renunciation of "the world" in favor of fantasy objects and for the purpose of personal salvation must be classified as a withdrawal of interest in collective life, regardless of whether the society places a value on such withdrawal.

[51] Although always less limited than we imagine them to be. See C. N. Parkinson, *Parkinson's Law and Other Studies in Administration* (Boston: Houghton Mifflin, 1957), in which many profound sociological insights are presented in humorous guise.

between society and the individual, Durkheim also treats this relationship as variable—altering in time and from collectivity to collectivity.

### Synergy

This approach is more highly developed in a recent paper by Maslow, drawing on unpublished (and seemingly atypical) ideas of Benedict. Benedict compared a group of what seemed to her anxious, aggressive, "surly" societies with another group that seemed cooperative, affectionate, and secure, but could find few principles of classification that would distinguish them. She finally arrived at the concept of synergy to account for the differences. Societies with high synergy (the cooperative ones) *"have social orders in which the individual by the same act and at the same time serves his own advantage and that of the group . . .* Non-aggression occurs [in these societies] not because people are unselfish and put social obligations above personal desires, but when social arrangements make these two identical." [52] In low-synergy societies, on the other hand, an advantage for one man "becomes a victory over another." In high-synergy societies wealth tends to be diffused, while in low-synergy societies it tends to be funneled or concentrated. Gods or ghosts in high-synergy societies are viewed as helpful, those in low-synergy societies as malevolent and terrifying.

Maslow points out that low-synergy institutions reflect an assumption of limited or scarce resources. [53] This does not necessarily mean that the resources in question are actually scarce by some external criterion, but only that the institutions follow such an assumption. American economic institutions, for example, have been historically of the low-synergy variety, despite immense natural wealth. The trend from a production-oriented to a consumption-oriented society, however, reflects a move toward high-synergy institutions. As Maslow points out, the Judaeo-Christian tradition as a whole has oscillated between these approaches. Maslow illustrates his concept with academic grades—a perfect example of a low-synergy institution if grading is done or suspected of being done on a curve. Each person's good performance detracts from the rewards available to the next. This can easily be converted into a high-synergy institution, of course,

---

[52] A. H. Maslow, "Synergy in the Society and in the Individual," *Journal of Individual Psychology,* **20,** 156 (1964).

[53] See G. M. Foster, "Peasant Society and the Image of Limited Good," *American Anthropologist,* **67,** 293–315 (1965). For an extended discussion of the nature of high- and low-synergy situations, see M. Deutsch, "Cooperation and Trust: Some Theoretical Notes," in *Nebraska Symposium on Motivation* (Lincoln: University of Nebraska Press, 1962), pp. 275–319.

simply by changing the rules. In the Soviet Union, for example, competition is always between schools, or between groups within schools, so that an individual's grade redounds to the credit of the group.[54] Coleman points out that athletics are so organized in American schools, and suggests that this may account for their greater importance as a source of prestige and involvement in adolescent peer society.[55]

Some motives lend themselves more easily to one or another type of institution. Sexuality must be severely perverted to generate anything but a high-synergy institution, since normally that which gratifies one partner also gratifies the other. The desire for fame, on the other hand, can only with difficulty give rise to a high-synergy institution, since fame is inherently invidious (one person cannot by definition "stand out" if everyone else is in the same position). Social institutions are seldom embarrassed by logic, however, and there is no dearth of attempts at such incompatible combinations. Sexual relationships have frequently been transformed into competitive, exploitive interactions in the history of Western culture,[56] either through the custom of selecting partners to enhance social prestige, or by defining sexual activity as a game in which one sex wins and the other loses by participating. The persistence of colloquial usages such as "conquest" and "score" reflect this latter orientation.[57] On the other side, an institution like the village social column of a small-town newspaper may, if the village is small enough, enable everyone in the community to have his name regularly in print.

We might assume that power, like fame, is an inherently scarce resource,

[54] D. Mace and Vera Mace, *The Soviet Family* (Garden City, N.Y.: Doubleday, 1964), pp. 290–293. This system, of course, pervades Russian (not merely Soviet) culture. It accounts for the custom, which has always baffled and amused Americans, of a speaker or performer applauding along with his audience. This gesture is an expression of the idea that any achievement is a group achievement, and is symptomatic of Soviet discomfort with individual prominence.

[55] J. S. Coleman, "Academic Achievement and the Structure of Competition," *Harvard Educational Review*, **29**, 330–351 (1959).

[56] See, for example, W. Waller, "The Rating and Dating Complex," *American Sociological Review*, **2**, 727–734 (1937).

[57] While there is an attempt to move away from this approach in contemporary America, it is difficult to insulate one area of life from the achievement orientation which pervades the entire culture. The inability to approach even pleasure or intimacy as anything but a challenge or task to be mastered is revealed by such phrases as "making out," "making it with so-and-so," "making the marriage (or relationship) work," and so on. The concern with sexual "adequacy" is of the same stamp, implying that the seeking of physical pleasure is some sort of job to be performed well. Pleasure is also frequently translated into duty by those with an ideological commitment to sexual freedom. Puritanism dies hard, as do the sadomasochistic and invidious assumptions associated with it. We see this in D. H. Lawrence's rather pathetic attempts to achieve an unfettered sexual orientation, which, however, all dwindle in the end to the same kinds of sadomasochistic fantasies which dominate modern popular fiction.

but this depends largely on how power is defined. This is an exceedingly complex issue, which cannot be entered into here, except to point out that one can employ a model of power that is inherently invidious, or one that merely reflects the capacity of a given individual to influence his environment.[58] Students of industrial organization have been able to make a convincing case for the notion that under conditions of higher synergy (less competitiveness, more trust, less centralization, more delegation) everyone gains power in the latter sense. Conversely, the assumption that influence or power is a fixed and limited quantity, and the resulting effort to keep subordinates from exercising too much of it, may lead to a loss of power for everyone.[59]

This distinction is more transparent in the case of wealth. The desire for absolute wealth presents no barriers to high-synergy institutions, but wealth is frequently defined entirely in relative terms; that is, it is viewed as meaningless unless displayed against a less wealthy background.[60] The consequences of this tendency are detailed with unrelenting wit by Veblen.[61] When it occurs, however, we are usually talking about a desire for fame or power rather than wealth—wealth being desired not for its own sake, or for the goods and services it procures, but for the opportunity it provides to acquire prestige or manipulate others.

One reason for belaboring this point is that sociologists have frequently been unable to account for the positive or negative reactions of individuals to a given situation in terms of absolute increases or decreases in concrete benefits or status, but have been forced to employ the concepts of "relative

---

[58] Power is difficult to evaluate. As Stephens points out, deference customs do not necessarily reflect the power situation, and often are more inhibiting and controlling for the person deferred to than for those who defer. See W. N. Stephens, *The Family in Cross-Cultural Perspective* (New York: Holt, 1963), pp. 291 ff., 315–316. Freud pointed out the ambivalence expressed in deference behavior toward rulers, which has often involved paralyzing and painful restrictions. Sigmund Freud, *Totem and Taboo* (New York: Norton, 1962), pp. 41–51. The ambiguity of power is even more acutely displayed in the parent-child relationship, in which, on the one hand, the parent has absolute mastery and control over the helpless infant, and on the other, must cater to the infant's every need.

[59] R. Likert, *New Patterns of Management* (New York: McGraw-Hill, 1961), pp. 179–183; D. McGregor, *The Human Side of Enterprise* (New York: McGraw-Hill, 1960).

[60] The cartoonist Al Capp once presented the ultimate illustration of this attitude, in the person of General Bullmoose. The latter complained bitterly that his wealth gave him no pleasure since what it purchased (fine food, comfortable beds, beautiful women) could also be obtained by the less wealthy. His solution was to buy sole rights in a popular cartoonist, and every morning to read his single copy of the strip to himself in front of an angry mob of deprived citizens. Thus the invidious fantasy of Bullmoose was realized through the even more invidious fantasy of his creator that a comic strip be the most valuable possession in the world.

[61] T. Veblen, *The Theory of the Leisure Class* (New York: Modern Library, 1934).

deprivation" and "relative status" [62] to explain such a phenomenon as a man feeling himself slighted despite an improvement in his status because the improvement was less than that received by some reference group.

The concept of synergy provides another way of looking at Freud's theory of sexual repression and civilization. We suggested above that such repression may well be correlated with both cultural complexity and level of aggressiveness. We might also say that the social repression of sexual expression (in the broad sense of seeking pleasurable physical stimulation of any kind) [63] tends to bring about the replacement of high-synergy institutions with low-synergy ones: that the desire for absolute gains gives way to the desire for relative or invidious ones, and the desire for shareable joys—physical pleasure, comforts, and possessions (for their own sake)— gives way to the desire for unshareable ones—power, glory, prestige, fame.

But how can we reconcile the notion of synergy as a *variable* with the idea that different collectivities *must* compete with each other and individuals for limited resources? Are we not thereby positing an inherently "low-synergy" universe? The answer is that in stressing such competition we are merely emphasizing the limits of compatibility between systems. Total identity and total antithesis of interest are equally impossible. Furthermore, no resource is either totally incapable of being expanded nor infinitely expandable. The overlapping of two systems means *both* that they share an identity of interest and, at the same time and to the same degree, that they come into competition with one another. The concept of synergy reflects the great range of variability that remains between the limits just noted. This is an important point to keep in mind, since many authors seem to imply that problems in social organization would disappear if we could somehow transform all low-synergy institutions into high-synergy ones. Yet, competition is not eliminated by shifting the arena from intragroup to intergroup rivalry, and it would be a thin and diluted goal indeed that could be shared by all individuals and groups in the world.

We can perhaps best summarize our discussion of the various images

---

[62] S. A. Stouffer et al., *The American Soldier* (Princeton, N.J.: Princeton University Press, 1949); R. K. Merton, *Social Theory and Social Structure* (New York: Free Press, 1957), pp. 225–236.

[63] This is the way Freud meant it, and it is the way extreme puritanism has generally expressed itself—forbidding, with admirable consistency (since for the Christian variety at least, the only sins arousing any clerical interest were sexual ones) any form of spontaneity, even athletics—showing, thereby, an unconscious understanding of psychoanalytic theories several hundred years before they were advanced. See M. Weber (cited in footnote 37), pp. 156 ff., and G. R. Taylor (cited in footnote 34), pp. 162–174, 206 ff., and *passim*.

of the individual-society relationship by listing the three sets of contradictory assumptions on which they have traditionally been based.

1. Some theorists have viewed the individual as identified with his
society; others as in conflict with it.

2. Some theorists have viewed society in unitary terms; others have
viewed it as inherently divided against itself in some respects.

3. Some theorists have viewed the individual in unitary terms; others
as inherently divided against himself in some respects.

Now, however, we are in a position to see the limitation of all of these
views: they have relied upon an "either-or" rather than a dimensional
concept of each of these three variables. In fact, the individual can be more
or less identified with his society and more or less in conflict with it, but
must to some extent be both. Similarly, there must be some sense in which
a society or an individual is unitary in order for us even to be able to
identify it, but a society or an individual without internal contradictions
would be a static monstrosity—a corpse. Bearing these considerations in
mind, let us turn to the question of how unity and conflict are articulated,
both within and between the individual and his society.

## Roles and Role Induction

Gideon Sjoberg has pointed out that all social systems must meet contradictory functional requirements, which gives rise to the formation of
"mutually antagonistic structural arrangements that function to meet these
requirements." [64] In other words, the internal contradictions of a system are
not always historical accidents, hopefully to be swept away by the application of utopian logic, but may be essential to the maintenance of the
system itself.[65] We have already encountered some of these contradictions
—needs for change and stability,[66] for deviation and conformity, for creation and destruction, for cooperation and competition, and for individualism
and collectivism.

[64] G. Sjoberg, "Contradictory Functional Requirements and Social Systems," *Journal
of Conflict Resolution,* **4,** 199 (1960).
[65] Lewis Mumford has similarly argued that only the "laxity, corruption, and disorder"
in a system make it viable. L. Mumford, "The Fallacy of Systems," *Saturday Review
of Literature,* **32,** 8–9 (October, 1949).
[66] Western societies are somewhat overadapted to the need for innovation, and pay a
heavy social cost in unproductive deviance and diluted social relationships. Biological
organisms work with a similarly wide margin of random experimentation, however, in
the form of mutations. Fewer than one out of a hundred mutations are anything but
a nuisance or a tragedy, but that one occasionally rescues a species from extinction.

This should by no means be interpreted as positing some sort of "golden mean" concept of social systems. Compromise is, of course, the temporary outcome of most contradictions, but it does little to remove the tension of conflict.[67] There is no meaningful compromise (to use one of Sjoberg's examples) between adhering to scientific procedures and violating those procedures, although both behaviors have been essential to the growth of science. It is no solution to satisfy each contradictory requirement halfway, any more than it is a solution, when two men each need a quart of blood to survive and only one quart is available, to divide this quart between them.

The more successful and more frequently encountered empirical outcome is the emergence of separate institutions to realize the contradictory requirements. This, however, threatens to some extent the integrity of the whole, and the belief systems that emerge to counteract this threat tend to emphasize and idealize one of a contradictory pair over the other. (Satirists, for example, have always delighted in contrasting the one-sided Christian emphasis on amity and pacifism with the unrivaled bloodthirstiness of its proponents.) One of the pair thus tends to become overt, the other covert, one formal and official, the other informal and unofficial. Bootlegging, black markets, organized vice, and political machines are examples of institutions that derive from such one-sided belief systems.[68]

This creates a strain, however, between the belief system and the concrete institutions, between the need to suppress the covert or informal institutions and the need to maintain them. One can try either to modify the belief system to make it less contrary to reality (this will cause ideologues, both of the radical reformer stamp and of the conservative fundamentalist stamp, to cry out against the compromising of ethical standards) or to eradicate the unofficial institutions so that the reality conforms to the belief. Such eradication is often attempted during revolutions and reform movements (such as the Reformation, the Inquisition, or the reform governments that overturn urban political machines from time to time). The savagery often shown in essaying such consistency may occasionally mitigate the impermanence of the results but, sooner or later, in some form or another, the "repressed" aspect returns. Functional requirements that run counter to official ideology can be limited and suppressed for a time, but that time is finite.

---

[67] One frequent outcome of compromise is overelaboration. Freud showed how this occurred in the development of obsessive symptoms, and we can easily observe the same process at the organizational level. Unusual complexity in the rules of concentration and distribution, for example, is a handy index of both inter- and intradepartmental conflict in academic settings.

[68] See, for example, R. K. Merton (cited footnote 62), pp. 72–76.

Actually, these two ways of resolving strain are always taking place simultaneously.[69] Ideology can never precisely conform to reality, since to do so would imperil the solidarity of the collectivity. Neither can the devalued requirement of the system be altogether ignored, by definition. Consequently, we find social change represented less by a change in the contradictory functions themselves than by a change in the structural arrangements through which these contradictory functions are performed. This fact often converts idealists into cynics, since they are motivated by the vain hope that one of the contradictory requirements can be altogether dispensed with, and they are disappointed when they find some expression of it creeping back into the system in a new form, even though the new contradictory institutions may be vastly superior to the old pair in some respect.

### Contradiction Within the Individual

Similarly, in the study of individual personality we have learned to speak less of the presence or absence of traits such as aggressiveness, dependency, friendliness, or introversion, than of the way in which these traits express themselves. As awareness of unconscious motivation has gradually penetrated American psychology, it has become increasingly clear that to classify one individual as "aggressive" and another as "overtly affiliative but covertly hostile" essentially obliterates the variability and hence the usefulness of the trait concept "aggressiveness." As we learn the large area of identity between sadism and masochism, the frequency with which the goal of rebellion seems to be greater submission rather than true independence, the striking similarity of values between policeman and criminal, and between Communist and zealous anti-Communist—in short, between all pairs of apparent opposites—we realize that to a large extent the personality characteristics that we use to describe one another differentially are actually universal. What varies is (1) their mode of manifestation, (2) our belief systems regarding their presence or absence in ourselves, and (3) our consequent selection of a particular axis or axes along which to work out our ambivalence in interaction with others.

Ambivalence may be considered the keystone of individual motivation, just as contradictory functional requirements are central to social systems. We can never be totally committed to any action, or totally absorbed in a single feeling toward a person, an object, or a goal. There are always competing and contradictory feelings and wishes—hate mixed with our love,

---

[69] L. A. Coser, *The Functions of Social Conflict* (Glencoe, Ill.: Free Press, 1956).

love mixed with our hate.[70] As in the case of social systems, tension will arise insofar as our belief system ignores one half of our ambivalent response, yet some such ignoring seems necessary in order to make action possible, since action seems to require a certain minimum level of simplicity and constancy. At the level of communication this is obvious—statements like "I am well," "I am sick," "I love you," and "I hate you" are gross oversimplifications, but one does not give the passerby a catalogue of physical blemishes and minor malfunctionings, although no one is without them; nor does he recite to the doctor the numerous ways in which his body is still functioning brilliantly; nor does he qualify his declaration to his beloved with a description of the situations in which he is irritated, disdainful, enraged, frightened, or even indifferent toward her; nor, finally, does he point out to his enemy the fascination that the latter has for him, the frequency with which he thinks of and talks about him, and how excited and alive he becomes when he has an opportunity to fight with or over him.

But this holds true not only at the interpersonal level. It is by no means accidental that one who is too aware of the contrary forces operating within him is considered "indecisive," nor that many people considered "decisive" are also considered "capricious," because one side of their ambivalence is expressed one day and the other side the next. In order to act, we must exaggerate the differences between each feeling and its opposite. This is the basis of majority rule. The two-party system, precisely *because* it is a poorer reflection of the total complexity of popular sentiment than a multi-party system, seems to lend itself more easily to decisive action. In the individual, action is achieved in part through what the psychoanalysts call repression—that is, the discarding of the connections between one idea and another (in this case, the conceptualization of two antithetical feelings).

We can understand this process through a familiar analogy. After a national election in the United States, we say that the nation "went Democratic" or "went Republican." By this we may mean only that a dozen seats in Congress changed sides, or that a fraction of 1% of the population

[70] Many have pointed out that intense feelings of love and hate resemble one another in any case, and that this dichotomy is secondary to the more profound one of intensity versus indifference, or moving toward interaction versus moving away. See Sigmund Freud, "Instincts and Their Vicissitudes" (1915), in *Collected Papers* (London: Hogarth, 1953), Vol. IV, p. 76. Those who are bothered by this inveterate dualism need only be reminded that a relatively small number of independent bipolar dimensions permits a very large number of possible combinations, while on the other hand, any of these bipolar dimensions might be resolved into unity by assuming them ultimately to be curved. Love and hate would thus ultimately fuse, as would heat and cold, and even largeness and smallness—so that combinations of supergalaxies would form subatomic particles. In the present state of our knowledge of both physics and social psychology, either a linear or a curvilinear vision of these dimensions may equally well be entertained.

changed its vote from the previous election. We do not call attention to the fact that about 90% of the vote never changes, but remains more or less evenly divided. We treat the matter as in some sense finished, although the range of opinion on issues and candidates in the country is exactly as it was before. All that changes is that individuals who were previously in the role of candidates are now in the role of incumbents and, as such, will receive more support. In the case of the President of the United States the increase in support attributable solely to his election is usually from a little over 50% to about 70% of the population. The remaining 30% will presumably accept his authority, but will still regard him as a less desirable leader.

Notice that the 20% who change their opinion are responding to nothing in the personality of the individual, but only to a change in his *role*—a change from candidate to President. By virtue of his having assumed this new role their feelings toward him as a person change. Those individuals who do not change their opinion but accept the President's authority are making a distinction between personality and role, but those who change their opinion are not.

This change in opinion—this collapse of the ability to distinguish between personality and role—is analogous to what we call repression in the individual; that is, the inability to distinguish between deciding not to act on a feeling or desire or idea, and believing that the feeling, desire, or idea is not a part of oneself at all. Just as the newspapers will refer to a "Democratic congress," so all of us as individuals go about viewing and presenting ourselves as "extraverts," "intellectuals," "plain folks," "rebels," "kind," "frank," "easygoing," "orderly," or "dominant" and, to a lesser extent, accepting the similarly one-sided self-descriptions of others.

To some extent this is a convenient shorthand, but it necessitates one form of gross distortion. In terms of the distribution of opinion and sentiment in the nation, an election that went 52% to 48% for the Democrats would resemble one that went 52% to 48% for the Republicans more than it would resemble one that went 80% to 20% for the Democrats; yet the outcomes of the first pair would be considered antithetical, and the outcomes of the second pair identical. This is even more marked on the individual-interpersonal level, where we seldom appreciate the similarity of two individuals who share a common ambivalence but have "elected" different sides of it to a position of manifest prominence. Since the closer the balance is to 50% the more it threatens to reverse, individuals in such a situation will tend to show more tension around this sentiment than any other—they will be preoccupied and absorbed with it, and will seek out other people with the same preoccupation, regardless of which side they have "elected."

A few concrete examples will clarify this point. Let us take, as one ambivalent pair, the desire for autonomy versus the desire for dependence, both of which are present in all human beings. Let us assume that many people have a more or less comfortably lopsided distribution (for instance, 70% to 30%) of these desires, so that they can view themselves with some consistency, and act or make choices with relatively little difficulty. The "minority" need is expressed at specific times and in specific relationships without threatening the individual's overall or "majority" view of himself. Individuals with opposite "majorities" resemble each other in seeming "unconflicted," that is, able to behave contrary to their "majority" tendencies when the situation demands it.[71]

Now consider two individuals in whom these traits are distributed on a 52% to 48% basis. These individuals are obviously very similar, but one is a little higher on the dependent side, the other a little higher on the autonomous side. They are continually threatened with a reversal of this predominance, and hence with being unable to act or to maintain a constant self-image. Both types of individuals will be preoccupied with the problem of freedom. Those that have a dependent "majority" are chronically concerned with suppressing rebelliousness and deviance everywhere, and invest a great deal of energy in maintaining a consistent image of loyalty and devotion to authority. Those that have an autonomous "majority" are obsessed with combating authority wherever they find it, and invest their energies in upholding an image of rebelliousness. Both stances are naturally brittle because the "minorities" are so large. Since the "majority's" power must be constantly exercised to survive, both types of individual will often seek the other out in order to join in ideological dispute.[72] This has the additional function of permitting the dissident "minority" to express itself vicariously. The authoritarian will be attracted to situations in which there is deviance to be suppressed, while the rebel will seek situations in which he can be tyrannized over and nobly resist it. While the two may seem opposite, they are basically like-minded and share an identical problem. We should not be surprised, therefore—although we usually are—when they occasionally "convert," going to what seems like the opposite extreme. We can be sure that the new position will be just as brittle and exaggerated as the old.

[71] This entire discussion of dependency-autonomy is an elaboration of ideas drawn from Erich Fromm, *Escape from Freedom* (New York: Rinehart, 1941); F. Redl, "Group Emotion and Leadership," *Psychiatry*, 5, 573–596 (1942); W. C. Schutz, *FIRO: A Three-Dimensional Theory of Interpersonal Behavior* (New York: Holt, 1958); and W. G. Bennis and H. A. Shepard, "A Theory of Group Development," *Human Relations*, 9, 415–437 (1956).

[72] They will also seek out those on the *same* side (which is, after all, scarcely any different) to "join forces" with them. This creates the ideal conditions for what is usually called "covert culture"—the emergence of institutions reflecting sentiments or assumptions which cannot be acknowledged.

One can see a similar process operating in individuals from backgrounds in which sexual expression has been severely prohibited, and who are consequently in conflict over this issue. Some will become puritanical, seeking and seeing sexuality everywhere and trying to suppress it; others will become ideological hedonists, interested primarily in sexual behavior which is conspicuous. The puritans may become censors, which enables them to spend more time engrossed in pornography than the population at large. The ideological hedonists prefer public debate over sexual restrictions to circumvention of those restrictions, which enables them more easily to be restricted.

## Temporal and Spatial Compartmentalization

What keeps most people, most of the time, and on most dimensions of feeling, from either a brittle absolutism or from being paralyzed with indecision, is the convenient fact that contradictory tendencies in the individual can be expressed through temporal or spatial separation. Thus a college student may reject his parents' values but send his laundry home or write for money. Different relationships, different groups, and different occasions will be used to express contrary tendencies. Indeed, all cultures contain built-in institutions for such separation: relationships that require and others that forbid the same behavior (hostility, sexuality), spatial areas and special times of license, and other areas and times of taboo. The phrase "there is a time and place for everything" is not merely a tight-lipped New England reproof, but in its most literal sense is a profound cross-cultural generalization. There is no conceivable kind of human behavior that is not socially acceptable somewhere at some times under some conditions. Many societies have a special time of the year in which all of the usual rules do not apply and "anything goes." The "Feast of Fools" (of which the Christmas office party, New Year's Eve, Mardi Gras, and April Fool's Day are in one way or another lineal descendants), which was popular for more than a thousand years in Europe, was this kind of a festival, and involved such usually forbidden behavior as public ridicule of the clergy, transvestitism, and public copulation in the church.[73]

Less dramatic but more important are the short-term temporal rhythms—working in the day and playing in the evening, "sinning" and confessing, parties and hangover. Usually these temporal separations also involve spatial ones—we work or play, are active or passive, in different places and in different relationships. The nuclear family of husband, wife, and children

[73] G. R. Taylor (cited in footnote 34), pp. 271–274.

is, in our society, an exception to this rule; its relationships are "diffuse" and all feelings and desires tend to converge there, no matter how contradictory they may be. For this reason most tragic dramas are set within the home and center around family relationships—ambivalent conflict, the heart of drama, always seems a little less necessary in other settings. But even here some splitting of the antithetical tendencies is possible, particularly for males, who can more easily establish work-home dichotomies in their behavior. The manager who is dominant on the job but submissive to his wife, for example, is a familiar phenomenon, as is the browbeaten clerk who plays domestic tyrant. Recent studies of the adjustment problems of the elderly, however, have made us more aware of the shattering impact that compulsory retirement can have on these elaborate systems of compartmentalization, and on the families who collude in maintaining them.

### Role

Since all collectivities have contradictory functional requirements, and all individuals have contradictory needs and desires, it might seem to be a simple matter to mesh one with the other. Since both also have needs for unity, consistency, and homogeneity, however, the problem becomes highly complicated. Every group requires the performance of certain roles whose existence it cannot admit, and initiation into these roles must therefore be subtle. At the same time, there are roles that no individual can admit he is able to perform. Furthermore, there is likely to be a correlation between the function denied by the group and the behavioral tendencies denied by the individual, so that generalized "shortages" may emerge.

Before examining these relationships, some discussion of the concept of "role" is necessary. It is a difficult concept to use in a manner both rigorous and fruitful, but it is one which it is almost impossible to get along without, at least for descriptive purposes.

The need arises from two opposite directions (which accounts for part of the confusion). Starting from the standpoint of the individual, one must find some way of designating those consistencies in an individual's behavior which arise from his need to have a unified, simplified, and unambivalent definition of himself. Used in this way, the concept is often qualified as "assumed role," [74] "individual role," [75] or "interpersonal role." [76] This usage

[74] J. P. Spiegel, "The Social Roles of Doctor and Patient in Psychoanalysis and Psychotherapy," *Psychiatry,* **17**, 369–376 (1954).

[75] K. D. Benne and P. Sheats, "Functional Roles of Group Members," *Journal of Social Issues,* **4**, 41–49 (1948).

[76] T. Shibutani, *Society and Personality* (Englewood Cliffs, N.J.: Prentice-Hall, 1961), p. 326.

is exemplified by statements such as "He played an aggressive role in the group," "He always plays it pretty cool," "She's a real family matriarch," and "He always comes on like an elder statesman."

Sociologists more commonly use role—sometimes called "position," "status," or distinguished by the qualifier "social role"—to refer not to such a grouping of individual tendencies, but to a set of expectations associated with a position in a social system, expectations which normally determine behavior within specified limits regardless of the personality of the incumbent. It is in this sense that we refer to the role of President of the United States, the role of husband, wife, father, or mother, of bookkeeper, of doctor, of foreman, the sick role, the secretarial role, the leader role, the role of mediator. Sometimes the expectations are highly detailed, as in the case of many occupational specialties, sometimes broad and elastic, as in the case of familial roles.

In practice, the distinction between personal and social roles is somewhat difficult to maintain. Theoretically, for example, the *manner* in which an individual plays a social role should be distinguished from the role itself, from the normative expectations governing that position in the social system. When we talk of an individual's behavior in terms that connote evaluation, however, we immediately blur this boundary. When we say an individual made a "good president," we refer both to personality characteristics which affected the way he performed his role and the normative definition of the role itself. Since there are few variations in role behavior which do not arouse normative judgments, it is rarely possible to assign any given bit of stable behavior (and it is, of course, some stability or consistency in the behavior which allows us to apply the term role at all) to one category or the other. Further confusion arises when an individual seems in his behavior to anticipate his incumbency—when he "carves out a role for himself." To speak of such a role as a group of normative expectations is clearly a little absurd. The person who assumes leadership in an unstructured situation may be said to be responding to a group need for structure, but this is tautologous. He may in fact form a role where none existed, or create a position that overlaps with, competes with, and eventually undermines several others. One must therefore be cautious about embracing a model of social behavior which visualizes social systems as static arrangements of slots waiting for people to fall into them.

Why, then, do we use the concept of role at all in its social sense, when we cannot more easily distinguish it from its psychological usage? The concept is useful primarily as a mental lever to free us from the erroneous notion that the unit of a social system is a person. It serves to remind us that there is no group anywhere, nor has there ever been one, which includes the whole person—every aspect of his instinctual, emotional, and cognitive being. Some very primitive societies, with completely localized individuals, come much closer to such a condition than our own complex society, in which everyone belongs in a lifetime to an enormous number of different groups, each with a special claim on some aspect of his personality—but this difference is quantitative rather than qualitative. In most contemporary nonliterate societies nuclear families, unilineal clans, local village groups, age groups, and sex groups, create a sufficiently elaborate system of crosscutting relationships to tax the ingenuity of ethnographers. Even in the rare case where little social organization exists beyond the familial level, an irreducible minimum of multiple-group affiliation is produced by the incest taboo, which makes it necessary for a man to have two families, in one of which he has the role of child, while in the other he has the role of parent. No society (that is, group of more than one nuclear family) can, in fact, exist without an incest taboo or some equivalent; and no society involving large numbers of people can exist without some principle of relatedness other than a territorial one. Otherwise, an individual would interact only with his immediate neighbors, and large-scale cooperation would be impossible. Most kinship systems contain some clear nonterritorial principle such as local exogamy, or marriage outside a specific group, and the more complex a society becomes, the more crosscutting principles of affiliation are found.

## Role and Personality

Any group, then, is made up, on the one hand, of group functions to be performed and, on the other, of *pieces of people* performing them. It is not only that "one man in his time plays many parts," and in different groups, but also that he commits only the relevant and valued segments of his personality to a given group, while much of the remainder he excludes altogether. Every group, to an extent, violates the integrity of the individuals who participate in it, while at the same time restoring their integrity in other respects from the limitations imposed by other groups.

Some groups and roles permit a greater range of behavior than others—a man will have a wider range of behavior in his role of husband than in his role as bank president, for example—and we generally view these roles or groups as permitting us to relax and "be ourselves." Such an attitude cannot be taken at face value, however, since it may mean only that some aspect of the personality which is suppressed in most other roles is finally permitted to emerge. The sense of release that this entails blinds us to the manifold suppression of other tendencies which accompanies this release.

Nor should we imagine that we are "ourselves" when alone, since a vast range of our behavior is thereby made impossible. We are the sum total of our feelings, ideas, and behavior—regardless of what sort of truncated self-label we typically parade before our now indulgently gullible, now tactfully skeptical audiences—and neither any single group nor the lack of any group can embrace this totality.

Some roles—usually the more diffuse ones—will nevertheless show some tendency to be generalized into an "identity" or self-concept. When this takes place the contradictions between roles cannot easily be handled through temporal or spatial alternation. Thus a student who goes to college away from home will develop patterns of behavior that contrast sharply with his role in the family. To the extent that his student role becomes integrated with more generalized attitudes about becoming an adult, he will resist being reinducted into his familial role of child when he visits his family. To the extent that his resistance is effective, it will be experienced by other family members as rejection, while too conspicuous a resumption of his familial role will be experienced by the student as a humiliating regression. For students who do not generalize the new role, however, movement from one situation to another will be made easily so long as there is no overlap (for example, bringing a friend home from school and thus being subject to conflicting role expectations). A similar problem arises for the student who commutes from a working-class neighborhood to a middle-class college. If going to college is part of a generalized commitment to social mobility, he will resist reinduction into his old friendship groups, and will be subject to the same ridicule and resentment met in the family. ("Now he thinks he's too good for us" will be substituted for— or added to—"Now he thinks he's a man already.") Even if it is not such a commitment and he attempts to maintain his old ties, the proximity of the conflicting role contexts will cause some strain (for example, the problem of changing from middle-class to working-class garb before encountering neighborhood friends).

The degree of role generalization may be seen by noting, when contradictory roles overlap, the direction of our embarrassment: Are we more upset by being seen with $X$ (or treated by $X$ in a certain way) in front of $Y$, or by being seen with $Y$ in front of $X$? It is the least generalized role of which we will be most ashamed.

The more complex a society—the more groups, the more roles—the more limited a segment of the individual personality it is possible to include within a single role definition. Just as a society with so many crosscutting groups must with difficulty strive for a unitary definition of itself, and hence must be tempted to seek ever more oversimplified and unambivalent self-descriptions, so also must the individual. It is in fact with respect to the latter problem that Erikson developed his concept of identity.[77]

We must make a distinction, however, between having an integrated self-concept (accurate or inaccurate), having a sense of uniqueness (accurate or inaccurate), and having one's whole personality fulfilled in his role behavior.[78] These are not only distinct, but tend to contravene each other, at least as they are usually defined. A sense of identity is maximized in a small, simple society in which every group involves a large segment of the individual's personality, with a generous overlapping of segments between groups. It is minimized in a society like our own, in which each group involves a tiny segment, and overlap is hence inconsiderable. By the same token, however, *uniqueness* (or "individuality") is increased by social complexity. Durkheim observes this tendency with regard to the development of the division of labor in society, noting that the logical end of such specialization (although perhaps never reached) would be a situation in which everyone played an entirely unique role. Furthermore, since everyone would be different, there would be "much more place open for the free play of our initiative." [79]

Durkheim's rather primitive psychology blinded him, however, to one consequence of such specialization. Human beings vary in their instinctual, emotional makeup far less than in their role behavior and self-concepts. Everyone experiences hunger, thirst, fatigue, sexual excitement, anger, dependency, affection, jealousy, and pride in some form or other. Any behavioral situation which moves an individual toward uniqueness will thus tend to do violence to his emotional economy, and will be experienced not as freedom but as constraint. It is this paradox which generates so much confusion in modern discussions of "conformity," "identity," and "individual integrity." Strictly speaking, given the overpowering role of our culture in forming personality, and the basic instinctual uniformity of mankind, it is individuation rather than conformity that threatens the integrity of the human individual.

Uniqueness can be conceived in two ways, however. An individual can be different from others (1) because he does or does not do something in contradistinction to everyone else, or (2) because the *combination* of performances is different. Durkheim seems to have the first conception in mind, although more as a chimerical pole toward which a complex, dif-

[77] E. H. Erikson, *Childhood and Society* (New York: Norton, 1950), pp. 227 ff.; and "The Problem of Ego Identity," in M. R. Stein, A. J. Vidich, and D. M. White, eds., *Identity and Anxiety* (Glencoe, Ill.: Free Press, 1960).

[78] C. W. Smith, "Social Units and Collectivities," Unpublished doctoral dissertation, Brandeis University, 1966.

[79] Émile Durkheim, *The Division of Labor in Society* (cited in footnote 40), p. 131.

ferentiated society moves than as a conceivable reality. Each individual's combination of experiences and roles is automatically unique, however, and this kind of uniqueness need not violate his emotional integrity.

But even a strong sense of *this* kind of uniqueness, which is certainly made more manifest by social complexity such as we experience today, contributes negatively, if at all, to the development of a sense of identity, since it enhances awareness of the infinite fragments which must somehow be welded or twisted into a unitary self-concept.[80]

### Age and Sex Roles

Role and personality thus relate to one another in an extremely complex manner. An individual who performed a role perfectly would be regarded as a little inhuman—lacking the richness of normal human endowment—while a role that did not do violence to personality structure would be an emotional sinecure indeed. It is not merely that a servant's need to be dominant is frustrated, or a ruler's need to be submissive, private, or retiring, thwarted.[81] Even the most diffuse and vaguely defined roles would be crippling if they monopolized an individual's behavior. Fortunately, in most instances, compensatory mechanisms are present to moderate this effect—in the form of crosscutting roles, or latent contradictions built into the role itself, or some other process. A good example can be found in the traditional American sex roles (now undergoing substantial modification). Margaret

---

[80] The complexity of modern society not only makes it easier than ever before to be unique, but also maximizes the amount of choice which can be exercised in everyday life. It is difficult to decide which arouses more human aversion, even in a society like ours which places a positive value on both. The development of culture may even be viewed as a device for minimizing the exercise of free choice in daily life. To be utterly unroutinized, so that every act and motion of every day involved a new decision, would be a burdensome freedom, indeed. For discussions of the avoidance of freedom and choice, see Erich Fromm (cited in footnote 25) and J. Huizinga, *Homo Ludens* (Boston: Beacon Press, 1950).

[81] It might be argued that these needs do not exist, since individuals are socialized from birth to accept these limitations. But it does not really matter whether one assumes that an individual is born with a potentially full interpersonal repertoire and then learns to inhibit portions of it, or whether he starts with a *tabula rasa*, for even in the latter case the variety of roles that a person must learn quickly produces a full range of needs. The ruler learns submissiveness in relation to his parents, the servant dominance in his childhood peer group. It is, paradoxically, the very need of a society to inculcate proper attitudes of superiority and inferiority which makes it impossible for them to be developed to their extreme, since stratification into endogamous classes—the principal device for ensuring such attitudes—greatly increases the individual's exposure to peers, and hence to interpersonal responses other than those appropriate to interaction with class inferiors and superiors. Conceivably, a person who from birth experienced nothing but domination or submission from others might lack this response himself, but as yet no documented case of such a person has been found.

Mead long ago pointed out that few of the characteristics that we feel are inherently masculine or feminine are so regarded in all cultures, while most are even assigned to the opposite sex in some society or other.[82] Hall similarly notes [83] that in our culture men traditionally have been expected to be unemotional, undemonstrative, and practical, with women being regarded as inherently sensitive, intuitive, susceptible, excitable, and affectionate, but that the exact opposite distribution of "traits" is found in Iran. Leaving aside that large part of the world which takes it for granted that a woman is "by nature" practical and earth-bound, what does a woman do with her common sense in a culture like ours, which has often regarded woman as "by nature" impractical and delicate? What does a man do with his aspirations for elegance in a culture in which it is obligatory for a "real man" to be clumsy? [84] The answer is simply that the manifest definition of the desired personality of the role incumbent and the behavior actually required by that incumbency do not necessarily coincide. A man of the pre–World War II generation could be as graceful, surefooted, and elegant as he liked on a football field and, indeed, could strut about like a seventeenth-century fop if he wished, so long as he fell over his feet and looked sheepish in the living room. Even in Victorian England women were assigned most of the practical care of the household, despite their alleged vaporousness; and they retained their monopoly over the management of illness and death, despite their alleged squeamishness. The constrictions imposed on personality by sex-role definitions nevertheless create problems of one kind or another in every culture and, as Mead points out, are extremely wasteful of individual potential.[85]

Even more dramatic are the constraints imposed by age roles, which might at first glance seem to be even broader and less well defined. But this is only because we assume, as in the case of sex roles, that the behavior enjoined by the role encumbency is somehow natural or biological. Everyone is, of course, familiar with the injunction, "Act your age," but few are conscious of the extensive limitations that it places on behavior in all age groups. This is most striking in the case of the elderly, who must relinquish patterns of behavior that have been ingrained for decades, and which may have formed the core of their self-concepts. A man of eighty may still think

---

[82] Margaret Mead, *Sex and Temperament in Three Primitive Societies* (New York: Mentor, 1950); and *Male and Female* (New York: Mentor, 1955).

[83] E. T. Hall (cited in footnote 17), p. 67.

[84] This has created the anomalous situation in America that changes in men's clothing styles have almost always been initiated either by homosexuals or by members of lower-class minority groups who have a tradition of masculine display.

[85] Margaret Mead, *Sex and Temperament in Three Primitive Societies* (cited in footnote 82), p. 211.

of himself privately as he did when he was twenty, but if he were to behave along these familiar lines he would probably be hospitalized. Athletes and movie stars seem to have particular difficulty with this problem.

What is amazing is that these drastic changes do not cause more difficulty than they do. Most people effect the transition so well that children often cannot grasp the fact that old people were once young. The secret is, of course, in the gradualness of the change. As people grow older they drop certain modes of behavior bit by bit—in part modeling themselves on parents and other older people they knew when younger, in part being "inducted" into older age roles by those around them, who caution them to "slow down," take "better care" of themselves "at your age," and gently ridicule the persistence of too-youthful behavior and interests. One must learn to be decrepit, just as one must learn to talk, even if the physical capacity is already present.

Such drastic changes in behavior, however, are characteristic of all role induction. People often become disillusioned at how little effect a change in Presidents has on, for instance, American foreign policy, and how much more the remarks of different incumbents sometimes resemble each other than they resemble their own statements and beliefs out of office. The fun-loving Prince Hal becomes the coldly ambitious Henry V; the married man no longer seems congenial to his bachelor friends. We even find such changes in small and informal collectivities—when a member has sharply specialized in some bit of behavior useful to the group and subsequently departs, we are often surprised to see how quickly someone else ( or perhaps several) slips into the gap, and becomes the joker, the idea man, or the re-strainer.

## Marital and Family Roles

Vogel and Bell describe a particularly instructive form of personality change through role induction in the context of the family. They note that parents who have severe tensions in their own relationship which are not expressed directly often induct one of their offspring into the role of "problem child"—obliquely rewarding him for the very behavior of which they complain. By maintaining emotional distance from each other, avoiding confrontation in areas of conflict, and scapegoating the child, the parents are able to preserve a fragile equilibrium. Sometimes each parent will pressure the child to behave in opposite ways, thus permitting "one spouse to express annoyance to the other indirectly without endangering the marital relationship." When a child's problem shows signs of responding to therapeutic treatment, the latent marital conflict often erupts violently, and threatens to lead to the breakup of the marriage or to personality disturbances in one of the spouses.[86]

As we would expect, the initial attraction of the parents in cases of this kind is based partly on "the fact that they shared many of the same conflicts and understood each other quite well. Not long after marriage, however, they seemed to have become polarized in their conflicts, so that one parent represented one side of the conflict and the other represented the other side." [87] Thus the induction of the child is really derived from the mutual polar induction of the parents.

This is not to say, of course, that the personality of the child plays no part in the induction process. Vogel and Bell observe that although a child (rather than an adult) is selected for the "scapegoat" role precisely because his personality structure is more malleable, and because the child performs no essential task functions in the family, not every child is equally likely to fall into the role. Eldest children are preferred, presumably out of urgency, but the relationship of the child's sex and birth order to the parents' own childhood experiences is often compelling, as is the presence in the child of any physical defects. (Generally, only one child is chosen as a scapegoat, while the others are free from pathology.) But Vogel and Bell observe that the number of available candidates for scapegoating is severely limited, and on occasion no child is an appropriate selection. In such a case "there must be considerable cognitive distortion in order to permit the most appropriate one available to be used. . . ." The authors cite as an example a son who responded to parental preoccupation with his quite adequate school performance by working harder and doing better, in response to which "the mother stoutly maintained that her son didn't deserve those grades, that he must have cheated, and she continued to criticize him for his school performance." [88] This is a good example of a failure in role induction, followed by renewed pressure.

Vogel and Bell's discussion of the marital relationship reminds us that marriage is a particularly fruitful laboratory for the study of role induction. The most familiar type of role induction is what we usually refer to as "role specialization" or "role differentiation." We have noted Durkheim's remark that the division of labor provided the individual with more "individuality," but we also observed that this individuality, based as it was on limiting one's range of behavior, thereby violated the rich complexity

---

[86] E. F. Vogel and N. W. Bell, "The Emotionally Disturbed Child as the Family Scapegoat," in N. W. Bell and E. F. Vogel, eds., *A Modern Introduction to the Family* (Glencoe, Ill.: Free Press, 1960), pp. 382–397.
[87] *Ibid.*, p. 389.
[88] *Ibid.*, pp. 386–390.

of the human organism. All of us are familiar with informal role specialization in marriage relationships ("So-and-so is a different person when his wife [her husband] isn't around")—one spouse tells the jokes, the other fills in contexts, one is expressive, one judicious, one initiates new social contacts, the other provides excuses for withdrawal by being prone to illness, chronically busy, and so on. In some cases this distribution of traits and behavioral responses is regulated by sex roles or occupational roles: thus women usually manage social arrangements and the expression of emotion in our society, while husbands are expected to be the authorities in business matters. In some cases, however, there are few external guidelines and the matter tends to be settled in terms of whose proclivities are most intense. If both husband and wife are eager and able storytellers, the most eager is likely to develop the skill to new heights, while the other permits it to atrophy. A new husband may abandon his bachelorhood culinary skills, or he may accentuate them and become the "fancy cook," with his wife falling into the role of "plain cook." Gradually the traits and abilities are sorted out and assigned (usually, but not always, quite unconsciously), atrophying or hypertrophying as the case may be, and eventually achieving an almost stereotypic rigidity ("He's the smart one of the family," "She's always right about people"). Widowhood and divorce often produce what appear to be startling personality changes as the structural conditions for suppressing or overdeveloping some characteristic are suddenly removed. A retiring, dependent wife suddenly becomes competent and forceful upon losing a dominant husband, while the dour spouse of a vivacious girl reveals a humorous facet when separated from her.[89] Unsuspected talents suddenly emerge or are revived, and many other relationships must be readjusted. Those who experience this phenomenon often describe it as a kind of self-rediscovery, albeit a very painful and disruptive one.

### Mechanical and Organic Solidarity

But what leads people so to distort themselves in the first place? Why can they not retain all of their capacities and traits?

The principal reason is economic: specialization, up to a point, reduces

---

[89] This phenomenon is usually called "object loss identification" by psychoanalysts, and it cannot be denied that people tend to take on the characteristics of those they have recently lost. Indeed, Freud, who is often accused of underestimating the importance of interpersonal factors argued that individual personality is a "precipitate" of past relationships. Some of these changes, however, clearly reflect the recovery of an aspect of the individual's *own* personality long sacrificed to the solidarity of the pair. See Sigmund Freud, *The Ego and the Id* (London: Hogarth, 1927), pp. 36–37.

the amount of energy that must be committed to maintaining the solidarity of a relationship. The more interaction is ritualized through specialization, the more predictable, obviously, it becomes; and the more that skills are divided, the less competition will occur. If each spouse seeks rewards and approval in different areas, interaction will flow smoothly and relatively effortlessly. Durkheim, in making this point for societies as a whole, uses a biological analogy, pointing out that where resources are limited, and competition is thus likely, a great diversity of species will develop, each using different resources, or in a different way.[90]

Yet it is easy to overdraw this picture. Durkheim's analogy breaks down when we realize that individual human beings do not permanently shed their overlapping characteristics the way species do in biological evolution, but suppress them at some measurable cost. If the cost is too great, the energy saved in the interaction of the couple may be expended by each individual in maintaining internal balance. Furthermore, we must not assume that specialization eliminates conflict, since one of the natural concomitants of a division of labor is ritualized conflict: the expressive wife complains that the controlled husband is too cold, while he complains that she is too temperamental. This kind of running quarrel derives in part from the strain each experiences in suppressing that portion of his personality which is assigned to the other. Finally, we must remember that understanding is facilitated by similarity of experience and feeling—those who desire the same thing will compete, but will also share a sympathy and acceptance of one another. This will be lacking where polarizations of the type described exist.

It should be emphasized here that Durkheim, while placing so much emphasis on the division of labor, also pointed out the existence of another principle of solidarity—one based on similarity rather than complementarity. He called this, rather confusingly, "mechanical solidarity" as opposed to the "organic solidarity" of the division of labor, and regarded it as characterizing primitive societies. Whereas organic solidarity "suggests two beings mutually dependent because they are each incomplete," mechanical solidarity "consists in an agglutination. The two representations become solidary because, being indistinct . . . they confound each other, and become no more than one. . . ."[91] Durkheim saw mechanical solidarity as an inherently "low-synergy" mechanism, since it was strong only to the extent that "individuality" was obliterated, while organic solidarity, on the other hand, *depended* upon individual differences: "the individuality of all grows

[90] Émile Durkheim, *The Division of Labor in Society* (cited in footnote 40), pp. 266–267.
[91] *Ibid.*, pp. 61–62.

at the same time as that of its parts." [92] As we have seen, however, Durkheim's optimistic notion that organic solidarity occasions less violation of the individual personality is based on the assumption that human beings are more conspicuously different than they are similar, an assumption which is at best meaningless. Insofar as society inhibits *or* exaggerates differences between people the individual personality is violated, and feelings of alienation will be engendered.

Interestingly enough, Durkheim's distinction is precisely reproduced in psychoanalytic theory, so that we are able to form a concept of these principles of organization in their psychological inception. Freud and Flugel distinguished between "narcissistic" love, based on resemblances between oneself and another, and "anaclitic" love, based on dependency: "The lover is here attracted towards his object because he finds in it something that is essential to the fulfillment of his own bodily or mental needs." [93] Narcissistic love is thus an extension of the self-love of the infant, while anaclitic love is an extension of the infant's helpless dependence on its mother. One emphasizes similarities, the other differences. A group based on "narcissistic" bonds would then be characterized by mechanical solidarity, while one based on "anaclitic" ties (note the emphasis on *incompleteness* in anaclitic love) would be characterized by organic solidarity. Since all relationships are an admixture of these two modes of loving, all collectivities presumably involve both kinds of solidarity. It is therefore increasingly clear that Durkheim's equation—qualified though it was—of mechanical solidarity with primitive societies and organic solidarity with modern societies was still considerably overdrawn. [94]

---

[92] *Ibid.*, p. 131.

[93] J. C. Flugel, *The Psychoanalytic Study of the Family* (London: Hogarth, 1921), pp. 103–104. See also Sigmund Freud, "On Narcissism: An Introduction," in *Collected Papers,* Vol. IV (London: Hogarth, 1953), pp. 30–59.

[94] Although the field of role theory is generally beset with terminological confusion, one particularly confusing set of usages is germane to this distinction. The terms "reciprocity" and "complementarity" are often used synonymously, although reciprocity should imply a response in kind and complementarity a response which differs from the behavior which elicited it. The problem arises in part from the unfortunate practice of discussing role behavior in terms of rigid two-part sequences, in which a given act can produce one and only one "appropriate" response to complete the sequence. Whether the response is in kind or different, it is seen as both "reciprocal" (since both participants are playing the same game) and "complementary" (since it completes the sequence). The definition of the "appropriate" sequence is of course totally arbitrary. If one man punches another in the nose, a sociologist might define the "appropriate" response as punching him back, falling to the ground, running away, or expressing submission, depending upon the context. All are "complementary" in the sense of completing an interaction unit, but it would seem preposterous to say that when a fighter collapses to the canvas he is "denying reciprocity."

## Techniques of Role Induction: Socialization

Thus far we have seen rather dramatically how mutable is the human [95] personality, within certain limits, and how inextricably woven into the fabric of social interaction. Let us now consider the mechanisms through which role induction actually takes place.

Two separate problems can be distinguished: the way in which an individual *learns* to play a given role, and what *motivates* him to mold himself in this manner. To understand both of these processes we must consider a special case of role induction—the socialization of the child, which, as we shall see, forms the model for all role induction, particularly those types which seek drastic personality alteration in a short period of time.

Social learning takes place almost entirely through imitation. This imitation has been variously conceived and explained, but the core is always the same—we learn to act like human beings (no matter how "inhuman" this may at times seem), or like members of a given society or subgroup, or like males or females, or like teenagers or like adults, by observing how other members of these social categories behave and mimicking them. We even learn how to be individualists or nonconformists by imitating other individualists and nonconformists, which accounts for the paradoxical fact that individuals of unconventional persuasions cluster together to form their own conventions.

In our society, our value on individualism leads us to regard this natural process with some uneasiness. Children are called "copycats" or are ridiculed with phrases like "monkey see, monkey do" when they imitate others too closely, but originality in behavior can, after all, only consist in new and complex combinations of imitations, and cannot transcend mere negativism (which is hardly original, either) until a large repertory of behavioral skills is acquired. The correlation between intelligence and imitative capacity is, in any case, extremely high.

The process of imitation is complex. The child must form an accurate mental representation of the act and then correctly relate each of the parts of its own body to that representation in order to reproduce it. For the social psychologist G. H. Mead, this *internal* process was the keystone of social learning. Mead saw that the ability to reproduce the behavior in action was a mere corollary of the ability to "take the role of the other"

---

[95] Studies made by Norbett Mintz a few years ago at Harvard University suggest that this mutability is not restricted to humans. By manipulating early socialization conditions, Mintz raised cats who were "doglike" (dependent, obedient, affectionate, and so on) and vice versa.

in a symbolic sense. This ability he viewed as based on the responses of others toward the individual—responses which communicate to him a viewpoint other than his own. In time, the individual generalizes this "role-taking ability" and becomes aware of the position of his own role in the larger system of roles. Mead uses the example of the baseball game, in which a player perceives the action not only in terms of his own role, but in terms of all of the other players, and of the organized game as a whole.[96]

### Identification

Why does an individual wish to imitate others, or to adopt the viewpoint of another? Or, since these two tendencies have usually been grouped under the term "identification," we may ask: What motivates an individual to identify with another?

Although the theory and research surrounding this concept reflect its ambiguity as well as its importance, it seems safe to say that dependency and the need for the love of other human beings play a central role in generating identification. When we compare species we find that the more "advanced" or intelligent they are, the longer is the period of childhood dependence on the mother; this is usually explained as being necessary for the replacement of "instinctive" behavior by learned behavior in the higher animals. By and large, an "independent" young animal is a stupid one.

Prolonged physical dependency automatically provides for more contact and interaction between child and adult, but it also establishes an emotional condition of peculiar intensity. The human infant is helpless—other human beings are a matter of life and death to it for years, and the deprivation of human contact eventually produces emotional and intellectual starvation even in adults.[97] The moment the child becomes aware

[96] G. H. Mead, *Mind, Self and Society* (Chicago: University of Chicago Press, 1934).
[97] Part of this need is for stimulation pure and simple. Among many mammals, offspring not washed by the mother are lethargic and die, and studies of laboratory animals show that animals which are not in some way stimulated in early infancy—whether by handling or by electric shocks—do not develop adequately, show less exploratory behavior, more anxiety, exaggerated and maladaptive stress responses, lower resistance to infection, and slower physical development. S. Levine, "Stimulation in Infancy," *Scientific American*, May, 1960. Landauer and Whiting have shown that among humans, also, early stimulation is related to growth. T. K. Landauer and J. W. M. Whiting, "Infantile Stimulation and Adult Stature of Human Males," *American Anthropologist*, 66, 1007–1028 (1964). In recent years, furthermore, the "sensory deprivation" experiments have demonstrated impressively that adult humans are incapable of maintaining an internal equilibrium in the absence of any sensory input and after only a few hours begin to

of its separateness from the mother, a sense of the danger of abandonment arises and becomes a dominant issue in the emotional economy
of the child. Along with this awareness goes another: the feeling that this
danger is maximized when the child behaves in ways of which the mothering
one disapproves, and is minimized when the child's actions are approved.

At this point one might say merely that this constellation is generalized
into a pervasive need for love and approval from others. Such a formulation would work rather well for many purposes, especially in dealing with
many primitive societies in which social control is based on shame rather
than guilt. Such societies are usually characterized by "diffusion of
nurturance"—that is, the presence of many relatives and neighbors who
perform parental functions for the child, and the threat of exclusion or
ridicule from the immediate community is an overwhelming sanction
(although by no means overwhelming as a preventive).

For other purposes it is necessary to call into play a more complex model,
a function that at present is best performed, although somewhat uncertainly, by psychoanalytic theory. Crudely stated, Freud's theory argues
that to avoid the threatened loss of the parent or of the parent's love,
the child sets up a replica of the parent within itself to which all normative
questions are then referred. Thus a two-year-old child who touches a
forbidden object will say "No, no" to himself, or even slap his own hand.
We then say that he has begun to *internalize* parental norms, and when
this internalization has proceeded a little further the psychoanalytic theorist
begins to talk about "superego development."

Several complexities arise here, however. First, it seems at times as if
the internalization of the parent is "all of a piece"—that the child sets
up this "normative" parent within himself in completely undigested form,
without integrating it with the rest of the child's own personality, that is,
with those characteristics which are constitutional, have developed out
of other relationships, or have arisen in *complementary* interaction with
the parent. When this occurs, we are less apt to talk about "identification,"
which implies some blending or fusing of personalities or at least traits.
We are more likely to speak instead of an "archaic superego," with the
implication that the internalized image gradually becomes digested
(although perhaps never entirely so) in the normal person as he grows
older, so that some parts are retained and others discarded.

A second complexity derives from the fact that the "fear-of-loss" model
of identification, even in all of its variant forms, does not exhaust the

hallucinate. P. Solomon et al., eds., *Sensory Deprivation* (Cambridge, Mass.: Harvard
University Press, 1961). The human organism is a dynamic one, and requires a constant intake of social and intellectual "fuel" in order not to atrophy.

interpretations of this process.[98] Psychoanalytic theory also provides an alternative model—poorly integrated with the first—which has been most clearly isolated in Whiting's "status envy hypothesis." This model sees identification as deriving from the power and prestige of the parent (or other object): ". . . identification consists of the covert practice of the role of an envied status." [99] The child envies the position of the parent and attempts to gain this advantageous position by copying the behavior that seems to go with it. While it is not possible here to explore the ramifications and interrelationships of these two models, it seems clear that love and salience are both of crucial importance in identification.[100] The child must feel sufficiently loved so that the threat of losing this love is powerful enough to evoke identification, and must feel that the object of identification is prominent enough to warrant the desire to acquire his status. Studies of identification have shown (1) that children tend to identify most with the parent who is seen as most powerful or effective in the family, and (2) that children are most likely to identify with a parent who is affectionate.[101]

Of particular relevance to our present discussion are the studies showing the effects on internalization of different methods of discipline. These studies emphasize the technical superiority of what are usually referred to as "love-oriented" techniques (reasoning, praise, withdrawal of love) over the more traditional "fear-oriented" methods like physical punishment.[102] The development of internalized controls on behavior seems to depend strongly upon having nurturance and discipline come from the same source. This is unnecessary in small, stable societies in which an individual spends his entire life in the same social context, since external controls are always

---

[98] R. F. Winch, *Identification and Its Familial Determinants* (New York: Bobbs-Merrill, 1962).

[99] R. V. Burton and J. W. M. Whiting, "The Absent Father and Cross-Sex Identity," *Merrill-Palmer Quarterly*, **7**, 85 (1961).

[100] J. Kagan, "Acquisition and Significance of Sex Typing and Sex Role Identity," in M. L. Hoffman and Lois W. Hoffman, eds., *Review of Child Development Research* (New York: Russell Sage Foundation, 1964), Vol. I, p. 147.

[101] Susan W. Gray and R. Klaus, "The Assessment of Parental Identification," *Genetic Psychology Monographs*, **54**, 87–114 (1956); J. Kagan (cited in footnote 100), pp. 148–150; P. H. Mussen, "Some Antecedents and Consequences of Masculine Sex Typing in Adolescent Boys," *Psychological Monographs*, **75**, 1–24 (1961); P. H. Mussen and L. Distler, "Masculinity, Identification, and Father-Son Relationships," *Journal of Abnormal and Social Psychology*, **59** (1959); D. E. Payne and P. H. Mussen, "Parent-child Relations and Father Identification among Adolescent Boys," *Journal of Abnormal and Social Psychology*, **52** (1956); R. F. Winch (cited in footnote 98).

[102] W. C. Becker, "Consequences of Different Kinds of Parental Discipline," in M. L. Hoffman and Lois W. Hoffman, *Review of Child Development Research* (cited in footnote 100), pp. 176–189; L. Kohlberg, "Development of Moral Character and Moral Ideology," *ibid.*, pp. 409–414.

present.[103] But it becomes important in large, complex, changing societies like our own, in which people move from one setting to another, and external controls are uncertain and shifting.

The development of internalized controls and restraints is usually associated closely with the handling of aggression. Individuals who have internalized controls, and hence a strong capacity to experience guilt, are said to respond to anger-arousing situations by turning their anger against themselves rather than directing it outward. Research studies have shown this variable to be related, on the one hand, to physiological functions and, on the other, to the pattern of parental training. The tendency to discharge anger toward others in response to experimental stress is associated with a norepinephrine type of cardiovascular activity, while self-blame in the same situation is tied to an epinephrine type of cardiovascular activity. Subjects characterized by the first type of response reported their fathers to be the principal disciplinarians in the family, while the second group assigned this role to their mothers.[104] Similar results were obtained in an attitudinal experiment.[105] The reason for these results seems to be that fathers are less likely than mothers to use love-oriented techniques of discipline (particularly when they are the principal disciplinarians) and are more likely to be "specialists" in discipline, leaving the provision of affection and nurturance to the mother; mothers, on the other hand, are far more likely to present discipline in the context of an affectionate relation.[106]

---

[103] An example of the operation of external controls where internalization is not expected to be strong can be found in the many societies in which a very high value is placed on male aggressiveness, physical courage, and "honor." A man is expected to respond to any insult with blows, and it is the responsibility of bystanders to prevent those blows from falling. In group situations (which is, of course, where such situations always arise) this system of control is usually effective in preventing injury, but occasionally a man is forced to kill or be killed simply because bystanders are too slow to provide a much-desired restraint. Another example of a completely external system of controls is chaperonage. In most cultures with elaborate chaperon systems, it is assumed that a man and woman left together will copulate, or that if a woman smiles at a man in the marketplace she is inviting him to her bed. There is never any question of restraining one's own impulses. Neither, consequently, is there much frigidity. On the other hand, it is a somewhat cumbersome system for a modern industrial society where women work in offices. See E. T. Hall (cited in footnote 17), pp. 114–115. It is in part due to the need for flexible internal controls in a mobile society that Americans are such virtuosi in sexual self-control, with their complex gradations of "so far, no farther."

[104] S. H. King and A. F. Henry, "Aggression and Cardiovascular Reactions Related to Parental Control over Behavior," *Journal of Abnormal and Social Psychology*, **50**, 206–210 (1955).

[105] A. F. Henry, "Family Role Structure and Self-Blame," *Social Forces*, **25**, 34–38 (1956).

[106] Lois W. Hoffman, "The Father's Role in the Family and the Child's Peer-Group Adjustment," *Merrill-Palmer Quarterly*, **7**, 102 (1961); U. Bronfenbrenner, "The Changing American Child—A Speculative Analysis," *Merrill-Palmer Quarterly*, **7**, 73–84

The fusion of affection and discipline, then, has profound effects, both physiological and psychological. Most important for our immediate interest is that it facilitates, deepens, and intensifies the process of identification in general, and of the internalization of social norms in particular. Differences between groups, societies, and cultures are maintained by differences in the socialization process, and there are few spheres of human activity which have failed to show some correlation with child-rearing patterns. But some of these differences are not only qualitative but also quantitative, that is, identification with parents and consequent internalization of social norms may be greater or less in some groups.

This seems to be the case with social-class differences in our own society, for example. The fact that middle-class individuals have an easier time than working-class persons in adjusting to school, achieving success in the occupational sphere, and so on, is due not only to the enormous material advantages they enjoy, but also to the head start afforded them by the kind of socialization they are likely to have received, and the personality traits resulting from it. Studies have shown that (1) middle-class parents are more permissive than working-class parents, and use "love-oriented" techniques; (2) middle-class parents are more affectionate than working-class parents; (3) middle-class parents are less differentiated than working-class parents, with the father and mother sharing the giving of *both* nurturance and discipline.[107] The middle-class tendencies are all such as would be expected to increase parental identification and the internalization of social norms. As Bronfenbrenner observes, the middle-class techniques are not merely different but more "compelling." [108] They

(1961). This is one of several respects in which the father's role generates duality. Sex role differentiation has also been shown to be something primarily brought about by the father: if he plays a weak or unimportant role in the family, boys and girls will both experience difficulty in assuming the roles culturally designated as appropriate to their own sex. The mother-child relationship, on the other hand, seems to blur all distinctions and antedate all dualities. See U. Bronfenbrenner, *op. cit.*, p. 79; Lois W. Hoffman, *op. cit.*, p. 98.

[107] W. C. Becker (cited in footnote 102), pp. 170–171; U. Bronfenbrenner (cited in footnote 106); Bettye M. Caldwell, "The Effects of Infant Care," in M. L. and Lois W. Hoffman, *Review of Child Development Research*, pp. 67–75; Lois W. Hoffman (cited in footnote 106); M. L. Kohn and Eleanor E. Carroll, "Social Class and the Allocation of Parental Responsibilities," *Sociometry*, 23, 372–392 (1960). These differences will probably diminish in the future, since "the gap between social classes in their goals and methods of childrearing appears to be narrowing, with working-class parents beginning to adopt both the values and techniques of the middle class." U. Bronfenbrenner, *op. cit.*, p. 73. If so, much of the change must be attributed to the mass media, particularly television, which has exposed the entire country to urban middle-class values, assumptions, and techniques of childrearing.

[108] U. Bronfenbrenner (cited in footnote 106), p. 75; see also L. Kohlberg (cited in footnote 102), pp. 407–408.

engender such characteristics in the middle-class child as will facilitate his successful adaptation to our society.[109]

## Initiation

The most striking characteristic of the techniques used for role induction among adults is their tendency to mimic the process of socialization of children. In gradual induction procedures this may involve nothing more than making the inductee feel a little childish and ignorant (calling him "tenderfoot," or "greenhorn"), and presenting him with a conspicuous role model—but we can see it rather clearly in sudden and extreme inductions such as puberty rites and other initiation ceremonies, entrance into what Goffman calls "total institutions," [110] and the process popularly known as "brainwashing."

All of these situations are alike in their attempts to recreate the helpless dependency of infancy and foster identification with the representatives of the new group. The techniques differ only in emphasis from one situation to another. Thus Goffman is able to give a description of induction procedures which shows great consistency although his examples are drawn from such superficially varied sources as mental hospitals, prisons, monasteries, concentration camps, army training barracks, boarding schools, and ships.

The first step in an induction procedure is the reduction of the individual to a childlike state—the destruction of his previous sense of identity and self-respect. Goffman gives vivid examples of the mortification and degradation undergone by those who enter the institutions he describes: the loss of status, freedom, personal property, and privilege, the demand

[109] This relationship is one which lends itself all too well to chicken-and-egg controversies. One can argue that the childrearing differences produce the class differences or that they are caused by them, since both are probably true. The problem is even more complicated when we introduce belief systems. Lambert, Triandis, and Wolf found in a crosscultural study that societies which were more nurturant and less rigid, punitive, and demanding toward their children tended to believe in more benevolent gods than those with a reversed socialization pattern. One could see the harsh practices as both caused by and causing the belief in malevolent gods, or either in turn as affecting or dependent upon the low-synergy institutions presumably obtaining in such cultures. W. W. Lambert, Leigh M. Triandis, and Margery Wolf, "Some Correlates of Beliefs in the Malevolence and Benevolence of Supernatural Beings: A Cross-Societal Study," *Journal of Abnormal and Social Psychology*, **58**, 162–169 (1959). For an interesting attempt to unravel such problems of direction of causality, see J. W. M. Whiting, "Socialization Process and Personality," in F. L. K. Hsu, ed., *Psychological Anthropology* (Homewood, Ill.: Dorsey, 1961).

[110] "A total institution may be defined as a place of residence and work where a large number of like-situated individuals, cut off from the wider society for an appreciable period of time, together lead an enclosed, formally administered round of life." E. Goffman, *Asylums* (Garden City, N.Y.: Doubleday, 1961), p. xiii.

for the performance of humiliating or meaningless tasks, the loss of contact with the outside world, the demand for slavish subservience and deference, the elimination of differentiated characteristics, the violation of privacy, the compulsion to perform acts which violate deep personal values, and so on. But to a very large extent this degradation involves being returned to the status of a very small, if unusually regimented, child. According to Goffman,

> . . . one of the most telling ways in which one's economy of action can be disrupted is the obligation to request permission or supplies for minor activities that one can execute on one's own on the outside, such as smoking, shaving, going to the toilet, telephoning, spending money, or mailing letters. This obligation not only puts the individual in a submissive or suppliant role "unnatural" for an adult but also opens up his line of action to interceptions by staff. Instead of having his request immediately and automatically granted, the inmate may be teased, denied, questioned at length, not noticed. . . .[111]

Goffman further observes that compliance is ensured by the manipulation of a few rewards or privileges consisting of trivial items whose availability had previously been taken for granted, together with an elaborate punishment system entirely alien to normal civilian life. That sadism is rife in the institutions Goffman describes is perhaps well-known —his contribution is to make clear that such sadism is an essential rather than an accidental feature of these systems.

In addition to placing the individual in the role of child by enforcing dependency and submission and taking the satisfaction of even his physical needs out of his control, acute induction procedures usually contain unlearning or disorienting mechanisms. Goffman describes beautifully the loss of cultural items and the invasion of personal rhythms that occurs in institutional life, and we may also note the use of darkness, isolation, silence, fasting, and torture in the initiation rites of primitive tribes, college fraternities, and the like. We have noticed how sensory deprivation tends to produce hallucinations; this phenomenon was the foundation of puberty rites for some American Indian tribes. Combined with starvation, which is also hallucinogenic, prolonged isolation eventually produced visions that indicated the nature of a man's individual totem. Children's camps and fraternities still use the vigil as a technique of initiation. Ancient Greek mystery cults also utilized prolonged exposure to total darkness as a prelude to initiation.

Another disorienting device is the use of ambiguous stimuli. A great deal of ritual hocus-pocus accompanies initiations: strange noises, flashing lights, or unpleasant smells and tastes (often accompanied by blindfolding),

[111] *Ibid.*, p. 41.

which serve to make the neophyte doubt his own perceptions. Various physical tortures and tests of endurance may serve the same purpose, as does the use of intoxicants.

Often the attempt to induce a state of childlike dependency is accompanied by symbols of death and rebirth. In one sense, of course, the entire initiation procedure is such a symbol—the individual is stripped of his former identity, is disoriented, suffers physical pain, enters darkness, and emerges into light, is greeted joyfully by the group, and given sustenance or some other expression of nurturance. In some primitive societies, however, this symbolism is elaborated considerably, particularly where male puberty rites signify a transition for the young boy from the world of women to the world of men. Thus the boy's sponsor may dress like a woman and pretend to be pregnant, the boys may walk through the legs of the men while the men grunt as if in childbirth, and the men may later carry the boys about like babies and hand-feed them. The initiates may "pretend to be as disoriented as one might expect a newborn infant to be. When they return to their homes, they act as if they had forgotten how to walk, tottering and entering the house backward. If food is given to them, they hold the plate upside down." In some cases they are not allowed to move even to urinate or defecate.[112]

All of this has the effect not only of obliterating the previous identity of the neophyte, but also of magnifying the stature of the members of the group he is entering. They appear mysterious and all-powerful, partly because they are in a position to gratify essential needs and remove severe discomforts and pain (which, of course, they have themselves created), and partly because the disorientation procedures are successful in themselves in making the neophyte feel lost and childlike and hence making him view his tormentors as parental figures. Since, in addition, their immediate post-initiation behavior tends to be nurturant, the ideal conditions for identification are established.

These observations help us to understand what is perhaps the most dramatic form of acute role induction—"brainwashing." Few phenomena have so captured the imagination of Americans as the "confessions" and defections of American prisoners captured by the Chinese in the Korean War. That this should have been perceived as mysterious and startling is testimony to the entrenchment of individualism in modern Western life—there is little that would seem remarkable to most peoples of the world, who have lived in a far more collective manner throughout history and prehistory. Perhaps the fact that the public had been bombarded for years with movies, plays, and novels depicting individuals heroically

---

[112] B. Bettelheim, *Symbolic Wounds* (London: Thames and Hudson, 1955), pp. 212–219.

withstanding some rather mild and unimaginative tortures at the hands of sadistic but strangely ineffectual Nazis (most of the tortures actually used in such situations could not even be hinted at given the movie codes of the period) had something to do with it. But complete resistance either to conventional torture or to the more sophisticated technique associated with "brainwashing" requires a fanaticism which few human beings possess (usually at the expense of most other attributes generally considered desirable). Perhaps the rapid colloquial adoption of the term "brainwashing" for the most varied and mild forms of role induction reveals some unconscious awareness of its lack of novelty.

It is a sad but repeatedly documented fact [113] of American law enforcement systems, for example, that thousands of confessions, many of them entirely false, are forcibly extracted from ignorant lower-class prisoners in every part of the country every year, both with and without the aid of the superior techniques supposedly developed by Soviet and Chinese Communists. Sometimes old-fashioned, physical methods are employed: whipping, beating with rubber hoses, and, occasionally, more exotic and imaginative measures. The use of psychological techniques, however, is also a long-standing police tradition. The "third degree," for example, has always been considered an indigenous procedure, yet it involves many of the same techniques used by the Chinese: prolonged questioning, lack of sleep, attempt at disorientation, and the manipulation of light and darkness, of isolation and belonging. The prisoner is alternately isolated in a cell and surrounded by questioners, first in darkness and then in a glare of light (usually with his questioners obscured). Like Goffman's inmates or the neophyte in an initiation, the prisoner alternates between utter aloneness and a total loss of privacy. As in initiations and in the Chinese prison camp, the accused prisoner will often find that one of his questioners has assumed the role of one who is sympathetic toward him and wants to be helpful, to protect him against the other "unfriendly" interrogators. If the prisoner would only be reasonable and confess, he argues, every one would be happy and the unpleasantness would cease —he is interested only in the prisoner's redemption.

Another common facet of initiations, brainwashing, and police interrogations is the attempt to invade the individual's psyche by getting him to commit, or showing that he already has committed, acts that violate his own value system, or by pointing out inconsistencies and contradictions

113 See, for example, National Commission on Law Observance and Enforcement, *Report on Lawlessness in Law Enforcement*, U.S. Government Printing Office, Washington, D.C., 1931; United States Commission on Civil Rights, *1961 Report*, Book 5, "Justice," U.S. Government Printing Office, Washington, D.C., 1961. I am grateful to Nancy Stoller Shaw for calling my attention to this material.

within that system. Part of the initiation into the Nazi party was the commission of a crime, while the Chinese technique of "thought reform" was vastly accelerated by seducing prisoners into attempting to make false confessions (only sincere ones were acceptable) or denouncing loved ones.[114] Fraternity initiations often involve the commission of similar acts.[115]

The Hungarian Communist interrogation of an American businessman who "confessed" after two months of questioning shows many of the above themes. The prisoner was isolated for several days, then was given a friendly welcome with an attempt to establish common bonds of experience. Stimulants were used, prolonged and uninterrupted questioning, bright lights, darkness, ambiguous stimuli (opening and closing the cell door as if having entered by mistake, and constant whispering outside), and solitary confinement.[116]

The only contribution of the Chinese has been the more sophisticated use of groups and the emphasis on total conversion and "reform" rather than mere confession. Some of the Chinese techniques have been compared with group therapy and, indeed, from the Chinese point of view, this is precisely what they are. They were also able to play effectively upon the prisoners' genuine guilt over their middle-class prejudices, the more unfortunate facets of American foreign policy, and their contribution to existing injustices at home. The use of cellmates involved the prisoner in a genuine desire to establish some kind of emotional unity with these people with whom his whole waking life was so closely bound.[117] But these again are simply rearrangements of induction procedures that have been used for centuries.

One final mechanism involved in initiation techniques is related to the theory of "cognitive dissonance." [118] A study by Aronson and Mills [119] confirmed a prediction that individuals confronted with the contradiction between (1) having undergone a "severe" initiation to a group and (2) the undesirability of the group, would in some cases resolve the contradiction, not by writing off their unpleasant experience as a mistake but by

---

[114] E. H. Schein, "Brainwashing," in W. G. Bennis, E. H. Schein, D. E. Berlew, and F. I. Steel, *Interpersonal Dynamics* (Homewood, Ill.: Dorsey, 1964), p. 463.

[115] See also E. Goffman (cited in footnote 110).

[116] J. C. Moloney, "Psychic Self-Abandon and Extortion of Confessions," in Bennis et al., *Interpersonal Dynamics*, pp. 446–447.

[117] E. H. Schein (cited in footnote 114); see also R. J. Lifton, " 'Thought Reform' of Western Civilians in Chinese Communist Prisons," *Psychiatry*, 19, 173–195 (1956).

[118] L. Festinger, H. Riecken, and S. Schachter, *When Prophecy Fails* (Minneapolis, Minn.: University of Minnesota Press, 1956).

[119] E. Aronson and J. Mills, "The Effect of Severity of Initiation on Liking for a Group," *Journal of Abnormal and Social Psychology*, 59, 177–181 (1959).

distorting, in a positive direction, the value of the group (compare the earlier discussion regarding the two methods of resolving strain). The individual's need for some consistent self-perception as a rational being thus forces him into an irrational position. Although there are flaws in Aronson and Mills' procedure, the phenomenon is a highly familiar one.[120] How many individuals have retained a fervent loyalty to fraternities simply out of an unwillingness to face the absurdity of their having undergone humiliation, ridicule, degradation, and discomfort for very little reason? How many have become doctors, lawyers, or professors rather than admit that tedious learning, boring information, and difficult examinations were a waste of time? How many wars have been expanded in order to impart meaning to the deaths of soldiers?

Thus the mechanisms of conversion, initiation, confession, defection, and other forms of role induction are not at all mysterious. All play upon the simple needs and vulnerabilities of human beings to generate new loyalties and allegiances. But in their more extreme and exaggerated forms they play upon human ignorance as well—particularly our self-delusions about autonomy, consistency, and self-sufficiency. Human beings are all social, vulnerable, incomplete, and interconnected—it is because of these characteristics that we have become intelligent, human, adaptable, and creative. Denial of them makes us brittle and manipulable, for it makes it possible for us to be surprised by ourselves, and there is no one so susceptible to social influence as an individual who is unfamiliar with his own constituents.

## Summary

We have discussed how embedded man is in his society, how much he is created and molded by it, and how his humanness derives from it. We noticed that this dependence does not prohibit conflict, since the individual and society as entities share elastic but finite resources, and consequently must compete as well as reflect one another. We considered the amount of internal contradiction and ambivalence that is found both within the society and within the individual, and the necessity for both to deny this complexity in order to achieve unified self-conceptions and actions. We examined the ways of effecting the expression of this complexity along with their impact on the relationship of individual to group. We explored the articulation of role and personality, and briefly reviewed some of the ways in which personality is molded, and in which individuals are inducted into social roles.

[120] E. Goffman (cited in footnote 110).

*11*

# DEVIANT
# BEHAVIOR

*Stanton Wheeler**

* Kai Erikson worked jointly with me on much of this chapter, and we would have written it together if time had allowed it. As it is, much of the first section reflects his formulation and style, although he is not responsible for its final form. I am also indebted to Alex Inkeles and Anne Romasco for a close reading of an earlier draft.

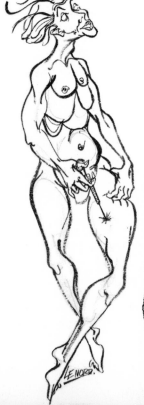

# LAXITY REPORTED IN JERSEY ASYLUM

## Sex Offenders Have Full Run of Greystone Park, Trenton Inquiry Hears

### By RONALD SULLIVAN
Special to The New York Times

TRENTON, Sept. 10—A legislative committee was told today that convicted sex offenders in a state mental institution went to tea dances, ran a floating numbers and loan-shark operation, had affairs with college girls and mixed drinks in their ward.

Three Morris County detectives testified before the Assembly Committee on Institutions, Public Health and Welfare that attendants at Greystone Park, the state's largest mental hospital, sold master keys to sex offenders for $20 each.

A young Florham Park mother testified later behind closed doors that her 9-year-old daughter had been repeatedly molested by a sex offender when she went to the institution to visit her son. She said that at least one molestation took place on a day when several offenders were assigned to a work detail in the children's section of the hospital.

Detective Edward O'Brien startled the committee in the sultry Assembly chamber when he declared softly:

"It's my opinion that I could work inside Greystone for six

# DEVIANT
# BEHAVIOR

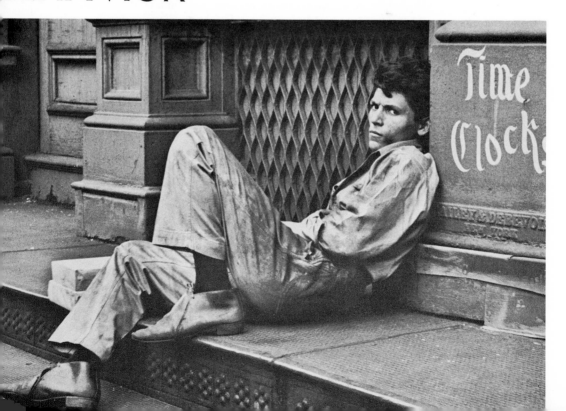

## Introduction

Every human society makes a distinction between behavior that conforms to the prevailing conventions of social life and behavior that deviates in one way or another from those conventions. Every human society, too, maintains a set of institutions for dealing with people whose behavior comes to be regarded as deviant. These two observations provide the field of sociology with one of its most interesting subject matters and bring into focus a number of issues that reflect on the very nature of man as a social being. The purpose of this chapter is to introduce some of these issues.

To deal intelligently with deviant behavior, we must begin with a working idea of what is meant when we say that most people, most of the time, manage to conform. Every society is characterized by an elaborate scaffolding of rules and precepts that help to organize the activities of the people who live within the society's domain. Some of these rules are formally stated as laws; others are embedded in that body of custom and usage which a people accepts as its special way of doing things; and still others are vaguely sensed understandings about how people should behave, which are absorbed into the texture of social life without being articulated directly at all. All of these rules and precepts, together, make up a cultural stance—a shared conception of what is fitting and proper—on the basis of which the people of a society judge whether the behavior of their fellows is reasonable or unreasonable, moral or immoral, proper or improper.

Sociologists usually refer to these rules by their Latin name, "norms." A norm is a rule of conduct, a standard, shared by participants in any patterned social interaction. Norms may vary, of course, in the degree to which they clearly demarcate the boundaries of appropriate behavior in particular circumstances, and in the degree to which they are genuinely and widely shared by those to whom they apply. When there are literally no agreed-upon standards to guide conduct in particular contexts, we have a condition of normlessness or anomie.

The term "norm" is a short and perhaps an oversimple designation for something that cannot be seen or touched or even described very accurately, but something that every student of society knows exists because he can observe its effects on human behavior. The problem, however, is that norms are very difficult to portray as separate threads in the fabric of culture: the moment we lift a norm out of its context to see how it works as a guide to behavior, we are apt to discover that we have detached it from that shared body of experience which gives it whatever meaning it has to the persons whose lives are touched by it. Actually, the authority of any par-

604

ticular norm is hedged in by so many conditions and qualifications that it would be easier (and probably a good deal more accurate) simply to say that the social setting in which people act is governed by a moral climate, a normative temper, which cannot be broken up into its constituent parts. We shall consider norms throughout this chapter as if they were discrete items in the structure of society, but it should be understood that this usage is a kind of sociological shorthand.

Men are constantly surrounded by a thick tissue of rules, and it is important to appreciate how complex this tissue can be. The life of any given person is guided by several different clusters of rules at once: he must act in reference to family traditions, ethnic ways, state laws, neighborhood customs, regional mores, occupational norms, and a vast array of other pressures and demands imposed upon him by the various groups to which he belongs. It is only natural that some of these normative pressures will be contradictory and that others will be confusing; but, somehow, each of us is expected to fashion a way of life that pays sufficient attention to all of them at the same time. Consider the case of a second-generation immigrant living in one of the more crowded urban slums. Suppose he comes from a Polish family that respects the traditional peasant values of hard work, piety, thrift, and a low personal ceiling on aspiration. He lives in a neighborhood where open defiance of the law is considered an important measure of masculinity by the young. He expects to move out into a society where mobility, success, and a fairly bland style of conformity are valued. Around him he hears the voices of parents representing the older virtues, of schoolteachers and television performers representing a newer American ethic, of teen-age comrades representing the special morality of the streets, of police officers and priests, politicians and social workers, each holding up a somewhat different set of values for him to conform to. And out of all these materials he is to build a consistent life.

Obviously this is an extreme case, but it is only a more sharply etched illustration of something that all of us encounter as we try to sort out the various competing demands on our attention. In one sense, people always run the risk of deviating from one standard of performance in the very act of conforming to another, and everyone devotes a good deal of energy to the job of picking out a reasonably consistent path among the pressures imposed upon him. Still, it is important to notice that some persons respond to this dilemma by acting in ways that the rest of society views as deviant while others do not, and the problem of finding some meaningful way to distinguish between the two is a remarkably complicated one. The difficulties begin at the very moment we try to describe what deviation is.

Deviant behavior, ordinarily, is defined as conduct that runs afoul of social norms. But norms are not blueprints outlining in compulsory detail how people should act; they are abstract standards of conduct that people are expected to *approximate* in their daily activities, and this means that there are many varieties of behavior, many shades of difference, which fit within the compass of the norm. In this sense, the norm itself is a midpoint in a range of behavior, and when we say that someone has violated the norm we are saying that his behavior has passed over some cut-off point at the edges of the norm's jurisdiction. In trying to distinguish between the behavior known as deviant and the behavior accepted as conventional, then, it is more important to look at the cut-off point than at the letter of the norm itself. Yet, how do we learn where these cut-off points are located? It is one thing to observe, for instance, that the norms of American life require people to respect one another's property and to remain loyal to the national government, but it is quite another thing to specify where, along the continuum of human conduct, borrowing shades over into stealing and criticism into sedition—or, for that matter, where gossip becomes slander, eccentricity becomes illness, seduction becomes rape, and so on.

Among the difficulties of learning where these cut-off points are located on the normative map is the fact that they are apt to vary from time to time, from place to place, and from strata to strata. In American society, again, it is generally agreed that public intoxication is improper, and this moral sentiment is backed by legal ordinances as well as by a wide variety of other sanctions. But this information does not necessarily tell us what degree of intoxication will qualify an individual for deviant censure. A moderate display of drunken behavior would probably provoke more critical reactions in Salt Lake City than in Las Vegas and would probably reflect more harshly on the person of a clergyman than on the person of a merchant seaman, and this means, in effect, that it is difficult to keep track of all the conditions and qualifications that enter into the process by which people are judged to be deviant. In this sense, the people of society are always a little in doubt about the edges of the norm, no matter how strongly they may feel about the values at its center. And it might be noted, too, that this doubt is institutionalized in the various procedures that we develop in society to ascertain whether a particular set of behavior is deviant. Thus, the ladies of the sewing circle may be quite positive that schoolteachers should not act in a provocative fashion, but these ladies spend many hours among themselves trying to decide whether the conduct of this or that individual falls within the scope of that stricture. In the same way, the kinds of deliberation that take place in jury rooms, psychiatric staff conferences, or any other location in society where judgments of this sort are made, all have this character—because the people of society are constantly reviewing where the edges of the norms should be. Indeed, the formal mechanisms of courts and judges have the business of establishing cut-off points in difficult cases.

These remarks suggest something of the subtleties and complexities that are encountered as we attempt to apply the concepts of norms and deviation, and there remains still another point that requires a brief discussion before we can introduce the specific subject matter of the field. It seems simple enough to agree that a deviant is one who violates social norms but, in practice, two different strategies have developed for the actual process of deciding who is deviant. The first strategy assumes that an observer looking in at the behavior of people in society can detect which of it constitutes deviancy and which of it does not.[1] After all, deviant behavior is conduct that violates the norms, and if the observer knows what the norms require he should be able to judge what kinds of behavior constitute a transgression. The second strategy assumes that the range of conduct that falls within the authority of the norm is so illusive and so subject to shifts in the social climate that the observer can do little more than note how other people in society react to the deviancies of their fellows and use this as his guide.[2] According to the first strategy, then, deviant behavior is conduct that *objectively appears* to violate a norm. According to the second strategy, deviant behavior is conduct that is *perceived by others* as contrary to the norms. The distinction is pointed out because most of the important writings on deviant behavior in sociology derive from one or the other of these positions and depend heavily on them. For example, the widely admired work of Robert K. Merton illustrates the use to which the first strategy can be put.[3]

In Merton's analysis of deviant behavior (which we discuss in more detail later), he discusses persons who fail to live up to culturally valued goals as a type of deviant, without worrying too much about whether other people in society actually think of them in this way. The equally admired works of Edwin M. Lemert and Howard S. Becker illustrate the second strategy.[4] In their conception, less attention is paid to abstract standards, and more atten-

---

[1] This strategy is the focal point of the work of Robert K. Merton and Talcott Parsons, for example, and through their influence in the work of quite a few others.

[2] This strategy is reflected in the work of Howard S. Becker, Kai T. Erikson, Erving Goffman, John I. Kitsuse, Edwin M. Lemert, Thomas J. Scheff, and others.

[3] Robert K. Merton, *Social Theory and Social Structure* (Glencoe, Ill.: The Free Press, 1957).

[4] Edwin M. Lemert, *Social Pathology* (New York: McGraw-Hill, 1951); Howard S. Becker, *Outsiders: Studies in the Sociology of Deviance* (Glencoe, Ill.: The Free Press, 1963).

tion is paid to the actual social definitions of conduct by members of on-going social groups. For them, deviants are persons who are socially treated as such.

The usage in this chapter comes closer to the second than the first definition. We define deviant behavior as conduct that the people of a society generally regard as abberant, disturbing, improper or immoral, and for which specific social control efforts are likely to be found. And with this discussion of norms, deviation, and social control as background, we turn to the substantive problems that most interest the student of this subject matter.

The questions and issues that concern the sociologist can be conveniently sorted into three general categories.

1. The first set of questions involves the way in which social norms and deviant behavior fit into the life of society. How do norms function in social life? Are they necessary at all? Do they operate in such a way as to expand the potential range of human expression, or do they primarily serve to narrow and to contract the freedom of anyone who lives under their jurisdiction? We can only deal with these matters in a most provisional way, but they lead us into important questions about the role of deviant behavior in the overall context of society. For example, if a structure of norms is valuable to society, does this mean that deviation is by definition harmful or dysfunctional? Or is there a sense in which society can gain from the occasional misconduct of its members? Does deviant behavior become a stable feature of the social landscape in much the same way that other institutions and other forms of behavior become routinized and patterned? And, basic to all of these questions, is this one: Why do the members of a society bother to define certain forms of behavior as deviant at all?

The last question is a more serious one than it seems, since it is probably accurate to say at the outset that no behavior is inherently deviant. If we look across the world at the various cultures into which mankind is divided, or if we look backward in time at the various historical periods that have preceded our own, we can find an extraordinary diversity in the kinds of behavior that have been singled out as deviant. Activities that one society tries to suppress with all its resources may turn out to be wholly acceptable to another society, even when conditions of life in the two societies are much the same; and this means, in effect, that every society develops a conception of deviation that is local to its own history and circumstances. Now some forms of behavior are regarded as deviant because they constitute a clear danger to the survival of the group. Other forms of behavior are regarded as deviant because they seem to be generated by states of mind that are so far outside of the experience of ordinary men that they appear erratic, capricious, and dangerous in their very unpredictability. Beyond this, however, every society takes action against behavior which has no apparent liabilities except that it happens to offend the sensitivities of other people, and this brings us back to the original question: Why?

All of these questions are addressed to the larger social setting in which deviant behavior occurs, and deal only in the most marginal way with the situation of those persons who themselves become deviants.

2. Our second set of questions is concerned with the problem of deviant persons. In a society in which certain activities are generally thought to be deviant and in which a considerable number of people are censured for engaging in these activities, why is it that some kinds of individuals find their way into the deviant ranks and others do not? What properties can we discover in human society or in the human mind that distinguish between the persons who manage to conform and the persons who drift off into one form or another of deviant expression? At first glance, it seems quite reasonable to assume that every deviant act is the product of some confusion or perversity local to the actor's personality or to the conditions of his life and, to that extent, it makes good sense to insist that every deviant act is a unique human story, an individual case, which should be considered in its own terms. Fortuitously, however, sociologists have discovered some stubborn facts about deviant behavior. There is a pattern—a structure—to the way in which deviant behavior appears in social life; and this is partly because the various social strains that seem to produce deviant behavior are unequally distributed over the surface of society. The sociologist is principally interested in knowing where these sensitive zones are located and how they function as breeding grounds for deviant behavior. Why are some areas of society more likely than others to produce particular styles of deviation? What kinds of persons are most susceptible to the strains or temptations found in these areas? What social experiences provoke people to test the deviant edges of society and what social experiences tend to confirm them in a deviant way of life?

3. The third set of questions involves the reactions of society to the deviant conduct of its members. Every society devotes a considerable portion of its organizational resources to the task of suppressing the deviant leanings of the persons who live within it. To begin with, of course, every society has its own methods for encouraging people to act within the jurisdiction of the norm; but, beyond this, every society also develops an institutional machinery for controlling the behavior of those individuals who do venture off in deviant directions. Now the nature of this control machinery varies widely from one society to another, and the questions that we ask in this connection cover a wide range. How does a society go about the critical business of detecting acts of deviation? What test or

concept does a society use to determine whether a person should be considered responsible for his own misconduct? In what ways does a society deal with people who are adjudged to be deviant? What strategies are available to a society for reforming or remotivating the persons whose behavior becomes problematic?

These three sets of questions provide the main content of our discussion. We shall comment on (1) social definitions of deviation, (2) the process of becoming a deviant, and (3) the machinery of social control.

## Social Definitions of Deviation

Persons, in their first exposure to sociological ways of thinking, are sometimes offended by the fact that sociologists pay so much attention to the norms governing social life and seem so committed to the notion that human lives are shaped and molded by the influence of the social structure. If the behavior of men is dictated by external forces to the degree that sociologists seem to feel is the case, does this mean that there is no room in our calculus for concepts such as free will or individual creativity? If the people of society are sealed away in a tight envelope of rules, does this mean that they are really mindless creatures being hauled this way and that by forces that they can neither control nor understand? It may be true that sociologists have lent more plausibility to this point of view than most of them intended—if only because it is their job to point out that the social structures that men build around themselves have a profound effect on the scope of human action—but the study of social life does not, by any means, lead to this conclusion.

Therefore, let us presume that men have an extraordinary capacity for creativity and imagination, and that human lives can be spontaneous, adventurous, inventive, and free. But let us also ask where these qualities come from. One tradition of Western thought would have us assume that the finer instincts of human life are more or less inhibited by any increase in the complexities of social organization—as though society were of such nature as to destroy whatever is fresh and original in the human spirit. This line of reasoning has led to a compelling vision of man's condition and has provided one of the major themes of Western thought and literature; but it is the substance of metaphor, not of social science. When sociologists argue that men are subject to the influence of an orderly social system, they are referring to the context *in which* men express whatever freedoms we can reasonably assume them to have, and it is difficult to pursue any sociological subject intelligently if we begin with the suspicion (so large a part of our theological and philosophical heritage) that societies do little more than repress the more natural inclinations of the people who live in them and limit their potential range of action.[5] It is true, certainly, that the rules men invent to govern themselves can become too brittle and tight, restricting their capacity for invention and change, but this is neither an inherent property of rules nor their most evident function. Since the point is quite important to any discussion of conformity and deviation, let us consider a rather extensive illustration.

One of the most remarkable achievements of society (although we generally take it for granted) is that society permits great masses of men to live together in a narrow space without trampling all over one another. In cities like London or Tokyo, millions of people are pressed together in an area of a few square miles. They shift back and forth across the surface of this area, enter into countless transactions with each other, swarm through narrow doorways and along crowded streets—and, in general, manage to weave in and out of the elaborate architecture of the city with a minimum of collisions, either physical or emotional. Now all of this seems perfectly ordinary; but imagine the intricate structure of rules necessary for coordinating this stir of activity so that organized movement is possible at all. Within a few minutes, hundreds of people can pass through a single passageway without causing so much as a bruise; thousands of automobiles can pass through an intersection with no more than an occasional dent; and millions of people can be in motion at the same time without serious hazard to any of them. If each of these people were circulating through space at random, mindful only of his own errands and governed only by some inner sense of urgency, the ensuing crush and confusion would be beyond imagination.

But we have rules. Automobiles and pedestrians manage their way across the city by responding to an extraordinary variety of signals, by being constantly alert to the movement of others, by giving and receiving gestures, and by acting in terms of an immensely complex grammar of rules. Insofar as we know, men are not aided in their efforts to coordinate such a complex social situation by anything that resembles programmed instincts—as is, for example, a colony of ants—and this means that we are dealing with something that men must teach each other. The pertinent point is that the rules and norms regulating the movement of traffic represent an enormous number of constraints on human behavior. For instance, men exercise very few options

---

[5] For two strong statements of this tradition (both cast in a psychoanalytic framework), see Herbert Marcuse, *Eros and Civilization* (Boston: Beacon Press, 1955); and Norman O. Brown, *Life Against Death* (Middletown, Conn.: Wesleyan University Press, 1959).

when they drive an automobile—so few that we can almost program the whole process on a computer—but the important question for us (and presumably for the motorist) concerns the ostensible purpose of this activity in the first place. Is the motorist on his way home to dine with his family? Is he on his way to read poetry in a coffee house? To study in a university? To join friends at a poker table? No matter what his purpose is, he will encounter another screen of rules as elaborate as the one through which he just passed, but the options that he has exercised in choosing his destination and in electing to conform to that system of norms and values represent his freedoms as a social being. Social life is never that simple, of course, but the general point should be clear: the rules of the social order sometimes act to restrict the range of a person's activity, but they also serve to extend that range by permitting him to move through the intricate machinery of society with a minimum of friction and stoppage.

Granted, then, that some rules may be necessary and even beneficial for social life, how do we know which particular rules are most important to establish? Stated differently: On what basis do the people of society decide to regard one form of behavior as deviant and not another? The answer is that we do not know for sure. But at least three different lines of argument have been made on this problem in the sociological literature, and we shall consider them briefly.

First, it seems sensible to begin our inquiry by asking whether certain forms of behavior are treated as deviant simply because society cannot afford to tolerate them. That is, every social system requires certain kinds of behavior from the people who live within it in order to survive from one generation to the next, and any activities that interefere too drastically with the performance of these necessary tasks are likely to be regarded as deviant and treated accordingly. It is reasonable, for example, that every society must make some arrangements for an orderly replacement of its members if it is to persist, must inspire something akin to what we call "loyalty" in its members if the energies of the whole group are to be mobilized in moments of emergency, must make provisions for the distribution of property, sexual favor, prestige, and so on. In the language of sociology, some forms of behavior are "functional" for society because they contribute to its coherence, while other forms of behavior are "dysfunctional" because they disrupt the normal processes of the group and jeopardize its chances for survival.[6]

Within certain limits, then, we can argue that the people of society elect to define certain forms of conduct as deviant because they know (somehow) that the behavior in question is harmful and dysfunctional; and

[6] Robert K. Merton, *op. cit.*

we can continue the list of deviancies that belong in this category almost endlessly. The problem is that this procedure has a limited explanatory value since, as a general rule, people *always* assume that the behavior they are willing to censure is harmful—because it violates the rules of good hygiene, or risks the displeasure of the gods, or causes the fish not to run, or gives comfort to the enemy, or turns the young against their elders, or reduces one's prospects in the afterlife, or something else. But it is quite another matter to ask what forms of behavior *really are* dangerous on an objective scale of measurement. Obviously, no society can afford to lose whole generations of young men in indiscriminate brawling and murder, and thus it would seem that norms governing homicide are necessary for survival, but it is by no means so clear that the norms restricting marihuana use or prostitution, for example, are in the same category. Although marihuana use may be injurious, neither the medical nor the sociological evidence of its danger is at all clearcut. On this score alone, a visitor from another culture might be curious to know why we take such a dim view of this activity and yet allow one another to climb mountains, smoke cigarettes, race automobiles, or engage in other pursuits that are demonstrably more dangerous. Émile Durkheim, one of the most outstanding figures in the history of sociological thought, stated the point this way in a discussion of life in primitive societies:

  . . . there are many acts which have been and still are regarded as criminal (read "deviant") without in themselves being harmful to society. What social danger is there in touching a tabooed object, an impure animal or man, in letting the sacred fire die down, in eating certain meats, in failure to make the traditional sacrifice over the grave of parents, in not exactly pronouncing the ritual formula, in not celebrating holidays, etc.? [7]

The difficulty of trying to equate deviation with danger, then, is that we can find many kinds of human behavior that pose a frightening threat to survival without ever coming under the limiting influence of deviant controls, and many kinds of human behavior that are treated as deviant without constituting the slightest threat to the security of the group.

    This issue has led several sociologists (most notably Howard S. Becker) to take a somewhat different view of the matter.[8] Becker is not at all impressed by the argument that people impose deviant sanctions on certain kinds of conduct in a more or less rational effort to protect society from harmful influences. He assumes, instead, that a community is made up of

[7] Émile Durkheim, *The Division of Labor in Society*, translated by George Simpson (Glencoe, Ill.: The Free Press, 1947, p. 72). See also the classic paper by George Herbert Mead, "The Psychology of Punitive Justice," *American Journal of Sociology*, **23**, 577–602 (1918).

[8] Howard S. Becker (cited in footnote 4).

competing power blocs, each of which is trying to impose its own peculiar brand of morality on the others by taking over and managing the existing machinery of control. What Becker is adding to our understanding of deviant processes is the notion that a kind of moral politics is always going on within the framework of social life in which definitions of deviation are negotiated and contested like any other resource of power. Although the notion can easily be taken too far, the point is an important one. In recent years, for example, a number of commentators have argued that the laws governing premarital sex relations, prostitution, the use of marihuana, homosexuality, and other activities—not to mention the prevailing medical view as to what constitutes mental illness [9]—represent little more than the tastes and attitudes of certain vested interests, which happen to be in a position of power. Historically, we can find support for this notion in several quarters. There is little question that the establishment of prohibition laws earlier in the century and the laws prohibiting the sale of marihuana were engineered by groups of resourceful and energetic "moral entrepreneurs" who managed to bring about a formal change in the normative structure of society without—in the beginning at least—representing anything like the majority of the people concerned.

The third perspective found in the sociological literature relating to the basis for regarding one form of behavior as deviant and not another was suggested about seventy years ago by Émile Durkheim and remains one of the most interesting statements on the subject.[10] Durkheim was concerned with the problem of group cohesiveness throughout his life and gradually began to develop the idea that deviant behavior may play an important role in society by providing a target around which people could organize into communities. In other words, crime (and, by extension, other forms of deviation) may actually perform a needed service to society by drawing people together in a common posture of anger and indignation. The deviant violates rules of conduct that the rest of the community hold in high regard, and when the people in the community come together to bear witness against the offender and to express their outrage over the offense, they develop a tighter bond of solidarity than existed earlier. In other words, the excitement generated by the deviant offense quickens the tempo of interaction in the group and creates a climate in which the private feelings of many separate persons are fused into a common sense of morality.

---

[9] The most energetic criticism along these lines in recent years has been by Thomas Szasz, *The Myth of Mental Illness* (New York: Harper and Row, 1961).
[10] See, particularly, Émile Durkheim's *The Division of Labor in Society, op. cit.,* and *The Rules of Sociological Method,* translated by S. A. Solovay and J. H. Meuller (Glencoe, Ill.: The Free Press, 1958).

Crime brings together upright consciences and concentrates them. We have only to notice what happens, particularly in a small town, when some moral scandal has just been committed. They stop each other on the street, they visit each other, they seek to come together to talk of the event and to wax indignant in common. From all these similar impressions which are exchanged, for all the temper that gets itself expressed, there emerges a unique temper . . . which is everybody's without being anybody's in particular. That is the public temper.[11]

Thus the deviant act creates a sense of mutuality among the people of the community by supplying a focus for group feeling. Like a war, a flood, or some other emergency, deviance makes people more alert to the interests they share in common and draws attention to those basic values which Durkheim called the "collective conscience" of the community. Unless the rhythm of social life is punctuated by occasional moments of deviant behavior, presumably, the stability of society would be seriously threatened.

In recent years, sociologists have begun to develop this theme first introduced by Durkheim and have begun to consider in fuller detail what its implications might be for the study of society.[12] A review of this material is not relevant here, but we point out that in many ways it reverses the logic of the first of the three points that we are discussing—since one assumption of Durkheim's thesis is that deviant behavior may be positively functional for society, and another assumption may be that societies actually *need* a fairly constant volume of deviation in order to remain intact.

Of course, these contrasting perspectives are difficult to test empirically, since it is difficult to understand how any one of them could be specifically invalidated. Indeed, each may contain a portion of the truth, as our discussion is intended to suggest. Some forms of conduct appear to be proscribed in just about every society; some forms show the work of special interest groups; and no society has yet managed to eliminate deviant behavior.

One of the fruitful sources of further knowledge about these alternatives may be found in longitudinal or comparative studies in which efforts are made to establish rates of deviance for whole societies. Information recently accumulated by the Norwegian sociologist, Nils Christie, provides an interesting illustration.[13] Using historical data, Christie has been able to calculate the rate of officially registered criminals for Norway from 1834 to 1960. This rate (although not, of course, the total amount) is surprisingly

[11] Émile Durkheim, *The Division of Labor in Society, op. cit.,* p. 102.
[12] Lewis A. Coser, "Some Functions of Deviant Behavior and Normative Flexibility," *American Journal of Sociology,* **68,** 174–82 (September, 1962); Robert A. Dentler and Kai T. Erikson, "The Functions of Deviance in Groups," *Social Problems,* **9,** 207–214 (spring, 1962).
[13] Nils Christie (personal communication with the author).

consistent across that span of time, and it appears that there are fairly stable upper and lower limits to the volume of crime experienced in any given period. The specific acts with which people were charged vary considerably over the period under study: in 1860 there were many arrests for a crime called concubinage and in 1960 there were many arrests for auto theft, but regardless of the shifts taking place in the kinds of activity attracting police attention, the total rate of crime remained quite constant.

The fact that the rate itself remains stable and that its peaks and valleys occur at fairly regular intervals leads one to ask why these regularities exist at all. There is no reason to expect, for example, that the persons managing the control apparatus in Norway were somehow interested in producing a constant rate of deviation, and there are no theories that would lead us to guess that there is a consistent feature in human populations—a genetic flaw, a psychological quirk—that would predispose a particular quota of people to engage in deviant activities. As we shall see later, there are other corners of the social structure in which we might look for the sources of this stability; but, here, we should note that one property of deviant behavior that needs to be accounted for in our analysis is the fact that this kind of behavior seems to appear in society in fairly constant dosages.

The above findings concern the fairly remote country of Norway. Perhaps other patterns might be found in other regions which have been characterized by a different political structure, a different rate of industrialization, a different religious and ideological climate, but the thin yield of data available to us from other studies tends to indicate that the Norwegian experience is more likely the rule than the exception. Interested readers should consult *Psychosis and Civilization* by Goldhamer and Marshall,[14] which is concerned with mental illness rates over an extended period of Massachusetts history, or *Wayward Puritans* by Erikson, which suggests that crime rates tended to remain quite stable in colonial New England.[15] At this point in the development of the field of deviant behavior, one can at least say that the ideas are intriguing, even if they still fall far short of adequate empirical support.

## The Process of Becoming a Deviant

Perhaps the most frequently asked question about deviant behavior is simply: Why? Why do individuals engage in deviant lines of conduct?

[14] Herbert Goldhamer and Andrew Marshall, *Psychosis and Civilization* (Glencoe, Ill.: The Free Press, 1953).
[15] Kai T. Erikson, *Wayward Puritans: A Study in the Sociology of Deviance* (New York: Wiley, 1966).

What is it about some people that makes them do the things they do? Or—to emphasize sociological as distinct from psychological features of the process—what accounts for the way in which particular forms of deviation are distributed throughout a social unit? Why, for example, does the incidence of schizophrenia appear to be higher among members of the lower social classes than among those farther up the socioeconomic ladder? [16] Why is it that high crime rates are concentrated among the youth of the society and decline with age? [17] In a more limited social sphere, why is it that classroom cheating on some college campuses seems more frequently to be found among members of fraternities than among non-members? [18]

All of these questions relate to the general problem of understanding the genesis of deviant behavior. The difficulties in even beginning to answer them are vast, and our progress to date is quite small. Among other problems, deviant behavior varies so greatly in the kinds of social units in which it is expressed and in the concrete forms which it takes that it is not easy to identify the most basic or important causal processes. Before discussing what many sociologists agree to be basic elements in the creation of deviant behavior patterns, let us comment in detail on the varying social units in which deviation may be studied and the variety of forms and types that it may take.

## Deviation in Varying Levels of Social Unit

Social norms may be generated within any kind of concrete social unit: between a married pair, a small group of friends, within the neighborhood or business organization, within the broader community and, of course, in the culture as a whole. Since norms may be generated at any of these levels, it follows that conformity and deviation might be examined in any one of them. A crucial question concerning the general field is whether these processes operate similarly at the different levels.

Historically, much of the concern for deviant behavior arose in the context of the primary group, the kinship system, the neighborhood, the small community, and other restricted social spheres. In the early sociological writings on norms and deviation, much concern was expressed for the

[16] August B. Hollingshead and Frederick C. Redlich, *Social Class and Mental Illness* (New York: Wiley, 1958).
[17] Walter B. Miller, "The Impact of a 'Total-Community' Delinquency Control Project," *Social Problems*, **10**, 168–191 (1962).
[18] John Harp and Philip Taietz, "Academic Integrity and Social Structure: A Study of Cheating Among College Students," *Social Problems*, **13**(4), 365–373 (1966).

informally established standards referred to as the folkways (or, in their stronger form, the mores) by scholars such as William Graham Sumner.[19] Persons who violated the folkways or mores of their group were likely to be met with ostracism, ridicule, or other unpleasant and negative sanctions; furthermore, these sanctions might be expressed by any member of the group and did not necessarily require an official charged with the task of social control.

It is these informal social processes that appear to be important in helping children learn the norms of their playmates and in keeping other community members roughly in line with community standards. Today, in most modern societies, these processes still occupy an important place, but something else has been added to them. Forms of deviation are not just informally recognized by the community, but political officials make rules and establish statutes and procedures for dealing officially with conduct felt to be deviant. Much of the work of courts of law is devoted to the processing of deviants, and we have a wide range of social agencies defined as responsible for the prevention, detection, and control of social deviation. Police, psychiatrists, social workers, judges, probation officers, and a vast array of correctional and mental-health workers reflect the extent to which social control has become a formally recognized function of the society. In addition, the agencies and institutions for the handling of deviance are permanent features of any community or state.

These agencies are not entirely new, of course, nor were they generated solely by the processes that brought about industrialization and modernization. Any relatively complex culture is characterized by a differentiation of roles so that some individuals are given the power or authority to pass judgment on the behavior of others—to sanction them, and in other ways to engage in the control of deviance. Thus, at least at the level of a total community, the control of deviance is rarely if ever a completely informal function. But our point is that the degree of importance attached to the formal agencies of control has grown greatly in modern societies. The forms of deviation that occupy most of our attention—crime, delinquency, mental illness, drug addiction, and the like—are recognized, in part, precisely because we have an elaborate mechanism for detecting them and handling them.

Here, we shall be concerned primarily with the forms of deviation that are recognized at the level of the broader community—the forms that have received attention from public officials and are important enough to require special administrative machinery that operates at the community level for the definition, detection, adjudication, and control of the deviant be-

19 William Graham Sumner, *Folkways* (New York: Blaisdell, 1940).

havior in question. But we can learn much by reviewing briefly a few of the salient findings and conclusions that emerge from the study of conformity and deviation in small group settings. In these settings it is possible to observe interaction as it unfolds, and to catch (in miniature, at least) some of the features that appear to operate also at the level of the broader society. We shall discuss results flowing from experimental research conducted by Solomon Asch and others in social psychology.[20]

Asch and other writers following his example have chosen a central theme for their research: What does an individual do when he is confronted with others who are agreed upon an answer to a question, when the individual personally believes that answer to be wrong? Will he continue to hold onto his own opinion in the face of unanimous group disagreement, or will he give in to the group pressure of the majority? Although these studies are usually thought of as dealing with social influence and the effects of group pressure, they also help to illustrate processes of deviance and social control.

The basic procedure employed in the Asch experiments is to place an individual in a relation of radical conflict with other members of a group and then to observe the individual's reaction. A group of eight individuals are instructed to match the length of a particular line with one of three unequal lines. Each member announces aloud which line he thinks is the best match. All of the eight members, except one, have been previously instructed by the experimenter to give the same incorrect answer. The one naïve member, then, who is usually placed near the end of the line so that he has heard the other responses first, faces a direct conflict between what his own experience tells him and the unanimous judgment of a group of equals. This procedure allows us to see how persons respond to being a minority of one in the midst of a unanimous majority.

The findings using this procedure illustrate some important points about deviant behavior. First, conformity to social norms ordinarily brings rewards in the form of social approval, and these rewards are not likely to be foregone easily. Fear of being a deviant is strong, and there is a tremendously powerful pull of group consensus. In the first experiment that Asch conducted with the use of this technique, one third of the naïve subjects (all of them college men) yielded to the power of the majority in giving their answers. In contrast, a control group of persons who recorded their estimates in writing showed a virtual absence of errors, suggesting that the differences, indeed, resulted from the sensed group pres-

[20] Solomon Asch, "Effects of Group Pressure Upon the Modification and Distortion of Judgments," in Dorwin Cartwright and Alvin Zander, eds., *Group Dynamics: Research and Theory* (Evanston, Ill.: Row, Peterson, 1953).

sure. Only about one fourth of the experimental subjects adhered completely to their own perceptions and continued to give correct responses throughout, and even among them the signs of discomfort in the face of the opposing majority were often great, with tension being displayed in a variety of ways.

We can refer to the persons who gave in to the group majority as "conformists," of course, only from the perspective of the group standard that preceded their judgment, since each, in a sense, was deviating from his own values. But the main point illustrated by the experiment is that conforming to the group has its own apparent rewards, and many individuals find it threatening and disagreeable to go against the group judgment, even when their own cognition tells them to do this. We can imagine that in a less clear-cut stimulus situation, it might be even easier to side with the majority. In any event, the force of group consensus appears strong enough in this circumstance so that individuals do not find it easy to deviate from group standards. Nor is it necessary for the group to be large in order for this effect to take place. Although Asch conducted his basic experiments with eight persons, he introduced as an important variation some differences in the size of the group. He found that a majority of three is enough to produce about the same effect as a majority of any larger size. Increasing the group to six, eight, ten, twelve, or sixteen does not produce an added increment of conformity in the naïve subjects.

A variation of the Asch experiment illustrates a second significant point: the importance of companions in nonconformity. In the Asch experiments, the effects of group opinion become most powerfully evident when the individual is faced with a unanimous group in opposition. If we give the naïve subject one fellow creature who supports his perspective, the rate of yielding decreases rapidly. The frequency of yielding dropped to 10% when a second naïve subject was introduced, and to 5% when, instead of a second subject, another member of the group was instructed always to answer correctly. Similarly, when a "true partner" returns in the middle of a series of judgments to side with the majority, the number of subjects who again begin yielding increases dramatically. These observations are certainly sufficient to prove the importance of group support. Indeed, a large portion of all the types of deviation that we study are ones in which deviation takes a collective form—the deviant religious sect, the street gang, and the group of drug users are prominent examples.

The Asch experiments are only one instance of the kinds of experimental research that is being done in small-group settings, but this research may yield fruitful evidence on problems of conformity and deviation. A wide assortment of things may be learned by careful observation of naturally occurring groups and social processes. One example is the observations on the relation between the deviant and the group made by Dentler and Erikson.[21] By close observation of the way in which a unit of army men protected a psychotic soldier from detection by the officers, Dentler and Erikson were led to important observations about the way in which social deviants may be useful and functional for group members.

## Varieties of Deviants

Social deviation may take a bewildering and seemingly an endless variety of forms. This is only to be expected, because of the nature of the process by which various categories of acts and qualities come to be defined as deviant. But the endless forms of deviation affect, in important ways, our efforts to arrive at a generic explanation of deviant behavior, since we must naturally assume that the conditions producing deviant persons differ according to the kind of deviant that a person is in the process of becoming. Although it is impossible to provide an exhaustive list of the various attributes and variables that are important in distinguishing different types of deviation, some of the important dimensions are outlined briefly.

Social deviants differ greatly, for example, in the degree of planning and thought that precedes their acts of deviance. At one extreme are the kind of bank or armored-car robberies that we find celebrated in the press, where months of very careful planning and organization are necessary to make the enterprise successful. This careful planning contrasts with the many violations of norms that are set off by some immediate scene or incident—for example, an argument in a tavern that leads quickly into a fight and a charge of assault.

Also, acts of deviance differ greatly in the extent to which their performance requires the support of a constellation of other deviants. The narcotics addict and pusher are caught up in a symbiotic system where the presence of each one is a requirement for engaging in the deviant behavior. Similarly, the woman who wishes to end an unwanted pregnancy requires an abortionist; the burglar requires a fence; and the prostitute requires a pimp. In these instances, the very act of deviation requires a supporting cast of others who are intertwined in a social fabric. A lone thief, on the other hand, may manage to work successfully in relative privacy although, of course, he may depend on criminal contacts just for sheer company.

Some forms of deviation present constantly recurring problems for the deviant—problems that he can avoid only momentarily. This is usually true

[21] Robert A. Dentler and Kai T. Erikson (cited in footnote 12).

of people addicted to narcotics, alcohol, or barbiturates. There is a constant problem of maintaining a source of supply, and the deviation has the aspect of being a condition that the person almost always seems to carry with him. In contrast, there are persons whose deviant careers are focused around a small number of acts spaced over a long period of time and who therefore may not have the same daily management problems that are faced by the alcoholic or the drug addict.

Still another important basis for differentiating types of deviance is whether the deviation is in the form of overt behavior or in the form of stated values and attitudes. Many persons are deviant only because they express values and beliefs that are at odds with those that are accepted in their social world. Indeed, this is a potent and troublesome type of deviation, as anyone who espouses alien political beliefs is likely to find out. The sociologist, Robert K. Merton, refers to the distinction being made here as a distinction between aberrant forms of deviant behavior and nonconformity.[22] The nonconformist is likely to broadcast word of his deviation instead of attempting to hide it. And among the persons whose deviance takes an aberrant form, we are likely to find important differences that relate to the nature of the target of the deviant act. For example, the kinds of criminals who are engaged in offenses against property usually differ in systematic ways from criminals who engage in offenses directly against other people. They are more likely to be urban dwellers, to have longer past criminal records, and to be less successful when released on probation or parole.

We could recite indefinitely the ways in which deviants may differ from one another. However, our intent is simply to illustrate the range and diversity of elements that may have to be considered if we are to work out an adequate explanation of the process by which persons become deviant, depending upon the qualities of the deviant act itself, the qualities of the persons who commit it, the context in which it is committed, and the social response of other individuals to it.

## Deviant Types and Typologies

Our task here would be simpler if there were a method of reducing the number of elements that seemingly are important ways of differentiating types of deviance, so that we could deal with only two or three fundamental

[22] Robert K. Merton, "Social Problems and Sociological Theory," in Robert K. Merton and Robert A. Nisbet, eds., *Contemporary Social Problems* (New York: Harcourt, Brace and World, 1961), pp. 697–773.

ones. The problem is that what seems important for one purpose may not be important for another, and there is little agreement among students of the subject regarding the most appropriate bases for classifying forms of deviation.

Nevertheless, several efforts have been made to develop meaningful classifications of deviant behavior, and we shall discuss three of them. The first two classifications are useful primarily because they lead us to detect important facets of the problem of deviance that are not often dealt with systematically. The third way of classifying deviants is significant for this reason also, but it is of further importance because it is the most often-discussed and often-utilized typology of deviance. Moreover, it is formulated in such a way as to lead to direct claims about the distribution of types of deviance in different social systems and about variations in the rates of deviant behavior to be found within any one type.

## The Distinction between Deviant Motives and Deviant Acts

Judith Blake and Kingsley Davis have recently argued that students of deviant behavior should deal with the fact that motives and desires are not always congruent with actual behavior. By thinking of the desire or motive behind acts as either conforming or deviant, on the one hand, and actual behavior as either conforming or deviant, on the other, these writers have compiled a simple fourfold table (Table 11.1) presenting the possibilities shown.[23]

Table 11.1  The Relations between Motives and Behavior

| Desire or Motive | Behavior | |
|---|---|---|
| | Conforming | Deviating |
| Conforming | (1) + + | (2) + − |
| Deviating | (3) − + | (4) − − |

Two of the combinations noted by Blake and Davis (the two where motives and behavior are congruent) are not particularly intriguing. But

[23] Judith Blake and Kingsley Davis, "Norms, Values, and Sanctions," in Robert E. L. Faris, ed., *Handbook of Modern Sociology* (Chicago: Rand McNally, 1964), p. 468.

the other two types are most instructive. It is natural to think of deviant behavior as being generated by deviant motivations: the person has some inner need or desire to engage in a given deviant act, and does so. But Cell 2 in the Blake and Davis table reminds us that there may be circumstances when behavior may be perceived by others as deviant despite the fact that it is not based upon any deviant motives. Quite apart from motives, for example, some persons might become confused about the rules of the system in question, or there may be no systematic procedure by which they can become instructed about these rules. The result is that their behavior may diverge from the norms without any apparent intent or motivation for deviance on their part. Indeed, when a person moves into a new social setting, there are likely to be systematic procedures to train him in the rules of the setting or, if such procedures are lacking, he is likely to be given more leeway than other members of the organization in his behavior, until a reasonable time has passed so that he can be presumed to "know the ropes."

As social systems become more complex and more demanding on their members, there is likely to be an increase in unintentional forms of deviation. In particular, as societies become increasingly complex and demanding, we are likely to see an increase in that form of unintentional deviance called "error"—misreading of the rules, lack of knowledge of proper procedure, and the like.

But as Blake and Davis note further, unintentional deviance need not be based on incapacity or lack of knowledge. Complex social systems place such demands on their members that there literally are occasions when the members cannot conform even if they want to. These occasions usually involve ambiguities or conflicts in definitions of appropriate behavior. Persons may avoid conflicting demands by conforming to one set of demands, thereby necessarily deviating from the other set. There are, of course, some principles for ordering the demands so that some are felt to take precedence over others, but there are occasions when these orderings, in turn, break down and deviances are engendered through no one's intent or desire.[24]

The other interesting cell in Table 11.1 is Cell 3 in which deviant motives and desires are present, but have not eventuated in deviant conduct. We cannot discuss the sources of deviant motivation in detail here but, instead, we shall consider another interesting set of questions raised by Blake and Davis. Under what conditions will deviant motivations be converted into deviant acts, and under what conditions will these acts not follow the motives? We have already mentioned briefly one of the important reasons for the failure to convert motives into actions in our discussion of the way in

[24] *Ibid.*

which conformity to group norms is socially rewarding. Since people can presumably keep motives and desires to themselves but are often less able to conceal behavior patterns, the price of expressing deviant leanings in deviant actions is likely to be a loss of approval and esteem in the group. This alone should be a powerful restraining force.

In addition to this general force, formal negative sanctions may be imposed for converting deviant motives into deviant actions. A very important premise (although not the only one) underlying the criminal law is that persons will be deterred from crime by the fear of penalties. We should include here the fear of detection itself, for if the deviant behavior is unlikely to be detected no penalty could be imposed. Although most analyses of political force and power suggest that systems which depend heavily upon the threat of force and punishment for deviant conduct are likely to be unstable, no one really knows how the social system would operate where such sanctions were completely unavailable.

Another explanation for failing to convert motives into actions is the lack of opportunity. Just as opportunities must be available for conforming behavior, so must they be available for persons to engage in deviance. As Richard Cloward noted in an important theoretical article several years ago, the opportunities for deviant behavior are not spread evenly across the social order.[25] Negro Americans, for example, may have higher rates of theft and burglary than whites, but the rate of Negro embezzlement is correspondingly low; and one might seriously propose as a measure of the full integration of Negroes in American life that the rate of white-collar crime among Negroes be as high as it is among whites. The simple but important fact is that it requires position and status to be employed in a job where one can successfully embezzle, and this form of deviant behavior is unavailable to persons who cannot obtain the necessary positions.

Thus, many important problems in the study of deviant behavior depend on making a distinction between deviant motives and deviant acts.

### Distinctions between the Perception and the Fact of Deviance

Although the Blake and Davis typology clarifies somewhat the relation of motives to behavior within the individual deviant, an equally important distinction for the systematic study of deviance concerns the way in which a person's conduct is evaluated by others. To say that an act is deviant presumes some audience in terms of which that judgment is made, and there may be many occasions where such judgments are in error. Let us

---

[25] Richard Cloward, "Illegitimate Means, Anomie and Deviant Behavior," *American Sociological Review,* **24,** 164–176 (April, 1959).

examine the relationship between behavior and the labels placed upon it by means of a simple typology introduced by Howard S. Becker (Table 11.2).[26]

**Table 11.2    The Relations between Perceptions and Behavior**

|  | Conforming Behavior | Deviant Behavior |
|---|---|---|
| Perceived as deviant | Falsely accused | Pure deviant |
| Not perceived as deviant | Conforming | Secret deviant |

As was true of the Blake and Davis typology, there are two cells in Becker's table that are relatively unintriguing, since they point to a congruence between behavior and perception. These are the cells labeled "conforming" and "pure deviant." The importance of the typology lies in the questions that it forces us to raise about the relation between the social responses to patterns of conduct and the conduct itself. For example, almost all of what we know about most forms of deviant behavior has been learned from persons who, at some point, are caught and treated as deviant— the "pure deviant" or the "falsely accused" in Becker's language. Almost nothing is known about secret deviation, its forms and varieties. Particularly important here are likely to be those forms of deviation in which there is no true victim or sufferer and therefore no one who has a strong interest in reporting the behavior in question or finding out about it. This is typically the case of "nonvictim" crimes such as abortion and homosexuality.[27] In these two cases, whatever is known usually has been learned from a biased sample of participants: those who have been caught or officially treated as persons with problems. In rare instances where access has been gained by researchers to participants who are not known to officials, a different sort of pattern may be found. Evelyn Hooker, who has made extensive investigations of the world of male homosexuality, finds clearly that male homosexuals who have not sought out help for their problems and are not under treatment or surveillance by psychiatrists, police, or other social control agents appear very normal in every respect (except for their homosexuality) and do not have the burdens, problems, and neuroses associated with the clinical population of homosexuals.[28]

---

[26] Howard S. Becker (cited in footnote 4), p. 20.

[27] Edwin M. Schur, *Crimes Without Victims* (Englewood Cliffs, N.J.: Prentice-Hall, 1965).

[28] See the works of Evelyn Hooker, "The Adjustment of the Male Overt Homosexual," *Journal of Projective Techniques*, 21, 1–31 (1957); "Male Homosexuality in the Rorschach," *Journal of Projective Techniques*, 22, 33–54 (1958); and "The Homosexual

Similarly, much of what we know about the criminal population has been learned from studies of men in prison—clearly a biased sample of all who have committed criminal acts.

Deviant forms of sexual conduct are particularly likely to be found in the category of the secret deviant. Becker gives us reasons to believe, for example, that the population of fetishists in the United States is by no means small,[29] and it is likely that most Peeping Toms are able to keep their deviance secret from others for long periods of time.

But we can raise a broader question about deviance by asking under what conditions of society secret deviance is likely to flourish, and under what conditions it is apt to wither away. The city, for example, has long been recognized as a haven for deviants, and especially for all sorts of patterns of deviation known in other communities. The opportunity for the deviant to be anonymous, to lose his past and begin a new future, furnishes him a chance to convert from a pure deviant to a secret deviant, not by changing his behavior but by changing the knowledge of it on the part of relevant audiences. Furthermore, the very safeguards that protect our value system by providing us with a sense of privacy and freedom may, in the nature of the case, increase the proportion of all deviants whose deviant patterns of behavior are not known to others. An important problem that we shall examine later in our comment on social control concerns the process of detection which, in one sense, is part of the problem of secret deviance.

The situation of the falsely accused (as Becker calls the other interesting cell in his table) is found in the cases of persons who are tried and convicted of offenses and are later found to be innocent of them. Within the legal structure itself, many of the safeguards are obviously designed to protect against giving the official stamp of legitimacy to false accusations. In a jury trial, for example, the requirement of unanimity for a verdict of guilty is a clear indication of the relative value placed upon catching possible deviants versus the possibility of getting the wrong ones into the net. But in organizations where administrative procedure is not as preoccupied with the civil rights of individuals as criminal law, the likelihood of false accusation is much higher than in the courts.

Most important, the whole distinction between behavior and the interpretation placed upon it forces us to examine deviant behavior as an interaction process, and always to treat as problematic the relation between the actor and members of the responding system.

Community," in *Proceedings of the XIV International Congress of Applied Psychology* (Copenhagen: Munksgaard, 1961), pp. 40–59.

[29] Howard S. Becker (cited in footnote 4).

### The Distinction between Cultural Goals and Institutionalized Means

One of the most influential sets of ideas about deviant behavior has been developed by the sociologist Robert K. Merton,[30] who derived the impetus for some of his observations from the early French sociologist, Émile Durkheim.[31]

Merton's aim was to explain the nature and distribution of deviant behavior in societies. Why—he wanted to know—is the rate of various types of deviant behavior likely to be higher in some countries than in others? And within a given society, why is the rate likely to be higher for some segments of that society than for others? His answers to these questions devoted little attention, at least initially, to deviant behavior itself, but rather to the societal conditions that might generate it.

The main idea here involves a distinction between cultural goals and the institutionalized and legitimate means by which they may be achieved. The goal is what is worth striving for—the item or condition of value toward which we direct our activity. The legitimate means are the various procedures by which we can seek to achieve the goal without violating social or legal norms.

Merton's argument derives from this distinction in two ways. First, societies differ in the relative emphasis that they give to the goals themselves, or to the institutionalized means for achieving them. Some societies, which we might think of as "rule-oriented," stress proper and correct procedures most heavily—the norms revealing how an individual is allowed to compete for the goals. Other societies place the emphasis on the goals rather than on the means for their achievement. Second, people *within* a society differ in their proximity to the legitimate means for achieving the goals. Some individuals are in positions that provide easy access to the goals through legal means for achieving them; others are in positions where access to such means is difficult. The main concept here is one of *differential* opportunity or access. By examining the various combinations of attachment to and emphasis on cultural goals versus institutionalized means, Merton develops typology shown in Table 11.3.[32] The modes of adaptation are ways of dealing with the strains created by disjunction between goals and means.

In Merton's formulation, then, there are four important forms of deviant

[30] Robert K. Merton, "Social Structure and Anomie," *American Sociological Review,* 3, 672–682 (1938).
[31] Émile Durkheim, *Suicide, A Study in Sociology,* translated by John A. Spaulding and George Simpson (Glencoe, Ill.: The Free Press, 1951), pp. 241–277.
[32] Robert K. Merton (cited in footnote 30).

**Table 11.3   A Typology of Modes of Adaptation**

| Modes of Adaptation | Cultural Goals | Institutionalized Means |
|---|---|---|
| I. Conformity | + [a] | + |
| II. Innovation | + | − |
| III. Ritualism | − [b] | + |
| IV. Retreatism | − | − |
| V. Rebellion | ± [c] | ± |

[a] The plus signs signify acceptance.
[b] The minus signs signify rejection.
[c] The minus and plus signs signify rejection of prevailing values and substitutions of new values.

behavior. Innovation occurs when persons bypass the available means in order to aim for the ends in question. A good and simple example is almost any form of crime for personal economic gain, where the person is using an illegal but effective means of getting what others hopefully try to achieve through legitimate means such as compensation for work. Ritualists are those who scale down their ambitions and hopes to the point where they can be easily realized by even limited means, which denotes in effect that they continue to abide most compulsively by the institutional norms. Every organization has its stickler for detail, for the proper procedure, who has lost sight of what the goals are all about but who organizes his life around the rules. These persons, of course, will be recognized by some of us as conformists in the sense that they do, indeed, live within the rules of the system. For example, these persons are not usually subjected to the formal sanctions of confinement to a prison or mental hospital, nor are they likely to meet even less powerful sanctions. Merton calls them deviant, however, in the sense that they represent a departure from the culturally supported value that persons are obliged to strive onward and upward, setting increasingly lofty aims and desires as a basis for individual motivation. Retreatists are those who have forsaken both the lofty aspirations and the legitimate means for their attainment, turning instead to escape from the system through alcoholism, drug use, and the like. Finally, rebellion is a desire to replace both goals and means by a new set—in effect, a rejection of the culture and an effort to start a new system in its place.

Predictions about variations in the rates and types of deviance both within and between societies can be made in terms of this typology. Its value may be illustrated by summarizing the use usually made of the theory in helping to explain crime and other forms of "innovating" behavior. In comparing different societies, for example, the prediction must be that societies placing emphasis on personal goal attainment, without similar emphasis on the legitimate means for achieving the goals, will tend to have generally high rates of crime and other forms of "innovating" behavior designed to achieve the goals by whatever means. Merton has argued that the United States is such a society—that we have extolled the value of success without a balance of attention being given to the legitimate means for achieving it. If opportunities were easily accessible to all individuals, there would be no problem, since it would be possible to achieve the goals by legitimate means. But no society has so eliminated the struggle, and it is questionable whether the goal would be worth striving for if everyone could easily attain it. It is, of course, difficult to test these notions because we have no measure of the extent to which a society emphasizes, in its cultural values, goals versus means. No thorough attempt has been made to rate societies on these dimensions. Nevertheless, this idea is one of the important bases for explaining differential rates of crime among societies.

This line of reasoning is applied more frequently to individuals within the same society. Here the argument is straightforward; crime rates will differ according to the extent of "disjuncture" between the goals that persons internalize and the socially structured opportunities for achieving them. In American society, where the goal of material success seems dominant, and where the legitimate means to this success usually require high levels of education and professional training, we would expect high crime rates among the persons least able to obtain good vocational or professional training.

Notice, particularly, that this prediction does not imply that, anywhere and everywhere, persons of lower socioeconomic standing will have higher rates of crime. This will only be true, so the argument goes, when a cultural goal is set for these persons and is therefore in most instances internalized by them as an important aim in life, at the same time that their position makes it difficult to compete for this goal. If the society stresses some other goal (for instance, spirituality) and if lower-status persons are in no worse position to compete for this goal than others, the differences should disappear. Or (to take a more familiar case) if the goals held out to the members of the society differ depending on their social position (as in some caste systems), we would not necessarily expect the same result. For it is where people stand in relation to the goals which they seek that we use to predict their rate of deviant behavior, not where they stand in any absolute sense.

This reasoning, as a plausible account, goes far in helping us interpret some of the usual findings on crime rates. It is certainly true that persons in the lower part of the social order are at a disadvantage in their capacity to compete for monetary success. And since that success, on the basis of other values in American society, is expected to be won primarily by males rather than females, we would expect the male crime rates to be higher than the female rates. Indeed, we might expect relatively well-organized paths of criminal behavior to emerge as routes to financial success for the persons less likely to attain it through legitimate patterns. These paths are suggested by the disproportionate ties of political corruption and organized crime to lower-status ethnic groups in our society.

This theme has been criticized, modified, and extended since its original publication in the 1930s. Some writers have questioned whether the cultural goal of success is indeed held out to all or even to a large percentage of persons across the social strata; they have pointed to the evidence that persons in lower social strata do not necessarily expect their children to proceed far up the educational ladder, are less likely to expect them to hold professional jobs, and so forth.[33] The question concerns the number of positions that are available relative to the number of aspirants; the balance between the two is difficult to judge.

A closely related issue is the extent to which upward mobility is closed to persons near the bottom social stratum. Current programs that provide support for poor but talented students, that provide retraining for school dropouts, that provide special nursery-school training as a preparation for entering elementary school, are all designed to achieve greater equality of opportunity. To the extent that these programs are successful, and to the extent that this theory is correct, crime rates should decrease as more persons are given access to opportunities for developing their skills and talents. In any event, the problem here is primarily one of magnitude, since there is little question that some persons, because of their ethnic, cultural, or personal family backgrounds, are in poorer positions to struggle for success than others. And it is largely in these groups that relatively high official crime rates are found.

Another modification relates to our previous discussion of the conversion

[33] Herbert Hyman, "The Value Systems of Different Classes: A Social-Psychological Contribution of the Analysis of Stratification," in Reinhard Bendix and Seymour M. Lipset, eds., *Class, Status and Power: A Reader in Social Stratification* (Glencoe, Ill.: The Free Press, 1953), pp. 190–203.

of deviant motivation into action. The Merton theory helps us to understand why a person may want to turn to crime or some other illegitimate
activity, but it does not deal very effectively with the realistic difficulties
of moving from one form of adaptation to another. Crime is not a simple
reflex action emitted without any prior training or preparation. Most crimes
are not of that form, and many persons are not in positions where they
can learn to use effectively the necessary means for committing a crime.
How many students can "hotwire" a car, or find a fence for stolen property?
How many have the audacity to be a successful con man, have the manual
dexterity and training to be a successful pickpocket or safecracker, or
have the social ties to gain entry to organized gambling syndicates? These
questions are not as silly as they may seem. Many students would find it
difficult to acquire these skills, even if they were motivated to learn them.
To draw any clear predictions about the probable rates of crime in differing
social statuses, we need to know what access the various statuses provide
their occupants for both legitimate and illegitimate opportunities.[34]

These (and other) qualifying ideas suggest that the theory of illegitimate
or deviant means has been rich in its capacity to create new thought, leading to refinements and modifications in the theory. Unfortunately, evidence
providing efficient tests of these ideas is more difficult to come by. Hopefully, evidence will emerge from current efforts to provide equal opportunities and the associated effort to evaluate these programs.

Thus the typology provides a useful and significant way of examining
how individuals under strain may respond, when the strain has to do with
the relation of means to goals. Many research studies provide evidence
bearing in varying degrees on the Merton formulation, and the concept of
anomie, in particular, remains at the core of sociological thought.

Yet the closer we get into the contents of various patterns of deviant behavior, the less helpful is the scheme. This is only appropriate, since the
scheme is formulated at a high level of abstraction and was not designed to
expose some of the more immediate and concrete ways in which forms of
deviance differ. But it presents a major problem to the student of deviant
phenomena. Once we set aside the special case of ritualism, we are left with
innovation, retreatism, and rebellion as the three categories in which to
compress all of the concrete variations and types of deviation mentioned
above. The significance of group forms versus individual forms, the significance of intentionality, and of the variations in the target of deviant acts—
these and many other meaningful elements are not easy to include systematically.

Thus, although Merton's analysis is the chief one that claims a systematic

[34] Richard Cloward (cited in footnote 25).

theory of deviant behavior in which general propositions are formed regarding conditions under which the rates and types of deviance will vary,
it is similar to the other two classification schemes introduced above in
that each illuminates different aspects of the problem but neither is likely
to be appropriate for all purposes. The three ways of classifying concrete
types of deviation are directed toward different sets of critical factors:
Merton's way involves the strain between means and ends; Blake and
Davis's analysis is directed toward the relation of deviant motives and
deviant acts; and Becker's study involves the relation between the deviant
and those who may respond to him. Each one is an effort to simplify—to
lay bare—the underlying structure and processes related to deviance, and
each one encounters the immense variety of deviant forms as a constant
problem.

If each analysis seems unsatisfactory from some point of view, we might
ask: Why not give up the whole enterprise, return to specific concrete
forms of deviant behavior, and strive for separate explanations of each?
Indeed, much of the literature of deviation is constructed in just these
terms, and we have one or more theories of delinquency, suicide, embezzlement, aggression, withdrawal, schizophrenia, neurosis, pornography,
white-collar crime, and drug addiction (to name but a few). But this, too,
seems highly unsatisfactory. For one thing, such an approach is simply
inelegant and cumbersome. Furthermore, it is lacking in parsimony.
Finally, it suggests greater discreteness to the varied forms than is war-
ranted by the evidence since, despite the uniqueness that each concrete
type of deviance offers, there are clearly some common problems and
processes that appear to cut across many of these forms. Indeed, specific
persons often shift back and forth between deviant styles—as if they, at
least, could see common properties there. Thus the search for creative new
ways of ordering the types of deviation is likely to continue because the
alternative is simply intellectually unsatisfying.

## Basic Causal Processes

Despite the lack of complete agreement on the most feasible way to
split up the field of deviant behavior for purposes of studying why persons
become deviants, there is a common set of elements that most investigators
feel are relevant to the study of almost any particular form of deviation.
These components are likely to be stressed in varying degrees by different
students of deviant behavior, but it is difficult if not impossible to give a
coherent description of the process of becoming a deviant without devoting
at least some attention to each. These basic components include (1) devia-

tion and location in the social structure, (2) patterns of socialization, (3) situational forces and deviation, (4) the drift from deviant acts to deviant roles, and (5) the development of deviant collectivities and subcultures. We shall discuss each of these categories in the abstract, and then we shall give an extended illustration of their relevance and application by referring to work on one particular type of deviant behavior—delinquency. Delinquency is a good choice because it is recognized as an important social problem and is complex enough to illustrate many different features of the process of becoming deviant.

## Deviation and Location in the Social Order

The location of people in the society makes a difference in how they behave. It would be surprising, indeed, if this general fact did not also hold true for deviant behavior. In fact, the majority of all systematic studies of social deviation are probably directed toward establishing the relationship between location in the society and various forms of deviant behavior. We use the term social *location* in a broad sense to include a person's position in the stratification system, his position in the age and sex structure of the society, and his position in the spacial arrangements of the society, especially the character of his place of residence.

Individuals who occupy a particular position are likely to face a common set of problems, and their life chances in various respects will be distributed differently from the life chances of people in other positions. To this extent, a person's position provides varying opportunities and pressures for engaging in deviant behavior. The most general idea is simply that recruitment to patterns of deviation begins with a person's location in the social order, which provides structural inducement for engaging in certain forms of deviation and limitations on other forms.

## Patterns of Socialization

In order to make accurate predictions regarding deviance, however, more is required than knowledge of a person's location in a social order. A most important additional element is clearly the specific patterns of socialization to which persons have been exposed. Although these patterns are, in turn, related to positions in the social structure in some respects, such positions are not solely determinative of socialization patterns, and a closer examination of family interaction and primary group life is required to observe these patterns in detail.

In particular, the development of a moral sense (to the extent that deviance has a moral quality) is important in the control of deviance, and this appears to be related to patterns of family interaction. The formation of internalized controls, whether expressed in the language of psychiatry as "superego" controls or in some other sense, is clearly a basic part of the process. Many studies of systematic deviation show some relationship between patterns of the child's family interaction and socialization and his later conduct. Families filled with conflict and disharmony seem to produce more than their share of children who engage in certain forms of deviance, and families in which the children are raised solely by the mother (because of divorce or absence of the father from the home) may contribute to the rates of deviant conduct. In any event, in the search for an explanation of deviant behavior, it is only natural that many sociologists have turned to the immediate conditions of early socialization in the family in an effort to find its major sources.

But our concept of socialization need not be limited to early family experiences. In this context, schools become a very important sorting station (at least, in modern societies) where patterns of social position may join with patterns of family socialization and create new socialization possibilities within the context of the school. And it is a basic premise of most sociological work that socialization is a continuous process reaching into adulthood and does not stop with early family and school experiences.

### Situational Forces and Deviation

Regardless of the strength of deep underlying forces rooted in the social order, or in the psyche as a result of socialization patterns, a good portion of the genesis of deviant behavior relates to more immediate situational factors. Indeed, even such a dramatic event as the commission of a suicide often has chance elements. Consider the case where a woman, whose husband was almost never late in his arrival at home, apparently planned a gesture of suicide in order to win his sympathy and attention. The woman placed herself in a closed garage and turned on the motor of a car to produce carbon monoxide fumes. She did this just a few moments before her husband was expected to arrive home in the other car so that he could pull her—unconscious—from the garage. On this particular occasion the husband was delayed and therefore could not rescue her before the deed was done. This is an instance of what psychiatrist Edwin Schneideman calls "premeditated nondeath," and it appropriately illustrates the role of situational contingencies in deviant actions and careers.[35]

[35] Edwin Schneideman, "Orientations toward Death: A Vital Aspect of Study of Lives," in R. W. White, ed., *The Study of Lives* (New York: Atherton Press, 1963), pp. 200–227.

The systematic study of situational contingencies in relationship to deviant behavior is only currently gaining a great deal of attention, but investigators are forced to consider it, in part, because of the amount of unexplained variation that is left after one has tried to "control for" social position and factors of socialization and personality.

### The Movement from Deviant Acts to Deviant Roles

Thus far, we have discussed the possible conditions that contribute to the commission of a deviant act. It might seem, from our previous comment, that a deviant actor is simply one who engages in a deviant act at some point in time. But, as much of our earlier discussion suggests this interpretation, it may not be an entirely satisfactory way of looking at the problem. Almost all of us experiment with deviance of some form or another at some point in time, and to say that a deviant is anyone who has ever committed a deviant act would be to include nearly the total population of society. A more useful way of thinking about much of the phenomena of deviance is to examine the emergence of deviant roles.

We use the term deviant role when there is an organized and fairly systematic conception of a particular kind of deviation held by the public, where the deviation has appeared to be not merely a fleeting or passing thing but seems to "belong" to particular persons as part of their character, where the pattern in question is given a name or label so that it is easy to talk about it and easy to carry the concept in our minds, and where the category in question usually entails a whole series of acts or qualities that form a coherent whole, rather than a single characteristic.[36] The category of the addict provides a good, if extreme, example. Public stereotypes of narcotic addicts set them apart from other humans as a special breed, untrustworthy, unable to be reclaimed, likely to commit sex crimes and of course crimes of monetary gain in order to help support the habit. And although many may be addicted, only some will be assigned the role of an addict. For example, medical doctors may have all the physiological and psychological conditions of addiction, but may be able to avoid the role of addict because they have access to the drug and typically can avoid public identification. That identification, in turn, has a self-fulfilling character, in that those who are cast into that mold may find restrictions on their employment, may find that others withdraw from interaction with them, refuse to let their daughters date them, and so forth.

Thus the conversion of deviant acts into deviant roles involves more

[36] S. F. Nadel, *The Theory of Social Structure* (Glencoe, Ill.: The Free Press, 1957), pp. 20–62.

than the sheer frequency of commission of deviant conduct. The emergence of deviant roles involves the study of the systematic ways in which persons respond to deviance and therefore cast other individuals into a particular image. Furthermore, the clear assumption is that once a person who is engaged in a given line of deviant conduct is cast into a deviant role, his orientation to the conventional world and to himself is likely to change in important ways. In particular, his deviation is likely to become an important part of his self-conception and therefore, a very important part of the way in which he thinks about himself and his relation to others.

## The Development of Deviant Collectivities and Subcultures

A fundamental fact of social deviation is that it often occurs in the context of group support, as we noted earlier. Although we may speak of the development of a deviant role without necessarily involving the concept of deviant subculture or deviant subcommunity, it is often the case that persons who occupy these roles are formed together into such a community. A very important part of the study of deviant behavior relates to our understanding of the conditions under which a deviant subculture is likely to form and to flourish.

By deviant subculture we refer to a set of shared understandings, values, and ways of doing things that are at odds with conventional society and, yet, are accepted in common by members of a particular collectivity. Where such a subculture exists, the persons who participate in it gain some of the gratifications and rewards that they would obtain from participation in any culture, but they may do this at the cost of rejection by the conventional world. We may anticipate that such a culture will form wherever a relatively large number of individuals share a common problem of adjustment to conventional society and find difficulty in solving that problem within a conventional framework.[37]

Deviant collectivities and subcultures, like deviant individuals, come in a variety of forms. Some are formal organizations designed to accomplish a specific purpose, such as the overthrow of the dominant political regime. Others are more loosely knit groups like religious sects focused around generalized patterns of belief. Still others may exist in part because each member is supporting his own relatively personal deviant habit, but needs the others for both emotional and instrumental support. An example is the subculture of drug addicts. Each of these different forms will occur under differing structural conditions, are likely to bear varying relationships to those in power who attempt to control them, and are likely to recruit to

[37] Albert K. Cohen, *Delinquent Gangs* (Glencoe, Ill.: The Free Press, 1955), pp. 49–73.

them persons of widely varying types. Although we have discussed the concept of deviant subcultures as the last topic on our brief list, it is by no means clear that this concept is last in any temporal sense. Some persons may be introduced to deviation through their participation in a deviant subculture and others may be deviant first and only learn of the subculture through the fleeting and chance relations that they have had with deviant others.

## Juvenile Delinquency

Each year, approximately 2% of the children who are 10 to 18 years old are likely to appear in juvenile court. This is not a large figure, but it gets much bigger when we examine the proportion of all persons who reach their 18th birthday with at least one appearance in juvenile court on their record. The best estimate for the United States, as a whole, is about 10%, and for boys alone about 17%. This means that approximately 1 out of 6 boys may appear in court at some time during his adolescence.[38] Of course, if we use a different criterion of delinquency (for example, private self-reports of delinquent acts), the numbers would be much higher.[39] The problem is to explain which youths will be found among the delinquents and which will not.

### Delinquency and Social Position

The heart of the delinquency problem in the United States is found among lower-class male adolescents living in the more deteriorated housing areas of our largest central cities. Unquestionably, girls engage in delinquency as well, and so do male youths in small towns or rural areas. In addition, when we study self-reported delinquency (in contrast to delinquency that has been officially registered by the police), many of these different factors seem to be less clear. It remains generally true, however, that the highest rates of delinquency are found in just those sectors that we referred to.[40]

---

[38] Thomas P. Monahan, "On the Incidence of Delinquency," *Social Forces*, **39**, 66–72 (October, 1960); Leonard Savitz, "Delinquency and Migration," in Marvin E. Wolfgang, Leonard Savitz, and Norman Johnson, eds., *The Sociology of Crime and Delinquency* (New York: Wiley, 1962), pp. 199–205; and John C. Ball, "Incidence and Estimated Prevalence of Recorded Delinquency in a Metropolitan Area," *American Sociological Review*, **29**, 91–93 (February, 1964).
[39] Harwin L. Voss, "Socio-Economic Status and Reported Delinquent Behavior," *Social Problems*, **13**(3), 314–324 (1966).
[40] Walter B. Miller, "Lower Class Culture as a Generating Milieu of Gang Delinquency," *The Journal of Social Issues*, **14**(3), 5–19 (1958).

An immediate question, of course, is this: What is there about a poor male youth living in the central and deteriorated areas of a city that produces a relationship to delinquency? For example, is it the sheer hardships faced by the urban poor, the instability and disorganization sometimes found to characterize low-income districts, or what? Efforts to disentangle the possibilities have proceeded along a number of lines. One of the most prominent procedures is the use of a special statistical method called factor analysis. This method is used in conjunction with census data about the characteristics of urban subareas in order to try to find out which characteristics are most closely related.

There has been clear interest, for example, in locating something that resembles the concept of anomie as a possible cause of delinquency—a concept that might operate separately from socioeconomic status. One possible set of indicators of anomie are those things that suggest a highly unstable population base—a base in which it would be difficult to generate a consistent set of normative standards and, consequently, a base that is prone to normlessness. In Lander's well-known investigation, delinquency in Baltimore seemed to be strongly related to such a factor.[41] His indicators of anomie were the percentage of nonwhite residents in a census tract, and the percentage of residents who did not own their own homes. Delinquency was more closely correlated with these indicators than it was with socioeconomic indicators such as average rent or educational level.

The dangers of generalizing these results too far from a narrow empirical base became clear much later, when Chilton re-examined Lander's findings, added to them similar analyses for several other cities, and broadened the range of indicators included in the study.[42] In Chilton's analysis, transiency, low income, and poor housing show consistent relationships to delinquency, but there is no clear and easy separation of anomie from economic factors. The whole bundle of characteristics associated with the urban poor seem bound up with delinquency and, as yet, no one has shown that certain characteristics are clearly dominant in impact relative to others.

In the absence of further data that enable us to disentangle the possible causal features associated with delinquency, researchers have organized their observations and knowledge of urban lower-class life in an effort to provide a coherent theoretical interpretation of it. There are two general lines of interpretation, but there are many subtle distinctions within both.

[41] Bernard Lander, *Toward an Understanding of Juvenile Delinquency* (New York: Columbia University Press, 1954).

[42] Roland J. Chilton, "Continuity in Delinquency Area Research: A Comparison of Studies for Baltimore, Detroit and Indianapolis," *American Sociological Review,* **29(1),** 71–83 (1964). See also David J. Bordua, "Juvenile Delinquency and 'Anomie': An Attempt at Replication," *Social Problems,* **6(3),** 230–238 (1958–59).

One line of interpretation draws very heavily on anthropological observations about lower-class culture. The general argument has been well stated by anthropologist Walter Miller, who has spent many years studying city gangs in the Boston metropolitan area.[43] He observes that there is a core set of values and problems in lower-class culture that distinguishes it from other strata in society and increases the probability that anyone raised in lower-class culture will engage in violations of the law. He speaks of the "focal concerns" of lower-class culture—trouble, toughness, smartness, excitement, and others—all of which may help to create situations in which unlawful activity is likely to emerge. Stress on toughness, for example, leads one to respond to verbal insult with physical attack. Any youth growing up in a tough area, subject to its influences and surrounded by others who are responding to them, is likely to engage in the prohibited conduct himself. By virtue of the normal process of association with these persons the youth will come to adopt their attitudes, feelings, and behavior patterns.

A second line of interpretation does not consider the delinquent conduct of lower-class male youths as a direct expression of the values of lower-class culture but as a reaction against the problems created by a middle-class way of life. Most arguments here derive, in some respect, from the Merton scheme given earlier. Lower-class youths, lacking the opportunities and life chances provided by middle- and upper-class youths, but still incorporating the goals of economic success, may convert into delinquency the frustration caused by that incongruence. In this view, most lower-class delinquency is a form of reaction against the frustrations imposed by middle-class standards in the absence of achievement opportunities, while in the first line of reasoning delinquency does not represent so much a rejection of middle-class standards as an acceptance and enactment of lower-class standards.[44]

We shall comment on these alternatives more fully when we discuss the role of deviant collectivities and subcultures. Here, it is important simply to realize that no matter which alternative is correct, or which combination of both alternatives is correct, the fact still remains that a fairly large number of youths living in lower-class slum conditions do not become delinquents. In the highest delinquency-rate areas of our principal cities, no more than about 20% of the youths become delinquent in any one year, and perhaps two thirds to three fourths of them will have gone to court for delinquency by the time they reach the age of 18. We would still have to explain, then, why the remainder did not go.

[43] Walter B. Miller (cited in footnote 40).
[44] Albert K. Cohen, *Delinquent Boys* (Glencoe, Ill.: The Free Press, 1955).

## Patterns of Socialization

Numerous studies have been conducted that attempt to relate socialization patterns in the family to delinquency. Typically, these studies compare delinquent and nondelinquent youths with regard to the relationships maintained between them and family members. In a classic instance, Healy and Bronner studied delinquent and nondelinquent siblings, thus ruling out the effect of broad factors such as position in the social order, which had to be similar for children of the same parents.[45] Their findings suggested marked differences between delinquent and nondelinquent siblings. The most important finding was that more than 90% of the delinquents, compared to 13% of their nondelinquent siblings, had unhappy home lives and felt discontented with their life circumstances. Some delinquents felt rejected by parents; others felt inadequate or inferior; others were jealous of the siblings; and still others were affected by more deep-seated mental conflict. Delinquency was considered to be a solution to these problems. It brought attention to individuals who suffered from parental neglect, provided support from peers for individuals who felt inadequate, and brought on punishment and therefore reduced guilt feelings.

In a much more recent study, some of these same themes are repeated and new ones are developed. Bandura and Walters gathered detailed interview data from adolescents with records of aggressive action and compared these data with a control sample of nondelinquents.[46] Their investigations suggested that the delinquent youths differed from the nondelinquent controls in having much less identification with their fathers. The delinquent boys failed to internalize a set of moral values, apparently (in part) because of the absence of good role models in their fathers. In addition, discipline was meted out in a harsher manner.

In still another study, McCord, McCord, and Zola showed that delinquency, in addition to being related to such things as poor disciplinary practices, was also found more often in children of parents who were themselves engaging in deviant behavior.[47] Records of drunkenness, promiscuity, or crime on the part of the parents were found more often in cases of delinquents than in cases of nondelinquents from the same general areas.

[45] William Healy and Augusta Bronner, *New Light on Delinquency* (New Haven, Conn.: Yale University Press, 1936).
[46] Albert Bandura and David Walters, *Adolescent Aggression* (New York: Ronald Press, 1959). For another approach, see also Fritz Redl and David Wineman, *Children Who Hate* (Glencoe, Ill.: The Free Press, 1951).
[47] William McCord, Joan McCord, and Irving Zola, *Origins of Crime* (New York: Columbia University Press, 1959).

These studies are not without limitations, but they do establish the general point that patterns of socialization within the family are likely to have some effect upon adolescent conduct. Furthermore, it is interesting to notice the parallel between the interpretations here and those in the previous section. Some adolescents are believed to become delinquent because they are reacting *against* poor parental practices, while others may become delinquent because they are directly learning from deviant-role models. The interpretation that delinquency results from learning directly from deviant-role models takes approximately the same form as the cultural interpretation of delinquency and social position, while the interpretation that delinquency results from a reaction against poor parental practices is similar to the idea of reaction to frustration.

Most of these investigations show the effects of either social position or socialization, but we learn more when their combined effects can be examined. In a recent study, Stanfield has managed to accomplish this.[48] Four variables are crucial to his analysis. The first—delinquency—is measured simply by distinguishing between boys who have appeared and have not appeared one or more times in a court for one or more juvenile offenses. The three variables that are related to delinquency include (1) the father's occupational status (one indicator of social location of the boy), (2) the father's disciplinary methods (one indication of socialization practices), and (3) the frequency with which the boy was involved in peer group activity (a second indicator of some circumstances regarding his socialization experiences). Each of these three variables is related to delinquency in the common-sense manner that we might expect: low occupational status of the father, erratic or lax discipline, and frequent peer activity produce higher rates of delinquency than their opposites.

But the interesting findings occur when we examine the joint effect of these variables. The effect of the father's discipline, for example, appears to depend on the social position that the family occupies. If the father's occupation is one of high status, it makes relatively little difference whether his discipline is lax or consistent. If the father's discipline is lax, 21% of the boys become delinquent, and if the father's discipline is consistent, 13% of the boys become delinquent—a difference of 8%. But in families with low social position, the father's disciplinary practices make considerably more difference. If the father is consistent, about 17% of the boys become delinquent, and if the father is erratic or lax, 39% become delinquent. Thus, it is the combination of low family status and an erratic or lax disciplinary

[48] Robert Edward Stanfield, "The Interaction of Family Variables and Gang Variables in the Aetiology of Delinquency," *Social Problems*, **13**(4), 411–17 (1966).

style that leads to a relatively high rate of delinquency; neither one, acting alone, has nearly as much effect as the two acting together.

The relationship of peer activity to the family's socioeconomic status is quite different. Differences in peer group activities among boys from low-status families do not considerably alter their rates of delinquency. The data show 31% delinquent boys among families with frequent peer activity, and 27% delinquent boys among families with occasional or less peer activity—a difference of 4%. Among the boys from higher-status families, the parallel figures are 28% delinquent among families with frequent peer activity and 8% delinquent among families with occasional or less peer activity—a difference of 20%.

The combined effect of all three variables shows that for boys in families of low status, where the father's discipline is lax or erratic and where peer group activity is frequent, 46% have been found to be delinquent by the court. At the other extreme, among the higher-status families where the father's discipline is consistent and peer activity is infrequent, only 6% of the boys become delinquent.

This study illustrates the increased efforts to examine the combined and interacting effects of different factors. But it is only one effort, and it is limited, since it refers to delinquency several years ago and to delinquents in the Cambridge-Somerville area of Massachusetts. The other studies cited have similar limitations on their generality, but they are intended to demonstrate the sorts of research and findings that are relevant to the general processes of becoming deviant. They are not intended to give a precise descriptive account of the conditions in any particular community.

## Situational Forces and Delinquency

Emphasis on family and on sociocultural inducements to delinquency need not convince us that delinquency is always a deeply rooted trait. A close analysis of the actual ongoing context in which delinquent acts occur suggests that no matter what other facts may operate, situational forces operate also. Wilkins has noted, for example, that probably the best predictor of the auto-theft rate (usually, a youth crime) is not some characteristic of the youths in question but, instead, the number of available automobiles in an area.[49] Youths fashion their lives, make plans, and resolve problems by working with the materials and circumstances at hand.

The situational context does not mean that the events precipitating delinquency are random chance events. Briar and Piliavin have pointed out, for instance, that a slum boy, in the normal course of his life, runs into

[49] Leslie T. Wilkins, *Social Deviance* (Englewood Cliffs, N.J.: Prentice-Hall, 1965).

immediate opportunities for delinquency not easily made available to others.[50] Slum boys are more likely to encounter drunks on the streets who are candidates for rolling, and to be close to business and shopping areas where available articles for theft may be found. Regardless of the impetus provided by broad features of the sociocultural background and by socialization practices, the immediate environmental contacts will show their influence—sometimes toward delinquent modes of expression, and sometimes toward nondelinquent modes.

The concept of risk seems paramount to an understanding of situational features in relation to delinquency. In the interesting work on delinquency by sociologists James Short and Fred Strodtbeck, the problem of risk is subject to a close analysis.[51] They consider the case of a youth in a gang-fight situation deciding whether to "join the action" with gun in hand (thus, running the risk of violence), or whether to remain aloof. The youth's choice depends on his estimate of the probability that violence will occur. If the probability that violence will occur is low, he would rather join the action than remain aloof, perhaps getting credit for stopping the fight and thus increasing his status in the gang or, at least, maintaining it. But if the risk of violence is high, he would prefer not to join the action. If the threatening of his enemies with a gun is successful, there will be no violence and he will be a hero; but if his threat is not successful, someone may be hurt and he might be arrested. When he enters the situation, he may have no intention of using the gun unless he is "forced to." The situational element is in the various contingencies that determine whether he is forced to or not. If certain of these contingencies occur, he may have a jail record; if they do not occur, he may have renewed status with his gang. The difference in official statistics between delinquents and nondelinquents is partly a function of these situational contingencies.

### The Movement from Delinquent Acts to Delinquent Roles

Many youths flirt with delinquency and fail to engage in it; many others engage in it sporadically, but it fails to become a stable part of their character or self-image. Presumably, the transformation of a boy from one who commits delinquencies to a delinquent boy is an important feature of the process by which mature delinquents and criminals are formed. And

[50] Scott Briar and Irving Piliavin, "Delinquency, Situational Inducements and Commitment to Conformity," *Social Problems,* **13**(1), 35–45 (1965).
[51] James F. Short, Jr., and Fred L. Strodtbeck, *Group Process and Gang Delinquency* (Chicago: The University of Chicago Press, 1965) especially pp. 248–264 on aleatory risks.

clearly, too, this process involves events and considerations that cannot be reduced to the three areas already discussed.

In a recent study, inmates of an institution for juvenile delinquents were asked whether a series of other persons—parents, teachers, police, and others—thought of them as troublemakers and, if so, when and how these other persons started to think of them that way.[52] Here is one boy's response to the question as it concerned teachers.

> Well, it was when I entered the eighth grade. You know how other kids look all neat and clean and wear short hair, like they were ready to study. Well, I came in in tight pants and real long hair and everything and pointed shoes, and cigarettes sticking out of my pocket. One teacher said to me, "Oh! a young punk, heh!" I guess when they see me looking like that, they start thinking of me as a juvenile delinquent right off. I don't see as people should think of you that way just because of the way you dress, but I guess they do. And most of the time they are probably right.

This boy had been toying with the symbols of delinquency but apparently had not incorporated them into a systematic image. The teacher's instructions to him on how the traits hang together in the eyes of others helped to accomplish this. Indeed, the same study documents a fact concerning delinquents that is found in other research on the development of self-conceptions: the boys who are most likely to think of themselves as troublemakers are those who believe others think of them that way.

But the assumption of a delinquent role entails more than a mere shift in labels and self-references. Being cast in the role of a delinquent, like being cast in the role of a deviant of any kind, involves a complex array of norms, perceptions, and expectations. In the present case, we know from further talks with the boy that the teachers thoroughly expected him to be a bully—mean, scornful of their efforts to teach him, and prepared to disrupt the class at the slightest opportunity. Similarly, when certain articles were stolen in his neighborhood the police were more than ready to question him about the thefts because it is expected, after all, that young delinquents will steal. And both teachers and police, as well as other agents of the society, were prepared to consider the boy's family as inadequate and harmful for producing a son that behaved that way.

Official pronouncements of delinquency by police or courts are likely to be particularly decisive in the shaping of delinquent roles. Despite efforts by workers in the juvenile-court movement to avoid the stigma usually associated with an official record as a delinquent, a boy with such a record

---

[52] Taken from research in progress. One report of the study from which these materials were drawn is Martha Baum and Stanton Wheeler, "Becoming an Inmate," in Stanton Wheeler, ed., *Controlling Delinquents,* to be published in 1967 by Wiley, New York.

is still likely to find that his legitimate opportunities for school and work are limited, and that he remains under close surveillance. Indeed, these possibilities are part of what sociologist Edwin Lemert calls the development of "secondary deviance"—the deviant behavior that is produced in response to the whole process of labeling and casting a youth in a deviant role.[53] Thus far, empirical research on delinquency has failed to establish clearly the extent to which these processes actually occur, and there is a counterargument to the theme of secondary deviation, which maintains that until the delinquent is caught, charged, and forced to face directly the fact of his delinquency, he will not be motivated to put an end to it. Also, it is clear that many of the individuals who are cast into a delinquent role in adolescence lose that role as they move into the demands of adulthood, including marriage, child rearing, and holding a job. In the Stanfield study mentioned earlier, only about one third of the persons who had juvenile court records were also found to have criminal records as adults for offenses other than traffic violations. Therefore, it is clearly possible to move out of delinquency. But these processes, at the moment, are very poorly understood.

### The Development of Delinquent Collectivities and Subcultures

The bulk of juvenile delinquency has always been group-supported activity. One of the first sociological monographs on delinquency (written in 1927) was Thrasher's *The Gang*, a study of 1313 gangs in the city of Chicago.[54] We simply cannot begin to appreciate the nature of delinquency without being highly sensitive to its group character. There are suggestions from some studies that the delinquents who engage in their crimes with other youths are clearly healthier, in terms of personality, than young persons who are engaged in individual forms of delinquency.

Thrasher's work was largely descriptive, and it was not until the 1950s that serious theoretical questions were raised about the form and structure of delinquent collectivities and subcultures. Until then, researchers took fairly much for granted the existence of a delinquent subculture, and studied why this or that particular boy might happen to participate in it. In addition to the analyses that we have dealt with above, Sutherland's theory of differential association was a prominent explanation.[55] Stated briefly and oversimply, the theory maintains that boys will become de-

[53] Edwin M. Lemert, *Social Pathology* (New York: McGraw-Hill, 1951).
[54] Frederick M. Thrasher, *The Gang* (Chicago: University of Chicago Press, 1927).
[55] Edwin H. Sutherland and Donald R. Cressey, *Principles of Criminology*, sixth edition (Philadelphia: J. B. Lippincott, 1960).

linquent in direct ratio to the intensity, priority, duration, and frequency of their contacts with delinquent ideas or techniques.

Albert Cohen offered one of the first systematic treatments of the genesis of deviant subcultures, and applied his general theory to the development of specifically *delinquent* subcultures.[56] Again oversimplifying, in Cohen's view the delinquent subculture arises chiefly as a means of adapting to the status frustrations and problems found whenever lower-class youths are competing in an essentially middle-class world. The cultural and family backgrounds of lower-class boys leave them unprepared for such things as the delay of gratification, obtaining an education, the importance of study, and the like. Faced with these problems, lower-class boys wind up at the bottom of the heap in the status systems of the school. They do not like being at the bottom and are, therefore, in the market for a solution to their status problems. Through subtle interactive processes, they locate other youths who have the same problems and, together, establish a system that rewards them for the characteristics they do possess rather than denies them status for attributes they cannot easily obtain. Aggressiveness, fighting, attacking the school, all become part of the valued activity of the sub-culture. The important point is that if each child were acting independently, he could not find a solution to the problem, since the solution lies in status and requires the establishment of an alternative status system to the one provided by the conventional social order. And to have status in the eyes of others, there must be mutual consensus on the terms in which status will be awarded.

This theme has been modified and elaborated upon in other studies. Cloward and Ohlin, for example, have detailed three different delinquent subcultures: one organized around fighting and attacks by rival gangs, another around predatory theft, and a third around narcotics and other forms of escapist activity.[57] Although all of these subcultures have roots in the same kind of conditions noted by Cohen and, in part, in the Merton scheme, each subculture has its own distinctive conditions under which it flourishes. Cloward and Ohlin argue that the criminal subculture is found most often where there are strong ties between the adolescent and adult worlds in the urban slum so that youths who get involved in organized crime and the rackets may move upward to higher positions. The conflict subculture, on the other hand, is likely to arise where there are few ties to the adult world, the conflict giving expression to the frustration brought on by lack of either legitimate opportunity or the illegitimate

[56] Albert Cohen (cited in footnote 44).
[57] Richard Cloward and Lloyd Ohlin, *Delinquency and Opportunity* (Glencoe, Ill.: The Free Press, 1960).

channels made possible through organized theft and crime. The narcotic subculture, according to Cloward and Ohlin, is likely to be found among individuals who are "double failures"—those who, failing to be successful in conventional terms, are also failures in the world of illegitimate opportunities. In a recent effort to test these ideas systematically, Short and Strodtbeck examined gangs in the city of Chicago. They found clear evidence of what looked like subcultures built around gang conflict and narcotics, but found little evidence of gangs systematically organized around theft.[58]

### The Blending of Processes

Within a single chapter, it is impossible to convey adequately the way in which each of the five features that we have discussed blend together to give us a fuller understanding of delinquency. Although it is important to divide these influences into their component parts in some fashion (such as we have done), all of the influences are likely to blend together in a single causal process, even though the weight or importance attached to any one component may differ, depending upon the kind of delinquency or delinquent that we are concerned with.

Conditions of social background, for example, broadly locate persons in social space and thus influence the sorts of situational contingencies in which they find themselves. If this is combined with parental laxity so the youth in question spends most of his time on the street-corner, he is more readily available for recruitment into deviant groups, and may more easily be seen by policemen, teachers and others as falling into a delinquent mold. But if some of these elements are different, they may offset the effects of the others. A continued finding, for example, is that Japanese children are less prone to delinquency than either their Caucasian or Negro counterparts in our largest urban areas, one apparent reason being the strength and traditions of family life in the Japanese community.

We have used urban lower-class delinquency as a convenient example to illustrate the kinds of empirical research and theoretical formulation that may develop around a particular form of deviation. In order to clarify the utility of these various forms of analysis, let us suggest very briefly how some other types of deviant behavior might look when examined in similar fashion.

The relevance of early socialization in the family to later deviant careers is clearly more important for some forms of deviance than for others. It

[58] James F. Short, Jr., and Fred L. Strodtbeck (cited in footnote 51).

is likely to be important in any form of deviant behavior expressed among youths, and has been a prominent feature of most efforts to understand severe mental illness such as schizophrenia, where the nature of the parent-child and family relations is a very prominent focus of attention.[59]

We might find other elements much more important if we had chosen to examine deviant religious sects or extremist political movements. Indeed, those forms of collective deviation in which conventional standards are attacked and movements organized to establish new sets of values, whether political or religious, typically cannot be understood at all in terms of early childhood experience. Conditions for emergence of a value-oriented social movement typically have much to do with conditions in the society, less with particular individual characteristics. Smelser summarized some of the characteristics of situations in which value-oriented social movements seem to arise and take hold, and found them most frequently among politically disinherited peoples, such as recent migrants, among colonially dominated peoples, and among persecuted minorities. Furthermore, such movements were most likely in the context of an inflexible political structure that provided little room for legitimate forms of dissent and thus little opportunity for the formation of organized and legitimate means of pressing for reforms.[60]

This is simply to indicate, then, that a different blend of causal factors will be found when one shifts to different types of deviant behavior. If we were examining deviation within the setting of a concrete formal organization such as an office or a workplace, the relation of subordinates to superiors would be extremely important.[61] Finally, there are a number of forms of deviance, recruitment to which begins at positions in the social order other than within urban lower-class slums. Participation in groups using hallucinogenic drugs, for example, would be hard to understand in those terms, as would participation in ultraconservative political movements or white collar crime.

Indeed, a full and scientifically adequate perspective on the process of becoming a deviant requires that increased attention be given to the social conditions underlying the formation of a whole variety of deviant practices. As in the case of some other fields of study, we have developed the social

[59] Gregory Bateson, Don D. Jackson, Jay Haley and John Weakland, "The Genesis of Mental Disorders and Social Deviance," *Behavioral Science,* 1, 251–264 (1956); August B. Hollingshead and Frederick C. Redlich (cited in footnote 16); and J. Myers and B. Roberts, *Family and Class Dynamics in Mental Illness* (New York: Wiley, 1959).
[60] Neil J. Smelser, *Theory of Collective Behavior* (New York: The Free Press, 1963). See particularly Chapter 10 on "The Value-Oriented Movement."
[61] Theodore D. Kemper, "Representative Roles and the Legitimation of Deviance," *Social Problems,* 13(3), 288–297 (1966).

psychology of deviation far beyond the sociology of it. We are able to begin to answer the question: Why does this or that person become a deviant? But we must learn to answer other questions: What accounts for the emergence and patterning of different types of deviant activities? What are the characteristic interrelationships between different types of deviant collectivities and movements? These questions are currently being considered in the research on deviance, and answers to them will often require that we use as our chief unit of analysis the deviant group or movement itself, instead of the deviant individual within it.

## The Machinery of Social Control

Now we consider the third set of problems to be dealt with in this chapter: problems concerning the machinery of social control. Complex social systems have developed an elaborate set of mechanisms for the processing of social deviants, and we shall examine how these mechanisms are linked together, how they function, and what their effects are.

The most basic part of the social-control apparatus in any system, however, is not the network of agencies that comprise the formal social-control apparatus. Instead, it is an invisible part of daily social life. If the society is functioning effectively, most of its members will be guided by internalized standards of conduct that they share with others and that fall within the normative boundaries of the system, and will feel uncomfortable at even the thought of violating those standards. Thus the most basic social-control mechanism is the internalization of social norms. The society plans ahead, in effect, preparing individuals to guide their conduct without the need for invoking the heavy machinery of social control.

Even when internalized controls do not operate, informal social processes function continuously to keep people in line with conventional standards. Talcott Parsons stated the matter well:

Actors are continually doing and saying things which are more or less "out of line," such as by insinuation impugning someone's motives or presuming too much. Careful observation will show that others in the situation often without being aware of it, tend to react to these minor deviances in such a way as to bring the deviant back "into line," by tactfully disagreeing with him, by a silence which underlines the fact that what he said was not acceptable, or very often by humor as a tension-release, as a result of which he comes to see himself more nearly as others see him. These minor control mechanisms are, it may be maintained, the way in which the institutionalized values are implemented in behavior. They are, on a certain level, the most fundamental mechanisms of all, and only when they break down does it become necessary for more elaborate and specialized mechanisms to come into play.[62]

The social-control machinery, then, is a little like the part of the iceberg that shows above the surface. The great bulk of deviant thoughts are not converted into deviant actions, and most deviant actions do not get caught up in the formal control processes. This does not mean, however, that the formal machinery is only important in the particular instances in which it is actually invoked. The mere presence of this machinery may be felt in two important ways. First, it may be effective in a straightforward manner as a deterrent: knowledge of the reaction system may prevent some deviant acts even where internal mechanisms and interpersonal influences are not effective. And second, the machinery itself, by pointing to the normative boundaries of the system, may serve as an educative and socializing influence.[63]

When we begin examining the actual operation of social-control processes at the level of complex social units, it is necessary to break down the global concept of social control into its component stages. At one time this perhaps would not have been necessary, since social-control mechanisms were believed to operate in almost a reflex manner in response to acts of deviation. Indeed, Durkheim described homogeneous social systems guided by a broad consensus among their members as social systems characterized by "mechanical solidarity" in which the response to deviation was, indeed, unthinking and mechanical because any deviant act offended the common conscience to such an extent that an immediate controlling response was automatic.[64]

This image of a homogeneous community response may have been overdrawn even as it applied to primitive societies, and it is certainly overdrawn for the largest portion of social control in modern societies. In the remainder of this chapter, we shall describe these component stages in the abstract; we shall raise what seem to be significant questions about them; and we shall then apply these questions to our concrete illustration of delinquency.

The social-control machinery begins with the *definition of conduct as deviant*. In American society, formal and official definitions of acts as deviant occur largely in the legislative process at state, local, and national levels. These legislative groups, in turn, are subject to the influence of a vast array of interest groups that are concerned with promulgating their own definition of deviance. Many members of the interest groups may be

[62] Talcott Parsons, *The Social System* (Glencoe, Ill.: The Free Press, 1951), p. 303.
[63] Johs Andenas, "General Prevention, Illusion or Reality?" *Journal of Criminal Law, Criminology and Police Science*, 43(2), 176–198 (1952).
[64] Émile Durkheim, *The Division of Labor in Society*, op. cit.

persons who are experts in the particular area of conduct being considered. States periodically revise their criminal codes, for example, and establish new sets of penal sanctions. At these intervals, basic questions must be faced as to what ought to be defined as criminal and why. Legislative study groups, subcommittees of bar associations, voluntary associations with special interests in crime, all contribute to the process of shaping the new definitions.

A variety of exciting questions must be raised about these processes. Under what conditions, for example, will social systems tend to define many different areas of conduct as deviant and under what conditions will they define relatively few? It has been argued (at least since Tocqueville) that American society has always placed great reliance upon the formal definition of conduct as deviant, as reflected in the vast number of laws regarding what, in some other societies, are regarded as relatively private matters. The regulation of sexual conduct in the United States is particularly striking, with a multitude of statutes in most states giving expression to the moral sentiments of a portion of the population. What are the consequences of shrinking the number of acts defined as deviant and of reducing the severity of sanctions attached to them? What is the relation between the actual standards and informed public opinion? [65] What are the social conditions that generate the creation and modification of normative standards? [66] Here, we can merely raise these questions, note their importance for developing an understanding of social control, and note that some important work on the problems has already been done but that a vast amount remains.[67]

The various statutes found in criminal law and the statutes and administrative procedures that define mental illness may be conceived as laying down the minimum conditions for participation in a society for any person who has reached maturity. Inability or incapacity to meet these minimal conditions is treated as legitimate grounds for the removal of a person from full participation in the society, and this removal is both physically and symbolically represented by the presence of prisons and

[65] Julius Cohen, A. H. Reginald and Alan Bates, *Parental Authority: The Community and the Law* (New Brunswick: Rutgers University Press, 1958). See also Arnold M. Rose and Arthur F. Press, "Does the Punishment Fit the Crime: A Study in Social Valuation," *American Journal of Sociology,* **61**, 247–259 (November, 1955).

[66] For a case study see Jerome Hall, *Theft, Law and Society* (Boston: Little, Brown, 1935), and William Chambliss, "A Sociological Analysis of the Law of Vagrancy," *Social Problems,* **12**, 67–77 (summer, 1964).

[67] Much of this work is included in the study of the Sociology of Law. For a review see, Jerome H. Skolnick, "The Sociology of Law in America: Overview and Trends," supplement to *Social Problems,* **13(1)**, 4–38 (summer, 1965).

mental hospitals. But a great deal of the norm setting, in an increasingly complex social order, occurs around specialized and differentiated activities. Participation in the society in a specialized way requires more than a meeting of minimum conditions. Conformity and deviation within the sphere of occupational roles are particularly crucial, and much social-control machinery centers around occupations. All of the licensing and standard-setting organizations and associations related to occupations and professions are part of the machinery for producing definitions of deviant conduct. These organizations determine the standards that must be met if a person legally is to practice a trade or profession. Thus, a person cannot cut hair for profit without a barber's license, nor can a person practice medicine, law, accounting, psychology, or engage in electrical wiring without the approval of accrediting agencies. Indeed, any conduct that requires, for its legality, a license given by an administrative board automatically defines a broad category of potential deviants: all those persons who would like to engage in the conduct but who do not have the means to obtain the license. And, in addition to the norm setting that occurs around occupational spheres, there are a vast array of quasi-legislative operations, all of which have something to do with the definition of conduct as deviant. The Securities and Exchange Commission, for example, regulates the marketing of securities and establishes conditions under which this marketing is illegal.

It should be evident, then, that the definition of conduct as deviant and the establishing of sanctions for misconduct is a general and basic feature of social systems—one that requires both energy and enterprise. Therefore, in addition to the questions raised earlier in this chapter regarding the social definition of deviance, an appropriate and important subject for sociological inquiry concerns the nature and functioning of all of the social agencies that are responsible for generating the definitions.

But definitions of deviant conduct are not enough. The concrete process of social control usually begins when the abstract definitions are applied in concrete cases, and a prime requirement for their application is the *detection* of actual deviants. Only in the limiting case of full and open observability of all conduct and attitudes is the detection of deviation unproblematic. It is certainly not so in modern societies. On the contrary, modern societies usually have made a heavy investment in the detection of social deviation.

By detection we mean all those agencies and processes that lead persons to become aware of and knowledgeable about the deviant behavior that occurs in society. Recognition and awareness are perhaps more neutral terms, and characterize the informal process of discovering deviant patterns of conduct. For example, a fairly elaborate set of informal cues leads to recognition that a person is a homosexual.[68] But, to the extent that complex systems maintain differentiated units whose *job* it is to become aware of deviant behavior, the word detection seems appropriate. In American society the major work of detection, with respect to forms of deviance that involve breaking the law, is performed by the public and private police. Indeed, the public police are second only to teachers in the number of service persons that are on the typical public payroll. And the average citizen, after leaving school, is probably more likely to have contact with the police than with any other single branch of public officials. There are also vast numbers of private police, of course, who perform detective and other functions related to the private sector. A great bulk of all employee theft and theft from commercial establishments such as department stores is processed by private policing mechanisms.[69]

Although the police are the most visible agency involved in the detection of deviation, they are by no means the only ones involved. With respect to forms of deviation closer to the concept of mental illness, an enormous number of guidance personnel—school counselors, social workers, psychiatrists, and others—become involved in the detection process. Citizens may also detect deviance, and report to official agencies.

A question of great importance to the study of detection processes is this: What conditions determine the extent to which the persons who engage in acts of deviation are detected? In the case of the police, for example, less than one quarter of all offenses that become known to the police are actually resolved by the arrest of someone, and thus the "detection" rate is quite low. But it is undoubtedly different in various departments, and little is known about the social organization of police systems and about how police systems might be organized to produce higher rates of detection. Other important general questions about detection processes include these: When will deviants make their detection easier by their own possible conscious or unconscious desire to be caught? Are there particular personality types who like to "stick their nose in other people's business" and, therefore, play an informal detective role for the society? Do recruits to occupations that involve detection and surveillance display particular personality components? In view of the problematic character of deviant behavior, are there particular organizational problems facing any organization that must deal systematically with the detection of deviation? [70]

---

[68] John I. Kitsuse, "Societal Reaction to Deviant Behavior: Problems of Theory and Method," in Howard S. Becker, ed., *The Other Side: Perspectives on Deviance* (New York: The Free Press of Glencoe, 1964), pp. 87–102.

[69] Mary Owen Cameron, *The Booster and the Snitch* (New York: The Free Press, 1964).

[70] An important recent source for material on the organization of police systems is Jerome H. Skolnick, *Justice Without Trial: Law Enforcement in a Democratic Society* (New York: Wiley, 1966).

Detection itself is by no means the last step in the process of social control. The *decision to control*—especially in complex systems—is itself problematic, and does not automatically follow detection. Questions of the efficiency of the social-control mechanism are always balanced against problems of justice, since most social-control processes involve deprivation of individual liberty for the persons who are caught up in them. Thus, we have an elaborate adjudicative machinery to establish an official pronouncement regarding the deviant conduct in question, and we do not merely automatically ratify the detecting agency's operations. In a criminal court process, there is the presumption of innocence, the availabilty of defense counsel, the jury system, and other related mechanisms to assure that the decision to control is not taken lightly but meets standards of legality and due process of law. When the form of deviant behavior comes closer to mental illness, there are usually requirements that the potential patient be studied by persons who are presumed to be experts, and courts generally are unable to confine mental patients without certification.

The actual standards governing the formal pronouncement of deviance and the decision to control are, of course, themselves subject to debate, and these standards change with varying social conditions. Indeed, in the United States today there is a broad wave of concern and interest in these standards. This concern is apparent in Supreme Court decisions designed to increase the degree to which a potential offender is justly processed— important questions are raised involving the right to counsel, the admission of evidence, and the role of confessions. This concern also appears in conjunction with processes of admission to mental hospitals; we recognize that admissions are sometimes given on a perfunctory basis and that the definitions of illness are themselves vague and unreliable; and, more generally, we recognize that procedures for civil commitment may often be used as an unjust invasion of privacy and deprivation of liberty.[71]

Similar procedures operate within the sphere of commerce in order to pass judgment on persons who might be considered deviant in connection with their occupational life—for example, disbarment proceedings for lawyers, civil service hearings for persons charged with malfeasance of some kind, and court martial procedures in the military. Vital questions in the comparative study of social-control processes are thus raised by examination of the formal decision-making apparatuses. Under what conditions will systems surrender part of their efficiency in order to "protect the innocent?" What is the balance of power between the potential deviant and the persons who represent the official agencies? What limitations will agencies

[71] Thomas Szasz, *Psychiatric Justice* (New York: Macmillan, 1965). See also Thomas Szasz, *Law, Liberty, and Psychiatry* (New York: Macmillan, 1963).

place upon their legitimate domain of control? [72] These and related questions occupy an increasingly important role in the developing field of the sociology of law, and are obviously important to anyone who is studying social-control processes.

When the formal decision to control has been made, we usually enter a phase of what (for lack of a better term) can be called by its medical analogue: *diagnosis.* In this context we simply mean the effort to determine the nature of the problem that characterizes the deviant. For, before some determinative action can be taken, it is necessary to decide what sort of a problem the deviant presents. And, by diagnosis, we explicitly do not mean to limit the concept to expert opinion, but would include any concept of the causes of a deviant's problem that may be relevant to the actions to be taken. Thus, there are included all of the implicit and explicit conceptions of deviant behavior that influence the reactive mechanisms. [73] Perhaps the most important distinction is whether the deviant is viewed as having intended his deviant actions, and therefore ought to be held responsible for them, or whether the assumption is that the deviant is not responsible for his deviant acts because he was *incapable* of conformity under the circumstances. This distinction is approximately the same as the distinction between persons who will not behave in conventional fashion and those who cannot, and more generally in the distinction between the criminal and the sick. [74] This is a powerful means by which the society divides people— as is indicated in the existence of separate procedures for commitment, separate legal structures, and separate institutions for those judged to be criminal, on the one hand, and those diagnosed as sick, on the other hand. Samuel Butler illustrated the power of the distinction in Erewhon, the mythical country where illness was treated as a moral lapse for which the miscreant was punished, and crime was treated as a pathological condition requiring tender care and concern. [75]

Other perspectives on the deviant's condition are also important. If he was brought to the deviant act through some natural causal process, are the reasons conceived to be primarily biological, psychological, or sociocul-

[72] Theodore M. Millis, "Equilibrium and the Processes of Deviance and Control," *American Sociological Review,* **24,** 671–679 (1959).

[73] For an extended discussion of some conceptions of deviance that influence reactions see Eliot Freidson in "Disability as Social Deviance," in Marvin B. Sussman, ed., *Sociology and Rehabilitation* (Washington, D.C.: American Sociological Association and Vocational Rehabilitation Administration, 1965).

[74] Vilhelm Aubert and Sheldon Messinger, "The Criminal and the Sick," *Inquiry,* pp. 137–160 (autumn, 1958).

[75] Samuel Butler, *Erewhon and Erewhon Revisited* (New York: Modern Library, Random House, 1955).

tural? Is it presumed that he could not behave differently? Is the deviant conduct symptomatic of some deeper problem or disturbance? These and many other similar questions may be raised in an effort to arrive at a definition of the person's problem, and an elaborate network of agents may be invoked to find the appropriate answer. Social workers, probation officers, guidance personnel, participants in psychiatric court clinics, the clergy, and others may be involved in evolving a diagnosis. In the administrative structure of the courts, for example, presentence investigations by the probation staff are designed to provide the judge with information of this sort and, thus, to enable him to make an appropriate disposition of the case.

The comparative study of this stage in the social-control process is greatly needed if we are to understand fully the process of social control. Under what social conditions, for example, do persons interpret the actions of other persons as being caused by impersonal events, and under what conditions do they interpret the actions of others as being caused by their own wish or desire? Problems of the phenomenology of causality are raised here, as are questions about preferred cultural definitions.[76] Some societies are more likely to interpret a given act as a symptom of sickness rather than sin, while other societies are less likely to make this interpretation. Certainly, the major trend in modern nations is to bring to bear the power of science on the diagnostic process but, even here, many extrascientific considerations enter into the picture and help to determine which group will be able to have its diagnoses accepted by those in power.

A final stage in this problem-solving process is reached with the disposition—by which we mean simply the way in which the detected deviant, who falls within the legitimate control of the agencies in question, is dealt with by those agencies. The disposition may range from doing nothing to a wide set of alternatives available within the official repertoire of responses. Fines, outpatient treatment, confinement to prison, probation, requirement of restitution to victims, and an infinite variety of other responses are likely to be available in modern societies. We could order these dispositions in many ways. Perhaps the most important way, from the point of view of the individual involved, is the degree to which the disposition interferes with the individual's normal life circumstances. Probation, for example, probably would seem to interfere less than imprisonment, since probation leaves the offender in the community. A distinct but related way of ordering the dispositions is in terms of the amount of social stigma that they carry. Apparently, for example, a requirement that a person

[76] Fritz Heider, "Phenomenal Causality," *Psychological Bulletin* (1944).

must consult a psychiatrist is more stigmatizing than a requirement that he must consult the clergy.[77]

Just as each of the other steps in the process has its own causes and determinants, so do dispositions, and the determinants of variations in dispositions should be studied. There are known to be enormous variations, for example, in the length and severity of sentences meted out to offenders processed by different courts. What are some of the causes of these differences? Are they attributed to the personality of the judges, the structure of the courts, differences in the types of offenders passing through the courts, or what? We can probably anticipate stable relationships between the nature of the decision-making stages and the diagnostic procedures, on the one hand, and the dispositions actually arrived at, on the other. Individual differences in disposition are likely to be maximized in systems that depend on expertise and individual clinical judgment, while the dispositions are likely to be more uniform in systems where the concept of justice is given greater emphasis. Indeed, different lines of study of the processing of criminals suggest that the move toward a more scientific, psychiatric, and therapeutic concern brought with it increasing individual variation in sentencing.

The five stages that we have outlined—definition, detection, decision, diagnosis, and disposition—are analytically distinct, and refer to separate functions that occur in the process of social control. However, the actual concrete processes involving police, psychiatrists, court officials and the like can be sorted only crudely into these separate analytic stages. And often, of course, the concrete practices blend together in a single process of social control. In fact, a number of points should be made about the process as a whole.

1. Social systems may vary greatly in the degree to which each of these stages is differentiated and organized around separate roles. A limiting case is an individual who engages consciously in self-control. A student, for example, may have a definite concept of how much work is required to get a passing grade in a course. He observes that on the last examination he did not meet this standard, and decides that it was not fate but that he can do something about it. He diagnoses the problem as one of having studied too many nights in a row, and prescribes a movie for himself as the most effective way of bringing his performance back to standard. But it is typical in modern societies to find that these steps are differentiated and that different agents are important at different stages. Even

[77] Derek L. Phillips, "Rejection: A Possible Consequence of Seeking Help for Mental Disorders," *American Sociological Review,* **28(6),** 693–672 (December, 1963).

here, however, there is immense variation, depending on the type of deviation in question. For example, psychiatrists are likely to be involved in *all* of the stages in the processing of mental illness. They help to write the statutes; they are asked to pass judgment on whether the person is ill; they are asked to sign papers exerting legal control, to diagnose the nature of the illness, and to prescribe the treatment. In contrast, a person passing through the system of criminal adjudication will find that the statutes have been written by lawyers, that he is arrested by the police, that judges guide the decision process, that probation officers, psychiatrists, and others may have a hand in the diagnosis, and that an administrative tribunal may be responsible for setting a sentence. These variations are likely to produce corresponding differences in the feelings that persons have about the processing mechanisms through which they pass.

2. Although we have described the five stages as logical steps in a problem-solving sequence, it is very clear that the order often does not follow the logic. A policeman may decide whether to pick up alcoholics and vagrants partly on his estimate of what the court will, in fact, do. The starting of a new open ward in a mental hospital may force a re-diagnosis of patients so that the nature of the problem for some patients is changed and allows them an open-ward status.[78] Overcrowded conditions at a state hospital or prison may lead judges to refuse to commit inmates. These and other processes suggest a little about the nature of the feedbacks that may operate within the system of social control.

3. The whole structure of the system may depend heavily on the broader values that the process of social control is designed to fulfill. In some systems, emphasis may be placed on *protecting the system,* while in others it may be placed on restoration of the *deviant member* of the system. Where emphasis is placed on protecting the system, actions may be justified on the grounds of community protection and safety that could never be justified on the grounds of therapeutic benefit. Where emphasis is placed on restoration of the deviant member of the system, there may be instances in which adequate therapeutic benefits are believed to require a more severe deprivation of liberty than is necessary for community protection or for justice to be achieved. Also, where the primary concern is for the system rather than for the individual deviant, we may find acts being considered for their deterrent effect on other members of this system, rather than for immediate protection from the deviant in question.

4. A very important factor in determining the character of actions at each stage of the social-control process is whether we presume the system to be based on consensus and *harmony,* or whether we presume that the

[78] Harley Frank, unpublished Ph.D. dissertation on Mental Hospitals.

system is one in which conflicting interests are dominant. In a system in which conflicting interests are dominant, there may be controls at each step in the process to assure fair and just treatment and to protect against the imposition of unjust penalties or sanctions. In a system based on consensus and harmony, the need for such protection will be less, because of the presumed benevolence of the guiding authorities in the system. A clear instance of the relevance of this distinction for university life is the handling of dismissals of students from colleges and universities. In one analysis, the dispute between the students and the administration at Berkeley was conceived largely in these terms.[79] Is the relationship one of child to benevolent father, in which the sanctions meted out should not be examined for qualities of legality, or is it one of prosecution and defense, in which the student should be afforded the protections usually reserved for defendants in criminal trials?

5. In the typical social-control process, a cycle of stages may operate so that the disposition of one agency triggers off the definition and detection apparatus of the next, and so on. Thus, although the primary function of the police is detection, the police themselves have a variety of disposition alternatives available; they may exercise discretion in the use of these alternatives, and may well be guided by common-sense conceptions of the causes of the deviations in question in making their choices. A person who behaves in an "unreasonable" fashion may be booked for disorderly conduct, or taken to a hospital and put under observation for mental illness.[80] Thus the total process of social control is likely to involve several sequences of definition, detection, decision, diagnosis, and disposition.

6. Although we have described social-control processes as though they were applied only to individuals, it is very clear that the model applies to collectivities as well. Congressional investigations bring to light, for example, the extent of deviant conduct among members of the Ku Klux Klan (deviance now being judged against the norms of the nation as whole, and not against particular regional values). One result is the large commitment of federal resources for the detection of violence by the Klan, and special efforts to secure justice through the courts when Klan members come to trial. The social consequences of certain forms of collective deviation are believed to be great enough to justify special procedures for processing and control. For example, pressures have been brought to bear to make wire tapping legal, in efforts to fight organized crime and gambling syndicates.

[79] Jerome H. Skolnick, pp. 25–27 (cited in footnote 67).
[80] Egon Bittner, "Police Discretion in Emergency Apprehension of Mentally Ill Persons," to be published in *Social Problems*.

7. Finally, a highly differentiated social-control system (such as is found in our modern societies) creates clear problems of integration of the differentiated parts. Since prospective deviants are handed along from one agent to another, any differences in the modes of dealing with the problems we have discussed are likely to be communicated to the deviant, and he may get a very unclear conception of the process through which he is moving. Furthermore, there may be outright conflict between the various components, leading to further difficulties within the system. Perhaps the most prominent example in our current control networks is the conflict between persons who approach deviation within a punitive moralistic framework and persons who are more permissive and deterministically oriented.

## The Control of Juvenile Delinquency

Juvenile delinquency as a new form of deviance was established in American society around 1899. During that year, in the state of Illinois (and, later, in other jurisdictions), statutes were passed that distinguished delinquency from adult criminal conduct, and provided for special administrative procedures for the processing of delinquents. The statutory definitions of delinquency were broad and often vague—unlike the precise specifications of criminal conduct found in most criminal codes. In addition to acts that would be considered as crimes if they were committed by adults, the delinquency laws usually included such things as ungovernability, habitual truancy, and the like.

The most important forces leading to the new legislation were clearly humanitarian. There was a strong desire to separate youthful offenders from adult criminals, an unmistakable feeling that delinquents were not fully responsible for their conduct, and a belief in therapy or rehabilitation as the goal of remedial efforts, rather than condemnation and punishment. Increasingly, however, persons have sensed a wide gap between the ideology underlying the original creation of delinquency as a new form of deviance and the realities that have emerged in practice.[81]

One of the evident problems concerns detection. The hazy and open-ended character of delinquency legislation means that wide areas of discretion are opened to the police in deciding which youths ought to be picked up and charged with delinquency. Many police systems have

[81] The practical side of these issues is treated in Stanton Wheeler, Leonard S. Cottrell, Jr., and Anne Romasco, *Juvenile Delinquency Its Prevention and Control* (New York: Russell Sage Foundation, 1966).

developed specialized juvenile bureaus (composed of police) to deal with this problem. In one investigation in which two of these bureaus were compared, it was found that (contrary to anticipation) the department whose juvenile officers had more advanced and professional training (and, thus, were more prepared to consider delinquents as problem children) actually had much higher rates of arrest for juveniles than a department in which these conditions did not hold true.[82] Although the apparent causes were complex, two elements seemed clear: (1) the more sophisticated ideology of the more professionalized juvenile-bureau operation led to a greater sensitivity to delinquent conduct as a problem and hence to more stringent intervention policies; and (2) the more professionalized department was organized so that the juvenile bureau was housed in a central administrative unit, while in the more traditional force juvenile work was arranged through precinct stations where standard police work was the dominant activity. It seemed apparent to the researcher that juvenile officers were much more willing to bring in youths in the centralized system (as contrasted with the decentralized system) because the juvenile officers were less likely to meet with sarcasm and mocking from officers who dealt with adult criminals and consequently felt that juvenile work was for sissies. In any event, it seemed clear that the rate of detection and arrest for juveniles in these two communities depended at least as much on the organization of the detection apparatus as it did on the behavior of the youths in question.

Similar problems have been evident in the actual operation of the juvenile court itself, and therefore in the decision process. Clearly, the philosophy of the juvenile court is that it acts in the interest of the child, rather than in the interest of pronouncing moral condemnation on the community. The judge is considered as acting in lieu of the parents—as a firm but kind father who knows what is best for children in trouble. Efforts were thus made to strip away the standard regimen of the criminal court process and its stigmatizing features. The incorporation of the rehabilitative idea in behalf of the child has meant that the formal austerity of the criminal courtroom is not found in most juvenile hearings. Questions and problems are likely to concern such matters as the nature of the boy's character, his family upbringing, and parental disharmony, and there is a withdrawal of systematic attention from the specific conduct leading to the youth's appearance in court. Indeed, little formal effort may be exerted to establish that the youth has actually committed a specific offense. Actually,

---

[82] James Q. Wilson, "The Police and the Delinquent in Two Cities," in Stanton Wheeler, ed., *Controlling Delinquents,* to be published in 1967 by Wiley, New York.

because the court is presumed to act in benevolent fashion, less evidence and less due process are required to label a juvenile a delinquent than to label an adult a criminal.[83]

The changed conception of the decision process has its strict analogies in both diagnosis and disposition of delinquency. In view of the concern for rehabilitation and for the individual delinquent, judges have had a wide range of discretion in prescribing sanctions for juvenile offenders. Juveniles who have committed minor crimes (but who, in the judge's opinion, present severe problems) may be sent to a youth institution, while others who have committed more serious offenses may be released. The dispositions actually handed out by the judge apparently are often based at least as much on the judge's ideology, training, and his studying of the delinquent's record as on the seriousness of the offense in question and its resultant danger to the community. Indeed, in one study there is some evidence that the very judges who adopted a social-welfare attitude actually handed out more severe dispositions. Judges who read the social-work literature, who rarely wear robes in court, and who appear to be less punitive on attitude measures actually place more youths in institutions than do other judges. An apparent reason is that commitment to an institution is itself considered as a form of therapeutic response rather than punishment and, therefore, can be justified more easily by the more therapeutically oriented judges than by judges with a more austere judicial outlook. Conditions and programs in most youth institutions, however, lend little support to this image.[84]

As a result of the interaction of all of these factors, many persons have become increasingly concerned because the outcomes of the juvenile court process do not really match the ideology initially intended. Although the legal safeguards usually attached to adult criminal court proceedings have been withdrawn, it is evident that this withdrawal has not always been accompanied by benefits to the juvenile. This is especially true in view of the lack of really effective therapies since, at the moment, there is no verified proof that any particular program of correction or rehabilitation actually works.[85] The result is that many analysts feel that juveniles have not been given justice and fairness when they have met with the juvenile court. As a recent Supreme Court decision states: "There is evidence, in fact, that there may be grounds for concern that the child receives the worst of both

[83] Francis A. Allen, *The Borderland of Criminal Justice: Essays in Law and Criminology* (Chicago: University of Chicago Press, 1964).
[84] Stanton Wheeler, Leonard S. Cottrell, Jr., and Anne Romasco, *op. cit.*
[85] *Ibid.*

worlds: that he gets neither the protections accorded to adults nor the solicitous care and regenerative treatment postulated for children." [86]

This illustration suggests the complexities to be found when we examine the actual stages in the social control of a concrete form of deviant conduct. The case of delinquency is particularly interesting because the conclusions are by no means common-sense conclusions and, yet, they are of fundamental importance. But the case of delinquency can receive systematic and extended examination because the institutional procedures have been established for a long time and have been under scrutiny, study, and investigation for many years. Mental illness is a somewhat similar case. But, again, it has only been recently that studies have documented the extent to which the processes of detection, decision, diagnosis, and disposition are subject to a whole set of contingencies that are only marginally related to the state of the patient. For example, the study of paths of admission to the mental hospital suggests that whether a patient gets there through contacts with doctors or with police (or, indeed, whether one gets there at all) depends somewhat on his social background and interpersonal contacts.[87] And with regard to the various illnesses that bring persons to the emergency centers of a hospital, it has recently been established that cultural definitions of illness have a great deal to do with when a person sees the doctor and what his complaints are. In this instance, Irish patients are found to complain much more often of eye, ear, nose, and throat problems, while Italian patients complain more often about other parts of the body.[88] This is a case where the control process owes less to the vagaries of the official controlling mechanisms themselves, and more to the person's own recognition of particular problems as being the ones that require help.

The social-control networks for forms of deviance that are less routine than mental illness, delinquency, and crime are likely to be more subject to social change and to a variety of social constraints. From the standpoint of conventional society, for example, the use of LSD by students or others is probably a form of deviant conduct. But its new character, its frequent association with college and university life, and the claim that it may bring genuinely new experiences and insight mean that potential

[86] Morris A. Kent, Jr., Petitioner, v. United States, *Supreme Court Reporter* [St. Paul, Minn.: West Publishing Co., 86 (104), 1054 (April, 1966)]. A sophisticated analysis of the problems surrounding justice and the juvenile court, as well as many other aspects of delinquency, is given in David Matza, *Delinquency and Drift* (New York: Wiley, 1964).
[87] Elliot G. Mishler and Nancy E. Waxler, "Decision Processes in Psychiatric Hospitalization," *American Sociological Review,* 28(4), 576–587 (August, 1963).
[88] Irving Kenneth Zola, "Culture and Symptoms—An Analysis of Patients' Presenting Complaints," *American Sociological Review,* 31(5), 615–630 (October, 1966).

agents and agencies of social control have been relatively slow in developing a standard response and reaction. It is still undecided whether the use of LSD and other hallucinogenic drugs should be legally defined as deviant; it has not been determined what an appropriate detection mechanism would be, and through what decisional, diagnostic and dispositional channels users should be put. Unlike more traditional forms of deviation, both the social definition and the social reaction to the use of hallucinogenic drugs remain to be established and, today, are open to the interplay of competing moralities and interest groups.

## Conclusion

Sociology is on the growing edge of the social sciences, and the study of deviation and social control occupies an important part of sociological inquiry. It is a particularly difficult part to cover adequately in the short space of a chapter, because so many different perspectives have been brought to bear upon it, and the possible illustrative materials are so diverse. Instead of attempting to summarize the available knowledge, we have attempted to raise the most significant questions that confront the area of deviant behavior and social control, and to give, through brief examples, some indication of the kinds of answers that may emerge.

In doing this, we have remained substantially within the mainstream of sociological analysis. Now, in conclusion, it is important to point out two other approaches that should be examined by those who desire a fuller understanding of this domain of inquiry. One approach is the very direct and practical concern for deviant behavior and social control. We have underplayed this side of the problem here. What is the relative effectiveness of alternative treatment strategies for deviants? What is a responsible social policy toward "nonvictim" forms of deviation such as marihuana use, alchoholism, narcotics, and abortion? What can be done to improve the society's capacity to deal with criminals and mental patients, to upgrade the conditions found in hospitals and prisons, and to improve the quality of the total social control apparatus? These and related questions concern the pragmatics of social control, and the linkage between sociology and social policy. Many investigators who envision a contribution for sociological analysis envision it primarily in these terms—a direct and practical payoff value for the running of the society. Clearly, we had to make a choice, and we chose not to emphasize this orientation in this chapter.

An alternative formulation would have brought us closer to the humanistic study of society and to social criticism. Many scholars consider that the most important consequence of modern society is the increasing alienation of man from his work, from others, and from himself. Humanistically oriented sociologists and social critics would have given more emphasis to the dangers and limitations of conformity, the debilitating effects of conventional institutions, and the extent to which our mass educational and welfare bureaucracies produce a sense of alienation from the system among many of its members. Indeed, alienation, despair, a sense of powerlessness, and an estrangement from society might be examined as the most important consequences of our current social organization. This clearly suggests a different approach to social problems and a different definition of what the main intellectual issues are.

Finally, a closing reminder: the terms conformity and deviation often carry excess meaning and assume a particular value position. It cannot be overemphasized that the judgment of conformity and deviation is a technical one, made in terms of the norms and actions of members of an ongoing system, and made in reference to that system. Although most persons who are socially defined as deviants will be given a negative evaluation by those who adhere to that definition, a student of the society need not join group members in that judgment. Indeed, the student must be prepared to recognize that such judgments are often highly limited and time-bound, and that some of the great men of history were judged as deviants in their time. Certainly, the study of social deviation leads directly into questions of innovation and social change. Some forms of creative innovations are institutionalized in social systems, and men are rewarded for breaking the barriers and limited horizons that were set by their forebears. For instance, this is undoubtedly true with respect to the institutionalized structure of scientific activity.[89] But as any student of American society surely knows, other forms emerge from revolt and revolution. A suspension of evaluative judgment is a necessary part of the scientific process, and it is probably of vital importance in areas so tinged with moral and emotional meaning as those included in the study of deviation and social control.

[89] Robert K. Merton, "Priorities in Scientific Discovery: A Chapter in the Sociology of Science," *American Sociological Review*, **22**(6), 635–659 (December, 1957).

# IV

# SOCIAL CHANGE

SOCIAL CHANGE

# 12

# PROCESSES OF SOCIAL CHANGE

*Neil J. Smelser*

# PROCESSES OF
# SOCIAL CHANGE

B y one index, the study of social change is a solidly established subdivision of sociology. Almost all introductory textbooks—and this one is no exception—include a chapter toward the end on change. In addition, many texts and symposia are titled *Social Change* or some variation of it. Almost all undergraduate curricula have an upper-division course on the subject. And doctoral candidates are frequently examined on social change as one of their specialized fields of interest. All of this indicates that social change is a definite thing, with tangible subject matter to be taught and learned.

Yet, if we move behind the apparent reality bestowed on the subject by its fixed place in institutions of higher learning, we find that the topic is very difficult to define. Its core is evasive, and its boundaries are fuzzy. It occupies a kind of no-man's land between sociology and history and, depending on how we define it, is forever threatening to absorb—or be absorbed by—one or both of these fields. Insofar as social change is defined as the systematic study of variations in social life, it does not seem to differ from sociology in general; insofar as it is defined as the study of the unfolding of man's social arrangements through time, it appears to be indistinguishable from social history.

Instead of attempting, at the outset, a formal definition of this amorphous and possibly nonexistent field, let us begin in a very concrete way. I shall describe and analyze a series of dramatic social changes revolving around the lively issue of liquor sales in a little community that I studied as a graduate student ten years ago. The community is a real one, but I shall give it a fictitious name, Beachtown. On the basis of this account, I shall raise a number of questions involving what we want to find out when we study situations of this kind. Having raised these questions, I shall be in a position to specify some of the formal ingredients of the systematic study of social change. Then, having built a scaffolding for the study of change, I shall review a number of theories of change and give a sample of research in the field.


## Beachtown: A Case Study in Community Change

Professor Samuel A. Stouffer of Harvard, during the few years before his death in 1960, became interested in community conflict.[1] His interest grew partly from an intriguing finding that had emerged from his earlier studies on the social bases of anti-Communist and pro-McCarthy atti-

---

[1] For a survey of the field of community conflict, and an effort to develop generalizations, see James S. Coleman, *Community Conflict* (Glencoe, Ill.: The Free Press, 1957).

674

tudes: [2] the finding that a selected sample of community and other leaders were, on the average, more liberal in their attitudes on civil liberties than the general public. Stouffer wondered whether this relative liberalism might have anything to do with the way that leaders behave when controversy breaks out in local communities. For example, would leaders tend to be more tolerant of both sides in a conflict, and thus be in a favorable position to mediate between the warring parties? In Stouffer's research on conflict, he became preoccupied with the kinds of issues that people fight about in communities, the kinds of social cleavages—economic, political, religious, and the like—that nourish these fights, and the kinds of behavior that community leaders display when conflicts erupt.

Stouffer, as part of his research, engaged a number of assistants—I was one—as a kind of firehouse brigade to study conflict in communities while it was happening. We would keep an eye on the press for reports of explosions in nearby communities, and would go into these communities, almost like anthropologists, to try to find out why the conflict had erupted when it did, what kinds of people had initiated it and were being drawn into it, how the conflict was developing, how leaders were behaving, and how (if at all) things were being resolved. Relying mainly on interviews for our information, we first approached people who were in a position to know about the community—for instance, newspaper reporters or the town librarian—and then spoke with principals in the conflict and community leaders. In all, we interviewed about fifteen persons for as many as three hours each to obtain as clear a picture as possible of the community and its recent events. We could not probe too deeply into the situation on the basis of this limited research, but we were able to uncover a great deal about the causes, course, and consequences of the conflicts.

### The Conflict in Beachtown

I was assigned to conduct a study of Beachtown, a New England coastal town noted for its popular beach and summer recreation. This little town, which had voted to permit the sale of liquor in 1933—at the time that national prohibition ended—had, in November 1956, voted by referendum to go dry. This vote, a very close 778 to 776, immediately closed about 40 bars, nightclubs, and package liquor stores. Apparently the vote also took much of the community by surprise, since the campaign against liquor had not been given much publicity. In fact, it was described by a daily

---

[2] Samuel A. Stouffer, *Communism, Conformity and Civil Liberties: A Cross-Section of the Nation Speaks Its Mind* (Garden City, N.Y.: Doubleday, 1955, Chapter 2).

newspaper in a nearby metropolis as a "one-man campaign" waged by Fred Phillips (depicted by the newspaper as a mason, a family man, and a temperant), who had been fighting for 6 years to get the town dry, but who was "backed by no group."

After the referendum, the little town erupted into boiling conflict, which raged for 18 months. The hottest phase of the conflict was during the 4 or 5 months after the referendum. The town crystallized into two warring factions, the "wets" and the "drys," who spared one another no accusations. The wets first demanded and got a recount, which reversed the referendum vote and showed a tally of 776 to 762 in favor of the liquor interests. However, a superior court ruled this recount faulty, and reversed it to 776 to 770 in favor of the drys. In great consternation the liquor interests appealed to a higher court, but without success. Next they attempted to arrange a special-referendum election (by state law the next election on liquor licensing was not scheduled until the fall of 1958), but this effort was denied by the state legislature. As a desperate last move, the wets started an agitation to set up the beach area as a separate township, but this misfired after a short time. The regular town election in March 1957 also was fought mainly on the wet-dry issue, and in this election a dry candidate was elected to the town's governing board of selectmen. In the next regular town election in the spring of 1958, however the town voted by special referendum to permit liquor sales again, and to establish a special five-man liquor commission to be responsible for licensing liquor stores, bars, and nightclubs.

Before tracing the course of the wet-dry controversy and related issues in more detail, let me briefly characterize Beachtown. As we approach it from the western, landward side, we enter a town square that is not unlike those of a hundred New England villages—a couple of churches, a bright white town hall, a number of nicely kept traditional houses, and one or two diners down the main road from the square. When I first went to the town, after the referendum, it had an outwardly sleepy appearance—an appearance accentuated by the boarded liquor stores not far from the center of the town. As we move east through the center, we pass through about one mile of marshy terrain and reach the beach area, which stands in lavish contrast to the traditional town. The few streets here are lined with fun houses, popcorn stands, bars, and nightclubs. Stretching along the beach are long strings of cheap, jerry-built houses, obviously constructed for the holiday accommodation of low-income people. In the middle of the entertainment houses and bars stands Beachtown's police station. When I first visited the beach area in the winter, it struck me almost as a ghost town, both because winter is a quiet time of year and because all places serving liquor were closed by the referendum. Only one diner in the entire beach area was open for business.

This picture reveals a great deal about the economy of the town. The permanent population of 3000 expands every summer to more than 10,000, as thousands of workers and clerks from several nearby industrial towns pour into Beachtown for holidays and summer fun. Many of the town's permanent citizens find various kinds of employment on the beach during the active summer period. Most people in Beachtown are not wealthy, but there are not many poor, either. Houses in the town are of medium size and quality. A small group of landowning families live in the northern part of the town, but they are not too prosperous, since land in this part of the country is not very productive. The liquor merchants are the wealthiest group although, during the dry period, they were in financial difficulties. The only industry is a small shoe factory. A handful of the town's citizens commute to larger cities.

The town's government is typical of many New England communities—an annual town meeting, with a governing three-man board of selectmen, elected once a year. The selectmen are responsible for conducting the official business of the town, and for making appointments to various welfare boards, to the police and fire departments, and other municipal bureaus. The town has two churches: one Methodist, established as the parish church in 1834 when the town changed from Congregational to Methodist, and one Catholic, established more recently. I did not make an actual survey, but it appeared that the town is about half Protestant and half Catholic. The Protestants are made up of old Yankee families and some others who have migrated more recently from neighboring towns. The Catholics are a mixture of Irish, Italians, and French Canadians.

After the town voted to permit liquor in 1933, there gradually developed an extensive system of concessions and liquor establishments on the beach, which grew rapidly as a summer vacationland for working people. The board of selectmen was responsible for issuing and revoking liquor licenses. Toward the end of World War II, complaints of scandals in the beach area began to grow. The greatest numbers of complaints concerned house parties, sale of liquor to minors, and violation of closing-time laws by liquor establishments. The scandal that received the most publicity was the so-called "toll-road" scandal, in which policemen were exposed for arresting love-making couples on a certain road near the beach, then dropping the charges for a bribe. A captain of police and a patrolman had lost their jobs and had been sentenced to jail after this scandal. The town was also shaken by the death of a teenage girl—"a known drinker"—in an automobile accident. As community dissatisfaction and resentment against the liquor interests mounted, the vote on liquor sales (repeated, remember, every two years as required by law) grew closer and closer, and in 1956 the balance tipped—the town became dry. Phillips, leader of the dry forces, apparently expressed the sentiments of his supporters when he predicted that as a result of the referendum the beach would now become a "family beach" and cater to people of "higher standards."

An attack on the police department had accompanied the attack on the liquor interests. At the time of the November 1956 referendum, the board of selectmen was made up of three men—George Hart, Raymond Martin, and Gerald Marsh. Marsh was also the town's chief of police. During the period before the referendum, a number of charges of laxity and corruption were directed against the police. After the referendum, Phillips stated that the town could now reduce the size of its police force, since it did not have to police liquor establishments any longer, and that the saving in expenditures would permit Beachtown to own its sewage and water system. In the general town election in March 1957, the police also were involved. Three special items appeared on the ballot. The first item (obviously sponsored by the friends of Gerald Marsh) was a measure permitting Marsh to be police chief for life. The second item (sponsored by antipolice forces) would have changed the police recruitment system from an appointive one to one based on civil service. The third item (sponsored by the opponents of Marsh) would have prohibited the same individual from holding the offices of selectman and chief of police simultaneously.

In the March 1957 election, the voters did not vote to prohibit a selectman from simultaneously being chief of police, and did not vote to introduce the civil-service system for police. But they did vote to deny Marsh the possibility of lifetime tenure as police chief. And, although Marsh and Hart were reelected as selectmen, Martin—well known as a friend and political supporter of Marsh—was defeated, and Richard White, a "dry" and critic of the police, was elected to the board in his place. Mrs. Edna Sterling, another "dry," also almost won a selectman's seat. Shortly after the election, Hart and White joined forces to remove Marsh as chief of police, and replaced him with Michael Day, Hart's nephew. Then, one year later, when the town went wet again, Marsh, Martin, and White were elected as selectmen. Shortly after this election, Marsh and Martin voted (over White's opposition) to appoint Marsh as police chief once again and Martin as police sergeant. I hardly need observe that the police issue was of critical political importance in Beachtown.

### The Structure of Beachtown, and Its Relation to the Conflict

In order to better understand the peculiar importance of the wet-dry and police controversies in Beachtown, let us examine the manner in which these issues ramified into the town's social structure. Let me begin by locating the town's various social groupings according to two overlapping but distinguishable dimensions.

(1) *Town-area interests versus beach-area interests.* The town-area interests are those of most American communities—for instance, to carry on work and life, to raise children, to see that they are educated and exposed to religious values, and to protect life and property. Although the various beach merchants may have respect for these interests, they are certainly not their major interests in Beachtown. Many of these merchants do not reside in the town, and their main concern is to conduct beach businesses.

(2) *The interests of old residents versus the interests of new residents.* This dimension overlaps with town-area versus beach-area interests, since the residents with beach interests are mainly newcomers. But the new-versus-old dimension is more than this. Within the town areas itself, people distinguish between old and new residents mainly in terms of religious and ethnic memberships. By and large, the old residents are Protestant, Anglo-Saxon (or "Yankee"), and Republican (although some of the Protestants are more recent migrants from nearby towns), whereas the Irish, Italian, and French-Canadian Catholics are regarded and regard themselves as newcomers.

These two dimensions, and the relative social distance among the various social groupings, are shown in Figure 12.1. If a given group falls into any

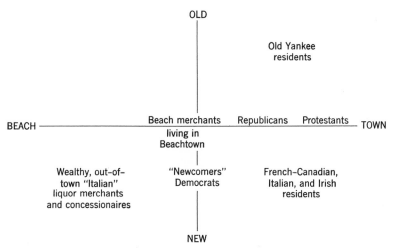

Figure 12.1   Social groupings in Beachtown.

one quadrant, its interests are different from and potentially in conflict with any group in any other quadrant. Thus there is potentiality of conflict between old and new residents within the town, and between all town residents and the beach interests. The upper left quadrant is almost empty,

since most beach residents are newcomers. The greatest social distance
and the greatest potential conflict are between the old-resident Yankees on
the one hand, and the new wealthy beach merchants (many of whom are
Italian, at least by reputation) on the other.

Despite the great cleavages and potential conflicts in Beachtown, the
fact remains that the town had lived for several decades in relative peace
before the explosion concerning liquor and the police. The reason for this
harmony lies in two peculiar bifurcations in the beach-town relations, and
in the peculiar political symbiosis that had grown up between the two areas
of the township.

The first bifurcation in beach-town relations is economic. Most of the
revenue for the town government is raised by property taxes. Moreover,
property is assessed in two ways: first, in terms of the percentage of market
value assigned to it and, second, in terms of the tax rate itself. Thus, if a
piece of property is valued at $500 on the market, and is valued at one half
of its market value by the assessor ($250) and taxed at a rate of 1%, $2.50
per year is collected in taxes. In Beachtown, an anomalous situation has
developed over the years. The actual tax rate is the same for property in
the beach area and property in the town area, but because the beach land
is judged by the tax authorities to be "income generating," it is assessed at
100% of its market value. By contrast, land in the town area, which is not
considered "income generating," is assessed at only 20% of its market value.
As a result, the beach area contributes about 70% of the town's revenue,
and the town area contributes about 30%.

The second bifurcation (a political one) produces an opposite kind of
imbalance. The qualified voters—full-time residents—from the beach area
do not exceed 150 in number, even though the transient summer population
of the beach is about 10,000 persons. The beach area is an empty shell
during the winter months. However, the town area has about 1600 qualified
voters, more than 10 times the number of beach-area voters. Political (voting) control of the whole township—including the beach area—clearly remains in the town area. Considering these two bifurcations, the town area
is high on political control but low on economic contribution to town govm-
ment, while the beach is low on political control but high on economic contribution to the town government.

The political and economic inbalances in Beachtown constitute a natural
setting for patronage to flourish. Because the town area exercises political
control over revenue from the beach, it has access to a comfortable source
of public funds that can be used to supply jobs for townspeople without
raising the tax rate. In most towns, patronage begins to irritate its citizens
sooner or later because they find out that they have to pay for the patronage
in the end. But, in Beachtown, the very prospersous beach area yields a

very large supply of patronage funds through taxes, liquor license fees, and similar sources. Furthermore, the police chief (who is often a select-man, too) has the statutory right to decide whether a bar or liquor estab-lishment requires police protection. Moreover, the arrangement in Beach-town is that the bar and liquor establishments themselves—not the town government—must pay the salaries of policemen assigned to their places of business. The liquor businesses accept this arrangement, because they are dependent on the town government for their liquor permits.

In view of such a natural opportunity for patronage, we would expect an invasion of relatives and friends of political leaders into politically ap-pointive jobs—especially jobs on the police force—in Beachtown. I was unable to make a complete study of the network of kinship and friendship ties among Beachtown's town employees. I did, however, obtain a list of all town officials and employees. I showed this list to several inhabitants of Beachtown who knew the town well, and asked them if they could identify who was related to whom. I discovered that George Hart (the selectman) had at least 23 relatives on the public payroll—including two brothers, a sister, and two nephews—which is quite an impressive total in a government of a town of 3000. For another family, I found 10 close relatives scattered through the fire department. And many other miscellaneous family ties were mentioned by my informants. In light of this kind of evidence, we would imagine that friendship as well as kinship operated in filling positions on the public payroll.

In this political-economic symbiosis between beach and town areas, the selectmen and chief of police play a key role. As between selectmen and beach, the selectmen are responsible for licensing food and liquor busi-nesses on the beach (or were, at least, before the establishment of the liquor commission in 1958). Furthermore, the selectmen, through the chief of police, determine the numbers of police necessary to regulate the beach in the summer, and thus can engage freely in a kind of legalized protection racket. Additionally, the selectmen and police adopt a permissive attitude toward the beach as long as they continue to contribute taxes, license fees (and, perhaps, other forms of payment), and jobs for relatives. As between selectmen and town, a similar kind of symbiosis exists. The townspeople donate their political support to the selectmen and, in return, are given a very sizeable distribution of patronage—sizeable because of the revenue supplied by the beach. Figure 12.2 illustrates the role played by the selec-ment in balancing beach and town interests (and, to some degree, the in-terests of old and new residents). The diagram shows why the issue of simultaneous occupancy of the jobs of selectman and police chief is so important in Beachtown. It also shows the significance of Gerald Marsh's request for lifetime tenure as police chief.

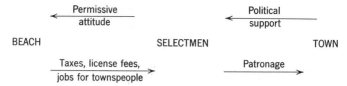

Figure 12.2   Selectmen's role in balancing beach and town interests.

To complete the story of conflict and change in Beachtown, let us re-examine the liquor and police controversies, and characterize them in terms of their relations to the social structure as I have outlined it. During the decade before the momentous referendum election of November 1956, Beachtown witnessed a gradual shift in the delicate balance of social forces in the direction of the beach-area interests. In the eyes of the citizenry the police were becoming too permissive of—indeed, too involved in—the affairs of the beach, and the resulting scandals were threatening the moral values of the community. In the first instance, then, the vote to go dry was a slap at the beach interests (and at the town officials who had formed such a close alliance with these interests). In addition, however, the battle between beach and town opened a number of the more latent cleavages in Beachtown, in the following ways.

First, the controversy was related to various kinds of ethnic prejudice. During the hottest part of the fight it was whispered frequently that the out-of-town merchants were mainly Italians, and that new Italian wealth was taking over the town. I did not undertake a systematic investigation of the ethnic background of the beach merchants, but it did appear that most of them were not of Yankee extraction; some had Irish names, some Italian, and some Syrian.

Second, latent religious cleavages in the community were opened, to a degree, by the controversy. The major Protestant interest in the community was Methodism, a religion with a tradition unfriendly to drinking, dancing, and other temporal pleasures. In fact, the town's Methodist minister was a very important behind-the-scenes worker for the dry forces. He joined company with Mrs. Sterling and Fred Phillips (both Protestants) and, actually, Phillips' "one-man campaign" was given much support by several influential Yankee Protestant families. This support was given mainly in secret, however. To many townspeople, it did not appear that the religion was involved in the wet-dry issue.

Finally and ironically, the wet-dry controversy opened a minor cleavage among the liquor merchants themselves. Notice in Figure 12.1 that one category—beach merchants living in Beachtown—overlaps all four quadrants. Some of these are old residents, some new; and they represent both beach and town interests. In fact, the townspeople themselves distinguish sharply between liquor merchants and concessionaires who reside in Beachtown and those who reside elsewhere. The liquor merchants and concessionaires who reside in Beachtown are regarded with much less suspicion. During the period of the wet-dry controversy, a few of the liquor merchants and package liquor dealers—those living in Beachtown—actually expressed some support for the drys, and therefore went against their own immediate economic interests. Because they were long-time residents in the town, they were very hostile to the outside beach interests, and were willing to sacrifice themselves, perhaps with the hope of driving away some of the outsiders who had set up establishments in the beach area.

The wet-dry controversy and the related police issue, then, were "over-determined" because the antagonists had so many different interests at stake in the battle. The controversy was manifestly between those townspeople concerned with the moral values of the community and the liquor interests. But beneath the surface there were a number of political, economic, ethnic, and religious cleavages, all of which added fuel to the flames of controversy. Moreover, because people were fighting for so many different reasons—only some of them conscious reasons—diffuse personal antagonisms were much higher than if the conflict had been simply a limited conflict of interest.

Because of the way things stood in Beachtown in 1956, the voters had little choice other than to define the various issues facing the community in wet-dry terms. But the referendum vote that year did much more than merely prohibit liquor sales. It upset the whole political and economic structure of the town. Let me illustrate this in terms of Figure 12.2, which (as already mentioned) depicts the intimate relations among selectmen, police, beach, and town. When the town went dry, the selectman-police-beach relationship also threatened to dry up. The police were no longer in a position to insist that the beach needed "protection," because all liquor establishments and most nightclubs were not in operation. Furthermore, the beach could not be expected to continue to provide its enormous revenue to the town, for two reasons. First, beach liquor establishments were no longer paying license fees, and this amounted, I was told, to a loss of $18,000 a year in revenue; and, second, since business in general fell off at the beach in the summer of 1957 (one merchant told me that business was only 60% of total business in the summer of 1956, but he may have been exaggerating), fewer employment opportunities existed on the beach for townspeople. In these ways the past politico-economic balance between selectmen, town, and beach was thrown off. To make matters worse, the decline in revenue meant that the selectmen were no longer in a position to provide jobs on the public payroll for so many relatives, friends, and other townspeople. Consequently, within several months after the town went dry, the political and economic structure, which was so much in the lifeblood of the town, came under great strain. This strain manifested itself tangibly in late 1956 and during 1957 when talk of a rise in property tax rates circulated through the town.

During the year after the dry vote, therefore, it began to look as if the town had gotten more than it had bargained for. By voting to go dry, the people had threatened to destroy those happy politico-economic arrangements between beach and town whereby so many townspeople had been able to prosper without seeing their income disappear out of the other pocket via the tax rate. During this year, many people began to have second thoughts. In fact, the election of March 1957 revealed a growing sense of moderation on the part of the townspeople. In this election, remember, the townspeople declined to convert the police system into a civil-service one, and declined to abolish the very important dual office of selectman and police chief. They merely threw out one of the selectmen—Raymond Martin—who was suspected of being a party to some of the permissiveness on the beach; and they denied lifetime tenure to Gerald Marsh. In a way, the voters were saying that somehow they wanted to rid the town of the excesses on the beach but did not want to abolish the comfortable balance between politics, economics, kinship, and friendship that the relations between beach and town had provided for many years.

The general town election of March 1958 showed more than moderation; in that election the swing of the pendulum brought the town almost back to where it had been immediately before November 1956. The people voted by an overwhelming majority (1010 to 651) to go wet again. By a similar majority (1019 to 515), they once again turned down the proposal to put police recruitment on a civil-service basis. And, finally, they reelected Gerald Marsh (by 1053 votes—the largest number of votes for a selectman in the town's history) and Raymond Martin as selectmen. Marsh and Martin promptly fired George Hart's nephew as chief of police, and appointed themselves, respectively, as chief and sergeant of police. Despite these restorations, however, the townspeople of Beachtown showed some wariness of the past. They voted by a large majority (1048 to 565) to establish a five-man liquor licensing commission, thus taking licensing from the hands of the selectmen (but the selectmen retained the power to appoint the commission's members). This measure promised at least the possibility of curbing some of the excesses that had arisen when the selectmen and the liquor establishments were more intimately entangled with one another. Finally, in the election of March 1958, it was stipulated that the liquor issue would come up again on the ballot in November 1958. This stipulation gave a kind of club to the townspeople, to be wielded the following November if the selectmen, licensing commission, police, and beach interests did not behave themselves during the summer of 1958. Aside from providing for the licensing commission and the revote six months hence, however, it appeared that the people of Beachtown were prepared in early 1958 to return to business and pleasure as usual.

## General Questions Arising from the Case Study

We have before us a general description of Beachtown and an account of the conflict that consumed it for about one year and a half. As social investigators, we now wish to increase our understanding of what transpired there. In doing this, it is possible to move in two directions.

1. We might become more microscopic in our focus on the community itself. For example, we might uncover more historical detail about the conflict and the events leading up to it; we might study the role of persons who tried to act as mediators between the town and beach interests during the heat of the controversy; we might study leaders like Gerald Marsh and Fred Phillips, intensively, to discover how their personalities affected their behavior before and during Beachtown's turmoil. By pursuing these lines of inquiry our understanding of the causes and courses of the conflict would surely become deeper and richer.

2. We might ask what general social processes are manifested in this particular incident. For example, we might compare Beachtown with 15 or 20 other towns with similar controversies to see if background factors and developmental processes are similar; or, if we were even more ambitious, we might analyze the conflict in Beachtown not as a subject of interest in itself but only as a particular manifestation of the principles of social change in general.

In this section, I shall move in the second direction. I shall pose a number of questions that arise from the case study and, in this manner, pave the way for describing the general characteristics of the subject of social change.

The most basic question that arises when we review the Beachtown story from the standpoint of the study of social change is: *Did anything change?* Or, to put the question another way: *Does this case constitute data for the study of social change?* In considering this question we arrive at several different answers. On the one hand, there is a case for the argument that nothing essential changed during the two-year period from mid-1956 to mid-1958. True, Beachtown gave off a great deal of heat, but if we examine the social situations at the beginning and at the end of the period, they are much the same, except for the presence of a five-man liquor commission which, after all, might have been controlled by the board of selectmen. On the other hand, when we focus on events *within* the two-year period, we see a great deal of change. People were elected to office and were thrown out of office; the flow of funds into the town's treasury fluctuated; laws were passed and were repealed by referendum; and social movements and countermovements rose and fell. Our answer to the question, then, depends on the time perspective and social scope within which the investigator reads the data. From the standpoint of Beachtown's history during the entire twentieth century—to say nothing of the history of New England or of the United States as a whole—Beachtown's controversy scarcely qualifies as an item of change; from the standpoint of the history of this community in the years of the mid-1950's, however, it is a very profound instance of change.

Suppose, for the moment, that our focus is sufficiently narrow to conclude that some changes took place in Beachtown during the period under consideration. The next question is: *What is it that changed?* At first glance the answer is simply a matter of determining the facts. For example, it is clear that in the period between the end of World War II and 1956 public attitudes toward liquor underwent a gradual shift; later, the laws governing the sale of liquor were modified; and the composition of the board of selectmen and the police force changed. But, in addition, part of the answer must be conceptual. For example, the investigator must ask: Of all the things that were changing during this period, which are to be considered the most important? Is it fair to assume that changes in the composition of the board of selectmen constituted power shifts in the community, or were new faces merely reflecting the same old power balance? These kinds of questions boil down to a general one: By what criteria does the investigator decide to identify and study what is changing?

Suppose, again, that the investigator has decided that some changes in social life are occurring, and that appropriate terms for identifying important changes have been devised. The next question is: *How do we extract, from the flow of history, definite points at which changes begin and end?* In the case of Beachtown, the logic of historical events provides the investigator with a number of "natural" junctures of change—for example, the passing of referendum votes and the election of officials, which are located at definite points in time. Thus it makes sense to start the story when the town went dry, and end it when the town voted to return to the sale of liquor. But history does not always oblige by providing such definite landmarks. It does not mark off starting points and stopping points for subtle and gradual shifts of public opinion, modifications of the institutional structure, and things of this kind. In these cases the investigator must assign sometimes seemingly arbitrary beginning and end points of change.

Moreover, an occurrence that is a historical landmark for some kinds of change is not necessarily a landmark for other kinds. The assassination of Abraham Lincoln, for instance, was a very important event from the standpoint of changes in Negro-white relations in the United States, but probably was not very important from the standpoint of American foreign policy; the assassination of John F. Kennedy, by contrast, was probably a more significant landmark in the conduct of American foreign policy than in the history of race relations.

The questions raised thus far deal mainly with the problem of describing change. But the social scientist must raise another, more complex question: *What are the causes of change?* The reason for the complexity is that the causes of change are found at so many different levels and operate in so many different ways. Some of the "causes" of change are not causes in an active sense, but are more in the nature of permissive conditions. To illustrate from the Beachtown story: the fact that state law required that a referendum on liquor be held every two years constituted a condition that permitted the town to go either wet or dry. If state law prohibited such referenda, or specified that they be held only every ten years, the course of change and controversy in Beachtown clearly would have been much different. These permissive conditions, however, account for only the broad directions of change, not for its specific course. It is necessary to locate more immediate and specific causes as well. For example, it appears reasonable to locate the proximate causes of change in Beachtown in the changing balance of power: the various forces favoring prohibition of liquor sales grew stronger and were able to win the day, at least temporarily. But it is necessary to go behind this immediate set of causes and inquire into factors that led to this shift in power. And this search leads us to analyze other social forces in Beachtown, and to assess the effect of various precipitating events (such as the "toll-road" scandal) that sharpened cleavages and highlighted issues. Evidently, unless the investigator is prepared to be overwhelmed by long lists of different kinds of causes that enter into any episode of social change, he must be prepared to organize his interpretations of causes—to try to assess the distinctive contribution of each cause to the change, and to relate the various causes to one another within a coherent explanatory framework.

This need to organize the explanation of why change occurs leads directly to another question: *Are there any general principles, mechanisms, or models that can be used to interpret sequences of change?* It seems plausible, for instance, to interpret the events in Beachtown between the early 1950's and 1958 as moving first in one direction away from an equilibrium position, next in an opposite direction away from the position, and finally back to the initial position. The equilibrium position, established firmly during the period between 1933 and the end of World War II, is represented by the politico-economic symbiosis shown in Figure 12.2 (p. 682). In the years leading up to the dry vote in 1956, affairs in the township had drifted too much toward the beach interests, at the expense of the town's moral concerns. Although the dry vote corrected this drift, it overshot the mark, and created another imbalance, this time by eroding the general political and economic relations between the town and beach areas. Finally, the election of 1958 marked a return to the previous state of affairs, restoring the politico-economic symbiosis but also giving the townspeople a few safeguards that would work to prevent past excesses. Withholding judgment, for the moment, on whether it is helpful to view the sequence of change in this way, it is clear that to do this constitutes an effort to incorporate as large a number of the events as possible into a single explanatory scheme, and thus to simplify the otherwise overwhelmingly complex mass of operating factors.

A final question arises from the Beachtown story: *Upon what general assumptions about men and their social surroundings is an explanation based?* In my own version of conflict and change in Beachtown, I assumed that people's social memberships (ethnic, religious, and economic) are important determinants of their behavior—more important, in fact, than their personality characteristics. Also I assumed that the parties to the conflict were moved mainly by self-interest (if not selfishness), since they appeared to be so loath to give up those happy arrangements that linked the politics and economics of the beach and town so closely. Yet I did not assign absolute predominance to this principle of self-interest, since I assumed that at a certain point the moral standards of the people in the community would eventually determine their actions, sometimes even at the expense of economic and political self-interest. Again, without considering the relative merits of these particular assumptions, it should be apparent that any account of social change rests on a number of quite general—although sometimes implicit—assumptions about man's nature and his relations to his society. To grasp these background assumptions, moreover, we must consider the fundamentals of the explanation itself.


## The Components of a Theory of Social Change

Even the events in Beachtown—no matter how insignificant they may be in the broad sweep of history—pose several general theoretical and empirical issues for the student of social change. In considering the problems that a social scientist must face in explaining change, my discussion will be explicit, formal, and abstract. I shall be guided in part by the questions that

I raised about Beachtown, but I shall introduce some other considerations as well. I shall simultaneously state the *issues* that are to be faced in analyzing social change, the *components* of a theory of change, and the *criteria* by which the scientific adequacy of such a theory may be assessed.

The first task facing any investigator is to specify *what he wishes to explain.* To put it another way, he must raise a problem about a *dependent variable.* Moving from specific to general examples, the following are sample problems: Why did Beachtown vote dry? Why has the divorce rate in America showed a steady upward climb during the past century? What social conditions are associated with the rise of totalitarian social movements? In these questions the dependent variables—changes for which we wish to account—are the dry vote, the divorce rate, and totalitarian movements. The first component of a theory of change, then, is a scientific problem, or a "why" question about some variation in a dependent variable. Furthermore, if an investigator of change fails to specify a scientific problem, his approach may be legitimately criticized as being scientifically inadequate.

Analysts of social change focus their interest on temporal variations of one or more of the following types of dependent variables.

1. Changes in *aggregated attributes* of the population of a social unit. Examples of these attributes are the proportions of persons of different ages in a population, persons holding various occupations, persons professing various religious beliefs, and illiterate persons. To pose scientific questions is to ask under what conditions changes in these aggregated attributes may be expected.

2. Changes in *rates of behavior* in a population over time. Here I have in mind changes such as variations in rates of voting, religious attendance, crime, suicide, and collective protest. To pose scientific questions is to ask under what conditions changes in these rates may be expected. In Beachtown, for instance, I was interested in explaining, among other things, variations in voting in referendum and general elections. While questions of this sort deal with the aggregated properties of individual members, they are conceptualized as a *flow* of behavior within a specified period of time rather than a *stock* of attributes characterizing the population at a given point in time. The difference between the two variables is illustrated in this way: to enumerate the proportion of Ph.D.'s in a population is to identify an aggregated attribute; to calculate the number of graduate students attaining Ph.D.'s in 1966 is to identify a behavior rate.

3. Changes in *social structure,* or patterns of interaction among individuals. To pose scientific questions is to ask under what conditions changes in structure may be expected. In Beachtown, for example, I was interested in

explaining why the particular politico-economic symbiosis between beach and town had arisen. In one sense the notion of social structure is very close to the first two variables, since we often identify social structure by pointing to regularities in attributes and rates of behavior. In using the term "family structure," for instance, we refer to the empirical facts that the same people—an adult male categorized as husband and father, an adult female categorized as wife and mother, and several young persons categorized as son, daughter, brother, and sister—regularly sleep under the same roof, share economic goods, and otherwise behave in repetitive ways. Social structure, however, differs from the other two variables in that it is characterized on the basis of the relations (for example, authority relations) among members of a social unit, not on some aggregated versions of attributes or behavior of its individual members. Moreover, in conceptualizing social structure, we assume that the relations among members are not merely fortuitous or statistical, but are regulated by two types of social forces: *sanctions,* including both rewards and deprivations, and *norms,* or standards of conduct that indicate the occasions on which various sanctions are applied.

4. Changes in *cultural patterns.* Cultural patterns—including, for instance, values, world views, knowledge, and expressive symbols—supply systems of meaning and legitimacy for patterned social interaction. Examples of cultural patterns are the Judaic-Christian religious heritage, the values of democratic constitutional government, and the baroque musical style. To pose scientific questions is to ask under what conditions changes in these kinds of patterns may be expected.

These dependent variables are constituent parts of any theory of change. Without specifying some question about a dependent variable, the investigator is in the embarrassing position of not knowing what he wishes to explain. In addition, it is necessary to set some limits on the scope of his attempted explanation. Surely the investigator of changes in social structure cannot hope to explain all of these changes everywhere. He must first indicate the type of social structure to which his theory applies—whether political, religious, economic, educational, medical, or some relation among these. In Beachtown I focused mainly on political and economic variables. Finally, the investigator must specify the kind of social unit to which his theory applies—an experimental small group, a formal organization, a community, a society, or the international order. In Beachtown my focus was on the local community, but I did have occasion to note that changes on the local level were influenced by the community's involvement in the laws and courts of the state. Of course, the social scientist may frame his theory in very general terms so that it will apply to many types of structural change in many different settings; but if this is the case, it must be translated into more specific terms when an application of the theory to a particular social setting is desired.

Suppose, now, that the invetigator has identified one or more dependent variables, has asked a scientific question about them, and has specified a social context for their study. Next he is confronted with a number of serious problems involved in *describing* the process of change. The first of these problems, already mentioned, concerns the establishment of beginning and end points for any given process of change. Parsons notes that in order for there to be any theory of change "there must be an initial and terminal pattern to be used as points of reference." [3] If the investigator is interested in accounting for changes in the American family system over the past 100 years, for example, he must make some kind of family arrangements (for instance, the typical frontier family) as a starting point and another kind of family arrangement (for instance, the urban family) as a terminal point. And, sooner or later, if he is going to explain what happened historically, he must make a judgment about when and where these family arrangements were predominant. But, as I indicated earlier, history does not provide the analyst of social change with many obvious clues. If only it could be said that the nineteenth-century frontier family gave way to the twentieth-century urban family on New Year's Day in 1900, the investigator's problem would be much easier. But history is very stingy in providing such obvious transition points; in the main, it rolls along in continuous flux. The result is that the investigator is often forced to select his own initial and terminal points and thus artificially "freeze" history by describing social arrangements as though they existed in fixed form at these moments. [4]

In connection with depicting the states of affairs at the initial and terminal points—as well as at various intermediate points between them—three related methodological problems arise. The first deals with the necessity of having proper concepts to describe both the initial and the terminal states. Suppose we wish to explain the development of modern bureaucratic forms of political administration, and we wish to go clear back to feudal times when monarchs and lords relied on household staffs and groups of retainers for political counsel and service. What kind of concept is sufficiently general to encompass both the feudal and modern arrangements? Surely the concept of civil service is unsatisfactory, because it is so intimately

---

[3] Talcott Parsons, *The Social System* (Glencoe, Ill.: The Free Press, 1961), p. 483.

[4] The student interested in the methodological problems involved in describing unique historical situations in general terms should read Max Weber, " 'Objectivity' in Social Science and Social Policy," *The Methodology of the Social Sciences,* translated and edited by Edward A. Shils and Henry A. Finch (Glencoe, Ill.: The Free Press, 1949), pp. 49–112.

linked with the modern form that it cannot be used to characterize social arrangements in periods prior to the development of a formal governmental apparatus. The concept of administration is somewhat superior, since it is not so closely tied to a particular form of bureaucracy, but this term is time-bound, too. Max Weber's concept of staff is even more helpful, since it can encompass various political arrangements based on kinship and other forms of personal loyalty.[5] The first rule of thumb, then, in comparing a society with its own past—as in comparing one society with another—is to avoid concepts that are so rooted in particular social circumstances that no instance of the concepts can be located in other times and places.

The second problem deals with the necessity for concepts to describe the direction of change over time. When the investigator is dealing with readily quantifiable variables such as a population's attributes or rates of behavior, his task is relatively easy. He is usually interested in either increases and decreases of some distinctive combination of these, such as a cycle. When he attempts to characterize changes in social structure and cultural patterns, however, his task is more complex. It is not very helpful—in fact, it may even be nonsensical—to say that a society has quantitatively *more* social structure or *fewer* esthetic symbols than before. It is necessary, instead, to turn to more qualitative indicators of direction of change. For example, in considering the modernization of traditional societies, it is important to trace the ways in which social structure grows more complex and specialized—the ways, for instance, that local tribal political arrangements give way to complex central national governments. To measure this process, however, involves more than simple counting; it requires a detailed account of the kinds of activities performed in various roles and organizations. To characterize directions of cultural change poses even greater difficulties. Some changes in culture—for example, the rise of the renaissance—bring qualitatively new cultural contents. Sometimes, too, the investigator is interested in judging whether one cultural item or pattern is of higher quality than another.[6] Or he may be interested in describing the breakdown or disintegration of cultural patterns. The systematic description and classification of these qualitative directions of change—to say nothing of their explanation—is one of the least developed aspects of the study of social change.

The third problem deals with the adequacy of the actual measures to be applied to the beginning, intermediate, and terminal points of change. Suppose an investigator wishes to trace the rate at which economic produc-

---

[5] Max Weber, *The Theory of Social and Economic Organization*, translated by A. M. Henderson and Talcott Parsons (New York: Oxford University Press, 1947), pp. 329 ff.
[6] See Gertrude Jaeger and Philip Selznick, "A Normative Theory of Culture," *American Sociological Review*, **29**, 653–669 (1964).

tion has increased during the past 150 years. How does he measure the change? The obvious answer is that he traces the course of some monetary index of production. Even if he is able to correct for inflationary or deflationary effects on the value of money itself, serious problems arise in connection with such a measure. In the early nineteenth century the family farm was the rule, whereas today it is coming to be the exception. Furthermore, on the family farm many of the products were consumed in the household and were never brought to the market to be sold for money. The result is that with the growth of modern agriculture a larger proportion of agricultural goods has entered the market and is measured in money terms than before. All of this means that if the monetary index of production is used, the growth rate for production is artificially inflated by the fact that much nonmonetized productive activity has been transformed into monetized productive activity. To take another example, suppose an investigator wishes to trace the course of the crime rate during the past 50 years, using court convictions as data. Is this obvious measure an adequate one? Surely the social definition of a crime has changed over the past 50 years, since criminal laws themselves and attitudes of judges and juries toward criminals have been modified. Is the investigator justified, then, in using the same measure for crime in 1915 as he does in 1965? If not, what sort of measure should he use? Such problems can be overcome only if the investigator faces the difficult task of taking into account the different social contexts in which measures are available.

Now let us suppose that these several thorny problems have been attacked more or less satisfactorily, and that we are able to describe and measure beginning, intermediate, and end states of change adequately. We are still far from a complete theory of change. We know only the beginning, middle, and final scenes of the drama, but we do not know how or why the plot unfolded the way it did. Or, to put it in the language of social change, we have a comparative picture of a number of static states, but we have little knowledge of the dynamics of change. To learn about the dynamics of change we must ask about the determinants (causes) of change and the way that these determinants are organized into explanatory models.

The determinants of processes of change can be divided conveniently into the following four broad classes.

*1. The structural setting for change.* What implications does the existing structure of a social unit have for future changes of the unit? The concept of structural setting includes both an opportunity and an obstacle aspect. Suppose we wish to estimate the probabilities of a speculative boom and collapse on the stock market. If 90% of the securities are possessed by individual holders who can dispose of them quickly, the opportunities for rapid changes in the market are great. If, however, 90% of the securities are held by trust companies, whose managers must clear big transactions with their boards of directors before undertaking them, the obstacles to wild buying and selling sprees are considerable. To take another example, suppose we wish to estimate the probabilities of orderly change through reform in a society. If, like contemporary Great Britain, the society possesses numerous channels for the effective expression of grievances—channels such as elections, petitions, and demonstrations—the probabilities for this kind of change are high. If, like contemporary South Africa, the society possesses few channels of this kind, the probabilities of repressive perpetuation or violent revolutionary overthrow of the status quo are higher. In considering the structural opportunities for and obstacles to change, it is also important to consider the power balance among different social groups (including vested interests) in the society.

2. *The impetus to change.* A conducive structural setting alone does not guarantee that change will occur. The social unit must be under some kind of pressure (which is called by many names, such as strain, tension, imbalance, and disequilibrium) that provides a more definite push toward change. The origins of these pressures for change are numerous. Pressure may accumulate as people go about their business in normal ways. For example, the fact that thousands of commuters pour in and out of a metropolis every day may create such problems of highway congestion that changes in public transport policy may result. Or pressures to change may result from events external to the society itself, such as foreign wars and natural catastrophes, which influence the internal balance of the society. Or a social system may generate pressure through different rates of change in its different parts. For example, the fact that an underdeveloped country, upon achieving national independence, institutes some version of universal suffrage tends to create a crisis in education—a need to create a responsible mass electorate—in these countries.

3. *Mobilization for change.* If the structural setting is conducive and pressures have accumulated, the probability that *some* sort of social change will occur is high. But these two determinants by themselves are too general to indicate what specific direction change will take. This direction depends on the ways in which resources are mobilized and are brought to bear on modifying the elements of social action. For some kinds of change, this mobilization may involve only a very routine operation. For example, suppose the executives of a business firm perceive that a potential demand exists for some new product. After a period of planning, they decide to invest some financial reserves in the manufacturing and marketing of the product, to hire a number of new employees, and perhaps to create a new subdivision of the research branch to develop the product. As these de-

cisions are implemented, the firm undergoes a number of changes in finance, personnel, and social structure. For other kinds of change the agents may not be so well "programmed" regarding the direction of change, and may not have such immediate access to resources. Consider, for example, how an inchoate demand for social reform comes to be translated into a concrete, effective proposal for change. Before change can be effected, it is necessary for some sort of belief in a specific kind of reform to crystallize and disseminate; for leaders to form an organization or pressure group; and for workers to collect funds, publish propaganda, and organize demonstrations. As these examples show, leadership plays a very important role in the processes of mobilization for change.

4. *The operation of social controls.* As leaders of reform movements well know, their efforts to mobilize do not automatically result in change, but encounter a variety of resistances. Various authorities—for instance, government officials, courts, community leaders, religious agencies, and the press—are not indifferent to efforts of groups to change society. They may be hostile to the aims of the reform movement, or they may be exposed to countermovements to the proposed change. Moreover, the behavior of these agents of social control determines, in part, the direction of change. For example, if governmental authorities are persistently hostile and repressive toward modest demands for reform, the persons desiring reform may be driven into underground organizations, may become more extreme in their demands for change, and may even begin to challenge the legitimacy of the political authorities. If this happens, the agents of social control themselves have been influential in transforming a reform movement into a revolutionary movement.

Simply to list the several types of variables influencing the course of social change is not sufficient to create a theory of change. These variables must be organized into some sort of explanatory model. A model, defined simply, is a conceptual apparatus that states that if a given number of determinants are combined in a certain way, a definite outcome (type of change) is to be expected. In one sense, a model is nothing more than an explanation; but it differs from *ad hoc* explanations of particular historical situations in that it is organized in explicit, formal, and general terms. However, because the field of social change—indeed, sociology in general—is not a very mature field from a scientific standpoint, many of its models are incomplete, implicit, and not properly validated.

One of the simplest types of model explanations in the field of social change is called the "natural history" approach. This approach involves the claim that a particular kind of social change unfolds according to a distinct number of stages. A classic model of the natural stages of a social movement is that developed by Carl A. Dawson and Warner E.

Gettys. The movement begins with a "preliminary stage of social unrest," passes through a "popular stage of collective excitement" and a "stage of formal organization," and finally reaches a kind of terminal point of "institutionalization." The entire sequence introduces some new institutional form—a religious sect, a law, a new kind of family structure, or a political reform.[7] A comparable model for revolution is found in Crane Brinton's analysis of the French Revolution of 1789, the American Revolution, the British Revolution of 1642, and the Russian Revolution of 1917. In the first stage, the society is in a state of general prosperity but has a government suffering from economic troubles and political weakness. In this atmosphere, various groups (especially intellectuals) become progressively disaffected with the old regime. The next stage is the actual revolution, during which a transfer of power takes place. For a while the moderates among the revolutionaries hold power, but thereafter the extremists seize the reigns of power and institute a period of bloody terrorism. This period also is limited in duration, and after a time the excesses of the revolution diminish; some of its aims are institutionalized, but in many other respects the society returns to its prerevolutionary ways.[8]

The basic organizing principle of the natural history model is *time*—the principle that, as a matter of historical fact, the various phases follow one another in temporal order. Such a principle does organize the variables of an episode of social change in a simple way, and thus reduces the randomness of their occurrence. But the model provides a general description rather than an explanation, since writers taking the natural history approach seldom inquire into the reasons why one stage gives way to the next, or why one particular sequence of stages instead of another should be expected.

Another, more formal way of organizing the determinants of change is what I have termed the "value-added" approach.[9] An analogy will reveal the logic of this approach. In the manufacture of automobiles, iron ore is converted into finished cars by a number of stages of processing. Relevant stages are mining, smelting, tempering, shaping, combining the steel with other parts, painting, delivering to retailer, and selling. Each stage "adds its value" to the final cost of the finished product. The key element in the value-added sequence is that no single stage can contribute its particular value until the prior stages are finished. It is of no use, for example, to

---

[7] Carl A. Dawson and Warner E. Gettys, *An Introduction to Sociology* (New York: The Ronald Press, 1929), pp. 787–803.

[8] Crane Brinton, *The Anatomy of Revolution* (New York: Vintage Books, 1958).

[9] This approach is spelled out in my book, *Theory of Collective Behavior* (New York: The Free Press of Glencoe, 1963), pp. 12–21. An earlier statement of the approach, with reference to the causes of industrial development is found in my book, *Social Change in the Industrial Revolution* (Chicago: University of Chicago Press, 1959), pp. 60–62.

paint iron ore; painting, to be effective, must "wait" for the completion of the earlier processes. Every stage, therefore, is a necessary condition for the final production of the automobile, but no single stage can be effective unless it occurs at a single point in the sequence.

Apply this analogy to a process of social change. Suppose we are interested in explaining the rise of the industrial method of production. Clearly, one of the necessary conditions for this rise in production is adequate technological know-how. But unless the know-how is applied in a certain structural setting—a setting that includes, for instance, an allocation system for resources and products, a medium of exchange, and a requisite level of skill in the labor force—it cannot possibly become effective as a determinant of the industrial method of production. Or, to take an example mentioned earlier, a sense of opportunity and profit is a necessary determinant for a speculative craze in the stock market; but unless this occurs in a setting in which it is possible to acquire and dispose of financial assets rapidly, it cannot be effective as a determinant of a craze. A value-added model is created when a number of these determinants are combined in a systematic way to produce an explanation for a particular type of social change.

An even more elaborate and sufficient model would involve not only a statement of the combinations of variables that are necessary to produce change but also a statement of the actual sequence by which they do combine. Such models scarcely exist in the field of social change, but a good approximation is found in the disaster research of Anthony F. C. Wallace.[10] His empirical work was limited to the analysis of the social and psychological effects of a tornado that had stricken Worcester, Massachusetts, but he also developed a fairly general equilibrium model to characterize the patterns of behavior during and after the disaster. His first step in creating the model was to posit a sequence of temporal stages of a disaster. The sequence begins with a steady equilibrium state of community interaction. After warning and threat, the disaster agent makes its impact. The stricken community is isolated at first, but this phase gives way to rescue and rehabilitation phases. The final phase is termed "irreversible change," and refers to the establishment of a new equilibrium state of community interaction. Wallace's next step in creating the model was to construct a map of concentric rings around the geographical center of the stricken community. His purpose in constructing these coordinates was to permit him to locate the variables that affect behavior during and after a disaster in time and space.

[10] Anthony F. C. Wallace, *Tornado in Worcester: An Exploratory Study of Individual and Community Behavior in an Extreme Situation* (Washington, D.C.: National Academy of Sciences—National Research Council, 1956).

Next, Wallace develops the notions of a "disaster syndrome" and a "counterdisaster syndrome" which, taken together, constitute a kind of moving equilibrium of forces in opposition, the balance among which determines the state of the social system at each stage. The disaster syndrome includes those kinds of behavior that arise in response to the destructive agent. In the stage immediately after impact, for instance, people are dazed and apathetic; this initial response gives way to suggestibility and dependency, and then several more stages of adaptation. The counterdisaster syndrome is illustrated in the hyperactive rescue behavior that counteracts the numbed, apathetic responses in the early stages after impact. At each stage, then, the exact state of the system is a function of the balance of disaster and counterdisaster forces. This notion of an equilibrium moving through time is only partially developed in Wallace's work, but it is a step in the direction of constructing a theoretically adequate model of social change.

In this section I have identified a number of ingredients of an adequate theory of social change: a scientific problem concerning one or more dependent variables; a language to describe, classify, and measure changes; and a number of determinants of change, organized into some kind of formal explanatory model. The final essential ingredient of any theory of social change, of course, is its empirical application; it must be actually brought to bear on the data of the social world in order to test its explanatory utility. The acid test of any scientific theory is: Are the outcomes that theoretical models lead us to expect in evidence in the real world? To answer this question the investigator must turn to his armory of research methods and locate historical data that will lead him to confirm, modify, or reject his theory.

## Some Approaches to Social Change

To specify the ingredients of a theory of change is simultaneously to provide standards by which such a theory may be criticized. If, for example, a theory of change fails to specify a distinctive scientific problem, it is the less adequate for this omission; if it attempts to account for a wide variety of changes by reference to a single determinant (for example, the factor of leadership in a "great man" theory of change), it is vulnerable because of its oversimple approach to the causes of change.

In this section I shall review and criticize several theories of change, using the criteria developed in the preceding section. In a limited space I naturally cannot exhaust the dozens of approaches by hundreds of theorists that are found in the history of sociological thought. Moreover, I shall not in every case choose theorists whose work plays an important role in contemporary thinking about change, since these authors are often considered elsewhere in this book. For example, I shall not review Karl Marx and Max Weber, whose theories conflict over the relative importance of material and cultural determinants of social change; the works of these men are treated in the chapters on stratification and religion. I shall only give an illustrative sample of approaches to change, and demonstrate how these approaches can be criticized.

## Classical Evolutionary Theory

One dominant characteristic of nineteenth-century social thought was the notion that civilization had progressed from a backward to an advanced state. Although some social evolutionary theories predate Charles Darwin's work on biological evolution, they resemble his theory that the history of organisms is one of the progressive evolution from lower to higher forms. The backward state of society was identified by most social evolutionists as being in early history or among contemporary "primitives," such as the aborigines of Australia, or the Indians of America; and the advanced societies were the Western European nations.

Theorists taking the evolutionary approach differed in many particulars. August Comte (1798–1857) viewed society as passing through three main epochs: (1) the theological and military epoch, in which supernatural preoccupations dominate the culture, and military conquest and slavery are the major social goals; (2) the metaphysical and juridical epoch, which is a transitional epoch between the first and third; and (3) the scientific and industrial epoch, in which positivism displaces religious speculation and peaceful economic production displaces war-making as the dominant aim of social organization.[11] Sir Henry Sumner Maine (1822–1888) viewed the progress of civilization as a series of stages between early forms of social order based on patriarchy and status and later forms based on freedom and contract.[12] Rather than survey the different varieties of social evolutionary theory, however, I shall summarize briefly a single case—*Ancient Society*, by Lewis Henry Morgan (1818–1881).[13]

The subtitle of *Ancient Society* reveals its essence: *Researches in the*

---

[11] August Comte, *System of Positive Polity* (London: Longmans, Green, 1877), Volume IV.

[12] Sir Henry Sumner Maine, *Ancient Law* (New York: Henry Holt, 1885).

[13] *Ancient Society* was first published in 1877. A convenient modern edition is published in paperback as a Meridian book (Cleveland and New York: The World Publishing Company, 1963), edited, with an introduction and annotations, by Eleanor Burke Leacock. All references in this chapter are to this edition.

*Lines of Human Progress from Savagery through Barbarism to Civilization.*
Morgan regarded human history as advancing through several stages. These
stages, moreover, constitute "a natural as well as a necessary sequence of
progress." [14] The main defining characteristics of each stage is the type
of inventions that man used to gain his subsistence. Thus, the lower status
of savagery extends from the beginnings of the human race to the time that
man began to rely on fish for subsistence; the middle status of savagery
began with the acquisition of a fish subsistence and the use of fire, and
moved into the upper status of savagery with the invention of the bow
and arrow; and so on through three stages of barbarism to the state of
civilization, which began with the use of a written alphabet. [15] In addition
to technology, man's other institutions also developed by stages. In the
period of savagery, government was organized into gentes, or clans, and
"followed down, through the advancing forms of this institution, to the
establishment of political society." [16] And a parallel story of progress is to
be found for religion, architecture, property, kinship, and other institutions.
In fact, most of Morgan's scholarly efforts were devoted to presenting
evidence of "human progress . . . through successive . . . periods, as it
is revealed by inventions and discoveries, and by the growth of the ideas
of government, of the family, and of property." [17] For evidence he relied
mainly on historical accounts of earlier civilizations and anthropological
accounts of contemporary civilizations.

Subsequent students of social change have found little difficulty in
criticizing such a simple view of how human society has changed through
the ages. The following criticisms are the most pertinent ones.

1. The classification scheme of savagery, barbarism, and civilization is
lacking in theoretical sophistication. Such terms abound in vague connotations, and thus deviate from the scientific canon that the subject matter
under study should be defined as precisely as possible. In addition, terms
like "barbarism" carry implications of moral inferiority, which contradict
another scientific canon—that concepts should be as free as possible from
the value preferences of the theorist.

2. Even though Morgan claimed that the sequential stages were both
"natural" and "necessary," little in his theory indicates why it is necessary
that society everywhere and always should have passed through these

[14] Lewis Henry Morgan, *Ancient Society* (cited in footnote 13), p. 3.
[15] *Ibid.*, pp. 9–18.
[16] *Ibid.*, p. 5.
[17] *Ibid.*, p. 6. For an example of the way that Morgan proceeded, see his account of
how different familial institutions fitted into the several substages of savagery, barbarism, and civilization in Part III, Chapter 6.

stages, and that one stage should have given rise to the next. Insofar as his theory is lacking in any statement of mechanisms, it shares with the natural-history approach the deficiency of being descriptive rather than explanatory. Insofar as he relied on some general notion of a "grand design" or "moving force" to account for the movement through the various stages, his theory assumes a mystical cast. And insofar as he claimed that the various inventions themselves—fire, pottery, and iron manufacture, for instance—propelled society from one stage to the next, his theory suffers from being an oversimple materialist interpretation of history.

3. Empirically minded anthropologists have pointed out that the asserted correlations between levels of technology, religion, government, family, and so on, in each stage, simply do not square with the facts. According to Julian Steward:

> Morgan had lumped together in the stage of middle barbarism the Pueblo Indians, who were simple farmers, and the peoples of Mexico, who had cities, empires, monumental architecture, metallurgy, astronomy, mathematics, phonetic writing, and other accomplishments unknown to the Pueblo. Field research rapidly disclosed that one tribe after another had quite the wrong cultural characteristics to fit the evolutionary niche assigned it by Morgan. Eventually the general scheme of evolution postulated by the nineteenth-century theorists fell apart completely.[18]

4. To assume that a single sequence of development characterizes all societies runs counter to another line of empirical evidence—that societies grow not only from forces within, but also by borrowing ideas and institutions from other societies. If this is the case, then backward societies could skip various stages of development as cultural elements diffuse from more advanced societies. To choose a modern example of this, a relatively underdeveloped country like Indonesia has access to an externally accumulated technology that it can apply directly to its economy; it does not have to "invent" it all as it was invented in the West during the past three centuries.

5. Finally and most generally, it might be asked whether the evolutionists were posing the right kinds of questions for social science. How much is the understanding of an institution increased by simply tracing its origins? Would it not be more profitable to study societies as they are currently functioning, in order to discover the ways that the various institutions influence one another and contribute to the working of society as a whole?

With objections so formidable as these, there is little wonder that by the end of World War I, "evolutionism in the social sciences was com-

---

[18] Julian H. Steward, "Cultural Evolution," *Scientific American*, **194** (5), 70 (1956).

pletely defunct." [19] In its place, moreover, there grew up a number of more modest approaches to the study of social change. Each of these approaches attempted to overcome one or more of the objections that proved so fatal to evolutionary theory, but each accumulated some new, distinctive short-comings. Let us review some of these alternatives to classical evolutionary thought.

## Alternatives to Evolutionism

### *The Cultural Lag Theory*

In the 1920's American sociology came under the strong influence of scientific positivism, which emphasizes the pursuits of truth through data that are readily available to the senses, that are measurable, and that are subject to quantitative analysis. One of the leading spokesmen of positivism in this period was William Fielding Ogburn (1886–1959),[20] who applied this approach, moreover, in his theory of social change.

With respect to evolutionary theory, Ogburn laid down the verdict in 1922 that "the inevitable series of stages in the development of social institutions has not only not been proven but has been disproven." [21] Ogburn argued further that the basis for the disproof is found in the hard facts of history and ethnography, which had shown that the evolutionists' generalizations were faulty. Furthermore, any conclusions about evolution must rest not on impressionistic history and anthropology but on a review of the "actual facts of early evolution." [22]

After a careful account of some of the history of inventions, Ogburn concluded that, with some exceptions, "material culture accumulates." Discoveries and uses of bronze build on these of stone, and those of iron build on both. In this way "the stream of material culture grows bigger." This peculiarity of material culture, however, does not apply to "other parts of culture, such as religion, art, law and custom," which tend to replace rather than build on one another.[23] On the basis of this fact, plus

[19] George Peter Murdock, *Social Structure* (New Haven: Yale University Press, 1948), p. xiii.
[20] For a forceful statement of Ogburn's positivistic views, see William F. Ogburn, "Presidential Address: The Folkways of a Scientific Sociology," *Studies in Quantitative and Cultural Sociology*, Papers Presented at the Twenty-fourth Annual Meeting of the American Sociological Society, held at Washington, D.C., December 27–30, 1929 (Chicago: University of Chicago Press, 1930), pp. 1–11.
[21] William Fielding Ogburn, *Social Change: With Respect to Culture and Original Nature* (New York: B. W. Huebsch, 1922), p. 57.
[22] *Ibid.*, p. 66.
[23] *Ibid.*, pp. 73–79, 103–118.

the fact that civilization has had many forces—such as habits, traditions, and vested interests—that resist change, Ogburn ventured his basic hypothesis of the cultural lag. This hypothesis states that changes in material culture proceed at a faster rate than changes in adaptive culture—customs, beliefs, philosophies, laws, and governments—and the result is continuous social maladjustment between the two types of culture. For example, the destruction of forests by economic exploitation precedes and indeed causes enlightened public policy concerning forest conservation; machinery and working conditions leading to industrial accidents precede workmen's compensation laws; and so on. Using this principle, Ogburn attempted to explain why modern society suffers from its great burden of unresolved social problems; in every case, the cause is found in the lag of adaptive culture behind material culture.

What are the characteristics of this theory as compared with classical evolution? Certainly it is more manageable, since it is addressed to the explanation of a limited range of phenomena—social maladjustments—rather than the whole history of civilization. In addition, its hypotheses are more easily brought to bear on empirical facts that are the vague generalizations of the evolutionists. And, finally, Ogburn's theory does contain some account of a mechanism—the lead and lag relations between various parts of culture—that explains why society experiences certain social problems at certain times; for this reason, it goes beyond mere description.

Despite these advantages, the theory of cultural lag falls victim to criticisms of the following sort.

1. The theory rests on a very simple dichotomy between material culture (which includes technological and economic factors) and adaptive culture (which includes every other aspect of social organization). Enough is known about the complexity of institutional interrelations to lead us to suspect that Ogburn had an oversimple notion of a social system. In addition, insofar as Ogburn claims without qualification that social maladjustments in, for instance, family organization, are the product solely of changes in the economic order, he appears to be advancing an oversimple materialistic view of society.[24]

2. It is difficult to know how widely the theory of cultural lag applies. On the one hand, since it is rooted in the facts of evolution in general, we would expect it to apply as a universal law. On the other hand, Ogburn qualified his position by saying that "the lags in adaptive culture are expected to be a problem of only modern times. In very early times changes

---

[24] Ogburn qualified his view by admitting that "it is hard to describe just how much of the family organization is subject to variation because of change in the economic system. *Ibid.*, p. 256.

were not sufficiently numerous and frequent to give rise often to any significant problem of this nature." [25] In view of this major qualification, the critic may wonder whether Ogburn was venturing a major theory or merely a characterization of selected instances of social change in recent times.

3. Despite the fact that Ogburn's concepts are more readily measured than those of the classical evolutionists, problems of measurement do persist. How can increases of economic exploitation of forest lands be made commensurable with changes in conservation policy? By what units are the two comparable? Without a common measure, it is difficult to trust the assertion that one changes faster than the other.

4. Ogburn seemed to overemphasize resistances to change in the area of adaptive culture and underemphasize resistances in the area of material culture. From a technological point of view, for example, the United States is probably ready to embark on large-scale investment in nuclear power plants. But one of the main areas of resistance to a really ambitious program has been the resistance of established power interests—coal, electricity, water, oil, and others.

5. While much of Ogburn's empirical evidence from the modern West —especially America—seems to illustrate the cultural lag, it is not difficult to produce contrary evidence from other societies. For example, in many of the African societies emerging from colonial rule, massive new education programs are being undertaken before the societies have begun to grow rapidly in the economic sector. In this case, educational advances are preceding the economic ones; indeed, educational advances are putting pressure on the societies to develop their economies so that the educated and trained personnel may be absorbed. These societies may be described as experiencing a lag, but the lag is just the reverse of that postulated by Ogburn.

## The Classical Diffusion Theory

As we have seen, classical evolutionary theory rests on the notion that a cultural item or complex appears when a given society is "ripe" for it—that is, when it has reached the appropriate stage of evolution. According to this view, causation is internal to the society; even if a backward society were exposed to more advanced technology and customs, this society, proceeding on its evolutionary path, would not be prepared to incorporate them. But such a view neglects the obvious interaction among societies through history.

[25] *Ibid.*, p. 265.

Soon after the formulation of classical evolutionary theories, a number of anthropologists began to challenge this single-line, immanent view of cultural change. The main line of challenge was to demonstrate that many cultural items did not develop independently in various cultures, but were borrowed from abroad, sometimes at a very great geographical distance. Very painstaking studies were made, showing how myths, costume styles, maize cultivation, and similar things have traveled in intricate paths around the world.[26] The author of one study—that of the material culture of the Blackfoot Indians—even argued that all current items in the culture had originated elsewhere and had been borrowed in one way or another.[27] Kroeber summarized the force of the principle of diffusion as follows.

The vast majority of culture elements have been learned by each nation from other peoples, past and present . . . even savages shift their habitations and acquire new neighbors. At times they capture women and children from one another. Again they intermarry; and they almost invariably maintain some sort of trade relations with at least some of the adjacent peoples. . . . There is thus every *a priori* reason why diffusion could be expected to have had a very large part in the formation of primitive and barbarous as well as advanced culture.[28]

Diffusionists, possibly because they wanted to avoid the errors of the grand theories of evolutionism, and possibly because they were influenced by positivism, proceeded modestly in their research, tracing such concrete and relatively measurable items and artifacts as the number zero, fire, calendars, and agricultural complexes. They often gave only descriptive accounts of the geographical distribution of these items over time. While their research was thus less vulnerable to criticism, it provided only limited insight into the character of social change. They seldom asked why certain items diffused and others did not; how items were modified after being incorporated into a new cultural setting; or what new internal changes were stimulated by borrowed items.[29] Diffusionists, in short, built their research mainly on the movement of *things* from society to society, and inquired very little into the *social-system contexts* of either the originating or the borrowing cultures. Because of these limitations, classical diffusionism has by and large been discredited as being mainly descriptive and un-

---

[26] For a review of these early studies, see Alexander Goldenweiser, "Diffusionism and the American School of Historical Ethnology," *American Journal of Sociology*, 31, 27–33 (1925–1926). See also Robert H. Lowie, *The History of Ethnological Theory* (New York: Rinehart and Co., 1937).

[27] Clark Wissler, "Material Culture of the Blackfoot Indians," *Anthropological Papers, American Museum of Natural History*, Vol. V, Part I (1910).

[28] Alfred L. Kroeber, *Anthropology* (New York: Harcourt, Brace, 1923), pp. 197–198.

[29] Many of the early anthropologists were aware of these problems. See Robert H. Lowie (cited in footnote 26), pp. 150–151. But their empirical research was seldom directed toward them.

interesting, and more recent studies of diffusion attempt more often to explain the movement of cultural items by reference to standard sociological variables.[30]

## Classical Functionalism

Both cultural lag theory and diffusionist theory criticized the classical evolutionists for being careless historians. A third school of thought that arose partly in reaction to evolutionism—classical functionalism—not only shared this criticism but also held that the evolutionists were asking the wrong kinds of questions. It is not important, some functionalists argued, to know about the historical origin of a particular social structure; this tells us nothing about how the structure fits into and contributes to the ongoing life of the society. It tells us little about the structure's current *functions*.

To grasp the approach of functionalism, it is convenient to begin with a biological analogy, as many functionalists themselves did.[31] If an organism is to survive, a number of functions have to be performed—for instance, it must take in food and oxygen, transform these into energy, and dispose of waste products. To perform these functions, organisms have developed various structures. For example, mammals have a nose, mouth, and lungs geared to the intake of oxygen; the gills of fish constitute a somewhat more primitive structure to perform the same function; and some lower forms of life take in oxygen through the pores of their body surface. Anatomy is the study of the structures alone; physiology is the study of the processes and mechanisms by which these structures perform their vital functions; and paleontology and biological evolution involve the study of how the structures came to be as they are.

Functionalists, although they were not the first social thinkers to do so, stressed that social life resembles the life of organisms. Social life requires that certain needs, or functions, be fulfilled; among the most obvious of these are the provision of material subsistence, the socialization of the dependent young, and the control of conflict that is destructive to organized society. Man's institutional arrangements contribute to the fulfillment of these functions; religion, for example, is a specialized social organization that provides, among other things, a basis for the integration of society

---

[30] For an excellent account of developments of the diffusionist school since its early days, see Elihu Katz, Martin L. Levin, and Herbert Hamilton, "Traditions of Research on the Diffusion of Innovation," *American Sociological Review*, **28**, 237–252 (1963).

[31] In this abbreviated account of functionalist theory I must neglect many differences among scholars who are known as functionalists. My summary follows the lines of thought of one of the most famous scholars, A. R. Radcliffe-Brown (1881–1955).

through social control. Radcliffe-Brown stated the functionalist argument in general terms as follows.

Individual human beings . . . are connected by a definite set of social relations into an integrated whole. The continuity of the *social structure*, like that of an organic structure, is not destroyed by changes in the units. Individuals may leave the society, by death or otherwise; others may enter it. The continuity of structure is maintained by the process of social life, which consists of the activities and interactions of the individual human beings and of the organized groups into which they are united. The social life of the community is here defined as the *functioning* of the social structure. The *function* of any recurrent activity, such as the punishment of a crime or a funeral ceremony, is the part it plays in the social life as a whole and therefore the contribution it makes to the maintenance of the structural continuity.[32]

A functionalist explanation is one that accounts for a given pattern of activities (such as religious ritual) by referring to its contribution to the social system of which it is a part.

The functionalist approach has been frequently criticized on logical grounds.[33] The criticisms of most concern to us, however, are those relating to social change. If the main focus of functional analysis is on the positive contribution of activities and structures to the current functioning of a social system, why, it might be asked, should we ever expect anything to change in that system? If the functionalist emphasis is on the current or momentary significance of a given pattern of activities, why would functionalists ever bother to study the past or future in relation to the present? These considerations have led to the charge that functionalists are unable or unwilling—perhaps both—to study processes of social change. As one critic has expressed it:

[The functionalists] were primarily concerned with maintaining a stable, integrated, and harmonious social equilibrium. By taking as their research problem the task of explaining how it is that various social institutions of preliterate societies function interdependently in an integrated whole, these earlier anthropologists either neglected the question of change . . . or studied social change as evidence of breakdown in social control and consequently studied means by which control was restored . . . Interest in the stability and order of . . . communities tended to preclude study of social and political change, and particularly, changes in the distribution of power.[34]

[32] A. R. Radcliffe-Brown, *Structure and Function in Primitive Society* (Glencoe, Ill.: The Free Press, 1952), p. 180. Italics added.
[33] See, for example, Ernest Nagel, *The Structure of Science: Problems in the Logic of Scientific Explanation* (New York: Harcourt, Brace and World, 1961), pp. 522–534.
[34] Wayne Hield, "The Study of Change in Social Science," *British Journal of Sociology,* 5, 1–2 (1954).

Insofar as the early functionalists were distrustful of history and limited their research to societies as they currently functioned, this charge has some merit. It is a valid criticism of their research emphases. But critics cannot correctly claim that the study of change is logically impossible in functional theory. There is no inherent reason why the functionalist approach precludes the study of the growth of civilizations, any more than physiology—the study of functioning organisms—precludes the study of embryology and paleontology.[35] There is no inherent reason why the notion of a functioning system precludes the study of conflict and disorganization, any more than the notion of a biological organism precludes the study of disease. But, again, it is true that as a matter of research emphasis, classical functionalists tended to neglect the study of conflict, structural change, and disorganization.

In recent times, scholars who call themselves—or are called—functionalists, have begun to supplement and modify the framework of the classical functionalists in ways that facilitate the study of change. For example, they have invented concepts such as "dysfunction" and "strain" in an effort to describe conditions of imbalance that predispose a social system to change.[36] They have revived categories such as structural differentiation to characterize processes of change.[37] They have attempted to formulate principles of equilibrium that are more useful for analyzing social systems in flux than were the relatively static formulations of the earlier functionalists.[38] And they have even revived an interest in social evolution.[39] These new approaches themselves are being criticized and debated in the current literature; [40] regardless of their particular merits, however, they represent a swing of the pendulum back toward the serious and systematic study of social change, following its swing away from this kind of study during the era of classical functionalism between the two World Wars.

[35] Radcliffe-Brown himself made this point. A. R. Radcliffe-Brown, "On the Concept of Function in Social Science," *American Anthropologist,* **37**, 395–397, 401 (1935).
[36] See, for example, Robert K. Merton, *Social Theory and Social Structure,* revised and enlarged edition (Glencoe, Ill.: The Free Press, 1957), Chapters 1, 4, and 5.
[37] See, for example, Talcott Parsons, "Some Considerations on the Theory of Social Change," *Rural Sociology,* **26**, 219–239 (1961). Reprinted as "A Functional Theory of Change," in Amitai Etzioni and Eva Etzioni, *Social Change: Sources, Patterns, and Consequences* (New York: Basic Books, 1964), Chapter 12. See also Neil J. Smelzer, *Social Change in the Industrial Revolution* (Chicago: University of Chicago Press, 1959).
[38] See Wilbert E. Moore, *Social Change* (Englewood Cliffs, N.J.: Prentice Hall, 1963), Chapter 1.
[39] See Talcott Parsons, "Evolutionary Universals in Society," Robert N. Bellah, "Religious Evolution" and S. N. Eisenstadt, "Social Change, Differentiation, and Evolution," *American Sociological Review,* **29**, 339–386 (1964).
[40] See, for example, George C. Homans, "Bringing Men Back In," *American Sociological Review,* **29**, 809–818 (1964).

*Multilineal Evolution*

Despite the assault on evolutionary theory from many sides, interest in the broad sweep of evolutionary history is not entirely dead—even among functionalists, as we have just noted. A few other authors, notably Leslie White and V. Gordon Childe,[41] have maintained an interest in evolutionary universals of the same order of generality as the nineteenth-century writers. Still another school of thought, which goes under the name of multilineal evolution, has been advanced by Julian H. Steward.[42]

Steward accepted many of the attacks on classical evolutionary theory —that it had an oversimple unilinear view of history unfolding by some sort of grand design, that it ignored the omnipresent historical facts of diffusion, and that its notions of causality were crude and erroneous. Nevertheless, Steward argued, important parallel patterns of development exist in different civilizations, and it is important to isolate and analyze these patterns. Recognizing the vulnerability of too-general assertions, however, Steward was relatively modest in his assertions of parallels. In addition, he was hesitant to accept any single view of causality, and rejected the notion that changes in subsistence or technology are the prime movers in cultural evolution.[43] In practice, therefore, the multilineal approach boils down to a descriptive search for repeated sequences in the long sweep of history.

A typical evolutionary sequence found in the Middle East, Asia, and America is the growth of large-scale irrigation agriculture, followed by the development of permanent cities and communities. This set the stage for new levels of technology, and the need for bureaucratic and national political organization. But this sequence is not the only source of modern nation-states, since the feudal empires of Europe and Japan also gave rise to this particular political form. These diverse origins of the modern nation-state illustrate Steward's basically multilineal approach.

Another example of a parallel pattern is illustrated in the growth of the Great Basin Shoshonean Indian civilization:

The Shoshoneans developed a higher level of sociocultural integration only after the whites entered their country and horses were introduced. The multifamily, mounted, predatory bands depended upon raiding the resources brought by the whites. In this respect they differed from the mounted Plains tribes, which sub-

[41] Leslie A. White, *The Science of Culture* (New York: Farrar, Strauss, 1949); and V. Gordon Childe, *Social Evolution* (New York: H. Schuman, 1951).
[42] Julian H. Steward, *Theory of Culture Change: The Methodology of Multilinear Evolution* (Urbana: University of Illinois Press, 1963).
[43] *Ibid.,* p. 41.

sisted by hunting bison, and resembled such peoples as the Apache, whose forays made them the scourge of the Southwest, the Puelche and certain tribes of the southern Gran Chaco in South America, and perhaps some of the Asiatic horse nomads, whose existence was at least quasiparasitic through raiding activities.[44]

To uncover these relatively modest parallel patterns certainly leaves Steward in a less vulnerable position than the classical evolutionists. But at the same time his modesty creates the same dilemma—although in somewhat less extreme form—that was created by the diffusionist reaction. The critic may wonder whether Steward has not abandoned a social-scientific approach to social change and retreated to essentially descriptive history. True, he is interested in parallels, but he has no theoretical basis for suggesting that any particular line of evolutionary development is more important than another. Every historical process that parallels another appears to qualify. Thus, the end result of Steward's approach would be a sort of count of typical processes in history, which is not very enlightening —no matter how interesting it may be as data—to the theoretically oriented student of social change.

### Two Theories of the Rise and Fall of Civilization

As we have seen, classical evolutionism portrayed the history of civilization as progressing from a low point to a high point. But not all general theories of cultural change share the optimism implied by this model of simple growth. Some are built on the additional notion that after a period of growth and maturity, stagnation and decline overtake a civilization. In the past century a number of these theories—associated with the names of Oswald Spengler, Arnold Toynbee, F. S. C. Northrup, Pitirim Sorokin, Alfred Louis Kroeber, and others—have commanded the attention of some serious scholars.[45] While most of these theories have fallen into disrepute among social scientists, they manifest a sufficient number of issues in the large-scale analysis of cultural change to merit our attention, no matter how brief it must be.

For illustrative purposes I shall consider only two theorists—Alfred Louis Kroeber (1876–1960) and Pitirim Alexandrovitch Sorokin (1889–  ) —and, for these, only one work of each.[46] I shall first summarize the work of each, then offer some comparisons and criticisms.

---

[44] *Ibid.*, p. 121.

[45] A review and criticism of a number of these theories is found in Pitirim A. Sorokin, *Social Philosophies in an Age of Crisis* (Boston: The Beacon Press, 1951).

[46] A. L. Kroeber, *Configurations of Culture Growth* (Berkeley and Los Angeles: University of California Press, 1944); and Pitirim A. Sorokin, *Social and Cultural Dynamics* (New York: American Book Company, 1937), four volumes.

Although Kroeber's approach to the rise and fall of civilization is ambitious enough in itself, he proceeded in a modest way. He was interested in simply trying to describe the "frequent habit of societies to develop their cultures to their highest levels spasmodically: especially in their intellectual and aesthetic aspects, but also in more material and practical respects. The cultures grow, prosper, and decline . . ." [47] Kroeber affirmed that his approach was "behavioristically factual rather than explanatory." [48]

Immediately, however, Kroeber faced enormous problems of measurement. Taking cultural patterns as his dependent variable in itself presented a headache, since these are notoriously difficult to quantify and measure. But, in addition, Kroeber wished to measure their qualities of superior and inferior development, which involves so many subjective judgments. Is modern jazz a high or low form of culture? Was George Bernard Shaw a genius or not? A million questions of this kind plague the investigator of culture. How did Kroeber face these questions? He again took a modest, inductive approach and followed the judgments of textbooks and encyclopedias on genius and cultural excellence, and, in his estimation, "[the consensus of the books was] fairly close." [49]

Kroeber, using this method of relying mainly on the judgments of historians and biographers, found remarkable agreement on what were considered to be the peaks of civilization, and who were the geniuses representing these peaks. But his sources fell into disagreement in judging the exact level of attainment of a civilization at a given time, and in judging whether a civilization was rising or falling at a given moment. So serious were these differences of opinion that Kroeber found himself unable to outline any universal contour of change beyond the very general pattern of alternate rises and falls of civilizations. Thus, still proceeding inductively, he described a number of different contours—for example, slow growth and fast decline; fast growth and slow decline; pulsated growth; growth at the periphery of a civilization; and insular growth—each illustrated by historical examples.

Kroeber did not venture much of an explanation of why civilizations wax and wane. But at one point he offered a general rationale for cultural cycles. Cultural patterns that are capable of growth, he asserted, are those that initially select from the myriad of possibilities of life experience for a civilization. We might call this distinctive pattern the basic premises on which the civilization is built. "Such patterns," Kroeber said, "must be selective and somehow differentiated or specialized. . . . This very selec-

---

[47] A. L. Kroeber, *Configurations of Culture Growth* (cited in footnote 46), p. 5.
[48] *Ibid.*, p. 7.
[49] *Ibid.*, p. 23.

tion which at the outset is necessary if a distinctive pattern is to be produced, is almost certain later on to become a limitation . . . with successful development it accordingly becomes exhausted. . . . It is then often or normally too late to go back and widen the scope of the pattern without undoing the entire growth which it has achieved . . . there must be a breakdown or abandonment and reformulation of patterns before the culture can go on to new high achievement." [50] To speak anthropomorphically, civilization chooses certain options, builds social structures and cultural forms around them, and then later finds that these very patterns limit further growth.

Sorokin's approach to cultural changes is more ambitious than Kroeber's. Not only did he attempt to locate and describe the rise and fall of cultures, but he attempted to interpret these fluctuations within a single typology of cultural mentalities. As we shall see presently, his general and deductive approach avoids some of the problems faced by Kroeber, but creates a different set of problems.

Sorokin began his analysis with a comprehensive classification of cultural changes—changes that are unique in time and space; recurring patterns; and a variety of unilinear, oscillating, spiralling, and branching patterns.[51] But the type of change that interested Sorokin most is what he called the "variably or creatively recurrent pattern." He considered this the "broadest and richest" type of cultural change. It cannot be reduced to a simple repetitive cycle—even though there may be recurrent elements—because it is always likely to veer off in a creative, exploratory direction. The creatively recurrent pattern is not influenced so much by forces external to the culture as by the implications of the culture itself. The causes of change are built into the basic premises of the culture; this is what Sorokin calls the "principle of immanent causation." [52]

The principle of internal cultural causation leads us directly to Sorokin's description of cultural mentalities. The basic dimension underlying his typology is the distinction between external, sense data and internal, spiritual concerns. A *Sensate* culture is one that emphasizes things readily available to the senses, and an *Ideational* culture is one that emphasizes things readily available to the spirit. An *Idealistic* culture is one that is built on a rich mixture of the Sensate and Ideational extremes. These mentalities constitute the basic premises of a culture and pervade all its particular manifestations. Thus, in terms of the criteria for truth, a Sensate

---

[50] *Ibid.*, p. 840.
[51] Pitirim A. Sorokin, *Social and Cultural Dynamics* (cited in footnote 46), Vol. I, Chapter IV.
[52] *Ibid.*, pp. 186–189.

culture stresses science and empiricism, whereas an Ideational culture stresses rationalism or mysticism; in terms of its ethics, a Sensate culture is hedonistic, an Ideational culture ascetic.

Sorokin outlined numerous combinations of Sensate, Ideational, and Idealistic cultures, but in the main he focused on a type of cycle—"the alternation of the domination of the Ideational, Sensate, and Idealistic types of cultural mentality and culture system" in the Western world from about 600 B.C. to the present time.[53] He considered the extremes of Ideational and Sensate as inherently temporary, sooner or later giving way to the opposite extreme, with an Idealistic period intervening between the two. Most of Sorokin's multivolume study is devoted to illustrating this general pattern with respect to fluctuations of art, philosophy, law, war, and revolution. Thus, in the field of painting, the medieval Catholic period represents an Ideational, spiritual phase; the renaissance of the thirteenth to the fifteenth centuries, an Idealistic mixture; and the modern period, a phase of Sensate excess.

Sorokin also analyzed fluctuations in forms of music. First he specified what types of music represent his general cultural categories. Thus, Ideational music is not judged in terms of its sounds, but in terms of its symbolization of some spiritual or religious state. Gregorian plain chant is a good example. Sensate music, by contrast, emphasizes the beauty of the musical sounds themselves, and any inner meanings are secondary. Sorokin also mentioned that Sensate music emphasizes sensual themes —for instance, love, dreams, and clouds. The music of Wagner, Mahler, and Debussy are examples. The Idealistic or intermediary phase is represented by the baroque and classical periods—Bach and Mozart, for example.

As with art and other cultural forms, Sorokin found the broad sweep in music to be an alternation between Ideational in the medieval period and Sensate in the modern period, with Idealistic in between. To illustrate, he pointed to several kinds of evidence of the increasingly Sensate quality of modern music: a decline in the proportion of religious composers during the past few centuries; and in easing theatricalization of music—for example, operas, program music, and musical comedies—that appeals to the senses; a growth in size and colossalism of performances; and a greater professionalism of criticism of music for its own sake (as opposed to earlier censorship in the name of religious values). Sorokin regarded the twentieth century as manifesting "all the symptoms of disorganization, demoralization, and degeneration. . . . It witnesses on the one hand an utter degrada-

[53] *Ibid.*, p. 190.

tion, vulgarization, 'jazzing,' and modernistic-impressionistic musical anarchy and impotency (in spite of the gigantic technical skill and complexities of many a modern composition); on the other hand, it exhibits the first signs of the efforts to seek new, anti-Sensate forms of music." [54] As his language shows, Sorokin is no friend of the twentieth century; indeed, he views it as being on the verge of a catastrophic Sensate collapse, to be followed by a reassertion of more spiritual values.

How might the approaches of Kroeber and Sorokin be compared? The most general observation to be made is that Kroeber's work shows the strengths and weaknesses of a particular, descriptive, inductive approach to cultural change, whereas Sorokin's work shows the strengths and weaknesses of a general, comprehensive, deductive approach. Kroeber's theory, that is, can be criticized for not rising to a scientific level of generality. He was so hesistant to describe general patterns, so ready to admit all kinds of variant patterns, and so wary of attempting systematic explanations that his work is a historical catalogue rather than a scientific account. Kroeber's conclusions are relatively free from criticism, but this is mainly because he was so cautious in venturing them. Sorokin, by contrast, built an ambitious explanatory system from a definite starting point, and attempted to apply his general concepts to a vast number of cultural products. And while his notion of immanent causation is largely implicit and rather mystical, it is more of an explanation than Kroeber made. But having exposed himself by venturing these general, sweeping assertions, Sorokin is more vulnerable to damaging criticisms. The following are samples.

1. The application of the Sensate and Ideational principle leads to apparent contradictions. The concepts are defined in terms of the distinction between external, sense data and inner, spiritual matters. But in one application of the concepts, Sorokin said that, with respect to continuity of values, the Sensate mentality stresses volatility and flux, whereas the Ideational mentality stresses eternity and stability. However, when we examine a specific cultural product—the Newtonian world view of the eighteenth century—we find it Sensate in that it focuses on the external world, but Ideational in that it rests on notions of harmony and order. A similar problem arises in judging the music of Richard Wagner, which is Sensate from the standpoint of theatricalism and massiveness, but Ideational in that it symbolizes a number of philosophical and national values. Applying Sorokin's general concepts leads at least to ambiguity and confusion, at most to outright contradiction.

[54] *Ibid.,* p. 568.

2. Some of the ways Sorokin identified his general concepts show a lack of scholarly care. At one point in his analysis Sorokin wished to demonstrate that the traits of culture mentalities are distributed unevenly among different social groups. In this connection he presented a table, classifying a large number of Roman Catholic popes and Russian, Austrian, English and French kings according to whether they represented "Very Sensate, Sensate, Mixed, Ideational, or Very Ideational" qualities.[55] The table was carefully percentaged. But Sorokin provided no criteria by which his kings and popes were classified, above and beyond the footnote stating that "a large body of literature was consulted. It is not detailed here in order to save overburdening the work with bibliographies which are secondary in importance and are otherwise not unknown or difficult of access." [56] Clearly, Sorokin demanded too much faith on the part of his readers by such a procedure, and the conclusions drawn from his calculations are correspondingly weakened.

3. In his zeal for locating general patterns, Sorokin tended to brush over items that might embarrass his theory. For example, he noted that the Idealistic period in music was the sixteenth to eighteenth centuries, and that the Idealistic period in art was the twelfth and thirteenth centuries.[57] This discrepancy is an important one. If we accept Sorokin's assertion that a definite cultural principle pervades and integrates the whole culture, we would expect the various specific cultural forms—art, music, and others— to move along at approximately the same rate. If they did not, the culture would experience some kind of malintegration. But Sorokin neglected to consider this theoretical difficulty posed by the several-century lag of music behind art.

To summarize the comparison between Kroeber and Sorokin, let us recall the relations between classical evolutionary theory, on the one hand, and diffusionism and multilinear evolutionary theory, on the other. The theorist basing his approach on a general, pervasive scheme (the classical evolutionists and Sorokin) comes closer to meeting the scientific desideratum of general applicability, but is more easily criticized for his erroneous conclusions and distortions. The theorist basing his approach on a more modest, cataloguing operation (the diffusionists, the multilinear evolutionists, and Kroeber) makes fewer mistakes because he is less ambitious, but may legitimately be criticized for being a descriptive historian rather than a social scientist. This tension between the historical, particular approach and the scientific, generalizing approach constitutes one of the major dilemmas in the field of social change.

---

[55] *Ibid.*, p. 106.
[56] *Ibid.*

[57] *Ibid.*, pp. 504, 568.

## Interrelations among Different Processes of Change: The Example of Modernization

If I were writing a whole book rather than a single chapter on social change, I would now develop several chapters, each devoted to a type of social change. Representative types might be (1) social cycles, including, for instance, business cycles, cycles of fashions, and alterations of liberalism and conservatism in public policy; (2) the breakdown and reconstitution of the social order under the impact of crises, such as wars, natural disasters, and famines; (3) the creation of new value systems, which would include analyses of the growth of religions and of revolutionary movements and revolutionary regimes; and (4) the integration of smaller social units into large ones, which would include the study of customs unions and other international federations and organizations. I would review the literature to indicate what we know and do not know about each type of change. Toward the end of the book I would attempt to show how the various types are related to one another.

Because there is not space for such a comprehensive approach, I must rely on a substitute. I shall choose a single type of change—economic development or modernization—specify some of the processes that typically enter this type of change, and indicate some of the ways that these processes are related to one another.[58] I cannot be exhaustive, but I do hope to give an idea of the complexity of modernization, and to show the theoretical and empirical challenges that confront the analyst attempting to fathom whole societies in flux.

The riddles of the development of industrial society have perplexed sociologists since the very inception of the field. The great classical figures— Spencer, Marx, Weber, and Durkheim, for example [59]—were preoccupied in different ways with the causes and consequences of what we now call

[58] Much of the material in this last section was originally prepared as a lecture for broadcast in the Voice of America's Forum Series on Modernization, recorded in the spring of 1965. My lecture was entitled "The Modernization of Social Relations." It subsequently appeared in a volume entitled *Modernization: The Dynamics of Growth*, edited by Myron Weiner (New York: Basic Books, 1966), pp. 110–121.

[59] Herbert Spencer, *The Principles of Sociology* (London: Williams and Norgate, 1897), Vol. III; Karl Marx, *Capital*, translated by Samuel Moore and Edward Aveling and edited by Friederick Engels (London: George Allen and Unwin, 1946); Max Weber, *The Theory of Social and Economic Organization*, translated by A. M. Henderson and Talcott Parsons (New York: Oxford University Press, 1947); Max Weber, *The Protestant Ethic and the Spirit of Capitalism*, translated by Talcott Parsons (London: George Allen and Unwin, 1935); and Émile Durkheim, *The Division of Labor in Society*, translated by George Simpson (Glencoe, Ill.: The Free Press, 1949).

economic development. The ideas of these men still dominate much sociological thinking about change. In addition, interest in development has
been heightened in recent decades by a profound world revolution that
has forced itself on the attention of social scientists. This revolution is the
dissolution of the Western countries' colonial empires, the emergence of
the former colonies as new nations, and the attempts of these nations to
introduce marked and rapid economic social changes in their societies.
Since World War II, many sociologists, economists, anthropologists, and
political scientists have applied their skills to an understanding of the
changes shaking these developing areas of the world.

Because the idea of economic development has become such an everyday
notion in our mid-twentieth-century outlook, we are likely to be tempted
to think of it as a simple, unitary type of process. But economic development
is neither simple nor unitary. When we employ the term, we usually have
at least four distinct but interrelated processes implicitly in mind:

1. In the realm of technology, a developing society is changing *from*
simple and traditionalized techniques *toward* the application of scientific
knowledge.

2. In agriculture, the developing society evolves *from* subsistence farming *toward* the commercial production of agricultural goods. This means
specialization in cash crops, purchase of nonagricultural products in the
market, and often agricultural wage-labor.

3. In industry, the developing society undergoes a transition *from* the use
of human and animal power *toward* industrialization proper, or men working for wages at power-driven machines, which produce commodities
marketed outside the community of production.

4. In ecological arrangements, the developing society moves *from* the
farm and village *toward* urban concentrations.

Furthermore, while these four processes often occur simultaneously during development, they need not necessarily do so. Agriculture may become
commercialized without any appreciable changes in the industrial sector,
as was the case in the colonial countries in which the dominant powers
strove to increase production of primary products. Industrialization may
occur in villages, as was the case in early British industrialization and in
some Southeast Asian societies. And cities may proliferate even where there
is no significant industrialization, as had happened in some Asian and
African societies. The conclusion to be drawn from these observations is
that the causes, courses, and consequences of economic development must
be expected to vary widely from nation to nation.

Economic development, moreover, is only one aspect of the complex of
social change experienced by the emerging nations. The term "moderniza-

tion"—a conceptual cousin of the term "economic development" but more comprehensive in scope—refers to the fact that technical, economic, and ecological changes ramify through the whole social and cultural fabric. In an emerging nation we may expect profound changes in these spheres: in the *political* sphere as simple tribal or village authority systems give way to systems of suffrage, political parties, representation, and civil-service bureaucracies; in the *educational* sphere as the society strives to reduce illiteracy and increase economically productive skills; in the *religious* sphere as secularized belief systems begin to replace traditionalistic religions; in the *familial* sphere as extended kinship units lose their pervasiveness; and in the *stratificational* sphere, as geographical and social mobility tend to loosen fixed, ascriptive hierarchical systems. Furthermore, these various changes begin at different times and proceed at different rates in a developing nation. A modernizing country, then, displays a multiplicity of institutional changes; and no matter how carefully social change is planned, some institutional changes will always lead the way, while others will always lag behind. Thus a developing society, if it could be depicted graphically, would resemble a large, awkward animal lumbering forward by moving each of its parts, sometimes in partial coordination and sometimes in opposition to one another.

I shall begin by describing some of the typical institutional changes and discontinuities that are part of the modernizing process, limiting my attention to three areas—work relations, family relations, and community relations. I shall necessarily deal with generalities, thus doing some injustice to national differences in the developmental process. Then I shall note some relations among the various institutional changes and discontinuities, and suggest some of the reasons for a high potential for social and political unrest in the developing nations. Finally, I shall explore the reasons why unrest is manifested sometimes in withdrawal behavior, sometimes in modest reform movements, and sometimes in violent revolutionary movements.

### Changing Work Relations

In preindustrial societies, production is typically located in kinship units. Subsistence farming predominates; other industry, such as domestic manufacture, is supplementary to farming but still attached to kin and village. In some cases, occupational position is determined by an extended group, such as the caste. Exchange relations are also determined by traditional kinship and community obligations. In short, economic activities are relatively undifferentiated from the traditional family-community setting.

Economic development means, above all, the segregation of economic activities from this traditional setting. In agriculture, the introduction of money crops means that—unlike subsistence farming—the goods are consumed in households different from those in which they are produced. Agricultural wage labor, in which individuals rather than families are likely to be hired, often undermines the family production unit. In industry, handicraft production and cottage industry—like commercial farming—means that individual families do not produce for themselves but for other, unknown families somewhere in the market. And when manufacturing and factory systems arise, the worker is segregated not only from the control of his capital but also from other members of his family, since he is placed side by side with individual workers recruited in the labor market. In these ways, modernization separates economic activities from family and community activities.

As a result of these changes, the worker's relations to economic life are greatly altered. He now receives cash for services performed and spends this cash for goods and services in the market. More and more of his income and welfare comes to depend on the pay envelope, and less and less on the traditional rights and obligations expected from and owed to kinspeople and neighbors. This means that the worker in a modernizing market faces a number of problems of adjustment.

First, he finds that a new basis of calculation is foisted upon him. From the standpoint of allocating his productive time, he may no longer work at his own pace; he must adjust to the notion of a work day and a work week and, on the job, he must adjust to the rhythm of the machine rather than the rhythm of his own mind and body. From the standpoint of allocating his wealth, he must think in terms of budgeting a weekly bundle of cash; on the face of it, this would not appear to be much of an adjustment, but when we contrast the requisite level of calculation required with the day-by-day flow of economic activities in the traditional setting—in which cash payments scarcely figure—it is possible to appreciate the significant changes in outlook required of the new urban industrial worker.

Second, he finds the definition of his economic security greatly changed. In a traditional system of agriculture or domestic manufacture, a worker is likely to be underemployed rather than unemployed as a result of market fluctuations. In this case he works somewhat less, and turns to kinsmen, tribesmen, and neighbors for help. In the urban industrial setting, however, the worker is likely to be laid off and totally unemployed when economic activity is slack. In the new setting, then, the worker is subject to sharper, more severe changes in welfare and security, even though his average income may be higher than it was in the traditional setting.

Third, with respect to consumption, the worker in the modernizing market is faced with continuously changing standards. The urban market provides a veritable flood of new items—sweets, beer, gadgets, bicycles, transistor radios, and the like. As the worker is simultaneously drifting away from traditional expenditures—such as the dowry—and being exposed to new forms of gratification, he is likely to experience confusions and disorientations. Obviously, opportunities abound for merchants to market shabby products and to swindle inexperienced and uncertain consumers.

A fourth need for adjustment is imposed on the traditional sector. Many urban industrial workers visit or migrate back to the countryside. When in the urban industrial setting they are probably ambivalent about its demands and opportunities; but they surely often paint a beautiful picture of city life to their kinsmen and former neighbors who have remained in the countryside. Insofar as this occurs, it is likely to prove unsettling to the traditional way of life—especially if conditions are not good in the countryside—and to augment social conflicts between urban and rural sectors, as well as between younger migrating generations and older generations who remain in the country.

I do not mean to exaggerate the differences and discontinuities between the traditional and modern sectors. Many halfway arrangements between the two sectors are worked out in the modernizing process. Migratory labor, for instance, is a kind of compromise between full membership in a wage-labor force and attachment to an old community life. Cottage industry introduces extended markets but retains the family-production fusion. The employment of families in factories—which is a more frequent phenomenon than is commonly appreciated—maintains a version of family production. The expenditure of wages on traditional items also manifests the half-entry into the full urban industrial structure. The social and psychological reasons for these halfway houses are many; but no matter what the reasons are, the adjustments and discontinuities just discussed are lessened accordingly in the compromise arrangements.

### Changing Family Relations

One consequence of the removal of economic activities from the family-community setting is that the family itself loses some of its previous functions and becomes a more specialized agency. As the family ceases to be an economic unit of production, one or more members leave the household to seek employment in the labor market. The family's activities become more concentrated on emotional gratification and socialization.

The social implications of these changes in family life are enormous. The most fundamental of these implications—imposed mainly by the demands for mobility of the family—is the individuation and isolation of the nuclear family. If the family has to move about through the labor market, it cannot afford to carry all of its relatives with it, or even to maintain close, diffuse ties with extended kin. Thus the ties with collateral kinsmen begin to erode; few generations live in the same household; newly married couples set up new households, and leave the elders behind. One of the social problems that arise as a consequence of these kinship changes concerns the place of the aged. No longer cushioned by a protective kinship unit, the aged are thrown onto the community or the state as "charges" in greater numbers than before. Because of the social isolation of the aged, new institutional arrangements, such as pensions and social security programs, become imperative.

I do not want to oversimplify the process of decline of the extended kinship unit. In many cases—Japan is a good example—it survives intact for quite a long period of industrialization; in other cases, some features of extended kinship (for example, reciprocal working) erode, but other features (for example, mutual visiting) survive. Even the most advanced industrial societies still show some viable extended kinship structures. Despite these qualifications, however, it must be remembered that advanced urban industrial market conditions and full-scale extended kinship systems are inimical to one another in many respects.

Simultaneously the relations between parents and children undergo a transformation. The father, who now has to leave the household for employment in a separate establishment, necessarily loses many of the economic training functions that he previously enjoyed over his children. Correspondingly, apprenticeship systems which require the continuous presence of father and son decline as specialized factory production arises. Often, it is claimed, this decline in economic authority spreads to a decline in *general* paternal authority, although these claims have proved difficult to substantiate empirically. The mother, often being the only adult in the presence of young children during most of the day, develops a more intensive emotional relationship with them. Her role in socialization thus becomes more crucial, since she has almost sole responsibility for shaping the early emotional life of the children.

No matter how concentrated the relations are between mother and children in the early years, this period is short-lived. An advancing urban industrial society demands more complex technical skills than the family is able to provide. Hence the family tends to surrender many of its training functions to formal educational systems. The nuclear family very early loses control of its children to primary school (or even nursery school); by adolescence the child has outside contacts not only with education but also with some parts of the labor market. Furthermore, children may have married by their late teens or early 20's, may have set up a new household of their own, and may have become even more independent of their parents.

One ramification of these changing relations between parents and children is the "gap of adolescence," when the youth has been freed from the intensive parental ties of his early years but has not yet become fully engaged in adult occupational, marital, and civic roles. He thereby experiences a few years of loose role involvements. Psychologically, this is a period of uncertainty for the young person; and this uncertainty usually produces a number of symptoms of disturbance, such as random protest, compulsive search for love and security, faddism and experimentation, and lethargy and apathy. Many commentators have noted the historical fact that urban industrial societies invariably witness a growth of adolescent protest and delinquency. The explanation for this historical fact cannot be appreciated, however, until we grasp the simultaneous and interrelated changes that occur among the economic, educational, and familial structures in a modernizing society.

A further ramification of the revolution in kinship relations in the urban industrial setting concerns the formation of new families. In many traditional settings, marriage is closely regulated by elders; the tastes and sentiments of the couple to be married are relatively unimportant. The basis for marriage, then, lies not in love, but rather in more practical arrangements, such as the availability of a substantial dowry or the promise of marrying into a choice parcel of land. With the decay of extended kinship ties and the redefinition of parental authority, youth becomes emancipated with respect to choosing a spouse. This emancipation, however, simultaneously produces a "vacuum." If some variety of arranged marriage is not available as an institutional mechanism for forming new families, what criteria are available? Having posed the question in this way, we may better appreciate the social importance of "romantic love" as the dominant basis for marriage in urban industrial societies. The feeling of being in love provides an alternative criterion for choice in an uncertain situation in which other institutional arrangements are lacking.

In sum, modernization tends to foster the rise of a family unit that is formed on emotional attraction and built on a limited sexual-emotional basis. The family has been removed from other major social spheres except for the segmental, external ties of individual family members. The family, being thus isolated and specialized, impinges less on these other social spheres; nepotism as a basis for recruitment into other social roles tends to become at most corrupt and at least suspect, whereas in traditional society it was the legitimate basis for recruitment into roles. Finally, within the family the complex and multifunctional relations of family members to one another tend to be pared down to more exclusively emotional ties.

## Changes in Community and Associational Life

In the simplified model of traditional society that we have been using, community and associational life are closely knit with the ascribed bases of social existence—kinship, clanship, tribal, and caste affiliations. Formal organizations such as trade unions, social clubs, voluntary associations, and special interest groups seldom develop. Most of social life and its problems are worked through in the multifunctional ascribed groupings themselves.

These traditional bases for community and associational life retain much vitality even as the urban and industrial complex begins to emerge. When industrialization occurs in villages, for example, or when villages are built around paternalistic industrial enterprises, many ties of community and kinship can be maintained under industrial conditions. Furthermore, some evidence shows that migrants to cities display what might be called the "brother-in-law" syndrome; they seek out relatives or tribesmen, reside with them while searching for employment and sometimes after finding it, and limit their social life primarily to them. The invariable development of racial, tribal, and ethnic "ghettos" in the growing cities of the world is probably the result of both outright residential discrimination and a search for community in cities.

The persistence of exclusively traditional ties in the urban industrial setting, however, appears not to be a sufficient basis for community and associational life. After a time, these traditional ties come to be supplemented by more specialized organizations, football clubs, and chapel or church societies. The names of these groups—which would suggest special purposes for each—should not obscure the fact, however, that especially in the early days of their formation, they are frequently multifunctional organizations. The friendly societies of eighteenth century England, for example, were simultaneously trade unions, insurance societies, and drinking clubs. Many of the loose formal organizations among African urban migrants are simultaneously tribal associations, trade unions, football clubs, and social centers. Furthermore, these organizations tend to be quite unstable in their early days. They may begin as a tribal association, turn next into a saving association, and then take an interest in nationalism. As time passes, however, the fluidity of these organizations diminishes, and more "functional" groupings, based on economic or political interest, begin to replace them.

## Discontinuities in Modernization and the Genesis of Social Unrest

The various economic and social changes that I have described are disruptive to the social order for several reasons.

First, structural change is, above all, uneven during periods of modernization, as I stressed at the beginning. In colonial societies, for instance, the
European powers frequently revolutionized the economic and political
framework by exploiting economic resources and establishing colonial administrations, but at the same time encouraged or imposed a conservatism
in traditional religious, class, and family systems. In a society undergoing
postcolonial modernization, similar discontinuities appear. Within the economy itself, rapid industrialization bites unevenly into established social and
economic structures. Social institutions also display a pattern of growth
that produces leads, lags, and bottlenecks. For example, most of the colonial
nations, upon attaining independence, more or less immediately established
some form of universal suffrage, thus entering instantaneously into the
modern era. This action promptly created a crisis in education, since a mass
electorate rests upon the assumption of a literate electorate with a sense
of citizenship and an ability to participate in the polity. Social change thus
moves ahead by a complicated leapfrog process, creating recurrent crises of
adjustment. The first paradox of development, then, is that a developing
society must change in all ways at once, but cannot conceivably plan such
a regular, coordinated pattern of growth. A certain amount of social unrest inevitably is created.

Second, the development of new kinds of social and economic activities
creates conflicts with traditional ways of life. For example, when factories
begin to mass-produce items that compete with the same items produced
domestically, the market is flooded with cheap goods, depriving the domestic workers of their means of livelihood. In theory, this should drive
domestic workers into more remunerative lines of wage labor. In practice,
however, the process of converting domestic labor into wage labor is a very
slow and painful one, sometimes taking several generations to complete. To
take another example, the growth of a class of highly trained doctors poses a threat to traditional medicine men and magicians, as well as
to many revered domestic cures. The second paradox of modernization
then, is that when economic and social advances take place, many people
in the society turn out to be at least ambivalent and possibly openly hostile
toward these advances. This continuing conflict between modern and traditional ways is a further source of social unrest.

Third, efforts on the part of governments of the new nations to contain
and handle social unrest often creates the conditions for even further unrest. Most of the effective efforts to integrate and to develop societies rest
with the centralized governments. In view of the severe and pervasive
problems of integration faced by these nations, it could scarcely be otherwise. But insofar as central authorities establish themselves as viable governments, they simultaneously become threats to local, caste, regional, and

other traditional types of authority. These threats underlie the apparent tendencies toward Balkanization in some of the developing countries. The third paradox of development, then, is that even the effective exercise of authority creates unrest and conflict with competing authority systems.

The conclusion to be drawn is that developing nations face a danger if they conceive of economic development simply in terms of developing as fast as possible. To focus unduly on this criterion is likely to create social costs—expressed in terms of unmanageable levels of social unrest and political instability—that may in the end defeat the effort to develop, itself. If speed is the only criterion, the developing nation may destroy too rapidly various forms of integration and unleash explosive levels of unrest. Furthermore, if too much speed is fostered in any one institutional sphere—for example, the economic—the society is likely to create an unbalanced pattern of growth, which is also a source of social unrest. It seems to me that the key problem in successful development is not to focus on a single criterion of growth, but rather to balance and measure development according to several different economic and social criteria.

### Different Manifestations of Social Unrest

Modernization, then, no matter how much a society may desire to achieve it, is a trying thing, and generally is accompanied by much social unrest. But this fact alone does not reveal very much about the specific forms that this unrest may take. Will it be expressed in individual form—crime, alcohol and drug addiction, suicide, and mental illness? Or will it be collective? And if collective, will it be religious or political? If political, will it be manifested in peaceful and modest movements for reform or in revolutionary threats to the legitimacy of the existing government?

The answers to these questions are bound to be complicated, since so many factors influence the channeling of social unrest. Foreign influence on social unrest plays a part. For example, the strategy and tactics of Communist youth movements in a Latin American country differ according to whether they are under the influence of the Soviet, Chinese, or Cuban model, or under the influence of no specific foreign party. The character of leadership of protest also plays a part. If a country is still essentially tribal and illiterate, leaders who can provide an articulate ideological base for organized protest are in short supply. (In this connection, notice that many of the leaders of African and Asian movements for independence from the colonial powers were not strictly "from the land," but were intellectuals educated in the universities of Oxford, London, and Paris, where they were exposed to the ideas and ideologies of the West.) Instead of attempting to catalogue all of the factors influencing protest in developing countries, however, I shall concentrate on the part played by the governing authorities themselves in determining the form of protest.

The agencies of social control, especially political leaders, are seldom neutral toward social unrest in their societies, since unrest is always potentially disruptive of the social order and is threatening to the political regime itself. Consequently, part of the legal and constitutional structure of a society is related to the management of unrest. The important point is that the very posture taken by the governing authorities will itself influence the direction of protest. Consider the following examples.

If the political authorities do not enjoy legitimacy, and if they do not have control over the police and the military, unrest will tend to take the forms of uncontrolled violence, successful defiance of governmental action, and periodic *coups d'etat*. These reactions occur mainly because the government itself is incapable of preventing them. This pattern of constitutionally unviable, politically ineffective authority, on the one hand, and simple, nonideological defiance of political authorities, on the other, is best illustrated in many of the Latin American republics in the nineteenth and early twentieth centuries.

Suppose, however, that political leaders have the constitutional and military means to prevent outright defiance of their authority. The way in which they use these means also influences the form of protest. If the society has institutionalized a variety of meaningful channels for expressing protest—for instance, democratic elections, the opportunity for petition and demonstration, a free press, and a court system to check political invasions of citizens' rights—protest will probably take the form of peaceful and lawful agitation designed to influence the policies of the governing authorities. (If, however, a group feels that it has been consistently excluded from the political decision-making process, it may adopt more militant means such as civil disobedience or outright subversive activity.) The combination of a constitutionally viable but flexible government, on the one hand, and peaceful protest and agitation for reform, on the other, is illustrated by some of the long-established Western democracies.

If a society lacks these channels to express protest, and if the political leaders are repressive toward its expression, social unrest is likely to take another form. Because of harassment by the authorities, it is frequently driven underground. In addition, being frustrated in action, it tends to develop elaborate fantasies and ideologies of social regeneration. Many of these fantasies and ideologies are hostile to the political system but, because of the strength and repressiveness of the regime, they remain latent. Such underground organizations often develop elaborate rituals and initiation ceremonies. The pattern of a strong and repressive government, on the one hand, and protest through withdrawal and fantasy, on the other, is illustrated by the cults and clubs that appear in societies under colonial rule or totalitarian dictatorship.

Finally, if a period of harsh repression is followed by a period of increasingly ineffective government, still another type of protest is manifested. The source of the ineffectiveness need not concern us here; it may, for example, result from the government's involvement in a losing war, or from the accession of a weak leader to power. During the first period, we would expect the pattern just discussed—protest through withdrawal and fantasy. As the authorities lose their power to repress, however, the hostile and potentially revolutionary fantasies emerge from underground and become the basis for outright attacks on the government. If this protest goes far, it develops into a full-scale ideological revolutionary movement. If successful, this kind of revolution is different from the simple *coup d'etat* mentioned above, which is often little more than a changeover in governing personnel; an ideological revolution involves the overthrow of a government, but it does so in the name of a fantasy of national and perhaps even world regeneration. Consequently its motivation to reconstruct the social order and rid itself of its enemies is very great.[60]

Without building a full theory of modernization, I have attempted in this final section to indicate some of the interrelations among different types of social change—change in various quantitative indices such as per capita production and literacy rates; change in social structures such as the family and community; and change in the level and kinds of social unrest. In the present state of social-scientific knowledge, it is not possible to formalize these interrelations into a theory that will meet effectively all of the requirements that I laid out earlier.[61] But perhaps I have indicated some directions that the persons who eventually construct such a theory might take.

## Summary

In this chapter I approached the subject of social change from a number of different angles. First, in order to be as specific as possible, I described and analyzed an individual case, and attempted to demonstrate the way that a sociologist might approach an instance of change. Then I considered some important theoretical issues raised even by this relatively minute case.

[60] A historically documented discussion of these relations between social control and protest is found in my book, *Theory of Collective Behavior* (cited in footnote 9), especially Chapters IX and X.
[61] *Supra*, pp. 688–698.

Building on these issues, I developed a formal statement of the ingredients of an adequate theory of change. These ingredients simultaneously constitute criteria by which the strengths and weaknesses of existing theories of change might be assessed. Next I reviewed a small sample of these theories, and criticized their theoretical and empirical adequacy. Finally, I considered the problem of modernization, illustrating especially the important interrelations among different process of change. I hope that the diversity of my approach has not obscured the fact that this chapter has been devoted to a single objective: to provide a vivid if not exhaustive appreciation of the problems that arise when social scientists undertake to explain, in a systematic way, the flux of the social world.

# Author Index *

Acquaviva, Sabina, 379n
Adams, Henry, 446
Allen, Francis A., 663n
Allen, V. L., 495
Alford, Robert, 459n, 480n, 481n
Almond, Gabriel, 449n, 460n
Andenas, Johs, 651n
Anderson, C. A., 394n, 425(t)
Anderson, Marian, 209
Andrews, F. Emerson, 316n
Anton, Thomas J., 234
Aoyama, H., 461n
Arendt, Hannah, 453n
Arensberg, Conrad, 311n
Aristotle, 65, 449, 450
Aronson, E., 599–600
Asch, Solomon, 619, 620
Ash, Ellis, 92n
Ashby, Sir Eric, 405n
Asher, Robert, 449n
Aubert, Vilhelm, 656n
Aveling, Edward, 716n
Axelrod, Morris, 140, 141(t)

Back, Kurt W., 42n, 48n, 78
Bailyn, Bernard, 388
Bailey, F. G., 245n
Baker, A., 92n
Bales, Robert Freed, 78, 540n
Ball, John C., 638n
Bandura, Albert, 641
Banfield, Edward, 168n, 192n, 453n
Barber, Bernard, 318n, 494n
Barnard, C. I., 70n, 71n
Bass, B. M., 78
Bastice, Henri, 177(t)
Bateman, J. Fremont, 92n
Bates, Alan, 652n
Bateson, Gregory, 551n, 649n

Baum, Martha, 645n
Bazelon, David T., 217
Beach, Frank A., 533
Becker, Howard S., 607, 613–614, 626n,
    627, 633, 654n
Becker, W. C., 592n, 594n
Belden, A. D., 476n
Bell, Daniel, 450n, 451n, 471n
Bell, N. W., 585n
Bellah, Robert N., 708n
Belshaw, Cyril S., 305n, 306
Bendix, Reinhard, 226n, 267, 343n, 462n,
    631n
Benedict, Ruth, 548, 556, 566
Benne, K. D., 577n
Benney, Mark, 457n
Bennis, W. G., 78, 575n, 599n
Bensman, Joseph, 367n
Bentley, Arthur, 438
Berelson, Bernard, 457n
Berger, Peter, 9, 17, 19, 358n, 359n, 375n
Berlew, D. E., 78, 599n
Bernstein, B., 399n, 422n
Bettelheim, Bruno, 549n, 597n
Birnbaum, N., 219n
Bittner, Egon, 660n
Blackmar, Frank, 439
Blake, Judith, 623–624, 625, 626, 633
Blau, Peter, 41n, 78, 168, 169n, 195n, 494n
Blauner, Robert, 154n, 167n, 190(t), 187,
    190(t)
Blondel, Jean, 249, 250n, 251, 252n
Boas, Franz, 306n
Bogue, Donald J., 109n
Bonner, H., 78
Bonner, J. T., 555n
Borgatta, E. F., 78
Boulding, Kenneth, 173n
Braidwood, Robert J., 116n

* The abbreviation "n" refers to a page footnote, and (t) refers to a table.

Braunias, Karl, 441n
Briar, Scott, 643, 644n
Brinton, Crane, 696n
Brodbeck, Arthur J., 168n, 492n
Bronfenbrenner, Urie, 540n, 593n, 594
Bronner, Augusta, 641
Broom, Leonard, 105n
Brown, Norman O., 560n, 611n
Brown, R. W., 554n
Browne, C. G., 78
Bryce, James, 454n
Burchinal, Lee, 142
Burdick, Eugene, 168n, 492n
Burton, R. V., 592n
Butler, Samuel, 656n

Caldwell, Bettye M., 594n
Cameron, Mary Owen, 654n
Campbell, Angus, 475n
Campbell, Ernest, 368n
Caplow, Theodore, 92
Capp, Al, 568n
Cardinal Newman, 406n, 411
Carnegie, Andrew, 209, 256
Carpenter, David B., 104
Carr-Saunders, A. M., 410n
Carroll, Eleanor E., 594n
Cartwright, Dorwin, 78, 619n
Castro, Fidel, 445, 462n
Catlin, George E. G., 93n
Caudill, William, 92n
Cayton, Horace, 240, 241n
Centers, Richard, 255, 470n
Chambliss, William, 652n
Childe, V. Gordon, 709
Chilton, Roland J., 638
Christenson, Harold T., 142n
Christie, Nils, 615
Clark, Burton R., 399, 402n
Clark, Colin, 100, 297
Clark, John Maurice, 168n
Clemmer, Donald, 92n
Clinard, Marshall B., 146n
Cloward, Richard, 625, 632n, 647, 648
Cohen, Albert K., 637, 640n, 647
Cohen, Julius, 652n
Cohn, T. S., 78
Cole, Allan, 461n
Cole, G. D. H., 250
Coleman, James S., 91, 185n, 186, 397–398,
    449n, 460n, 492n, 567, 674n
Comte, August, 699
Converse, Philip, 489, 490n
Copernicus, 554

Coser, Lewis A., 572n, 615n
Cottrell, Leonard S., Jr., 105n, 661n, 663n
de Coulanges, Fustel, 346n
Cressey, Donald R., 646n
Curle, Adam, 416n

Dahl, Robert, 234n
Dahrendorf, Rolf, 217, 218
Dalton, Melville, 194n, 473n, 475n
Darwin, Charles, 200, 554, 699
Davis, Kingsley, 118(t), 121, 207n, 229,
    529, 541n, 549, 550, 623–624, 625, 626,
    636
Dawson, Carl A., 695, 696n
Debelius, W., 412n
De Gaulle, Charles, 445
Dentler, Robert A., 615n, 621
Deutsch, M., 566n
Deutscher, Isaac, 476n
De Vore, I., 551n., 552n
Dewey, John, 454n
De Witt, N., 410n, 411n
Dickson, William J., 195n
Distler, L., 592n
Dornbusch, Sanford, 372n
Douglas, J. W. B., 422n
Drake, St. Clair, 240, 241n
Draper, Theodore, 462n
Drucker, Peter F., 168n, 409
Dubinsky, David, 496
Duncan, Beverly, 124, 125(t)
Duncan, Otis Dudley, 104, 110n, 124,
    125(t)
Dunham, H. Warren, 92n
Durkheim, Émile, 14n, 145, 146n, 304,
    333–334, 339–340, 343, 346n, 356–357,
    387, 405. 450n, 528, 560–564, 565–566,
    581, 587–588, 613, 614–615, 628, 651,
    716
Duverger, Maurice, 441n, 495

Eckstein, Harry, 496n
Eggan, Fred, 514, 515n
Eibl-Eibesfeldt, I., 551n
Eisenhower, Dwight, 467, 489–490
Eisenstadt, S. N., 708n
Eliade, Mircea, 337, 346
Ellis, Albert, 528
Emerson, Rupert, 264
Engel, Ernst, 315n
Engels, Friedrich, 716n
Erikson, Erik H., 581
Erikson, Kai T., 9, 16, 21, 22, 602, 607n,
    615n, 616, 621

Etzioni, Amitai, 169, 708n
Etzioni, Eva, 708n

Faris, Robert E. L., 402n
Feldman, Arnold S., 315n, 311n
Festinger, Leon, 42n, 46n, 48n, 78, 599n
Fichter, Joseph, 367n
Finch, Henry A., 691n
Firth, Raymond, 509n
Flexner, Abraham, 407n
Floud, Jean, 394n, 400n, 422–423, 425(t), 428n
Flugel, J. C., 588n
Ford, Clellan, 533
Ford, Henry, 158
Fortes, Meyer, 387
Foster, G. M., 566n
Frank, Harley, 659n
Fraser, W. R., 404n
Frazier, E. Franklin, 96n, 242
Freeman, Thomas, 92n
Freidson, Eliot, 656n
Fremont-Smith, Marion R., 304n
Freud, Sigmund, 18, 254, 548, 554, 558–559, 560–562, 568n, 569, 573n, 586n, 569, 573n, 586n, 588n, 591
Friedrich, Carl J., 86n, 90n
Fromm, Erich, 556, 575n, 582n

Galbraith, John K., 168n
Galenson, Walter, 154n
Gans, Herbert, 96n
y Gasset, José Ortega, 453n
Gee, Wilson, 85n
Geertz, Clifford, 173n
Gehlen, Arnold, 369n, 370n
Gerth, H. H., 221n, 348n, 367n, 396n, 407n, 412n, 443n
Gettys, Warner E., 695–696
Gibbs, Jack P., 120(t)
Giddings, Franklin, 438, 439
Girard, Alain, 177(t), 423n, 429(t)
Glass, David, 291n
Glenn, Norval D., 242
Goffman, Erving, 56n, 78, 92n, 595–596, 599n, 600n, 607n
Goffman, Irwin W., 256
Golden, Hilda Hertz, 118(t), 121
Goldenweiser, Alexander, 705n
Goldhamer, Herbert, 616
Goldsen, Rose, 332n
Goldwater, Barry, 371
Golombiewski, R. T., 78

Goode, William J., 91, 327n, 536n, 540n, 541n
Gordon, Margaret, 418n
Gough, E., Kathleen, 526n
Gould, Julius, 87n, 106n
Gouldner, Alvin W., 494n, 495
Grant, Nigel, 394n
Gras, Norman Scott Brien, 108
Gray, A. P., 457n
Gray, Susan W., 592n
Grigg, Charles M., 146
Guest, Robert H., 187
Gulick, Charles, 478n
Guttsman, W. L., 250–252, 253n

Hagen, Everett, 449n
Hagstrom, Warren O., 93n
Haire, Mason, 198n
Halbwachs, Maurice, 339n
Haley, Jay, 649n
Hall, E. T., 553–554, 583n, 593n
Hall, Jerome, 652n
Halleck, Seymour L., 92n
Halsey, A. H., 6, 9, 394n, 399n, 413(t), 417n, 423n, 425(t)
Hamill, Hugh M., Jr., 444n
Hamilton, Alexander, 445
Hamilton, Herbert, 706n
Hamilton, M. A., 412n
Hare, A. Paul, 78
Harlow, H. F., 550n
Harlow, Margaret K., 550n
Harp, John, 617n
Harrington, Michael, 239
Harrison, Paul M., 49n, 363n
Hartley, Eugene L., 540n, 553n, 554n
Harwitz, Mitchell, 293n
Hatt, Paul K., 104n, 237, 238
Hauser, Philip M., 110n, 127n, 133n, 134n, 144n
Haviland, H. Field, Jr., 93n
Havighurst, R. J., 430
Hawley, Amos H., 85–86, 94, 95, 111
Hayner, Norman S., 92n
Healy, William, 641
Hegel, Georg Wilhelm Friedrich, 439
Heider, Fritz, 46n, 78, 657
Henderson, A. M., 2n, 169n, 692n, 716n
Henry, Andrew F., 593n
Henrysson, S., 404n
Herberg, Will, 343n, 359n, 492
Hermens, F. A., 441n
Herskovits, Melville J., 293n
Hertz, Hilda, *see* Golden, Hilda Hertz

Heyns, R. W., 50–51, 78
Hield, Wayne, 707n
Hillery, George A., Jr., 84n, 90–91, 92n, 93n, 94
Hitler, Adolf, 448, 479
Hobbes, Thomas, 550, 555–557, 562–563
Hoffa, Jimmy, 496
Hoffman, Lois W., 592n, 593n, 594n
Hoffman, M. L., 592n, 594n
Hofstadter, Richard, 266, 406, 407n, 408
Hollander, E. P., 75n, 78
Hollingshead, August B., 259–260, 398, 617n, 649n
Holmberg, A. R., 560n
Homans, George, 2n, 4, 5, 7, 14, 16, 17–18, 33n, 49n, 67n, 75n, 78, 708n
Hooker, Evelyn, 626
Horkheimer, Max, 453n
Hoselitz, Bert F., 305n, 315n
Hsu, F. L. K., 595n
Hughes, Everett C., 318n
Huizinga, J., 582n
Hunter, Floyd, 361n
Husen, T., 404n
Hutton, J. H., 246, 247
Hyash, C., 461n
Hyman, Herbert, H., 137, 138(t), 243, 631n

Inkeles, Alex, 602

Jackson, Don D., 649n
Jacobs, H. Lee, 142n
Jacques, Elliott, 186n
Jaeger, Gertrude, 692n
James, William, 336
Janowitz, Morris, 195n
Jefferson, Thomas, 445
Jennings, H. H., 78
Johnson, Benton, 487, 488(t)
Johnson, Norman, 638n
Jones, Maxwell, 92n

Kagan, J., 592n
Kahin, George M., 477n
Katz, Elihu, 706n
Kautsky, John H., 462n
Keller, Suzanne, 265
Kelley, H. M., 42n, 53n, 78
Kemper, Theodore D., 649n
Kennedy, John F., 490, 491, 687
Kent, Morris A., Jr., 664n
Kerr, Clark, 168n, 406n, 494n
Kido, Kotaro, 454n

Killian, Lewis M., 146
King, Martin Luther, 371
King, S. H., 593n
Kirchheimer, Otto, 468n
Kitsuse, John I., 607n, 654n
Klaus, R., 592n
Klausner, Samuel, 372n
Klein, J., 78
Kluckhohn, Clyde, 528
Kohlberg, L., 592n, 594n
Kohn, M. L., 594n
Kolaja, Jiri, 87n
Kolb, William L., 87n, 105n, 106n
Kolko, Gabriel, 235, 236
Kornhauser, William, 325n, 453n
Kroeber, Alfred Louis, 705, 710–712, 714, 715
Kuhn, A., 78
Kuznets, Simon, 235, 315n, 316n

Ladd, John, 90
Lambert, W. W., 595n
Landauer, T. K., 590n
Landecker, Werner S., 113n
Lander, Bernard, 639
Lawrence, D. H., 567
Lazarsfeld, Paul F., 183, 184, 457n
Leacock, Eleanor Burke, 699n
Lederer, Emil, 453n
van der Leeuw, Gerardus, 337, 347
Lemert, Edwin M., 607, 646
Lenin, V. I., 191, 445
Lenneberg, E. H., 554n
Lenski, Gerhard, 343n, 359n, 471, 473n
Lepawsky, Albert, 438n, 439n
Lerner, Daniel, 450n, 455, 456n
Lerner, Max, 361n
Lessa, William, 335n
Levin, Martin L., 706n
Levine, S., 590n
Levy, Marion J., 277n
Lewis, John L., 496
Lewis, Oscar, 144
Lifton, R. J., 599n
Likert, R., 568n
Lincoln, Abraham, 209, 687
Linden, Franz, 476n
Linton, Ralph, 562n
Lipset, Seymour M., 5, 16, 17, 19, 91, 154n, 186, 207n, 226n, 230, 267, 282n, 392, 393, 449n, 459n, 461n, 462n, 466n, 476n, 478n, 492n, 495n, 631n
Little, A., 428n
**Litwak, Eugene**, 538n

Locke, John, 548, 549–552, 555
Lockwood, David, 196n
Loeb, Martin B., 92n
Lorenz, K. Z., 551
Lowie, Robert H., 528, 705n
Luckman, Thomas, 369n, 376n
Lunt, Paul S., 223n
Lynn, Kenneth S., 318n

McCarthy, Joseph, 183n
Maccoby, Eleanor E., 540n, 553n, 554n
McCord, Joan, 641
McCord, William, 641
Machiavelli, N., 347, 359
Mace, D., 567n
Mace, Vera, 567n
Machlup, F., 400n
MacIver, Robert M., 84n, 96
Mack, Raymond W., 93n
McKenzie, Robert D., 108, 109, 495
McKinney, John C., 306n
McPhee, William, 457n
Maine, Henry Sumner, 699
Malinowski, Bronislaw, 305, 562n
Malthus, T. R., 291
de Man, Henri, 154
Manners, R. A., 559n
Mannheim, Karl, 453n
Mao Tse-tung, 445
March, James, 157n
Marcuse, Herbert, 560n, 611n
Marder, Rene, 156(t)
Marshall, Andrew, 616
Marshall, T. H., 462, 463n
Massing, Paul, 467n
Martin, F. M., 423n
Martindale, Don, 2n, 91
Marx, Karl, 5, 15, 144, 167n, 179–180, 185,
   211 ff., 253, 282, 288–290, 316, 439,
   451, 699, 716
Maslow, A. H., 566
Mason, W., 402n
Masumi, Jennosuke, 461n
Matusita, K., 461n
Mayer, Kurt B., 239
Mead, George Herbert, 589, 590n, 613n
Mead, Margaret, 582–583
Mendel, Douglas, 461n
Mercer, Blaine E., 86
Merriam, Alan P., 93n
Merry, Julius, 92n
Merton, Robert K., 105n, 339, 569n, 571n,
   607, 612n, 622, 628, 632–633, 640, 666n,
   708n

Messinger, Sheldon, 656n
Meuller, J. H., 614n
Michels, Robert, 438, 493, 495, 497–498
Miller, Herman P., 236
Miller, S. M., 252
Miller, Walter B., 617n, 638n, 640
Millis, Theodore M., 656n
Mills, C. Wright, 221n, 232, 233, 348n,
   367n, 396n, 407n, 412n. 443n, 462n, 498
Mills, J., 599–600
Mintz, Norbett, 589n
Mishler, Elliot G., 664n
Moberg, David, 359n, 368n
Moe, Edward O., 93–94
Mogey, John, 142n
Moloney, J. C., 599n
Moment, D., 78
Monahan, Thomas P., 638n
Moore, Samuel, 716n
Moore, Wilbert E., 6, 7, 9, 15, 18, 207n,
   229, 282n, 293n, 297n, 300n, 305n,
   306n, 309n, 311n, 315n, 316n, 320n,
   708n
Morgan, Lewis Henry, 699–700, 701
Morse, Nancy C., 190(t)
Morse, Richard M., 444n
Mosca, Gaetano, 438, 493
Mumford, Lewis, 570n
Murdock, George Peter, 514, 515n, 516,
   517, 520, 527n, 528, 532, 533, 559n,
   702n
Mussen, P. H., 592n
Myers, J., 649n
Myrdal, Gunnar, 236, 451n

Nadel, S. F., 636n
Naegele, K. D., 556n
Nagel, Ernest, 707n
Nakanishi, Naomichi, 461n
Nasser, Gamel Abdel, 445
Needler, Martin C., 447n
Neumann, Sigmund, 495
Newcomb, Theodore M., 78, 540n, 553n,
   554n
Nisbet, Robert A., 622n
Northrup, F. S. C., 710

O'Dea, Thomas, 351n
Ogburn, William F., 549n, 702–704
Ohlin, Lloyd, 647, 648
Olmsted, M. S., 78
Orenstein, Alan M., 149
Otto, Rudolf, 336–337, 347

Pareto, Vilfredo, 438
Park, Robert E., 85
Parkinson, C. N., 565n
Parsons, Talcott, 2n, 6n, 86, 87, 94, 95,
    154n, 168n, 169n, 173n, 211, 225–229,
    278n, 304n, 318n, 358n, 394–397, 420–
    421, 492, 497, 539n, 540, 543n, 556,
    607n, 650, 651n, 691n, 692n, 708n, 716n
Payne, D. E., 592n
Peabody, Robert, 192
Pear, R. H., 457n
Pearson, Harry, 311n
Pedley, R., 404n
Perón, Juan D., 460
Pettigrew, Thomas, 368n
Phillips, Derek L., 658n
Piliavin, Irving, 643, 644n
Pitts, J. R., 556n
Plato, 548
Polanyi, Karl, 311n
Polsby, Nelson W., 234
Pomryn, B. A., 92n
Pope, Liston, 351n
Pope John XXIII, 357
Press, Arthur F., 652n
Proudhon, P. J., 439

Queen, Stuart A., 104

Radcliffe-Brown, A. R., 707, 708n
Redl, Fritz, 575n, 641n
Redlich, Frederick C., 259–260, 617n, 649n
Reginald, A. H., 652n
Reiss, Albert J., Jr., 104n, 106n, 237n
Reissman, Leonard, 5, 8, 9, 15, 18, 21n,
    136, 237n, 258n
Rheinstein, Max, 168n
Rice, Stuart, 439
Richards, Audrey, 385n
Riecken, H., 599n
Riesman, David, 233, 410
Roberts, Bertram H., 649n
Roberts, Leigh M., 92n
Roethlisberger, Fritz J., 195n
Rogoff, Natalia, 423–424, 431
Rokkan, Stein, 461n, 464n
Romasco, Anne, 602, 661n, 663n
Roosevelt, Franklin D., 496
Rose, Arnold M., 652n
Ross, Edward A., 438
Ross, Lawrence H., 96n
Rousseau, J. J., 555, 562

Saint-Simon, Claude Henri de, 439
Sandler, Joseph, 92n

Savitz, Leonard, 638n
Scalapino, Robert A., 461n
Schachter, S., 42n, 48n, 78, 599n
Schattschneider, E. E., 441n
Scheff, Thomas J., 607n
Schein, E. H., 78, 599n
Schelling, T. C., 57n
Schelsky, Helmut, 369n
Schneideman, Edwin, 635
Schneider, Louis, 372n
Schnore, Leo F., 9, 10–11, 14, 18, 103n,
    120(t), 122n, 126(t), 127n, 128(t),
    133n, 134n, 144n
Schulze, Robert O., 135–136
Schumpeter, Joseph A., 287, 449, 492n
Schur, Edwin M., 626n
Schutz, W. C., 575n
Scott, J. P., 550n, 551, 552n
Scott, W. Richard, 168n
Seeley, John, 372n
Selznick, Philip, 161n, 196n, 198n, 453n,
    692n
Senn, Milton J. E., 527n
Seton-Watson, Hugh, 462n
Sewell, William H., 147–149
Shaw, George Bernard, 249, 711
Sheats, P., 577n
Sheatsley, Paul B., 243
Shepard, H. A., 575n
Shepherd, C. R., 78
Sherif, C. W., 78
Sherif, Muzafer, 78
Shibutani, T., 577n
Shils, Edward A., 6n, 168n, 195n, 410n,
    462n, 556n, 691n
Short, James F., Jr., 644, 648
Simpson, George, 14n, 304n, 613n, 628n,
    716n
Simpson, Richard L., 150n
Sjoberg, Gideon, 87, 105n, 117, 570, 571
Skinner, B. F., 33n
Sklare, Marshall, 363n
Skolnick, Jerome H., 652n, 654n, 660n
Slater, Philip E., 4, 9, 21n, 530
Small, Albion, 438, 439n
Smelser, Neil J., 207n, 278n, 282n, 304n,
    495n, 649n, 708n
Smith, Adam, 296
Smith, C. W., 581n
Smith, G. H., 454n
Smith, M. G., 20
Solomon, P., 591n
Solovay, S. A., 614n
Solow, Robert M., 452n

Sorel, George, 493
Sorokin, Pitirim A., 103, 106, 710, 712–714, 715
Spaulding, John A., 628n
Spencer, Herbert, 716
Spengler, Oswald, 710
Spiegel, J. P., 577n
Spitz, R. A., 550
Srinivas, M. N., 248n
Staats, A. W., 33n, 78
Staats, C. K., 33n, 78
Stalin, Joseph, 445
Stanfield, Robert Edward, 642
Starbuck, William, 157n, 198n
Steele, F. I., 78, 599n
von Stein, Lorenz, 439
Stein, Maurice R., 88, 89, 134, 581n
Stephens, William N., 4, 9, 21n, 515n, 527n, 531n, 532n, 533n, 542n, 568n
Steward, Julian H., 701, 709, 710
Stinchcombe, Arthur L., 5n, 9, 15–18, 156(t), 167n
Stockhammer, Morris, 145n
Stogdill, R. M., 78
Stokes, Anson Phelps, 360n
Stoller, Nancy, 598n
Stouffer, Samuel A., 20, 195n, 454n, 569n, 674–675
Strodtbeck, Fred L., 644, 648
Stuart, Grace, 561
Suetuna, Z., 461n
Sugi, Masataka, 454n
Sumner, William Graham, 438, 618
Sussman, Marvin B., 142, 538n, 656n
Sutherland, Edwin H., 646
Sykes, Gresham M., 92n
Szasz, Thomas, 614n, 655n

Taeuber, Alma, 129–130, 131(t), 132(t)
Taeuber, Karl E., 129–130, 131(t), 132(t)
Taietz, Philip, 617n
Taylor, G. R., 559, 569n, 576n
Thibaut, J. W., 42n, 53n, 78
Thielens, Wagner F., 183, 184
Thrasher, Frederick M., 646
Tillich, Paul, 378
Tisdale, Hope, 107
de Tocqueville, Alexis, 452, 453
Tomeh, Aida K., 143
Torsvik, Per, 464n
Toynbee, Arnold, 710
Triandis, Leigh M., 595n
Trotsky, Leon, 185

Trow, Martin A., 91, 186, 403n, 454n, 492n
Trumen, David, 494n
Tumin, Melvin, 207n
Turner, Ralph, 399
Tuxford, Joy, 92n
Tylor, Edward B., 529

Udy, Stanley H., Jr., 167n, 294, 295n
Underwood, Kenneth, 367n
Unwin, J. D., 559n

Veblen, Thorstein, 317, 361, 408–409, 568
Verney, Douglas V., 494n
Vidich, Arthur, 367n, 581n
Voegelin, Eric, 356n
Vogel, E. F., 585
Vogt, Evon, 335n
Voss, Harwin L., 638n
de Vyver, Frank T., 306n

Wach, Joachim, 367n
Wagner, Helmut R., 2n
Walker, Charles R., 187
Walker, E. L., 50–51, 78
Wallace, Anthony F. C., 697, 698
Waller, W., 567n
Walters, David, 641
Ward, Lester, 438
Warner, W. Lloyd, 222 ff., 253, 341, 469n
Warren, Roland L., 89–90, 134
Washburn, S. L., 551n, 552n
Washington, George, 445
Watanuki, Joji, 461n
Watnick, Morris, 462n
Waxler, Nancy E., 664n
Weakland, John, 649n
Wearmouth, Robert F., 476n
Webber, Melvin M., 88–89
Weber, Max, 2–3, 5, 17, 133, 168n, 169, 173n, 211, 216, 218 ff., 253, 334, 339, 341, 343–344, 346n, 348–352, 353, 354, 367n, 369, 396, 407, 411–412, 438, 440, 443, 449, 465, 469, 479, 492, 560, 569n, 691n, 692n, 699, 716
Weiss, Robert S., 190(t)
Westergaard, J., 428n
Westermarck, Edvard A., 528
Wheeler, Stanton, 9, 16, 21, 22, 645n, 661n, 662n, 663n
White, D. M., 581n
White, Leslie, 709
White, R. W., 635n

Whiting, John W. M., 527n, 533n, 590n, 592, 595n
Whorf, Benjamin Lee, 552–553
Whyte, W. H., 409
Wilcox, Francis O., 93n
Wilensky, Harold L., 320n
Wilkens, Leslie T., 643
Willey, Gordon R., 116n
Wilson, Bryan, 351n, 400n
Wilson, James Q., 192n, 662n
Winch, Robert F., 536n, 592n
Wineman, David, 641n
Wingo, Lowdon, Jr., 89n
Wirth, Louis, 85, 105, 106, 137
Wissler, Clark, 705n
Wolf, Charles, Jr., 449n
Wolf, Margery, 595n

Wolfgang, Marvin E., 638n
Wolfle, Dael, 423n, 427(t)
Wright, Charles R., 137, 138(t)
Wright, Quincy, 93n
Wrong, Dennis, 548, 556n, 557, 559n, 562n

Yelyutin, V. P., 394
Young, Michael, 265, 266n, 432

Zaleznik, A., 78
Zander, Alvin, 78, 619n
Zeitlin, Maurice, 462n
Zimmer, Basil G., 138, 139, 140n
Zimmerman, Carle C., 103, 106, 315n
Zinkin, Taya, 245n
Zola, Irving Kenneth, 641, 664n

# Subject Index *

Academic freedom, 183–185
*Academic Mind, The,* 184
Adaption, typology of modes of, 629(t)
Adolescence, 397–398
  American extension of, 542–543
*Adolescent Society,* 397
Advertising, 308–309
Aggression, animal, 550–552
  human, 558–560
  individual internalized controls of, 593
  and synergy, 566–570
Alienation, 18–19
  and community, 82–83
  and planned work, 179, 180(t)
  and urbanization, 144–145
Ambivalence, and individual motivation, 572–576
*Ancient Society,* 699–700
Anomie, and urbanization, 145–146
Authority, and discipline, 165–166, 167, 175(t)
  and leadership, 68–72
  legitimation of, 169–172
  and responsibility, 164–165, 167, 175(t), 186
  and supervision, 165, 167, 175(t), 186

Balance theory, 46–47
"Beachtown," 674–688
Behavior, human, changes in rates of, 689
  learned nature of, 34–35
  as social behavior, 30–32
  social influences on, 15–17
  subjective meaning of, 2–4
Behavior, social, *see* Behavior, human; Social action; and Social process
Brainwashing, 595, 597–600
Buddhism, 333, 335, 349, 351, 353

Bureaucracy, and attitudes toward planning, 183(t)
  characteristics of, 133
  effects on community organization, 133–136
  and labor, 299–300
  as organizational type, 169, 171, 174–175(t)
  and religion, 361–367
  and working hours, 180, 181(t), 182

Calvinism, 285, 344, 355
  and political parties, 476–477
  *see also* Religion
*Cameralists, The,* 438
*Capital,* 289
Caste, 343
  and Indian stratification, 244–249
  system, 8, 9, 31
Catholicism, 355, 357, 367–368
  and political parties, 459–460, 474–475, 476–477
  and recent U.S. elections, 489–492
  *see also* Religion
Charisma, 169–170, 174–175(t), 396
  and political legitimacy, 442–443, 444–445
  and religion, 350–352
"Chicago school," 85, 86
Church, and interrelations of religious and economic, 277
Cities, growth rates for, 119(t)
  preconditions for development of, 116–118
  segregation in, 124–133
  *see also* Community; Metropolitanization; Urbanism; and Urbanization
*Civilization and Its Discontents,* 548, 558

* The (t) in parentheses indicates a table.

Class, social, in community study, 223–224
  in England vs United States, 249–253
  in Marxian theory, 213–216
  membership and educational opportunities, 427–432
  and mental health, 259–260
  and occupational prestige, 237–240
  role of middle class in developing nations, 262–264
  and social participation, 260–261
  and socialization, 257–259
  and voting behavior, 451–453, 461–473, 480–492
Class consciousness, effect on behavior, 254–256
  in England, 249, 255
Cognitive dissonance, 599–600
Cohesion, group, and deviance, 614–615
Communism, and economic activity, 283–285, 449
*Communist Manifesto, The,* 217
Community, case study in social change in, 674–685
  changes in, 723
  classical views of, 84–87
  contemporary view of, 82–84
  defined, 94–96
  demographic aspects of, 110–111, 116–122
  and deviant behavior, 617–619
  dynamics of, 115–150
  ecological aspects of, 111–112, 122–133
  forms and functions, 100–102
  geographical vs aggregate usage, 90 ff.
  metropolitan, 108–110
  new perspectives on, 87–90
  power structure of, 233–234
  psychological dimension of, 86–87, 88–89, 91
  and rural-urban dimension, 103–108
  size and interdependence, 98(t)
  social psychological aspects of, 114–115, 144–150
  social stratification of, 223–225
  structure and organization of, 112–114, 133–144
  structure and relation to conflict, 678–685
  types of, 96–110
Competition, 51
Conflict, community, 674–685
  intergenerational, 397–398

Conformity, and group interation, 47–51
  small group experiments on, 619–620
  and status, 75–77
  *see also* Deviant behavior; Norms
Confucianism, 349
Conservativism, dilemma of, 462–468
  and political parties, 459–462
Consumption, changing standards of, 719–720
  and income distribution, 316–317
  institutions of, 317–318
  in rich nations vs poor nations, 315–316
  types of consumers, 313–315
Contract and trust, 303–305
Creativity, 610–611
Credit, 312
Crime, *see* Deviant behavior
Cultural lag, 702–704
Culture, changes in patterns of, 690, 711–712
  classification of, 712–714, 715
  "failure" of, 561–563
  and language, 552–555

Deferential behavior, 63
Democracy, 492–499
  and economic development, 449–456
  economic development and education, 392(t)
  and voting behavior, 456–462
Demography, and community, 110–111
  and social process, 193–194, 198
  and urbanization, 116–122
  *see also* Population
Deprivation-satiation, basic proposition of, 37–39, 42, 44, 49, 55, 73
Deviant behavior, 21–22
  acts to roles, 636–638, 644–646
  acts vs motives, 623–625
  creation of patterns of, 616–617, 633–638
  and cultural goals vs institutionalized means, 628–633
  and development of subcultures, 637–638, 646–648
  and juvenile delinquency, 638–650
  and norms, 604–610
  perception vs fact of, 625–627
  and situational forces, 635–636, 643–644
  and social control, 609–610, 618, 650–666
  social definitions of, 610–616
  and social position, 634, 638–640, 642
  and sociological patterns, 634–635, 641–643

Deviant behavior, types and typologies, 622–623
  varieties of, 621–622
  in varying levels of social unit, 617–621
Dictatorship, *see* Oligarchy
*Dictionary of Occupational Titles,* 178, 295–296
*Dictionary of the Social Sciences, A,* 87
Diffusion theory, 704–706
Disasters, research in, 697–698
Discrimination, process of, 34
Distribution, institutions of, 311–313
  traditional and modern, 315 ff.
  Western vs Soviet, 310–311
"Distributive justice," 17–18, 63–67
Division of labor, 294–295, 301, 302–303
  and marriage, 534–535
  and solidarity, 586–588
  and stratification, 225

*Eclipse of Community, The,* 87–88
Ecology, human, and the community, 111–112
  and community studies, 86
  and urbanization, 122–133
Economic activity, as analytical structure, 276–277
  common features in, 285–286
  consumption category of, 313–318
  distribution category of, 305–313
  identification of, 278–281
  and political systems, 449–456
  production category of, 286–305
  professions, as example of, 318–328
  and religion, 360–361, 371
  social setting of, 284–285
  sources and types of variability in, 281–284
Economic determinism, 15–16
  and stratification, 211–229
Economic development, as social change, 716–720
  *see also* Industrialization
Economic Opportunity Act of 1964, 209, 218
Education, aspirations for, and urbanization, 147(t)
  as cultural transmission, 385, 388–389
  and democracy, 454–456
  English, 251–252, 403, 411–414, 426(t), 427(t), 429(t)
  equality of opportunity for, 420–421, 423–427
Education, family status and aspirations for, 425(t)
  functions of, 385–399
  and personality formation, 385–387, 390–393
  and power, 419–420
  and residential segregation, 126(t)
  social determinants of educability, 421–422
  as social integration, 393–399
  Soviet, 394, 403, 410–411
  and stratification, 414–418
  structure of, 399–414
  trends in class chances for higher, 427–432
  and U.S. population, 384
  university enrollment and degrees conferred, 413(t)
  *see also* Schools
Effectiveness, as basis of legitimacy, 446–448
  economic, and political systems, 449–456
Elites, and changes in developed nations, 265–266
  education and formation of new, 419–420
  in England, 250–251
  political, economic, military, 230–234
  theories of, 493
Engel's law, 315
England, education in, 251–252, 403, 411–414, 426(t), 427(t), 429(t)
  stratification system of, 249–253

Family, American, 535–543
  changing relations of, 720–722
  and contemporary religion, 372–374
  and deviant behavior, 635
  nuclear, polygynous and extended, 516–518
  roles, 584–586
  social position and delinquency, 641–643
  *see also* Kinship
Field investigations, and formal organizations, 198–199
*First New Nation, The,* 230
Frustration-aggression, basic proposition of, 39–41, 44, 63
Function, manifest vs latent, 339
Functionalism, and social change, 706–708

*General Sociology,* 438
Generalization, process of, 34

Groups, social, 4–5
  interaction of, 47–51

Hinduism, 349, 353
Homosexuality, 626
Human condition, scarcity in, 279

Identification, 590–595
Ideology, and economic activity, 285
Imitation, 595–600
Income distribution, and styles of life, 316–317
  trends in, 234–236
India, caste system of, 244–249
Individualism, 562–563
Inequality, social, 206–211, 240–244
Industrial society, education in, 385–389, 390–393, 399–414
  social integration in, 393–399
Industrialization, effect on Indian caste system, 247–249
  universities and emergence of, 406–411
Institutions, and human action, 32
  *see also* under specific institutions
Interaction, analysis of, 41–45
  elaboration of, 45–47
  and equality, 72–75
  role, 5–6
  within groups, 47–51
Islam, 349, 351, 353
Isolation, social, 549–550

Judaism, 349
Juvenile delinquency, from acts to roles, 644–646
  blending of processes, 648–650
  control of, 661–666
  development of subcultures, 646–648
  and situational forces, 643–644
  and social position, 638–640, 642
  and socialization patterns, 641–643

Kinship, 579
  and avoidance rules, 513–515
  function of rules, 508–511
  and joking relationships, 515–516
  larger groups, 518–523, 538–539
  and marriage, 530–535
  marriage and incest taboos, 524–530
  types of deference customs, 511–513
  *see also* Family
Ku Klux Klan, 660

Labor, characteristics of, by community size, 102(t)

Labor, organization of, 297–300
  as production factor, 292–300
  *see also* Division of labor; Work
Language, and perception, 552–555
Leadership, as cause and effect of status, 68–72
Learning, and experience, 34–35
Legitimacy, of political systems, 441–448
Leisure vs work, 154, 176–177
Liberalism, and political parties, 459–462
Literacy, distribution of, 393(t)
  and economic development, 455

Management, legal powers of, United States vs USSR, 162(t)
Marriage, 530–535
  American, 536–537, 541
  and incest taboos, 524–530
Marxian theory, 276, 278, 285, 288–289
McCarthyism, 20, 183–184
Mental health, and social class, 259–260
Meritocracy, 266, 419, 432
Metropolitanization, 108–110
  levels and measures of, 120(t)
Middle ages, religion in, 355–356, 359–360
Mobility, England vs United States, 252–253
  in United States, 267–268
Models, *see* Sociological models
Modernization, discontinuities in, 723–725
  as social change, 716–728
Motives, and deviant behavior, 623(t)

Nationalism, and social change, 263–265
Negroes, 604–608, 617
  and anomie, 146
  and deviant behavior, 625
  and educational opportunities, 421–423
  effects of recent militancy of, 242–244
  and mobility, 267–268
  political and economic inequality of, 240–241
  and race consciousness, 255
  and residential segregation, 129–133
  values shared with whites, 241–242
*Negroes in Cities*, 129
New nations, social development in, 262–265
Norms, 16, 604–610
  defined, 7, 45

Occupation, aspirations in, and urbanization, 149(t)

Occupation, and level of responsibility and overtime, 188–189(t)
  as measure of class, 237–240
  *see also* Labor; Work
Occupational communities, 91–94
*Of Civil Government,* 548
Oligarchy, 492–499
  and economic development, 449
Opinion polls, on integration, 243
Organizations, formal, and authority systems, 164–167
  classifications of, 167–169
  and corruption, 196–197
  and creation of vested interests, 196
  defined, 155–156
  demographic structure of, 193–194, 198
  effects on daily life, 173–189
  main types of, 169–172, 174–175(t)
  and primary groups, 194–196
  resources for, 160–164, 166–167
  societal variation in, 172–173
  studying, 197–201
  theories in planning, 157–160, 166
  and voluntary associations, 137–144, 189–192

Pattern variables, 394–395
*Patterns of Culture,* 548
Peer groups, 195
Perception, and deviant behavior, 626(t)
Personality, and role, 579–582
Planning, and formal organizations, 154–156
  work time spent in, 156(t)
Pluralism, and economic activity, 283–285
Political parties, conservative, 459–462, 462–468
  of the left, 458–459
  liberal, 459–462
  and lower-class support, 451
  religious, 476–480
  and voting behavior, 456–462
Political sociology, defined, 440–442
  history of, 438–440
  and voting behavior, 456–462
Political stability, and conservative dilemma, 462–463
  and legitimacy, 446–448
Political systems, and economic effectiveness, 449–456
Politics, United States, interplay of class and religion in recent, 480–492
Polity, defined, 441
  legitimacy of, 441–448

Population, and age and sex composition, 99–100
  and capital accumulation, 291–292
  and community types, 97–100
  density, 98
  percent living in cities, 118(t)
  *see also* Demography
Poverty, and income distribution, 235–236
  structural, 239–240
Power, on community level, 233–234
  and education, 419–420
  individual and group, 49–56
  legitimation of, 341–342
  and minorities, 497–498
  political, 221–222
  role in stratifying society, 219–220
  and status, 220–221
  in U.S. society, 230–234
Primary groups, 194–196
Primitive society, *see* Society, preindustrial
Private sphere, of contemporary religion, 369–374
*Process of Government, The,* 438
Production, and capital formation, 289–292
  factors of, 287–288
  institutions of, 301–305
  and labor input, 292–300
  Marxist reformulation of, 288–289
  and political power, 301
  and values in, 300–301
Professions, as communities, 91–94
  criteria of professionalism, 318–320
  institutions of, 327–328
  and role relations, 320–327
Property, 301–302
Protestantism, and rise of capitalism, 344, 560
  transformations of function of, 352–361
Psychoanalytic theory, and identification, 591–592
*Psychosis and Civilization,* 616
Psychology, behavioral, basic propositions of, 32–41
Psychology, dynamic, and nature of man, 556
*Pygmalion,* 249

Race, and social stratification, 240–244
  *see also* Negroes
Religion, contemporary situation of, 369–379
  demonopolization of, 374–376, 378
  and economics, 277, 360–361, 371

Religion, phenomenon of, defined, 335–338

and politics, 347–348, 357, 359–360, 371

in premodern societies, 344–352

and social control, 341–343, 358–359, 706–707

social functions of, 338–344

and social structuration, 343–344, 359

sociological study of, 332–335

status and party preference, 484(t)

and symbolic integration, 339–341, 357

transformation of functions of, 352–361

transformation of structures of, 361–369

and voting behavior, 459–460, 473–480, 480–492

Representation, political, 492–499

Residential segregation, by education, 126(t)

of nonwhites, 131(t)

by region, 132(t)

by socioeconomic status, 125(t), 128(t)

*see also* Segregation

Resources, organizational, control of, 160, 164, 167, 174(t)

creation of, 160–161, 166

defense of, 160, 161–162, 166

replenishment of, 160, 163–164, 166–167, 174(t)

*Rites de passage,* 385

Roles, age and sex, 582–584

American familial, 537–538, 541–542

as compartmentalization, 576–579

defined, 5–6, 72

delinquent, 644–646

deviant, 636–637

familial, 395, 584–586

generalization of, 580

induction techniques of, 589–600

and personality, 579–582

of professionals, 320–327

and role induction, 570–576

Rural communities, 103–108

Rural-urban continuum, 104


Sanctions, 16

defined, 7

Schools, English university, 411–414

primary and secondary, 402–404

and role of teacher, 400–402

as social systems, 395–397

universities in industrial societies, 404–406

Schools, universities and emergence of industrialism, 406–411

*see also* Education

Secularization, 356–358

Segregation, of groups and activities, 122–133

residential, 124–133

Sexuality, and societal forms, 567, 569, 576

Social action, defined, 2–3

Social change, and ascription vs achievement criteria of stratification, 209–210

a case study in, 674–685

causes of, 687–688

classical diffusion theory of, 704–706

classical evolutionary theory of, 699–702

classical functionalists approach to, 706–708

components of theory of, 688–698

cultural lag theory of, 702–704

dependent variables of, 689–690

describing, 685–687

determinants of processes of, 693–695

and education, 389

evaluating case study in, 685–688

interrelations among processes of, 716–728

in Marxian theory, 215–218

multilineal evolution theory of, 709–710

natural history approach to, 696 ff.

as rise and fall of civilization, 710–715

and stratification in developing nations, 261–268

Social controls, 16, 22, 399

defined, 7–8

group, 49–50

of juvenile delinquency, 661–666

machinery of, 650–661

religion as, 706–707

and social change, 695

Social order, and nature of man, 555–558

Social organization, of the community, 112–114

identifying economic elements in, 276–286

as precondition for city life, 117

and results of urbanization, 133–144

Social process, and bargaining, 56–58

basic propositions of, 32–41

and conformity, 75–77

discovery and explanation of, 30–32

and distributive justice, 63–67

and equality, 72–75

and interaction, 41–47

and leadership, 68–72

Social process, of organizations, 193–197
  and power, 49–56
  and status, 58–60
  *see also* Behavior, human; Social action
Social psychology, 14–15
  of the community, 114–115
  and results of urbanization, 144–150
Social stratification, basic features of, 206–211
  and behavior, 253–261
  cohesive element in, 210–211
  and deviance, 634
  and education, 414–418, 420–421, 423–432
  functional theory of, 225–229
  and juvenile delinquency, 638–640, 642
  Marxian theory of, 212–218
  and political behavior, 451–453, 461–473, 480–492
  and social change, 261–268
  and social structure, 229–253
  theory of community, 223–225
  and urbanization, 136
  Weber's theory of, 218–222
  *see also* Class, social
Social structure, changes in, 689–690
  defined, 6
  influence on behavior, 15–17
  relations of polity to, 441, 442
  role of religion to, 343–344
  *see also* Social organization; Social stratification
Social system, contradictory functional requirements of, 570–588
  defined, 6
  school class as, 395–397
Social unrest, genesis of, 723–725
  manifestations of, 725–727
Socialization, disruption of normal, 549–550, 552
  and education, 385, 387–388, 394–397
  as function of class, 257–259
  patterns of, and delinquency, 641–643
  patterns of, and deviancy, 634–635
  as role induction technique, 589–600
Society, competing structures within, 564–566
  contradictory functional requirements of, 570–588
  and the individual, 548–570
  meaning of existence in, 552
  norms and deviant behavior, 604–610

Society, preindustrial, education in, 385–389
  religion in, 344–352
Socioeconomic status, and city-suburban differentials, 128(t)
  and residential segregation, 125(t)
  *see also* Status
Sociological models, 17–22
Sociological hypotheses, 13–17, 22
Sociological thought, history of, 13–14
Sociology, conceptual framework of, 3–12, 83
  defined, 2
  empirical terms of, 83
  methodology of, 9–12, 83
  subdivisions of, 2
  substance of, 2–12
Solidarity, organic vs mechanical, 586–588
Specialization, economic, 283–284
  of interaction, 586–588
  in labor productivity, 293–297
  in professions, 323–324
"State of nature" theory, 549–555
Status, bases of, 58–60
  and conformity, 75–77
  family, and educational aspirations and achievement, 425(t), 426(t)
  inconsistency, 256–257
  and party preference, 484(t)
  and political behavior, 470–471
  and power, 220–221, 223
  symbolism of, 60–63, 317–318
  *see also* Socioeconomic status
Stimulus, basic proposition of, 33–35, 42, 43, 45, 51, 56, 61, 68
Subcultures, delinquent, 646–648
  deviant, 637–638
Success, basic proposition of, 33, 43, 68
Suicide, 563–564, 565
Symbols, of status, 60–63, 317–318
Synergy, 566–570, 587

Taoism, 353
Technological society, *see* Industrial society
Technology, as precondition for city life, 116
Theories, of distribution of benefits, 158–159
  nonsociological, 13–14
  of personnel, 159–160
  of social change, 215–218, 695–715
  and sociological models, 17–22

Theories, of stratification, 211–229
    of technical costs, 157–158

United States, families in, 535–543
    marriage in, 536–537, 541
    mobility in, 267–268
    power in, 230–244
    social stratification of, 230–244
    *see also* Politics, United States
Unions, 185, 186(fig.), 496–497
Urban communities, 103–108
    *see also* Urbanism
Urbanism, classic conception of, 105
    features of, 106–107
*Urbanism as a Way of Life,* 105, 137
Urbanization, and behavioral changes, 144–
    150
    and community structural changes, 133–
    144
    defined, 107–108
    and demographic changes, 116–122
    and ecological changes, 122–133
    and economic development, 455
    effect on Indian caste system, 247–249
    and metropolitanization, 108–110
    *see also* Cities; Urbanism

Value, basic proposition of, 35–37, 42, 43,
    52–53, 68
    defined, 8
    orientations, 16

Variables, and basic propositions of social
    processes, 32–41
    dependent, 8–9, 10–12, 17–22
    independent, 13, 16, 19
    and sociological models, 17–22
Voluntary associations, dynamics of, 189–
    192
    membership in, 138(t), 139(t), 141(t)
    and urbanization, 137–144
Voting behavior, 456–462
    and ambivalence, 573–574
    and class membership, 451–453, 461–
    468
    and religious membership, 459–460,
    473–492
    in United States, by religion and occu-
    pation, 486(t), 488(t)
    in United States, by class and religion,
    482–483(t)

*Wayward Puritans,* 616
Women, pressures toward employment,
    177(t)
Work, and alienation, 144–145, 179, 180(t)
    changing relations in, 718–720
    and job satisfaction, 187–189, 190(t)
    versus leisure, 154, 176–177
    pressures on women toward, 177(t)
    *see also* Labor; Occupations; and Pro-
    fessions

"Yankee City," 223–224, 253